Contemporary
Moral
Problems

Third Edition

Contemporary Moral Problems

James E. White
St. Cloud State University

West Publishing Company
St. Paul   New York   Los Angeles   San Francisco

Copyeditor: *Susan Ecklund*
Interior Design: *David J. Farr,*
                  Imagesmythe, Inc.
Cover Design: *Diane Beasley*
Cover Image: *Robert Motherwell* Elegy to the
               Spanish Republic No. 34,
               1953–54. *Albright–Knox Art*
               Gallery, Buffalo, New York. Gift
               of Seymour H. Knox, 1957.

Library of Congress Cataloging-in-Publication
Data

Contemporary Moral Problems / [edited by]
James E. White.—3rd ed. p. cm.
  Includes bibliographical references and index.
  ISBN 0-314-77301-0
  1. Ethical problems. 2. Civilization, Modern
—1950–   I. White, James E.
BJ1031.C6 1991   90–40482
170–dc20   CIP

Contents

Chapter 6
Corporate Responsibility 225

Chapter 7
Job Discrimination and Affirmative Action 249

Chapter 8
Sexual Issues 291

Chapter 9
Animals and the Environment 337

Chapter 10
Nuclear Deterrence 413

Preface

The choice of topics for the third edition of this text was dictated largely by student interest. Students in a class called Contemporary Moral Problems were surveyed to see what moral issues they wished to discuss. Abortion was at the top of the list, followed by the environment and animal rights. Abortion has been of interest since the surveys were first given five years ago, but the interest in the environment and animal rights is new. Perhaps the untiring work of environmentalists and animal rights activists is finally having an effect. Third on the most recent list was euthanasia, followed by sexual issues, hunger and welfare, the death penalty, corporate responsibility, and discrimination. Recent classes have shown less interest in nuclear deterrence than in the past. No doubt this is due to the dramatic democratic revolution in Eastern Europe and the Soviet Union, and the general perception that the cold war with the Soviet Union has ended. Students feel that conventional or nuclear war with the Russians is now unlikely, and that nuclear deterrence is no longer very important. They seem to be more interested in personal and domestic issues. Nevertheless, the chapter on nuclear deterrence is still included.

A new chapter on ethical theories has been added at the beginning of the text. Many reviewers of the first and second editions thought some attempt should be made to introduce students to the basic theories in ethics, or at least to the theories most often appealed to in the readings. After a careful review, it was decided that the most important theories for the purposes of the book were utilitarianism, Kant's theory, Rawls' theory of justice, and theory of rights. Obviously this chapter is not intended to provide a comprehensive review of all the important theories in ethics. To do that, one would need a whole book, or even several books.

The choice of particular readings on each topic was influenced by a variety of considerations. First there was an attempt to find readings of high quality. As a result, many of the articles included are semiclassics such as Mary Anne Warren's "On the Moral and Legal Status of Abortion," and none are previously unpublished. Some of the readings were chosen for their historical importance, e.g., the Supreme Court decisions on abortion and the death penalty. Also, there was an attempt to balance the readings, to have different points of view expressed. On most of these issues, it is possible to discern what might be called, loosely speaking, a conservative view and a more liberal view opposed to it. For example, in the first chapter on abortion, John T. Noonan defends the conservative view that abortion is killing an innocent human being, and as such it is almost always wrong; while Mary Anne Warren expounds the liberal view that abortion is not the killing of a person with a right to life, and that women have a right to get an abortion when they want to. Whenever possible, a moderate view, relatively speaking, has been included as well. For example, in the chapter on abortion, Jane English expresses a more or less moderate view that allows abortions in some cases where the abortion is justified by an appeal to self-defense, but certainly not in all cases.

The final consideration in choosing these readings, and by no means the least important, was their suitability for undergraduate instruction. This book is intended to be an introductory level textbook that can be read and understood by most college students. Many of the readings were assigned in class, but some of these readings may be more difficult than others for students to grasp easily. The following student aids have proved helpful:

1. *Chapter Introductions.* Each chapter begins with a general introduction that explains the issue and gives background information. When it is necessary, there is a brief survey of the main philosophical issues, arguments, and theories relevant to the moral issue.

2. *Reading Introductions.* Each reading is preceded by an author biography and a short summary of the author's main conclusions and arguments.

3. *Study Questions.* After each reading, there are study questions of two kinds. First, there are rather detailed and pedestrian review questions that test the student's grasp of the main points in the reading. They are directed towards the student who has had trouble following the text. Second, there are more difficult discussion questions that probe deeper into the reading. They are aimed at the person who has understood the reading and is ready to discuss it.

4. *Problem Cases.* At the end of each chapter, there are problem cases that require the student to apply the concepts, principles, arguments, and theories discussed in the chapter to a hard case, either actual or hypothetical. This case-study method (as they call it in law schools and business schools) produces lively discussion, and it is a good way to get the students to think about the moral issues from a moral point of view. Also the problem cases can be assigned as short paper topics or used on essay tests. For this edition, there is a supplement with additional problem cases. These are mostly factual cases gathered from recent magazines and newspapers.

5. *Suggested Readings.* Specific suggestions are made for further reading. Usually they are books and articles that might have been included in the chapter. They are not intended to take the place of a comprehensive bibliography.

6. *Philosophical Glossary.* There is a glossary of philosophical terms at the end of the book. The glossary also covers some of the philosophers mentioned in the text. It is not supposed to take the place of a standard dictionary; it merely supplements a dictionary.

In revising the book for the third edition, I have benefited from the help and advice of many people. In particular, I am heavily indebted to my faithful colleague Myron Anderson. For more than twenty years, he has been an unfailing source of good advice and articles. The following people were also of help with their reviews of this book: Peter Amato, Marist College; Dr. Mary Angelec Cooksey, Ball State/Indiana University; Barry Curtis, University of Hawaii at Hilo; John Godbey, Marymount University; Dr. Stephen Infantino, College of Lake County; Laura Lyn Inglis, Buena Vista College; Emilio M. Kosrovani, Humboldt State University; Joseph Paul Porter, University of Missouri; Dr. Winslow Shea, University of Miami; Peter K. Steinfeld, Buena Vista College; and Joseph Chuman William Paterson College. Finally, I received helpful recommendations and encouragement from Nancy E. Crochiere, my editor at West Publishing Company.

Contemporary Moral Problems

Chapter 1

Ethical Theories

Introduction

The purpose of this chapter is to introduce students to the ethical theories that are the most important for understanding the readings in the rest of the book. Two such philosophical theories stand out: utilitarianism and Kant's theory. The readings contain frequent appeals to rights (see the chapter on abortion, for example); this makes it appropriate to include Ronald Dworkin's helpful explanation and defense of the notion of rights. Finally, John Rawls' theory of justice has been included because it is a **social contract theory** that has been very influential in current discussions of justice and rights.

Utilitarianism   The classical statement of the theory of utilitarianism is found in the writings of the English philosophers **Jeremy Bentham** (1748–1832) and John Stuart Mill (1806–1873). In the reading, Mill gives a succinct statement of the basic principle of utilitarianism, the Principle of Utility: "Actions are right in proportion as they tend to promote happiness, wrong as they tend to produce the reverse of happiness." But what is happiness? Mill answers: "By happiness is intended pleasure, and the absence of pain."

The most obvious feature of the theory is that it determines the rightness or wrongness of an action by its *consequences,* by the happiness or unhappiness it produces. An ethical theory that looks at consequences is classified as a **teleological theory,** and is distinguished from a **deontological theory** (such as Kant's theory) that does not consider consequences.

In considering the happiness or unhappiness produced, utilitarianism counts

1

everyone equally (including nonhuman animals). No one's happiness is to be considered more important than anyone else's. This means that utilitarianism rejects **ethical egoism,** a rival teleological theory holding that people should consider only their own happiness and not anyone else's happiness.

Utilitarianism and Conventional Morality

Determining rightness or wrongness by considering consequences and nothing else is a very radical idea that leads to the rejection of certain features of conventional morality. In deciding what is right or wrong, people sometimes refer to the beliefs of their society and assume the truth of **cultural relativism,** the view that acts generally approved by society are right, and acts disapproved are wrong. But utilitarians reject this view for the simple reason that the moral beliefs of a society can be mistaken. In Mill's time, it was believed that women were inferior to men in intelligence and ability, and that women should not be allowed to enter certain occupations such as law and medicine. But as Mill pointed out in his classic feminist work, *The Subjection of Women,* these beliefs are mistaken. Women are capable of being doctors and lawyers, and should have the opportunity to do so.

Another feature of conventional morality is that people sometimes consult their feelings in deciding what is right or wrong; that is, they accept **subjectivism,** the view that an act is right if a person approves of it, and wrong if a person disapproves of it. This view is similar to cultural relativism, but instead of saying that moral values are relative to the beliefs of society, the subjectivist holds that moral values are relative to subjective feelings. Thus a subjectivist might say, "All abortions are wrong because I very strongly disapprove of them." But utilitarians reject subjectivism for the same reason they reject cultural relativism—people can be mistaken in their moral beliefs. The person who believes that

abortion is wrong because of negative feelings about it could be mistaken. If a woman with a tubal pregnancy has a lifesaving abortion, and this produces more happiness than unhappiness for her and her family, then according to the utilitarian the abortion is right. The fact that the abortion makes some other person unhappy can be taken into account, of course, but if this unhappiness is outweighed by the happiness of the mother and her family, then on the utilitarian view the abortion is morally right.

Objections to Utilitarianism

We have seen that utilitarianism sometimes conflicts with conventional morality and can be used as a basis for social criticism and social reform. But these conflicts with conventional morality are also a major source of objections to utilitarianism. These criticisms of utilitarianism are discussed by Rachels in the reading. The basic complaint is that utilitarianism (in either a hedonistic or a nonhedonistic form) goes too far in its rejection of conventional morality and results in obviously wrong or unjust acts such as punishing an innocent person, violating a person's rights, breaking promises, failing to consider merit, and so on.

As Rachels points out in the reading, at least two replies are available to utilitarians. They can take the radical reformist line that these acts are not really wrong or unjust even though they are conventionally considered to be so. Or they can switch from Act Utilitarianism (which judges individual acts to be right or wrong) to Rule Utilitarianism (which uses the Principle of Utility to judge rules of action rather than individual acts).

Utilitarianism and Religion

Utilitarianism is compatible with belief in God. In fact, Bentham argued that if God is benevolent, then God would command us to follow the Principle of Utility, since this is the best way to be benevolent. But utilitarians cannot accept the **Divine Command Theory,** the deontological theory which says that an act is right if and only if God commands it. Utilitarians do not find the commands commonly attributed to God to be acceptable. For example, consider the basic moral command "Thou shalt not kill." It is easy for a utilitarian to find cases where killing is justified—for example, killing the terrorist who is threatening to blow up an airplane packed with innocent people, or even killing an innocent person in order to save many other lives.

Utilitarianism and Moral Problems The use of utilitarianism for moral criticism and social reform becomes even clearer when we consider how utilitarianism is used in the readings to deal with moral problems, particularly euthanasia, capital punishment, and animal rights. Let us see what the utilitarians have to say about these problems.

The conventional moral rule is that it is wrong to kill innocent people, and this implies that euthanasia is wrong. But in our readings for Chapter 3, Rachels, Singer, and Brandt argue on utilitarian grounds that euthanasia can be morally justified in some cases. Rachels argues that if we allow passive euthanasia (mercifully letting people die), as the American Medical Association does, then we should allow active euthanasia (mercifully killing people) as well, for there is no important moral difference between passive and active euthanasia—both have the same consequences. Singer's argument is more straightforward. According to preference utilitarianism, it is right to maximize the satisfaction of people's preferences; but voluntary euthanasia does this in some cases, namely in those cases where people want to die. So euthanasia is right in some cases. Brandt uses the utilitarian theory to justify the termination of newborn infants whose lives will be unhappy.

What is the justification of capital punishment? On the utilitarian view, killing a criminal can be justified only by appealing to consequences, and the main relevant consequence of capital punishment is the deterrence of other criminals from committing crimes. But does the death penalty deter? In Chapter 4, both Amsterdam and Glover argue that this has not been established, and thus that the death penalty has no utilitarian justification.

The view that nonhuman animals should be given equal moral consideration (accepted by Singer and Regan in Chapter 9) is a radical utilitarian idea, found in the writings of Bentham (who is quoted by Singer). Remember that everyone's happiness or unhappiness is to be equally considered, and since nonhuman animals do have the capacity to be happy or unhappy, or at least to feel pleasure and pain, they have a moral standing equal to humans.

Kant's Theory The main rival to utilitarianism in the readings is Kant's theory. Unlike utilitarianism and ethical egoism, it is a deontological theory that does not consider consequences. Kant believes that by reasoning we can discover one supreme moral principle that is binding on all rational beings. He calls this principle the Categorical Imperative because it commands absolutely, as distinguished from hypothetical imperatives which command only if you have certain desires.

Kant formulates the Categorical Imperative in several different ways, but commentators usually focus on two distinct versions. The first one is that you should "act only on that maxim which you can at the same time will that it should become a universal law." This principle gives you a way of deciding whether an act is wrong or not. You ask yourself what rule you would be following if you did something; this rule is the maxim of your act. If you are not willing to have this rule become a universal law that everyone follows, then the act falling under the rule is wrong. To take one of Kant's examples, suppose you want to lie to someone. The rule you would be following, the maxim of your act, would be "It is not wrong to lie to someone." But you would not be willing to have everyone follow this rule, Kant claims, because this would be self-defeating. If everyone lied at will, then lying would be pointless because nobody would believe you. According to Kant, these considerations prove that lying is always wrong.

Many philosophers have thought that this first formulation of the Categorical Imperative is problematic. One problem is that you can formulate the rule under which an act falls in different ways, and some of these rules might be universalizable and others not. For example, instead of a general rule about lying, you could have a more specific rule about lying such as "It is not wrong to lie to save someone's life." This seems to be a rule about lying that we would be willing to accept as a universal law.

Kant formulated the Categorical Imperative in a second way that avoids this problem. His second formulation, called the Formula of the End in Itself, is that you should "act in such a way that you always treat humanity, whether in your own person or in the person of any other, never simply as a means, but always at the same time as an end."

This principle is explained by Onora O'Neill in our readings. According to O'Neill, treating someone as a mere means is treating them in a way to which they could not in principle consent, e.g., deceiving them. Treating someone as an end in himself or herself requires that we not treat the person as a mere means, but help them with their plans and activities. This gives us a duty to help or a duty of beneficence.

Kant's Theory and Moral Problems Kant's theory and utilitarianism can be used to arrive at similar conclusions in some issues. Both Singer (a utilitarian) and O'Neill (a Kantian) agree that we have a moral obliga-

tion to help starving people in other countries (although in Chapter 5 Hardin gives utilitarian reasons for not helping). On other matters, however, Kant's theory is opposed to utilitarianism. The difference between the two theories is most clear in the case of capital punishment. In the reading in Chapter 4, Kant condemns the "serpent-windings of Utilitarianism," and insists that murderers must die because they deserve to die; they must be paid back for their crimes, and the consequences of the punishment are irrelevant.

Kant also rejects the utilitarian view of nonhuman animals. In the reading in Chapter 9, Tom Regan accurately puts Kant in the anthropocentric tradition that excludes animals from moral concern because they are not supposed to be rational. According to Kant, we do not have any direct duties to animals, but we do have indirect duties based on the effect the treatment of animals has on our treatment of humans. Thus we should not be cruel to animals since this makes us cruel to humans.

Kant does not discuss euthanasia, but in view of the fact that he believed that human life is always valuable, even when it is full of suffering, it seems likely that he would have condemned euthanasia. He does say that suicide is always wrong because it treats a human life as an animal life, that is, as a life having little or no value in itself.

Rights Many readings in the book do not appeal to utilitarianism or Kant's theory but to rights. We find references to the rights of fetuses, newborn infants, the terminally ill, animals, future generations, the needy, and the environment. There are debates about who has rights and what rights they have. But what is a right? On Dworkin's analysis, a person has a right if it is wrong to interfere with the exercise of the right. Usually it is persons who are said to be the bearers of rights; to show that fetuses or animals have rights, then, it seems necessary to demonstrate that they are persons. According to Dworkin, in the United States citizens have certain fundamental rights (such as the rights to free speech and free press) that they hold against their government; these are moral rights that have been turned into legal rights by the Constitution. Dworkin thinks that the basis of these moral rights is the Kantian idea that humans who are members of the moral community should be treated with respect, and also the utilitarian idea of political equality.

Traditional Theories of Rights   What is the basis for moral rights? The traditional view of **Locke** and Jefferson is that they are given to us by God. But most philosophers today do not want to appeal to God; they want a theory that appeals to nonbelievers too. A traditional secular view is the social contract theory of **Hobbes** and **Rousseau.** On this theory it is in everyone's self-interest to live in a society rather than as hermits in a state of nature. But to live in a society, people must agree to follow certain rules (Don't steal, Don't murder, etc.), and these rules imply corresponding rights. Every citizen tacitly makes such an agreement, the social contract, in order to get the benefits of living in society. Without this social contract, society would not be possible.

Rawls' Theory of Justice   Rawls' theory is a kind of social contract theory. He imagines that the social contract is made by self-interested but free and rational persons. In order to insure impartiality or fairness, he imagines that the contractors make the agreement in a hypothetical original position where they are ignorant of all the particular facts about themselves, but they do know general facts about social theory and psychology. According to Rawls, the rational contractors in the original position would agree upon two principles of justice. The first says that "each person is to have an equal right to the most extensive basic liberty compatible with a similar liberty for others." The second says that "social and economic inequalities are to be arranged so that they are both (a) reasonably expected to be to everyone's advantage, and (b) attached to positions and offices open to all."

This theory is relevant to moral problems about distribution of goods and resources such as the problems of world hunger, welfare, job discrimination, and affirmative action. It is also relevant to problems involving the rights of citizens. In our readings for Chapter 8, for example, David A.J. Richards appeals to Rawls' theory in his discussion of the impact laws against obscenity have on the constitutional rights of free speech and free press.

John Stuart Mill

Utilitarianism

John Stuart Mill (1806–1873) was one of the most important and influential British philosophers. His

From John Stuart Mill, Utilitarianism (1861), Chapters 12 and 14

most important works in ethics are On Liberty *and* Utilitarianism, *from which the reading is taken.*

Mill sets forth the basic principles of utilitarianism including the Principle of Utility (or the Greatest Happiness Principle) and the hedonistic principle that happiness is pleasure. He explains the theory by replying to various objections, and concludes with an attempt to prove the Principle of Utility.

The creed which accepts as the foundation of morals, Utility, or the Greatest Happiness

Principle, holds that actions are right in proportion as they tend to promote happiness, wrong as they tend to produce the reverse of happiness. By happiness is intended pleasure, and the absence of pain; by unhappiness, pain, and the privation of pleasure. To give a clear view of the moral standard set up by the theory, much more requires to be said; in particular, what things it includes in the ideas of pain and pleasure; and to what extent this is left an open question. But these supplementary explanations do not affect the theory of life on which this theory of morality is grounded—namely, that pleasure, and freedom from pain, are the only things desirable as ends; and that all desirable things (which are as numerous in the utilitarian as in any other scheme) are desirable either for the pleasure inherent in themselves, or as means to the promotion of pleasure and the prevention of pain.

Now, such a theory of life excites in many minds, and among them in some of the most estimable in feeling and purpose, inveterate dislike. To suppose that life has (as they express it) no higher end than pleasure—no better and nobler object of desire and pursuit—they designate as utterly mean and grovelling; as a doctrine worthy only of swine, to whom the followers of **Epicurus** were, at a very early period, contemptuously likened; and modern holders of the doctrine are occasionally made the subject of equally polite comparisons by its German, French, and English assailants.

When thus attacked, the **Epicureans** have always answered, that it is not they, but their accusers, who represent human nature in a degrading light; since the accusation supposes human beings to be capable of no pleasures except those of which swine are capable. If this supposition were true, the charge could not be gainsaid, but would then be no longer an imputation; for if the sources of pleasure were precisely the same to human beings and to swine, the rule of life which is good enough for the one would be good enough for the other. The comparison of the Epicurean life to that of beasts is felt as degrading, precisely because a beast's pleasures do not satisfy a human being's conceptions of happiness. Human beings have faculties more elevated than the animal appetites, and when once made conscious of them, do not regard anything as happiness which does not include their gratification. I do not, indeed, consider the Epicureans to have been by any means faultless in drawing out their scheme of consequences from the utilitarian principle. To do this in any sufficient manner, many **Stoic,** as well as Christian elements require to be included. But there is no known Epicurean theory of life which does not assign to the pleasures of the intellect, of the feelings and imagination, and of the moral sentiments, a much higher value as pleasures than to those of mere sensation. It must be admitted, however, that utilitarian writers in general have placed the superiority of mental over bodily pleasures chiefly in the greater permanency, safety, uncostliness, etc., of the former—that is, in their circumstantial advantages rather than in their intrinsic nature. And on all these points utilitarians have fully proved their case; but they might have taken the other, and, as it may be called, higher ground, with entire consistency. It is quite compatible with the principle of utility to recognise the fact, that some *kinds* of pleasure are more desirable and more valuable than others. It would be absurd that while, in estimating all other things, quality is considered as well as quantity, the estimation of pleasures should be supposed to depend on quantity alone.

If I am asked, what I mean by difference of quality in pleasures, or what makes one pleasure more valuable than another, merely as a pleasure, except its being greater in amount, there is but one possible answer. Of two pleasures, if there be one to which all or almost all who have experience of both give a decided preference, irrespective of any feeling of moral obligation to prefer it, that is the more desirable pleasure. If one of the two is, by those who are competently acquainted with both, placed so far above the other that they prefer it, even though knowing it to be attended with a greater amount of discontent, and would not resign it for any quantity of the other pleasure which their nature is capable of, we are justified in ascribing to the preferred enjoyment a superiority in quality, so far outweighing quantity as to render it, in comparison, of small account.

Now it is an unquestionable fact that those who are equally acquainted with, and equally capable of appreciating and enjoying, both, do give a most marked preference to the manner of existence which employs their higher faculties. Few human creatures would consent to be changed into any of the lower animals, for a promise of the fullest allowance of a beast's pleasures; no intelligent human being would consent to be a fool, no instructed person would be an ignoramus, no person of feeling and conscience would be selfish and base, even though they should be persuaded that the fool, the dunce, or the rascal is better satisfied with his lot than they are with theirs. They would not resign what they possess more than he for the most complete satisfaction of all the desires which they have in common with him. If they ever fancy they would, it is only in cases of unhappiness so extreme, that to escape from it they would exchange their lot for almost any other, however undesirable in their own eyes. A being of higher faculties requires more to make him happy, is capable probably of more acute suffering, and certainly accessible to it at more points, than one of an inferior type; but in spite of these liabilities, he can never really wish to sink into what he feels to be a lower grade of existence. We may give what explanation we please of this unwillingness; we may attribute it to pride, a name which is given indiscriminately to some of the most and to some of the least estimable feelings of which mankind are capable: we may refer it to the love of liberty and personal independence, an appeal to which was with the Stoics one of the most effective means for the incul-

cation of it; to the love of power, or to the love of excitement, both of which do really enter into and contribute to it: but its most appropriate appellation is a sense of dignity, which all human beings possess in one form or other, and in some, though by no means in exact, proportion to their higher faculties, and which is so essential a part of the happiness of those in whom it is strong, that nothing which conflicts with it could be, otherwise than momentarily, an object of desire to them. Whoever supposes that this preference takes place at a sacrifice of happiness—that the superior being, in anything like equal circumstances, is not happier than the inferior—confounds the two very different ideas, of happiness, and content. It is undisputable that the being whose capacities of enjoyment are low, has the greatest chance of having them fully satisfied; and a highly endowed being will always feel that any happiness which he can look for, as the world is constituted, is imperfect. But he can learn to bear its imperfections, if they are at all bearable; and they will not make him envy the being who is indeed unconscious of the imperfections, but only because he feels not at all the good which those imperfections qualify. It is better to be a human being dissatisfied than a pig satisfied; better to be **Socrates** dissatisfied than a fool satisfied. And if the fool, or the pig, are of a different opinion, it is because they only know their own side of the question. The other party to the comparison knows both sides.

It may be objected, that many who are capable of the higher pleasures, occasionally, under the influence of temptation, postpone them to the lower. But this is quite compatible with a full appreciation of the intrinsic superiority of the higher. Men often, from infirmity of character, make their election for the nearer good, though they know it to be the less valuable; and this no less when the choice is between two bodily pleasures, than when it is between bodily and mental. They pursue sensual indulgences to the injury of health, though perfectly aware that health is the greater good. It may be further objected, that many who begin with youthful enthusiasm for everything noble, as they advance in years sink into indolence and selfishness. But I do not believe that those who undergo this very common change, voluntarily choose the lower description of pleasures in preference to the higher. I believe that before they devote themselves exclusively to the one, they have already become incapable of the other. Capacity for the nobler feelings is in most natures a very tender plant, easily killed, not only by hostile influences, but by mere want of sustenance; and in the majority of young persons it speedily dies away if the occupation to which their position in life has devoted them, and the society into which it has thrown them, are not favourable to keeping that higher capacity in exercise. Men lose their high aspirations as they lose their intellectual tastes, because they have not time or opportunity for indulging them; and they addict themselves to inferior pleasures, not because they deliberately prefer them, but because they are either the only ones to which they have access, or the only ones which they are any longer capable of enjoying. It may be questioned whether any one who has remained equally susceptible to both classes of pleasures, ever knowingly and calmly preferred the lower; though many, in all ages, have broken down in an ineffectual attempt to combine both.

From this verdict of the only competent judges, I apprehend there can be no appeal. On a question which is the best worth having of two pleasures, or which of two modes of existence is the most grateful to the feelings, apart from its moral attributes and from its consequences, the judgment of those who are qualified by knowledge of both, or, if they differ, that of the majority among them, must be admitted as final. And there needs be the less hesitation to accept this judgment respecting the quality of pleasures, since there is no other tribunal to be referred to even on the question of quantity. What means are there of determining which is the acutest of

two pains, or the intensest of two pleasurable sensations, except the general suffrage of those who are familiar with both? Neither pains nor pleasures are homogeneous, and pain is always heterogeneous with pleasure. What is there to decide whether a particular pleasure is worth purchasing at the cost of a particular pain, except the feelings and judgment of the experienced? When, therefore, those feelings and judgment declare the pleasures derived from the higher faculties to be preferable *in kind,* apart from the question of intensity, to those of which the animal nature, disjoined from the higher faculties, is susceptible, they are entitled on this subject to the same regard.

I have dwelt on this point, as being a necessary part of a perfectly just conception of Utility or Happiness, considered as the directive rule of human conduct. But it is by no means an indispensable condition to the acceptance of the utilitarian standard; for that standard is not the agent's own greatest happiness, but the greatest amount of happiness altogether; and if it may possibly be doubted whether a noble character is always the happier for its nobleness, there can be no doubt that it makes other people happier, and that the world in general is immensely a gainer by it. Utilitarianism, therefore, could only attain its end by the general cultivation of nobleness of character, even if each individual were only benefited by the nobleness of others, and his own, so far as happiness is concerned, were a sheer deduction from the benefit. But the bare enunciation of such an absurdity as this last, renders refutation superfluous.

According to the Greatest Happiness Principle, as above explained, the ultimate end, with reference to and for the sake of which all other things are desirable (whether we are considering our own good or that of other people), is an existence exempt as far as possible from pain, and as rich as possible in enjoyments, both in point of quantity and quality; the test of quality, and the rule for measuring it against quantity, being the preference felt by those who in their opportunities of experience, to which must be added their habits of self-consciousness and self-observation, are best furnished with the means of comparison. This, being, according to the utilitarian opinion, the end of human action, is necessarily also the standard of morality; which may accordingly be defined, the rules and precepts for human conduct, by the observance of which an existence such as has been described might be, to the greatest extent possible, secured to all mankind; and not to them only, but, so far as the nature of things admits, to the whole sentient creation. . . .

I must again repeat, what the assailants of utilitarianism seldom have the justice to acknowledge, that the happiness which forms the utilitarian standard of what is right in conduct, is not the agent's own happiness, but that of all concerned. As between his own happiness and that of others, utilitarianism requires him to be as strictly impartial as a disinterested and benevolent spectator. In the golden rule of Jesus of Nazareth, we read the complete spirit of the ethics of utility. To do as you would be done by, and to love your neighbour as yourself, constitute the ideal perfection of utilitarian morality. As the means of making the nearest approach to this ideal, utility would enjoin, first, that laws and social arrangements should place the happiness, or (as speaking practically it may be called) the interest, of every individual, as nearly as possible in harmony with the interest of the whole; and secondly, that education and opinion, which have so vast a power over human character, should so use that power as to establish in the mind of every individual an indissoluble association between his own happiness and the good of the whole; especially between his own happiness and the practice of such modes of conduct, negative and positive, as regard for the universal happiness prescribes; so that not only he may be unable to conceive the possibility of happiness to himself, consistently with conduct opposed to the general good, but also that a direct impulse to promote the general good

may be in every individual one of the habitual motives of action, and the sentiments connected therewith may fill a large and prominent place in every human being's sentient existence. If the impugners of the utilitarian morality represented it to their own minds in this its true character, I know not what recommendation possessed by any other morality they could possibly affirm to be wanting to it; what more beautiful or more exalted developments of human nature any other ethical system can be supposed to foster, or what springs of action, not accessible to the utilitarian, such systems rely on for giving effect to their mandates. . . .

OF WHAT SORT OF PROOF THE PRINCIPLE OF UTILITY IS SUSCEPTIBLE

It has already been remarked, that questions of ultimate ends do not admit of proof, in the ordinary acceptation of the term. To be incapable of proof by reasoning is common to all first principles; to the first premises of our knowledge, as well as to those of our conduct. But the former, being matters of fact, may be the subject of a direct appeal to the faculties which judge of fact—namely, our senses, and our internal consciousness. Can an appeal be made to the same faculties on questions of practical ends? Or by what other faculty is cognisance taken of them?

Questions about ends, in other words, question what things are desirable. The utilitarian doctrine is, that happiness is desirable, and the only thing desirable, as an end; all other things being only desirable as means to that end. What ought to be required of this doctrine—what conditions is it requisite that the doctrine should fulfil—to make good its claim to be believed?

The only proof capable of being given that an object is visible, is that people actually see it. The only proof that a sound is audible, is that people hear it: and so of the other sources of our experience. In like manner, I apprehend, the sole evidence it is possible to produce that anything is desirable, is that people do actually desire it. If the end which the utilitarian doctrine proposes to itself were not, in theory and in practice, acknowledged to be an end, nothing could ever convince any person that it was so. No reason can be given why the general happiness is desirable, except that each person, so far as he believes it to be attainable, desires his own happiness. This, however, being a fact, we have not only all the proof which the case admits of, but all which it is possible to require, that happiness is a good: that each person's happiness is a good to that person, and the general happiness, therefore, a good to the aggregate of all persons. Happiness has made out its title as one of the ends of conduct, and consequently one of the criteria of morality.

But it has not, by this alone, proved itself to be the sole criterion. To do that, it would seem, by the same rule, necessary to show, not only that people desire happiness, but that they never desire anything else. Now it is palpable that they do desire things which, in common language, are decidedly distinguished from happiness. They desire, for example, virtue, and the absence of vice, no less really than pleasure and the absence of pain. The desire of virtue is not as universal, but it is as authentic a fact, as the desire of happiness. And hence the opponents of the utilitarian standard deem that they have a right to infer that there are other ends of human action besides happiness, and that happiness is not the standard of approbation and disapprobation.

But does the utilitarian doctrine deny that people desire virtue, or maintain that virtue is not a thing to be desired? The very reverse. It maintains not only that virtue is to be desired, but that it is to be desired disinterestedly, for itself. Whatever may be the opinion of utilitarian moralists as to the original conditions by which virtue is made virtue; however they may believe (as they do) that actions and dispositions are only virtuous because they promote another end than virtue; yet this being granted, and it having been decided, from considerations of this description,

what *is* virtuous, they not only place virtue at the very head of the things which are good as means to the ultimate end, but they also recognise as a psychological fact the possibility of its being, to the individual, a good in itself, without looking to any end beyond it; and hold, that the mind is not in a right state, not in a state conformable to Utility, not in the state most conducive to the general happiness, unless it does love virtue in this manner—as a thing desirable in itself, even although, in the individual instance, it should not produce those other desirable consequences which it tends to produce, and on account of which it is held to be virtue. This opinion is not, in the smallest degree, a departure from the Happiness principle. The ingredients of happiness are very various, and each of them is desirable in itself, and not merely when considered as swelling an aggregate. The principle of utility does not mean that any given pleasure, as music, for instance, or any given exemption from pain, as for example health, is to be looked upon as means to a collective something termed happiness, and to be desired on that account. They are desired and desirable in and for themselves; besides being means, they are a part of the end. Virtue, according to the utilitarian doctrine, is not naturally and originally part of the end, but it is capable of becoming so; and in those who love it disinterestedly it has become so, and is desired and cherished, not as a means to happiness, but as a part of their happiness.

To illustrate this farther, we may remember that virtue is not the only thing, originally a means, and which if it were not a means to anything else, would be and remain indifferent, but which by association with what it is a means to, comes to be desired for itself, and that too with the utmost intensity. What, for example, shall we say of the love of money? There is nothing originally more desirable about money than about any heap of glittering pebbles. Its worth is solely that of the things which it will buy; the desires for other things than itself, which it is a means of gratifying. Yet the love of money is not only one of the strongest moving forces of human life, but money is, in many cases, desired in and for itself; the desire to possess it is often stronger than the desire to use it, and goes on increasing when all the desires which point to ends beyond it, to be compassed by it, are falling off. It may, then, be said truly, that money is desired not for the sake of an end, but as part of the end. From being a means to happiness, it has come to be itself a principal ingredient of the individual's conception of happiness. The same may be said of the majority of the great objects of human life—power, for example, or fame; except that to each of these there is a certain amount of immediate pleasure annexed, which has at least the semblance of being naturally inherent in them; a thing which cannot be said of money. Still, however, the strongest natural attraction, both of power and of fame, is the immense aid they give to the attainment of our other wishes; and it is the strong association thus generated between them and all our objects of desire, which gives to the direct desire of them the intensity it often assumes, so as in some characters to surpass in strength all other desires. In these cases the means have become a part of the end, and a more important part of it than any of the things which they are means to. What was once desired as an instrument for the attainment of happiness, has come to be desired for its own sake. In being desired for its own sake it is, however, desired as *part* of happiness. The person is made, or thinks he would be made, happy by its mere possession; and is made unhappy by failure to obtain it. The desire of it is not a different thing from the desire of happiness, any more than the love of music, or the desire of health. They are included in happiness. They are some of the elements of which the desire of happiness is made up. Happiness is not an abstract idea, but a concrete whole; and these are some of its parts. And the utilitarian standard sanctions and approves their being so. Life would be a poor thing, very ill provided with

sources of happiness, if there were not this provision of nature, by which things originally indifferent, but conducive to, or otherwise associated with, the satisfaction of our primitive desires, become in themselves sources of pleasure more valuable than the primitive pleasures, both in permanency, in the space of human existence that they are capable of covering, and even in intensity.

Virtue, according to the utilitarian conception, is a good of this description. There was no original desire of it, or motive to it, save its conduciveness to pleasure, and especially to protection from pain. But through the association thus formed, it may be felt a good in itself, and desired as such with as great intensity as any other good; and with this difference between it and the love of money, of power, or of fame, that all of these may, and often do, render the individual noxious to the other members of the society to which he belongs, whereas there is nothing which makes him so much a blessing to them as the cultivation of the disinterested love of virtue. And consequently, the utilitarian standard, while it tolerates and approves those other acquired desires, up to the point beyond which they would be more injurious to the general happiness than promotive of it, enjoins and requires the cultivation of the love of virtue up to the greatest strength possible, as being above all things important to the general happiness.

It results from the preceding considerations, that there is in reality nothing desired except happiness. Whatever is desired otherwise than as a means to some end beyond itself, and ultimately to happiness, is desired as itself a part of happiness, and is not desired for itself until it has become so. Those who desire virtue for its own sake, desire it either because the consciousness of it is a pleasure, or because the consciousness of being without it is a pain, or for both reasons united; as in truth the pleasure and pain seldom exist separately, but almost always together, the same person feeling pleasure in the degree of virtue attained, and pain in not having attained more. If one of these gave him no pleasure, and the other no pain, he would not love or desire virtue, or would desire it only for the other benefits which it might produce to himself or to persons whom he cared for. . . .

Review Questions

1. State and explain the Principle of Utility. Show how it could be used to justify actions that are conventionally viewed as wrong, such as lying and stealing.

2. How does Mill reply to the objection that Epicureanism is a doctrine only worthy of swine?

3. How does Mill distinguish between higher and lower pleasures?

4. According to Mill, whose happiness must be considered?

5. Carefully reconstruct Mill's proof of the Principle of Utility.

Discussion Questions

1. Is happiness nothing more than pleasure, and the absence of pain? What do you think?

2. Does Mill convince you that the so-called higher pleasures are better than the lower ones? What about the person of experience who prefers the lower pleasures over the higher ones?

3. Mill says, "In the golden rule of Jesus of Nazareth, we read the complete spirit of the ethics of utility." Is this true or not?

4. Many commentators have thought that Mill's proof of the Principle of Utility is defective. Do you agree? If so, then what mistake or mistakes does he make? Is there any way to reformulate the proof so that it is not defective?

James Rachels

The Debate over Utilitarianism

James Rachels is University Professor of Philosophy at the University of Alabama at Birmingham. He is the author of The End of Life: Euthanasia and Morality *and articles on the right to privacy, reverse discrimination, and the treatment of nonhuman animals. The reading is taken from his textbook* The Elements of Moral Philosophy.

Rachels presents the main objections to utilitarianism and the replies given by defenders of utilitarianism. His own view is that utilitarianism is correct in telling us to consider the consequences of actions, and in advising us to be impartial, but incorrect in

ignoring other important moral considerations such as merit.

The utilitarian doctrine is that happiness is desirable, and the only thing desirable, as an end; all other things being desirable as means to that end.
    John Stuart Mill, Utilitarianism *(1861)*

Man does not strive after happiness; only the Englishman does that.
    Friedrich Nietzsche, Twilight of the Idols *(1889)*

THE RESILIENCE OF THE THEORY

Classical Utilitarianism—the theory defended by Bentham and Mill—can be summarized in three propositions:

First, actions are to be judged right or wrong solely in virtue of their consequences. Nothing else matters. Right actions are, simply, those that have the best consequences.

Second, in assessing consequences, the only thing that matters is the amount of happiness or unhappiness that is caused. Everything else is irrelevant. Thus right actions are those that produce the greatest balance of happiness over unhappiness.

The Elements of Moral Philosophy, James Rachels, 1986, McGraw-Hill Publishing Company. Reprinted by permission.

Third, in calculating the happiness or unhappiness that will be caused, no one's happiness is to be counted as more important than anyone else's. Each person's welfare is equally important. As Mill put it in his *Utilitarianism*,

the happiness which forms the utilitarian standard of what is right in conduct, is not the agent's own happiness, but that of all concerned. As between his own happiness and that of others, utilitarianism requires him to be as strictly impartial as a disinterested and benevolent spectator.

Thus right actions are those that produce the greatest possible balance of happiness over unhappiness, with each person's happiness counted as equally important.

The appeal of this theory to philosophers, economists, and others who theorize about human decision making has been enormous. The theory continues to be widely accepted, even though it has been challenged by a number of apparently devastating arguments. These antiutilitarian arguments are so numerous, and so persuasive, that many have concluded the theory must be abandoned. But the remarkable thing is that so many have *not* abandoned it. Despite the arguments, a great many thinkers refuse to let the theory go. According to these contemporary utilitarians, the antiutilitarian arguments show only that the classical theory needs to be *modified;* they say the basic idea is correct and should be preserved, but recast into a more satisfactory form.

In what follows, we will examine some of these arguments against Utilitarianism, and consider whether the classical version of the theory may be revised satisfactorily to meet them. These arguments are of interest not only for the assessment of Utilitarianism but for their own sakes, as they raise some additional fundamental issues of moral philosophy.

IS HAPPINESS THE ONLY THING THAT MATTERS?

The question *What things are good?* is different from the question *What actions are right?* and Utilitarianism answers the second question by referring back to the first one. Right actions, it says, are the ones that produce the most good. But what is good? The classical utilitarian reply is: one thing, and one thing only, namely happiness. As Mill put it, "The utilitarian doctrine is that happiness is desirable, and the only thing desirable, as an end; all other things being desirable as means to that end."

The idea that happiness is the one ultimate good (and unhappiness the one ultimate evil) is known as **Hedonism**. Hedonism is a perennially popular theory that goes back at least as far as the ancient Greeks. It has always been an attractive theory because of its beautiful simplicity, and because it expresses the intuitively plausible notion that things are good or bad only on account of the way they make us *feel.* Yet a little reflection reveals serious flaws in the theory. The flaws stand out when we consider examples like these:

1. A promising young pianist's hands are injured in an automobile accident so that she can no longer play. Why is this a bad thing for her? Hedonism would say it is bad because it causes her unhappiness. She will feel frustrated and upset whenever she thinks of what might have been, and *that* is her misfortune. But this way of explaining the misfortune seems to get things the wrong way around. It is not as though, by feeling unhappy, she has made an otherwise neutral situation into a bad one. On the contrary, her unhappiness is a rational response to a situation that *is* unfortunate. She could have had a career as a concert pianist, and now she cannot. *That* is the tragedy. We could not eliminate the tragedy just by getting her to cheer up.

2. You think someone is your friend, but really he ridicules you behind your back. No one ever tells you, so you never know. Is this situation unfortunate for you? Hedonism would have to say no, because you are never caused any unhappiness by the situation. Yet

we do feel that there is something bad going on here. You *think* he is your friend, and you are "being made a fool," even though you are not aware of it and so suffer no unhappiness.

Both these examples make the same basic point. We value all sorts of things, including artistic creativity and friendship, for their own sakes. It makes us happy to have them, but only because we *already* think them good. (We do not think them good *because* they make us happy—this is what I meant when I said that Hedonism "gets things the wrong way around.") Therefore we think it a misfortune to lose them, independently of whether or not the loss is accompanied by unhappiness.

In this way, Hedonism misunderstands the nature of happiness. Happiness is not something that is recognized as good and sought for its own sake, with other things appreciated only as means of bringing it about. Instead, happiness is a response we have to the attainment of things that we recognize *as* goods, independently and in their own right. We think that friendship is a good thing, and so having friends makes us happy. That is very different from first setting out after happiness, then deciding that having friends might make us happy, and then seeking friends as a means to this end.

Today, most philosophers recognize the truth of this. There are not many contemporary hedonists. Those sympathetic to Utilitarianism have therefore sought a way to formulate their view without assuming a hedonistic account of good and evil. Some, such as the English philosopher G.E. Moore (1873–1958), have tried to compile short lists of things to be regarded as good in themselves. Moore suggested that there are three obvious **intrinsic goods**—pleasure, friendship, and aesthetic enjoyment—and that right actions are those that increase the world's supply of such things. Other utilitarians have tried to bypass the question of how many things are good in themselves, leaving it an open question and saying only that right ac-

tions are the ones that have the best results, *however* goodness is measured. (This is sometimes called **Ideal Utilitarianism.**) Still others try to bypass the question in another way, holding only that we should act so as to maximize the satisfaction of people's *preferences*. (This is called **Preference Utilitarianism.**) It is beyond the scope of this book to discuss the merits or demerits of these varieties of Utilitarianism. I mention them only in order to note that although the hedonistic assumption of the classical utilitarians has largely been rejected, contemporary utilitarians have not found it difficult to carry on. They do so by urging that Hedonism was never a necessary part of the theory in the first place.

ARE CONSEQUENCES ALL THAT MATTER?

The claim that only consequences matter *is*, however, a necessary part of Utilitarianism. The most fundamental idea underlying the theory is that in order to determine whether an action would be right, we should look at *what will happen as a result of doing it.* If it were to turn out that some *other* matter is also important in determining rightness, then Utilitarianism would be undermined at its very foundation.

The most serious antiutilitarian arguments attack the theory at just this point: they urge that various other considerations, in addition to utility, are important in determining whether actions are right. We will look briefly at three such arguments.

1. *Justice.* Writing in the academic journal *Inquiry* in 1965, H.J. McCloskey asks us to consider the following case:

Suppose a utilitarian were visiting an area in which there was racial strife, and that, during his visit, a Negro rapes a white woman, and that race riots occur as a result of the crime, white mobs, with the connivance of the police, bashing and killing Negroes, etc. Suppose too that our utilitarian is in the area of the crime when it is committed such that his testimony would bring about the conviction of a particular Negro. If he knows that a quick arrest will stop the riots and lynchings, surely, as a utilitarian, he must conclude that he has a duty to bear false witness in order to bring about the punishment of an innocent person.

This is a fictitious example, but that makes no difference. The argument is only that *if* someone were in this position, then on utilitarian grounds he should bear false witness against the innocent person. This might have some bad consequences—the innocent man might be executed—but there would be enough good consequences to outweigh them: the riots and lynchings would be stopped. The best consequences would be achieved by lying; therefore, according to Utilitarianism, lying is the thing to do. But, the argument continues, it would be wrong to bring about the execution of the innocent man. Therefore, Utilitarianism, which implies it would be right, must be incorrect.

According to the critics of Utilitarianism, this argument illustrates one of the theory's most serious shortcomings: namely, that it is incompatible with the ideal of justice. Justice requires that we treat people fairly, according to their individual needs and merits. The innocent man has done nothing wrong; he did not commit the rape and so he does not deserve to be punished for it. Therefore, punishing him would be unjust. The example illustrates how the demands of justice and the demands of utility can come into conflict, and so a theory that says utility is the *whole* story cannot be right.

2. *Rights.* Here is a case that is *not* fictitious; it is from the records of the U.S. Court of Appeals, Ninth Circuit (Southern District of California), 1963, in the case of *York v. Story:*

In October, 1958, appellant [Ms. Angelynn York] went to the police department of Chino for the purpose of filing charges in connection with an assault upon her. Appellee Ron Story, an officer of that police department, then acting under color of his authority as such, advised appellant that it was necessary to take photographs of her. Story then took appellant to a room in the police station, locked the door, and directed her to undress, which she did. Story then directed appellant to assume various indecent positions, and photographed her in those positions. These photographs were not made for

any lawful purpose.
Appellant objected to undressing. She stated to Story that there was no need to take photographs of her in the nude, or in the positions she was directed to take, because the bruises would not show in any photograph....
Later that month, Story advised appellant that the pictures did not come out and that he had destroyed them. Instead, Story circulated these photographs among the personnel of the Chino police department. In April, 1960, two other officers of that police department, appellee Louis Moreno and defendant Henry Grote, acting under color of their authority as such, and using police photographic equipment located at the police station made additional prints of the photographs taken by Story. Moreno and Grote then circulated these prints among the personnel of the Chino police department....

Ms. York brought suit against these officers and won. Her *legal* rights had clearly been violated. But what of the *morality* of the officers' behavior?

Utilitarianism says that actions are defensible if they produce a favorable balance of happiness over unhappiness. This suggests that we consider the amount of unhappiness caused to Ms. York and compare it with the amount of pleasure taken in the photographs by Officer Story and his cohorts. It is at least possible that more happiness than unhappiness was caused. In that case, the utilitarian conclusion apparently would be that their actions were morally all right. But this seems to be a perverse way to approach the case. Why should the pleasure afforded Story and his cohorts matter at all? Why should it even count? They had no right to treat Ms. York in that way, and the fact that they enjoyed doing so hardly seems a relevant defense.

To make the point even clearer, consider an (imaginary) related case. Suppose a Peeping Tom spied on Ms. York by peering through her bedroom window, and secretly took pictures of her undressed. Further suppose that he did this without ever being detected and that he used the photographs entirely for his own amusement, without showing them to anyone. Now under these circumstances, it seems clear that the *only* consequence of his action is an increase in his own happiness. No one else, including Ms. York, is caused any unhappiness at all. How, then, could Utilitarianism deny that the Peeping Tom's actions are right? But it is evident to moral common sense that they are not right. Thus, Utilitarianism appears to be an incorrect moral view.

The moral to be drawn from this argument is that Utilitarianism is at odds with the idea that people have *rights* that may not be trampled on merely because one anticipates good results. This is an extremely important notion, which explains why a great many philosophers have rejected Utilitarianism. In the above cases, it is Ms. York's right to privacy that is violated; but it would not be difficult to think of similar cases in which other rights are at issue—the right to freedom of religion, to free speech, or even the right to life itself. It may happen that good purposes are served, from time to time, by ignoring these rights. But we do not think that our rights *should* be set aside so easily. The notion of a personal right is not a utilitarian notion. Quite the reverse: it is a notion that places limits on how an individual may be treated, regardless of the good purposes that might be accomplished.

3. *Backward–Looking Reasons.* Suppose you have promised someone you will do something—say, you promised to meet him downtown this afternoon. But when the time comes to go, you don't want to do it—you need to do some work and would rather stay home. What should you do? Suppose you judge that the utility of getting your work accomplished slightly outweighs the inconvenience your friend would be caused. Appealing to the utilitarian standard, you might then conclude that it is right to stay home. However, this does not seem correct. The fact that *you promised* imposes an obligation on you that you cannot escape so easily. Of course, if the consequences of not breaking the promise were *great*—if, for example, your mother had just been stricken with a heart attack and you had to rush her to the hospital—you would be justified in breaking it. But a *small* gain in

utility cannot overcome the obligation imposed by the fact that you promised. Thus Utilitarianism, which says that consequences are the only things that matter, seems mistaken.

There is an important general lesson to be learned from this argument. Why is Utilitarianism vulnerable to this sort of criticism? It is because the only kinds of considerations that the theory holds relevant to determining the rightness of actions are considerations having to do with the *future*. Because of its exclusive concern with consequences, Utilitarianism has us confine our attention to what *will happen* as a result of our actions. However, we normally think that considerations about the *past* also have some importance. The fact that you promised your friend to meet him is a fact about the past, not the future. Therefore, the general point to be made about Utilitarianism is that it seems to be an inadequate moral theory because it excludes what we might call backward-looking considerations.

Once we understand this point, other examples of backward-looking considerations come easily to mind. The fact that someone did not commit a crime is a good reason why he should not be punished. The fact that someone once did you a favor may be a good reason why you should now do him a favor. The fact that you did something to hurt someone may be a reason why you should now make it up to her. These are all facts about the past that are relevant to determining our obligations. But Utilitarianism makes the past irrelevant, and so it seems deficient for just that reason.

THE DEFENSE OF UTILITARIANISM

Taken together, the above arguments form an impressive indictment of Utilitarianism. The theory, which at first seemed so progressive and commonsensical, now seems indefensible: it is at odds with such fundamental moral notions as justice and individual rights, and seems unable to account for the place of backward-looking reasons in justifying conduct. The combined weight of these arguments has prompted many philosophers to abandon the theory altogether.

Many thinkers, however, continue to believe that Utilitarianism, in some form, is true. In reply to the arguments, three general defenses have been offered.

The First Line of Defense

The first line of defense is to point out that the examples used in the antiutilitarian arguments are unrealistic and do not describe situations that come up in the real world. Since Utilitarianism is designed as a guide for decision making in the situations we actually face, the fanciful examples are dismissed as irrelevant....

The Second Line of Defense

The first line of defense contains more bluster than substance. While it can plausibly be maintained that *most* acts of false witness and the like have bad consequences in the real world, it cannot reasonably be asserted that *all* such acts have bad consequences. Surely, in at least some real-life cases, one can bring about good results by doing things that moral common sense condemns. Therefore, in at least some real-life cases Utilitarianism will come into conflict with common sense. Moreover, even if the antiutilitarian arguments had to rely exclusively on fictitious examples, those arguments would nevertheless retain their power; for showing that Utilitarianism has unacceptable consequences in hypothetical cases is a perfectly valid way of pointing up its theoretical defects. The first line of defense, then, is weak.

The second line of defense admits all this and proposes to save Utilitarianism by giving it a new formulation. In revising a theory to meet criticism, the trick is to identify precisely the feature of the theory that is causing the trouble and to change *that,* leaving the rest of the theory undisturbed as much as possible.

The troublesome aspect of the theory was this: the classical version of Utilitarianism implied that *each individual action* is to be evaluated by reference to its own particular consequences. If on a certain occasion you are tempted to lie, whether it would be wrong is determined by the consequences of *that particular lie.* This, the theory's defenders said, is the point that causes all the trouble; even though we know that *in general* lying has bad consequences, it is obvious that sometimes particular acts of lying can have good consequences.

Therefore, the new version of Utilitarianism modifies the theory so that individual actions will no longer be judged by the Principle of Utility. Instead, *rules* will be established by reference to the principle, and individual acts will then be judged right or wrong by reference to the rules. This new version of the theory is called *Rule–Utilitarianism,* to contrast it with the original theory, now commonly called *Act–Utilitarianism.*

Rule–Utilitarianism has no difficulty coping with the three antiutilitarian arguments. An act-utilitarian, faced with the situation described by McCloskey, would be tempted to bear false witness against the innocent man because the consequences of *that particular act* would be good. But the rule-utilitarian would not reason in that way. He would first ask, "What *general rules of conduct* tend to promote the greatest happiness?" Suppose we imagine two societies, one in which the rule "Don't bear false witness against the innocent" is faithfully adhered to, and one in which this rule is not followed. In which society are people likely to be better off? Clearly, from the point of view of utility, the first society is preferable. Therefore, the rule against incriminating the innocent should be accepted, and *by appealing to this rule,* the rule-utilitarian concludes that the person in McCloskey's example should not testify against the innocent man.

Analogous arguments can be used to establish rules against violating people's rights, breaking promises, lying, and so on. We should accept such rules because following them, as a regular practice, promotes the general welfare. But once having appealed to the Principle of Utility to establish the rules, we do not have to invoke the principle again to determine the rightness of particular actions. Individual actions are justified simply by appeal to the already-established rules.

Thus Rule–Utilitarianism cannot be convicted of violating our moral common sense, or of conflicting with ordinary ideas of justice, personal rights, and the rest. In shifting emphasis from the justification of acts to the justification of rules, the theory has been brought into line with our intuitive judgments to a remarkable degree.

The Third Line of Defense

Finally, a small group of contemporary utilitarians has had a very different response to the antiutilitarian arguments. Those arguments point out that the classical theory is at odds with ordinary notions of justice, individual rights, and so on; to this, their response is, essentially, "So what?" In 1961 the Australian philosopher J.J.C. Smart published a monograph entitled *An Outline of a System of Utilitarian Ethics;* reflecting on his position in that book, Smart said:

Admittedly utilitarianism does have consequences which are incompatible with the common moral consciousness, but I tended to take the view "so much the worse for the common moral consciousness." That is, I was inclined to reject the common methodology of testing general ethical principles by seeing how they square with our feelings in particular instances.

Our moral common sense is, after all, not necessarily reliable. It may incorporate various irrational elements, including prejudices absorbed from our parents, our religion, and the general culture. Why should we simply assume that our feelings are always correct? And why should we reject a plausible, rational theory of ethics such as Utilitarianism simply because it conflicts with those feelings? Perhaps it is the feelings, not the theory, that should be discarded.

In light of this, consider again McCloskey's example of the person tempted to bear false witness. McCloskey argues that it would be wrong to have a man convicted of a crime he did not commit, because it would be unjust. But wait: such a judgment serves *that man's* interests well enough, but what of the *other* innocent people who will be hurt if the rioting and lynchings are allowed to continue? What of them? Surely we might hope that we never have to face a situation like this, for the options are all extremely distasteful. But if we *must* choose between (a) securing the conviction of one innocent person and (b) allowing the deaths of several innocent people, is it so unreasonable to think that the first option, bad as it is, is preferable to the second?

On this way of thinking, Act–Utilitarianism is a perfectly defensible doctrine and does not need to be modified. Rule–Utilitarianism, by contrast, is an unnecessarily watered-down version of the theory, which gives rules a greater importance than they merit. Act–Utilitarianism is, however, recognized to be a radical doctrine which implies that many of our ordinary moral feelings may be mistaken. In this respect, it does what good philosophy always does—it challenges us to rethink matters that we have heretofore taken for granted.

WHAT IS CORRECT AND WHAT IS INCORRECT IN UTILITARIANISM

There is a sense in which no moral philosopher can completely reject Utilitarianism. The consequences of one's actions—whether they promote happiness, or cause misery—must be admitted by all to be extremely important. John Stuart Mill once remarked that, insofar as we are benevolent, we must accept the utilitarian standard; and he was surely right. Moreover, the utilitarian emphasis on impartiality must also be a part of any defensible moral theory. The question is whether these are the *only* kinds of considerations an adequate theory must acknowledge. Aren't there *other* considerations that are also important?

If we consult what Smart calls our "common moral consciousness," it seems that there are *many* other considerations that are morally important. (In section 8.3 above, we looked at a few examples.) But I believe the radical act-utilitarians are right to warn us that "common sense" cannot be trusted. Many people once felt that there is an important difference between whites and blacks, so that the interests of whites are somehow more important. Trusting the "common sense" of their day, they might have insisted that an adequate moral theory should accommodate this "fact." Today, no one worth listening to would say such a thing. But who knows how many *other* irrational prejudices are still a part of our moral common sense? At the end of his classic study of race relations, *An American Dilemma* (1944), the Swedish sociologist Gunnar Myrdal reminds us:

There must be still other countless errors of the same sort that no living man can yet detect, because of the fog within which our type of Western culture envelops us. Cultural influences have set up the assumptions about the mind, the body, and the universe with which we begin; pose the questions we ask; influence the facts we seek; determine the interpretation we give these facts; and direct our reaction to these interpretations and conclusions.

The strength of Utilitarianism is that it firmly resists "corruption" by possibly irrational elements. By sticking to the Principle of Utility as the *only* standard for judging right and wrong, it avoids all danger of incorporating into moral theory prejudices, feelings, and "intuitions" that have no rational basis.

The warning should be heeded. "Common sense" can, indeed, mislead us. At the same time, however, there might be at least some nonutilitarian considerations that an adequate theory *should* accept, because there *is* a rational basis for them. Consider, for example, the matter of what people deserve. A person who has worked hard in her job may deserve a promotion more than someone who has loafed, and it would be unjust for the loafer to be promoted first. This is a point that we would expect any fair-minded em-

ployer to acknowledge; we would all be indignant if we were passed over for promotion in favor of someone who had not worked as hard or as well as we. Now utilitarians might agree with this, and say that it can be explained by their theory—they might argue that it promotes the general welfare to encourage hard work by rewarding it. But this does not seem to be an adequate explanation of the importance of desert. The woman who worked harder has a superior claim to the promotion, *not* because it promotes the general welfare for her to get it, but *because she has earned it.* The reason she should be promoted has to do with *her* merits. This does not appear to be the kind of consideration a utilitarian could admit.

Does this way of thinking express a mere prejudice, or does it have a rational basis? I believe it has a rational basis, although it is not one that utilitarians could accept. We ought to recognize individual desert as a reason for treating people in certain ways—for example, as a reason for promoting the woman who has worked harder—because that is the principal way we have of treating individuals as autonomous, responsible beings. If in fact people have the power to choose their own actions, in such a way that they are *responsible* for those actions and what results from them, then acknowledging their deserts is just a way of acknowledging their standing as autonomous individuals. In treating them as they deserve to be treated, we are responding to the way they have freely chosen to behave. Thus in some instances we will not treat everyone alike, because people are not just members of an undifferentiated crowd. Instead, they are individuals who, by their own choices, show themselves to deserve different kinds of responses....

Review Questions

1. Rachels says that classical utilitarianism can be summed up in three propositions. What are they?

2. Explain the problem with hedonism. How do defenders of utilitarianism respond to this problem?

3. What are the objections about justice, rights, and promises?

4. Distinguish between Rule- and Act-Utilitarianism. How does Rule-Utilitarianism reply to the objections?

5. What is the third line of defense?

Discussion Questions

1. Smart's defense of utilitarianism is to reject common moral beliefs when they conflict with utilitarianism. Is this acceptable to you or not? Explain your answer.

2. A utilitarian is supposed to give moral consideration to all concerned. Who must be considered? What about nonhuman animals? How about lakes and streams?

3. Rachels claims that merit should be given moral consideration independent of utility. Do you agree?

Immanuel Kant

The Categorical Imperative

Immanuel Kant (1724–1804), a German, was one of the most important philosophers of all time. He made significant contributions to all areas of philosophy. He wrote many books; the most important ones are Critique of Pure Reason, Prolegomena to All Future Metaphysics, Critique of Practical Reason, Critique of Judgment, *and* The Foundations of the Metaphysics of Morals, *from which the reading is taken.*

Kant believes that our moral duty can be formulated in one supreme rule, the Categorical Imperative, from which all our duties can be derived. Although he says that there is just one rule, he gives different versions of it, and two of them seem to be distinct. He arrives at the supreme rule or rules by considering the nature of the good will and duty.

THE GOOD WILL

It is impossible to conceive anything at all in the world, or even out of it, which can be taken as good without qualification, except a *good will.* Intelligence, wit, judgement, and any other *talents* of the mind we may care to name, or courage, resolution, and constancy of purpose, as qualities of *temperament,* are without doubt good and desirable in many respects; but they can also be extremely bad and hurtful when the will is not good which has to make use of these gifts of nature, and which for this reason has the term '*character*' applied to its peculiar quality. It is exactly the same with *gifts of fortune.* Power, wealth, honour, even health and that complete well-being and contentment with one's state which goes by the name of '*happiness*', produce boldness, and as a consequence often over-boldness as well, unless a good will is present by which their influence on the mind—and so too the whole principle of action—may be corrected and adjusted to universal ends; not to mention that a rational and impartial spectator can never feel approval in contemplating the uninterrupted prosperity of a being graced by no touch of a pure and good will, and that consequently a good will seems to constitute the indispensable condition of our very worthiness to be happy.

Some qualities are even helpful to this good will itself and can make its task very much easier. They have none the less no inner unconditioned worth, but rather presuppose a good will which sets a limit to the esteem in which they are rightly held and

The reading is from *The Moral Law: Kant's Groundwork of the Metaphysic of Morals*, trans. H. J. Paton (New York, NY: Barnes & Noble, Inc., 1948), pp. 61–62, 64–66, 69–70, 88–91, 95–96.

does not permit us to regard them as absolutely good. Moderation in affections and passions, self-control, and sober reflexion are not only good in many respects: they may even seem to constitute part of the *inner* worth of a person. Yet they are far from being properly described as good without qualification (however unconditionally they have been commended by the ancients). For without the principles of a good will they may become exceedingly bad; and the very coolness of a scoundrel makes him, not merely more dangerous, but also immediately more abominable in our eyes than we should have taken him to be without it.

THE GOOD WILL AND ITS RESULTS

A good will is not good because of what it effects or accomplishes—because of its fitness for attaining some proposed end: it is good through its willing alone—that is, good in itself. Considered in itself it is to be esteemed beyond comparison as far higher than anything it could ever bring about merely in order to favour some inclination or, if you like, the sum total of inclinations. Even if, by some special disfavour of destiny or by the niggardly endowment of step-motherly nature, this will is entirely lacking in power to carry out its intentions; if by its utmost effort it still accomplishes nothing, and only good will is left (not, admittedly, as a mere wish, but as the straining of every means so far as they are in our control); even then it would still shine like a jewel for its own sake as something which has its full value in itself. Its usefulness or fruitlessness can neither add to, nor subtract from, this value. Its usefulness would be merely, as it were, the setting which enables us to handle it better in our ordinary dealings or to attract the attention of those not yet sufficiently expert, but not to commend it to experts or to determine its value. . . .

THE GOOD WILL AND DUTY

We have now to elucidate the concept of a will estimable in itself and good apart from any further end. This concept, which is already present in a sound natural understanding and requires not so much to be taught as merely to be clarified, always holds the highest place in estimating the total worth of our actions and constitutes the condition of all the rest. We will therefore take up the concept of *duty,* which includes that of a good will, exposed, however, to certain subjective limitations and obstacles. These, so far from hiding a good will or disguising it, rather bring it out by contrast and make it shine forth more brightly.

THE MOTIVE OF DUTY

I will here pass over all actions already recognized as contrary to duty, however useful they may be with a view to this or that end; for about these the question does not even arise whether they could have been done *for the sake of duty* inasmuch as they are directly opposed to it. I will also set aside actions which in fact accord with duty, yet for which men have *no immediate inclination,* but perform them because impelled to do so by some other inclination. For there it is easy to decide whether the action which accords with duty has been done *from duty* or from some purpose of self-interest. This distinction is far more difficult to perceive when the action accords with duty and the subject has in addition an *immediate* inclination to the action. For example, it certainly accords with duty that a grocer should not overcharge his inexperienced customer; and where there is much competition a sensible shopkeeper refrains from so doing and keeps to a fixed and general price for everybody so that a child can buy from him just as well as anyone else. Thus people are served *honestly;* but this is not nearly enough to justify us in believing that the shopkeeper has acted in this way from duty or from principles of fair dealing; his interests required him to do so. We cannot assume him to have in addition an immediate inclination towards his customers, leading him, as it were out of love, to give no man preference over another in the matter of price. Thus the action was done neither from duty nor from immediate inclination, but solely from purposes of self-interest.

On the other hand, to preserve one's life is a duty, and besides this every one has also an immediate inclination to do so. But on account of this the often anxious precautions taken by the greater part of mankind for this purpose have no inner worth, and the maxim of their action is without moral content. They do protect their lives *in conformity with duty,* but not *from the motive of duty.* When on the contrary, disappointments and hopeless misery have quite taken away the taste for life; when a wretched man, strong in soul and more angered at his fate than faint-hearted or cast down, longs for death and still preserves his life without loving it—not from inclination or fear but from duty; then indeed his maxim has a moral content.

To help others where one can is a duty, and besides this there are many spirits of so sympathetic a temper that, without any further motive of vanity or self-interest, they find an inner pleasure in spreading happiness around them and can take delight in the contentment of others as their own work. Yet I maintain that in such a case an action of this kind, however right and however amiable it may be, has still no genuinely moral worth. It stands on the same footing as other inclinations—for example, the inclination for honour, which if fortunate enough to hit on something beneficial and right and consequently honourable, deserves praise and encouragement, but not esteem; for its maxim lacks moral content, namely, the performance of such actions, not from inclination, but *from duty.* Suppose then that the mind of this friend of man were overclouded by sorrows of his own which extinguished all sympathy with the fate of others, but that he still had power to help those in distress, though no longer stirred by the need of others because sufficiently occupied with his own; and suppose that, when no longer moved by any inclination, he tears himself out of this deadly insensibility and does the action without any inclination for the sake of duty alone; then for the first time his action has its genuine moral worth. Still further: if nature had implanted little sympathy in this or that man's heart; if (being in other respects an honest fellow) he were cold in temperament and indifferent to the sufferings of others—perhaps because, being endowed with the special gift of patience and robust endurance in his own sufferings, he assumed the like in others or even demanded it; if such a man (who would in truth not be the worst product of nature) were not exactly fashioned by her to be a philanthropist, would he not still find in himself a source from which he might draw a worth far higher than any that a good-natured temperament can have? Assuredly he would. It is precisely in this that the worth of character begins to show—a moral worth and beyond all comparison the highest—namely, that he does good, not from inclination, but from duty....

Thus the moral worth of an action does not depend on the result expected from it, and so too does not depend on any principle of action that needs to borrow its motive from this expected result. For all these results (agreeable states and even the promotion of happiness in others) could have been brought about by other causes as well, and consequently their production did not require the will of a rational being, in which, however, the highest and unconditioned good can alone be found. Therefore nothing but the *idea of the law* in itself, *which admittedly is present only in a rational being*—so far as it, and not an expected result, is the ground determining the will—can constitute that preeminent good which we call moral, a good which is already present in the person acting on this idea and has not to be awaited merely from the result.

THE CATEGORICAL IMPERATIVE

But what kind of law can this be the thought of which, even without regard to the results expected from it, has to determine the will if this is to be called good absolutely and without qualification? Since I have robbed the will of every inducement that might arise for it as a consequence of obeying any particular law, nothing is left but the conformity of actions to universal law as such, and this alone must serve the will as its principle. That is to say, I ought never to act except in such a way *that I can also will that my maxim should become a universal law.* Here bare conformity to universal law as such (without having as its base any law prescribing particular actions) is what serves the will as its principle, and must so serve it if duty is not to be everywhere an empty delusion and a chimerical concept. The ordinary reason of mankind also agrees with this completely in its practical judgements and always has the aforesaid principle before its eyes. . . .

When I conceive a *hypothetical* imperative in general, I do not know beforehand what it will contain—until its condition is given. But if I conceive a *categorical* imperative, I know at once what it contains. For since besides the law this imperative contains only the necessity that our maxim [1] should conform to this law, while the law, as we have seen, contains no condition to limit it, there remains nothing over to which the maxim has to conform except the universality of a law as such; and it is this conformity alone that the imperative properly asserts to be necessary.

There is therefore only a single categorical imperative and it is this: *'Act only on that maxim through which you can at the same time will that it should become a universal law'.*

Now if all imperatives of duty can be derived from this one imperative as their principle, then even although we leave it unsettled whether what we call duty may not be an empty concept, we shall still be able to show at least what we understand by it and what the concept means. . . .

ILLUSTRATIONS

We will now enumerate a few duties, following their customary division into duties towards self and duties towards others and into perfect and imperfect duties.[2]

1. A man feels sick of life as the result of a series of misfortunes that has mounted to the point of despair, but he is still so far in possession of his reason as to ask himself whether taking his own life may not be contrary to his duty to himself. He now applies the test 'Can the maxim of my action really become a universal law of nature?' His maxim is 'From self-love I make it my principle to shorten my life if its continuance threatens more evil than it promises pleasure'. The only further question to ask is whether this principle of self-love can become a universal law of nature. It is then seen at once that a system of nature by whose law the very same feeling whose function (*Bestimmung*) is to stimulate the furtherance of life should actually destroy life would contradict itself and consequently could not subsist as a system of nature. Hence this maxim cannot possibly hold as a universal law of nature and is therefore entirely opposed to the supreme principle of all duty.

2. Another finds himself driven to borrowing money because of need. He well knows that he will not be able to pay it back; but he sees too that he will get no loan unless he gives a firm promise to pay it back within a fixed time. He is inclined to make such a promise; but he has still enough conscience to ask 'Is it not unlawful and contrary to duty to get out of difficulties in this way?' Supposing, however, he did resolve to do so, the maxim of his action would run thus: 'Whenever I believe myself short of money, I will borrow money and promise to pay it back, though I know that this will never be done'. Now this principle of self-love or personal advantage is perhaps quite compatible with my own entire future welfare; only there remains the question 'Is it right?' I therefore transform the demand of self-love into a universal law and frame my question thus: 'How would things stand if my maxim became a universal law?' I then see straight away that this maxim can never rank as a universal law of nature and be self-

consistent, but must necessarily contradict itself. For the universality of a law that every one believing himself to be in need can make any promise he pleases with the intention not to keep it would make promising, and the very purpose of promising, itself impossible, since no one would believe he was being promised anything, but would laugh at utterances of this kind as empty shams.

3. A third finds in himself a talent whose cultivation would make him a useful man for all sorts of purposes. But he sees himself in comfortable circumstances, and he prefers to give himself up to pleasure rather than to bother about increasing and improving his fortunate natural aptitudes. Yet he asks himself further 'Does my maxim of neglecting my natural gifts, besides agreeing in itself with my tendency to indulgence, agree also with what is called duty?' He then sees that a system of nature could indeed always subsist under such a universal law, although (like the South Sea Islanders) every man should let his talents rust and should be bent on devoting his life solely to idleness, indulgence, procreation, and, in a word, to enjoyment. Only he cannot possibly *will* that this should become a universal law of nature or should be implanted in us as such a law by a natural instinct. For as a rational being he necessarily wills that all his powers should be developed, since they serve him, and are given him, for all sorts of possible ends.

4. Yet a *fourth* is himself flourishing, but he sees others who have to struggle with great hardships (and whom he could easily help); and he thinks 'What does it matter to me? Let every one be as happy as Heaven wills or as he can make himself; I won't deprive him of anything; I won't even envy him; only I have no wish to contribute anything to his well-being or to his support in distress!' Now admittedly if such an attitude were a universal law of nature, mankind could get on perfectly well—better no doubt than if everybody prates about sympathy and goodwill, and even takes pains, on occasion, to practise them, but on the other hand cheats where he

can, traffics in human rights, or violates them in other ways. But although it is possible that a universal law of nature could subsist in harmony with this maxim, yet it is impossible to *will* that such a principle should hold everywhere as a law of nature. For a will which decided in this way would be in conflict with itself, since many a situation might arise in which the man needed love and sympathy from others, and in which, by such a law of nature sprung from his own will, he would rob himself of all hope of the help he wants for himself. . . .

THE FORMULA OF THE END IN ITSELF

The will is conceived as a power of determining oneself to action *in accordance with the idea of certain laws.* And such a power can be found only in rational beings. Now what serves the will as a subjective ground of its self-determination is an *end;* and this, if it is given by reason alone, must be equally valid for all rational beings. What, on the other hand, contains merely the ground of the possibility of an action whose effect is an end is called a *means* . . . .

Now I say that man, and in general every rational being, *exists* as an end in himself, *not merely as a means* for arbitrary use by this or that will: he must in all his actions, whether they are directed to himself or to other rational beings, always be viewed *at the same time as an end.* All the objects of inclination have only a conditioned value; for if there were not these inclinations and the needs grounded on them, their object would be valueless. Inclinations themselves, as sources of needs, are so far from having an absolute value to make them desirable for their own sake that it must rather be the universal wish of every rational being to be wholly free from them. Thus the value of all objects that can *be produced* by our action is always conditioned. Beings whose existence depends, not on our will, but on nature, have none the less, if they are non-rational beings, only a relative value as means and are consequently called *things*. Rational beings, on the other hand, are called *persons* because their nature already marks them out as ends in themselves—that is, as something which ought not to be used merely as a means—and consequently imposes to that extent a limit on all arbitrary treatment of them (and is an object of reverence). Persons, therefore, are not merely subjective ends whose existence as an object of our actions has a value *for us:* they are *objective ends* —that is, things whose existence is in itself an end, and indeed an end such that in its place we can put no other end to which they should serve *simply* as means; for unless this is so, nothing at all of *absolute* value would be found anywhere. But if all value were conditioned—that is, contingent—then no supreme principle could be found for reason at all.

If then there is to be a supreme practical principle and—so far as the human will is concerned—a categorical imperative, it must be such that from the idea of something which is necessarily an end for every one because it is an *end in itself* it forms an *objective* principle of the will and consequently can serve as a practical law. The ground of this principle is: *Rational nature exists as an end in itself.* This is the way in which a man necessarily conceives his own existence: it is therefore so far a *subjective* principle of human actions. But it is also the way in which every other rational being conceives his existence on the same rational ground which is valid also for me; hence it is at the same time an *objective* principle, from which, as a supreme practical ground, it must be possible to derive all laws for the will. The practical imperative will therefore be as follows: *Act in such a way that you always treat humanity, whether in your own person or in the person of any other, never simply as a means, but always at the same time as an end....*

Endnotes

1. A *maxim* is a subjective principle of action and must be distinguished from an *objective principle*—namely, a practical law. The former contains a practical rule determined by reason in accordance with the conditions of the subject (often his ignorance or again his inclinations): it is thus a principle on which the subject *acts.* A law, on the other hand, is an objective principle valid for every rational being; and it is a principle on which he *ought to act*—that is, an imperative.

2. It should be noted that I reserve my division of duties entirely for a future *Metaphysic of Morals* and that my present division is therefore put forward as arbitrary (merely for the purpose of arranging my examples). Further, I understand here by a perfect duty one which allows no exception in the interests of inclination, and so I recognize among *perfect duties,* not only outer ones, but also inner. This is contrary to the accepted usage of the schools, but I do not intend to justify it here, since for my purpose it is all one whether this point is conceded or not.

Review Questions

1. Explain Kant's account of the good will.

2. Distinguish between hypothetical and categorical imperatives.

3. State the first formulation of the Categorical Imperative (using the notion of a universal law) and explain how Kant uses this rule to derive some specific duties towards self and others.

4. State the second version of the Categorical Imperative (using the language of means and end), and explain it.

Discussion Questions

1. Are the two different versions of the Categorical Imperative just different expressions of one basic rule, or are they two different rules? Defend your view.

2. Kant claims that an action which is not done from the motive of duty has no moral worth. Do you agree or not? If not, give some counter-examples.

3. Some commentators think that the Categorical Imperative (particularly the first formulation) can be used to justify nonmoral or immoral actions. Is this a good criticism?

Onora O'Neill

A Simplified Account of Kant's Ethics

Onora O'Neill teaches philosophy at the University of Essex in Colchester, England. She is the author of Acting on Principle *and, most recently,* Faces of Hunger.

O'Neill interprets and explains the formulation of the Categorical Imperative called the Formula of the End in Itself, and then compares the Kantian and utilitarian moral theories on the value of human life.

Kant's moral theory has acquired the reputation of being forbiddingly difficult to understand and, once understood, excessively demanding in its requirements. I don't believe that this reputation has been wholly earned, and I am going to try to undermine it.... I shall try to reduce some of the difficulties.... Finally, I shall compare Kantian and utilitarian approaches and assess their strengths and weaknesses.

The main method by which I propose to avoid some of the difficulties of Kant's moral theory is by explaining only one part of the theory. This does not seem to me to be an irresponsible approach in this case. One of the things that makes Kant's moral theory hard to understand is that he gives a number of different versions of the principle that he calls the Supreme Principle of Morality, and these different versions don't look at all like one another. They also don't look at all like the utilitarians' Greatest Happiness Principle. But the Kantian principle is supposed to play a similar role in arguments about what to do.

Kant calls his Supreme Principle the *Categorical Imperative;* its various versions also

"A Simplified Account of Kant's Ethics," by Onora O'Neill from *Matters of Life and Death,* ed. Tom Regan, 1986, McGraw-Hill Publishing Company. Reprinted by permission.

have sonorous names. One is called the Formula of Universal Law; another is the Formula of the Kingdom of Ends. The one on which I shall concentrate is known as the *Formula of the End in Itself.* To understand why Kant thinks that these picturesquely named principles are equivalent to one another takes quite a lot of close and detailed analysis of Kant's philosophy. I shall avoid this and concentrate on showing the implications of this version of the Categorical Imperative.

THE FORMULA OF THE END IN ITSELF

Kant states the Formula of the End in Itself as follows:

Act in such a way that you always treat humanity, whether in your own person or in the person of any other, never simply as a means but always at the same time as an end. [1]

To understand this we need to know what it is to treat a person as a means or as an end. According to Kant, each of our acts reflects one or more *maxims.* The maxim of the act is the principle on which one sees oneself as acting. A maxim expresses a person's policy, or if he or she has no settled policy, the principle underlying the particular intention or decision on which he or she acts. Thus, a person who decides "This year I'll give 10 percent of my income to famine relief" has as a maxim the principle of tithing his or her income for famine relief. In practice, the difference between intentions and maxims is of little importance, for given any intention, we can formulate the corresponding maxim by deleting references to particular times, places, and persons. In what follows I shall take the terms 'maxim' and 'intention' as equivalent.

Whenever we act intentionally, we have at least one maxim and can, if we reflect, state what it is. (There is of course room for self-deception here—"I'm only keeping the wolf from the door" we may claim as we wolf down enough to keep ourselves overweight, or, more to the point, enough to feed someone else who hasn't enough food.)

When we want to work out whether an act we propose to do is right or wrong, according to Kant, we should look at our maxims and not at how much misery or happiness the act is likely to produce, and whether it does better at increasing happiness than other available acts. We just have to check that the act we have in mind will not use anyone as a mere means, and, if possible, that it will treat other persons as ends in themselves.

USING PERSONS AS MERE MEANS

To use someone as a *mere means* is to involve them in a scheme of action *to which they could not in principle consent*. Kant does not say that there is anything wrong about using someone as a means. Evidently we have to do so in any cooperative scheme of action. If I cash a check I use the teller as a means, without whom I could not lay my hands on the cash; the teller in turn uses me as a means to earn his or her living. But in this case, each party consents to her or his part in the transaction. Kant would say that though they use one another as means, they do not use one another as *mere* means. Each person assumes that the other has maxims of his or her own and is not just a thing or a prop to be manipulated.

But there are other situations where one person uses another in a way to which the other could not in principle consent. For example, one person may make a promise to another with every intention of breaking it. If the promise is accepted, then the person to whom it was given must be ignorant of what the promisor's intention (maxim) really is. If one knew that the promisor did not intend to do what he or she was promising, one would, after all, not accept or rely on the promise. It would be as though there had been no promise made. Successful false promising depends on deceiving the person to whom the promise is made about what one's real maxim is. And since the person who is deceived doesn't know that real max-

im, he or she can't in principle consent to his or her part in the proposed scheme of action. The person who is deceived is, as it were, a prop or a tool—a mere means—in the false promisor's scheme. A person who promises falsely treats the acceptor of the promise as a prop or a thing and not as a person. In Kant's view, it is this that makes false promising wrong.

One standard way of using others as mere means is by deceiving them. By getting someone involved in a business scheme or a criminal activity on false pretenses, or by giving a misleading account of what one is about, or by making a false promise or a fraudulent contract, one involves another in something to which he or she in principle cannot consent, since the scheme requires that he or she doesn't know what is going on. Another standard way of using others as mere means is by coercing them. If a rich or powerful person threatens a debtor with bankruptcy unless he or she joins in some scheme, then the creditor's intention is to coerce; and the debtor, if coerced, cannot consent to his or her part in the creditor's scheme. To make the example more specific: If a moneylender in an Indian village threatens not to renew a vital loan unless he is given the debtor's land, then he uses the debtor as a mere means. He coerces the debtor, who cannot truly consent to this "offer he can't refuse." (Of course the outward form of such transactions may look like ordinary commercial dealings, but we know very well that some offers and demands couched in that form are coercive.)

In Kant's view, acts that are done on maxims that require deception or coercion of others, and so cannot have the consent of those others (for consent precludes both deception and coercion), are wrong. When we act on such maxims, we treat others as mere means, as things rather than as ends in themselves. If we act on such maxims, our acts are not only wrong but unjust: such acts wrong the particular others who are deceived or coerced.

TREATING PERSONS AS ENDS IN THEMSELVES

Duties of justice are, in Kant's view (as in many others'), the most important of our duties. When we fail in these duties, we have used some other or others as mere means. But there are also cases where, though we do not use others as mere means, still we fail to use them as ends in themselves in the fullest possible way. To treat someone as an end in him or herself requires in the first place that one not use him or her as mere means, that one respect each as a rational person with his or her own maxims. But beyond that, one may also seek to foster others' plans and maxims by sharing some of their ends. To act beneficently is to seek others' happiness, therefore to intend to achieve some of the things that those others aim at with their maxims. If I want to make others happy, I will adopt maxims that not merely do not manipulate them but that foster some of their plans and activities. Beneficent acts try to achieve what others want. However, we cannot seek everything that others want; their wants are too numerous and diverse, and, of course, sometimes incompatible. It follows that beneficence has to be selective.

There is then quite a sharp distinction between the requirements of justice and of beneficence in Kantian ethics. Justice requires that we act on *no* maxims that use others as mere means. Beneficence requires that we act on *some* maxims that foster others' ends, though it is a matter for judgment and discretion which of their ends we foster. Some maxims no doubt ought not to be fostered because it would be unjust to do so. Kantians are not committed to working interminably through a list of happiness-producing and misery-reducing acts; but there are some acts whose obligatoriness utilitarians may need to debate as they try to compare total outcomes of different choices, to which Kantians are stringently bound. Kantians will claim that they have done nothing wrong if none of their acts is unjust, and that their duty is complete if in addition their life plans have in the circumstances been reasonably beneficent.

In making sure that they meet all the demands of justice, Kantians do not try to compare all available acts and see which has the best effects. They consider only the proposals for action that occur to them and check that these proposals use no other as mere means. If they do not, the act is permissible; if omitting the act would use another as mere means, the act is obligatory. Kant's theory has less scope than utilitarianism. Kantians do not claim to discover whether acts whose maxims they don't know fully are just. They may be reluctant to judge others' acts or policies that cannot be regarded as the maxim of any person or institution. They cannot rank acts in order of merit. Yet, the theory offers more precision than utilitarianism when data are scarce. One can usually tell whether one's act would use others as mere means, even when its impact on human happiness is thoroughly obscure.

THE LIMITS OF KANTIAN ETHICS: INTENTIONS AND RESULTS

Kantian ethics differs from utilitarian ethics both in its scope and in the precision with which it guides action. Every action, whether of a person or of an agency, can be assessed by utilitarian methods, provided only that information is available about all the consequences of the act. The theory has unlimited scope, but, owing to lack of data, often lacks precision. Kantian ethics has a more restricted scope. Since it assesses actions by looking at the maxims of agents, it can only assess intentional acts. This means that it is most at home in assessing individuals' acts; but it can be extended to assess acts of agencies that (like corporations and governments and student unions) have decision-making procedures. It can do nothing to assess patterns of action that reflect no intention or policy, hence it cannot assess the acts of groups lacking decision-making procedures, such as the student movement, the women's movement, or the consumer movement.

It may seem a great limitation of Kantian

ethics that it concentrates on intentions to the neglect of results. It might seem that all conscientious Kantians have to do is to make sure that they never intend to use others as mere means, and that they sometimes intend to foster other's ends. And, as we all know, good intentions sometimes lead to bad results and correspondingly, bad intentions sometimes do no harm, or even produce good. If Hardin [2] is right, the good intentions of those who feed the starving lead to dreadful results in the long run. If some traditional arguments in favor of capitalism are right, the greed and selfishness of the profit motive have produced unparalleled prosperity for many.

But such discrepancies between intentions and results are the exception and not the rule. For we cannot just *claim* that our intentions are good and do what we will. Our intentions reflect what we expect the immediate results of our action to be. Nobody credits the "intentions" of a couple who practice neither celibacy nor contraception but still insist "we never meant to have (more) children." Conception is likely (and known to be likely) in such cases. Where people's expressed intentions ignore the normal and predictable results of what they do, we infer that (if they are not amazingly ignorant) their words do not express their true intentions. The Formula of the End in Itself applies to the intentions on which one acts—not to some prettified version that one may avow. Provided this intention—the agent's real intention—uses no other as mere means, he or she does nothing unjust. If some of his or her intentions foster others' ends, then he or she is sometimes beneficent. It is therefore possible for people to test their proposals by Kantian arguments even when they lack the comprehensive causal knowledge that utilitarianism requires. Conscientious Kantians can work out whether they will be doing wrong by some act even though it blurs the implications of the theory. If we peer through the blur, we see that the utilitarian view is that lives may indeed be sacrificed for the

sake of a greater good even when the persons are not willing. There is nothing wrong with using another as a mere means provided that the end for which the person is so used is a happier result than could have been achieved any other way, taking into account the misery the means have caused. In utilitarian thought, persons are not ends in themselves. Their special moral status derives from their being means to the production of happiness. Human life has therefore a high though derivative value, and one life may be taken for the sake of greater happiness in other lives, or for ending of misery in that life. Nor is there any deep difference between ending a life for the sake of others' happiness by not helping (e.g., by triaging) and doing so by harming. Because the distinction between justice and beneficence is not sharply made within utilitarianism, it is not possible to say that triaging is a matter of not benefiting, while other interventions are a matter of injustice.

Utilitarian moral theory has then a rather paradoxical view of the value of human life. Living, conscious humans are (along with other sentient beings) necessary for the existence of everything utilitarians value. But it is not their being alive but the state of their consciousness that is of value. Hence, the best results may require certain lives to be lost—by whatever means—for the sake of the total happiness and absence of misery that can be produced.

KANT AND RESPECT FOR PERSONS

Kantians reach different conclusions about human life. Human life is valuable because humans (and conceivably other beings, e.g., angels or apes) are the bearers of rational life. Humans are able to choose and to plan. This capacity and its exercise are of such value that they ought not to be sacrificed for anything of lesser value. Therefore, no one rational or autonomous creature should be treated as mere means for the enjoyment or even the happiness of another. We may in

Kant's view justifiably—even nobly—risk or sacrifice our lives for others. For in doing so we follow our own maxim and nobody uses us as mere means. But no others may use either our lives or our bodies for a scheme that they have either coerced or deceived us into joining. For in doing so they would fail to treat us as rational beings; they would use us as mere means and not as ends in ourselves.

It is conceivable that a society of Kantians, all of whom took pains to use no other as mere means, would end up with less happiness or with fewer persons alive than would some societies of complying utilitarians. For since the Kantians would be strictly bound only to justice, they might without wrongdoing be quite selective in their beneficence and fail to maximize either survival rates or happiness, or even to achieve as much of either as a strenuous group of utilitarians, who they know that their foresight is limited and that they may cause some harm or fail to cause some benefit. But they will not cause harms that they can foresee without this being reflected in their intentions.

UTILITARIANISM AND RESPECT FOR LIFE

From the differing implications that Kantian and utilitarian moral theories have for our actions towards those who do or may suffer famine, we can discover two sharply contrasting views of the value of human life. Utilitarians value happiness and the absence or reduction of misery. As a utilitarian one ought (if conscientious) to devote one's life to achieving the best possible balance of happiness over misery. If one's life plan remains in doubt, this will be because the means to this end are often unclear. But whenever the causal tendency of acts is clear, utilitarians will be able to discern the acts they should successively do in order to improve the world's balance of happiness over unhappiness.

This task is not one for the faint-hearted. First, it is dauntingly long, indeed interminable. Second, it may at times require the sacrifice of happiness, and even of lives, for the sake of a greater happiness. Such sacrifice may be morally required not only when the person whose happiness or even whose life is at stake volunteers to make the sacrifice. It may be necessary to sacrifice some lives for the sake of others. As our control over the means of ending and preserving human life has increased, analogous dilemmas have arisen in many areas for utilitarians. Should life be preserved at the cost of pain when modern medicine makes this possible? Should life be preserved without hope of consciousness? Should triage policies, because they may maximize the number of survivors, be used to determine who should be left to starve? Should population growth be fostered wherever it will increase the total of human happiness—or on some views so long as average happiness is not reduced? All these questions can be fitted into utilitarian frameworks and answered *if* we have the relevant information. And sometimes the answer will be that human happiness demands the sacrifice of lives, including the sacrifice of unwilling lives. Further, for most utilitarians, it makes no difference if the unwilling sacrifices involve acts of injustice to those whose lives are to be lost. It might, for example, prove necessary for maximal happiness that some persons have their allotted rations, or their hard-earned income, diverted for others' benefit. Or it might turn out that some generations must sacrifice comforts or liberties and even lives to rear "the fabric of felicity" for their successors. Utilitarians do not deny these possibilities, though the imprecision of our knowledge of consequences often somehow make the right calculations. On the other hand, nobody will have been made an instrument of others' survival or happiness in the society of complying Kantians.

Endnotes

1. [See the end of the reading from Kant—Ed.]
2. [See the reading by Garett Hardin in Chapter 5—Ed.]

1. According to O'Neill, what is involved in using someone as a mere means? Give some examples. Why is this wrong?

2. On O'Neill's interpretation, how does one treat people as ends in themselves? Give examples.

3. Distinguish between the requirements of justice and beneficence.

4. According to O'Neill, how does Kantian ethics differ from utilitarian ethics?

1. Does Kantian ethics require us to help strangers or people in other countries? Why or why not?

2. As O'Neill explains it, Kant's view is that a life is valuable because it is rational. This seems to imply that the life of a fetus or a comatose person is not valuable because it is not rational—it involves no choosing or planning. Do you agree with this or not?

3. Which theory is more acceptable to you, utilitarianism or Kant's theory? Why?

Ronald Dworkin

Taking Rights Seriously

Ronald Dworkin is University Professor of Jurisprudence, Oxford University, and Professor of Law, New York University. He is the author of A Matter of Principle, Law's Empire, *and* Taking Rights Seriously, *from which our reading is taken.*

On Dworkin's view, if a people have a right to do something, then it is wrong to interfere with them. For example, if citizens have a right to free speech, then it is wrong for the government to interfere with the exercise of this right (unless this is necessary to protect other rights). This notion of rights, Dworkin believes, rests on the Kantian idea of treating people with dignity as members of the moral community, and also on the idea of political equality.

THE RIGHTS OF CITIZENS

The language of rights now dominates political debate in the United States. Does the Government respect the moral and political rights of its citizens? Or does the Govern-

ment's foreign policy, or its race policy, fly in the face of these rights? Do the minorities whose rights have been violated have the right to violate the law in return? Or does the silent majority itself have rights, including the right that those who break the law be punished? It is not surprising that these questions are now prominent. The concept of rights, and particularly the concept of rights against the Government, has its most natural use when a political society is divided, and appeals to co-operation or a common goal are pointless.

The debate does not include the issue of whether citizens have *some* moral rights against their Government. It seems accepted on all sides that they do. Conventional lawyers and politicians take it as a point of pride that our legal system recognizes, for example, individual rights of free speech, equality, and due process. They base their claim that our law deserves respect, at least in part, on that fact, for they would not claim that totalitarian systems deserve the same loyalty.

Some philosophers, of course, reject the idea that citizens have rights apart from what the law happens to give them. Bentham thought that the idea of moral rights was 'nonsense on stilts'. But that view has never been part of our orthodox political theory, and politicians of both parties appeal to the rights of the people to justify a great part of what they want to do. I shall not be concerned, in this essay, to defend the thesis that citizens have moral rights against their governments; I want instead to explore the implications of that thesis for those, including the present United States Government, who profess to accept it.

It is much in dispute, of course, what *particular* rights citizens have. Does the acknowledged right to free speech, for example, include the right to participate in nuisance demonstrations? In practice the Government will have the last word on what an individual's rights are, because its police will do what its officials and courts say. But that does not mean that the Government's view is necessarily the correct view; anyone who thinks it does must believe that men and women have only such moral rights as Government chooses to grant, which means that they have no moral rights at all.

All this is sometimes obscured in the United States by the constitutional system. The American Constitution provides a set of individual *legal* rights in the First Amendment, and in the due process, equal protection, and similar clauses. Under present legal practice the Supreme Court has the power to declare an act of Congress or of a state legislature void if the Court finds that the act offends these provisions. This practice has led some commentators to suppose that individual moral rights are fully protected by this system, but that is hardly so, nor could it be so.

The Constitution fuses legal and moral issues, by making the validity of a law depend on the answer to complex moral problems, like the problem of whether a particular statute respects the inherent equality of all men. This fusion has important consequences for the debates about civil disobedience; .... But it leaves open two prominent questions. It does not tell us whether the Constitution, even properly interpreted, recognizes all the moral rights that citizens have, and it does not tell us whether, as many suppose, citizens would have a duty to obey the law even if it

did invade their moral rights....

Even if the Constitution were perfect, of course, and the majority left it alone, it would not follow that the Supreme Court could guarantee the individual rights of citizens. A Supreme Court decision is still a legal decision, and it must take into account precedent and institutional considerations like relations between the Court and Congress, as well as morality. And no judicial decision is necessarily the right decision. Judges stand for different positions on controversial issues of law and morals and, as the fights over Nixon's Supreme Court nominations showed, a President is entitled to appoint judges of his own persuasion, provided that they are honest and capable.

So, though the constitutional system adds something to the protection of moral rights against the Government, it falls far short of guaranteeing these rights, or even establishing what they are....

RIGHTS AND THE RIGHT TO BREAK THE LAW

... In most cases when we say that someone has 'right' to do something, we imply that it would be wrong to interfere with his doing it, or at least that some special grounds are needed for justifying any interference. I use this strong sense of right when I say that you have the right to spend your money gambling, if you wish, though you ought to spend it in a more worthwhile way. I mean that it would be wrong for anyone to interfere with you even though you propose to spend your money in a way that I think is wrong.

There is a clear difference between saying that someone has a right to do something in this sense and saying that it is the 'right' thing for him to do, or that he does no 'wrong' in doing it. Someone may have the right to do something that is the wrong thing for him to do, as might be the case with gambling. Conversely, something may be the right thing for him to do and yet he may have no right to do it, in the sense that it would not be wrong for someone to interfere with his trying. If our army captures an enemy soldier, we might say that the right thing for him to do is to try to escape, but it would not follow that it is wrong for us to try to stop him. . . .

These distinctions enable us to see an ambiguity in the orthodox question: Does a man ever have a right to break the law? Does that question mean to ask whether he ever has a right to break the law in the strong sense, so that the Government would do wrong to stop him, by arresting and prosecuting him? Or does it mean to ask whether he ever does the right thing to break the law, so that we should all respect him even though the Government should jail him? . . .

Conservatives and liberals do agree that sometimes a man does not do the wrong thing to break a law, when his conscience so requires. They disagree, when they do, over the different issue of what the State's response should be. Both parties do think that sometimes the State should prosecute. But this is not inconsistent with the proposition that the man prosecuted did the right thing in breaking the law. . . .

I said that in the United States citizens are supposed to have certain fundamental rights against their Government, certain moral rights made into legal rights by the Constitution. If this idea is significant, and worth bragging about, then these rights must be rights in the strong sense I just described. The claim that citizens have a right to free speech must imply that it would be wrong for the Government to stop them from speaking, even when the Government believes that what they will say will cause more harm than good. The claim cannot mean, on the prisoner-of-war analogy, only that citizens do no wrong in speaking their minds, though the Government reserves the right to prevent them from doing so.

This is a crucial point, and I want to labour it. Of course a responsible government must be ready to justify anything it does, particularly when it limits the liberty of its citizens. But normally it is a sufficient justification, even for an act that limits liberty, that the act is calculated to increase what the philosophers call general utility—that it is calculated to produce more over-all benefit than harm. So, though the New York City government needs a justification for forbidding motorists to drive up Lexington Avenue, it is sufficient justification if the proper officials believe, on sound evidence, that the gain to the many will outweigh the inconvenience to the few. When individual citizens are said to have rights against the Government, however, like the right of free speech, that must mean that this sort of justification is not enough. Otherwise the claim would not argue that individuals have special protection against the law when their rights are in play, and that is just the point of the claim.

Not all legal rights, or even Constitutional rights, represent moral rights against the Government. I now have the legal right to drive either way on Fifty-seventh Street, but the Government would do no wrong to make that street one-way if it thought it in the general interest to do so. I have a Constitutional right to vote for a congressman every two years, but the national and state governments would do no wrong if, following the amendment procedure, they made a congressman's term four years instead of two, again on the basis of a judgment that this would be for the general good.

But those Constitutional rights that we call fundamental like the right of free speech, are supposed to represent rights against the Government in the strong sense; that is the point of the boast that our legal system respects the fundamental rights of the citizen. If citizens have a moral right of free speech, then governments would do wrong to repeal the First Amendment that guarantees it, even if they were persuaded that the majority would be better off if speech were curtailed.

I must not overstate the point. Someone who claims that citizens have a right against the Government need not go so far as to say that the State is *never* justified in overriding that right. He might say, for example, that although citizens have a right to free speech, the Government may override that right when necessary to protect the rights of others, or to prevent a catastrophe, or even to obtain a clear and major public benefit (though if he acknowledged this last as a possible justification he would be treating the right in question as not among the most important or fundamental). What he cannot do is to say that the Government is justified in overriding a right on the minimal grounds that would be sufficient if no such right existed. He cannot say that the Government is entitled to act on no more than a judgment that its act is likely to produce, overall, a benefit to the community. That admission would make his claim of a right pointless, and would show him to be using some sense of 'right' other than the strong sense necessary to give his claim the political importance it is normally taken to have. . . .

I said that any society that claims to recognize rights at all must abandon the notion of a general duty to obey the law that holds in all cases. This is important, because it shows that there are no short cuts to meeting a citizen's claim to right. If a citizen argues that he has a moral right not to serve in the Army, or to protest in a way he finds effective, then an official who wants to answer him, and not simply bludgeon him into obedience, must respond to the particular point he makes, and cannot point to the draft law or a Supreme Court decision as having even special, let alone decisive, weight. Sometimes an official who considers the citizen's moral arguments in good faith will be persuaded that the citizen's claim is plausible, or even right. It does not follow, however, that he will always be persuaded or that he always should be.

I must emphasize that all these propositions concern the strong sense of right, and they therefore leave open important questions about the right thing to do. If a man believes he has the right to break the law, he must then ask whether he does the right thing to exercise that right. He must remember that reasonable men can differ about whether he has a right against the Govern-

ment, and therefore the right to break the law, that he thinks he has; and therefore that reasonable men can oppose him in good faith. He must take into account the various consequences his acts will have, whether they involve violence, and such other considerations as the context makes relevant; he must not go beyond the rights he can in good faith claim, to acts that violate the rights of others. . . .

CONTROVERSIAL RIGHTS

The argument so far has been hypothetical: if a man has a particular moral right against the Government, that right survives contrary legislation or adjudication. But this does not tell us what rights he has, and it is notorious that reasonable men disagree about that. There is wide agreement on certain clearcut cases; almost everyone who believes in rights at all would admit, for example, that a man has a moral right to speak his mind in a non-provocative way on matters of political concern, and that this is an important right that the State must go to great pains to protect. But there is great controversy as to the limits of such paradigm rights, and the so-called 'anti-riot' law involved in the famous Chicago Seven trial of the last decade is a case in point.

The defendants were accused of conspiring to cross state lines with the intention of causing a riot. This charge is vague—perhaps unconstitutionally vague—but the law apparently defines as criminal emotional speeches which argue that violence is justified in order to secure political equality. Does the right of free speech protect this sort of speech? That, of course, is a legal issue, because it invokes the free-speech clause of the First Amendment of the Constitution. But it is also a moral issue, because, as I said, we must treat the First Amendment as an attempt to protect a moral right. It is part of the job of governing to 'define' moral rights through statutes and judicial decisions, that is, to declare officially the extent that moral rights will be taken to have in law. Congress faced this task in voting on the anti-riot bill, and the Supreme Court has faced it in countless cases. How should the different departments of government go about defining moral rights?

They should begin with a sense that whatever they decide might be wrong. History and their descendants may judge that they acted unjustly when they thought they were right. If they take their duty seriously, they must try to limit their mistakes, and they must therefore try to discover where the dangers of mistake lie.

They might choose one of two very different models for this purpose. The first model recommends striking a balance between the rights of the individual and the demands of society at large. If the Government *infringes* on a moral right (for example, by defining the right of free speech more narrowly than justice requires), then it has done the individual a wrong. On the other hand, if the Government *inflates* a right (by defining it more broadly than justice requires) then it cheats society of some general benefit, like safe streets, that there is no reason it should not have. So a mistake on one side is as serious as a mistake on the other. The course of government is to steer to the middle, to balance the general good and personal rights, giving to each its due....

The first model, described in this way, has great plausibility, and most laymen and lawyers, I think, would respond to it warmly. The metaphor of balancing the public interest against personal claims is established in our political and judicial rhetoric, and this metaphor gives the model both familiarity and appeal. Nevertheless, the first model is a false one, certainly in the case of rights generally regarded as important, and the metaphor is the heart of its error.

The institution of rights against the Government is not a gift of God, or an ancient ritual, or a national sport. It is a complex and troublesome practice that makes the Government's job of securing the general benefit more difficult and more expensive, and it would be a frivolous and wrongful practice unless it served some point. Anyone who professes to take rights seriously, and who praises our Government for respecting them, must have some sense of what that point is. He must accept, at the minimum, one or both of two important ideas. The first is the vague but powerful idea of human dignity. This idea, associated with Kant, but defended by philosophers of different schools, supposes that there are ways of treating a man that are inconsistent with recognizing him as a full member of the human community, and holds that such treatment is profoundly unjust.

The second is the more familiar idea of political equality. This supposes that the weaker members of a political community are entitled to the same concern and respect of their government as the more powerful members have secured for themselves, so that if some men have freedom of decision whatever the effect on the general good, then all men must have the same freedom. I do not want to defend or elaborate these ideas here, but only to insist that anyone who claims that citizens have rights must accept ideas very close to these.[1]

It makes sense to say that a man has a fundamental right against the Government, in the strong sense, like free speech, if that right is necessary to protect his dignity, or his standing as equally entitled to concern and respect, or some other personal value of like consequence. It does not make sense otherwise.

So if rights make sense at all, then the invasion of a relatively important right must be a very serious matter. It means treating a man as less than a man, or as less worthy of concern than other men. The institution of rights rests on the conviction that this is a grave injustice, and that it is worth paying the incremental cost in social policy or efficiency that is necessary to prevent it. But then it must be wrong to say that inflating rights is as serious as invading them. If the Government errs on the side of the individual, then it simply pays a little more in social efficiency than it has to pay; it pays a little more, that is, of the same coin that it has already decided must be spent. But if it errs against the individual it inflicts an insult upon him that, on its own reckoning, it is worth a great deal of that coin to avoid. . . .

It cannot be an argument for curtailing a right, once granted, simply that society would pay a further price for extending it. There must be something special about that further cost, or there must be some other feature of the case, that makes it sensible to say that although great social cost is warranted to protect the original right, this particular cost is not necessary. Otherwise, the Government's failure to extend the right will show that its recognition of the right in the original case is a sham, a promise that it intends to keep only until that becomes inconvenient.

How can we show that a particular cost is not worth paying without taking back the initial recognition of a right? I can think of only three sorts of grounds that can consistently be used to limit the definition of a particular right. First, the Government might show that the values protected by the original right are not really at stake in the marginal case, or are at stake only in some attenuated form. Second, it might show that if the right is defined to include the marginal case, then some competing right, in the strong sense I described earlier, would be abridged. Third, it might show that if the right were so defined, then the cost to society would not be simply incremental, but would be of a degree far beyond the cost paid to grant the original right, a degree great enough to justify whatever assault on dignity or equality might be involved. . . .

But what of the individual rights of those who will be destroyed by a riot, of the passerby who will be killed by a sniper's bullet or the shopkeeper who will be ruined by looting? To put the issue in this way, as a question of competing rights, suggests a principle that would undercut the effect of uncertainty. Shall we say that some rights to protection are so important that the Government is justified in doing all it can to maintain them?

Shall we therefore say that the Government may abridge the rights of others to act when their acts might simply increase the risk, by however slight or speculative a margin, that some person's right to life or property will be violated?

Some such principle is relied on by those who oppose the Supreme Court's recent liberal rulings on police procedure. These rulings increase the chance that a guilty man will go free, and therefore marginally increase the risk that any particular member of the community will be murdered, raped, or robbed. Some critics believe that the Court's decisions must therefore be wrong.

But no society that purports to recognize a variety of rights, on the ground that a man's dignity or equality may be invaded in a variety of ways, can accept such a principle. If forcing a man to testify against himself, or forbidding him to speak, does the damage that the rights against self-incrimination and the right of free speech assume, then it would be contemptuous for the State to tell a man that he must suffer this damage against the possibility that other men's risk of loss may be marginally reduced. If rights make sense, then the degrees of their importance cannot be so different that some count not at all when others are mentioned.

Of course the Government may discriminate and may stop a man from exercising his right to speak when there is a clear and substantial risk that his speech will do great damage to the person or property of others, and no other means of preventing this are at hand, as in the case of the man shouting 'Fire!' in a theater. But we must reject the suggested principle that the Government can simply ignore rights to speak when life and property are in question. So long as the impact of speech on these other rights remains speculative and marginal, it must look elsewhere for levers to pull.

WHY TAKE RIGHTS SERIOUSLY?

I said at the beginning of this essay that I wanted to show what a government must do that professes to recognize individual rights. It must dispense with the claim that citizens never have a right to break its law, and it must not define citizens' rights so that these are cut off for supposed reasons of the general good. Any Government's harsh treatment of civil disobedience, or campaign against vocal protest, may therefore be thought to count against its sincerity.

One might well ask, however, whether it is wise to take rights all that seriously after all. America's genius, at least in her own legend, lies in not taking any abstract doctrine to its logical extreme. It may be time to ignore abstractions, and concentrate instead on giving the majority of our citizens a new sense of their Government's concern for their welfare, and of their title to rule.

That, in any event, is what former Vice-President Agnew seemed to believe. In a policy statement on the issue of 'weirdos' and social misfits, he said that the liberals' concern for individual rights was a headwind blowing in the face of the ship of state. That is a poor metaphor, but the philosophical point it expresses is very well taken. He recognized, as many liberals do not, that the majority cannot travel as fast or as far as it would like if it recognizes the rights of individuals to do what, in the majority's terms, is the wrong thing to do.

Spiro Agnew supposed that rights are divisive, and that national unity and a new respect for law may be developed by taking them more skeptically. But he is wrong. America will continue to be divided by its social and foreign policy, and if the economy grows weaker again the divisions will become more bitter. If we want our laws and our legal institutions to provide the ground rules within which these issues will be contested then these ground rules must not be the conqueror's law that the dominant class imposes on the weaker, as Marx supposed the law of a capitalist society must be. The bulk of the law—that part which defines and implements social, economic, and foreign policy—cannot be neutral. It must state, in its greatest part, the majority's view of the common good. The institution of rights is therefore crucial, because it represents the majority's promise to the minorities that their dignity and equality will be respected. When the divisions among the groups are most violent, then this gesture, if law is to work, must be most sincere.

The institution requires an act of faith on the part of the minorities, because the scope of their rights will be controversial whenever they are important, and because the officers of the majority will act on their own notions of what these rights really are. Of course these officials will disagree with many of the claims that a minority makes. That makes it all the more important that they take their decisions gravely. They must show that they understand what rights are, and they must not cheat on the full implications of the doctrine. The Government will not re-establish respect for law without giving the law some claim to respect. It cannot do that if it neglects the one feature that distinguishes law from ordered brutality. If the Government does not take rights seriously, then it does not take law seriously either.

Endnotes

1. He need not consider these ideas to be axiomatic. He may, that is, have reasons for insisting that dignity or equality are important values, and these reasons may be utilitarian. He may believe, for example, that the general good will be advanced, *in the long run,* only if we treat indignity or inequality as very great injustices, and never allow our *opinions* about the general good to justify them. I do not know of any good arguments for or against this sort of 'institutional' utilitarianism, but it is consistent with my point, because it argues that we must treat violations of dignity and equality as special moral crimes, beyond the reach of ordinary utilitarian justification.

Review Questions

1. What does Dworkin mean by right in the strong sense? What rights in this sense are protected by the U.S. Constitution?

2. Distinguish between legal and moral rights. Give some examples of legal rights that are not moral rights, and moral rights that are not legal rights.

3. What are the two models of how a government might define the rights of its citizens? Which does Dworkin find more attractive?

4. According to Dworkin, what two important ideas are behind the institution of rights?

Discussion Questions

1. Does a person have a right to break the law?

Why or why not?

2. Are rights in the strong sense compatible with Mill's utilitarianism? (See the footnote about institutional utilitarianism.)

3. Do you think that Kant would accept rights in the strong sense or not?

John Rawls
A Theory of Justice

John Rawls is Professor of Philosophy at Harvard University. Our reading is taken from his well-known book A Theory of Justice.

Rawls' theory states that there are two principles of justice: The first principle involves equal basic liberties, and the second principle concerns the arrangement of social and economic inequalities. According to Rawls' theory, these are the principles that free and rational persons would accept in a hypothetical original position where there is a veil of ignorance hiding from the contractors all the particular facts about themselves.

THE MAIN IDEA OF THE THEORY OF JUSTICE

My aim is to present a conception of justice which generalizes and carries to a higher level of abstraction the familiar **theory of the social contract** as found, say, in Locke, Rousseau, and Kant.[1] In order to do this we are not to think of the original contract as one to enter a particular society or to set up a particular form of government. Rather, the guiding idea is that the principles of justice for the

Reprinted by permission of the publishers from *A Theory of Justice* by John Rawls, Cambridge, Mass.: The Belnap Press of Harvard University Press, © 1971 by the President and Fellows of Harvard College.

basic structure of society are the object of the original agreement. They are the principles that free and rational persons concerned to further their own interests would accept in an initial position of equality as defining the fundamental terms of their association. These principles are to regulate all further agreements; they specify the kinds of social cooperation that can be entered into and the forms of government that can be established. This way of regarding the principles of justice I shall call justice as fairness.

Thus we are to imagine that those who engage in social cooperation choose together, in one joint act, the principles which are to assign basic rights and duties and to determine the division of social benefits. Men are to decide in advance how they are to regulate their claims against one another and what is to be the foundation charter of their society. Just as each person must decide by rational reflection what constitutes his good, that is, the system of ends which it is rational for him to pursue, so a group of persons must decide once and for all what is to count among them as just and unjust. The choice which rational men would make in this hypothetical situation of equal liberty, assuming for the present that this choice problem has a solution, determines the principles of justice.

In justice as fairness the original position of equality corresponds to the state of nature in the traditional theory of the social contract. This original position is not, of course, thought of as an actual historical state of affairs, much less as a primitive condition of culture. It is understood as a purely hypothetical situation characterized so as to lead to a certain conception of justice.[2] Among the essential features of this situation is that no one knows his place in society, his class position or social status, nor does any one know his fortune in the distribution of natural assets and abilities, his intelligence, strength, and the like. I shall even assume that the parties do not know their conceptions of the good or their special psychological propensities. The principles of justice are chosen behind a veil of ignorance. This ensures that no one is advantaged or disadvantaged in the choice of principles by the outcome of natural chance or the contingency of social circumstances. Since all are similarly situated and no one is able to design principles to favor his particular condition, the principles of justice are the result of a fair agreement or bargain. For given the circumstances of the original position, the symmetry of everyone's relations to each other, this initial situation is fair between individuals as moral persons, that is, as rational beings with their own ends and capable, I shall assume, of a sense of justice. The original position is, one might say, the appropriate initial status quo, and thus the fundamental agreements reached in it are fair. This explains the propriety of the name "justice as fairness": it conveys the idea that the principles of justice are agreed to in an initial situation that is fair. The name does not mean that the concepts of justice and fairness are the same, any more than the phrase "poetry as metaphor" means that the concepts of poetry and metaphor are the same.

Justice as fairness begins, as I have said, with one of the most general of all choices which persons might make together, namely, with the choice of the first principles of a conception of justice which is to regulate all subsequent criticism and reform of institutions. Then, having chosen a conception of justice, we can suppose that they are to choose a constitution and a legislature to en-act laws, and so on, all in accordance with the principles of justice initially agreed upon. Our social situation is just if it is such that by this sequence of hypothetical agreements we would have contracted into the general system of rules which defines it. Moreover, assuming that the original position does determine a set of principles (that is, that a particular conception of justice would be chosen), it will then be true that whenever social institutions satisfy these principles those engaged in them can say to one another that they are cooperating on terms to which they would agree if they were free and equal persons whose relations with respect to one another were fair. They could all view their arrangements as meeting the stipulations which they would acknowledge in an initial situation that embodies widely accepted and reasonable constraints on the choice of principles. The general recognition of this fact would provide the basis for a public acceptance of the corresponding principles of justice. No society can, of course, be a scheme of cooperation which men enter voluntarily in a literal sense; each person finds himself placed at birth in some particular position in some particular society, and the nature of this position materially affects his life prospects. Yet a society satisfying the principles of justice as fairness comes as close as a society can to being a voluntary scheme, for it meets the principles which free and equal persons would assent to under circumstances that are fair. In this sense its members are autonomous and the obligations they recognize self-imposed.

One feature of justice as fairness is to think of the parties in the initial situation as rational and mutually disinterested. This does not mean that the parties are egoists, that is, individuals with only certain kinds of interests, say in wealth, prestige, and domination. But they are conceived as not taking an interest in one another's interests. They are to presume that even their spiritual aims may be opposed, in the way that the aims of those of different religions may be opposed.

Moreover, the concept of rationality must be interpreted as far as possible in the narrow sense, standard in economic theory, of taking the most effective means to given ends. I shall modify this concept to some extent ... but one must try to avoid introducing into it any controversial ethical elements. The initial situation must be characterized by stipulations that are widely accepted.

In working out the conception of justice as fairness one main task clearly is to determine which principles of justice would be chosen in the original position. To do this we must describe this situation in some detail and formulate with care the problem of choice which it presents.... It may be observed, however, that once the principles of justice are thought of as arising from an original agreement in a situation of equality, it is an open question whether the principle of utility would be acknowledged. Offhand it hardly seems likely that persons who view themselves as equals, entitled to press their claims upon one another, would agree to a principle which may require lesser life prospects for some simply for the sake of a greater sum of advantages enjoyed by others. Since each desires to protect his interests, his capacity to advance his conception of the good, no one has a reason to acquiesce in an enduring loss for himself in order to bring about a greater net balance of satisfaction. In the absence of strong and lasting benevolent impulses, a rational man would not accept a basic structure merely because it maximized the algebraic sum of advantages irrespective of its permanent effects on his own basic rights and interests. Thus it seems that the principle of utility is incompatible with the conception of social cooperation among equals for mutual advantage. It appears to be inconsistent with the idea of reciprocity implicit in the notion of a well-ordered society. Or, at any rate, so I shall argue.

I shall maintain instead that the persons in the initial situation would choose two rather different principles: the first requires equality in the assignment of basic rights and duties, while the second holds that social and economic inequalities, for example inequalities of wealth and authority, are just only if they result in compensating benefits for everyone, and in particular for the least advantaged members of society. These principles rule out justifying institutions on the grounds that the hardships of some are offset by a greater good in the aggregate. It may be expedient but it is not just that some should have less in order that others may prosper. But there is no injustice in the greater benefits earned by a few provided that the situation of persons not so fortunate is thereby improved. The intuitive idea is that since everyone's well-being depends upon a scheme of cooperation without which no one could have a satisfactory life, the division of advantages should be such as to draw forth the willing cooperation of everyone taking part in it, including those less well situated. Yet this can be expected only if reasonable terms are proposed. The two principles mentioned seem to be a fair agreement on the basis of which those better endowed, or more fortunate in their social position, neither of which we can be said to deserve, could expect the willing cooperation of others when some workable scheme is a necessary condition of the welfare of all.[3] Once we decide to look for a conception of justice that nullifies the accidents of natural endowment and the contingencies of social circumstance as counters in quest for political and economic advantage, we are led to these principles. They express the result of leaving aside those aspects of the social world that seem arbitrary from a moral point of view.

The problem of the choice of principles, however, is extremely difficult. I do not expect the answer I shall suggest to be convincing to everyone. It is, therefore, worth noting from the outset that justice as fairness, like other contract views, consists of two parts: (1) an interpretation of the initial situation and of the problem of choice posed there, and (2) a set of principles which, it is argued, would be agreed to. One may accept the first part of the theory (or some variant thereof), but not the other, and conversely. The concept of the initial contractual situation may seem reasonable although the particular principles proposed are rejected. To be sure, I want to maintain that the most appropriate conception of this situation does lead to principles of justice contrary to utilitarianism and perfectionism, and therefore that the contract doctrine provides an alternative to these views....

A final remark. Justice as fairness is not a complete contract theory. For it is clear that the contractarian idea can be extended to the choice of more or less an entire ethical system, that is, to a system including principles for all the virtues and not only for justice. Now for the most part I shall consider only principles of justice and others closely related to them; I make no attempt to discuss the virtues in a systematic way. Obviously if justice as fairness succeeds reasonably well, a next step would be to study the more general view suggested by the name "rightness as fairness." But even this wider theory fails to embrace all moral relationships, since it would seem to include only our relations with other persons and to leave out of account how we are to conduct ourselves toward animals and the rest of nature. I do not contend that the contract notion offers a way to approach these questions which are certainly of the first importance; and I shall have to put them aside. We must recognize the limited scope of justice as fairness and of the general type of view that it exemplifies. How far its conclusions must be revised once these other matters are understood cannot be decided in advance....

TWO PRINCIPLES OF JUSTICE

I shall now state in a provisional form the two principles of justice that I believe would be chosen in the original position. In this section I wish to make only the most general comments, and therefore the first formulation of these principles is tentative. As we go on I shall run through several formulations and

approximate step by step the final statement to be given much later. I believe that doing this allows the exposition to proceed in a natural way.

The first statement of the two principles reads as follows.

First: each person is to have an equal right to the most extensive basic liberty compatible with a similar liberty for others.
Second: social and economic inequalities are to be arranged so that they are both (a) reasonably expected to be to everyone's advantage, and (b) attached to positions and offices open to all....

By way of general comment, these principles primarily apply, as I have said, to the basic structure of society. They are to govern the assignment of rights and duties and to regulate the distribution of social and economic advantages. As their formulation suggests, these principles presuppose that the social structure can be divided into two more or less distinct parts, the first principle applying to the one, the second to the other. They distinguish between those aspects of the social system that define and secure the equal liberties of citizenship and those that specify and establish social and economic inequalities. The basic liberties of citizens are, roughly speaking, political liberty (the right to vote and to be eligible for public office) together with freedom of speech and assembly; liberty of conscience and freedom of thought; freedom of the person along with the right to hold (personal) property; and freedom from arbitrary arrest and seizure as defined by the concept of the rule of law. These liberties are all required to be equal by the first principle, since citizens of a just society are to have the same basic rights.

The second principle applies, in the first approximation, to the distribution of income and wealth and to the design of organizations that make use of differences in authority and responsibility, or chains of command. While the distribution of wealth and income need not be equal, it must be to everyone's advantage, and at the same time, positions of authority and offices of command must be accessible to all. One applies the second principle by holding positions open, and then, subject to this constraint, arranges social and economic inequalities so that everyone benefits.

These principles are to be arranged in a serial order with the first principle prior to the second. This ordering means that a departure from the institutions of equal liberty required by the first principle cannot be justified by, or compensated for, by greater social and economic advantages. The distribution of wealth and income, and the hierarchies of authority, must be consistent with both the liberties of equal citizenship and equality of opportunity.

It is clear that these principles are rather specific in their content, and their acceptance rests on certain assumptions that I must eventually try to explain and justify. A theory of justice depends upon a theory of society in ways that will become evidence as we proceed. For the present, it should be observed that the two principles (and this holds for all formulations) are a special case of a more general conception of justice that can be expressed as follows.

All social values—liberty and opportunity, income and wealth, and the bases of self-respect—are to be distributed equally unless an unequal distribution of any, or all, of these values is to everyone's advantage.

Injustice, then, is simply inequalities that are not to the benefit of all. Of course, this conception is extremely vague and requires interpretation.

As a first step, suppose that the basic structure of society distributes certain primary goods, that is, things that every rational man is presumed to want. These goods normally have a use whatever a person's rational plan of life. For simplicity, assume that the chief primary goods at the disposition of society are rights and liberties, powers and opportunities, income and wealth. ... These are the social primary goods. Other primary goods such as health and vigor, intelligence and imagination, are natural goods; although their possession is influenced by the basic structure, they are not so directly under its control. Imagine, then, a hypothetical initial arrangement in which all the social primary goods are equally distributed: everyone has similar rights and duties, and income and wealth are evenly shared. This state of affairs provides a benchmark for judging improvements. If certain inequalities of wealth and organizational powers would make everyone better off than in this hypothetical starting situation, then they accord with the general conception.

Now it is possible, at least theoretically, that by giving up some of their fundamental liberties men are sufficiently compensated by the resulting social and economic gains. The general conception of justice imposes no restrictions on what sort of inequalities are permissible; it only requires that everyone's position be improved. We need not suppose anything so drastic as consenting to a condition of slavery. Imagine instead that men forego certain political rights when the economic returns are significant and their capacity to influence the course of policy by the exercise of these rights would be marginal in any case. It is this kind of exchange which the two principles as stated rule out; being arranged in serial order they do not permit exchanges between basic liberties and economic and social gains. The serial ordering of principles expresses an underlying preference among primary social goods. When this preference is rational so likewise is the choice of these principles in this order.

In developing justice as fairness I shall, for the most part, leave aside the general conception of justice and examine instead the special case of the two principles in serial order. The advantage of this procedure is that from the first the matter of priorities is recognized and an effort made to find principles to deal with it. One is led to attend throughout to the conditions under which the acknowledgment of the absolute weight of liberty with respect to social and economic advantages, as defined by the lexical order of the two principles, would be reasonable. Offhand, this ranking appears extreme and too special a case to be of much interest; but there is more justification for it than would appear at first sight. Or at any rate, so I shall maintain.... Furthermore, the distinction between fundamental rights and liberties and economic and social benefits marks a difference among primary social goods that one should try to exploit. It suggests an important division in the social system. Of course, the distinctions drawn and the ordering proposed are bound to be at best only approximations. There are surely circumstances in which they fail. But it is essential to depict clearly the main lines of a reasonable conception of justice; and under many conditions anyway, the two principles in serial order may serve well enough. When necessary we can fall back on the more general conception.

The fact that the two principles apply to institutions has certain consequences. Several points illustrate this. First of all, the rights and liberties referred to by these principles are those which are defined by the public rules of the basic structure. Whether men are free is determined by the rights and duties established by the major institutions of society. Liberty is a certain pattern of social forms. The first principle simply requires that certain sorts of rules, those defining basic liberties, apply to everyone equally and that they allow the most extensive liberty compatible with a like liberty for all. The only reason for circumscribing the rights defining liberty and making men's freedom less extensive than it might otherwise be is that these equal rights as institutionally defined would interfere with one another.

Another thing to bear in mind is that when principles mention persons, or require that everyone gain from an inequality, the reference is to representative persons holding the various social positions, or offices, or whatever, established by the basic structure. Thus in applying the second principle I assume that it is possible to assign an expecta-tion of well-being to representative individuals holding these positions. This expectation indicates their life prospects as viewed from their social station. In general, the expectations of representative persons depend upon the distribution of rights and duties throughout the basic structure. When this changes, expectations change. I assume, then, that expectations are connected: by raising the prospects of the representative man in one position we presumably increase or decrease the prospects of representative men in other positions. Since it applies to institutional forms, the second principle (or rather the first part of it) refers to the expectations of representative individuals. As I shall discuss below, neither principle applies to distributions of particular goods to particular individuals who may be identified by their proper names. The situation where someone is considering how to allocate certain commodities to needy persons who are known to him is not within the scope of the principles. They are meant to regulate basic institutional arrangements. We must not assume that there is much similarity from the standpoint of justice between an administrative allotment of goods to specific persons and the appropriate design of society. Our common sense intuitions for the former may be a poor guide to the latter.

Now the second principle insists that each person benefit from permissible inequalities in the basic structure. This means that it must be reasonable for each relevant representative man defined by this structure, when he views it as a going concern, to prefer his prospects with the inequality to his prospects without it. One is not allowed to justify differences in income or organizational powers on the ground that the disadvantages of those in one position are outweighed by the greater advantages of those in another. Much less can infringements of liberty be counterbalanced in this way. Applied to the basic structure, the principle of utility would have us maximize the sum of expectations of representative men (weighted by the number of persons they represent, on the classical view);

and this would permit us to compensate for the losses of some by the gains of others. Instead, the two principles require that everyone benefit from economic and social inequalities. It is obvious, however, that there are indefinitely many ways in which all may be advantaged when the initial arrangement of equality is taken as a benchmark. How then are we to choose among these possibilities? The principles must be specified so that they yield a determinate conclusion. I now turn to this problem. . . .

Endnotes

1. As the text suggests, I shall regard Locke's *Second Treatise of Government,* Rousseau's *The Social Contract,* and Kant's ethical works beginning with *The Foundations of the Metaphysics of Morals* as definitive of the contract tradition. For all of its greatness, Hobbes's *Leviathan* raises special problems. A general historical survey is provided by J.W. Gough, *The Social Contract,* 2nd ed. (Oxford, The Clarendon Press, 1957), and Otto Gierke, *Natural Law and the Theory of Society,* trans. with an introduction by Ernest Barker (Cambridge, The University Press, 1934). A presentation of the contract view as primarily an ethical theory is to be found in G.R. Grice, *The Grounds of Moral Judgment* (Cambridge, The University Press, 1967). See also § 19, note 30. [The footnotes have been renumbered—Ed.]

2. Kant is clear that the original agreement is hypothetical. See *The Metaphysics of Morals,* pt. I (*Rechtslehre*), especially §§ 47, 52; and pt. II of the essay "Concerning the Common Saying: This May Be True in Theory but It Does Not Apply in Practice," in *Kant's Political Writings,* ed. Hans Reiss and trans. by H.B. Nisbet (Cambridge, The University Press, 1970), pp. 73–87. See Georges Vlachos, *La Pensée politique de Kant* (Paris, Presses Universitaires de France, *1962),* pp. 326–335; and J.G. Murphy, *Kant: The Philosophy of Right* (London,

Macmillan, 1970), pp. 109–112, 133–136, for a further discussion.

3. For the formulation of this intuitive idea I am indebted to Allan Gibbard.

Review Questions

1. Carefully explain Rawls' conception of the original position.

2. State and explain Rawls' first principle of justice.

3. State and explain the second principle. Which principle has priority such that it cannot be sacrificed?

Discussion Questions

1. On the first principle, each person has an equal right to the most extensive basic liberty as long as this does not interfere with a similar liberty for others. What does this allow people to do? Does it mean, for example, that people have a right to engage in homosexual activities as long as they don't interfere with others? Can people produce and view pornography if it does not restrict anyone's freedom? Are people allowed to take drugs in the privacy of their homes?

2. Is it possible for free and rational persons in the original position to agree upon different principles than those given by Rawls? For example, why wouldn't they agree to an equal distribution of wealth and income rather than an unequal distribution? That is, why wouldn't they adopt socialism rather than capitalism? Isn't socialism just as rational as capitalism?

Problem Cases

1. Breaking a Promise and Lying Jane Rachel has been reading about people suffering from famine in Africa and she wants to help. But what can she do? She is unemployed at the moment, having lost her part-time job teaching Introduction to Ethics because of poor student evaluations. (Students complained that she was too demanding and gave low grades.) Despite the fact that Jane has no spare money, she decides to contrib-

ute to a famine-relief fund. To do this, she asks John, one of the full-time professors of philosophy, to loan her one thousand dollars. She tells him she needs the money for food and rent because her unemployment compensation has run out (actually this is not true—she is still getting unemployment compensation checks), and she promises to pay the money back as soon as she can (although she really has no intention of paying the money back—she figures that John can afford a thousand dollars because he is a full professor with tenure). John feels sorry for Jane, and he feels guilty because he voted to have her dismissed from her job, so he gives her the money. Jane promptly gives the money to famine relief, and the money is used to provide food for starving children in Africa. Did Jane do the right thing or not? What would Mill say? How about Kant? What do you think and why?

2. Protective Punishment Genetic research done on violent male criminals in prison, men convicted of violent crimes like assault and murder, reveals that they all have a certain genetic defect, namely a missing Y chromosome. Routine blood tests on men in the army show that one hundred of these men have the genetic defect, making it likely that they will commit violent crimes. Furthermore, clinical studies of these men reveal that in fact they are very aggressive and prone to violence. The genetic researchers and psychologists petition a judge to have these men imprisoned, arguing that they are very likely to commit violent crimes. The judge rules that they are a danger to society, even though they have not yet committed any crimes, and the one hundred men are given life sentences in a maximum-security prison. While in prison, thirty of these men commit a murder, and forty have to be placed in solitary confinement because of numerous fights with other inmates. But thirty of the men commit no crimes at all, and are eventually released because of their good behavior. Do you agree that

these men should have been imprisoned or not? Explain your view.

3. Should Smoking Be Legal? In the United States, it is legal for adults to smoke tobacco in cigars, cigarettes, and pipes even though it is unhealthy to do so. Tobacco contains nicotine, a poisonous drug that is as addictive as cocaine and is clearly associated with coronary heart disease and peripheral vascular disease. In addition, the tar in tobacco smoke damages lung tissue and causes lung cancer. Given these facts, do smokers have a right to smoke? If so, should they be allowed to smoke in public? If not, does this mean that smokers do not have a right to smoke in private?

In the United States, it is illegal to smoke marijuana. When smoked, marijuana produces physical effects such as a dry mouth, mild reddening of the eyes, slight clumsiness, and increased appetite. The main psychological effects are feelings of well-being and calmness, and more vivid visual and auditory perceptions. In large doses, it may cause panicky states and illusions. In rare cases, large doses may cause psychosis, or loss of contact with reality. Prolonged use has been associated with apathy and loss of motivation. But all things considered, marijuana seems to be no more dangerous or unhealthy than tobacco, and perhaps less so. If you agree that it should be legal for adults to smoke tobacco, then why not legalize marijuana for adults? On the other hand, if you think that marijuana should be illegal, then why shouldn't tobacco be illegal too?

Suggested Readings

(1) Jeremy Bentham's classical statement of utilitarianism is found in his book *An Introduction to the Principles of Morals and Legislation* (New York: Hafner, 1948).

(2) G.E. Moore's nonhedonistic version of utilitarianism is presented in his *Ethics* (London: Oxford University Press, 1912) and his *Principia Ethica* (Cambridge: Cambridge University Press, 1959).

(3) J.J.C. Smart defends Act-Utilitarianism and Bernard Williams attacks it in J.J.C. Smart and Bernard Williams, *Utilitarianism: For and Against* (Cambridge: Cambridge University Press, 1973).

(4) A. Sen and Bernard Williams, eds., *Utilitarian-*

ism and Beyond (Cambridge: Cambridge University Press, 1973), is a collection of recent articles on utilitarianism.

(5) Kant's work in ethics is difficult. A good place to begin is his *Lectures on Ethics,* trans. Louis Infield (New York: Harper, 1963). His ethical theory is developed in *Critique of Practical Reason,* trans. Lewis White Beck (Indianapolis: Bobbs–Merrill, 1956); *The Metaphysical Elements of Justice,* trans. John Ladd (Indianapolis: Bobbs–Merrill, 1965); and *The Metaphysical Principles of Virtue,* trans. James Ellington (Indianapolis: Bobbs–Merrill, 1964).

(6) For commentaries on Kant's moral philosophy, see H.J. Paton, *The Categorical Imperative* (New

York: Harper, 1967) and H.B. Acton, *Kant's Moral Philosophy* (London: Macmillan, 1970).

(7) Onora O'Neill discusses Kantian ethics in her article "Kant After Virtue," *Inquiry* 26 (1983), pp. 387–405, and in her book, written under the name Onora Nell (instead of O'Neill) *Acting on Principle: An Essay on Kantian Ethics* (New York: Columbia University Press, 1975).

(8) The classical formulations of the social contract theory are Thomas Hobbes' *Leviathan* (1651), John Locke's *The Second Treatise of Government* (1690), and Jean–Jacques Rousseau's *The Social Contract* (1762). These books are available in different editions.

(9) Since it first appeared in 1971, Rawls' theory of justice has been widely discussed. One of the first books on the theory to appear was Brian Barry, *The Liberal Theory of Justice* (Oxford: Oxford University Press, 1973). Another useful critical discussion is Robert Paul Wolff, *Understanding Rawls* (Princeton, N.J.: Princeton University Press, 1977).

(10) The journal *Ethics* devoted its entire July 1989 issue to a symposium on recent developments in Rawlsian theory of justice.

Chapter 2

Abortion

Introduction

Factual Background Abortion is the termination of pregnancy involving the death of the fetus. The word *fetus* is often used as a general term covering the prenatal organism from conception to birth, but strictly speaking, the prenatal organism is an *embryo* before the eighth week and a *zygote* when it is a fertilized egg or ovum.

In the past, most abortions performed before the tenth week were done by a medical procedure called *dilation and curettage.* In this procedure, the cervix is dilated and the fetus is removed from the interior lining of the uterus by scraping it with a curette, a spoonlike instrument. Abortions are now usually done by vacuum aspiration, where a suction device rather than a scraping instrument is used to remove the fetus. This involves less risk of internal bleeding than scraping the lining of the uterus.

Legal abortion performed by a qualified doctor is a very safe procedure for the mother, particularly if it is performed in the early stages of pregnancy. According to the Centers for Disease Control of the Public Health Service, in 1984 the number of women dying from complications in pregnancy, childbirth, and the aftermath was 7.8 per 100,000; by contrast, the number of women dying from abortions was only 0.7 per 100,000. In other words, having an abortion is roughly seven times safer than bearing a child.

Most abortions are performed early in pregnancy. The Centers for Disease Control reports that nine out of ten abortions are done before the twelfth week of pregnancy. At this stage, the fetus is about two inches long and weighs less than an ounce.

47

Abortion is now a common medical procedure. According to the latest statistics available, in 1985 there were 1,588,550 abortions performed in the United States. This was more than one abortion for every three babies born alive.

Legal Background In the 1960s, most states had laws restricting abortion, but all fifty states and the District of Columbia allowed abortion to save the life of the mother, and Colorado and New Mexico permitted abortion to prevent serious harm to the mother. In the landmark decision of *Roe* v. *Wade* (1973), the Supreme Court overturned these abortion laws. In this case, the Court ruled that restrictive abortion laws, except in certain narrowly defined circumstances, are unconstitutional. This decision made abortion legally available to women who could afford it. (The average cost of an abortion in 1986 was $213.)

The decision has been controversial, and it has been repeatedly challenged. Opponents of the decision have proposed to amend the Constitution with the Human Life Bill, which affirms that human life begins at conception and that every human life has intrinsic worth and equal value under the Constitution. A recent legal challenge to the decision was the case of *Webster* v. *Reproductive Health Services* (1989). In a 5–4 decision, the Court did not overturn *Roe* v. *Wade,* but allowed as constitutional further restrictions placed on abortion by a Missouri law, namely (1) banning the use of public funds for abortion and abortion counseling, (2) banning abortions in public hospitals and clinics, and (3) forbidding public employees from assisting in the performance of an abortion. Perhaps in the future the Court will overturn *Roe* v. *Wade,* but for the moment it seems that the majority is willing to let it stand.

The Moral Issue We shall not be primarily concerned with the legal aspects of the abortion controversy; instead, we will concentrate on the moral issue. The basic moral issue, of course, is whether or not abortion is morally wrong.

Roughly three positions have been taken on this issue. The conservative view in its most simple form is that all abortions are wrong. But most conservatives are willing to make an exception in rare cases where abortion is necessary to save the mother's life—although they may not agree on particular cases. An example of such a case is a tubal or ectopic pregnancy. The zygote does not descend to the uterus, but remains lodged in the fallopian tube: The mother will die if an abortion is not performed in this situation, and there is no hope for the survival of the zygote. Almost everyone agrees that abortion is justified in this case.

But what about the more troublesome case where the fetus can be saved by sacrificing the life of the mother, as, for example, in the case of a pregnant woman who has a cardiac condition such that she will die if she carries the baby to term? Some conservatives might allow an abortion in that case, but John T. Noonan, the second author in our readings, would not. He accepts the traditional Roman Catholic position that a direct abortion, where the fetus is deliberately and intentionally killed, is never morally permissible. However, the fetus may be allowed to die as a consequence of an action intended to save the life of the mother, for example, the removal of a cancerous uterus. Noonan gives an additional reason for the mother to sacrifice her life for the sake of her child—such a self-sacrifice is meaningful in the Christian tradition because it is an expression of unselfishness and Christ-like love.

The second view, the liberal view, is that abortion is morally permissible whenever the mother chooses it. But other than to save her life, why would a pregnant woman want an abortion? There are various answers to this question. If a woman is pregnant due to rape, she may feel justified in getting an abortion. Incest is often cited as a good reason for getting an abortion. Another common reason is to avoid giving birth to a defective child. Or a woman may want an abortion because pregnancy interferes with her career. The liberal insists that abortion is permissible in all of these cases.

Liberals do not agree, however, about infanticide. Some liberals see little difference between abortion and killing newborn infants. But Mary Anne Warren, the representative of the liberal position in our readings, does not endorse infanticide. She claims that it does not follow from her liberal position that infanticide is morally permissible in our society. She believes that adoption is a better alternative in our society, where many people value the lives of infants.

The third view is the moderate one that abortion is justified in some cases but not in others. In which cases is it justified and in which not justified? Moderates do not agree on the answer to this question. The Supreme Court decision in *Roe* v. *Wade* allows abortion merely for the sake of convenience. But Judith Jarvis Thomson does not agree; she does not think that abortion is justified merely for the sake of convenience, say to avoid postponing a trip to Europe. Jane English, another moderate in our readings, agrees with Thomson that a woman who is seven months pregnant should not get an abortion merely to avoid postponing a trip to Europe, but she says that in the early months of pregnancy, abortion is permissible if it is in the interests of the pregnant woman or her family. This makes English's position slightly more liberal than that of Thomson. But English's view is slightly more conservative than that of Justice Blackmun in his opinion in *Roe* v. *Wade* because she thinks that we do have a serious obligation to not kill or harm the fetus in the later states of development when it is more like a baby.

Philosophical Issues   How can we resolve the moral issue about the wrongness of abortion? Most writers agree that settling this issue requires solving some difficult philosophical puzzles. Debate has most often centered on the nature and status of the fetus. Is it a person or not, and how do we tell if something is a person or not? Does the fetus have the full moral status of a person, a partial moral status, or none at all? One common approach to these problems is called line drawing, that is, making an attempt to find a morally significant point or dividing line in the development of the fetus that divides the period in which it is not a person with rights from the period in which it is a person with rights. Justice Blackmun, for example, thinks that viability is such a point. Viability occurs when the fetus is capable of surviving outside the womb. Just when this occurs is the subject of debate: Blackmun puts viability at the twenty-eighth week of pregnancy, but many doctors say it occurs earlier, at twenty-four weeks, or perhaps even as early as twenty weeks.

Other writers have chosen different points in the development of the fetus as significant dividing lines. Some say that the presence of brain waves, beginning at about the eighth week, is a significant dividing line because their presence marks the beginning of consciousness or the ability to feel pain. This is important for utilitarians who follow Bentham's view that all conscious beings should be given moral consideration. In European comman law, abortion is considered killing a person only after quickening, the time when a pregnant woman first feels the fetus move on its own.

Opponents of line drawing between conception and birth, such as Noonan, argue that these lines are always arbitrary and inadequate. Viability is a shifting point. The development of artificial incubation may make the fetus viable at any time, even shortly after conception. Furthermore, the time at which the fetus is viable varies according to circumstances such as its weight, age, and race. Opponents of line drawing often use what are called **slippery slope arguments** to argue that a line cannot be securely drawn at any point in the development of the fetus because such a line inevitably slides down the slope of development to conception; they insist that the only place to draw the line is at conception. These arguments are discussed by Thomson and John Finnis in our readings.

Noonan, Finnis, and other conservatives adopt a different approach to the problem of establishing the moral status of the fetus: Instead of trying to draw a line in the development of the fetus, they try to prove that the fetus is a human being with a right to life from the moment of conception. One argument depends upon the religious **doctrine of ensoulment.** This doctrine states that the soul enters the fetus at the moment of conception; anything with a soul is a person with a right to life; hence the fetus is a person with a right to life from the moment of conception. This may be the argument that persuades most conservatives, but Noonan avoids it because it appeals to religious doctrines not universally accepted in our pluralistic society. Instead he updates the traditional view by discussing the genetic coding of the zygote. At conception, the zygote receives the full genetic code, twenty-three pairs of chromosomes. Anything with full human genetic coding is a human being with a right to life; hence the zygote is a human being with a right to life from the moment of conception.

Liberals find it very hard to believe that a zygote, a single cell, is a human being with a right to life, that is, a person. For one thing, any human cell has the full genetic coding of a human being, but any given human cell is hardly a person. Saying that the zygote is a potential person is no help because the rights of an actual person, the mother, would always outweigh the rights of merely a potential person, assuming that potential persons have rights in the first place.

Warren thinks that conservatives like Noonan confuse two different senses of the word *human.* There is a genetic sense in which a being is human if it is a member of the biological species *Homo sapiens,* and a moral sense in which a being is human if it is a member of the moral community. Just because the zygote is genetically human does not mean that it is morally human or a member of the moral community. In order to be a person, a being must have at least some of the traits of persons, namely consciousness, reasoning, self-motivated activity, the capacity to communicate, and the presence of self-concepts. Warren contends that the fetus has none of these traits of a person, not even at the later stages of development, and hence it is not a person.

Conservative critics point out that Warren's position seems to imply that infants are not persons either, since they do not have all of the traits of a person, and thus it can be used to justify infanticide. Because the conservative thinks that babies are undeniably persons with rights, and that infanticide is morally wrong, they find Warren's position to be unacceptable.

An alternative approach to line drawing is to hold, as English does, that the concept of person has fuzzy borders, that is, there are borderline cases in which we cannot say whether an entity is a person or not. The fetus constitutes just such a case. Another alternative is to hold that the fetus is neither a full-fledged person nor merely an organism with no moral status at all; rather, it has some sort of partial moral status.

If we cannot conclusively determine the nature and moral status of the fetus, then how can we answer the moral question about abortion? The tactic of Thomson is to shift the focus of debate from the status of the fetus to the rights of the mother. She argues that even if the fetus is a person with a right to life, it still does not follow that abortions are never justified. The rights of the mother can justify an abortion. English adopts a similar tactic and uses it to attack both the conservative and the liberal views. Even if we assume that the fetus is a person, the mother's right of self-defense is sufficient to justify abortion in a number of cases including rape, serious harm, or great inconvenience. On the other hand, even if we assume that the fetus is not a person, it still has some rights because it is at least personlike. Therefore, we have an obligation to not kill it or harm it without a good reason.

The methods of Thomson and English are open to criticism, however. Both of them rely on puzzling imaginary cases, e.g., Thomson's case of the famous violinist who is plugged into another person, and English's case of the mad scientist who hypnotizes people to attack innocent passersby with knives. They ask us what we would say or think about these cases; that is, they appeal to our moral intuitions. Such an appeal does not always produce agreement, particularly when we are talking about abortion. The conservative John Finnis, for example, does not have the same intuitions about these cases as Thomson does. Another problem with appealing to intuitions is that these intuitions may merely reflect different backgrounds, e.g., the different backgrounds of Thomson and Finnis. If so, then they are not an infallible guide to moral conduct.

The Supreme Court

Excerpts from *Roe* v. *Wade* (1973)

Harry A. Blackmun is an associate justice of the United States Supreme Court. He is a graduate of Harvard Law School, and he was appointed to the Court in 1970.

Byron R. White is also an associate justice of the United States Supreme Court. He was appointed in 1962, and he is a graduate of Yale Law School.

In the case of Roe v. Wade, a pregnant single woman challenged a Texas abortion law making abortion (except to save the mother's life) a crime punishable by a prison sentence of two to five years. The Court invalidated this law.

The reading includes excerpts from the majority opinion written by Justice Blackmun (concurred in by six other justices), and from the dissenting opinion written by Justice White (concurred in by Justice

William H. Rehnquist).

Justice Blackmun argues that the abortion decision is included in the right of personal privacy. But this right is not absolute. It must yield at some point to the state's legitimate interest in protecting potential life, and this interest becomes compelling at the point of viability.

Justice White in his dissenting opinion holds that the Court has no constitutional basis for its decision, and that it values the convenience of the mother more than the existence and development of human life.

MAJORITY OPINION

A recent review of the common law precedents argues ... that even post-quickening abortion was never established as a common law crime. This is of some importance because while most American courts ruled, in holding or dictum, that abortion of an unquickened fetus was not criminal under their received common law, others followed Coke in stating that abortion of a quick fetus was a "misprison," a term they translated to mean "misdemeanor." That their reliance on Coke on this aspect of the law was uncritical and, apparently in all the reported cases, dictum (due probably to the paucity of common law prosecutions for post-quickening abortion), makes it now appear doubtful that abortion was ever firmly established as a common law crime even with respect to the destruction of a quick fetus....

It is thus apparent that at common law, at the time of the adoption of our Constitution, and throughout the major portion of the 19th century, abortion was viewed with less disfavor than under most American statutes currently in effect. Phrasing it another way, a woman enjoyed a substantially broader right to terminate a pregnancy than she does in most States today. At least with respect to the early stage of pregnancy, and very possibly without such a limitation, the opportunity to make this choice was present in this country well into the 19th century. Even later, the law continued for some time to treat less punitively an abortion procured in early pregnancy....

Three reasons have been advanced to explain historically the enactment of criminal abortion laws in the 19th century and to justify their continued existence.

It has been argued occasionally that these laws were the product of a Victorian social concern to discourage illicit sexual conduct. Texas, however, does not advance this justification in the present case, and it appears that no court or commentator has taken the argument seriously....

A second reason is concerned with abortion as a medical procedure. When most criminal abortion laws were first enacted, the procedure was a hazardous one for the woman. This was particularly true prior to the development of antisepsis. Antiseptic techniques, of course, were based on discoveries by Lister, Pasteur, and others first announced in 1867, but were not generally accepted and employed until about the turn of the century. Abortion mortality was high. Even after 1900, and perhaps until as late as the development

of antibiotics in the 1940s, standard modern techniques such as dilation and curettage were not nearly so safe as they are today. Thus it has been argued that a State's real concern in enacting a criminal abortion law was to protect the pregnant woman, that is, to restrain her from submitting to a procedure that placed her life in serious jeopardy.

Modern medical techniques have altered this situation. Appellants and various *amici* refer to medical data indicating that abortion in early pregnancy, that is, prior to the end of first trimester, although not without its risk, is now relatively safe. Mortality rates for women undergoing early abortions, where the procedure is legal, appear to be as low as or lower than the rates for normal childbirth. Consequently, any interest of the State in protecting the woman from an inherently hazardous procedure, except when it would be equally dangerous for her to forgo it, has largely disappeared. Of course, important state interests in the area of health and medical standards do remain. The State has a legitimate interest in seeing to it that abortion, like any other medical procedure, is performed under circumstances that insure maximum safety for the patient. This interest obviously extends at least to the performing physician and his staff, to the facilities involved, to the availability of aftercare, and to adequate provision for any complication or emergency that might arise. The prevalence of high mortality rates at illegal "abortion mills" strengthens, rather than weakens, the State's interest in regulating the conditions under which abortions are performed. Moreover, the risk to the woman increases as her pregnancy continues. Thus the State retains a definite interest in protecting the woman's own health and safety when an abortion is performed at a late stage of pregnancy.

The third reason is the State's interest—some phrase it in terms of duty—in protecting prenatal life. Some of the argument for this justification rests on the theory that a new human life is present from the moment of conception....

Parties challenging state abortion laws have sharply disputed in some courts the contention that a purpose of these laws, when enacted, was to protect prenatal life. Pointing to the absence of legislative history to support the contention, they claim that most state laws were designed solely to protect the woman. Because medical advances have lessened this concern, at least with respect to abortion in early pregnancy, they argue that with respect to such abortions the laws can no longer be justified by any state interest. There is some scholarly support for this view of original purpose. The few state courts called upon to interpret their laws in the late 19th and early 20th centuries did focus on the State's interest in protecting the woman's health rather than in preserving embryo and fetus....

The Constitution does not explicitly mention any right of privacy. In a line of decisions, however, going back perhaps as far as *Union Pacific R. Co.* v. *Botsford,* 141 U.S. 250, 251 (1891), the Court has recognized that a right of personal privacy, or a guarantee of certain areas or zones of privacy, does exist under the Constitution. In varying contexts the Court or individual Justices have indeed found at least the roots of that right in the First Amendment, ... in the Fourth and Fifth Amendments ... in the penumbras of the Bill of Rights ... in the Ninth Amendment ... or in the concept of liberty guaranteed by the first section of the Fourteenth Amendment.... These decisions make it clear that only personal rights that can be deemed "fundamental" or "implicit in the concept of ordered liberty," ... are included in this guarantee of personal privacy. They also make it clear that the right has some extension to activities relating to marriage, ... procreation, ... contraception, ... family relationships, ... and child rearing and education....

This right of privacy, whether it be founded in the Fourteenth Amendment's concept of personal liberty and restrictions upon state action, as we feel it is or, as the District Court

determined, in the Ninth Amendment's reservation of rights to the people, is broad enough to encompass a woman's decision whether or not to terminate her pregnancy....

... Appellants and some *amici* argue that the woman's right is absolute and that she is entitled to terminate her pregnancy at whatever time, in whatever way, and for whatever reason she alone chooses. With this we do not agree. Appellants' arguments that Texas either has no valid interest at all in regulating the abortion decision, or no interest strong enough to support any limitation upon the woman's sole determination, is unpersuasive. The Court's decisions recognizing a right of privacy also acknowledge that some state regulation in areas protected by that right is appropriate. As noted above, a state may properly assert important interests in safeguarding health, in maintaining medical standards, and in protecting potential life. At some point in pregnancy, these respective interests become sufficiently compelling to sustain regulation of the factors that govern the abortion decision. The privacy right involved, therefore, cannot be said to be absolute....

We therefore conclude that the right of personal privacy includes the abortion decision, but that this right is not unqualified and must be considered against important state interests in regulation.

We note that those federal and state courts that have recently considered abortion law challenges have reached the same conclusion....

Although the results are divided, most of these courts have agreed that the right of privacy, however based, is broad enough to cover the abortion decision; that the right, nonetheless, is not absolute and is subject to some limitations; and that at some point the state interests as to protection of health, medical standards, and prenatal life, become dominant. We agree with this approach.

The appellee and certain *amici* argue that the fetus is a "person" within the language and meaning of the Fourteenth Amendment.

In support of this they outline at length and in detail the well-known facts of fetal development. If this suggestion of personhood is established, the appellant's case, of course, collapses, for the fetus' right to life is then guaranteed specifically by the Amendment. The appellant conceded as much on reargument. On the other hand, the appellee conceded on reargument that no case could be cited that holds that a fetus is a person within the meaning of the Fourteenth Amendment.

All this, together with our observation, supra, that throughout the major portion of the 19th century prevailing legal abortion practices were far freer than they are today, persuades us that the word "person," as used in the Fourteenth Amendment, does not include the unborn.... Indeed, our decision in *United States* v. *Vuitch*, 402 U.S. 62 (1971), inferentially is to the same effect, for we there would not have indulged in statutory interpretation favorable to abortion in specified circumstances if the necessary consequence was the termination of life entitled to Fourteenth Amendment protection.

... As we have intimated above, it is reasonable and appropriate for a State to decide that at some point in time another interest, that of health of the mother or that of potential human life, becomes significantly involved. The woman's privacy is no longer sole and any right of privacy she possesses must be measured accordingly.

... We need not resolve the difficult question of when life begins. When those trained in the respective disciplines of medicine, philosophy, and theology are unable to arrive at any consensus, the judiciary, at this point in the development of man's knowledge, is not in a position to speculate as to the answer.

It should be sufficient to note briefly the wide divergence of thinking on this most sensitive and difficult question. There has always been strong support for the view that life does not begin until live birth. This was the belief of the Stoics. It appears to be the predominant, though not the unanimous, attitude of the Jewish faith. It may be taken to represent also the position of a large segment of the Protestant community, insofar as that can be ascertained; organized groups that have taken a formal position on the abortion issue have generally regarded abortion as a matter for the conscience of the individual and her family. As we have noted, the common law found greater significance in quickening. Physicians and their scientific colleagues have regarded that event with less interest and have tended to focus either upon conception or upon live birth or upon the interim point at which the fetus becomes "viable," that is, potentially able to live outside the mother's womb, albeit with artificial aid. Viability is usually placed at about seven months (28 weeks) but may occur earlier, even at 24 weeks....

In areas other than criminal abortion the law has been reluctant to endorse any theory that life, as we recognize it, begins before live birth or to accord legal rights to the unborn except in narrowly defined situations and except when the rights are contingent upon live birth.... In short, the unborn have never been recognized in the law as persons in the whole sense.

In view of all this, we do not agree that, by adopting one theory of life, Texas may override the rights of the pregnant woman that are at stake. We repeat, however, that the State does have an important and legitimate interest in preserving and protecting the health of the pregnant woman, whether she be a resident of the State or a nonresident who seeks medical consultation and treatment there, and that it has still *another* important and legitimate interest in protecting the potentiality of human life. These interests are separate and distinct. Each grows in substantiality as the woman approaches term and, at a point during pregnancy, each becomes "compelling."

With respect to the State's important and legitimate interest in the health of the mother, the "compelling" point, in the light of present medical knowledge, is at approximately the end of the first trimester. This is so because of the now established medical fact ... that until the end of the first trimester mortality in abortion is less than mortality in normal childbirth. It follows that, from and after this point, a State may regulate the abortion procedure to the extent that the regulation reasonably relates to the preservation and protection of maternal health. Examples of permissible state regulation in this area are requirements as to the qualifications of the person who is to perform the abortion; as to the licensure of that person; as to the facility in which the procedure is to be performed, that is, whether it must be a hospital or may be a clinic or some other place of less-than-hospital status; as to the licensing of the facility; and the like.

This means, on the other hand, that, for the period of pregnancy prior to this "compelling" point, the attending physician, in consultation with his patient, is free to determine, without regulation by the State, that in his medical judgment the patient's pregnancy should be terminated. If that decision is reached, the judgment may be effectuated by an abortion free of interference by the State.

With respect to the State's important and legitimate interest in potential life, the "compelling" point is at viability. ... State regulation protective of fetal life after viability thus has both logical and biological justifications. If the State is interested in protecting fetal life after viability, it may go so far as to proscribe abortion during that period except when it is necessary to preserve the life or health of the mother. ...

To summarize and repeat:

1. A state criminal abortion statute of the current Texas type, that excepts from criminality only a *life-saving* procedure on behalf of the mother, without regard to pregnancy stage and without recognition of the other interests involved, is violative of the Due Process Clause of the Fourteenth Amendment.

   (a) For the stage prior to approximately the end of the first trimester, the abortion decision and its effectuation must be left to the medical judgment of the pregnant woman's attending physician.

(b) For the stage subsequent to approximately the end of the first trimester, the State, in promoting its interest in the health of the mother, may, if it chooses, regulate the abortion procedure in ways that are reasonably related to maternal health.

(c) For the stage subsequent to viability the State, in promoting its interest in the potentiality of human life, may, if it chooses, regulate, and even proscribe, abortion except where it is necessary, in appropriate medical judgment, for the preservation of the life or health of the mother.

2. The State may define the term "physician," as it has been employed in the preceding numbered paragraphs of this Part XI of this opinion, to mean only a physician currently licensed by the State, and may proscribe any abortion by a person who is not a physician as so defined.

... The decision leaves the State free to place increasing restrictions on abortion as the period of pregnancy lengthens, so long as those restrictions are tailored to the recognized state interests. The decision vindicates the right of the physician to administer medical treatment according to his professional judgment up to the points where important state interests provide compelling justifications for intervention. Up to those points the abortion decision in all its aspects is inherently, and primarily, a medical decision, and basic responsibility for it must rest with the physician. If an individual practitioner abuses the privilege of exercising proper medical judgment, the usual remedies, judicial and intraprofessional, are available. ...

DISSENT

At the heart of the controversy in these cases

are those recurring pregnancies that pose no danger whatsoever to the life or health of the mother but are nevertheless unwanted for any one or more of a variety of reasons—convenience, family planning, economics, dislike of children, the embarrassment of illegitimacy, etc. The common claim before us is that for any one of such reasons, or for no reason at all, and without asserting or claiming any threat to life or health, any woman is entitled to an abortion at her request if she is able to find a medical advisor willing to undertake the procedure.

The Court for the most part sustains this position: During the period prior to the time the fetus becomes viable, the Constitution of the United States values the convenience, whim or caprice of the putative mother more than the life or potential life of the fetus; the Constitution, therefore, guarantees the right to an abortion as against any state law or policy seeking to protect the fetus from an abortion not prompted by more compelling reasons of the mother.

With all due respect, I dissent. I find nothing in the language or history of the Constitution to support the Court's judgment.... As an exercise of raw judicial power, the Court perhaps has authority to do what it does today; but in my view its judgment is an improvident and extravagant exercise of the power of judicial review which the Constitution extends to this Court.

The Court apparently values the convenience of the pregnant mother more than the continued existence and development of the life or potential life which she carries....

It is my view, therefore, that the Texas statute is not constitutionally infirm because it denies abortions to those who seek to serve only their convenience rather than to protect their life or health....

Review Questions

1. Justice Blackmun discusses three reasons for the enactment of criminal abortion laws. Why doesn't he accept these reasons?

2. Where does the Constitution guarantee a right of privacy according to Justice Blackmun?

3. Is the fetus a person in the legal sense according to Justice Blackmun?

4. According to Justice Blackmun, when is the *compelling* point in the state's interest in the health of the mother?

5. When, according to Justice Blackmun, is the *compelling* point in the state's interest in potential life?

6. Explain Justice Blackmun's conclusions.

7. What are Justice White's objections?

Discussion Questions

1. What is the right of privacy? Try to define it.

2. What do you think is properly included in the right of privacy, and what is properly excluded?

3. Do you think that the fetus has any legal rights or any moral rights? Defend your view.

4. Justice White complains that Justice Blackmun's opinion allows a woman to get an abortion "without asserting or claiming any threat to life or health" provided she is able to find a doctor willing to undertake the procedure. Do you think that women should be allowed to get such abortions? Explain your answer. Do you believe that doctors have any obligation to perform such abortions? Why or why not?

John T. Noonan, Jr.

An Almost Absolute Value in History

John T. Noonan, Jr., is Professor of Law at the University of California, Berkeley. His books include Contraception: A History of Its Treatment by the Catholic Theologians and Canonists *(1965), (1970), and* Persons and Masks of the Law *(1976).*

Noonan begins with the question, How do you determine the humanity of a being? The answer he defends is what he says is the view of traditional Christian theology, namely that you are human if you are conceived by human parents. This view is compared to other alleged criteria of humanity such as viability, experience, feelings of adults, sensations of adults, and social visibility. Each of these is rejected as inadequate and arbitrary. In his defense of the traditional view, Noonan does not appeal to the medieval theory of ensoulment, that is, the theory that the soul enters the body at conception. Instead, he rests his case on the fact that at conception the fetus (or strictly speaking, the zygote) receives the full genetic code of a human being. He assumes that anything with human genetic coding is a human being with rights equal to those of other humans. It follows that the fetus is a human being with rights from the moment of conception. Once this has been granted, we can see that abortion is morally wrong except in rare cases where it is necessary to save the mother's life.

The most fundamental question involved in the long history of thought on abortion is: How do you determine the humanity of a being? To phrase the question that way is to put in comprehensive humanistic terms what the theologians either dealt with as an explic-

itly theological question under the heading of "ensoulment" or dealt with implicitly in their treatment of abortion. The Christian position as it originated did not depend on a narrow theological or philosophical concept. It had no relation to theories of infant baptism.[1] It appealed to no special theory of instantaneous ensoulment. It took the world's view on ensoulment as that view changed from Aristotle to Zacchia. There was, indeed, theological influence affecting the theory of ensoulment finally adopted, and, of course, ensoulment itself was a theological concept, so that the position was always explained in theological terms. But the theological notion of ensoulment could easily be translated into humanistic language by substituting "human" for "rational soul"; the problem of knowing when a man is a man is common to theology and humanism.

If one steps outside the specific categories used by the theologians, the answer they gave can be analyzed as a refusal to discriminate among human beings on the basis of their varying potentialities. Once conceived, the being was recognized as man because he had man's potential. The **criterion** for humanity, thus, was simple and all-embracing: if you are conceived by human parents, you are human.

The strength of this position may be tested by a review of some of the other distinctions offered in the contemporary controversy over legalizing abortion. Perhaps the most popular distinction is in terms of viability. Before an age of so many months, the fetus is not viable, that is, it cannot be removed from the mother's womb and live apart from her. To that extent, the life of the fetus is absolutely dependent on the life of the mother. This dependence is made the basis of denying recognition to its humanity.

There are difficulties with this distinction. One is that the perfection of artificial incubation may make the fetus viable at any time: it may be removed and artificially sustained. Experiments with animals already show that such a procedure is possible. This hypothetical extreme case relates to an actual difficulty:

there is considerable elasticity to the idea of viability. Mere length of life is not an exact measure. The viability of the fetus depends on the extent of its anatomical and functional development. The weight and length of the fetus are better guides to the state of its development than age, but weight and length vary. Moreover, different racial groups have different ages at which their fetuses are viable. Some evidence, for example, suggests that Negro fetuses mature more quickly than white fetuses. If viability is the norm, the standard would vary with race and with many individual circumstances.

The most important objection to this approach is that dependence is not ended by viability. The fetus is still absolutely dependent on someone's care in order to continue existence; indeed a child of one or three or even five years of age is absolutely dependent on another's care for existence; uncared for, the older fetus or the younger child will die as surely as the early fetus detached from the mother. The unsubstantial lessening in dependence at viability does not seem to signify any special acquisition of humanity.

A second distinction has been attempted in terms of experience. A being who has had experience, has lived and suffered, who possesses memories, is more human than one who has not. Humanity depends on formation by experience. The fetus is thus "unformed" in the most basic human sense.

This distinction is not serviceable for the embryo which is already experiencing and reacting. The embryo is responsive to touch after eight weeks and at least at that point is experiencing. At an earlier stage the zygote is certainly alive and responding to its environment. The distinction may also be challenged by the rare case where aphasia has erased adult memory: has it erased humanity? More fundamentally, this distinction leaves even the older fetus or the younger child to be treated as an unformed inhuman thing. Finally, it is not clear why experience as such confers humanity. It could be argued that certain central experiences such as loving or learning are necessary to make a man human. But then human beings who have failed to love or to learn might be excluded from the class called man.

A third distinction is made by appeal to the sentiments of adults. If a fetus dies, the grief of the parents is not the grief they would have for a living child. The fetus is an unnamed "it" till birth, and is not perceived as personality until at least the fourth month of existence when movements in the womb manifest a vigorous presence demanding joyful recognition by the parents.

Yet feeling is notoriously an unsure guide to the humanity of others. Many groups of humans have had difficulty in feeling that persons of another tongue, color, religion, sex, are as human as they. Apart from reactions to alien groups, we mourn the loss of a ten-year-old boy more than the loss of his one-day-old brother or his 90–year-old grandfather. The difference felt and the grief expressed vary with the potentialities extinguished, or the experience wiped out; they do not seem to point to any substantial difference in the humanity of baby, boy, or grandfather.

Distinctions are also made in terms of sensation by the parents. The embryo is felt within the womb only after about the fourth month. The embryo is seen only at birth. What can be neither seen nor felt is different from what is tangible. If the fetus cannot be seen or touched at all, it cannot be perceived as man.

Yet experience shows that sight is even more untrustworthy than feeling in determining humanity. By sight, color became an appropriate index for saying who was a man, and the evil of racial discrimination was given foundation. Nor can touch provide the test; a being confined by sickness, "out of touch" with others, does not thereby seem to lose his humanity. To the extent that touch still has appeal as a criterion, it appears to be a survival of the old English idea of "quickening"—a possible mistranslation of the Latin *animatus* used in the canon law. To that extent touch as a criterion seems to be dependent on the Aristotelian notion of ensoulment, and to fall when this notion is discarded.

Finally, a distinction is sought in social visibility. The fetus is not socially perceived as human. It cannot communicate with others. Thus, both subjectively and objectively, it is not a member of society. As moral rules are rules for the behavior of members of society to each other, they cannot be made for behavior toward what is not yet a member. Excluded from the society of men, the fetus is excluded from the humanity of men.[2]

By force of the argument from the consequences, this distinction is to be rejected. It is more subtle than that founded on an appeal to physical sensation, but it is equally dangerous in its implications. If humanity depends on social recognition, individuals or whole groups may be dehumanized by being denied any status in their society. Such a fate is fictionally portrayed in *1984* and has actually been the lot of many men in many societies. In the Roman empire, for example, condemnation to slavery meant the practical denial of most human rights; in the Chinese Communist world, landlords have been classified as enemies of the people and so treated as nonpersons by the state. Humanity does not depend on social recognition, though often the failure of society to recognize the prisoner, the alien, the heterodox as human has led to the destruction of human beings. Anyone conceived by a man and a woman is human. Recognition of this condition by society follows a real event in the objective order, however imperfect and halting the recognition. Any attempt to limit humanity to exclude some group runs the risk of furnishing authority and precedent for excluding other groups in the name of the consciousness or perception of the controlling group in the society.

A philosopher may reject the appeal to the humanity of the fetus because he views "humanity" as a secular view of the soul and because he doubts the existence of anything real and objective which can be identified as humanity. One answer to such a philosopher is to ask how he reasons about moral questions without supposing that there is a sense in which he and the others of whom he speaks are human. Whatever group is taken as the society which determines who may be killed is thereby taken as human. A second answer is to ask if he does not believe that there is a right and wrong way of deciding moral questions. If there is such a difference, experience may be appealed to: to decide who is human on the basis of the sentiment of a given society has led to consequences which rational men would characterize as monstrous.

The rejection of the attempted distinctions based on viability and visibility, experience and feeling, may be buttressed by the following considerations: Moral judgments often rest on distinctions, but if the distinctions are not to appear arbitrary *fiat*, they should relate to some real difference in probabilities. There is a kind of continuity in all life, but the earlier stages of the elements of human life possess tiny probabilities of development. Consider, for example, the spermatozoa in any normal ejaculate: There are about 200,000,000 in any single ejaculate, of which one has a chance of developing into a zygote. Consider the oocytes which may become ova: there are 100,000 to 1,000,000 oocytes in a female infant, of which a maximum of 390 are ovulated. But once spermatozoon and ovum meet and the conceptus is formed, such studies as have been made show that roughly in only 20 percent of the cases will spontaneous abortion occur. In other words, the chances are about 4 out of 5 that this new being will develop. At this stage in the life of the being there is a sharp shift in probabilities, an immense jump in potentialities. To make a distinction between the rights of spermatozoa and the rights of the fertilized ovum is to respond to an enormous shift in possibilities. For about twenty days after conception the egg may split to form twins or combine with another egg to form a chimera, but the probability of either event happening is very small.

It may be asked, What does a change in biological probabilities have to do with establishing humanity? The argument from probabilities is not aimed at establishing humanity but at establishing an objective discontinuity which may be taken into account in moral discourse. As life itself is a matter of probabilities, as most moral reasoning is an estimate of probabilities, so it seems in accord with the structure of reality and the nature of moral thought to found a moral judgment on the change in probabilities at conception. The appeal to probabilities is the most commonsensical of arguments; to a greater or smaller degree all of us base our actions on probabilities, and in morals, as in law, prudence and negligence are often measured by the account one has taken of the probabilities. If the chance is 200,000,000 to 1 that the movement in the bushes into which you shoot is a man's, I doubt if many persons would hold you careless in shooting; but if the chances are 4 out of 5 that the movement is a human being's, few would acquit you of blame. Would the argument be different if only one out of ten children conceived came to term? Of course this argument would be different. This argument is an appeal to probabilities that actually exist, not to any and all states of affairs which may be imagined.

The probabilities as they do exist do not show the humanity of the embryo in the sense of a demonstration in logic any more than the probabilities of the movement in the bush being a man demonstrate beyond all doubt that the being is a man. The appeal is a "buttressing" consideration, showing the plausibility of the standard adopted. The argument focuses on the decisional factor in any moral judgment and assumes that part of the business of a moralist is drawing lines. One evidence of the nonarbitrary character of the line drawn is the difference of probabilities on either side of it. If a spermatozoon is destroyed, one destroys a being which had a chance of far less than 1 in 200 million of developing into a reasoning being, possessed of the genetic code, a heart and other organs, and capable of pain. If a fetus is destroyed, one destroys a being already possessed of the genetic code, organs, and sensitivity to pain, and one which had an 80 percent chance of developing further into a baby outside the womb who, in time, would reason.

The positive argument for conception as the decisive moment of humanization is that at conception the new being receives the genetic code. It is this genetic information which determines his characteristics, which is the biological carrier of the possibility of human wisdom, which makes him a self-evolving being. A being with a human genetic code is man.

This review of current controversy over the humanity of the fetus emphasizes what a fundamental question the theologians resolved in asserting the inviolability of the fetus. To regard the fetus as possessed of equal rights with other humans was not, however, to decide every case where abortion might be employed. It did decide the case where the argument was that the fetus should be aborted for its own good. To say a being was human was to say it had a destiny to decide for itself which could not be taken from it by another man's decision. But human beings with equal rights often come in conflict with each other, and some decision must be made as to whose claims are to prevail. Cases of conflict involving the fetus are different only in two respects: the total inability of the fetus to speak for itself and the fact that the right of the fetus regularly at stake is the right to life itself.

The approach taken by the theologians to these conflicts was articulated in terms of "direct" and "indirect." Again, to look at what they were doing from outside their categories, they may be said to have been drawing lines or "balancing values." "Direct" and "indirect" are spatial metaphors; "line-drawing" is another. "To weigh" or "to balance" values is a metaphor of a more complicated mathematical sort hinting at the process which goes on in moral judgments. All the metaphors suggest that, in the moral judgments made, comparisons were necessary, that no value completely controlled. The principle of double effect was no doctrine fallen from heaven, but a method of analysis appropriate where two relative values were being compared. In Catholic moral theology, as it developed, life even of the innocent was not taken as an absolute. Judgments on acts affecting life issued from a process of weighing. In the weighing, the fetus was always given a value greater than zero, always a value separate and independent from its parents. This valuation was crucial and fundamental in all Christian thought on the subject and marked it off from any approach which considered that only the parents' interests needed to be considered.

Even with the fetus weighed as human, one interest could be weighed as equal or superior: that of the mother in her own life. The casuists between 1450 and 1895 were willing to weigh this interest as superior. Since 1895, that interest was given decisive weight only in the two special cases of the cancerous uterus and the ectopic pregnancy. In both of these cases the fetus itself had little chance of survival even if the abortion were not performed. As the balance was once struck in favor of the mother whenever her life was endangered, it could be so struck again. The balance reached between 1895 and 1930 attempted prudentially and pastorally to forestall a multitude of exceptions for interests less than life.

The perception of the humanity of the fetus and the weighing of fetal rights against other human rights constituted the work of the moral analysts. But what spirit animated their abstract judgments? For the Christian community it was the injunction of Scripture to love your neighbor as yourself. The fetus as human was a neighbor; his life had parity with one's own. The commandment gave life to what otherwise would have been only rational calculation.

The commandment could be put in hu-manistic as well as theological terms: Do not injure your fellow man without reason. In these terms, once the humanity of the fetus is perceived, abortion is never right except in self-defense. When life must be taken to save life, reason alone cannot say that a mother must prefer a child's life to her own. With this exception, now of great rarity, abortion violates the rational humanist tenet of the equality of human lives.

For Christians the commandment to love had received a special imprint in that the exemplar proposed of love was the love of the Lord for his disciples. In the light given by this example, self-sacrifice carried to the point of death seemed in the extreme situations not without meaning. In the less extreme cases, preference for one's own interests to the life of another seemed to express cruelty or selfishness irreconcilable with the demands of love.

Endnotes

1. According to Glanville Williams (*The Sanctity of Human Life supra* n. 169, at 193), "The historical reason for the Catholic objection to abortion is the same as for the Christian Church's historical opposition to infanticide: the horror of bringing about the death of an unbaptized child." This statement is made without any citation of evidence. As has been seen, desire to administer baptism could, in the Middle Ages, even be urged as a reason for procuring an abortion. It is highly regrettable that the American Law Institute was apparently misled by Williams' account and repeated after him the same baseless statement. See American Law Institute, *Model Penal Code: Tentative Draft No. 9* (1959), p. 148, n. 12.

2. ... Thomas Aquinas gave an analogous reason against baptizing a fetus in the womb: "As long as it exists in the womb of the mother, it cannot be subject to the operation of the ministers of the Church as it is not known to men" (*In sententias Petri Lombardi* 4.6 1.1.2).

Review Questions

1. According to Noonan, what is the simple Christian criterion for humanity?

2. Noonan discusses five different distinctions (starting with viability) used by defenders of abortion. Explain Noonan's critique of these distinctions.

3. State and explain Noonan's argument from probabilities.

4. What is Noonan's positive argument for saying that conception is "the decisive moment of humanization?"

5. In Noonan's view, why does the fetus have rights equal to those of other human beings?

6. According to Noonan, how do Christian theologians resolve conflicts of rights such as that between the mother's right to life and the fetus' right to life?

7. According to the traditional view defended by Noonan, in which cases do the fetus' right to life outweigh the mother's right to life?

Discussion Questions

1. Consider the following objection to Noonan's claim that "a being with a human genetic code is a man." A human cell also is a being with a human genetic code, but obviously it is not a man in the sense of being a human being; therefore, Noonan's claim is false. How could Noonan respond to this objection?

2. Is it possible for a nonhuman being, for example an angel or an intelligent alien being, to have rights equal to those of human beings? Defend your answer.

3. Noonan admits that abortion can be justified by appealing to the right of self-defense. Does this right justify an abortion in a case of rape? Why or why not?

Judith Jarvis Thomson

A Defense of Abortion

Judith Jarvis Thomson is Professor of Philosophy at Massachusetts Institute of Technology. She is the author of numerous articles on issues in ethics and the philosophy of mind.

Thomson assumes, just for the sake of argument, that the fetus is a person from the moment of conception. It does not follow, she argues, that the fetus' right to life always outweighs the mother's rights. Using a series of imaginary examples (such as being plugged into a famous violinist), she tries to convince us that the mother's right to control her own body and her right to self-defense are strong enough to justify abortion in cases of rape, in cases where the mother's life is threatened, and in cases in which the woman has taken reasonable precautions not to get pregnant.

Judith J. Thomson, "A Defense of Abortion," *Philosophy & Public Affairs*, Vol. 1, No. 1 (1978). Copyright © 1971 Princeton University Press. Reprinted by permission of Princeton University Press.

Most opposition to abortion relies on the premise that the fetus is a human being, a person, from the moment of conception. The premise is argued for, but, as I think, not well. Take, for example, the most common argument. We are asked to notice that the development of a human being from conception through birth into childhood is continuous; then it is said that to draw a line, to choose a point in this development and say "before this point the thing is not a person, after this point it is a person" is to make an arbitrary choice, a choice for which in the nature of things no good reason can be given. It is concluded that the fetus is, or anyway that we had better say it is, a person from the moment of conception. But this conclusion does not follow. Similar things might be said about the development of an acorn into an oak tree, and it does not follow that acorns are oak trees, or that we had better say they are. Arguments of this form are sometimes called "slippery slope arguments"—the phrase is perhaps self-explanatory—and it is dismaying that opponents of abortion rely on them so heavily and uncritically.

I am inclined to agree, however, that the prospects for "drawing a line" in the development of the fetus look dim. I am inclined to think also that we shall probably have to agree that the fetus has already become a human person well before birth. Indeed, it comes as a surprise when one first learns how early in its life it begins to acquire human characteristics. By the tenth week, for example, it already has a face, arms and legs, fingers and toes; it has internal organs, and brain activity is detectable.[1] On the other hand, I think that the premise is false, that the fetus is not a person from the moment of conception. A newly fertilized ovum, a newly implanted clump of cells, is no more a person than an acorn is an oak tree. But I shall not discuss any of this. For it seems to me to be of great interest to ask what happens if, for the sake of argument, we allow the premise. How, precisely, are we supposed to get from there to the conclusion that abortion is morally impermissible? Opponents of abortion commonly spend most of their time establishing that the fetus is a person, and hardly any time explaining the step from there to the impermissibility of abortion. Perhaps they think the step too simple and obvious to require much comment. Or perhaps instead they are simply being economical in argument. Many of those who defend abortion rely on the premise that the fetus is not a person, but only a bit of tissue that will become a person at birth; and why pay out more arguments than you have to? Whatever the explanation, I suggest that the step they take is neither easy nor obvious, that it calls for closer examination than it is commonly given, and that when we do give it this closer examination we shall feel inclined to reject it.

I propose, then, that we grant that the fetus is a person from the moment of conception. How does the argument go from here? Something like this, I take it. Every person has a right to life. So the fetus has a right to life. No doubt the mother has a right to decide what shall happen in and to her body; everyone would grant that. But surely a person's right to life is stronger and more stringent than the mother's right to decide what

happens in and to her body, and so outweighs it. So the fetus may not be killed; an abortion may not be performed.

It sounds plausible. But now let me ask you to imagine this. You wake up in the morning and find yourself back to back in bed with an unconscious violinist. A famous unconscious violinist. He has been found to have a fatal kidney ailment, and the Society of Music Lovers has canvassed all the available medical records and found that you alone have the right blood type to help. They have therefore kidnapped you, and last night the violinist's circulatory system was plugged into yours, so that your kidneys can be used to extract poisons from his blood as well as your own. The director of the hospital now tells you, "Look, we're sorry the Society of Music Lovers did this to you—we would never have permitted it if we had known. But still, they did it, and the violinist now is plugged into you. To unplug you would be to kill him. But never mind, it's only for nine months. By then he will have recovered from his ailment, and can safely be unplugged from you." Is it morally incumbent on you to accede to this situation? No doubt it would be very nice of you if you did, a great kindness. But do you *have* to accede to it? What if it were not nine months, but nine years? Or longer still? What if the director of the hospital says, "Tough luck, I agree, but you've now got to stay in bed, with the violinist plugged into you, for the rest of your life. Because remember this. All persons have a right to life, and violinists are persons. Granted you have a right to decide what happens in and to your body, but a person's right to life outweighs your right to decide what happens in and to your body. So you cannot ever be unplugged from him." I imagine you would regard this as outrageous, which suggests that something really is wrong with that plausible-sounding argument I mentioned a moment ago.

In this case, of course, you were kidnapped; you didn't volunteer for the operation that plugged the violinist into your kidneys. Can those who oppose abortion on the ground I mentioned make an exception for a pregnancy due to rape? Certainly. They can say that persons have a right to life only if they didn't come into existence because of rape; or they can say that all persons have a right to life, but that some have less of a right to life than others, in particular, that those who came into existence because of rape have less. But these statements have a rather unpleasant sound. Surely the question of whether you have a right to life at all, or how much of it you have, shouldn't turn on the question of whether or not you are the product of a rape. And in fact the people who oppose abortion on the ground I mentioned do not make this distinction, and hence do not make an exception in case of rape.

Nor do they make an exception for a case in which the mother has to spend the nine months of her pregnancy in bed. They would agree that would be a great pity, and hard on the mother; but all the same, all persons have a right to life, the fetus is a person, and so on. I suspect, in fact, that they would not make an exception for a case in which, miraculously enough, the pregnancy went on for nine years, or even the rest of the mother's life.

Some won't even make an exception for a case in which continuation of the pregnancy is likely to shorten the mother's life; they regard abortion as impermissible even to save the mother's life. Such cases are nowadays very rare, and many opponents of abortion do not accept this extreme view. All the same, it is a good place to begin; a number of points of interest come out in respect to it.

1. Let us call the view that abortion is impermissible even to save the mother's life "the extreme view." I want to suggest first that it does not issue from the argument I mentioned earlier without the addition of some fairly powerful premises. Suppose a woman has become pregnant, and now learns that she has a cardiac condition such that she will die if she carries the baby to term. What may be done for her? The fetus, being a person, has a right to life, but as the mother is a person too, so has she a right to life. Presum-

ably they have an equal right to life. How is it supposed to come out that an abortion may not be performed? If mother and child have an equal right to life, shouldn't we perhaps flip a coin? Or should we add to the mother's right to life her right to decide what happens in and to her body, which everybody seems to be ready to grant—the sum of her rights now outweighing the fetus' right to life?

The most familiar argument here is the following. We are told that performing the abortion would be directly killing [2] the child, whereas doing nothing would not be killing the mother, but only letting her die. Moreover, in killing the child, one would be killing an innocent person, for the child has committed no crime, and is not aiming at his mother's death. And then there are a variety of ways in which this might be continued: (1) But as directly killing an innocent person is always and absolutely impermissible, an abortion may not be performed. Or (2) as directly killing an innocent person is murder, and murder is always and absolutely impermissible, an abortion may not be performed.[3] Or (3) as one's duty to refrain from directly killing an innocent person is more stringent than one's duty to keep a person from dying, an abortion may not be performed. Or (4) if one's only options are directly killing an innocent person or letting a person die, one must prefer letting the person die, and thus an abortion may not be performed.[4]

Some people seem to have thought that these are not further premises which must be added if the conclusion is to be reached, but that they follow from the very fact that an innocent person has a right to life.[5] But this seems to me to be a mistake, and perhaps the simplest way to show this is to bring out that while we must certainly grant that innocent persons have a right to life, the theses in (1) through (4) are all false. Take (2), for example. If directly killing an innocent person is murder, and thus is impermissible, then the mother's directly killing the innocent person inside her is murder, and thus is impermissible. But it cannot seriously be thought to be murder if the mother performs an abortion on herself to save her life. It cannot seriously be said that she *must* refrain, that she *must* sit passively by and wait for her death. Let us look again at the case of you and the violinist. There you are, in bed with the violinist, and the director of the hospital says to you, "It's all most distressing, and I deeply sympathize, but you see this is putting an additional strain on your kidneys, and you'll be dead within the month. But you *have* to stay where you are all the same. Because unplugging you would be directly killing an innocent violinist, and that's murder, and that's impermissible." If anything in the world is true, it is that you do not commit murder, you do not do what is impermissible, if you reach around to your back and unplug yourself from that violinist to save your life.

The main focus of attention in writings on abortion has been on what a third party may or may not do in answer to a request from a woman for an abortion. This is in a way understandable. Things being as they are, there isn't much a woman can safely do to abort herself. So the question asked is what a third party may do, and what the mother may do, if it is mentioned at all, is deduced, almost as an afterthought, from what it is concluded that third parties may do. But it seems to me that to treat the matter in this way is to refuse to grant to the mother that very status of person which is so firmly insisted on for the fetus. For we cannot simply read off what a person may do from what a third party may do. Suppose you find yourself trapped in a tiny house with a growing child. I mean a very tiny house, and a rapidly growing child—you are already up against the wall of the house and in a few minutes you'll be crushed to death. The child on the other hand won't be crushed to death; if nothing is done to stop him from growing he'll be hurt, but in the end he'll simply burst open the house and walk out a free man. Now I could well understand it if a bystander were to say, "There's nothing we can do for you. We cannot choose between your life and his, we cannot be the

ones to decide who is to live, we cannot intervene." But it cannot be concluded that you too can do nothing, that you cannot attack it to save your life. However innocent the child may be, you do not have to wait passively while it crushes you to death. Perhaps a pregnant woman is vaguely felt to have the status of house, to which we don't allow the right of self-defense. But if the woman houses the child, it should be remembered that she is a person who houses it.

I should perhaps stop to say explicitly that I am not claiming that people have a right to do anything whatever to save their lives. I think, rather, that there are drastic limits to the right of self-defense. If someone threatens you with death unless you torture someone else to death, I think you have not the right, even to save your life, to do so. But the case under consideration here is very different. In our case there are only two people involved, one whose life is threatened, and one who threatens it. Both are innocent: the one who is threatened is not threatened because of any fault, the one who threatens does not threaten because of any fault. For this reason we may feel that we bystanders cannot intervene. But the person threatened can.

In sum, a woman surely can defend her life against the threat to it posed by the unborn child, even if doing so involves its death. And this shows not merely that the theses in (1) through (4) are false; it shows also that the extreme view of abortion is false, and so we need not canvass any other possible ways of arriving at it from the argument I mentioned at the outset.

2. The extreme view could of course be weakened to say that while abortion is permissible to save the mother's life, it may not be performed by a third party, but only by the mother herself. But this cannot be right either. For what we have to keep in mind is that the mother and the unborn child are not like two tenants in a small house which as, by an unfortunate mistake, been rented to both: the mother *owns* the house. The fact that she does

adds to the offensiveness of deducing that the mother can do nothing from the supposition that third parties can do nothing. But it does more than this: it casts a bright light on the supposition that third parties can do nothing. Certainly it lets us see that a third party who says "I cannot choose between you" is fooling himself if he thinks this is impartiality. If Jones has found and fastened on a certain coat, which he needs to keep him from freezing, but which Smith also needs to keep him from freezing, then it is not impartiality that says "I cannot choose between you" when Smith owns the coat. Women have said again and again "This body is *my* body!" and they have reason to feel angry, reason to feel that it has been like shouting into the wind. Smith, after all, is hardly likely to bless us if we say to him, "Of course it's your coat, anybody would grant that it is. But no one may choose between you and Jones who is to have it...."

3. Where the mother's life is not at stake, the argument I mentioned at the outset seems to have a much stronger pull. "Everyone has a right to life, so the unborn person has a right to life." And isn't the child's right to life weightier than anything other than the mother's own right to life, which she might put forward as ground for an abortion?

This argument treats the right to life as if it were unproblematic. It is not, and this seems to me to be precisely the source of the mistake.

For we should now, at long last, ask what it comes to, to have a right to life. In some views having a right to life includes having a right to be given at least the bare minimum one needs for continued life. But suppose that what in fact *is* the bare minimum a man needs for continued life is something he has no right at all to be given? If I am sick unto death, and the only thing that will save my life is the touch of Henry Fonda's cool hand on my fevered brow, then all the same, I have no right to be given the touch of Henry Fonda's cool hand on my fevered brow. It would be frightfully nice of him to fly in from the West Coast to provide it. It would be less nice, though no doubt well meant, if my friends flew out to the West Coast and carried Henry Fonda back with them. But I have no right at all against anybody that he should do this for me. Or again, to return to the story I told earlier, the fact that for continued life that violinist needs the continued use of your kidneys does not establish that he has a right to be given the continued use of your kidneys. He certainly has no right against you that *you* should give him continued use of your kidneys. For nobody has any right to use your kidneys unless you give him such a right; and nobody has the right against you that you shall give him this right—if you do allow him to go on using your kidneys, this is a kindness on your part, and not something he can claim from you as his due. Nor has he any right against anybody else that *they* should give him continued use of your kidneys. Certainly he had no right against the Society of Music Lovers that they should plug him into you in the first place. And if you now start to unplug yourself, having learned that you will otherwise have to spend nine years in bed with him, there is nobody in the world who must try to prevent you, in order to see to it that he is given something he has a right to be given.

Some people are rather stricter about the right to life. In their view, it does not include the right to be given anything, but amounts to, and only to, the right not to be killed by anybody. But here a related difficulty arises. If everybody is to refrain from killing that violinist, then everybody must refrain from doing a great many different sorts of things. Everybody must refrain from slitting his throat, everybody must refrain from shooting him—and everybody must refrain from unplugging you from him. But does he have a right against everybody that they shall refrain from unplugging you from him? To refrain from doing this is to allow him to continue to use your kidneys. It could be argued that he has a right against us that *we* shall allow him to continue to use your kidneys. That is, while he had no right against us that we should give him the use of your kidneys, it might be argued that he anyway has a right against us that we shall not now intervene and deprive him of the use of your kidneys. I shall come back to third-party interventions later. But certainly the violinist has no right against you that *you* shall allow him to continue to use your kidneys. As I said, if you do allow him to use them, it is a kindness on your part, and not something you owe him.

The difficulty I point to here is not peculiar to the right to life. It reappears in connection with all the other natural rights; and it is something which an adequate account of rights must deal with. For present purposes it is enough just to draw attention to it. But I would stress that I am not arguing that people do not have a right to life—quite to the contrary, it seems to me that the primary control we must place on the acceptability of an account of rights is that it should turn out in that account to be a truth that all persons have a right to life. I am arguing only that having a right to life does not guarantee having either a right to be given the use of or a right to be allowed continued use of another person's body—even if one needs it for life itself. So the right to life will not serve the opponents of abortion in the very simple and clear way in which they seem to have thought it would. . . .

Endnotes

1. Daniel Callahan, *Abortion: Law, Choice and Morality* (New York, 1970), p. 373. This book gives a fascinating survey of the available information on abortion. The Jewish tradition is surveyed in David M. Feldman, *Birth Control in Jewish Law* (New York, 1968), Part 5, the Catholic tradition in John T. Noonan, Jr., "An Almost Absolute Value in History," in *The Morality of Abortion*, ed. John T. Noonan, Jr. (Cambridge, Mass., 1970).

2. The term "direct" in the arguments I refer to is a technical one. Roughly, what is meant by "direct killing" is either killing as an end in itself, or killing as a means to some end, for example, the end of saving someone else's life. See note 5, below, for an example of its use.

3. Cf. *Encyclical Letter of Pope Pius XI on Christian Marriage*, St. Paul Editions (Boston, n.d.), p. 32: "however much we may pity the mother whose health and even life is gravely imperiled in the performance of the duty allotted to her by nature, nevertheless what could ever be a sufficient reason for excusing in any way the direct murder of the innocent? This is precisely what we are dealing with here." Noonan (*The Morality of Abortion*, p. 43) reads this as follows: "What cause can ever avail to excuse in any way the direct killing of the innocent? For it is a question of that."

4. The thesis in (4) is in an interesting way weaker than those in (1), (2), and (3): they rule out abortion even in cases in which both mother *and* child will die if the abortion is not performed. By contrast, one who held the view expressed in (4) could consistently say that one needn't prefer letting two persons die to killing one.

5. Cf. the following passage from Pius XII, *Address to the Italian Catholic Society of Midwives*: "The baby in the maternal breast has the right to life immediately from God. Hence there is no man, no human authority, no science, no medical, eugenic, social, economic or moral 'indication' which can establish or grant a valid juridical ground for a direct deliberate disposition of an innocent human life, that is, a disposition which looks to its destruction either as an end or as a means to another end perhaps in itself not illicit. The baby, still not born, is a man in the same degree and for the same reason as the mother" (quoted in Noonan, *The Morality of Abortion*, p. 45).

Review Questions

1. What are slippery slope arguments?

2. Why does Thomson reject them?

3. According to Thomson, does the fetus become a human person before birth or not? Does it become a person at conception?

4. Explain the example about the famous violinist.

5. What is the extreme view?

6. What argument is used to defend this view?

7. How does Thomson attack this argument?

8. What is the point of the example about the tiny house and the growing child?

9. Why do women say, "This body is *my* body?" (Do they say this?)

10. Explain the example about Henry Fonda's cool hand on my fevered brow.

Discussion Questions

1. Does a woman who is pregnant due to rape have a right to get an abortion? Defend your view.

2. Does a woman have a right to have an abortion to save her life? Why, or why not?

3. What are the limits, if any, to the right to self-defense?

4. What obligations, if any, do we have towards people who have a right to life? Do we have an obligation, for example, to take care of them and feed them?

John Finnis

The Rights and Wrongs of Abortion: A Reply to Judith Thomson

John Finnis is Fellow in Jurisprudence, University College, Oxford University, and Reader in Commonwealth and American Law, Oxford University, England. He is the author of Natural Law *and* Natural Rights.

Finnis makes several points in his reply to Thomson: She has misrepresented the traditional condemnation of abortion; she has ignored the child's rights which derive from it having a body; the violinist case is different in important respects from the case of lifesaving abortion; and zygotes are different than acorns.

... Let us look at this "traditional condemnation of abortion" a little more closely than Thomson does. It is not a condemnation of the administration of medications to a pregnant mother whose life is threatened by, say, a high fever (whether brought on by pregnancy or not), in an effort to reduce the fever, even if it is known that such medications have the side effect of inducing miscarriage. It is not a condemnation of the removal of the malignantly cancerous womb of a pregnant woman, even if it is known that the foetus

within is not of viable age and so will die. It is quite doubtful whether it is a condemnation of an operation to put back in its place the displaced womb of a pregnant woman whose life is threatened by the displacement, even though the operation necessitates the draining off of the amniotic fluids necessary to the survival of the foetus.[1]

But why are these operations not condemned? As Foot has remarked, the distinction drawn between these and other death-dealing operations "has evoked particularly bitter reactions on the part of non-Catholics. If you are permitted to bring about the death of the child, what does it matter how it is done?"[2] Still, she goes some way to answering her own question....

Foot recognizes that attention to "overriding aim" and "ultimate purpose" is not enough if we are to keep clear of moral horrors such as saving life by killing innocent hostages, etc. As a general though not exclusive and not (it seems) at-all-costs principle, she proposes that one has a duty to refrain from doing injury to innocent people and that this duty is stricter than one's duty to aid others; this enables her to see that "we might find" the traditional conclusion correct, that we must not crush the unborn child's skull in order to save the mother (in a case where the child could be saved if one let the mother die): "for in general we do not think that we can kill one innocent person to rescue another."[3] But what is it to "do injury to" innocent people? She does not think it an injury to blow a man to pieces, or kill and eat him, in order to save others trapped with him in a cave, *if he is certain to die soon anyway.*[4] So I suppose that, after all, she *would* be willing (however reluctantly) to justify the killing by D of hostages, V, V_1, V_2, whenever the black-

John Finnis, "The Rights and Wrongs of Abortion: A Reply to Judith Thomson," *Philosophy & Public Affairs,* Vol. 2, No. 2 (1973). Copyright © 1973 Princeton University Press. Reprinted with permission of Princeton University Press.

mailer P threatened to kill *them too,* along with Q, Q₁, Q₂, unless D killed them himself. One wonders whether this is not an unwarranted though plausible concession to consequentialism.

In any event, Foot was aware, not only that the "**doctrine of the double effect**" "should be taken seriously in spite of the fact that it sounds rather odd ...,"[5] but also of what Thomson has not recorded in her brief footnote (p. 50 n. 3) on the technical meaning given to the term "direct" by moralists using the "doctrine" to analyze the relation between choices and basic values, namely that the "doctrine" requires more than that a certain bad effect or aspect (say, someone's being killed) of one's deed be not intended either as end or as means. If one is to establish that one's death-dealing deed need not be characterized as directly or intentionally against the good of human life, the "doctrine" requires further that the good effect or aspect, which *is* intended, should be proportionate (say, saving someone's life), i.e. sufficiently good and important relative to the bad effect or aspect: otherwise (we may add, in our own words) one's choice, although not directly and intentionally to kill, will reasonably be counted as a choice inadequately open to the value of life.[6] And this consideration alone might well suffice to rule out abortions performed in order simply to remove the unwanted foetus from the body of women who conceived as a result of forcible rape, even if one were to explicate the phrase "intended directly as end or as means" in such a way that the abortion did not amount to a directly intended killing (e.g. because the mother desired only the removal, not the death of the foetus, and would have been willing to have the foetus reared in an artificial womb had one been available).[7] ...

Now the traditional condemnation of abortion[8] concerns the bystander's situation: a bystander cannot but be choosing to kill if (a) he rips open the mother, in a way foreseeably fatal to her, in order to save the child from the threatening enveloping presence of the mother (say, because the placenta has come adrift and the viable child is trapped and doomed unless it can be rescued, or because the mother's blood is poisoning the child, in a situation in which the bystander would prefer to save the child, either because he wants to save it from eternal damnation, or because the child is of royal blood and the mother low born, or because the mother is in any case sick, or old, or useless, or "has had her turn," while the child has a whole rich life before it); or if (b) he cuts up or drowns the child in order to save the mother from the child's threatening presence. "Things being as they are, there isn't much a woman can safely do to abort herself," as Thomson says (p. 52)—at least, not without the help of bystanders, who by helping (directly) would be making the same choice as if they did it themselves. But the unplugging of the violinist is done by the very person defending herself. Thomson admits (p. 52) that this gives quite a different flavor to the situation, but she thinks that the difference is not decisive, since bystanders have a decisive reason to intervene in favor of the *mother* threatened by her child's presence. And she finds this reason in the fact that the mother *owns* her body, just as the person plugged in to the violinist owns his own kidneys and is entitled to their unencumbered use (p. 53). Well, this too has always been accounted a factor in these problems, as we can see by turning to the following question.

Does the chosen action involve not merely a denial of aid and succor to someone but an actual intervention that amounts to an assault on the body of that person? Bennett wanted to deny all relevance to any such question,[9] but Foot[10] and Thomson have rightly seen that in the ticklish matter of respecting human life in the persons of others, and of characterizing choices with a view to assessing their respect for life, it *can* matter that one is directly injuring and not merely failing to maintain a life-preserving level of assistance to another. Sometimes, as here, it is the causal structure of one's activity that involves one willy-nilly in a choice for or against a basic value. The connection between one's activity and the destruction of life may be so close and direct that intentions and considerations which would give a different dominant character to mere nonpreservation of life are incapable of affecting the dominant character of a straightforward taking of life. This surely is the reason why Thomson goes about and about to represent a choice to have an abortion as a choice *not* to provide assistance or facilities, *not* to be a Good or at any rate a Splendid Samaritan; and why, too, she carefully describes the violinist affair so as to minimize the degree of intervention against the violinist's body, and to maximize the analogy with simply refusing an invitation to volunteer one's kidneys for his welfare (like Henry Fonda's declining to cross America to save Judith Thomson's life). "If anything in the world is true, it is that you do not commit murder, you do not do what is impermissible, if you reach around to your back and unplug yourself from that violinist to save your life" (p. 52). Quite so. It might nevertheless be useful to test one's moral reactions a little further: suppose, not simply that "unplugging" required a *bystander's* intervention, but also that (for medical reasons, poison in the bloodstream, shock, etc.) unplugging could not safely be performed unless and until the violinist had first been dead for six hours and had moreover been killed outright, say by drowning or decapitation (though not necessarily while conscious). Could one then be *so* confident, as a bystander, that it was right to kill the violinist in order to save the philosopher? But I put forward this revised version principally to illustrate *another* reason for thinking that, within the traditional casuistry, the violinist-unplugging in Thomson's version is *not* the "direct killing" which she claims it is, and which she *must* claim it is if she is to make out her case for rejecting the traditional principle about direct killing.

Let us now look back to the traditional rule about abortion. If the mother needs medical treatment to save her life, she gets it, subject to one proviso, even if the treatment is certain to kill the unborn child—for after all, her body is *her* body, as "women have said again and again" (and they have been heard by the traditional casuists!). And the proviso? That the medical treatment not be *via* a straightforward assault on or intervention against the child's body. For after all *the child's body is the child's body, not the woman's.* The traditional casuists have admitted the claims made on behalf of one "body" up to the very limit where those claims become *mere (understandable) bias, mere (understandable) self-interested* refusal to listen to the *very same* claim ("This body is *my* body") when it is made by or on behalf of another person.[11] Of course, a traditional casuist would display an utter want of feeling if he didn't most profoundly sympathize with women in the desperate circumstances under discussion. But it is vexing to find a philosophical Judith Thomson, in a cool hour, unable to see when an argument cuts both ways, and unaware that the casuists have seen the point before her and have, unlike her, allowed the argument to cut both ways impartially. The child, like his mother, has a "just prior claim to his own body," and abortion involves laying hands on, manipulating, that body. And here we have perhaps the decisive reason why abortion cannot be assimilated to the range of Samaritan problems and why Thomson's location of it within that range is a mere (ingenious) novelty.

But is the action against someone who had a duty not to be doing what he is doing, or not to be present where he is present? There seems no doubt that the "innocence" of the victim whose life is taken makes a difference to the characterizing of an action as open to and respectful of the good of human life, and as an intentional killing. Just how and why it makes a difference is difficult to unravel; I shall not attempt an unraveling here. We all, for whatever reason, recognize the difference and Thomson has expressly allowed its relevance (p. 52).

But her way of speaking of "rights" has a final unfortunate effect at this point. We can grant, and have granted, that the unborn child has no ... **claim-right** to be allowed to stay within the mother's body under all circumstances; the mother is not under a strict duty to allow it to stay under all circumstances. In *that* sense, the child "has no right to be there." But Thomson discusses also the case of the burglar in the house; and he, too, has "no right to be there," even when she opens the window! But beware of the equivocation! The burglar not merely has no claim-right to be allowed to enter or stay; he also has a strict duty *not* to enter or stay, ... and it is *this* that is uppermost in our minds when we think that he "has no right to be there": it is actually unjust for him to be there. Similarly with Jones who takes Smith's coat, leaving Smith freezing (p. 53). And similarly with the violinist. He and his agents had a strict duty not to make the hook-up to Judith Thomson or her gentle reader. Of course, the violinist himself may have been unconscious and so not himself at fault; but the whole affair is a gross injustice to the person whose kidneys are made free with, and the injustice to that person is not measured simply by the degree of moral fault of one of the parties to the injustice. Our whole view of the violinist's situation is colored by this burglarious and persisting wrongfulness of his presence plugged into his victim.

But can any of this reasonably be said or thought of the unborn child? True, the child had no *claim-right* to be allowed to come into being within the mother. But it was not in breach of any *duty* in coming into being nor in remaining present within the mother; Thomson gives no arguments at all in favor of the view that the child is in breach of duty in being present (though her counter examples show that she is often tacitly assuming this). (Indeed, if we are going to use the wretched analogy of owning houses, I fail to see why the unborn child should not with justice say of the body around it: "That is my house. No one *granted* me property rights in it, but equally no one *granted* my mother any property rights in it." The fact is that both persons

share in the use of this body, both by the same sort of title, viz., that this is the way they happened to come into being. But it would be better to drop this ill-fitting talk of "ownership" and "property rights" altogether.) So though the unborn child "had no right to be there" (in the sense that it never had a claim-right to be allowed to *begin* to be there), in another straightforward and more important sense it *did* "have a right to be there" (in the sense that it was not in breach of duty in being or continuing to be there). All this is, I think, clear and clearly different from the violinist's case. Perhaps forcible rape is a special case; but even then it seems fanciful to say that the child is or could be in any way at fault, as the violinist is at fault or would be but for the adventitious circumstance that he was unconscious at the time.

Still, I don't want to be dogmatic about the justice or injustice, innocence or fault, involved in a rape conception. (I have already remarked that the impermissibility of abortion in any such case, where the mother's life is not in danger, does not depend necessarily on showing that the act is a choice directly to kill.) It is enough that I have shown how in three admittedly important respects the violinist case differs from the therapeutic abortion performed to save the life of the mother. As presented by Thomson, the violinist's case involves (i) no bystander, (ii) no intervention against or assault upon the body of the violinist, and (iii) an indisputable injustice to the agent in question. Each of these three factors is absent from the abortion cases in dispute. Each has been treated as relevant by the traditional casuists whose condemnations Thomson was seeking to contest when she plugged us into the violinist....

I have been assuming that the unborn child is, from conception, a person and hence is not to be discriminated against on account of age, appearance or other such factors insofar as such factors are reasonably considered irrelevant where respect for basic human values is in question. Thomson argues against this assumption, but not, as I think, well. She thinks . . . that the argument in favor of treating a newly conceived child as a person is merely a "slippery slope" argument (p. 47), rather like (I suppose) saying that one should call all men bearded because there is no line one can confidently draw between beard and clean shavenness. More precisely, she thinks that a newly conceived child is like an acorn, which after all is not an oak! It is discouraging to see her relying so heavily and uncritically on this hoary muddle. An acorn can remain for years in a stable state, simply but completely an acorn. Plant it and from it will sprout an oak sapling, a new, dynamic biological system that has nothing much in common with an acorn save that it came from an acorn and is capable of generating new acorns. Suppose an acorn is formed in September 1971, picked up on 1 February 1972, and stored under good conditions for three years, then planted in January 1975; it sprouts on 1 March 1975 and fifty years later is a fully mature oak tree. Now suppose I ask: When did that oak begin to grow? Will anyone say September 1971 or February 1972? Will anyone look for the date on which it was first noticed in the garden? Surely not. If we know it sprouted from the acorn on 1 March 1975, that is enough (though a biologist could be a trifle more exact about "sprouting"); that is when *the oak* began. *A fortiori* with the conception of a child, which is no *mere* germination of a seed. Two sex cells, each with only twenty-three chromosomes, unite and more or less immediately fuse to become a new cell with forty-six chromosomes providing a unique genetic constitution (not the father's, not the mother's, and not a mere juxtaposition of the parents') which thenceforth throughout its life, however long, will substantially determine the new individual's makeup.[12] This new cell is the first stage in a dynamic integrated system that has nothing much in common with the individual male and female sex cells, save that it sprang from a pair of them and will in time produce new sets of them. To say that *this* is when a person's life began is not to work backwards

from maturity, sophistically asking at each point "How can one draw the line *here*?" Rather it is to point to a perfectly clear-cut beginning to which each one of us can look back and in looking back see how, in a vividly intelligible sense, "in my beginning is my end." Judith Thomson thinks she began to "acquire human characteristics" "by the tenth week" (when fingers, toes, etc. became visible). I cannot think why she overlooks the most radically and distinctively human characteristic of all—the fact that she was conceived of human parents. And then there is Henry Fonda. From the time of his conception, though not before, one could say, looking at his unique personal genetic constitution, not only that "by the tenth week" Henry Fonda would have fingers, but also that in his fortieth year he would have a cool hand. That is why there seems no rhyme or reason in waiting "ten weeks" until his fingers and so on actually become visible before declaring that he *now* has the human rights which Judith Thomson rightly but incompletely recognizes.

Endnotes

1. The three cases mentioned in this paragraph are discussed in a standard and conservative Roman Catholic textbook: Marcellino Zalba, *Theologiae Moralis Compendium* (Madrid, 1958), I, p. 885. [The footnotes have been renumbered—Ed.]

2. Philippa Foot, "The Problem of Abortion and the Doctrine of Double Effect," *The Oxford Review* 5 (1967): 6.

3. Foot, "The Problem of Abortion and the Doctrine of Double Effect," p. 15.

4. Ibid., p. 14.

5. Ibid., p. 8.

6. Ibid., p. 7. This is the fourth of the four usual conditions for the application of the "Doctrine of Double Effect"; see e.g. Grisez, *Abortion: the Myths, the Realities and the Arguments,* p. 329. G.E.M. Anscombe, "War and Murder," in *Nuclear Weapons and Christian Conscience,* ed. W. Stein, (London, 1961), p. 57, formulates the "principle of double effect," in relation to the situation where "someone innocent will die unless I do a wicked thing," thus: "you are no murderer if a man's death was neither your aim nor your chosen means, *and if you had to act in the way that led to it or else do something absolutely forbidden*" (emphasis added).

7. Grisez argues thus, *op. cit.,* p. 343; also in "Toward a Consistent Natural–Law Ethics of Killing," *American*

Journal of Jurisprudence 15 (1970): 95.

8. *Summa Theologiae* II, q. 64, arts. 2 and 3.

9. Bennett, " 'Whatever the Consequences.' "

10. Foot, "The Problem of Abortion and the Doctrine of Double Effect," pp. 11–13.

11. Not, of course, that they have used Thomson's curious talk of "owning" one's own body with its distracting and legalistic connotations and its dualistic reduction of subjects of justice to objects.

12. See Grisez, *Abortion: The Myth, the Realities and the Arguments,* chap. 1 and pp. 273–287, with literature there cited.

Review Questions

1. According to Finnis, why does the traditional condemnation of abortion allow certain exceptions?

2. State the doctrine of double effect, and explain how it can be used to justify acts of killing.

3. How does Finnis reply to the claim that a woman's body is *her* body?

4. According to Finnis, in what respects is the violinist case different from lifesaving abortion?

5. Explain Finnis' argument about acorns.

Discussion Questions

1. Critically examine the doctrine of double effect. Can you think of any good objections to this doctrine? What are they?

2. Do you agree that this doctrine rules out abortions in the case of forcible rape? Why or why not?

3. Has Finnis given any plausible arguments to support his assumption that "the unborn child is, from conception, a person and hence is not to be discriminated against?" If so, what are they?

4. Compare the views of Finnis and Noonan.

Mary Anne Warren

On the Moral and Legal Status of Abortion

Mary Anne Warren teaches at San Francisco State University. She is the author of several articles including "Do Potential People Have Moral Rights?" and "Secondary Sexism and Quota Hiring."

The first part of Warren's article is a response to Thomson. She argues that even though Thomson's argument from analogy is probably conclusive in showing that abortion is justified in the case of pregnancy due to rape, it does not show that abortion is permissible in numerous other cases where pregnancy is not due to rape and is not life threatening. Warren feels that more argument is needed to show the per-

From "On the Moral and Legal Status of Abortion," *The Monist,* vol. 57, no. 1 (January 1973), pp. 43–61. Reprinted with permission from *The Monist* and Dr. Mary Anne Warren, San Francisco State University.

missibility of abortion in those cases.

In the second part of the article, Warren presents her case for the liberal view that abortion can be justified in any case. Her argument depends on a distinction between two senses of the word human. *The first sense is a* genetic sense *where something is human if it is a member of the biological species* Homo sapiens; *the second is a* moral sense *where something is human if it is a member of the moral community. She claims that conservatives like Noonan confuse these two senses of human. They fallaciously argue from the fact that fetuses are genetically human to the conclusion that they are morally human, that is, persons with a right to life. But an analysis of the concept of person shows that fetuses are unlike persons in too many areas to have a significant right to life. There are five features central to personhood—consciousness, reasoning, self-motivated activity, the capacity to communicate, and self-awareness. The fetus lacks all of these features in the early stages of development and continues to lack most of them in the later stages. Furthermore, the fetus' potential for becoming a person does not provide us with a good reason for ascribing to it a significant right to life. The rights of merely a potential person, even assuming it has rights, would always be outweighed by the rights of an actual person, in this case, the mother. The mother's right to have an abortion, then, is absolute; it can never be outweighed by the rights of the fetus.*

In the postscript, Warren replies to the objection that her view would justify infanticide. She admits that infants do not have a significant right to life in her view, but she claims that it does not follow that infanticide is permissible for two reasons. First, there may be people willing to adopt the unwanted child and in that case it would be wrong to kill it. Second, many people in our country value infants and would prefer that they be preserved, even if foster parents are not available.

We will be concerned with both the moral status of abortion, which for our purposes we may define as the act which a woman performs in voluntarily terminating, or allowing another person to terminate, her pregnancy, and the legal status which is appropriate for this act. I will argue that, while it is not possible to produce a satisfactory defense of a woman's right to obtain an abortion without showing that a fetus is not a human being, in the morally relevant sense of that term, we ought not to conclude that the difficulties involved in determining whether or not a fetus is human make it impossible to produce any satisfactory solution to the problem of the moral status of abortion. For it is possible to show that, on the basis of intuitions which we may expect even the opponents of abortion to share, a fetus is not a person, and hence not the sort of entity to which it is proper to ascribe full moral rights.

Of course, while some philosophers would deny the possibility of any such proof,[1] others will deny that there is any need for it, since the moral permissibility of abortion appears to them to be too obvious to require proof. But the inadequacy of this attitude should be evident from the fact that both the friends and the foes of abortion consider their position to be morally self-evident. Because pro-abortionists have never adequately come to grips with the conceptual issues sur-

rounding abortion, most if not all, of the arguments which they advance in opposition to laws restricting access to abortion fail to refute or even weaken the traditional antiabortion argument, i.e., that a fetus is a human being, and therefore abortion is murder.

These arguments are typically one of two sorts. Either they point to the terrible side effects of the restrictive laws, e.g., the deaths due to illegal abortions, and the fact that it is poor women who suffer the most as a result of these laws, or else they state that to deny a woman access to abortion is to deprive her of her right to control her own body. Unfortunately, however, the fact that restricting access to abortion has tragic side effects does not, in itself, show that the restrictions are unjustified, since murder is wrong regardless of the consequences of prohibiting it; and the appeal to the right to control one's body, which is generally construed as a property right, is at best a rather feeble argument for the permissibility of abortion. Mere ownership does not give me the right to kill innocent people whom I find on my property, and indeed I am apt to be held responsible if such people injure themselves while on my property. It is equally unclear that I have any moral right to expel an innocent person from my property when I know that doing so will result in his death.

Furthermore, it is probably inappropriate to describe a woman's body as her property, since it seems natural to hold that a person is something distinct from her property, but not from her body. Even those who would object to the identification of a person with his body, or with the conjunction of his body and his mind, must admit that it would be very odd to describe, say, breaking a leg, as damaging one's property, and much more appropriate to describe it as injuring one*self*. Thus it is probably a mistake to argue that the right to obtain an abortion is in any way derived from the right to own and regulate property.

But however we wish to construe the right to abortion, we cannot hope to convince those who consider abortion a form of murder of the existence of any such right unless we are able to produce a clear and convincing refutation of the traditional antiabortion argument, and this has not, to my knowledge, been done. With respect to the two most vital issues which that argument involves, i.e., the humanity of the fetus and its implication for the moral status of abortion, confusion has prevailed on both sides of the dispute.

Thus, both pro-abortionists and antiabortionists have tended to abstract the question of whether abortion is wrong to that of whether it is wrong to destroy a fetus, just as though the rights of another person were not necessarily involved. This mistaken abstraction has led to the almost universal assumption that if a fetus is a human being, with a right to life, then it follows immediately that abortion is wrong (except perhaps when necessary to save the woman's life), and that it ought to be prohibited. It has also been generally assumed that unless the question about the status of the fetus is answered, the moral status of abortion cannot possibly be determined.

Two recent papers, one by B.A. Brody,[2] and one by Judith Thomson,[3] have attempted to settle the question of whether abortion ought to be prohibited apart from the question of whether or not the fetus is human. Brody examines the possibility that the following two statements are compatible: (1) that abortion is the taking of innocent human life, and therefore wrong; and (2) that nevertheless it ought not to be prohibited by law, at least under the present circumstances.[4] Not surprisingly, Brody finds it impossible to reconcile these two statements, since, as he rightly argues, none of the unfortunate side effects of the prohibition of abortion is bad enough to justify legalizing the *wrongful* taking of human life. He is mistaken, however, in concluding that the incompatibility of (1) and (2), in itself, shows that "the legal problem about abortion cannot be resolved independently of the status of the fetus problem"
....

What Brody fails to realize is that (1) embodies the questionable assumption that if a fetus is a human being, then of course abortion is morally wrong, and that an attack on *this* assumption is more promising, as a way of reconciling the humanity of the fetus with the claim that laws prohibiting abortion are unjustified, than is an attack on the assumption that if abortion is the wrongful killing of innocent human beings then it ought to be prohibited. He thus overlooks the possibility that a fetus may have a right to life and abortion still be morally permissible, in that the right of a woman to terminate an unwanted pregnancy might override the right of the fetus to be kept alive. The immorality of abortion is no more demonstrated by the humanity of the fetus, in itself, than the immorality of killing in self-defense is demonstrated by the fact that the assailant is a human being. Neither is it demonstrated by the *innocence* of the fetus, since there may be situations in which the killing of innocent human beings is justified.

It is perhaps not surprising that Brody fails to spot this assumption, since it has been accepted with little or no argument by nearly everyone who has written on the morality of abortion. John Noonan is correct in saying that "the fundamental question in the long history of abortion is, How do you determine the humanity of a being?"[5] He summarizes his own antiabortion argument, which is a version of the official position of the Catholic Church, as follows:

> ... *it is wrong to kill humans, however poor, weak, defenseless, and lacking in opportunity to develop their potential they may be. It is therefore morally wrong to kill Biafrans. Similarly, it is morally wrong to kill embryos.*[6]

Noonan bases his claim that fetuses are human upon what he calls the theologians' criterion of humanity: that whoever is conceived of human beings is human. But although he argues at length for the appropriateness of this criterion, he never questions the assumption that if a fetus is human then abortion is wrong for exactly the same reason that murder is wrong.

Judith Thomson is, in fact, the only writer I am aware of who has seriously questioned this assumption; she has argued that, even if we grant the antiabortionist his claim that a fetus is a human being, with the same right to life as any other human being, we can still demonstrate that, in at least some and perhaps most cases, a woman is under no moral obligation to complete an unwanted pregnancy.[7] Her argument is worth examining, since if it holds up it may enable us to establish the moral permissibility of abortion without becoming involved in problems about what entitles an entity to be considered human, and accorded full moral rights. To be able to do this would be a great gain in the power and simplicity of the pro-abortion position, since, although I will argue that these problems can be solved at least as decisively as can any other moral problem, we should certainly be pleased to be able to avoid having to solve them as part of the justification of abortion.

On the other hand, even if Thomson's argument does not hold up, her insight, i.e., that it requires *argument* to show that if fetuses are human then abortion is properly classified as murder, is an extremely valuable one. The assumption she attacks is particularly invidious, for it amounts to the decision that it is appropriate, in deciding the moral status of abortion, to leave the rights of the pregnant woman out of consideration entirely, except possibly when her life is threatened. Obviously, this will not do; determining what moral rights, if any, a fetus possesses is only the first step in determining the moral status of abortion. Step two, which is at least equally essential, is finding a just solution to the conflict between whatever rights the fetus may have, and the rights of the woman who is unwillingly pregnant. While the historical error has been to pay far too little attention to the second step, Ms. Thomson's suggestion is that if we look at the second step first we may find that a woman has a right to obtain an abortion *regardless* of what rights the fetus has.

Our own inquiry will also have two stages. In Section I, we will consider whether or not it is possible to establish that abortion is morally permissible even on the assumption that a fetus is an entity with a full-fledged right to life. I will argue that in fact this cannot be established, at least not with the conclusiveness which is essential to our hopes of convincing those who are skeptical about the morality of abortion, and that we therefore cannot avoid dealing with the question of whether or not a fetus really does have the same right to life as a (more fully developed) human being.

In Section II, I will propose an answer to this question, namely, that a fetus cannot be considered a member of the moral community, the set of beings with full and equal moral rights, for the simple reason that it is not a person, and that it is personhood, and not genetic humanity, i.e., humanity as defined by Noonan, which is the basis for membership in this community. I will argue that a fetus, whatever its stage of development, satisfies none of the basic criteria of personhood, and is not even enough *like* a person to be accorded even some of the same rights on the basis of this resemblance. Nor, as we will see, is a fetus's *potential* personhood a threat to the morality of abortion, since, whatever the rights of potential people may be, they are invariably overridden in any conflict with the moral rights of actual people.

I

We turn now to Professor Thomson's case for the claim that even if a fetus has full moral rights, abortion is still morally permissible, at least sometimes, and for some reasons other than to save the woman's life. Her argument is based upon a clever, but I think faulty, analogy. She asks us to picture ourselves waking up one day, in bed with a famous violinist. Imagine that you have been kidnapped, and your bloodstream hooked up to that of the violinist, who happens to have an ailment which will certainly kill him unless he is permitted to share your kidneys for a period of nine months. No one else can save him, since you alone have the right type of blood. He will be unconscious all that time, and you will have to stay in bed with him, but after the nine months are over he may be unplugged, completely cured, that is provided that you have cooperated.

Now then, she continues, what are your obligations in this situation? The antiabortionist, if he is consistent, will have to say that you are obligated to stay in bed with the violinist: for all people have a right to life, and violinists are people, and therefore it would be murder for you to disconnect yourself from him and let him die .... But this is outrageous, and so there must be something wrong with the same argument when it is applied to abortion. It would certainly be commendable of you to agree to save the violinist, but it is absurd to suggest that your refusal to do so would be murder. His right to life does not obligate you to do whatever is required to keep him alive; nor does it justify anyone else in forcing you to do so. A law which required you to say in bed with the violinist would clearly be an unjust law, since it is no proper function of the law to force unwilling people to make huge sacrifices for the sake of other people toward whom they have no such prior obligation.

Thomson concludes that, if this analogy is an apt one, then we can grant the antiabortionist his claim that a fetus is a human being, and still hold that it is at least sometimes the case that a pregnant woman has the right to refuse to be a Good Samaritan towards the fetus, i.e., to obtain an abortion. For there is a great gap between the claim that *x* has a right to life, and the claim that *y* is obligated to do whatever is necessary to keep *x* alive, let alone that he ought to be forced to do so. It is *y*'s duty to keep *x* alive only if he has somehow contracted a *special* obligation to do so; and a woman who is unwillingly pregnant, e.g., who was raped, has done nothing which obligates her to make the enormous sacrifice which is necessary to preserve the conceptus.

This argument is initially quite plausible,

and in the extreme case of pregnancy due to rape it is probably conclusive. Difficulties arise, however, when we try to specify more exactly the range of cases in which abortion is clearly justifiable even on the assumption that the fetus is human. Professor Thomson considers it a virtue of her argument that it does not enable us to conclude that abortion is *always* permissible. It would, she says, be "indecent" for a woman in her seventh month to obtain an abortion just to avoid having to postpone a trip to Europe. On the other hand, her argument enables us to see that "a sick and desperately frightened schoolgirl pregnant due to rape may *of course* choose abortion, and that any law which rules this out is an insane law" .... So far, so good; but what are we to say about the woman who becomes pregnant not through rape but as a result of her own carelessness, or because of contraceptive failure, or who gets pregnant intentionally and then changes her mind about wanting a child? With respect to such cases, the violinist analogy is of much less use to the defender of the woman's right to obtain an abortion.

Indeed, the choice of a pregnancy due to rape, as an example of a case in which abortion is permissible even if a fetus is considered a human being, is extremely significant; for it is only in the case of pregnancy due to rape that the woman's situation is adequately analogous to the violinist case for our intuitions about the latter to transfer convincingly. The crucial difference between a pregnancy due to rape and the *normal* case of an unwanted pregnancy is that in the normal case we cannot claim that the woman is in no way responsible for her predicament; she could have remained chaste, or taken her pills more faithfully, or abstained on dangerous days, and so on. If, on the other hand, you are kidnapped by strangers, and hooked up to a strange violinist, then you are free of any shred of responsibility for the situation, on the basis of which it could be argued that you are obligated to keep the violinist alive. Only when her pregnancy is due to rape is a woman clearly just as nonresponsible.[8]

Consequently, there is room for the antiabortionist to argue that in the normal case of unwanted pregnancy a woman has, by her own actions, assumed responsibility for the fetus. For if x behaves in a way which he could have avoided, and which he knows involves, let us say, a 1 percent chance of bringing into existence a human being, with a right to life, and does so knowing that if this should happen then that human being will perish unless x does certain things to keep him alive, then it is by no means clear that when it does happen x is free of any obligation to what he knew in advance would be required to keep that human being alive.

The plausibility of such an argument is enough to show that the Thomson analogy can provide a clear and persuasive defense of a woman's right to obtain an abortion only with respect to those cases in which the woman is in no way responsible for her pregnancy, e.g., where it is due to rape. In all other cases, we would almost certainly conclude that it was necessary to look carefully at the particular circumstances in order to determine the extent of the woman's responsibility, and hence the extent of her obligation. This is an extremely unsatisfactory outcome, from the viewpoint of the opponents of restrictive abortion laws, most of whom are convinced that a woman has a right to obtain an abortion regardless of how and why she got pregnant.

Of course a supporter of the violinist analogy might point out that it is absurd to suggest that forgetting her pill one day might be sufficient to obligate a woman to complete an unwanted pregnancy. And indeed it *is* absurd to suggest this. As we will see, the moral right to obtain an abortion is not in the least dependent upon the extent to which the woman is responsible for her pregnancy. But unfortunately, once we allow the assumption that a fetus has full moral rights, we cannot avoid taking this absurd suggestion seriously. Perhaps we can make this point more clear by altering the violinist story just enough to

make it more analogous to a normal unwanted pregnancy and less to a pregnancy due to rape, and then seeing whether it is still obvious that you are not obligated to stay in bed with the fellow.

Suppose, then, that violinists are peculiarly prone to the sort of illness the only cure for which is the use of someone else's bloodstream for nine months, and that because of this there has been formed a society of music lovers who agree that whenever a violinist is stricken they will draw lots and the loser will, by some means, be made the one and only person capable of saving him. Now then, would you be obligated to cooperate in curing the violinist if you had voluntarily joined this society, knowing the possible consequences, and then your name had been drawn and you had been kidnapped? Admittedly, you did not promise ahead of time that you would, but you did deliberately place yourself in a position in which it might happen that a human life would be lost if you did not. Surely this is at least a prima facie reason for supposing that you have an obligation to stay in bed with the violinist. Suppose that you had gotten your name drawn deliberately; surely *that* would be quite a strong reason for thinking that you had such an obligation.

It might be suggested that there is one important disanalogy between the modified violinist case and the case of an unwanted pregnancy, which makes the woman's responsibility significantly less, namely, the fact that the fetus *comes into existence* as the result of the woman's actions. This fact might give her a right to refuse to keep it alive, whereas she would not have had this right had it existed previously, independently, and then as a result of her actions become dependent upon her for its survival.

My own intuition, however, is that x has no more right to bring into existence, either deliberately or as a foreseeable result of actions he could have avoided, a being with full moral rights (y), and then refuse to do what he knew beforehand would be required to keep that being alive, than he has to enter into an agreement with an existing person, whereby he may be called upon to save that person's life, and then refuse to do so when so called upon. Thus, x's responsibility for y's existence does not seem to lessen his obligation to keep y alive, if he is also responsible for y's being in a situation in which only he can save him.

Whether or not this intuition is entirely correct, it brings us back once again to the conclusion that once we allow the assumption that a fetus has full moral rights it becomes an extremely complex and difficult question whether and when abortion is justifiable. Thus the Thomson analogy cannot help us produce a clear and persuasive proof of the moral permissibility of abortion. Nor will the opponents of the restrictive laws thank us for anything less; for their conviction (for the most part) is that abortion is obviously *not* a morally serious and extremely unfortunate, even though sometimes justified act, comparable to killing in self-defense or to letting the violinist die, but rather is closer to being a morally neutral act, like cutting one's hair.

The basis of this conviction, I believe, is the realization that a fetus is not a person, and thus does not have a full-fledged right to life. Perhaps the reason why this claim has been so inadequately defended is that it seems self-evident to those who accept it. And so it is, insofar as it follows from what I take to be perfectly obvious claims about the nature of personhood, and about the proper grounds for ascribing moral rights, claims which ought, indeed, to be obvious to both the friends and foes of abortion. Nevertheless, it is worth examining these claims, and showing how they demonstrate the moral innocuousness of abortion, since this apparently has not been adequately done before.

II

The question which we must answer in order to produce a satisfactory solution to the problem of the moral status of abortion is this: How are we to define the moral community, the set of beings with full and equal moral rights, such that we can decide whether a human fetus is a member of this community or not? What sort of entity, exactly, has the inalienable rights to life, liberty, and the pursuit of happiness? Jefferson attributed these rights to all *men*, and it may or may not be fair to suggest that he intended to attribute them *only* to men. Perhaps he ought to have attributed them to all human beings. If so, then we arrive, first, at Noonan's problem of defining what makes a being human, and, second, at the equally vital question which Noonan does not consider, namely, What reason is there for identifying the moral community with the set of all human beings, in whatever way we have chosen to define that term?

On the Definition of "Human"

One reason why this vital second question is so frequently overlooked in the debate over the moral status of abortion is that the term "human" has two distinct, but not often distinguished, senses. This fact results in a slide of meaning, which serves to conceal the fallaciousness of the traditional argument that since (1) it is wrong to kill innocent human beings, and (2) fetuses are innocent human beings, then (3) it is wrong to kill fetuses. For if "human" is used in the same sense in both (1) and (2) then, whichever of the two senses is meant, one of these premises is question-begging. And if it is used in two different senses then of course the conclusion doesn't follow.

Thus, (1) is a self-evident moral truth,[9] and avoids begging the question about abortion, only if "human being" is used to mean something like "a full-fledged member of the moral community." (It may or may not also be meant to refer exclusively to members of the species *Homo sapiens.*) We may call this the *moral* sense of "human." It is not to be confused with what we will call the *genetic* sense, i.e., the sense in which *any* member of the species is a human being, and no member of any other species could be. If (1) is acceptable only if the moral sense is intended, (2) is non-question-begging only if what is intended is the genetic sense.

In "Deciding Who Is Human," Noonan argues for the classification of fetuses with human beings by pointing to the presence of the full genetic code, and the potential capacity for rational thought . . . . It is clear that what he needs to show, for his version of the traditional argument to be valid, is that fetuses are human in the moral sense, the sense in which it is analytically true that all human beings have full moral rights. But, in the absence of any argument showing that whatever is genetically human is also morally human, and he gives none, nothing more than genetic humanity can be demonstrated by the presence of the human genetic code. And, as we will see, the *potential* capacity for rational thought can at most show that an entity has the potential for *becoming* human in the moral sense.

Defining the Moral Community

Can it be established that genetic humanity is sufficient for moral humanity? I think that there are very good reasons for not defining the moral community in this way. I would like to suggest an alternative way of defining the moral community, which I will argue for only to the extent of explaining why it is, or should be, self-evident. The suggestion is simply that the moral community consists of all and only *people,* rather than all and only human beings; [10] and probably the best way of demonstrating its self-evidence is by considering the concept of personhood, to see what sorts of entity are and are not persons, and what the decision that a being is or is not a person implies about its moral rights.

What characteristics entitle an entity to be considered a person? This is obviously not the place to attempt a complete analysis of the concept of personhood, but we do not need such a fully adequate analysis just to determine whether and why a fetus is or isn't a person. All we need is a rough and approximate list of the most basic criteria of personhood, and some idea of which, or how many, of these an entity must satisfy in order to properly be considered a person.

In searching for such criteria, it is useful to look beyond the set of people with whom we are acquainted, and ask how we would decide whether a totally alien being was a person or not. (For we have no right to assume that genetic humanity is necessary for personhood.) Imagine a space traveler who lands on an unknown planet and encounters a race of beings utterly unlike any he has ever seen or heard of. If he wants to be sure of behaving morally toward these beings, he has to somehow decide whether they are people, and hence have full moral rights, or whether they are the sort of thing which he need not feel guilty about treating as, for example, a source of food.

How should he go about making this decision? If he has some anthropological background, he might look for such things as religion, art, and the manufacturing of tools, weapons, or shelters, since these factors have been used to distinguish our human from our prehuman ancestors, in what seems to be closer to the moral than the genetic sense of "human." And no doubt he would be right to consider the presence of such factors as good evidence that the alien beings were people, and morally human. It would, however, be overly anthropocentric of him to take the absence of these things as adequate evidence that they were not, since we can imagine people who have progressed beyond, or evolved without ever developing, these cultural characteristics.

I suggest that the traits which are most central to the concept of personhood, or humanity in the moral sense, are, very roughly, the following:

1. consciousness (of objects and events external and/or internal to the being), and in particular the capacity to feel pain;
2. reasoning (the *developed* capacity to solve new and relatively complex problems);
3. self-motivated activity (activity which is relatively independent of either genetic or direct external control);
4. the capacity to communicate, by

whatever means, messages of an indefinite variety of types, that is, not just with an indefinite number of possible contents, but on indefinitely many possible topics;

5. the presence of self-concepts, and self-awareness, either individual or racial, or both.

Admittedly, there are apt to be a great many problems involved in formulating precise definitions of these criteria, let alone in developing universally valid behavioral criteria for deciding when they apply. But I will assume that both we and our explorer know approximately what (1)–(5) mean, and that he is also able to determine whether or not they apply. How, then, should he use his findings to decide whether or not the alien beings are people? We needn't suppose that an entity must have *all* of these attributes to be properly considered a person; (1) and (2) alone may well be sufficient for personhood, and quite probably (1)–(3) are sufficient. Neither do we need to insist that any one of these criteria is *necessary* for personhood, although once again (1) and (2) look like fairly good candidates for **necessary conditions,** as does (3), if "activity" is construed so as to include the activity of reasoning.

All we need to claim, to demonstrate that a fetus is not a person, is that any being which satisfies *none* of (1)–(5) is certainly not a person. I consider this claim to be so obvious that I think anyone who denied it, and claimed that a being which satisfied none of (1)–(5) was a person all the same, would thereby demonstrate that he had no notion at all of what a person is—perhaps because he had confused the concept of a person with that of genetic humanity. If the opponents of abortion were to deny the appropriateness of these five criteria, I do not know what further arguments would convince them. We would probably have to admit that our conceptual schemes were indeed irreconcilably different, and that our dispute could not be settled objectively.

I do not expect this to happen, however, since I think that the concept of a person is one which is very nearly universal (to people), and that it is common to both proabortionists and antiabortionists, even though neither group has fully realized the relevance of this concept to the resolution of their dispute. Furthermore, I think that on reflection even the antiabortionists ought to agree not only that (1)–(5) are central to the concept of personhood, but also that it is a part of this concept that all and only people have full moral rights. The concept of a person is in part a moral concept; once we have admitted that *x* is a person we have recognized, even if we have not agreed to respect, *x* 's right to be treated as a member of the moral community. It is true that the claim that *x* is a *human being* is more commonly voiced as part of an appeal to treat *x* decently than is the claim that *x* is a person, but this is either because "human being" is here used in the sense which implies personhood, or because the genetic and moral senses of "human" have been confused.

Now if (1)–(5) are indeed the primary criteria of personhood, then it is clear that genetic humanity is neither necessary nor sufficient for establishing that an entity is a person. Some human beings are not people, and there may well be people who are not human beings. A man or woman whose consciousness has been permanently obliterated but who remains alive is a human being which is no longer a person; defective human beings, with no appreciable mental capacity, are not and presumably never will be people; and a fetus is a human being which is not yet a person, and which therefore cannot coherently be said to have full moral rights. Citizens of the next century should be prepared to recognize highly advanced, self-aware robots or computers, should such be developed, and intelligent inhabitants of other worlds, should such be found, as people in the fullest sense, and to respect their moral rights. But to ascribe full moral rights to an entity which is not a person is as absurd as to ascribe moral obligations and responsibilities to such an entity.

Fetal Development and the Right to Life

Two problems arise in the application of these suggestions for the definition of the moral community to the determination of the precise moral status of a human fetus. Given that the paradigm example of a person is a normal adult human being, then (1) How like this paradigm, in particular how far advanced since conception, does a human being need to be before it begins to have a right to life by virtue, not of being fully a person as of yet, but of being *like* a person? and (2) To what extent, if any, does the fact that a fetus has the *potential* for becoming a person endow it with some of the same rights? Each of these questions requires some comment.

In answering the first question, we need not attempt a detailed consideration of the moral rights of organisms which are not developed enough, aware enough, intelligent enough, etc., to be considered people, but which resemble people in some respects. It does seem reasonable to suggest that the more like a person, in the relevant respects, a being is, the stronger is the case for regarding it as having a right to life, and indeed the stronger its right to life is. Thus we ought to take seriously the suggestion that, insofar as "the human individual develops biologically in a continuous fashion ... the rights of a human person might develop in the same way." [11] But we must keep in mind that the attributes which are relevant in determining whether or not an entity is enough like a person to be regarded as having some of the same moral rights are no different from those which are relevant to determining whether or not it is fully a person—i.e., are no different from (1)–(5)—and that being genetically human, or having recognizably human facial and other physical features, or detectable brain activity, or the capacity to survive outside the uterus, are simply not among these relevant attributes.

Thus it is clear that even though a seven- or eight-month fetus has features which make it apt to arouse in us almost the same power-ful protective instinct as is commonly aroused by a small infant, nevertheless it is not significantly more personlike than is a very small embryo. It is *somewhat* more personlike; it can apparently feel and respond to pain, and it may even have a rudimentary form of consciousness, insofar as its brain is quite active. Nevertheless, it seems safe to say that it is not fully conscious, in the way that an infant of a few months is, and that it cannot reason, or communicate messages of indefinitely many sorts, does not engage in self-motivated activity, and has no self-awareness. Thus, in the *relevant* respects, a fetus, even a fully developed one, is considerably less personlike than is the average mature mammal, indeed the average fish. And I think that a rational person must conclude that if the right to life of a fetus is to be based upon its resemblance to a person, then it cannot be said to have any more right to life than, let us say, a newborn guppy (which also seems to be capable of feeling pain), and that a right of that magnitude could never override a woman's right to obtain an abortion, at any stage of her pregnancy.

There may, of course, be other arguments in favor of placing legal limits upon the stage of pregnancy in which an abortion may be performed. Given the relative safety of the new techniques of artificially inducing labor during the third trimester, the danger to the woman's life or health is no longer such an argument. Neither is the fact that people tend to respond to the thought of abortion in the later stages of pregnancy with emotional repulsion, since mere emotional responses cannot take the place of moral reasoning in determining what ought to be permitted. Nor, finally, is the frequently heard argument that legalizing abortion, especially late in the pregnancy, may erode the level of respect for human life, leading, perhaps, to an increase in unjustified euthanasia and other crimes. For this threat, if it is a threat, can be better met by educating people to the kinds of moral distinctions which we are making here than by limiting access to abortion (which limitation may, in its disregard for the rights of women, be just as damaging to the level of respect for human rights).

Thus, since the fact that even a fully developed fetus is not person-like enough to have any significant right to life on the basis of its person-likeness shows that no legal restrictions upon the stage of pregnancy in which an abortion may be performed can be justified on the grounds that we should protect the rights of the older fetus; and since there is no other apparent justification for such restrictions, we may conclude that they are entirely unjustified. Whether or not it would be *indecent* (whatever that means) for a woman in her seventh month to obtain an abortion just to avoid having to postpone a trip to Europe, it would not, in itself, be *immoral,* and therefore it ought to be permitted.

Potential Personhood and the Right to Life

We have seen that a fetus does not resemble a person in any way which can support the claim that it has even some of the same rights. But what about its *potential,* the fact that if nurtured and allowed to develop naturally it will very probably become a person? Doesn't that alone give it at least some right to life? It is hard to deny that the fact that an entity is a potential person is a strong prima facie reason for not destroying it; but we need not conclude from this that a potential person has a right to life, by virtue of that potential. It may be that our feeling that it is better, other things being equal, not to destroy a potential person is better explained by the fact that potential people are still (felt to be) an invaluable resource, not to be lightly squandered. Surely, if every speck of dust were a potential person, we would be much less apt to conclude that every potential person has a right to become actual.

Still, we do not need to insist that a potential person has no right to life whatever. There may well be something immoral, and not just imprudent, about wantonly destroying potential people, when doing so isn't necessary to protect anyone's rights. But even if a potential person does have some **prima facie right** to life, such a right could not possibly outweigh the right of a woman to obtain an abortion, since the rights of any actual person invariably outweigh those of any potential person, whenever the two conflict. Since this may not be immediately obvious in the case of a human fetus, let us look at another case.

Suppose that our space explorer falls into the hands of an alien culture, whose scientists decide to create a few hundred thousand or more human beings, by breaking his body into its component cells, and using these to create fully developed human beings, with, of course, his genetic code. We may imagine that each of these newly created men will have all of the original man's abilities, skills, knowledge, and so on, and also have an individual self-concept, in short that each of them will be a bona fide (though hardly unique) person. Imagine that the whole project will take only seconds, and that its chances of success are extremely high, and that our explorer knows all of this, and also knows that these people will be treated fairly. I maintain that in such a situation he would have every right to escape if he could, and thus to deprive all of these potential people of their potential lives; for his right to life outweighs all of theirs together, in spite of the fact that they are all genetically human, all innocent, and all have a very high probability of becoming people very soon, if only he refrains from acting.

Indeed, I think he would have a right to escape even if it were not his life which the alien scientists planned to take, but only a year of his freedom, or, indeed, only a day. Nor would he be obligated to stay if he had gotten captured (thus bringing all these people-potentials into existence) because of his own carelessness, or even if he had done so deliberately, knowing the consequences. Regardless of how he got captured, he is not morally obligated to remain in captivity for *any* period of time for the sake of permitting any number of potential people to come into actuality, so great is the margin by which one actual person's right to liberty outweighs whatever right to life even a hundred thousand potential people have. And it seems reasonable to conclude that the rights of a woman will outweigh by a similar margin whatever right to life a fetus may have by virtue of its potential personhood.

Thus, neither a fetus's resemblance to a person, nor its potential for becoming a person provides any basis whatever for the claim that it has any significant right to life. Consequently, a woman's right to protect her health, happiness, freedom, and even her life,[12] by terminating an unwanted pregnancy, will always override whatever right to life it may be appropriate to ascribe to a fetus, even a fully developed one. And thus, in the absence of any overwhelming social need for every possible child, the laws which restrict the right to obtain an abortion, or limit the period of pregnancy during which an abortion may be performed, are a wholly unjustified violation of a woman's most basic moral and constitutional rights.[13]

POSTSCRIPT ON INFANTICIDE

Since the publication of this article, many people have written to point out that my argument appears to justify not only abortion, but infanticide as well. For a new-born infant is not significantly more person-like than an advanced fetus, and consequently it would seem that if the destruction of the latter is permissible so too must be that of the former. Inasmuch as most people, regardless of how they feel about the morality of abortion, consider infanticide a form of murder, this might appear to represent a serious flaw in my argument.

Now, if I am right in holding that it is only people who have a full-fledged right to life, and who can be murdered, and if the criteria of personhood are as I have described them, then it obviously follows that killing a new-born infant isn't murder. It does *not* follow, however, that infanticide is permissible, for

two reasons. In the first place, it would be wrong, at least in this country and in this period of history, and other things being equal, to kill a new-born infant, because even if its parents do not want it and would not suffer from its destruction, there are other people who would like to have it, and would, in all probability, be deprived of a great deal of pleasure by its destruction. Thus, infanticide is wrong for reasons analogous to those which make it wrong to wantonly destroy natural resources, or great works of art.

Secondly, most people, at least in this country, value infants, and would much prefer that they be preserved, even if foster parents are not immediately available. Most of us would rather be taxed to support orphanages than allow unwanted infants to be destroyed. So long as there are people who want an infant preserved, and who are willing and able to provide the means of caring for it, under reasonably humane conditions, it is, *ceteris parabis,* wrong to destroy it.

But, it might be replied, if this argument shows that infanticide is wrong, at least at this time and in this country, doesn't it also show that abortion is wrong? After all, many people value fetuses, are disturbed by their destruction, and would much prefer that they be preserved, even at some cost to themselves. Furthermore, as a potential source of pleasure to some foster family, a fetus is just as valuable as an infant. There is, however, a crucial difference between the two cases: so long as the fetus is unborn, its preservation, contrary to the wishes of the pregnant woman, violates her rights to freedom, happiness, and self-determination. Her rights override the rights of those who would like the fetus preserved, just as if someone's life or limb is threatened by a wild animal, his right to protect himself by destroying the animal overrides the rights of those who would prefer that the animal not be harmed.

The minute the infant is born, however, its preservation no longer violates any of its mother's rights, even if she wants it destroyed, because she is free to put it up for adoption. Consequently, while the moment of birth does not mark any sharp discontinuity in the degree to which an infant possesses the right to life, it does mark the end of its mother's right to determine its fate. Indeed, if abortion could be performed without killing the fetus, she would never possess the right to have the fetus destroyed, for the same reasons that she has no right to have an infant destroyed.

On the other hand, it follows from my argument that when an unwanted or defective infant is born into a society which cannot afford and/or is not willing to care for it, then its destruction is permissible. This conclusion will, no doubt, strike many people as heartless and immoral; but remember that the very existence of people who feel this way, and who are willing and able to provide care for unwanted infants, is reason enough to conclude that they should be preserved.

Endnotes

1. For example, Roger Wertheimer, who in "Understanding the Abortion Argument" (*Philosophy and Public Affairs,* 1, No. 1 [Fall 1971], 67–95), argues that the problem of the moral status of abortion is insoluble, in that the dispute over the status of the fetus is not a question of fact at all, but only a question of how one responds to the facts.

2. B.A. Brody, "Abortion and the Law," *The Journal of Philosophy,* 68, No. 12 (June 17, 1971), 357–69.

3. Judith Thomson, "A Defense of Abortion," *Philosophy and Public Affairs,* 1, No. 1 (Fall 1971), 47–66.

4. I have abbreviated these statements somewhat, but not in a way which affects the argument.

5. John Noonan, "Abortion and the Catholic Church: A Summary History," *Natural Law Forum,* 12 (1967), 125.

6. John Noonan, "Deciding Who Is Human," *Natural Law Forum,* 13 (1968), 134.

7. "A Defense of Abortion."

8. We may safely ignore the fact that she might have avoided getting raped, e.g., by carrying a gun, since by similar means you might likewise have avoided getting kidnapped, and in neither case does the victim's failure to take all possible precautions against a highly unlikely event (as opposed to reasonable precautions against a rather likely event) mean that he is morally responsible for what happens.

9. Of course, the principle that it is (always) wrong to kill innocent human beings is in need of many modifications, e.g., that it may be permissible to do so to save a greater number of other innocent human beings, but we may safely ignore these complications here.

10. From here on, we will use "human" to mean genetically human, since the moral sense seems closely connected to, and perhaps derived from, the assumption that genetic humanity is sufficient for membership in the moral community.

11. Thomas L. Hayes, "A Biological View," *Commonweal,* 85 (March 17, 1967), 677–78; quoted by Daniel Callahan, in *Abortion, Law, Choice, and Morality* (London: Macmillan & Co., 1970).

12. That is, insofar as the death rate, for the woman, is higher for childbirth than for early abortion.

13. My thanks to the following people, who were kind enough to read and criticize an earlier version of this paper: Herbert Gold, Gene Glass, Anne Lauterbach, Judith Thomson, Mary Mothersill, and Timothy Binkley.

Review Questions

1. What is the traditional antiabortion argument according to Warren?

2. According to Warren, why are the two typical pro-abortion arguments inadequate?

3. What difficulties does Warren raise in Thomson's argument?

4. Warren claims that the word *human* has two different senses, a *genetic sense* and a *moral sense.* Explain the distinction between the two.

5. Why does Warren think that it is obvious that a fetus is not a person, and why does she expect antiabortionists to agree with her?

6. Warren admits that she has two problems when it comes to applying her account of personhood to human fetuses. What are these two problems, and how does Warren solve them?

7. How does Warren reply to the objection that her position justifies infanticide as well as abortion?

Discussion Questions

1. Warren asserts that neither defective humans with little mental capacity nor permanently comatose humans are persons with moral rights. Do you agree? Why or why not?

2. Warren also claims that there can be nonhuman persons, for example, self-aware robots and alien beings from other planets. Is this possible? Explain your answer.

3. Warren says that an infant of a few months is

less personlike than the average fish. Is this true?

4. Warren says, in opposition to Thomson, that a woman in her seventh month of pregnancy ought to be permitted to have an abortion just to avoid postponing a trip to Europe. Do you agree with this judgment? Defend your answer.

Jane English

Abortion and the Concept of a Person

Jane English (1947–1978) taught at the University of North Carolina, Chapel Hill, and published several articles in ethics. She was the editor of Sex Equality *(1977).*

English argues that one of the central issues in the abortion debate, whether the fetus is a person or not, cannot be conclusively settled because of the nature of the concept of a person. This concept is said to be a cluster concept because it cannot be defined in terms of necessary and sufficient conditions. Given this lack of defining features, we cannot say whether a fetus is a person or not; it remains in a conceptually fuzzy borderline area.

English argues that regardless of whether or not the fetus is a person we must accept the moderate view that abortion is justified in some cases and not in others. Even if the fetus is a person, as the conservatives hold, it does not follow that abortion is never morally permissible. For the self-defense model not only justifies abortion to save the mother's life, but also justifies abortion to avoid serious harm or injury. On the other hand, the liberal view that the fetus is not a person does not warrant abortion on demand because we still have a duty to not harm or kill nonpersons that are sufficiently personlike. This duty makes late abortions for the sake of convenience (such as the woman who does not want to postpone a trip to Europe) morally wrong.

Reprinted with the permission of the editors from *Canadian Journal of Philosophy*, Vol. V, No. 2, October 1975, pp. 233–243.

The abortion debate rages on. Yet the two most popular positions seem to be clearly mistaken. Conservatives maintain that a human life begins at conception and that therefore abortion must be wrong because it is murder. But not all killings of humans are murders. Most notably, self defense may justify even the killing of an innocent person.

Liberals, on the other hand, are just as mistaken in their argument that since a fetus does not become a person until birth, a woman may do whatever she pleases in and to her own body. First, you cannot do as you please with your own body if it affects other people adversely.[1] Second, if a fetus is not a person, that does not imply that you can do to it anything you wish. Animals, for example, are not persons, yet to kill or torture them for no reason at all is wrong.

At the center of the storm has been the issue of just when it is between ovulation and adulthood that a person appears on the scene. Conservatives draw the line at conception, liberals at birth. In this paper I first examine our concept of a person and conclude that no single criterion can capture the concept of a person and no sharp line can be drawn. Next I argue that if a fetus is a person, abortion is still justifiable in many cases; and if a fetus is not a person, killing it is still wrong in many cases. To a large extent, these two solutions are in agreement. I conclude that our concept of a person cannot and need not bear the weight that the abortion controversy has thrust upon it.

I

The several factions in the abortion argument have drawn battle lines around various proposed criteria for determining what is and what is not a person. For example, Mary Anne Warren[2] lists five features (capacities for reasoning, self-awareness, complex communication, etc.) as her criteria for personhood and argues for the permissibility of abortion because a fetus falls outside this concept. Baruch Brody[3] uses brain waves. Michael Tooley[4] picks having-a-concept-of-self as his criterion and concludes that infanticide and abortion are justifiable, while the killing of adult animals is not. On the other side, Paul Ramsey[5] claims a certain gene structure is the defining characteristic. John Noonan[6] prefers conceived-of-humans and presents counterexamples to various other candidate criteria. For instance, he argues against viability as the criterion because the newborn and infirm would then be nonpersons, since they cannot live without the aid of others. He rejects any criterion that calls upon the sorts of sentiments a being can evoke in adults on the grounds that this would allow us to exclude other races as nonpersons if we could just view them sufficiently unsentimentally.

These approaches are typical: foes of abortion propose **sufficient conditions** for personhood which fetuses satisfy, while friends of abortion counter with necessary conditions for personhood which fetuses lack. But these both presuppose that the concept of a person can be captured in a strait jacket of necessary and/or sufficient conditions.[7] Rather, 'person' is a cluster of features, of which rationality, having a self concept and being conceived of humans are only part.

What is typical of persons? Within our concept of a person we include, first, certain biological factors: descended from humans, having a certain genetic makeup, having a head, hands, arms, eyes, capable of locomotion, breathing, eating, sleeping. There are psychological factors: sentience, perception, having a concept of self and of one's own interests and desires, the ability to use tools, the ability to use language or symbol systems, the ability to joke, to be angry, to doubt.

There are rationality factors: the ability to reason and draw conclusions, the ability to generalize and to learn from past experience, the ability to sacrifice present interests for greater gains in the future. There are social factors: the ability to work in groups and respond to peer pressures, the ability to recognize and consider as valuable the interests of others, seeing oneself as one among "other minds," the ability to sympathize, encourage, love, the ability to evoke from others the responses of sympathy, encouragement, love, the ability to work with others for mutual advantage. Then there are legal factors: being subject to the law and protected by it, having the ability to sue and enter contracts, being counted in the census, having a name and citizenship, the ability to own property, inherit, and so forth.

Now the point is not that this list is incomplete, or that you can find counterinstances to each of its points. People typically exhibit rationality, for instance, but someone who was irrational would not thereby fail to qualify as a person. On the other hand, something could exhibit the majority of these features and still fail to be a person, as an advanced robot might. There is no single core of necessary and sufficient features which we can draw upon with the assurance that they constitute what really makes a person; there are only features that are more or less typical.

This is not to say that no necessary or sufficient conditions can be given. Being alive is a necessary condition for being a person, and being a U.S. Senator is sufficient. But rather than falling inside a sufficient condition or outside a necessary one, a fetus lies in the penumbra region where our concept of a person is not so simple. For this reason I think a conclusive answer to the question whether a fetus is a person is unattainable.

Here we might note a family of simple fallacies that proceed by stating a necessary condition for personhood and showing that a fetus has that characteristic. This is a form of the **fallacy of affirming the consequent.** For example, some have mistakenly reasoned from the premise that a fetus is human (after all, it is a human fetus rather than, say, a canine fetus), to the conclusion that it is a human. Adding an **equivocation** on 'being', we get the fallacious argument that since a fetus is something both living and human, it is a human being.

Nonetheless, it does seem clear that a fetus has very few of the above family of characteristics, whereas a newborn baby exhibits a much larger proportion of them—and a two-year-old has even more. Note that one traditional anti-abortion argument has centered on pointing out the many ways in which a fetus resembles a baby. They emphasize its development ("It already has ten fingers ...") without mentioning its dissimilarities to adults (it still has gills and a tail). They also try to evoke the sort of sympathy on our part that we only feel toward other persons ("Never to laugh ... or feel the sunshine?"). This all seems to be a relevant way to argue, since its purpose is to persuade us that a fetus satisfies so many of the important features on the list that it ought to be treated as a person. Also note that a fetus near the time of birth satisfies many more of these factors than a fetus in the early months of development. This could provide reason for making distinctions among the different stages of pregnancy, as the U.S. Supreme Court has done.[8]

Historically, the time at which a person has been said to come into existence has varied widely. Muslims date personhood from fourteen days after conception. Some medievals followed Aristotle in placing ensoulment at forty days after conception for a male fetus and eighty days for a female fetus.[9] In European common law since the Seventeenth Century, abortion was considered the killing of a person only after quickening, the time when a pregnant woman first feels the fetus move on its own. Nor is this variety of opinions surprising. Biologically, a human being develops gradually. We shouldn't expect there to be any specific time or sharp dividing point when a person appears on the scene.

For these reasons I believe our concept of a person is not sharp or decisive enough to bear the weight of a solution to the abortion controversy. To use it to solve that problem is to clarify *obscurum per obscurius*.

II

Next let us consider what follows if a fetus is a person after all. Judith Jarvis Thomson's landmark article, "A Defense of Abortion," [10] correctly points out that some additional argumentation is needed at this point in the conservative argument to bridge the gap between the premise that a fetus is an innocent person and the conclusion that killing it is always wrong. To arrive at this conclusion, we would need the additional premise that killing an innocent person is always wrong. But killing an innocent person is sometimes permissible, most notably in self-defense. Some examples may help draw out our intuitions or ordinary judgments about self-defense.

Suppose a mad scientist, for instance, hypnotized innocent people to jump out of the bushes and attack innocent passers-by with knives. If you are so attacked, we agree you have a right to kill the attacker in self-defense, if killing him is the only way to protect your life or to save yourself from serious injury. It does not seem to matter here that the attacker is not malicious but himself an innocent pawn, for your killing of him is not done in a spirit of retribution but only in self-defense.

How severe an injury may you inflict in self-defense? In part this depends upon the severity of the injury to be avoided: you may not shoot someone merely to avoid having your clothes torn. This might lead one to the mistaken conclusion that the defense may only equal the threatened injury in severity; that to avoid death you may kill, but to avoid a black eye you may only inflict a black eye or the equivalent. Rather, our laws and customs seem to say that you may create an injury somewhat, but not enormously, greater than the injury to be avoided. To fend off an attack whose outcome would be as serious as rape, a severe beating or the loss of a finger, you may shoot; to avoid having your clothes torn, you may blacken an eye.

Aside from this, the injury you may inflict should only be the minimum necessary to deter or incapacitate the attacker. Even if you know he intends to kill you, you are not justified in shooting him if you could equally well save yourself by the simple expedient of running away. Self-defense is for the purpose of avoiding harms rather than equalizing harms.

Some cases of pregnancy present a parallel situation. Though the fetus is itself innocent, it may pose a threat to the pregnant woman's well-being, life prospects or health, mental or physical. If the pregnancy presents a slight threat to her interests, it seems self-defense cannot justify abortion. But if the threat is on a par with a serious beating or the loss of a finger, she may kill the fetus that poses such a threat, even if it is an innocent person. If a lesser harm to the fetus could have the same defensive effect, killing it would not be justified. It is unfortunate that the only way to free the woman from the pregnancy entails the death of the fetus (except in very late stages of pregnancy). Thus a self-defense model supports Thomson's point that the woman has a right only to be freed from the fetus, not a right to demand its death.[11]

The self-defense model is most helpful when we take the pregnant woman's point of view. In the pre-Thomson literature, abortion is often framed as a question for a third party: do you, a doctor, have a right to choose between the life of the woman and that of the fetus? Some have claimed that if you were a passer-by who witnessed a struggle between the innocent hypnotized attacker and his equally innocent victim, you would have no reason to kill either in defense of the other. They have concluded that the self defense model implies that a woman may attempt to abort herself, but that a doctor should not assist her. I think the position of the third party is somewhat more complex. We do feel some inclination to intervene on behalf of the victim rather than the attacker,

other things equal. But if both parties are innocent, other factors come into consideration. You would rush to the aid of your husband whether he was attacker or attackee. If a hypnotized famous violinist were attacking a skid row bum, we would try to save the individual who is of more value to society. These considerations would tend to support abortion in some cases.

But suppose you are a frail senior citizen who wishes to avoid being knifed by one of these innocent hypnotics, so you have hired a bodyguard to accompany you. If you are attacked, it is clear we believe that the bodyguard, acting as your agent, has a right to kill the attacker to save you from a serious beating. Your rights of self defense are transferred to your agent. I suggest that we should similarly view the doctor as the pregnant woman's agent in carrying out a defense she is physically incapable of accomplishing herself.

Thanks to modern technology, the cases are rare in which a pregnancy poses as clear a threat to a woman's bodily health as an attacker brandishing a switchblade. How does self defense fare when more subtle, complex and long-range harms are involved?

To consider a somewhat fanciful example, suppose you are a highly trained surgeon when you are kidnapped by the hypnotic attacker. He says he does not intend to harm you but to take you back to the mad scientist who, it turns out, plans to hypnotize you to have a permanent mental block against all your knowledge of medicine. This would automatically destroy your career which would in turn have a serious adverse impact on your family, your personal relationships and your happiness. It seems to me that if the only way you can avoid this outcome is to shoot the innocent attacker, you are justified in so doing. You are defending yourself from a drastic injury to your life prospects. I think it is no exaggeration to claim that unwanted pregnancies (most obviously among teenagers) often have such adverse life-long consequences as the surgeon's loss of livelihood.

Several parallels arise between various

views on abortion and the self defense model. Let's suppose further that these hypnotized attackers only operate at night, so that it is well known that they can be avoided completely by the considerable inconvenience of never leaving your house after dark. One view is that since you could stay home at night, therefore if you go out and are selected by one of these hypnotized people, you have no right to defend yourself. This parallels the view that abstinence is the only acceptable way to avoid pregnancy. Others might hold that you ought to take along some defense such as mace which will deter the hypnotized person without killing him, but that if this defense fails, you are obliged to submit to the resulting injury, no matter how severe it is. This parallels the view that contraception is all right but abortion is always wrong, even in cases of contraceptive failure.

A third view is that you may kill the hypnotized person only if he will actually kill you, but not if he will only injure you. This is like the position that abortion is permissible only if it is required to save a woman's life. Finally we have the view that it is all right to kill the attacker, even if only to avoid a very slight inconvenience to yourself and even if you knowingly walked down the very street where all these incidents have been taking place without taking along any mace or protective escort. If we assume that a fetus is a person, this is the analogue of the view that abortion is always justifiable, "on demand."

The self-defense model allows us to see an important difference that exists between abortion and infanticide, even if a fetus is a person from conception. Many have argued that the only way to justify abortion without justifying infanticide would be to find some characteristic of personhood that is acquired at birth. Michael Tooley, for one, claims infanticide is justifiable because the really significant characteristics of person are acquired some time after birth. But all such approaches look to characteristics of the developing human and ignore the relation between the fetus and the woman. What if, after birth, the

presence of an infant or the need to support it posed a grave threat to the woman's sanity or life prospects? She could escape this threat by the simple expedient of running away. So a solution that does not entail the death of the infant is available. Before birth, such solutions are not available because of the biological dependence of the fetus on the woman. Birth is the crucial point not because of any characteristics the fetus gains, but because after birth the woman can defend herself by a means less drastic than killing the infant. Hence self defense can be used to justify abortion without necessarily thereby justifying infanticide.

III

On the other hand, supposing a fetus is not after all a person, would abortion always be morally permissible? Some opponents of abortion seem worried that if a fetus is not a full-fledged person, then we are justified in treating it in any way at all. However, this does not follow. Nonpersons do get some consideration in our moral code, though of course they do not have the same rights as persons have (and in general they do not have moral responsibilities), and though their interests may be overridden by the interests of persons. Still, we cannot just treat them in any way at all.

Treatment of animals is a case in point. It is wrong to torture dogs for fun or to kill wild birds for no reason at all. It is wrong Period, even though dogs and birds do not have the same rights persons do. However, few people think it is wrong to use dogs as experimental animals, causing them considerable suffering in some cases, provided that the resulting research will probably bring discoveries of great benefit to people. And most of us think it all right to kill birds for food or to protect our crops. People's rights are different from the consideration we give to animals, then, for it is wrong to experiment on people, even if others might later benefit a great deal as a result of their suffering. You might volunteer to be a subject, but this would be supererogatory; you certainly have a right to refuse to be a medical guinea pig.

But how do we decide what you may or may not do to nonpersons? This is a difficult problem, one for which I believe no adequate account exists. You do not want to say, for instance, that torturing dogs is all right whenever the sum of its effects on people is good—when it doesn't warp the sensibilities of the torturer so much that he mistreats people. If that were the case, it would be all right to torture dogs if you did it in private, or if the torturer lived on a desert island or died soon afterward, so that his actions had no effect on people. This is an inadequate account, because whatever moral consideration animals get, it has to be indefeasible, too. It will have to be a general proscription of certain actions, not merely a weighing of the impact on people on a case-by-case basis.

Rather, we need to distinguish two levels on which consequences of actions can be taken into account in moral reasoning. The traditional objections to Utilitarianism focus on the fact that it operates solely on the first level, taking all the consequences into account in particular cases only. Thus Utilitarianism is open to "desert island" and "lifeboat" counterexamples because these cases are rigged to make the consequences of actions severely limited.

Rawls' theory could be described as a teleological sort of theory, but with teleology operating on a higher level.[12] In choosing the principles to regulate society from the original position, his hypothetical choosers make their decision on the basis of the total consequences of various systems. Furthermore, they are constrained to choose a general set of rules which people can readily learn and apply. An ethical theory must operate by generating a set of sympathies and attitudes toward others which reinforces the functioning of that set of moral principles. Our prohibition against killing people operates by means of certain moral sentiments including sympathy, compassion and guilt. But if these attitudes are to form a coherent set, they carry us

further: we tend to perform supererogatory actions, and we tend to feel similar compassion toward person-like nonpersons.

It is crucial that psychological facts play a role here. Our psychological constitution makes it the case that for our ethical theory to work, it must prohibit certain treatment of nonpersons which are significantly person-like. If our moral rules allowed people to treat some person-like nonpersons in ways we do not want people to be treated, this would undermine the system of sympathies and attitudes that makes the ethical system work. For this reason, we would choose in the original position to make mistreatment of some sorts of animals wrong in general (not just wrong in the cases with public impact), even though animals are not themselves parties in the original position. Thus it makes sense that it is those animals whose appearance and behavior are most like those of people that get the most consideration in our moral scheme.

It is because of "coherence of attitudes," I think, that the similarity of a fetus to a baby is very significant. A fetus one week before birth is so much like a newborn baby in our psychological space that we cannot allow any cavalier treatment of the former while expecting full sympathy and nurturative support for the latter. Thus, I think that anti-abortion forces are indeed giving their strongest arguments when they point to the similarities between a fetus and a baby, and when they try to evoke our emotional attachment to and sympathy for the fetus. An early horror story from New York about nurses who were expected to alternate between caring for six-week premature infants and disposing of viable 24-week aborted fetuses is just that—a horror story. These beings are so much alike that no one can be asked to draw a distinction and treat them so very differently.

Remember, however, that in the early weeks after conception, a fetus is very much unlike a person. It is hard to develop these feelings for a set of genes which doesn't yet have a head, hands, beating heart, response to touch or the ability to move by itself. Thus it seems to me that the alleged "slippery slope" between conception and birth is not so very slippery. In the early stages of pregnancy, abortion can hardly be compared to murder for psychological reasons, but in the latest stages it is psychologically akin to murder.

Another source of similarity is the bodily continuity between fetus and adult. Bodies play a surprisingly central role in our attitudes toward persons. One has only to think of the philosophical literature on how far physical identity suffices for personal identity or Wittgenstein's remark that the best picture of the human soul is the human body. Even after death, when all agree the body is no longer a person, we still observe elaborate customs of respect for the human body; like people who torture dogs, necrophiliacs are not to be trusted with people.[13] So it is appropriate that we show respect to a fetus as the body continuous with the body of a person. This is a degree of resemblance to persons that animals cannot rival.

Michael Tooley also utilizes a parallel with animals. He claims that it is always permissible to drown newborn kittens and draws conclusions about infanticide.[14] But it is only permissible to drown kittens when their survival would cause some hardship. Perhaps it would be a burden to feed and house six more cats or to find other homes for them. The alternative of letting them starve produces even more suffering than the drowning. Since the kittens get their rights second-hand, so to speak, *via* the need for coherence in our attitudes, their interests are often overridden by the interests of full-fledged persons. But if their survival would be no inconvenience to people at all, then it is wrong to drown them, *contra* Tooley.

Tooley's conclusions about abortion are wrong for the same reason. Even if a fetus is not a person, abortion is not always permissible, because of the resemblance of a fetus to a person. I agree with Thomson that it would be wrong for a woman who is seven months pregnant to have an abortion just to avoid having to postpone a trip to Europe. In the early months of pregnancy when the fetus hardly resembles a baby at all, then, abortion is permissible whenever it is in the interests of the pregnant woman or her family. The reasons would only need to outweigh the pain and inconvenience of the abortion itself. In the middle months, when the fetus comes to resemble a person, abortion would be justifiable only when the continuation of the pregnancy or the birth of the child would cause harms—physical, psychological, economic or social—to the woman. In the late months of pregnancy, even on our current assumption that a fetus is not a person, abortion seems to be wrong except to save a woman from significant injury or death.

The Supreme Court has recognized similar gradations in the alleged slippery slope stretching between conception and birth. To this point, the present paper has been a discussion of the moral status of abortion only, not its legal status. In view of the great physical, financial and sometimes psychological costs of abortion, perhaps the legal arrangement most compatible with the proposed moral solution would be the absence of restrictions, that is, so-called abortion "on demand."

So I conclude, first, that application of our concept of a person will not suffice to settle the abortion issue. After all, the biological development of a human being is gradual. Second, whether a fetus is a person or not, abortion is justifiable early in pregnancy to avoid modest harms and seldom justifiable late in pregnancy except to avoid significant injury or death.[15]

Endnotes

1. We also have paternalistic laws which keep us from harming our own bodies even when no one else is affected. Ironically, anti-abortion laws were originally designed to protect pregnant women from a dangerous but tempting procedure.

2. Mary Anne Warren, "On the Moral and Legal Status of Abortion," *Monist* 57 (1973), [*supra*, pp. 102–119].

3. Baruch Brody, "Fetal Humanity and the Theory of

Essentialism," in Robert Baker and Frederick Elliston (eds.), *Philosophy and Sex* (Buffalo, N.Y., 1975).

4. Michael Tooley, "Abortion and Infanticide," *Philosophy and Public Affairs* 2 (1971). [Revised version *supra*, pp. 120–134.]

5. Paul Ramsey, "The Morality of Abortion," in James Rachels, ed., *Moral Problems* (New York, 1971).

6. John Noonan, "Abortion and the Catholic Church: A Summary History," *Natural Law Forum* 12 (1967), pp. 125–131.

7. Wittgenstein has argued against the possibility of so capturing the concept of a game, *Philosophical Investigations* (New York, 1958), § 66–71.

8. Not because the fetus is partly a person and so has some of the rights of persons, but rather because of the rights of person-like non-persons. This I discuss in part III below.

9. Aristotle himself was concerned, however, with the different question of when the soul takes form. For historical data, see Jimmye Kimmey, "How the Abortion Laws Happened," *Ms.* 1 (April, 1973), pp. 48ff, and John Noonan, *loc. cit.*

10. J.J. Thomson, "A Defense of Abortion," *Philosophy and Public Affairs* 1 (1971). [*Infra*, pp. 173–187.]

11. Ibid. [p. 187].

12. John Rawls, *A Theory of Justice* (Cambridge, Mass., 1971), § 3–4.

13. On the other hand, if they can be trusted with people, then our moral customs are mistaken. It all depends on the facts of psychology.

14. Op. cit., pp. 40, 60–61.

15. I am deeply indebted to Larry Crocker and Arthur Kuflik for their constructive comments.

Review Questions

1. What is wrong with the conservative view according to English?

2. What two objections does she make to the liberal argument?

3. According to English, why do the various attempts to find the necessary and/or sufficient conditions for personhood all fail?

4. Explain English's own account of the concept of person including the biological, psychological, rationality, social, and legal factors.

5. According to English, in what cases does the self-defense model justify abortion, as distinguished from merely extracting the fetus and keeping it alive?

6. English discusses four different views of abortion and self-defense. Distinguish between these four different views.

7. According to English, why isn't abortion always morally permissible even if the fetus is not a person?

Discussion Questions

1. Is English's analysis of the concept of person correct? To find out, try to state necessary and sufficient conditions for being a person.

2. English never commits herself to one of the four views on abortion and self-defense. Which of these do you think is the most plausible? Why?

3. English asserts that it is wrong—period—to kill wild birds for no reason at all. Do you agree? Why or why not?

Problem Cases

1. Mrs. Sherri Finkbine and Thalidomide In 1962 Mrs. Sherri Finkbine, the mother of four normal children, became pregnant. During the pregnancy, Mrs. Finkbine had trouble sleeping, so without consulting her physician, she took some tranquilizers containing the drug thalidomide, which her husband had brought back from a trip to Europe. In Europe the sedative was widely used.

Later Mrs. Finkbine read that a number of severely deformed children had been born in Europe. These children's limbs failed to develop, or developed in malformed ways; some were born blind and deaf, or had seriously defective internal organs. The birth defects had been traced to the use in pregnancy of a widely used tranquilizer whose active ingredient was thalidomide, the very tranquilizer that she had taken.

Mrs. Finkbine went to her physician, and he confirmed her fears. The tranquilizer did contain thalidomide, and she had a very good chance of delivering a seriously deformed baby. The physician recommended an abortion. Mrs. Finkbine then presented her case to the three-member medical board of Phoenix, and they granted approval for the abortion.

In her concern for other women who might have taken thalidomide, Mrs. Finkbine told her story to a local newspaper. The story made the front page, and it wasn't long before reporters had discovered and published Mrs. Finkbine's identity. She became the object of an intense anti-abortion campaign, and she was condemned as a murderer by the Vatican newspaper.

As a result of the controversy, the medical board decided that their approval for an abortion would not survive a court test because the Arizona statute at that time allowed abortion only to save the mother's life. So the board withdrew their approval.

Eventually Mrs. Finkbine found it necessary to get an abortion in Sweden. After the abortion, Mrs. Finkbine asked if the fetus was a boy or a girl. The doctor could not say because the fetus was too badly deformed.

Do you think that Mrs. Finkbine acted wrongly in having an abortion or not? Explain your answer.

Do you think that the government has a right to prohibit abortions in such cases or not? Why or why not?

2. A Cancer Case (This is an actual case, but the name has been changed.) Mrs. Jones was a devout Catholic and was very religious. She was a wonderful wife and mother, and had eight children. She did not use any artificial method of birth control, and she became pregnant again. Tragically, it was discovered that she had cancer of the uterus. Rather than getting an abortion to save her life, she decided to have the child and risk dying of cancer. She delivered the child successfully and died a short time later, leaving her husband with nine children.

Do you think that Mrs. Jones made the morally correct decision or not? Explain your answer.

3. A Rape Case Suppose that a sixteen-year-old girl, an honor student, is living with her mother in New York City. One day while walking home from school, she is caught by a gang of thugs from a different neighborhood. She is raped and beaten in an alley one block from her apartment; nobody comes to her aid despite her screams and cries for help. She is left unconscious in the alley, and eventually she is discovered by the police and taken to the hospital. She has a concussion and a punctured lung, and she must stay in the hospital for three weeks. At the end of this time, just when she is about to be released, she finds out that she is pregnant. Her doctor advises her to have an abortion, but she is not sure what to do. She feels very angry, hurt, and depressed.

What would you advise this girl to do? Should she get an abortion or should she have the child?

4. A Minor In Alabama, state law forbids a minor (anyone under eighteen) to have an abortion without a parent's consent. Kathy is a seventeen-year-old woman who is accidentally pregnant after having sex once with her boyfriend. Her parents are divorced, and she lives with her mother and an alcoholic stepfather who frequently abuses Kathy and her mother. She does not want to tell her mother or her stepfather about the problem because she is afraid she will be beaten by the stepfather. She wants to have an abortion, so she goes to an abortion clinic. The people at the clinic are eager to challenge the law about minors, and they offer to give her free legal representation if she takes the case to court. She goes to court, but the judge rules against her—she cannot get a legal abortion without her parent's consent. Her lawyer wants to appeal the case to a higher court, but by the time Kathy gets to court again, the fetus will be viable, and she does not want to abort a viable fetus.

What should Kathy do? Should she get an illegal abortion or not? What is your advice?

5. The Punker Jane is a twenty-three-year-old lead singer in a punk rock band, and she loves it. With the other male members of the band she takes drugs, and when she feels like it, she has sex. Sometimes she uses contraceptives and sometimes she doesn't, particularly when she is on drugs. Despite her destructive life-style, she is very successful—after earning two gold records she has three new cars, two houses, and a couple of million dollars in the bank. During the recording sessions for her third record, she discovers that she is pregnant, father unknown. This is not a good time to be pregnant, for after the record she has a nationwide tour; if she cancels, she will take a big loss and also hurt the band. Besides, she thinks that motherhood is a drag, to say the least. So without giving it much thought, she has a quick abortion and then gets back to business.

Does Jane have a right to get an abortion or not? Explain your answer.

Suggested Readings

(1) Sissela Bok, "Ethical Problems of Abortion," *Hastings Center Studies* 2 (January 1974), pp. 33–52, rejects attempts to define humanity and suggests that various reasons for not getting an abortion become stronger as the fetus develops.

(2) Baruch Brody, "On the Humanity of the Foetus," in Robert L. Perkins, ed., *Abortion: Pro and Con* (Cambridge, MA: Schenkman, 1974), pp. 69–90. After critically examining various proposals for drawing the line on the humanity of the fetus, Brody suggests that the most defensible view is to draw the line at the point when fetal brain waves can be detected.

(3) Daniel Callahan, *Abortion: Law, Choice and Morality* (New York: Macmillan, 1970), provides factual material relevant to medical, social, and legal questions about abortion. He defends the moderate view that the fetus has a partial moral status.

(4) Marshall Cohen, Thomas Nagel, and Thomas Scanlon, eds., *The Rights and Wrongs of Abortion* (Princeton, NJ: Princeton University Press, 1974). This short anthology has five articles including two by Judith Jarvis Thomson; all originally appeared in the journal *Philosophy & Public Affairs*.

(5) Tristram H. Engelhardt, Jr., "The Ontology of Abortion," *Ethics* 84 (April 1974), pp. 217–234, deals with the question of whether or not the fetus is a person. Engelhardt decides that it is not, strictly speaking, a person until the later stages of infancy, but after viability the fetus can be treated as if it were a person.

(6) Joel Feinberg, ed., *The Problem of Abortion* (Belmont, CA: Wadsworth, 1984). This is one of the best anthologies available on the subject, with a wide range of good articles representing different points of view.

(7) Joel Feinberg, "Abortion," in Tom Regan, ed., *Matters of Life and Death*, 2nd ed. (New York: Random House, 1985), provides a sophisticated discussion of various issues connected to abortion including the status of the fetus. Feinberg ends up with a liberal position since he finds that fetuses are not people in the ordinary meaning of the term, and not moral persons either.

(8) Germain Grisez, *Abortion: The Myths, the Realities, and the Arguments* (New York: Corpus Books, 1970). This is a long and difficult book; Grisez defends the conservative view on abortion in Chapter 6.

(9) R.M. Hare, "Abortion and the Golden Rule," *Philosophy & Public Affairs* 4 (Spring 1975), pp. 201–222, attacks those who appeal to intuition such as Thomson, and relies on the Golden Rule as a basic ethical principle to support a roughly moderate view of abortion.

(10) James M. Humber, "Abortion: The Avoidable Moral Dilemma," *Journal of Value Inquiry* 9 (Winter 1975), pp. 282–302, asserts that abortion is immoral because it violates the fetus' right to life, and attacks defenses of abortion as merely after-the-fact rationalizations resulting from sympathy for the mother rather than for the fetus.

(11) Susan Nicholson, *Abortion and the Roman Catholic Church* (Knoxville, TN: Religious Ethics, 1974), explains the position of the Church.

(12) Robert L. Perkins, ed., *Abortion: Pro and Con* (Cambridge, MA: Schenkman, 1974). This anthology contains a variety of articles representing different positions on abortion.

(13) Peter Singer, *Practical Ethics* (Cambridge: Cambridge University Press, 1979). Chapter 6, discusses abortion from a utilitarian point of view. The version of utilitarianism that Singer accepts is preference utilitarianism.

(14) Michael Tooley, "Abortion and Infanticide," *Philosophy & Public Affairs* 1 (Fall 1971), pp. 47–66, presents a classical defense of the extreme liberal view that neither a fetus nor a newborn infant has a serious right to continued existence, and that both abortion and infanticide are morally acceptable.

(15) Alan Zaitchik, "Viability and the Morality of Abortion," *Philosophy & Public Affairs* 10, No. 1 (1981), pp. 18–24, defends the view that viability is a morally significant dividing line against criticisms made by conservatives.

Chapter 3

Euthanasia

Introduction

The term *euthanasia* is usually defined as mercy killing, or the killing of those who are incurably ill or in great pain in order to spare them further suffering.

It is customary to distinguish between different types of euthanasia. *Voluntary euthanasia* is mercy killing with the consent of the terminally ill person. For example, a patient suffering from a very painful and terminal cancer may ask to be killed with a fatal injection of morphine. *Nonvoluntary euthanasia,* by contrast, is mercy killing without the consent of the person who is ill (although the consent of others such as parents or relatives can be obtained). Authors who discuss nonvoluntary euthanasia usually have in mind the killing of those who are unable to give consent, for example a comatose person such as Karen Ann Quinlan or a defective infant. There is another possibility, however, and that is the mercy killing of a person who is able to give consent but is not asked. If the person killed does not wish to die, it might be more accurate to call this *involuntary euthanasia.*

A further distinction is often made between active and passive euthanasia, or between killing and letting die for the sake of mercy. Just how this distinction should be drawn is a matter of some debate. As Rachels explains it in the reading, active euthanasia is taking a direct action designed to kill the patient, for example, giving the patient a lethal injection. Passive euthanasia, by contrast, is withholding treatment and allowing the patient to die, for example, not performing lifesaving surgery on a defective infant.

Rachels believes that this distinction has no moral significance, and that using it

97

leads to confused moral thinking. But Tom L. Beauchamp defends the distinction, and argues that it can play an important role in our moral reasoning.

In the first reading for the chapter, J. Gay–Williams objects to making any distinction between active and passive euthanasia. He claims that the phrase passive euthanasia is misleading and mistaken. In his view, what is called passive euthanasia is not really euthanasia at all because it is not intentional killing. Either the killing is an unintended consequence, a side effect of the real intention—elimination of the suffering—or the cause of death is the person's injuries or disease, not the failure to receive treatment.

The traditional position that Gay–Williams adopts rests on a distinction between the intended consequence of an act and the foreseen but unintended consequence. Although Gay–Williams does not discuss it, it is worth noting that this distinction is part of the traditional doctrine of double effect, the doctrine that John Finnis appeals to in Chapter 2. You will recall that according to this doctrine, as long as the intended consequence of an act is good, a bad foreseen consequence (such as death) can be morally allowed provided it is not intended and it prevents a greater evil (such as great suffering). To use Gay–Williams' example, suppose that a doctor gives a terminal cancer patient an overdose of morphine, that is, an amount sufficient to kill the patient. If the doctor intends only to reduce or eliminate the patient's pain, and not to kill the patient, and if the death of the patient is not as bad as the patient's suffering, then according to the doctrine of double effect, the doctor's action is not wrong, even though the doctor foresees that the patient will die from the overdose.

The Moral Issue The moral issue is whether or not euthanasia is wrong. It is complicated by the fact that all parties do not agree about the meaning of the term *eutha-*

nasia. It seems safe to say that the traditional conservative view is that active euthanasia is always wrong. This is the view of Gay–Williams. But conservatives on euthanasia grant that patients may be morally allowed to die or even indirectly killed in some cases. As we have said, Gay–Williams allows indirect killing where death is not intended but is merely a side-effect—for example, the case where a patient is given an injection of a drug that is necessary to treat disease and instead the drug kills the patient. Gay–Williams also argues that allowing a patient with no chance of recovery to die by failing to treat his or her injuries or disease results in the cause of death being the injuries or disease, not the failure to provide treatment—so it is not properly regarded as passive euthanasia. The AMA position is somewhat different. It allows the cessation of extraordinary means of treatment, and in some cases this seems to be passive euthanasia, even though the AMA statement does not make any distinction between passive and active euthanasia.

The liberal view on euthanasia, as distinguished from what we are calling the traditional conservative view, is that active euthanasia can be morally right in some cases, and is even preferable to passive euthanasia when a quick and painless death avoids suffering by the patient. This view is defended by Rachels, Singer, and Brandt in the readings.

Philosophical Issues As far as voluntary euthanasia is concerned, one basic issue is whether or not terminally ill persons who are rational and fully informed should be free to decide to die, and then to bring about that decision by themselves or with another's help. Peter Singer argues that such active voluntary euthanasia is morally permissible, even in those cases where it is basically the same as assisted suicide. Gay–Williams does not agree. He argues that a person who chooses to die, whether by suicide or by active euthanasia, is acting contrary to nature and contrary to self-interest.

As we have seen, another issue is whether or not there is a morally significant difference between killing and letting die. There is also controversy about the doctrine of double effect. Critics complain that no clear distinction can be made between the two effects, the intended one and the unintended but foreseen one. Furthermore, assuming that a distinction between the two effects can be made, then it seems to follow that the doctrine can be used to defend any evil act provided it is merely foreseen and not intended. All that is required is an appropriate manipulation of intentions. Defenders of the doctrine insist that a clear distinction between the two effects in question can be made, in some important cases anyway, and that it does not allow any evil act, but only those that prevent an even greater evil.

Another matter of controversy is the distinction between ordinary and extraordinary means of prolonging life. This distinction is found in the AMA statement. Rachels thinks that the cessation of extraordinary means of treatment amounts to passive euthanasia because it is the intentional termination of life. But is this true? Perhaps the reason for stopping extraordinary treatment is to avoid

treatment that causes more discomfort than the disease. In that case, the reason for doing this is not to terminate life, but to avoid excessive suffering.

Finally, there is debate about how to make life-or-death decisions. One standard answer given by Rachels and Brandt is to appeal to the quality of a person's life: If a person will have a bad life, then her life should be ended; but if a person will have a good life, then his life should be continued. But how do we distinguish between good and bad lives? That is a classical problem in ethics that resists easy solution. One answer is that we should ask ourselves if we would want to live the life in question. But it seems unlikely that everyone will agree about which lives are or are not worth living. Taking surveys may not be the answer. Brandt's suggestion is that we use a happiness criterion. A life is good or worth living if over the whole lifetime there are more moments of happiness (moments of experience that are liked) than moments of unhappiness (moments of experience that are disliked). But is happiness the only thing to be considered? What about other things like knowledge and achievement? Perhaps an unhappy life could still be good because of achievements or knowledge.

J. Gay-Williams
The Wrongfulness of Euthanasia

J. Gay-Williams has requested that no biographical information be provided.

Gay-Williams defines "euthanasia" as intentionally taking the life of a presumably hopeless person. Suicide can count as euthanasia, but not "passive euthanasia" because the latter does not involve intentional killing. Three main arguments are presented to show that euthanasia is wrong: the argument from nature, the argument from self-interest, and the argument from practical effects.

My impression is that euthanasia—the idea, if

not the practice—is slowly gaining acceptance within our society. Cynics might attribute this to an increasing tendency to devalue human life, but I do not believe this is the major factor. The acceptance is much more likely to be the result of unthinking sympathy and benevolence. Well-publicized, tragic stories like that of Karen Quinlan elicit from us deep feelings of compassion. We think to ourselves, "She and her family would be better off if she were dead." It is an easy step from this very human response to the view that if someone (and others) would be better off dead, then it must be all right to kill that person.[1] Although I respect the compassion that leads to this conclusion, I believe the conclusion is wrong. I want to show that euthanasia is wrong. It is inherently wrong, but it is also wrong judged from the standpoints of self-interest and of practical effects.

Before presenting my arguments to support this claim, it would be well to define "euthanasia." An essential aspect of euthanasia is that it involves taking a human life, either one's own or that of another. Also, the person whose life is taken must be someone who is believed to be suffering from some disease or injury from which recovery cannot reasonably be expected. Finally, the action must be deliberate and intentional. Thus, euthanasia is intentionally taking the life of a presumably hopeless person. Whether the life is one's own or that of another, the taking of it is still euthanasia.

It is important to be clear about the deliberate and intentional aspect of the killing. If a hopeless person is given an injection of the wrong drug by mistake and this causes his death, this is wrongful killing but not euthanasia. The killing cannot be the result of accident. Furthermore, if the person is given an injection of a drug that is believed to be necessary to treat his disease or better his condition and the person dies as a result, then this is neither wrongful killing nor euthanasia. The intention was to make the patient well, not kill him. Similarly, when a patient's condition is such that it is not reasonable to hope that any medical procedures or treatments will save his life, a failure to implement the procedures or treatments is not euthanasia. If the person dies, this will be as a result of his injuries or disease and not because of his failure to receive treatment.

The failure to continue treatment after it has been realized that the patient has little chance of benefiting from it has been characterized by some as "passive euthanasia." This phrase is misleading and mistaken.[2] In such cases, the person involved is not killed (the first essential aspect of euthanasia), nor is the death of the person intended by the withholding of additional treatment (the third essential aspect of euthanasia). The aim may be to spare the person additional and unjustifiable pain, to save him from the indignities of hopeless manipulations, and to avoid increasing the financial and emotional burden on his family. When I buy a pencil it is so that I can use it to write, not to contribute to an increase in the gross national product. This may be the unintended consequence of my action, but it is not the aim of my action. So it is with failing to continue the treatment of a dying person. I intend his death no more than I intend to reduce the GNP by not using medical supplies. His is an unintended dying, and so-called "passive euthanasia" is not euthanasia at all.

THE ARGUMENT FROM NATURE

Every human being has a natural inclination to continue living. Our reflexes and responses fit us to fight attackers, flee wild animals, and dodge out of the way of trucks. In our daily lives we exercise the caution and care necessary to protect ourselves. Our bodies are similarly structured for survival right down to the molecular level. When we are cut, our capillaries seal shut, our blood clots, and fibrogen is produced to start the process of healing the wound. When we are invaded by bacteria, antibodies are produced to fight against the alien organisms, and their remains are swept out of the body by special cells designed for clean-up work.

Euthanasia does violence to this natural goal of survival. It is literally acting against nature because all the processes of nature are bent towards the end of bodily survival. Euthanasia defeats these subtle mechanisms in a way that, in a particular case, disease and injury might not.

It is possible, but not necessary, to make an appeal to revealed religion in this connection.[3] Man as trustee of his body acts against God, its rightful possessor, when he takes his own life. He also violates the commandment to hold life sacred and never to take it without just and compelling cause. But since this appeal will persuade only those who are prepared to accept that religion has access to revealed truths, I shall not employ this line of argument.

It is enough, I believe, to recognize that the organization of the human body and our patterns of behavioral responses make the continuation of life a natural goal. By reason alone, then, we can recognize that euthanasia sets us against our own nature.[4] Furthermore, in doing so, euthanasia does violence to our dignity. Our dignity comes from seeking our ends. When one of our goals is survival, and actions are taken that eliminate that goal, then our natural dignity suffers. Unlike animals, we are conscious through reason of our nature and our ends. Euthanasia involves acting as if this dual nature—inclination towards survival and awareness of this as an end—did not exist. Thus, euthanasia denies our basic human character and requires that we regard ourselves or others as something less than fully human.

THE ARGUMENT FROM SELF–INTEREST

The above arguments are, I believe, sufficient to show that euthanasia is inherently wrong. But there are reasons for considering it wrong when judged by standards other than reason. Because death is final and irreversible, euthanasia contains within it the possibility that we will work against our own interest if we practice it or allow it to be practiced on us.

Contemporary medicine has high standards of excellence and a proven record of accomplishment, but it does not possess perfect and complete knowledge. A mistaken diagnosis is possible, and so is a mistaken prognosis. Consequently, we may believe that we are dying of a disease when, as a matter of fact, we may not be. We may think that we have no hope of recovery when, as a matter of fact, our chances are quite good. In such circumstances, if euthanasia were permitted, we would die needlessly. Death is final and the chance of error too great to approve the practice of euthanasia.

Also, there is always the possibility that an experimental procedure or a hitherto untried technique will pull us through. We should at least keep this option open, but euthanasia closes it off. Furthermore, spontaneous remission does occur in many cases. For no apparent reason, a patient simply recovers when those all around him, including his physicians, expected him to die. Euthanasia would just guarantee their expectations and leave no room for the "miraculous" recoveries that frequently occur.

Finally, knowing that we can take our life at any time (or ask another to take it) might well incline us to give up too easily. The will to live is strong in all of us, but it can be weakened by pain and suffering and feelings of hopelessness. If during a bad time we allow ourselves to be killed, we never have a chance to reconsider. Recovery from a serious illness requires that we fight for it, and anything that weakens our determination by suggesting that there is an easy way out is ultimately against our own interest. Also, we may be inclined towards euthanasia because of our concern for others. If we see our sickness and suffering as an emotional and financial burden on our family, we may feel that to leave our life is to make their lives easier.[5] The very presence of the possibility of euthanasia may keep us from surviving when we might.

THE ARGUMENT FROM PRACTICAL EFFECTS

Doctors and nurses are, for the most part, totally committed to saving lives. A life lost is, for them, almost a personal failure, an insult to their skills and knowledge. Euthanasia as a practice might well alter this. It could have a corrupting influence so that in any case that is severe doctors and nurses might not try hard enough to save the patient. They might decide that the patient would simply be "better off dead" and take the steps necessary to make that come about. This attitude could then carry over to their dealings with patients less seriously ill. The result would be an overall decline in the quality of medical care.

Finally, euthanasia as a policy is a slippery slope. A person apparently hopelessly ill may be allowed to take his own life. Then he may be permitted to deputize others to do it for him should he no longer be able to act. The judgment of others then becomes the ruling factor. Already at this point euthanasia is not personal and voluntary, for others are acting "on behalf of" the patient as they see fit. This may well incline them to act on behalf of other patients who have not authorized them to exercise their judgment. It is only a short step, then, from voluntary euthanasia (self-inflicted or authorized), to directed euthanasia administered to a patient who has given no authorization, to involuntary euthanasia conducted as part of a social policy.[6] Recently many psychiatrists and sociologists have argued that we define as "mental illness" those forms of behavior that we disapprove of.[7] This gives us license then to lock up those who display the behavior. The category of the "hopelessly ill" provides the possibility of even worse abuse. Embedded in a social policy, it would give society or its representatives the authority to eliminate all those who might be considered too "ill" to function normally any longer. The dangers of euthanasia are too great to all to run the risk of approving it in any form. The first slippery step may well lead to a serious and harmful fall.

I hope that I have succeeded in showing why the benevolence that inclines us to give approval of euthanasia is misplaced. Euthanasia is inherently wrong because it violates the nature and dignity of human beings. But even those who are not convinced by this must be persuaded that the potential personal and social dangers inherent in euthanasia are sufficient to forbid our approving it either as a personal practice or as a public policy.

Suffering is surely a terrible thing, and we have a clear duty to comfort those in need and to ease their suffering when we can. But suffering is also a natural part of life with values for the individual and for others that we should not overlook. We may legitimately seek for others and for ourselves an easeful death, as Arthur Dyck has pointed out.[8] Euthanasia, however, is not just an easeful death. It is a wrongful death. Euthanasia is not just dying. It is killing.

Endnotes

1. For a sophisticated defense of this position see Philippa Foot, "Euthanasia," *Philosophy and Public Affairs* 6 (1977): 85–112. Foot does not endorse the radical conclusion that euthanasia, voluntary and involuntary, is always right.

2. James Rachels rejects the distinction between active and passive euthanasia as morally irrelevant in his "Active and Passive Euthanasia," *New England Journal of Medicine*, 292: 78–80. But see the criticism by Foot, pp. 100–103.

3. For a defense of this view see J.V. Sullivan, "The Immorality of Euthanasia," in *Beneficent Euthanasia*, ed. Marvin Kohl (Buffalo, NY: Prometheus Books, 1975), pp. 34–44.

4. This point is made by Ray V. McIntyre in "Voluntary Euthanasia: The Ultimate Perversion," *Medical Counterpoint* 2: 26–29.

5. See McIntyre, p. 28.

6. See Sullivan, "Immorality of Euthanasia," pp. 34–44, for a fuller argument in support of this view.

7. See, for example, Thomas S. Szasz, *The Myth of Mental Illness*, rev. ed. (New York: Harper & Row, 1974).

8. Arthur Dyck, "Beneficent Euthanasia and Benemortasia," Kohl, op. cit., pp. 117–129.

Review Questions

1. How does Gay-Williams define euthanasia?

2. Why does he object to the phrase passive eu-

thanasia?

3. Explain the three arguments he uses to show that euthanasia is wrong.

Discussion Questions

1. Is Gay-Williams' definition of euthanasia acceptable? Defend your view.

2. Are his arguments sound or not?

James Rachels

Active and Passive Euthanasia

For biographical information on Rachels, see his reading in Chapter 1.

Here Rachels attacks the distinction between active and passive euthanasia, and the doctrine apparently accepted by the American Medical Association that taking direct action to kill a patient (active euthanasia) is wrong, but withholding treatment and allowing a patient to die (passive euthanasia) is allowable. Rachels makes three criticisms of this doctrine. First, it results in unnecessary suffering for patients who die slowly and painfully rather than quickly and painlessly. Second, the doctrine leads to moral decisions based on irrelevant considerations. Third, the distinction between killing and letting die assumed by the doctrine is of no moral significance.

The distinction between active and passive euthanasia is thought to be crucial for medical ethics. The idea is that it is permissible, at least in some cases, to withhold treatment and allow a patient to die, but it is never permissible to take any direct action designed to kill the patient. This doctrine seems to be accepted by most doctors, and it is endorsed in a statement adopted by the House of Delegates of the American Medical Association on December 4, 1973:

From James Rachels, "Active and Passive Euthanasia," *The New England Journal of Medicine*, Vol. 292, No. 2, 9 January 1975, pp. 78–80.

The intentional termination of the life of one human being by another—mercy killing—is contrary to that for which the medical profession stands and is contrary to the policy of the American Medical Association. The cessation of the employment of extraordinary means to prolong the life of the body when there is irrefutable evidence that biological death is imminent is the decision of the patient and/or his immediate family. The advice and judgment of the physician should be freely available to the patient and/or his immediate family.

However, a strong case can be made against this doctrine. In what follows I will set out some of the relevant arguments, and urge doctors to reconsider their views on this matter.

To begin with a familiar type of situation, a patient who is dying of incurable cancer of the throat is in terrible pain, which can no longer be satisfactorily alleviated. He is certain to die within a few days, even if present treatment is continued, but he does not want to go on living for those days since the pain is unbearable. So he asks the doctor for an end to it, and his family joins in the request.

Suppose the doctor agrees to withhold treatment, as the conventional doctrine says he may. The justification for his doing so is that the patient is in terrible agony, and since he is going to die anyway, it would be wrong to prolong his suffering needlessly. But now notice this. If one simply withholds treatment, it may take the patient longer to die, and so he may suffer more than he would if more direct action were taken and a lethal injection given. This fact provides strong reason for thinking that, once the initial decision not to prolong his agony has been made, active euthanasia is actually preferable to passive euthanasia, rather than the reverse. To say otherwise is to endorse the option that leads to more suffering rather than less, and is contrary to the humanitarian impulse that prompts the decision not to prolong his life in the first place.

Part of my point is that the process of being "allowed to die" can be relatively slow and painful, whereas being given a lethal injection is relatively quick and painless. Let me give a different sort of example. In the United States about one in 600 babies is born with Down's syndrome. Most of these babies are otherwise healthy—that is, with only the usual pediatric care, they will proceed to an otherwise normal infancy. Some, however, are born with congenital defects such as intestinal obstructions that require operations if they are to live. Sometimes, the parents and the doctor will decide not to operate, and let the infant die. Anthony Shaw describes what happens then:

> ... When surgery is denied [the doctor] must try to keep the infant from suffering while natural forces sap the baby's life away. As a surgeon whose natural inclination is to use the scalpel to fight off death, standing by and watching a salvageable baby die is the most emotionally exhausting experience I know. It is easy at a conference, in a theoretical discussion, to decide that such infants should be allowed to die. It is altogether different to stand by in the nursery and watch as dehydration and infection wither a tiny being over hours and days. This is a terrible ordeal for me and the hospital staff—much more so than for the parents who never set foot in the nursery.[1]

I can understand why some people are opposed to all euthanasia, and insist that such infants must be allowed to live. I think I can also understand why other people favor destroying these babies quickly and painlessly. But why should anyone favor letting "dehydration and infection wither a tiny being over hours and days?" The doctrine that says that a baby may be allowed to dehydrate and wither, but may not be given an injection that would end its life without suffering, seems so patently cruel as to require no further refutation. The strong language is not intended to offend, but only to put the point in the clearest possible way.

My second argument is that the conventional doctrine leads to decisions concerning life and death made on irrelevant grounds.

Consider again the case of the infants with Down's syndrome who need operations for congenital defects unrelated to the syndrome to live. Sometimes, there is no operation, and the baby dies, but when there is no such defect, the baby lives on. Now, an operation such as that to remove an intestinal obstruction is not prohibitively difficult. The reason why such operations are not performed in these cases is, clearly, that the child has Down's syndrome and the parents and doctor judge that because of that fact it is better for the child to die.

But notice that this situation is absurd, no matter what view one takes of the lives and potentials of such babies. If the life of such an infant is worth preserving, what does it matter if it needs a simple operation? Or, if one thinks it better that such a baby should not live on, what difference does it make that it happens to have an unobstructed intestinal tract? In either case, the matter of life and death is being decided on irrelevant grounds. It is the Down's syndrome, and not the intestines, that is the issue. The matter should be decided, if at all, on that basis, and not be allowed to depend on the essentially irrelevant question of whether the intestinal tract is blocked.

What makes this situation possible, of course, is the idea that when there is an intestinal blockage, one can "let the baby die," but when there is no such defect there is nothing that can be done, for one must not "kill" it. The fact that this idea leads to such results as deciding life or death on irrelevant grounds is another good reason why the doctrine should be rejected.

One reason why so many people think that there is an important moral difference between active and passive euthanasia is that they think killing someone is morally worse than letting someone die. But is it? Is killing, in itself, worse than letting die? To investigate this issue, two cases may be considered that are exactly alike except that one involves killing whereas the other involves letting someone die. Then, it can be asked whether this difference makes any difference to the moral assessments. It is important that the cases be exactly alike, except for this one difference, since otherwise one cannot be confident that it is this difference and not some other that accounts for any variation in the assessments of the two cases. So, let us consider this pair of cases:

In the first, Smith stands to gain a large inheritance if anything should happen to his six-year-old cousin. One evening while the child is taking his bath, Smith sneaks into the bathroom and drowns the child, and then arranges things so that it will look like an accident.

In the second, Jones also stands to gain if anything should happen to his six-year-old cousin. Like Smith, Jones sneaks in planning to drown the child in his bath. However, just as he enters the bathroom Jones sees the child slip and hit his head, and fall face down in the water. Jones is delighted; he stands by, ready to push the child's head back under if it is necessary, but it is not necessary. With only a little thrashing about, the child drowns all by himself, "accidentally," as Jones watches and does nothing.

Now Smith killed the child, whereas Jones "merely" let the child die. That is the only difference between them. Did either man behave better, from a moral point of view? If the difference between killing and letting die were in itself a morally important matter, one should say that Jones's behavior was less reprehensible than Smith's. But does one really want to say that? I think not. In the first place, both men acted from the same motive, personal gain, and both had exactly the same end in view when they acted. It may be inferred from Smith's conduct that he is a bad man, although that judgment may be withdrawn or modified if certain further facts are learned about him—for example, that he is mentally deranged. But would not the very

same thing be inferred about Jones from his conduct? And would not the same further considerations also be relevant to any modification of this judgment? Moreover, suppose Jones pleaded, in his own defense, "After all, I didn't do anything except just stand there and watch the child drown. I didn't kill him; I only let him die." Again, if letting die were in itself less bad than killing, this defense should have at least some weight. But it does not. Such a "defense" can only be regarded as a grotesque perversion of moral reasoning. Morally speaking, it is no defense at all.

Now, it may be pointed out, quite properly, that the cases of euthanasia with which doctors are concerned are not like this at all. They do not involve personal gain or the destruction of normal healthy children. Doctors are concerned only with cases in which the patient's life is of no further use to him, or in which the patient's life has become or will soon become a terrible burden. However, the point is the same in these cases: the bare difference between killing and letting die does not, in itself, make a moral difference. If a doctor lets a patient die, for humane reasons, he is in the same moral position as if he had given the patient a lethal injection for humane reasons. If his decision was wrong— if, for example, the patient's illness was in fact curable—the decision would be equally regrettable no matter which method was used to carry it out. And if the doctor's decision was the right one, the method used is not in itself important.

The AMA policy statement isolates the crucial issue very well; the crucial issue is "the intentional termination of the life of one human being by another." But after identifying this issue, and forbidding "mercy killing," the statement goes on to deny that the cessation of treatment is the intentional termination of a life. This is where the mistake comes in, for what is the cessation of treatment, in these circumstances, if it is not "the intentional termination of the life of one human being by another?" Of course it is exactly that, and if it were not, there would be no point to it.

Many people will find this judgment hard to accept. One reason, I think, is that it is very easy to conflate the question of whether killing is, in itself, worse than letting die, with the very different question of whether most actual cases of killing are more reprehensible than most actual cases of letting die. Most actual cases of killing are clearly terrible (think, for example, of all the murders reported in the newspapers), and one hears of such cases every day. On the other hand, one hardly ever hears of a case of letting die, except for the actions of doctors who are motivated by humanitarian reasons. So one learns to think of killing in a much worse light than of letting die. But this does not mean that there is something about killing that makes it in itself worse than letting die, for it is not the bare difference between killing and letting die that makes the difference in these cases. Rather, the other factors—the murderer's motive of personal gain, for example, contrasted with the doctor's humanitarian motivation—account for different reactions to the different cases.

I have argued that killing is not in itself any worse than letting die; if my contention is right, it follows that active euthanasia is not any worse than passive euthanasia. What arguments can be given on the other side? The most common, I believe, is the following:

The important difference between active and passive euthanasia is that, in passive euthanasia, the doctor does not do anything to bring about the patient's death. The doctor does nothing, and the patient dies of whatever ills already afflict him. In active euthanasia, however, the doctor does something to bring about the patient's death: he kills him. The doctor who gives the patient with cancer a lethal injection has himself caused his patient's death; whereas if he merely ceases treatment, the cancer is the cause of the death.

A number of points need to be made here. The first is that it is not exactly correct to say that in passive euthanasia the doctor does nothing, for he does do one thing that is very important: he lets the patient die. "Letting someone die" is certainly different, in some respects, from other types of action—mainly in that it is a kind of action that one may perform by way of not performing certain other actions. For example, one may let a patient die by way of not giving medication, just as one may insult someone by way of not shaking his hand. But for any purpose of moral assessment, it is a type of action nonetheless. The decision to let a patient die is subject to moral appraisal in the same way that a decision to kill him would be subject to moral appraisal: it may be assessed as wise or unwise, compassionate or sadistic, right or wrong. If a doctor deliberately let a patient die who was suffering from a routinely curable illness, the doctor would certainly be to blame for what he had done, just as he would be to blame if he had needlessly killed the patient. Charges against him would then be appropriate. If so, it would be no defense at all for him to insist that he didn't "do anything." He would have done something very serious indeed, for he let his patient die.

Fixing the cause of death may be very important from a legal point of view, for it may determine whether criminal charges are brought against the doctor. But I do not think that this notion can be used to show a moral difference between active and passive euthanasia. The reason why it is considered bad to be the cause of someone's death is that death is regarded as a great evil—and so it is. However, if it has been decided that euthanasia—even passive euthanasia—is desirable in a given case, it has also been decided that in this instance death is no greater an evil than the patient's continued existence. And if this is true, the usual reason for not wanting to be the cause of someone's death simply does not apply.

Finally, doctors may think that all of this is only of academic interest—the sort of thing that philosophers may worry about but that has no practical bearing on their own work. After all, doctors must be concerned about the legal consequences of what they do, and active euthanasia is clearly forbidden by the law. But even so, doctors should also be concerned with the fact that the law is forcing upon them a moral doctrine that may well be indefensible, and has a considerable effect on their practices. Of course, most doctors are not now in the position of being coerced in this matter, for they do not regard themselves as merely going along with what the law requires. Rather, in statements such as the A.M.A. policy statement that I have quoted, they are endorsing this doctrine as a central point of medical ethics. In that statement, active euthanasia is condemned not merely as illegal but as "contrary to that for which the medical profession stands," whereas passive euthanasia is approved. However, the preceding considerations suggest that there is really no moral difference between the two, considered in themselves (there may be important moral differences in some cases in their *consequences,* but, as I pointed out, these differences may make active euthanasia, and not passive euthanasia, the morally preferable option). So, whereas doctors may have to discriminate between active and passive euthanasia to satisfy the law, they should not do any more than that. In particular, they should not give the distinction any added authority and weight by writing it into official statements of medical ethics.

Endnote

1. A. Shaw, "Doctor, Do We Have a Choice?" *The New York Times Magazine,* January 30, 1972, p. 54.

Review Questions

1. According to Rachels, what is the distinction between active and passive euthanasia?

2. Why does Rachels think that being allowed to die is worse in some cases than a lethal injection?

3. What is Rachels' second argument against the conventional doctrine?

4. According to Rachels, why isn't killing worse than letting die?

Discussion Questions

1. The AMA statement quoted by Rachels does not use the terminology of active and passive euthanasia. Furthermore, so-called passive euthanasia could be the intentional termination of life rejected by the AMA. Does the AMA really accept this distinction? Why or why not?

2. Is the distinction between killing and letting die morally relevant? What do you think?

3. Should the law be changed to allow active euthanasia or not? Defend your view.

Tom L. Beauchamp

A Reply to Rachels on Active and Passive Euthanasia

Tom L. Beauchamp is a member of the philosophy department at Georgetown University. He is the author of Philosophical Ethics *and coauthor of* Medical Ethics *and* Principles of Biomedical Ethics.

Beauchamp agrees with Rachels that the active/ passive distinction is sometimes morally insignificant. But it does not follow, he argues, that the distinction is always morally irrelevant in our moral thinking about euthanasia. He presents utilitarian arguments for saying that the best consequences for society might result (he is cautious about predicting consequences) if passive euthanasia is allowed and active euthanasia is not. The resulting ethical position is in substantial but not total agreement with the AMA position, which does seem to endorse a limited form of passive euthanasia.

James Rachels has recently argued that the distinction between active and passive euthanasia is neither appropriately used by the American Medical Association nor generally useful for the resolution of moral problems of euthanasia.[1] Indeed he believes this distinction—which he equates with the killing/ letting die distinction—does not in itself have any moral importance. The chief object of his attack is the following statement adopted by the House of Delegates of the American Medical Association in 1973:

The intentional termination of the life of one human being by another—mercy killing—is contrary to that for which the medical profession stands and is contrary to the policy of the American Medical Association.
The cessation of the employment of extraordinary means to prolong the life of the body when there is irrefutable evidence that biological death is imminent is the decision of the patient and/or his immediate family. The advice and judgment of the physician should be freely available to the patient and/or his immediate family (241).

Rachels constructs a powerful and interesting set of arguments against this statement. In this paper I attempt the following: (1) to challenge his views on the grounds that he does not appreciate the moral reasons which give weight to the active/passive distinction; and (2) to provide a constructive account of the moral relevance of the active/passive distinction; and (3) to offer reasons showing that Rachels may nonetheless be correct in urging that we *ought* to abandon the active/passive distinction for purposes of moral reasoning.

I would concede that the active/passive distinction is *sometimes* morally irrelevant. Of this Rachels convinces me. But it does not follow that it is *always* morally irrelevant. What we need, then, is a case where the distinction is a morally relevant one and an explanation why it is so. Rachels himself uses the method of examining two cases which are exactly alike except that "one involves killing whereas the other involves letting die" (243). We may profitably begin by comparing the kinds of cases governed by the AMA's doctrine with the kinds of cases adduced by Rachels in order to assess the adequacy and fairness of his cases.

The second paragraph of the AMA statement is confined to a narrowly restricted range of passive euthanasia cases, viz., those (a) where the patients are on extraordinary means, (b) where irrefutable evidence of imminent death is available, and (c) where patient or family consent is available. Rachels' two cases involve conditions notably different from these:

In the first, Smith stands to gain a large inheritance if anything should happen to his six-year-old cousin. One evening while the child is taking his bath, Smith sneaks into the bathroom and drowns the child, and then arranges things so that it will look like an accident.

In the second, Jones also stands to gain if anything should happen to his six-year-old cousin. Like Smith, Jones sneaks in planning to drown the child in his bath. However, just as he enters the bathroom Jones sees the child slip and hit his head, and fall face down in the water. Jones is delighted; he stands by, ready to push the child's head back under if it is necessary, but it is not necessary. With only a little thrashing about, the child drowns all by himself, "accidentally," as Jones watches and does nothing.
Now Smith killed the child, whereas Jones "merely" let the child die. That is the only difference between them (243).

Rachels says there is no moral difference between the cases in terms of our moral assessments of Smith and Jones' behavior. This assessment seems fair enough, but what can Rachels' cases be said to prove, as they are so markedly disanalogous to the sorts of cases envisioned by the AMA proposal? Rachels concedes important disanalogies, but thinks them irrelevant:

The point is the same in these cases: the bare difference between killing and letting die does not, in itself, make a moral difference. If a doctor lets a patient die, for humane reasons, he is in the same moral position as if he had given the patient a lethal injection for humane reasons (244).

Three observations are immediately in order. First, Rachels seems to infer that from such cases we can conclude that the distinction between killing and letting die is *always* morally irrelevant. This conclusion is fallaciously derived. What the argument in fact shows, being an analogical argument, is only that in all *relevantly similar* cases the distinction does not in itself make a moral difference. Since Rachels concedes that other cases are disanalogous, he seems thereby to concede that his argument is as weak as the analogy itself. Second, Rachels' cases involve two *unjustified* actions, one of killing and the other of letting die. The AMA statement distinguishes one set of cases of unjustified killing and another of *justified* cases of allowing to die. Nowhere is it claimed by the AMA that what makes the difference in these cases is the active/passive distinction itself. It is only implied that one set of cases, the justified set, *involves* (passive) letting die while the unjustified set *involves* (active) killing. While it is said that justified euthanasia cases are passive ones and unjustified ones active, it is not said either that what makes some acts justified is the fact of their being passive or that what makes others unjustified is the fact of their being active. This fact will prove to be of vital importance.

The third point is that in both of Rachels' cases the respective moral agents—Smith and Jones—are morally responsible for the death of the child and are morally blameworthy—even though Jones is presumably not causally responsible. In the first case death is caused by the agent, while in the second it is not; yet the second agent is no less morally responsible. While the law might find only the first homicidal, morality condemns the motives in each case as equally wrong, and it holds that the duty to save life in such cases is as compelling as the duty not to take life. I suggest that it is largely because of this equal degree of moral responsibility that there is no morally relevant difference in Rachels' cases. In the cases envisioned by the AMA, however, an agent is held to be responsible for taking life by actively killing but is not held to be morally required to preserve life, and so not responsible for death, when removing the patient from extraordinary means (under conditions a–c above). I shall elaborate this latter point momentarily. My only conclusion thus far is the negative one that Rachels' arguments rest on weak foundations. His cases are not relevantly similar to euthanasia cases and do not support his apparent conclusion that the active/passive distinction is *always* morally irrelevant.

I wish first to consider an argument that I believe has powerful intuitive appeal and probably is widely accepted as stating the main reason for rejecting Rachels' views. I will maintain that this argument fails, and so leaves Rachels' contentions untouched.

I begin with an actual case, the celebrated Quinlan case.[2] Karen Quinlan was in a coma, and was on a mechanical respirator which artificially sustained her vital processes and which her parents wished to cease. At least some physicians believed there was irrefutable evidence that biological death was imminent and the coma irreversible. This case, under this description, closely conforms to the passive cases envisioned by the AMA. During an interview the father, Mr. Quinlan, asserted that he did not wish to kill his daughter, but only to remove her from the machines in order to see whether she would live or would die a natural death.[3] Suppose he had said—to envision now a second and hypothetical, but parallel case—that he wished only to see her die painlessly and therefore wished that the doctor could induce death by an overdose of morphine. Most of us would think the second act, which involves active killing, morally unjustified in these circumstances, while many of us would think the first act morally justified. (This is not the place to consider whether in fact it is justified, and if so under what conditions.) What accounts for the apparent morally relevant difference?

I have considered these two cases

together in order to follow Rachels' method of entertaining parallel cases where the only difference is that the one case involves killing and the other letting die. However, there is a further difference, which crops up in the euthanasia context. The difference rests in our judgments of medical fallibility and moral responsibility. Mr. Quinlan seems to think that, after all, the doctors might be wrong. There is a remote possibility that she might live without the aid of a machine. But whether or not the medical prediction of death turns out to be accurate, if she dies then no one is morally responsible for directly bringing about or causing her death, as they would be if they caused her death by killing her. Rachels finds explanations which appeal to causal conditions unsatisfactory; but perhaps this is only because he fails to see the nature of the causal link. To bring about her death is by that act to preempt the possibility of life. To "allow her to die" by removing artificial equipment is to allow for the possibility of wrong diagnosis or incorrect prediction and hence to absolve oneself of moral responsibility for the taking of life under false assumptions. There may, of course, be utterly no empirical possibility of recovery in some cases since recovery would violate a law of nature. However, judgments of empirical impossibility in medicine are notoriously problematic—the reason for emphasizing medical fallibility. And in all the hard cases we do not *know* that recovery is empirically impossible, even if good *evidence* is available.

The above reason for invoking the active/passive distinction can now be generalized: Active termination of life removes all possibility of life for the patient, while passively ceasing extraordinary means may not. This is not trivial since patients have survived in several celebrated cases where, in knowledgeable physicians' judgments, there was "irrefutable" evidence that death was imminent.[4]

One may, of course, be entirely responsible and culpable for another's death either by killing him or by letting him die. In such cases, of which Rachels' are examples, there is no morally significant difference between killing and letting die precisely because whatever one does, omits, or refrains from doing does not absolve one of responsibility. Either active or passive involvement renders one responsible for the death of another, and both involvements are equally wrong for the same principled moral reason: it is (prima facie) morally wrong to bring about the death of an innocent person capable of living whenever the causal intervention or negligence is intentional. (I use causal terms here because causal involvement need not be active, as when by one's negligence one is nonetheless causally responsible.) But not all cases of killing and letting die fall under this same moral principle. One is sometimes culpable for killing, because morally responsible as the agent for death, as when one pulls the plug on a respirator sustaining a recovering patient (a murder). But one is sometimes not culpable for letting die because not morally responsible as agent, as when one pulls the plug on a respirator sustaining an irreversibly comatose and unrecoverable patient (a routine procedure, where one is *merely* causally responsible).[5] Different degrees and means of involvement assess different degrees of responsibility, and our assessments of culpability can become intricately complex. The only point which now concerns us, however, is that because different moral principles may govern very similar circumstances, we are sometimes morally culpable for killing but not for letting die. And to many people it will seem that in passive cases we are not morally responsible for causing death, though we are responsible in active cases.

This argument is powerfully attractive. Although I was once inclined to accept it in virtually the identical form just developed,[6] I now think that, despite its intuitive appeal, it cannot be correct. It is true that different degrees and means of involvement entail different degrees of responsibility, but it does not follow that we are *not* responsible and therefore are absolved of possible culpability in *any* case of intentionally allowing to die. We are responsible and *perhaps* culpable in either active or passive cases. Here Rachels' argument is entirely to the point: It is not primarily a question of greater or lesser responsibility by an active or a passive means that should determine culpability. Rather, the question of culpability is decided by the moral *justification* for choosing either a passive or an active means. What the argument in the previous paragraph overlooks is that one might be unjustified in using an active means or unjustified in using a passive means, and hence be culpable in the use of either; yet one might be justified in using an active means or justified in using a passive means, and hence not be culpable in using either. Fallibility might just as well be present in a judgment to use one means as in a judgment to use another. (A judgment to allow to die is just as subject to being based on *knowledge which is fallible* as a judgment to kill.) Moreover, in either case, it is a matter of what one knows and believes, and not a matter of a particular kind of causal connection or causal chain. If we kill the patient, then we are certainly causally responsible for his death. But, similarly, if we cease treatment, and the patient dies, the patient might have recovered if treatment had been continued. The patient might have been saved in either case, and hence there is no morally relevant difference between the two cases. It is, therefore, simply beside the point that "one is sometimes culpable for killing ... but one is sometimes not culpable for letting die"—as the above argument concludes.

Accordingly, despite its great intuitive appeal and frequent mention, this argument from responsibility fails.

There may, however, be more compelling arguments against Rachels, and I wish now to provide what I believe is the most significant argument that can be adduced in defense of the active/passive distinction. I shall develop this argument by combining (1) so-called wedge or slippery slope arguments with (2) recent arguments in defense of rule utilitarianism. I shall explain each in turn and show how in combination they may be used to defend the active/passive distinction.

(1) *Wedge arguments* proceed as follows: if killing were allowed, even under the guise of a merciful extinction of life, a dangerous wedge would be introduced which places all "undesirable" or "unworthy" human life in a precarious condition. Proponents of wedge arguments believe the initial wedge places us on a slippery slope for at least one of two reasons: (i) It is said that our justifying principles leave us with no principled way to avoid the slide into saying that all sorts of killings would be justified under similar conditions. Here it is thought that once killing is allowed, a firm line between justified and unjustified killings cannot be securely drawn. It is thought best not to redraw the line in the first place, for redrawing it will inevitably lead to a downhill slide. It is then often pointed out that as a matter of historical record this is precisely what has occurred in the darker regions of human history, including the Nazi era, where euthanasia began with the best intentions for horribly ill, non-Jewish Germans and gradually spread to anyone deemed an enemy of the people. (ii) Second, it is said that our basic principles against killing will be gradually eroded once some form of killing is legitimated. For example, it is said that permitting voluntary euthanasia will lead to permitting involuntary euthanasia, which will in turn lead to permitting euthanasia for those who are a nuisance to society (idiots, recidivist criminals, defective newborns, and the insane, e.g.). Gradually other principles which instill respect for human life will be eroded or abandoned in the process.

I am not inclined to accept the first reason (i).[7] If our justifying principles are themselves justified, then any action they warrant would be justified. Accordingly, I shall only be concerned with the second approach (ii).

(2) *Rule utilitarianism* is the position that a society ought to adopt a rule if its acceptance would have better consequences for the common good (greater social utility) than any comparable rule could have in that society.

Any action is right if it conforms to a valid rule and wrong if it violates the rule. Sometimes it is said that alternative rules should be measured against one another, while it has also been suggested that whole moral *codes* (complete sets of rules) rather than individual rules should be compared. While I prefer the latter formulation (Brandt's), this internal dispute need not detain us here. The important point is that a particular rule or a particular code of rules is morally justified if and only if there is no other competing rule or moral code whose acceptance would have a higher utility value for society, and where a rule's acceptability is contingent upon the consequences which would result if the rule were made current.

Wedge arguments, when conjoined with rule utilitarian arguments, may be applied to euthanasia issues in the following way. We presently subscribe to a no-active-euthanasia rule (which the AMA suggests we retain). Imagine now that in our society we make current a restricted-active-euthanasia rule (as Rachels seems to urge). Which of these two moral rules would, if enacted, have the consequence of maximizing social utility? Clearly a restricted-active-euthanasia rule would have *some* utility value, as Rachels notes, since some intense and uncontrollable suffering would be eliminated. However, it may not have the highest utility value in the structure of our present code or in any imaginable code which could be made current, and therefore may not be a component in the ideal code for our society. If wedge arguments raise any serious questions at all, as I think they do, they rest in this area of whether a code would be weakened or strengthened by the addition of active euthanasia principles. For the disutility of introducing legitimate killing into one's moral code (in the form of active euthanasia rules) may, in the long run, outweigh the utility of doing so, as a result of the eroding effect such a relaxation would have on rules in the code which demand respect for human life. If, for example, rules permitting active killing were introduced, it is not implausible to suppose that destroying defective newborns (a form of involuntary euthanasia) would become an accepted and common practice, that as population increases occur the aged will be even more neglectable and neglected than they now are, that capital punishment for a wide variety of crimes would be increasingly tempting, that some doctors would have appreciably reduced fears of actively injecting fatal doses whenever it seemed to them propitious to do so, and that laws of war against killing would erode in efficacy even beyond their already abysmal level.

A hundred such possible consequences might easily be imagined. But these few are sufficient to make the larger point that such rules permitting killing could lead to a general reduction of respect for human life. Rules against killing in a moral code are not *isolated* moral principles; they are pieces of a web of rules against killing which forms the code. The more threads one removes, the weaker the fabric becomes. And if, as I believe, moral principles against active killing have the deep and continuously civilizing effect of promoting respect for life, and if principles which allow passively letting die (as envisioned in the AMA statement) do not themselves cut against this effect, then this seems an important reason for the maintenance of the active/passive distinction. (By the logic of the above argument passively letting die would also have to be prohibited if a rule permitting it had the serious adverse consequence of eroding acceptance of rules protective of respect for life. While this prospect seems to me improbable, I can hardly claim to have refuted those conservatives who would claim that even rules which sanction letting die place us on a precarious slippery slope.)

A troublesome problem, however, confronts my use of utilitarian and wedge arguments. Most all of us would agree that both killing and letting die are justified under some conditions. Killings in self-defense and in "just" wars are widely accepted as justified because the conditions excuse the killing. If society can withstand these exceptions to moral rules prohibiting killing, then why is it not plausible to suppose society can accept another excusing exception in the form of justified active euthanasia? This is an important and worthy objection, but not a decisive one. The defenseless and the dying are significantly different classes of persons from aggressors who attack individuals and/or nations. In the case of aggressors, one does not confront the question whether their lives are no longer *worth living*. Rather, we reach the judgment that the aggressors' morally blameworthy actions justify counteractions. But in the case of the dying and the otherwise ill, there is no morally blameworthy action to justify our own. Here we are required to accept the judgment that their lives are no longer *worth living* in order to believe that the termination of their lives is justified. It is the latter sort of judgment which is feared by those who take the wedge argument seriously. We do not now permit and never have permitted the taking of morally blameless lives. I think this is the key to understanding why recent cases of intentionally allowing the death of defective newborns (as in the now famous case at the Johns Hopkins Hospital) have generated such protracted controversy. Even if such newborns could not have led meaningful lives (a matter of some controversy), it is the wedged foot in the door which creates the most intense worries. For if we once take a decision to allow a restricted infanticide justification or any justification at all on grounds that a life is not meaningful or not worth living, we have qualified our moral rules against killing. That this qualification is a matter of the utmost seriousness needs no argument. I mention it here only to show why the wedge argument may have moral force even though we *already* allow some very different conditions to justify intentional killing.

There is one final utilitarian reason favoring the preservation of the active/passive distinction.[8] Suppose we distinguish the following two types of cases of wrongly diagnosed patients:

1. Patients wrongly diagnosed as hopeless, and who will survive even if a treatment *is* ceased (in order to allow a natural death).
2. Patients wrongly diagnosed as hopeless, and who will survive only if the treatment is *not ceased* (in order to allow a natural death).

If a social rule permitting only passive euthanasia were in effect, then doctors and families who "allowed death" would lose only patients in class 2, not those in class 1; whereas if active euthanasia were permitted, at least some patients in class 1 would be needlessly lost. Thus, the consequence of a no-active-euthanasia rule would be to save some lives which could not be saved if both forms of euthanasia were allowed. This reason is not a *decisive* reason for favoring a policy of passive euthanasia, since these classes (1 and 2) are likely to be very small and since there might be counterbalancing reasons (extreme pain, autonomous expression of the patient, etc.) in favor of active euthanasia. But certainly it is *a* reason favoring only passive euthanasia and one which is morally relevant and ought to be considered along with other moral reasons....

There remains, however, the important question as to whether we *ought* to accept the distinction between active and passive euthanasia, now that we are clear about (at least one way of drawing) the moral grounds for its invocation. That is, should we employ the distinction in order to judge some acts of euthanasia justified and others not justified? Here, as the hesitant previous paragraph indicates, I am uncertain. This problem is a substantive moral issue—not merely a conceptual one—and would require at a minimum a lengthy assessment of wedge arguments and related utilitarian considerations. In important respects empirical questions are involved in this assessment. We should like to know, and yet have hardly any evidence to indicate, what the consequences would be for our society if we were to allow the use of active means to produce death. The best hope for making such an assessment has

seemed to some to rest in analogies to suicide and capital punishment statutes. Here it
may reasonably be asked whether recent liberalizations of laws limiting these forms of
killing have served as the thin end of a wedge
leading to a breakdown of principles protecting life or to widespread violations of moral
principles. Nonetheless, such analogies do
not seem to me promising, since they are still
fairly remote from the pertinent issue of the
consequences of allowing active humanitarian killing of one person by another.

It is interesting to notice the outcome of
the Kamisar–Williams debate on euthanasia—which is almost exclusively cast by both
writers in a consequential, utilitarian framework.[9] At one crucial point in the debate,
where possible consequences of laws permitting euthanasia are under discussion, they exchange "perhaps" judgments:

*I [Williams] will return Kamisar the compliment and
say: "Perhaps." We are certainly in an area where no
solution is going to make things quite easy and happy
for everybody, and all sorts of embarrassments may be
conjectured. But these embarrassments are not avoided by
keeping to the present law: we suffer from them
already.*[10]

Because of the grave difficulties which stand
in the way of making accurate predictions
about the impact of liberalized euthanasia
laws—especially those that would permit active killing—it is not surprising that those
who debate the subject would reach a point
of exchanging such "perhaps" judgments.
And that is why, so it seems to me, we are
uncertain whether to perpetuate or to abandon the active-passive distinction in our moral thinking about euthanasia. I think we *do*
perpetuate it in medicine, law, and ethics because we are still somewhat uncertain about
the conditions under which *passive* euthanasia
should be permitted by law (which is one
form of social *rule*). We are unsure about
what the consequences will be of the California "Natural Death Act" and all those similar
acts passed by other states which have followed in its path. If no untoward results oc-

cur, and the balance of the results seems
favorable, then we will perhaps be less concerned about further liberalizations of euthanasia laws. If untoward results do occur (on a
widespread scale), then we would be most
reluctant to accept further liberalizations and
might even abolish natural death acts.

In short, I have argued in this section that
euthanasia in its active and its passive forms
presents us with a dilemma which can be developed by using powerful consequentialist
arguments on each side, yet there is little
clarity concerning the proper resolution of
the dilemma precisely because of our uncertainty regarding proclaimed consequences. . . .

Endnotes

1. "Active and Passive Euthanasia," *New England Journal of Medicine* 292 (January 9, 1975), 78–80.

2. As recorded in the Opinion of Judge Robert Muir,
Jr., Docket No. C–201–75 of the Superior Court of
New Jersey, Chancery Division, Morris County (Novem-
ber 10, 1975).

3. See Judge Muir's Opinion, p. 18—a slightly different statement but on the subject.

4. This problem of the strength of evidence also
emerged in the Quinlan trial, as physicians disagreed
whether the evidence was "irrefutable." Such disagreement, when added to the problems of medical fallibility
and causal responsibility just outlined, provides in the
eyes of some one important argument against the *legalization* of active euthanasia, as perhaps the AMA would
agree.

5. Among the moral reasons why one is held to be responsible in the first sort of case and not responsible
in the second sort are, I believe, the moral grounds for
the active/passive distinction under discussion in this
section.

6. In *Social Ethics,* as cited in the permission note to
this article.

7. An argument of this form, which I find unacceptable
for reasons given below, is Arthur Dyck, "Beneficient
Euthanasia and Benemortasia: Alternative Views of
Mercy," in M. Kohl, ed., *Beneficient Euthanasia* (Buffalo:
Prometheus Books, 1975), pp. 120f.

8. I owe most of this argument to James Rachels,
whose comments on an earlier draft of this paper led
to several significant alterations.

9. Williams bases his pro-euthanasia argument on the
prevention of two consequences: (1) loss of liberty and
(2) cruelty. Kamisar bases his anti-euthanasia position
on three projected consequences of euthanasia laws:
(1) mistaken diagnosis, (2) pressured decisions by seriously ill patients, and (3) the wedge of the laws will

lead to legalized involuntary euthanasia. Kamisar admits that individual acts of euthanasia are sometimes justified. It is the rule that he opposes. He is thus clearly a rule-utilitarian, and I believe Williams is as well (cf. his views on children and the senile). Their assessments of wedge arguments are, however, radically different.

10. Glanville Williams, "Mercy–Killing Legislation—A Rejoinder," *Minnesota Law Review*, 43, no. 1 (1958), 5.

Review Questions

1. Beauchamp begins with three criticisms of Rachels. What are they?

2. What is the widely accepted argument for rejecting Rachels' position? Why doesn't Beauchamp accept it?

3. Explain the wedge or slippery slope argument that is used to defend the active/passive distinction.

4. Explain the utilitarian arguments that Beauchamp uses to defend the active/passive distinction.

Discussion Questions

1. Are Beauchamp's utilitarian arguments persuasive? Why or why not?

2. Should we accept the distinction between active and passive euthanasia or not? What is your view?

Peter Singer

Justifying Voluntary Euthanasia

Peter Singer is Professor of Philosophy at Monash University in Australia. He is the author of Animal Liberation *and* Practical Ethics, *from which our reading is taken.*

Singer argues that voluntary euthanasia and assisted suicide (which is very similar) are morally justified in cases where a patient is suffering from an incurable and painful or very distressing condition. In such cases, the fear of death, preference utilitarianism, the theory of rights, and respect for autonomy all provide reasons for allowing voluntary euthanasia or assisted suicide.

Voluntary Euthanasia

Most of the groups currently campaigning for changes in the law to allow euthanasia are

From Peter Singer, *Practical Ethics* (Cambridge: Cambridge University Press, 1979), pp. 128–129, and 140–146. © Cambridge University Press, 1979. Reprinted with permission of Cambridge University Press.

campaigning for voluntary euthanasia—that is, euthanasia carried out at the request of the person killed.

Sometimes voluntary euthanasia is scarcely distinguishable from assisted suicide. In *Jean's Way*, Derek Humphry has told how his wife Jean, when dying of cancer, asked him to provide her with the means to end her life swiftly and without pain. They had seen the situation coming and discussed it beforehand. Derek obtained some tablets and gave them to Jean, who took them and died soon afterwards.

In other cases, people wanting to die may be unable to kill themselves. In 1973 George Zygmaniak was injured in a motorcycle accident near his home in New Jersey. He was taken to hospital, where he was found to be totally paralysed from the neck down. He was also in considerable pain. He told his doctor and his brother, Lester, that he did not want to live in this condition. He begged them both to kill him. Lester questioned the doctor and hospital staff about George's prospects of recovery; he was told that they were nil. He then smuggled a gun into the hospital, and said to his brother: 'I am here to end your pain, George. Is it all right with you?' George, who was now unable to speak because of an operation to assist his breathing, nodded affirmatively. Lester shot him through the temple.

The Zygmaniak case appears to be a clear instance of voluntary euthanasia, although without some of the procedural safeguards that advocates of the legalization of voluntary euthanasia propose. For instance, medical opinions about the patient's prospects of recovery were obtained only in an informal manner. Nor was there a careful attempt to establish, before independent witnesses, that George's desire for death was of a fixed and rational kind, based on the best available information about his situation. The killing was not carried out by a doctor. An injection would have been less distressing to others than shooting. But these choices were not open to Lester Zygmaniak, for the law in New Jersey, as in most other places, regards mercy killing as murder, and if he had made his plans known, he would not have been able to carry them out.

Euthanasia can be voluntary even if a person is not able, as Jean Humphrey and George Zygmaniak were able, to indicate the wish to die right up to the moment the tablets are swallowed or the trigger pulled. A person may, while in good health, make a written request for euthanasia if, through accident or illness, she should come to be incapable of making or expressing a decision to die, in pain, or without the use of her mental faculties, and there is no reasonable hope of recovery. In killing a person who has made such a request, has re-affirmed it from time to time, and is now in one of the states described, one could truly claim to be acting with her consent....

JUSTIFYING VOLUNTARY EUTHANASIA

Under existing laws people suffering unrelievable pain or distress from an incurable illness who ask their doctors to end their lives are asking their doctors to become murderers. Although juries are extremely reluctant to convict in cases of this kind the law is clear that neither the request, nor the degree of suffering, nor the incurable condition of the person killed, is a defence to a charge of murder. Advocates of voluntary euthanasia propose that this law be changed so that a doctor could legally act on a patient's desire to die without further suffering.

The case for voluntary euthanasia has some common ground with the case for nonvoluntary euthanasia, in that the reason for killing is to end suffering. The two kinds of euthanasia differ, however, in that voluntary euthanasia involves the killing of a person, a rational and self-conscious being and not a merely conscious being. (To be strictly accurate it must be said that this is not always so, because although only rational and self-conscious beings can consent to their own deaths, they may not be rational and self-conscious at the time euthanasia is contemplated—the doctor may, for instance, be acting on a prior written request for euthanasia if, through accident or illness, one's rational faculties should be irretrievably lost. For simplicity we shall, henceforth, disregard this complication.)

We have seen that it is possible to justify nonvoluntary euthanasia, when the being killed lacks the capacity to consent. We must now ask in what way the ethical issues are different when the being is capable of consenting, and does in fact consent.

Let us return to the general principles about killing.... I [have] argued ... that the wrongness of killing a conscious being which is not self-conscious, rational or autonomous, depends on utilitarian considerations. It is on this basis that I have defended nonvoluntary euthanasia. On the other hand it is, as we saw, plausible to hold that killing a self-conscious being is a more serious matter than killing a merely conscious being. We found four distinct grounds on which this could be argued:

i. The classical utilitarian claim that since self-conscious beings are capable of fearing their own death, killing them has worse effects on others.

ii. The preference utilitarian calculation which counts the thwarting of the victim's desire to go on living as an important reason against killing.

iii. A theory of rights according to which to have a right one must have the ability to desire that to which one has a right, so that to have a right to life one must be able to desire one's own continued existence.

iv. Respect for the autonomous decisions of rational agents.

Now suppose we have a situation in which a person suffering from a painful and incurable disease wishes to die. If the individual were not a person—not rational or self-conscious—euthanasia would, as I have said, be justifiable. Do any of the four grounds for holding that it is normally worse to kill a person provide reasons against killing when the individual is a person?

The classical utilitarian objection does not apply to killing that takes place only with the genuine consent of the person killed. That people are killed under these conditions would have no tendency to spread fear or insecurity, since we have no cause to be fearful of being killed with our own genuine consent. If we do not wish to be killed, we simply do not consent. In fact, the argument from fear points in favour of voluntary euthanasia, for if voluntary euthanasia is not permitted we may, with good cause, be fearful that our deaths will be unnecessarily drawn-out and distressing.

Preference utilitarianism also points in favour of, not against, voluntary euthanasia. Just as preference utilitarianism must count a desire to go on living as a reason against killing, so it must count a desire to die as a reason for killing.

Next, according to the theory of rights we have considered, it is an essential feature of a right that one can waive one's rights if one so chooses. I may have a right to privacy; but I can, if I wish, film every detail of my daily life and invite the neighbours to my home movies. Neighbours sufficiently intrigued to accept my invitation could do so without violating my right to privacy, since the right has on this occasion been waived. Similarly, to say that I have a right to life is not to say that it would be wrong for my doctor to end my life, if she does so at my request. In making this request I waive my right to life.

Lastly, the principle of respect for autonomy tells us to allow rational agents to live their own lives according to their own autonomous decisions, free from coercion or interference; but if rational agents should autonomously choose to die, then respect for autonomy will lead us to assist them to do as they choose.

So, although there are reasons for thinking that killing a self-conscious being is normally worse than killing any other kind of being, in the special case of voluntary euthanasia most of these reasons count for euthanasia rather than against. Surprising as this result might at first seem, it really does no more than reflect the fact that what is special about self-conscious beings is that they can know that they exist over time and will, unless they die, continue to exist. Normally this continued existence is fervently desired; when the foreseeable continued existence is dreaded rather than desired however, the desire to die may take the place of the normal desire to live, reversing the reasons against killing based on the desire to live. Thus the case for voluntary euthanasia is arguably much stronger than the case for nonvoluntary euthanasia.

Some opponents of the legalization of voluntary euthanasia might concede that all this follows, if we have a genuinely free and rational decision to die; but, they add, we can never be sure that a request to be killed is the result of a free and rational decision. Will not the sick and elderly be pressured by their relatives to end their lives quickly? Will it not be possible to commit outright murder by pretending that a person has requested euthanasia? And even if there is no pressure of falsification, can anyone who is ill, suffering pain, and very probably in a drugged and confused state of mind, make a rational decision about whether to live or die?

These questions raise technical difficulties for the legalization of voluntary euthanasia, rather than objections to the underlying ethical principles; but they are serious difficulties nonetheless. Voluntary euthanasia societies in Britain and elsewhere have sought to meet them by proposing that euthanasia should be legal only for a person who:

i. is diagnosed by two doctors as suffering from an incurable illness expected to cause severe distress or the loss of rational faculties;

and

ii. has, at least 30 days before the proposed act of euthanasia, and in the presence of two independent witnesses, made a written request for euthanasia in the event of the situation described in (i) occurring.

Only a doctor could administer euthanasia, and if the patient was at the time still capable of consenting, the doctor would have to make sure that the patient still wished the declaration to be acted upon. A declaration could be revoked at any time.

These provisions, though in some respects cumbersome, appear to meet most of the technical objections to legalization. Murder in the guise of euthanasia would be far-fetched. Two independent witnesses to the declaration, the 30 day waiting period, and—in the case of a mentally competent person—the doctor's final investigation of the patient's wishes would together do a great deal to reduce the danger of doctors acting on requests which did not reflect the free and rational decisions of their patients.

It is often said, in debates about euthanasia, that doctors can be mistaken. Certainly some patients diagnosed by competent doctors as suffering from an incurable condition have survived. Possibly the legalization of

voluntary euthanasia would, over the years, mean the deaths of one or two people who would otherwise have recovered. This is not, however, the knockdown argument against euthanasia that some imagine it to be. Against a very small number of unnecessary deaths that might occur if euthanasia is legalized we must place the very large amount of pain and distress that will be suffered by patients who really are terminally ill if euthanasia is not legalized. Longer life is not such a supreme good that it outweighs all other considerations. (If it were, there would be many more effective ways of saving life—such as a ban on smoking, or on cars that can drive faster than 10 m.p.h.—than prohibiting voluntary euthanasia.) The possibility that two doctors may make a mistake means that the person who opts for euthanasia is deciding on the balance of probabilities, and giving up a very slight chance of survival in order to avoid suffering that will almost certainly end in death. This may be a perfectly rational choice. Probability is, as Bishop Butler said, the guide of life, and we must follow its guidance right to the end. Against this, some will reply that improved care for the terminally ill has eliminated pain and made voluntary euthanasia unnecessary. Elisabeth Kübler–Ross, whose *On Death and Dying* is perhaps the best-known book on care for the dying, has claimed that none of her patients request euthanasia. Given personal attention and the right medication, she says, people come to accept their deaths and die peacefully without pain.

Kübler–Ross may be right. It may be possible, now, to eliminate pain. It may even be possible to do it in a way which leaves patients in possession of their rational faculties and free from vomiting, nausea, or other distressing side-effects. Unfortunately only a minority of dying patients now receive this kind of care. Nor is physical pain the only problem. There can also be other distressing conditions, like bones so fragile they fracture at sudden movements, slow starvation due to a cancerous growth, inability to control one's bowels or bladder, difficulty in breathing and so on.

Take the case of Jean Humphry, as described in *Jean's Way*. This is not a case from the period before effective painkillers: Jean Humphry died in 1975. Nor is it the case of someone unable to get good medical care: she was treated at an Oxford hospital and if there were anything else that could have been done for her, her husband, a well-connected Fleet St journalist, would have been better placed than most to obtain it. Yet Derek Humphry writes:

when the request for help in dying meant relief from relentless suffering and pain and I had seen the extent of this agony, the option simply could not be denied . . . And certainly Jean deserved the dignity of selecting her own ending. She must die soon—as we both now realized—but together we would decide when this would be.

Perhaps one day it will be possible to treat all terminally ill patients in such a way that no one requests euthanasia and the subject becomes a non-issue; but this still distant prospect is no reason to deny euthanasia to those who die in less comfortable conditions. It is, in any case, highly paternalistic to tell dying patients that they are now so well looked after they need not be offered the option of euthanasia. It would be more in keeping with respect for individual freedom and autonomy to legalize euthanasia and let patients decide whether their situation is bearable—let them, as Derek Humphry puts it, have the dignity of selecting their own endings. Better that voluntary euthanasia be an unexercised legal right than a prohibited act which, for all we know, some might desperately desire.

Finally, do these arguments for voluntary euthanasia perhaps give too much weight to individual freedom and autonomy? After all, we do not allow people free choices on matters like, for instance, the taking of heroin. This is a restriction of freedom but, in the view of many, one that can be justified on paternalistic grounds. If preventing people becoming heroin addicts is justifiable pater-

nalism, why isn't preventing people having themselves killed?

The question is a reasonable one, because respect for individual freedom can be carried too far. John Stuart Mill thought that the state should never interfere with the individual except to prevent harm to others. The individual's own good, Mill thought, is not a proper reason for state intervention. But Mill may have had too high an opinion of the rationality of a human being. It may occasionally be right to prevent people making choices which are obviously not rationally based and which we can be sure they will later regret. The prohibition of voluntary euthanasia cannot be justified on paternalistic grounds, however, for voluntary euthanasia is, by definition, an act for which good reasons exist. Voluntary euthanasia occurs only when, to the best of medical knowledge, a person is suffering from an incurable and painful or distressing condition. In these circumstances one cannot say that to choose to die quickly is obviously irrational. The strength of the case for voluntary euthanasia lies in this combination of respect for the preferences, or autonomy, of those who decide for euthanasia; and the clear rational basis of the decision itself. . . .

Review Questions

1. Distinguish between the cases of Jean Humphry and George Zygmaniak.

2. What are the four grounds for holding that killing a person, a rational and self-conscious being, is wrong?

3. According to Singer, how do these grounds provide reasons for allowing voluntary euthanasia or assisted suicide?

4. What objections does Singer discuss? How does he reply to these objections?

Discussion Questions

1. Was Jean Humphry morally justified in committing suicide or not? Would it make any moral difference if her husband had killed her instead?

2. Was Lester Zygmaniak justified in killing his brother? Why or why not? If not, then should Lester be punished? Explain your view.

3. Do you think that the law should be changed to allow voluntary euthanasia or assisted suicide for terminally ill patients? Defend your answer.

Richard B. Brandt

Defective Newborns and the Morality of Termination

Richard B. Brandt is Professor of Philosophy at the University of Michigan. His most recent book on ethics is A Theory of the Good and the Right *(1979).*

Brandt argues that it is morally right to actively or passively terminate the life of a defective newborn if its life is bad according to a "happiness criterion". Consent is irrelevant; the infant cannot give consent, and it will be indifferent to continued life. But the cost of caring for the infant is relevant to the decision to terminate in addition to the quality of the prospective life.

The *legal* rights of a fetus are very different from those of a newborn. The fetus may be aborted, legally, for any reason or no reason up to twenty-four or twenty-eight weeks (U.S. Supreme Court, *Roe* v. *Wade*). But, at least in theory, immediately after birth an infant has all the legal rights of the adult, including the right to life.

The topic of this paper, however, is to identify the moral rights of the newborn, specifically whether *defective* newborns have a right to life. But it is simpler to talk, not about "rights to life," but about when or whether it is *morally right* either actively or passively (by withdrawal of life-supportive

From *Infanticide and the Value of Life*, ed. by Marvin Kohl (Prometheus Books, 1978). Reprinted with permission.

measures) to terminate defective newborns. It is also better because the conception of a right involves the notion of a sphere of autonomy—something is to be done or omitted, but only if the subject of the rights wants or consents—and this fact is apt to be confusing or oversimplifying. Surely what we want to know is whether termination is morally right or wrong, and nothing can turn on the **semantics** of the concept of a "right."[1]

What does one have to do in order to support some answers to these questions? One thing we can do is ask—and I think myself that the answer to this question is definitive for our purposes—whether rational or fully informed persons would, in view of the total consequences, support a moral code for a society in which they expected to live, with one or another, provision on this matter. (I believe a fully rational person will at least normally have some degree of benevolence, or positive interest in the welfare or happiness of others; I shall not attempt to specify how much.) Since, however, I do not expect that everyone else will agree that answering this question would show what is morally right, I shall, for their benefit, also argue that certain moral principles on this matter are coherent with strong moral convictions of reflective people; or, to use Rawls's terminology, that a certain principle on the matter would belong to a system of moral principles in "reflective equilibrium."

Historically, many writers, including Pope Pius XI in *Casti Connubii* (1930), have affirmed an absolute prohibition against killing anyone who is neither guilty of a capital crime nor an unjust assailant threatening one's life (self-defense), except in case of "extreme necessity." Presumably the prohibition is intended to include withholding of food or liquid from a newborn, although strictly speaking this is only *failing* to do something, not actually *doing* something to bring about a death. (Would writers in this tradition demand, on moral grounds, that complicated and expensive surgery be undertaken to save a life? Such surgery is going beyond normal care, and in some cases beyond what earlier writers even conceived.) However the intentions of these writers may be, we should observe that historically their moral condemnation of all killing (except for the cases mentioned) derives from the Biblical injunction, "Thou shalt not kill," which, as it stands and without interpretation, may be taken to forbid suicide, killing of animals, perhaps even plants, and hence cannot be taken seriously.

Presumably a moral code that is coherent with our intuitions and that rational persons would support for their society would include some prohibition of killing, but it is another matter to identify the exact class to which such a prohibition is to apply. For one thing, I would doubt that killing one's self would be included—although one might be forbidden to kill one's self if that would work severe hardship on others, or conflict with the discharge of one's other moral obligations. And, possibly, defective newborns would *not* be included in the class. Further, a decision has to be made whether the prohibition of killing is *absolute* or only **prima facie**, meaning by "prima facie" that the duty not to kill might be outweighed by some other duty (or right) stronger in the circumstances, which could be fulfilled only by killing. In case this distinction is made, we would have to decide whether defective newborns fall within the scope of even a prima facie moral prohibition against killing. I shall, however, not attempt to make this fine distinction here, and shall simply inquire whether, everything considered, defective newborns—or some identifiable group of them—are excluded from the moral prohibition against killing.

THE PROSPECTIVE QUALITY OF LIFE OF DEFECTIVE NEWBORNS

Suppose that killing a defective newborn, or allowing it to die, would not be an *injury*, but would rather be doing the infant a favor. In that case we should feel intuitively less opposed to termination of newborns, and presumably rational persons would be less inclined to support a moral code with a prohibition against such action. In that case we would feel rather as we do about a person's preventing a suicide attempt from being successful, in order that the person be elaborately tortured to death at a later stage. It is no favor to the prospective suicide to save his life; similarly, if the prospective life of defective newborns is bad we are doing them a favor to let them die.

It may be said that we have no way of knowing what the conscious experiences of defective children are like, and that we have no competence in any case to decide when or what kind of life is bad or not worth living. Further, it may be said that predictions about a defective newborn's prospects for the future are precarious, in view of possible further advances of medicine. It does seem, however, that here, as everywhere, the rational person will follow the evidence about the present or future facts. But there is a question how to decide whether a life is bad or not worth living.

In the case of *some* defective newborns, it seems clear that their prospective life is bad. Suppose, as sometimes happens, a child is hydrocephalic with an extremely low I.Q., is blind and deaf, has no control over its body, can only lie on its back all day and have all its needs taken care of by others, and even cries out with pain when it is touched or lifted. Infants born with spina bifida—and these number over two per one thousand births—are normally not quite so badly off, but are often nearly so.

But what criterion are we using if we say that such a life is bad? One criterion might be called a "happiness" criterion. If a person *likes* a moment of experience while he is having it, his life is so far good; if a person *dislikes* a moment of experience while he is having it, his life is so far bad. Based on such reactions, we might construct a "happiness curve" for a person, going up above the indifference axis when a moment of experience is liked—and how far above depending on how strongly it is liked—and dipping down below the line when a moment is disliked. Then this criterion would say that a life is worth living if there is a net balance of positive area under the curve over a lifetime, and that it is bad if there is a net balance of negative area. One might adopt some different criterion: for instance, one might say that a life is worth living if a person would *want* to live it over again given that, at the end, he could remember the whole of it with perfect vividness in some kind of grand intuitive awareness. Such a response to this hypothetical holistic intuition, however, would likely be affected by the state of the person's drives or moods at the time, and the conception strikes me as unconvincing, compared with the moment-by-moment reaction to what is going on. Let us, for the sake of the argument, adopt the happiness criterion.[2]

Is the prospective life of the seriously defective newborn, like the one described above, bad or good according to this criterion? One thing seems clear: that it is *less* good than is the prospective life of a normal infant. But is it bad?

We have to do some extrapolating from what we know. For instance, such a child will presumably suffer from severe sensory deprivation; he is simply not getting interesting stimuli. On the basis of laboratory data, it is plausible to think the child's experience is at best boring or uncomfortable. If the child's experience is painful, of course, its moments are, so far, on the negative side. One must suppose that such a child hardly suffers from disappointment, since it will not learn to expect anything exciting, beyond being fed and fondled, and these events will be regularly forthcoming. One might expect such a child to suffer from isolation and loneliness, but insofar as this is true, the object of dislike probably should be classified as just sensory deprivation; dislike of loneliness seems to depend on the deprivation of past pleasures of human company. There are also some positive enjoyments: of eating, drinking, elimination, seeing the nurse coming with food, and so on. But the brief enjoyments can hardly balance the long stretches of boredom, discomfort, or even pain. On the whole, the lives of such children are bad according to the happiness criterion.

Naturally we cannot generalize about the cases of all "defective" newborns; there are all sorts of defects, and the cases I have described are about the worst. A child with spina bifida may, if he survives the numerous operations, I suppose, adjust to the frustrations of immobility; he may become accustomed to the embarrassments of no bladder or bowel control; he may have some intellectual enjoyments like playing chess; he will suffer from observing what others have but he cannot, such as sexual satisfactions, in addition to the pain of repeated surgery. How does it all balance out? Surely not as very good, but perhaps above the indifference level.

It may fairly be said, I think, that the lives of some defective newborns are destined to be bad on the whole, and it would be a favor to them if their lives were terminated. Contrariwise, the prospective lives of many defective newborns are modestly pleasant, and it would be some injury to them to be terminated, albeit the lives they will live are ones some of us would prefer not to live at all.

CONSENT

Let us now make a second suggestion, not this time that termination of a defective newborn would be doing him a favor, but this time that he *consents* to termination, in the sense of expressing a rational deliberated preference for this. In that case I suggest that intuitively we would be *more* favorably inclined to judge that it is right to let the defective die, and I suggest also that for that case rational persons would be more ready to support a moral code permitting termination. Notice that we think that if an ill person has signified what we think a rational and deliberated desire to die, we are morally better justified in withdrawing life-supporting measures than we otherwise would be.

The newborn, however, is incapable of expressing his preference (giving consent) at all, much less expressing a rational deliberated preference. There could in theory be court-appointed guardians or proxies, presumably disinterested parties, authorized to give such consent on his behalf, but even so this would not be *his* consent.

Nevertheless, there is a fact about the mental life of the newborn (defective or not) such that, if he could understand the fact, it seems he would not object—even rationally or after deliberation, if that were possible—to his life being terminated, or to his parents substituting another child in his place. This suggestion may seem absurd, but let us see. The explanation runs along the lines of an argument I once used to support the morality of abortion. I quote the paragraph in which this argument was introduced.[3]

Suppose I were seriously ill, and were told that, for a sizeable fee, an operation to save "my life" could be performed, of the following sort: my brain would be removed to another body which could provide a normal life, but the unfortunate result of the operation would be that my memory and learned abilities would be wholly erased, and that the forming of memory brain traces must begin again from scratch, as in a newborn baby. Now, how large a fee would I be willing to pay for this operation, when the alternative is my peaceful demise? My own answer would be: None at all. I would take no interest in the continued existence of "myself" in that sense, and I would rather add the sizeable fee to the inheritance of my children.... I cannot see the point of forfeiting my children's inheritance in order to start off a person who is brand new except that he happens to enjoy the benefit of having my present brain, without the memory traces. It appears that some continuity of memory is a necessary condition for personal identity in an important sense.

My argument was that the position of a fetus, at the end of the first trimester, is essentially the same as that of the person contemplating this operation: he will consider that the baby born after six months will not be *he* in any *important* and *motivating* sense (there will be no continuity of memory, and, indeed, maybe nothing to have been remembered), and the later existence of this baby, in a sense bodily continuous with his present body, would be a matter of indifference to him. So, I argued, nothing is being done to the fetus that he would object to having done if he understood the situation.

What do I think is necessary in order for the continuation of my body with its conscious experiences to be worthwhile? One thing is that it is able to remember the events I can now remember; another is that it takes some interest in the projects I am now planning and remembers them as my projects; another is that it recognizes my friends and has warm feelings for them, and so on. Reflection on these states of a future continuation of my body with its experiences is what makes the idea motivating. But such motivating reflection for a newborn is impossible: he has no memories that he wants recalled later; he has no plans to execute; he has no warm feelings for other persons. He has simply not had the length of life necessary for these to come about. Not only that: the conception of these things cannot be motivating because the concept of some state of affairs being motivating requires roughly a past experience in which similar states of affairs were satisfying, and he has not lived long enough for the requisite conditioning to have taken place. (The most one could say is that the image of warm milk in his mouth is attractive; he might answer affirmatively if it could be put to him whether he would be aversive to the idea of no more warm milk.) So we can say not merely that the newborn does not want the continuation of himself as a subject of experiences (he has not the conceptual framework for this), he does not want *anything* that his own survival would promote. It is like the case of the operation: there is nothing I want that the survival of my brain with no memory would promote. Give the newborn as much *conceptual* framework as you like; the *wants* are not there, which could give significance to the continuance of his life.

The newborn, then, is bound to be *indifferent* to the idea of a continuation of the stream of his experiences, even if he clearly has the idea of that. It seems we can know this about him.

The truth of all this is still not for it to be the case that the newborn, defective or not, gives *consent* to, or expresses a preference for, the termination of his life. *Consent* is a performance, normally linguistic, but always requiring some conventional *sign.* A newborn, who has not yet learned how to signalize consent, cannot give consent. And it may be thought that this difference makes all the difference.

In order to see what difference it does make in this case, we should ask what makes adult consent morally important. Why is it that we think euthanasia can be practiced on an adult only if he gives his consent, at least his implied consent (e.g., by previous statements)? There seem to be two reasons. The first is that a person is more likely to be concerned with his own welfare, and to take steps to secure it, than are others, even his good friends. Giving an individual control over his own life, and not permitting others to take control except when he consents, is normally to promote his welfare. An individual may, of course, behave stupidly or shortsightedly, but we think that on the whole a person's welfare is best secured if decisions about it are in his hands; and it is best for society in the normal case (not for criminals, etc.) if persons' own lives are well-served. The second reason is the feeling of security a person can have if he knows the major decisions about himself are in his own hands. When they are not, a person can easily, and in some cases very reasonably, suppose that other persons may well be able to do something to him that he would very much like them not to do. He does not have to worry about that if he knows they cannot do it without his consent.

Are things different with the newborn? At least he, like the fetus, is not yet able to suffer from insecurity; he cannot worry about what others may do to him. So the second reason for requiring consent cannot have any importance in his case. His situation is thus very unlike that of the senile adult, for an adult can worry about what others may do to him if they judge him senile. And this worry can well cast a shadow over a lot of life. But how about the first reason? Here matters are more complex. In the case of children, we think their own lives are better cared for if certain decisions are in the hands of others; the child may not want to visit the dentist, but the parents know that his best interests are served by going, and they make him go. The same for compulsory school attendance. And the same for the newborn. But there is another point: that society has an interest, at certain crucial points, that may not be served by doing just exactly what is for the lifelong interest of the newborn. There are huge costs that are relevant, in the case of the defective newborn. I shall go into that problem in a moment. It seems, then, that in the case of the newborn, *consent* cannot have the moral importance that it has in the case of adults.

On the other hand, then, the newborn will not *care* whether his life is terminated, even if he understands his situation perfectly; and, on the other hand, consent does not have the moral importance in his case that it has for adults. So, while it seems true that we would feel better about permitting termination of defective newborns if only they could give rational and deliberated consent and gave it, nevertheless when we bear the foregoing two points in mind, the absence of consent does not seem morally crucial in their case. We can understand why rational persons deciding which moral code to support for their society would not make the giving of consent a necessary condition for feeling free to terminate an infant's life when such action was morally indicated by the other features of the situation.

REPLACEMENT IN ORDER TO GET A BETTER LIFE

Let us now think of an example owing to Derek Parfit. Suppose a woman wants a child, but is told that if she conceives a child now it will be defective, whereas if she waits three months she will produce a normal child. Obviously we think it would be wrong for the mother not to delay. (If she delays, the child she will have is not the *same* child as the one she would have had if she had not delayed, but it will have a better life.) This is the sole reason why we think she should delay and have the later-born child.

Suppose, however, a woman conceives but discovers only three months later that the fetus will become a defective child, but that she can have a normal child if she has an abortion and tries again. Now this time there is still the same reason for having the abortion that there formerly was for the delay: that she will produce a child with a better life. Ought she not then to have the abortion? If the child's life is bad, he could well complain that he had been injured by deliberately being brought to term. Would he complain if he were aborted, in favor of the later normal child? Not if the argument of the preceding section is correct.

But now suppose the woman does not discover until after she gives birth, that the child is severely defective, but that she could conceive again and have a normal child. Are things really different, in the first few days? One might think that a benevolent person would want, in each of these cases, the substitution of a normal child for the defective one, of the better life for the worse one.

THE COST AND ITS RELEVANCE

It is agreed that the burden of care for a defective infant, say one born with spina bifida, is huge. The cost of surgery alone for an infant with spina bifida has been estimated to be around $275,000.[4] In many places this cost must be met by the family of the child, and there is the additional cost of care in an institution, if the child's condition does not permit care at home—and a very modest estimate of the monthly cost at present is $1,100. To meet even the surgical costs, not to mention monthly payments for continuing care, the lives of members of the family must be at a most spartan level for many years. The psychological effects of this, and equally, if not more so, of care provided at home, are far-reaching; they are apt to destroy the marriage and to cause psychological problems for the siblings. There is the on-going anxiety, the regular visits, the continuing presence of a caretaker if the child is in the home. In one way or another the continued existence of the child is apt to reduce dramatically the quality of life of the family as a whole.

It can be and has been argued that such costs, while real, are irrelevant to the moral problem of what should be done.[5] It is obvious, however, that rational persons, when deciding which moral code to support, would take these human costs into account. As indeed they should: the parents and siblings are also human beings with lives to live, and any sacrifices a given law or moral system might call on them to make must be taken into account in deciding between laws and moral codes. Everyone will feel sympathy for a helpless newborn; but everyone should also think, equally vividly, of all the others who will suffer and just how they will suffer—and, of course, as indicated above, of just what kind of life the defective newborn will have in any case. There is a choice here between allowing a newborn to die (possibly a favor to it, and in any case not a serious loss), and imposing a very heavy burden on the family for many years to come.

Philosophers who think the cost to others is irrelevant to what should be done should reflect that we do not accept the general principle that lives should be saved at no matter what cost. For instance, ships are deliberately built with only a certain margin of safety; that could be built so that they would hardly sink in any storm, but to do so would be economically unfeasible. We do not think we should require a standard of safety for automobiles that goes beyond a certain point of expense and inconvenience; we are prepared to risk a few extra deaths. And how about the lives we are willing to lose in war, in order to assure a certain kind of economic order or democracy or free speech? Surely there is a point at which the loss of a life (or the abbreviation of a life) and the cost to others become comparable. Is it obvious that the continuation of a marginal kind of life for a child takes moral precedence over providing a college education for one or more of his siblings? Some comparisons will be hard to make, but continuing even a marginally pleasant life hardly has absolute priority.

DRAWING LINES

There are two questions that must be answered in any complete account of what is the morally right thing to do about defective newborns.

The first is: If a decision to terminate is made, how soon must it be made? Obviously it could not be postponed to the age of five, or of three, or even a year and a half. At those ages, all the reasons for insisting on consent are already cogent. And at those ages, the child will already care what happens to him. But ten days is tolerable. Doubtless advances in medicine will permit detection of serious prospective defects early in pregnancy, and this issue of how many days will not arise.

Second, the argument from the quality of the prospective life of the defective newborn requires that we decide which defects are so serious that the kind of life the defective child can have gives it no serious claim as compared with the social costs. This issue must be thought through, and some guidelines established, but I shall not attempt this here.

One might argue that, if the newborn cannot rationally care whether its life ends or not, the parents are free to dispose of a child irrespective of whether he is defective, if they simply do not want it. To this there are two replies. First, in practice there are others who want a child if the parents do not, and they can put it up for adoption. But second, the parents are *injuring* a child if they prevent it from having the good life it could have had. We do not in general accept the argument that a person is free to injure another, for no reason, even if he has that person's consent. In view of these facts, we may expect that rational, benevolent persons deciding which moral code to support would select one that required respect for the life of a normal child, but would permit the termination of the life of a seriously defective child.

ACTIVE AND PASSIVE PROCEDURES

There is a final question: that of a choice between withdrawal of life-supporting measures (such as feeding), and the active, painless taking of life. It seems obvious, however, that once the basic decision is made that an infant is not to receive the treatment necessary to sustain life beyond a few days, it is mere stupid cruelty to allow it to waste away gradually in a hospital bed—for the child to suffer, and for everyone involved also to suffer in watching the child suffer. If death is the outcome decided upon, it is far kinder for it to come quickly and painlessly.

Endnotes

1. Here I disagree with Michael Tooley, "Abortion and Infanticide," *Philosophy and Public Affairs* 2 (1972): 37–65, especially pp. 44–49.

2. Professor P. Foot has made interesting remarks on when a life is worth living. See her "Euthanasia," *Philosophy and Public Affairs*, 6 (1977): 85–112, especially pp. 95–96. She suggests that a good life must "contain a minimum of basic goods," although not necessarily a favorable balance of good over evil elements. When does she think this minimum fails? For one thing, in extreme senility or severe brain damage. She also cites as examples of conditions for minimal goods that "a man is not driven to work far beyond his capacity; that he has the support of a family or community; that he can more or less satisfy his hunger; that he has hopes for the future; that he can lie down to rest at night." Overwhelming pain or nausea, or crippling depression, she says, also can make life not worth living. All of these, of course, except for cases of senility and brain damage, are factors fixing whether stretches of living are highly unpleasant.

If a person thinks that life is not good unless it realizes certain human potentialities, he will think life can be bad even if liked—and so far sets a higher standard than the happiness criterion. But Foot and such writers may say that even when life is not pleasant on balance, it can still be good if human potentialities are being realized or these basic minimal conditions are met; and in that sense they set a lower standard.

3. Richard B. Brandt, "The Morality of Abortion," in an earlier form in *The Monist* 56 (1972): 504–526, and in revised form in R.L. Perkins, ed., *Abortion: Pro and Con* (Cambridge, MA: Schenkman Publishing Co., 1974).

4. See A.M. Shaw and I.A. Shaw, in S. Gorovitz, et al., *Moral Problems in Medicine* (Englewood Cliffs, NJ: Prentice-Hall, Inc., 1976), pp. 335–341.

5. See, for instance, Philippa Foot, "Euthanasia," especially pp. 109–111. She writes: "So it is not for their sake but to avoid trouble to others that they are allowed to die. When brought out into the open this seems unacceptable; at least we do not easily accept the principle that adults who need special care should be counted too burdensome to be kept alive." I would think that "to avoid trouble to others" is hardly the terminology to describe the havoc that is apt to be produced. I agree that adults should not be allowed to die, or actively killed, without their consent, possibly except when they cannot give consent but are in great pain; but the reasons that justify different behavior in the two situations have appeared in the section, "Consent."

Review Questions

1. According to Brandt, how should one answer questions about moral rightness?

2. According to Brandt, why can't the Biblical injunction "Thou shalt not kill" be taken seriously?

3. Explain Brandt's happiness criterion.

4. In Brandt's view, in what cases would the life of a defective infant be bad?

5. Why would a newborn be indifferent to continued life according to Brandt?

6. In Brandt's view, why is it better to replace a defective child with a normal one?

7. According to Brandt, why is active euthanasia better than passive euthanasia in some cases?

Discussion Questions

1. Is Brandt's happiness criterion acceptable? Defend your view.

2. Is the cost of caring for a defective infant morally relevant? Defend your position.

3. Do you agree that in some cases active euthanasia is better than passive euthanasia? Why or why not?

Problem Cases

1. An AIDS Patient James is a twenty-five-year-old man who is dying from AIDS. His doctors predict that he will die within six months or a year. He is not in a great deal of pain yet, but he is very depressed and suicidal. He tells his doctor that he needs very strong pills to help him sleep at night, but the doctor suspects that James intends to kill himself with an overdose. It is not illegal for the doctor to prescribe these pills, and since the 1961 Suicide Act, it is not a criminal offense to commit suicide or to attempt to do so.

Should the doctor prescribe these pills or not? Explain your view.

2. The Case of Karen Quinlan On the night of April 15, 1975, for reasons still unclear, Karen Quinlan ceased breathing. She had been at a birthday party, and after a few drinks, she had passed out. Her friends thought she must be

drunk and put her to bed. Later they found that she had stopped breathing. Her friends gave her mouth-to-mouth resuscitation and took her to the nearest hospital. There she had a temperature of 100 degrees, her pupils were unreactive, and she was unresponsive even to deep pain.

Blood and urine tests showed that Karen had not consumed a dangerous amount of alcohol. A small amount of aspirin and the tranquilizer Valium were present, but not enough to be toxic or lethal. Why Karen had stopped breathing was a mystery. It was clear that part of her brain had died from oxygen deprivation.

After a week of unconsciousness, she was moved to St. Clare's Hospital in nearby Denville, where she was examined by Dr. Robert J. Morse, a neurologist. Dr. Morse found that she was in a "chronic persistent vegetative state" but not brain dead by the ordinary medical standard. It was judged that no form of treatment could restore her to cognitive life.

Nevertheless, she was kept breathing by means of a respirator that pumped air through a tube in her throat, and fed by means of a nasal-gastro tube. Her condition began to deteriorate. Her weight dropped to seventy pounds, and her five-foot two-inch frame bent into a rigid fetal position about three feet in length. After a few months, her father, Joseph Quinlan, asked to be appointed her legal guardian with the expressed purpose of requesting that the use of the respirator be discontinued. Experts testified that there was a strong likelihood that death would follow the removal of the respirator. The lower court refused his request that the respirator be discontinued; it said that "to do so would be homicide and an act of euthanasia." But in a famous decision (Supreme Court of New Jersey 355 A.2d 647), the Supreme Court of New Jersey granted the request on the condition that (1) attending physicians of Joseph Quinlan's choice conclude that there was no reasonable possibility of Karen being restored to cognitive life, and (2) the ethics committee of the institution where Karen was hospitalized concurred in the physicians' judgment.

Do you agree with the Supreme Court of New Jersey decision or not? Why or why not?

3. The Case of Karen Quinlan Continued   Six weeks after the court decision, the respirator still had not been turned off because the attending physicians, Dr. Robert Morse, the neurologist, and Dr. Javed, a pulmonary internist, were reluctant to do so. After Mr. Quinlan demanded that they remove Karen from the respirator, they agreed to wean her slowly from the machine. Soon she was breathing without mechanical assistance, and she was moved to a chronic-care hospital. For about ten years Karen was kept alive in the Morris View Nursing Home with high-nutrient feedings and regular doses of antibiotics to prevent infections. During this time, she never regained consciousness, but sometimes she made reflexive responses to touch and sound. After about ten years of comatose existence, Karen Quinlan died.

Would it have been morally right, during this long comatose period, to not give Karen antibiotics so that she would die from infections?

Would it have been wrong to give her a fatal injection? Why or why not?

Was it a good idea to keep her alive all this time or not? Why or why not?

4. The Case of Baby Jane Doe   In October 1983, Baby Jane Doe (as the infant was called by the court to protect her anonymity) was born with spina bifida and a host of other congenital defects. According to the doctors consulted by the parents, the child would be severely mentally retarded and bedridden, and would suffer considerable pain. After consultations with doctors and religious counselors, Mr. and Mrs. A (as the parents were called in the court documents) decided not to consent to lifesaving surgery.

Did the parents make the right decision or not? Explain and defend your position.

5. The Baby Doe Case Continued   A right-to-life activist lawyer tried to legally force lifesaving surgery in the Baby Doe case, but two New York appeals courts and a state children's agency decided not to override the parents' right to make a decision in the case. At this point, the U.S. Justice Department intervened in the case. It sued to obtain records from the University Hospital in Stony Brook, New York, to determine if the hospital had violated a federal law that forbids discrimination against the handicapped. Dr. C. Everett Koop, the U.S. Surgeon General, appeared on television to express the view that the government has the moral obligation to intercede on behalf of such infants in order to protect their right to life.

Two weeks later, Federal District Judge Leonard Wexler threw out the Justice Department's unusual suit. Wexler found no discrimination. The hospital had been willing to perform the surgery, but had failed to do so because the parents refused to consent to it. Wexler found the parents' decision to be a reasonable one in view of the circumstances.

The day after the ruling, the Justice Department appealed. On January 9, 1984, federal regulations were issued preventing federally funded hospitals from withholding treatment in such cases.

Do parents have a right to make life-and-death decisions for their defective children or not? Why or why not?

Do you agree with Dr. Koop that the government has a moral obligation to save the lives of such infants, even when their parents do not wish it? Explain your position.

If the government forces us to save the lives of defective infants like Baby Doe, then should it assume the responsibility for the cost of surgery, intensive care, and so on? If so, then how much money should be spent on this program? If not, then who is going to pay the bills?

Suggested Readings

(1) Tristram H. Englehardt, Jr., "Ethical Issues in Aiding the Death of Young Children," in Marvin Kohl, ed. *Beneficent Euthanasia* (Buffalo, NY: Prometheus Books, 1975), pp. 180–192. Englehardt distinguishes between adult euthanasia and euthanasia of children. He assumes that adult euthanasia can be justified by the appeal to freedom. Adults have a right to choose to die. But, Englehardt claims, children do not have this right because they are not persons in a strict sense; they are persons only in a social sense. He argues that child euthanasia is justified when parents decide that the child has little chance of a full human life and a great chance of suffering, and the cost of prolonging life is great.

(2) Philippa Foot, "Euthanasia," *Philosophy & Public Affairs* 6 (Winter 1977), pp. 85–112. Foot defines euthanasia as producing a death (by act or omission) that is good for the one who dies. She distinguishes between voluntary and nonvoluntary euthanasia, and between active and passive euthanasia. The latter distinction is based on the right to life and the correlative duty of noninterference. This duty is usually violated by active euthanasia, but not by passive euthanasia. She finds that nonvoluntary active euthanasia is never justified; however, she allows that the other types can be justified in some cases.

(3) _____, "The Problem of Abortion and the Doctrine of the Double Effect," *Oxford Review*, no. 5, pp. 5–15. Foot gives a classical discussion of the doctrine of double effect. As Foot defines it, this is the doctrine that it is sometimes permissible to bring about by oblique intention (that is, to foresee as a consequence of action, but to not directly intend) what is wrong to directly intend. Appealing to this doctrine, conservatives hold that it is permissible to perform an abortion to save the mother's life since the direct intention is to save the mother's life and the death of the fetus is only indirectly or obliquely intended (to use Foot's example).

(4) Jonathan Glover, *Causing Death and Saving Lives* (Harmondsworth, Middlesex, England: Penguin, 1977), pp. 182–189. Glover applies utilitarianism to the problem of euthanasia and to other problems of killing such as abortion and capital punishment.

(5) Marvin Kohl, ed., *Beneficent Euthanasia* (Buffalo, NY: Prometheus Books, 1975). This anthology has a number of excellent articles on euthanasia.

(6) _____, ed., *Infanticide and the Value of Life* (Buffalo, NY: Prometheus Books, 1978). This anthology concentrates on the morality of euthanasia for severely defective newborns.

(7) John Ladd, "Positive and Negative Euthanasia," in John Ladd, ed., *Ethical Issues Relating to Life & Death* (Oxford: Oxford University Press, 1979), pp. 164–186. Ladd prefers to talk about positive euthanasia instead of active euthanasia, and negative euthanasia instead of passive euthanasia. He rejects two positions, the absolutist position that a clear-cut and absolute distinction can be made between killing and letting die, and the consequentialist position that the consequences of killing and letting die are the same, and so there is no significant moral difference between the two. His own position is called a contextual position; it is the view that the distinction always depends on the context.

(8) James Rachels, "Euthanasia," in Tom Regan, ed., *Matters of Life and Death*, 2d ed. (New York: Random House, 1986), pp. 35–76. Rachels discusses the history of euthanasia and the arguments for and against active euthanasia, and concludes with a proposal on how to legalize active euthanasia.

(9) _____, *The End of Life: Euthanasia and Morality* (Oxford: Oxford University Press, 1986). Rachels develops the liberal view on euthanasia and defends it from criticism.

(10) John A. Robertson, "Involuntary Euthanasia of Defective Newborns," *Stanford Law Review* 27 (January 1975), pp. 213–261. In opposition to Engelhardt, Brandt, and others, Robertson argues that the utilitarian or consequentialist defense of euthanasia for defective newborns does not succeed in showing that it is justified.

(11) Bonnie Steinbock, "The Intentional Termination of Life," *Ethics in Science and Medicine*, no. 315 (1979), pp. 59–64. Steinbock defends the AMA statement on euthanasia from the attacks made by Rachels. She claims that the AMA statement does not make any distinction between active and passive euthanasia. She argues that cessation of extraordinary means of treatment is not the same as passive euthanasia.

(12) Thomas D. Sullivan, "Active and Passive Euthanasia: An Impertinent Distinction?" *Human Life Review* 3 (Summer 1977), pp. 40–46, defends the AMA statement against Rachels' attack in "Active and Passive Euthanasia." He argues that Rachels' distinction between active and passive euthanasia is impertinent and irrelevant. Rachels' reply to Sullivan is entitled "More Impertinent Distinctions," in T.A. Mappes and J.S. Zembaty, eds., *Biomedical Ethics* (New York: MacGraw–Hill, 1981), pp. 355–359.

(13) Donald Van DeVeer, "Whither Baby Doe?" in Tom Regan, ed., *Matters of Life and Death*, 2d ed. (New York: Random House, 1986), pp. 213–255. Van DeVeer begins a detailed discussion of the famous Baby Doe case (see the Problem Cases). Then he examines various moral issues raised by the case, including the relevance of defects, the neonatal right to life, neonatal moral standing, and questions about public policy on the treatment or nontreatment of defective newborns.

(14) Robert Young, "Voluntary and Nonvoluntary Euthanasia," *The Monist* 59 (April 1976), pp. 264–282. Young reviews a number of arguments used to show that voluntary active euthanasia is not justified, and concludes that none of them is successful.

(15) Robert F. Weir, *Selective Nontreatment of Handicapped Newborns: Moral Dilemmas in Neonatal Medicine* (New York: Oxford University Press, 1984). Weir discusses moral issues relating to the care and treatment of defective or handicapped newborns.

Chapter 4

Capital Punishment

Introduction

Legal Background   The Eighth Amendment to the Constitution of the United States prohibits cruel and unusual punishment. For example, the medieval punishment of cutting off the hands of thieves seems to be cruel and unusual. Is the death penalty another example of cruel and unusual punishment, and thus unconstitutional? This is a matter of debate. In the case of *Furman* v. *Georgia* (1972), the Supreme Court ruled (by a five-to-four majority) that the death penalty was unconstitutional because it was being administered in an arbitrary and capricious manner. Juries were allowed to inflict the death sentence without any explicit guidelines or standards, and the result was that blacks were much more likely to receive the sentence than whites.

After the *Furman* decision, states wishing to retain the death sentence reacted in two ways. One way was to meet the objection about standardless discretion of juries by making the death penalty mandatory for certain crimes. But in *Woodson* v. *North Carolina* (1976), the court ruled (again by a mere five-to-four majority) that mandatory death sentences are unconstitutional.

The second approach to the objection raised in *Furman* was to provide standards for juries. Georgia specified in its law ten statutory aggravating circumstances, one of which had to be found by the jury to exist beyond reasonable doubt before a death sentence could be imposed. This second approach proved to be successful. For in *Gregg* v. *Georgia* (1976), the majority ruled, with only Justice Marshall and Justice Brennan dissenting, that the death penalty is not unconstitutional for the crime of murder, provided there are safeguards

131

against any arbitrary or capricious imposition by juries.

But why isn't the death penalty cruel and unusual? In their majority opinion, Justices Stewart, Powell, and Stevens answered this important question. First, they gave an explanation of the concept of cruel and unusual. In their view, a punishment is cruel and unusual if it either fails to accord with evolving standards of decency or fails to accord with the dignity of man that is the basic concept underlying the Eighth Amendment. This second stipulation rules out excessive punishment that involves unnecessary pain or is disproportionate to the crime. Second, they argued that the death penalty does not satisfy either of these stipulations. It is acceptable to the majority of the people, since thirty-five states have statutes providing for the death penalty, and it is not excessive because it achieves two important social purposes, retribution and deterrence.

Retribution   To fully understand the appeal to retribution, it is necessary to examine the theory on which it is based, namely retributivism. The classical formulation of this theory is given by Immanuel Kant. According to Kant, the only justification for punishing a person is guilt. If a person is guilty of a crime, then justice requires that he or she be punished; if a person is not guilty, then no punishment is justified. In other words, guilt is both a necessary and a sufficient condition for justified punishment. Furthermore, on Kant's view the punishment must fit the crime, or be proportionate to the crime, according to the traditional principle of retaliation (*lex talionis*) that says, "life for life, eye for eye, tooth for tooth." Now what punishment fits the crime of murder on this principle? Kant insists that death, and only death, is the proper punishment for murder; no other punishment will satisfy the requirements of legal justice.

But why must a criminal be punished? Why is it necessary for a criminal to pay for

his or her crime? After all, punishing the criminal causes suffering, and suffering is bad. Walter Berns tries to explain why criminals must be paid back for their crimes, and in particular why murderers must pay with their lives. On Bern's view, this punishment is an expression of anger, but this anger is morally right because it serves justice, and it acknowledges the humanity of the criminal by holding the criminal responsible for his or her actions.

Various objections have been made to the retributive view. Glover thinks that it is open to the objection that it leads to what he considers to be pointless suffering, that is, suffering without any real benefits, either to the person punished or to other people. But the retributivist can reply that punishment does provide an important benefit, namely that justice is served by giving the criminal the punishment he or she deserves. If punishment is not given, then people will not be held accountable for their actions nor will they realize the consequences of their deeds.

Anthony G. Amsterdam rejects the principle of strict retaliation according to which there must be "an eye for an eye, a life for a life." He claims that appealing to this principle does not justify capital punishment because of the simple fact that most murderers are not executed but just sent to prison. Obviously, we think that many crimes of murder do not deserve the death penalty; for example, we do not have the death sentence for homicides that are unpremeditated or accidental. Another objection to the strict principle of retaliation is that we do have the death sentence for nonhomicidal crimes such as treason. This shows that the death sentence can be justified for crimes other than murder.

The principle of strict retaliation can be revised to say that the punishment should fit the crime, so that serious crimes are severely punished. But as Amsterdam points out, this does not tell us how severely we ought to punish any particular crime. Should we punish vicious murderers by burning them at the stake or boiling them in oil? Now it seems that retributivism can be used to justify punishment that is indeed cruel.

But retributivism can be defended against the charge that it justifies cruel and unusual punishment. Perhaps it does not even justify the death sentence after all. We can agree with retributivism that criminals should be punished, but insist there are limits to the severity of the punishment. We shouldn't, for example, torture criminals. We must treat the criminal with the respect due to a member of the community (as Kant would say), and because of this requirement, it may be that we cannot deliberately kill a person because such a punishment might show a lack of respect for the moral worth and dignity of the person.

Deterrence   The appeal to deterrence is an appeal to the social benefits of punishment. The particular social benefits claimed for the death penalty by its defenders are deterrence and prevention: It deters other potential criminals from killing, and it prevents the criminal who is executed from committing further crimes. No doubt an executed criminal can commit no more crimes in this life, but does the death penalty actually deter other potential criminals? This is a factual question that is much debated.

Without going into the details, the Supreme Court Justices note that statistical attempts to prove that the death penalty is a deterrent have been inconclusive. However, the Justices think that the death penalty is undoubtedly a significant deterrent for some potential murderers, for example, those who carefully contemplate their actions.

Amsterdam reviews some of the evidence for the death penalty being a deterrent and finds it to be inconclusive—it does not show that the death penalty is a better deterrent than life imprisonment for murder. Amsterdam also discusses and rejects the appeal to intuition, namely, that the fear of death would intuitively seem to deter potential murderers.

Glover agrees that capital punishment has not been shown to be a substantial deterrent and that there is a strong presumption against it because of its special evils and bad side effects.

The Supreme Court
Gregg v. *Georgia* (1976)

Potter Stewart, Lewis F. Powell, Jr., and John Paul Stevens are Associate Justices of the United States Supreme Court. (Justices Stewart and Powell are no longer on the Court.) Justice Stewart, a graduate of Yale Law School, was appointed to the Court in 1958. Justice Powell, LL.M (Harvard), was appointed in 1971. Justice Stevens graduated from Northwestern University School of Law, and was *appointed to the Court in 1975. Thurgood Marshall, associate justice of the United States Supreme Court, was appointed in 1967; he was the first black person ever to be appointed.*

The main issue before the Court in the case of Gregg v. Georgia *(1976) was whether or not the death penalty violates the Eighth Amendment prohibition of cruel and unusual punishment. The majority of the Court, with Justice Marshall and Justice Brennan dissenting, held that the death penalty does not violate the Eighth Amendment because it is in accord with contemporary standards of decency. It serves both a deterrent and retributive purpose, and in the case of the Georgia law being reviewed, it is no longer arbitrarily applied.*

In his dissenting opinion, Justice Marshall objects that the death sentence is excessive because a less severe penalty—life imprisonment—would accomplish the legitimate purposes of punishment. In reply to the claim that the death sentence is necessary for deterrence, Marshall asserts that the available evidence shows that this is not the case. As for the appeal to retribution, Marshall argues that the purely retributive justification for the death penalty is not consistent with human dignity.

The issue in this case is whether the imposition of the sentence of death for the crime of murder under the law of Georgia violates the Eighth and Fourteenth Amendments.

I

The petitioner, Troy Gregg, was charged with committing armed robbery and murder. In accordance with Georgia procedure in capital cases, the trial was in two stages, a guilt stage and a sentencing stage....

... The jury found the petitioner guilty of two counts of armed robbery and two counts of murder.

At the penalty stage, which took place before the same jury, ... the trial judge instructed the jury that it could recommend either a death sentence or a life prison sentence on each count. ... The jury returned verdicts of death on each count.

The Supreme Court of Georgia affirmed the convictions and the imposition of the death sentences for murder. ... The death sentences imposed for armed robbery, however, were vacated on the grounds that the death penalty had rarely been imposed in Georgia for that offense. ...

II

... The Georgia statute, as amended after our decision in *Furman* v. *Georgia* (1972), retains the death penalty for six categories of crime: murder, kidnaping for ransom or where the victim is harmed, armed robbery, rape, treason, and aircraft hijacking. ...

III

We address initially the basic contention that the punishment of death for the crime of murder is, under all circumstances, "cruel and unusual" in violation of the Eighth and Fourteenth Amendments of the Constitution. In Part IV of this opinion, we will consider the sentence of death imposed under the Georgia statutes at issue in this case.

The Court on a number of occasions has both assumed and asserted the constitutionality of capital punishment. In several cases that assumption provided a necessary foundation for the decision, as the Court was asked to decide whether a particular method of carrying out a capital sentence would be allowed to stand under the Eighth Amendment. But until *Furman* v. *Georgia* (1972), the Court never confronted squarely the fundamental claim that the punishment of death always, regardless of the enormity of the offense or the procedure followed in imposing the sentence, is cruel and unusual punishment in violation of the Constitution. Although this issue was presented and addressed in *Furman,* it was not resolved by the Court. Four Justices would have held that capital punishment is not unconstitutional *per se;* two Justices would have reached the opposite conclusion; and three Justices, while agreeing that the statutes then before the Court were invalid as applied, left open the question whether such punishment may ever be imposed. We now hold that the punishment of death does not invariably violate the Constitution.

A

The history of the prohibition of "cruel and unusual" punishment already has been reviewed at length. The phrase first appeared in the English Bill of Rights of 1689, which was drafted by Parliament at the accession of William and Mary. The English version appears to have been directed against punishments unauthorized by statute and beyond the jurisdiction of the sentencing court, as well as those disproportionate to the offense involved. The American draftsmen, who adopted the English phrasing in drafting the Eighth Amendment, were primarily concerned, however, with proscribing "tortures" and other "barbarous" methods of punishment.

In the earliest cases raising Eighth Amendment claims, the Court focused on particular methods of execution to determine whether they were too cruel to pass constitutional muster. The constitutionality of the sentence of death itself was not at issue, and the criterion used to evaluate the mode of execution was its similarity to "torture" and other "barbarous" methods. . . .

But the Court has not confined the prohibition embodied in the Eighth Amendment to "barbarous" methods that were generally outlawed in the 18th century. Instead, the Amendment has been interpreted in a flexible and dynamic manner. The Court early recognized that "a principle to be vital must be capable of wider application than the mischief which gave it birth." Thus the clause forbidding "cruel and unusual" punishments "is not fastened to the obsolete but may acquire meaning as public opinion becomes enlightened by a humane justice." . . .

It is clear from the foregoing precedents that the Eighth Amendment has not been regarded as a static concept. As Mr. Chief Justice Warren said, in an oftquoted phrase, "[t]he Amendment must draw its meaning from the evolving standards of decency that mark the progress of a maturing society." Thus, an assessment of contemporary values concerning the infliction of a challenged sanction is relevant to the application of the Eighth Amendment. As we develop below more fully, this assessment does not call for a subjective judgment. It requires, rather, that we look to objective indicia that reflect the public attitude toward a given sanction.

But our cases also make clear that public perceptions of standards of decency with respect to criminal sanctions are not conclusive. A penalty also must accord with "the dignity of man," which is the "basic concept underlying the Eighth Amendment." This means, at least, that the punishment not be "excessive." When a form of punishment in the abstract (in this case, whether capital punishment may ever be imposed as a sanction for murder) rather than in the particular (the propriety of death as a penalty to be applied to a specific defendant for a specific crime) is under consideration, the inquiry into "excessiveness" has two aspects. First, the punishment must not involve the unnecessary and wanton infliction of pain. Second, the punishment must not be grossly out of proportion to the severity of the crime.

B

Of course, the requirements of the Eighth Amendment must be applied with an awareness of the limited role to be played by the courts. This does not mean that judges have no role to play, for the Eighth Amendment is a restraint upon the exercise of legislative power. . . .

But, while we have an obligation to ensure that constitutional bounds are not overreached, we may not act as judges as we might as legislators. . . .

Therefore, in assessing a punishment selected by a democratically elected legislature against the constitutional measure, we presume its validity. We may not require the legislature to select the least severe penalty possible so long as the penalty selected is not cruelly inhumane or disproportionate to the crime involved. And a heavy burden rests on those who would attack the judgment of the representatives of the people.

This is true in part because the constitutional test is intertwined with an assessment of contemporary standards and the legislative judgment weighs heavily in ascertaining such standards. "[I]n a democratic society legislatures, not courts, are constituted to respond to the will and consequently the moral values of the people."

The deference we owe to the decisions of the state legislatures under our federal system is enhanced where the specification of punishments is concerned, for "these are peculiarly questions of legislative policy." Caution is necessary lest this Court become, "under the aegis of the Cruel and Unusual Punishment Clause, the ultimate arbiter of the standards of criminal responsibility ... throughout the country." A decision that a given punishment is impermissible under the Eighth Amendment cannot be reversed short of a constitutional amendment. The ability of the people to express their preference through the normal democratic processes, as well as through ballot referenda, is shut off. Revisions cannot be made in the light of further experience.

C

In the discussion to this point we have sought to identify the principles and considerations that guide a court in addressing an Eighth Amendment claim. We now consider specifically whether the sentence of death for the crime of murder is a *per se* violation of the Eighth and Fourteenth Amendments to the Constitution. We note first that history and precedent strongly support a negative answer to this question.

The imposition of the death penalty for the crime of murder has a long history of acceptance both in the United States and in England. ...

It is apparent from the text of the Constitution itself that the existence of capital punishment was accepted by the Framers. At the time the Eighth Amendment was ratified, capital punishment was a common sanction in every State. Indeed, the First Congress of the United States enacted legislation providing death as the penalty for specified crimes. ...

For nearly two centuries, this Court, repeatedly and often expressly, has recognized that capital punishment is not invalid *per se*. ...

Four years ago, the petitioners in *Furman* and its companion cases predicated their argument primarily upon the asserted proposition that standards of decency had evolved to the point where capital punishment no longer could be tolerated. The petitioners in those cases said, in effect, that the evolutionary process had come to an end, and that standards of decency required that the Eighth Amendment be construed finally as prohibiting capital punishment for any crime regardless of its depravity and impact on society. This view was accepted by two Justices. Three other Justices were unwilling to go so far; focusing on the procedures by which convicted defendants were selected for the death penalty rather than on the actual punishment inflicted, they joined in the conclusion that the statutes before the Court were constitutionally invalid.

The petitioners in the capital cases before the Court today renew the "standards of decency" argument, but developments during the four years since *Furman* have undercut substantially the assumptions upon which their argument rested. Despite the continuing debate, dating back to the nineteenth century, over the morality and utility of capital punishment, it is now evident that a large proportion of American society continues to regard it as an appropriate and necessary criminal sanction.

The most marked indication of society's endorsement of the death penalty for murder is the legislative response to *Furman*. The legislatures of at least thirty-five States have enacted new statutes that provide for the death penalty for at least some crimes that result in the death of another person. And the Congress of the United States, in 1974, enacted a statute providing the death penalty for aircraft piracy that results in death. These recently adopted statutes have attempted to address the concerns expressed by the Court in *Furman* primarily (i) by specifying the factors to be weighed and the procedures to be followed in deciding when to impose a capital sentence, or (ii) by making the death penalty mandatory for specified crimes. But all of the post-*Furman* statutes make clear that capital punishment itself has not been rejected by the elected representatives of the people. ...

The jury also is a significant and reliable objective index of contemporary values because it is so directly involved. The Court has said that "one of the most important functions any jury can perform in making ... a selection [between life imprisonment and death for a defendant convicted in a capital case] is to maintain a link between contemporary community values and the penal system." It may be true that evolving standards have influenced juries in recent decades to be more discriminating in imposing the sentence of death. But the relative infrequency of jury verdicts imposing the death sentence does not indicate rejection of capital punishment *per se.* Rather, the reluctance of juries in many cases to impose the sentence may well reflect the humane feeling that this most irrevocable of sanctions should be reserved for a small number of extreme cases. Indeed, the actions of juries in many states since *Furman* are fully compatible with the legislative judgments, reflected in the new statutes, as to the continued utility and necessity of capital punishment in appropriate cases. At the close of 1974 at least 254 persons had been sentenced to death since *Furman,* and by the end of March 1976, more than 460 persons were subject to death sentences.

As we have seen, however, the Eighth Amendment demands more than that a challenged punishment be acceptable to contemporary society. The Court also must ask whether it comports with the basic concept of human dignity at the core of the amendment. Although we cannot "invalidate a category of penalties because we deem less severe penalties adequate to serve the ends of penology," the sanction imposed cannot be so totally without penological justification that it results in the gratuitous infliction of suffering.

The death penalty is said to serve two principal social purposes: retribution and deterrence of capital crimes by prospective offenders.[1]

In part, capital punishment is an expression of society's moral outrage at particularly offensive conduct. This function may be unappealing to many, but it is essential in an ordered society that asks its citizens to rely on legal processes rather than self-help to vindicate their wrongs.

The instinct for retribution is part of the nature of man, and channeling that instinct in the administration of criminal justice serves an important purpose in promoting the stability of a society governed by law. When people begin to believe that organized society is unwilling or unable to impose upon criminal offenders the punishment they "deserve," then there are sown the seeds of anarchy—if self-help, vigilante justice, and lynch law. Furman v. Georgia (Stewart, J., concurring).

"Retribution is no longer the dominant objective of the criminal law," but neither is it a forbidden objective nor one inconsistent with our respect for the dignity of men. Indeed, the decision that capital punishment may be the appropriate sanction in extreme cases is an expression of the community's belief that certain crimes are themselves so grievous an affront to humanity that the only adequate response may be the penalty of death.

Statistical attempts to evaluate the worth of the death penalty as a deterrent to crimes by potential offenders have occasioned a great deal of debate. The results simply have been inconclusive. ...

Although some of the studies suggest that the death penalty may not function as a significantly greater deterrent than lesser penalties, there is no convincing empirical evidence either supporting or refuting this view. We may nevertheless assume safely that there are murderers, such as those who act in passion, for whom the threat of death has little or no deterrent effect. But for many others, the death penalty undoubtedly is a significant deterrent. There are carefully contemplated murders, such as murder for hire, where the possible penalty of death may well enter into the cold calculus that precedes the decision to act. And there are some categories of murder, such as murder by a life prisoner, where other sanctions may not be adequate.

The value of capital punishment as a

deterrent of crime is a complex factual issue the resolution of which properly rests with the legislatures, which can evaluate the results of statistical studies in terms of their own local conditions and with a flexibility of approach that is not available to the courts. Indeed, many of the post-*Furman* statutes reflect just such a responsible effort to define those crimes and those criminals for which capital punishment is most probably an effective deterrent.

In sum, we cannot say that the judgment of the Georgia Legislature that capital punishment may be necessary in some cases is clearly wrong. Considerations of federalism, as well as respect for the ability of a legislature to evaluate, in terms of its particular State, the moral consensus concerning the death penalty and its social utility as a sanction, require us to conclude, in the absence of more convincing evidence, that the infliction of death as a punishment for murder is not without justification and thus is not unconstitutionally severe.

Finally, we must consider whether the punishment of death is disproportionate in relation to the crime for which it is imposed. There is no question that death as a punishment is unique in its severity and irrevocability. When a defendant's life is at stake, the Court has been particularly sensitive to insure that every safeguard is observed. But we are concerned here only with the imposition of capital punishment for the crime of murder, and when a life has been taken deliberately by the offender,[2] we cannot say that the punishment is invariably disproportionate to the crime. It is an extreme sanction, suitable to the most extreme of crimes.

We hold that the death penalty is not a form of punishment that may never be imposed, regardless of the circumstances of the offense, regardless of the character of the offender, and regardless of the procedure followed in reaching the decision to impose it.

IV

We now consider whether Georgia may impose the death penalty on the petitioner in this case.

A

While *Furman* did not hold that the infliction of the death penalty *per se* violates the Constitution's ban on cruel and unusual punishments, it did recognize that the penalty of death is different in kind from any other punishment imposed under our system of criminal justice. Because of the uniqueness of the death penalty, *Furman* held that it could not be imposed under sentencing procedures that created a substantial risk that it would be inflicted in an arbitrary and capricious manner. . . .

Furman mandates that where discretion is afforded a sentencing body on a matter so grave as the determination of whether a human life should be taken or spared, that discretion must be suitably directed and limited so as to minimize the risk of wholly arbitrary and capricious action.

It is certainly not a novel proposition that discretion in the area of sentencing be exercised in an informed manner. We have long recognized that "[f]or the determination of sentences, justice generally requires . . . that there be taken into account the circumstances of the offense together with the character and propensities of the offender." . . .

Jury sentencing has been considered desirable in capital cases in order "to maintain a link between contemporary community values and the penal system—a link without which the determination of punishment could hardly reflect 'the evolving standards of decency that mark the progress of a maturing society.' " But it creates special problems. Much of the information that is relevant to the sentencing decision may have no relevance to the question of guilt, or may even be extremely prejudicial to a fair determination of that question. This problem, however, is scarcely insurmountable. Those who have studied the question suggest that a bifurcated procedure—one in which the question of sentence is not considered until the determination of guilt has been made—is the best answer. ... When a human life is at stake and when the jury must have information prejudicial to the question of guilt but relevant to the question of penalty in order to impose a rational sentence, a bifurcated system is more likely to ensure elimination of the constitutional deficiencies identified in *Furman*.

But the provision of relevant information under fair procedural rules is not alone sufficient to guarantee that the information will be properly used in the imposition of punishment, especially if sentencing is performed by a jury. Since the members of a jury will have had little, if any, previous experience in sentencing, they are unlikely to be skilled in dealing with the information they are given. To the extent that this problem is inherent in jury sentencing, it may not be totally correctable. It seems clear, however, that the problem will be alleviated if the jury is given guidance regarding the factors about the crime and the defendant that the State, representing organized society, deems particularly relevant to the sentencing decision. ...

While some have suggested that standards to guide a capital jury's sentencing deliberations are impossible to formulate, the fact is that such standards have been developed. When the drafters of the Model Penal Code faced this problem, they concluded "that it is within the realm of possibility to point to the main circumstances of aggravation and of mitigation that should be weighed *and weighed against each other* when they are presented in a concrete case." [3] While such standards are by necessity somewhat general, they do provide guidance to the sentencing authority and thereby reduce the likelihood that it will impose a sentence that fairly can be called capricious or arbitrary. Where the sentencing authority is required to specify the factors it relied upon in reaching its decision, the further safeguard of meaningful appellate review is available to ensure that death sentences are not imposed capriciously or in a freakish manner.

In summary, the concerns expressed in *Furman* that the penalty of death not be imposed in an arbitrary or capricious manner can be met by a carefully drafted statute that ensures that the sentencing authority is given adequate information and guidance. As a general proposition these concerns are best met by a system that provides for a bifurcated proceeding at which the sentencing authority is apprised of the information relevant to the imposition of sentence and provided with standards to guide its use of the information.

We do not intend to suggest that only the above-described procedures would be permissible under *Furman* or that any sentencing system constructed along these general lines would inevitably satisfy the concerns of *Furman*, for each distinct system must be examined on an individual basis. Rather, we have embarked upon this general exposition to make clear that it is possible to construct capital-sentencing systems capable of meeting *Furman*'s constitutional concerns.

B

We now turn to consideration of the constitutionality of Georgia's capital-sentencing procedures. In the wake of *Furman*, Georgia amended its capital punishment statute, but chose not to narrow the scope of its murder provisions. Thus, now as before *Furman*, in Georgia "[a] person commits murder when he unlawfully and with malice aforethought, either express or implied, causes the death of another human being." All persons convicted of murder "shall be punished by death or by imprisonment for life."

Georgia did act, however, to narrow the class of murderers subject to capital punishment by specifying ten statutory aggravating circumstances, one of which must be found by the jury to exist beyond a reasonable doubt before a death sentence can ever be imposed. In addition, the jury is authorized to consider any other appropriate aggravating or mitigating circumstances. The jury is not required to find any mitigating circumstance in order to make a recommendation of mercy that is binding on the trial court, but it must find a *statutory* aggravating circumstance before recommending a sentence of death.

These procedures require the jury to consider the circumstances of the crime and the criminal before it recommends sentence. No longer can a Georgia jury do as Furman's jury did: reach a finding of the defendant's guilt and then, without guidance or direction, decide whether he should live or die. Instead, the jury's attention is directed to the specific circumstances of the crime: Was it committed in the course of another capital felony? Was it committed for money? Was it committed upon a peace officer or judicial officer? Was it committed in a particularly heinous way or in a manner that endangered the lives of many persons? In addition, the jury's attention is focused on the characteristics of the person who committed the crime: Does he have a record of prior convictions for capital offenses? Are there any special facts about this defendant that mitigate against imposing capital punishment (*e.g.*, his youth, the extent of his cooperation with the police, his emotional state at the time of the crime)? As a result, while some jury discretion still exists, "the discretion to be exercised is controlled by clear and objective standards so as to produce nondiscriminatory application."

As an important additional safeguard against arbitrariness and caprice, the Georgia statutory scheme provides for automatic appeal of all death sentences to the State's Supreme Court. That court is required by statute to review each sentence of death and determine whether it was imposed under the influence of passion or prejudice, whether the evidence supports the jury's finding of a statutory aggravating circumstance, and whether the sentence is disproportionate compared to those sentences imposed in similar cases.

In short, Georgia's new sentencing procedures require as a prerequisite to the imposition of the death penalty, specific jury findings as to the circumstances of the crime or the character of the defendant. Moreover, to guard further against a situation comparable to that presented in *Furman,* the Supreme Court of Georgia compares each death sentence with the sentences imposed on similarly situated defendants to ensure that the sentence of death in a particular case is not disproportionate. On their face these procedures seem to satisfy the concerns of *Furman.* No longer should there be "no meaningful basis for distinguishing the few cases in which [the death penalty] is imposed from the many cases in which it is not." ...

V

The basic concern of *Furman* centered on those defendants who were being condemned to death capriciously and arbitrarily. Under the procedures before the Court in that case, sentencing authorities were not directed to give attention to the nature or circumstances of the crime committed or to the character or record of the defendant. Left unguided, juries imposed the death sentence in a way that could only be called freakish. The new Georgia sentencing procedures, by contrast, focus the jury's attention on the particularized nature of the crime and the particularized characteristics of the individual defendant. While the jury is permitted to consider any aggravating or mitigating circumstances, it must find and identify at least one statutory aggravating factor before it may impose a penalty of death. In this way the jury's discretion is channeled. No longer can a jury wantonly and freakishly impose the death sentence; it is always circumscribed by the legislative guidelines. In addition, the review function of the Supreme Court of Georgia affords additional assurance that the concerns that prompted our decision in *Furman* are not present to any significant degree in the Georgia procedure applied here.

For the reasons expressed in this opinion, we hold that the statutory system under which Gregg was sentenced to death does not violate the Constitution. Accordingly, the judgment of the Georgia Supreme Court is affirmed.

DISSENTING OPINION

In *Furman* v. *Georgia* (1972) (concurring opinion), I set forth at some length my views on the basic issue presented to the Court in [this case]. The death penalty, I concluded, is a cruel and unusual punishment prohibited by the Eighth and Fourteenth Amendments. That continues to be my view.

I have no intention of retracing the "long and tedious journey" that led to my conclusion in *Furman*. My sole purposes here are to consider the suggestion that my conclusion in *Furman* has been undercut by developments since then, and briefly to evaluate the basis for my Brethren's holding that the extinction of life is a permissible form of punishment under the Cruel and Unusual Punishments Clause.

In *Furman* I concluded that the death penalty is constitutionally invalid for two reasons. First, the death penalty is excessive. And second, the American people, fully informed as to the purposes of the death penalty and its liabilities, would in my view reject it as morally unacceptable.

Since the decision in *Furman*, the legislatures of thirty-five States have enacted new statutes authorizing the imposition of the death sentence for certain crimes, and Congress has enacted a law providing the death penalty for air piracy resulting in death. I would be less than candid if I did not acknowledge that these developments have a significant bearing on a realistic assessment of the moral acceptability of the death penalty to the American people. But if the constitutionality of the death penalty turns, as I have urged, on the opinion of an *informed* citizenry, then even the enactment of new death statutes cannot be viewed as conclusive. In *Furman*, I observed that the American people are largely unaware of the information critical to a judgment on the morality of the death penalty, and concluded that if they were better informed they would consider it shocking, unjust, and unacceptable. A recent study, conducted after the enactment of the post-*Furman* statutes, has confirmed that the American people know little about the death penalty, and that the opinions of an informed public would differ significantly from those of a public unaware of the consequences and effects of the death penalty.

Even assuming, however, that the post-*Furman* enactment of statutes authorizing the death penalty renders the prediction of the views of an informed citizenry an uncertain basis for a constitutional decision, the enactment of those statutes has no bearing whatsoever on the conclusion that the death penalty is unconstitutional because it is excessive. An excessive penalty is invalid under the Cruel and Unusual Punishments Clause "even though popular sentiment may favor" it. The inquiry here, then, is simply whether the death penalty is necessary to accomplish the legitimate legislative purposes in punishment, or whether a less severe penalty—life imprisonment—would do as well.

The two purposes that sustain the death penalty as nonexcessive in the Court's view are general deterrence and retribution. In *Furman*, I canvassed the relevant data on the deterrent effect of capital punishment. The state of knowledge at that point, after literally centuries of debate, was summarized as follows by a United Nations Committee:

It is generally agreed between the retentionists and abolitionists, whatever their opinions about the validity of comparative studies of deterrence, that the data which now exist show no correlation between the existence of capital punishment and lower rates of capital crime.

The available evidence, I concluded in *Furman*, was convincing that "capital punishment is not necessary as a deterrent to crime in our society." ...

The evidence I reviewed in *Furman* remains convincing, in my view, that "capital punishment is not necessary as a deterrent to crime in our society." The justification for the death penalty must be found elsewhere.

The other principal purpose said to be served by the death penalty is retribution. The notion that retribution can serve as a moral justification for the sanction of death finds credence in the opinion of my Brothers Stewart, Powell, and Stevens. ... It is this notion that I find to be the most disturbing aspect of today's unfortunate [decision].

The concept of retribution is a multifaceted one, and any discussion of its role in the criminal law must be undertaken with caution. On one level, it can be said that the notion of retribution or reprobation is the basis of our insistence that only those who have broken the law be punished, and in this sense the notion is quite obviously central to a just system of criminal sanctions. But our recognition that retribution plays a crucial role in determining who may be punished by no means requires approval of retribution as a general justification for punishment. It is the question whether retribution can provide a moral justification for punishment—in particular, capital punishment—that we must consider.

My Brothers Stewart, Powell, and Stevens offer the following explanation of the retributive justification for capital punishment:

The instinct for retribution is part of the nature of man, and channeling that instinct in the administration of criminal justice serves an important purpose in promoting the stability of a society governed by law. When people begin to believe that organized society is unwilling or unable to impose upon criminal offenders the punishment they "deserve," then there are sown the seeds of anarchy—of self-help, vigilante justice, and lynch law.

This statement is wholly inadequate to justify the death penalty. As my Brother Brennan stated in *Furman*, "[t]here is no evidence whatever that utilization of imprisonment rather than death encourages private blood feuds and other disorders." It simply defies belief to suggest that the death penalty is necessary to prevent the American people from taking the law into their own hands.

In a related vein, it may be suggested that the expression of moral outrage through the imposition of the death penalty serves to reinforce basic moral values—that it marks some crimes as particularly offensive and

therefore to be avoided. The argument is akin to a deterrence argument, but differs in that it contemplates the individual's shrinking from antisocial conduct, not because he fears punishment, but because he has been told in the strongest possible way that the conduct is wrong. This contention, like the previous one, provides no support for the death penalty. It is inconceivable that any individual concerned about conforming his conduct to what society says is "right" would fail to realize that murder is "wrong" if the penalty were simply life imprisonment.

The foregoing contentions—that society's expression of moral outrage through the imposition of the death penalty preempts the citizenry from taking the law into its own hands and reinforces moral values—are not retributive in the purest sense. They are essentially utilitarian in that they portray the death penalty as valuable because of its beneficial results. These justifications for the death penalty are inadequate because the penalty is, quite clearly I think, not necessary to the accomplishment of those results.

There remains for consideration, however, what might be termed the purely retributive justification for the death penalty—that the death penalty is appropriate, not because of its beneficial effect on society, but because the taking of the murderer's life is itself morally good. Some of the language of the opinion of my Brothers Stewart, Powell, and Stevens ... appears positively to embrace this notion of retribution for its own sake as a justification for capital punishment. They state:

[T]he decision that capital punishment may be the appropriate sanction in extreme cases is an expression of the community's belief that certain crimes are themselves so grievous an affront to humanity that the only adequate response may be the penalty of death.

They then quote with approval from Lord Justice Denning's remarks before the British Royal Commission on Capital Punishment:

The truth is that some crimes are so outrageous that

society insists on adequate punishment, because the wrong-doer deserves it, irrespective of whether it is a deterrent or not.

Of course, it may be that these statements are intended as no more than observations as to the popular demands that it is thought must be responded to in order to prevent anarchy. But the implication of the statements appears to me to be quite different—namely, that society's judgment that the murderer "deserves" death must be respected not simply because the preservation of order requires it, but because it is appropriate that society make the judgment and carry it out. It is this latter notion, in particular, that I consider to be fundamentally at odds with the Eighth Amendment. The mere fact that the community demands the murderer's life in return for the evil he has done cannot sustain the death penalty, for as Justices Stewart, Powell, and Stevens remind us, "the Eighth Amendment demands more than that a challenged punishment be acceptable to contemporary society." To be sustained under the Eighth Amendment, the death penalty must "compor[t] with the basic concept of human dignity at the core of the Amendment;" the objective in imposing it must be "[consistent] with our respect for the dignity of [other] men." Under these standards, the taking of life "because the wrongdoer deserves it" surely must fail, for such a punishment has as its very basis the total denial of the wrongdoer's dignity and worth.

The death penalty, unnecessary to promote the goal of deterrence or to further any legitimate notion of retribution, is an excessive penalty forbidden by the Eighth and Fourteenth Amendments. I respectfully dissent from the Court's judgment upholding the [sentence] of death imposed upon the [petitioner in this case].

Endnotes

1. Another purpose that has been discussed is the incapacitation of dangerous criminals and the consequent prevention of crimes that they may otherwise commit in the future.

2. We do not address here the question whether the taking of the criminal's life is a proportionate sanction where no victim has been deprived of life—for example, when capital punishment is imposed for rape, kidnapping, or armed robbery that does not result in the death of any human being.

3. The Model Penal Code proposes the following standards:

"(3) Aggravating Circumstances.

"(a) The murder was committed by a convict under sentence of imprisonment.

"(b) The defendant was previously convicted of another murder or of a felony involving the use or threat of violence to the person.

"(c) At the time the murder was committed the defendant also committed another murder.

"(d) The defendant knowingly created a great risk of death to many persons.

"(e) The murder was committed while the defendant was engaged or was an accomplice in the commission of, or an attempt to commit, or flight after committing or attempting to commit robbery, rape or deviate sexual intercourse by force or threat of force, arson, burglary or kidnapping.

"(f) The murder was committed for the purpose of avoiding or preventing a lawful arrest or effecting an escape from lawful custody.

"(g) The murder was committed for pecuniary gain.

"(h) The murder was especially heinous, atrocious or cruel, manifesting exceptional depravity.

"(4) Mitigating Circumstances.

"(a) The defendant has no significant history of prior criminal activity.

"(b) The murder was committed while the defendant was under the influence of extreme mental or emotional disturbance.

"(c) The victim was a participant in the defendant's homicidal conduct or consented to the homicidal act.

"(d) The murder was committed under circumstances which the defendant believed to provide a moral justification or extenuation for his conduct.

"(e) The defendant was an accomplice in a murder committed by another person and his participation in the homicidal act was relatively minor.

"(f) The defendant acted under duress or under the domination of another person.

"(g) At the time of the murder, the capacity of the defendant to appreciate the criminality [wrongfulness] of his conduct or to conform his conduct to the requirements of law was impaired as a result of mental disease or defect or intoxication.

"(h) The youth of the defendant at the time of the crime." ALI Model Penal Code § 210.6 (Proposed Official Draft 1962).

Review Questions

1. How did the justices rule in *Furman* v. *Georgia* (1972), and by contrast, how do they rule in this case?

2. According to the justices, what is the basic concept underlying the Eighth Amendment?

3. According to the justices, in what two ways may a punishment be excessive?

4. According to the justices, why doesn't the death penalty violate contemporary standards of decency?

5. The justices say that the death penalty serves two principal social purposes. What are they, and how are they supposed to work?

6. What safeguards against the arbitrary and capricious application of the death sentence are suggested by the justices?

7. Explain Justice Marshall's objections and his criticisms of the majority opinion.

Discussion Questions

1. The Georgia statute retains the death penalty for six crimes, including rape, armed robbery, and treason. Do you agree that persons guilty of these crimes should receive the death sentence? Explain your view.

2. Try to give a precise definition of the phrase cruel and unusual. Can you do it?

3. How could it be conclusively proven that the death penalty deters potential criminals better than life imprisonment?

4. Should the instinct for retribution be satisfied? Defend your answer.

Immanuel Kant

The Retributive Theory of Punishment

For biographical information on Kant, see his reading in Chapter 1.

On Kant's retributive theory of punishment, punishment is not justified by any good results, but simply by the criminal's guilt. Criminals must pay for their crimes; otherwise an injustice has occurred. Furthermore, the punishment must fit the crime. Kant asserts that the only punishment that is appropriate for the crime of murder is the death of the murderer. As he puts it, "Whoever has committed a murder must die."

Judicial or juridical punishment (*poena forensis*) is to be distinguished from natural punishment (*poena naturalis*), in which crime as vice punishes itself, and does not as such come within the cognizance of the legislator.

Juridical punishment can never be administered merely as a means for promoting another good, either with regard to the criminal himself or to civil society, but must in all cases be imposed only because the individual on whom it is inflicted *has committed a crime.* For one man ought never to be dealt with merely as a means subservient to the purpose of another, nor be mixed up with the subjects of real right. Against such treatment his inborn personality has a right to protect him, even although he may be condemned to lose his civil personality. He must first be found guilty and *punishable,* before there can be any thought of drawing from his punishment any benefit for himself or his fellow-citizens. The penal law is a categorical imperative; and woe to him who creeps through the serpent-windings of utilitarianism to discover some advantage that may discharge him from the justice of punishment, or even from the due measure of it, according to the pharisaic maxim: 'It is better that *one* man should die than that the whole people should perish.' For if justice and righteousness perish, human life would no longer have any value in the world.— What, then, is to be said of such a proposal as to keep a criminal alive who has been

Immanuel Kant, *The Philosophy of Law,* Part II trans. W. Hastie (1887).

condemned to death, on his being given to understand that if he agreed to certain dangerous experiments being performed upon him, he would be allowed to survive if he came happily through them? It is argued that physicians might thus obtain new information that would be of value to the commonweal. But a court of justice would repudiate with scorn any proposal of this kind if made to it by the medical faculty; for justice would cease to be justice, if it were bartered away for any consideration whatever.

But what is the mode and measure of punishment which public justice takes as its principle and standard? It is just the principle of equality, by which the pointer of the scale of justice is made to incline no more to the one side than the other. It may be rendered by saying that the undeserved evil which any one commits on another, is to be regarded as perpetrated on himself. Hence it may be said: 'If you slander another, you slander yourself; if you steal from another, you steal from yourself; if you strike another, you strike yourself; if you kill another, you kill yourself.' This is the right of retaliation (*jus talionis*); and properly understood, it is the only principle which in regulating a public court, as distinguished from mere private judgment, can definitely assign both the quality and the quantity of a just penalty. All other standards are wavering and uncertain; and on account of other considerations involved in them, they contain no principle conformable to the sentence of pure and strict justice. It may appear, however, that difference of social status would not admit the application of the principle of retaliation, which is that of 'like with like.' But although the application may not in all cases be possible according to the letter, yet as regards the effect it may always be attained in practice, by due regard being given to the disposition and sentiment of the parties in the higher social sphere. Thus a pecuniary penalty on account of a verbal injury, may have no direct proportion to the injustice of slander; for one who is wealthy may be able to indulge himself in this offence for his own gratification. Yet the attack committed on the honour of the party aggrieved may have its equivalent in the pain inflicted upon the pride of the aggressor, especially if he is condemned by the judgment of the court, not only to retract and apologize, but to submit to some meaner ordeal, as kissing the hand of the injured person. In like manner, if a man of the highest rank has violently assaulted an innocent citizen of the lower orders, he may be condemned not only to apologize but to undergo a solitary and painful imprisonment, whereby, in addition to the discomfort endured, the vanity of the offender would be painfully affected, and the very shame of his position would constitute an adequate retaliation after the principle of like with like. But how then would we render the statement: 'If you *steal* from another, you steal from yourself'? In this way, that whoever steals anything makes the property of all insecure; he therefore robs himself of all security in property, according to the right of retaliation. Such a one has nothing, and can acquire nothing, but he has the will to live; and this is only possible by others supporting him. But as the state should not do this gratuitously, he must for this purpose yield his powers to the state to be used in penal labour; and thus he falls for a time, or it may be for life, into a condition of slavery.—But whoever has committed murder, must *die*. There is, in this case, no juridical substitute or surrogate, that can be given or taken for the satisfaction of justice. There is no *likeness* or proportion between life, however painful, and death; and therefore there is no equality between the crime of murder and the retaliation of it but what is judicially accomplished by the execution of the criminal. His death, however, must be kept free from all maltreatment that would make the humanity suffering in his person loathsome or abominable. Even if a civil society resolved to dissolve itself with the consent of all its members—as might be supposed in the case of a people inhabiting an island resolving to separate and scatter themselves throughout the whole world—the last murderer lying in the prison ought to be executed before the resolution was carried out. This ought to be done in order that every one may realize the desert of his deeds, and that bloodguiltiness may not remain upon the people; for otherwise they might all be regarded as participators in the murder as a public violation of justice.

The equalization of punishment with crime, is therefore only possible by the cognition of the judge extending even to the penalty of death, according to the right of retaliation.

Review Questions

1. According to Kant, who deserves juridical punishment?

2. Why does Kant reject the maxim "It is better that *one* man should die than that the whole people should perish"?

3. How does Kant explain the principle of retaliation?

Discussion Questions

1. Does Kant have any good reason to reject the "serpent-windings of utilitarianism"?

2. Is death always a just punishment for murder? Can you think of any exceptions?

Walter Berns

For Capital Punishment

Walter Berns teaches political science at Georgetown University. He is the author of For Capital Punishment.

Berns wants to explain the retributive view that requires us to pay criminals back for their crimes, and that requires us to make murderers pay for their crimes with their lives. Berns thinks that punishing criminals, including murderers, is an expression of anger. But this anger is morally right, he believes, because it acknowledges the humanity of the criminals, it holds them responsible for their actions, and it serves justice. A criminal who has violated the trust of a moral community has thereby injured it, therefore, the criminal must be punished for the sake of justice. Berns concludes with an interesting discussion of the views of capital punishment that he finds in Camus The Stranger *and Shakespeare's* Mac-

beth; he asserts that Shakespeare gives us a truer account of murder than Camus.

INTRODUCTION

Until recently, my business did not require me to think about the punishment of criminals in general or the legitimacy and efficacy of capital punishment in particular. In a vague way, I was aware of the disagreement among professionals concerning the purpose of punishment—whether it was intended to deter others, to rehabilitate the criminal, or to pay him back—but like most laymen I had no particular reason to decide which purpose was right or to what extent they may all have been right. I did know that retribution was held in ill repute among criminologists and jurists—to them, retribution was a fancy name for revenge, and revenge was barbaric—and, of course, I knew that capital punishment had the support only of policemen, prison guards, and some local politicians, the sort of people Arthur Koestler calls "hanghards" (Philadelphia's Mayor Rizzo comes to mind). The intellectual community denounced it as both unnecessary and immoral. It was the phenomenon of Simon Wiesenthal that allowed me to understand why the intellectuals were wrong and why the police, the politicians, and the majority of the voters were right: we punish criminals principally in order to pay them back, and we execute the worst of them out of moral necessity. Anyone who respects Wiesenthal's mission will be driven to the same conclusion.

Of course, not everyone will respect that mission. It will strike the busy man—I mean the sort of man who sees things only in the light cast by a concern for his own interests—as somewhat bizarre. Why should anyone devote his life—more than thirty years of it!—exclusively to the task of hunting down the Nazi war criminals who survived World War II and escaped punishment? Wiesenthal says his conscience forces him, "to bring the guilty ones to trial." But why punish them? What do we hope to accomplish now by punishing SS Obersturmbannführer Adolf Eichmann or SS Obersturmführer Franz Stangl or someday—who knows?—Reichsleiter Martin Bormann? We surely don't expect to rehabilitate them, and it would be foolish to think that by punishing them we might thereby deter others. The answer, I think, is clear: We want to punish them in order *to pay them back*. We think they must be made to pay for their crimes with their lives, and we think that we, the survivors of the world they violated, may legitimately exact that payment because we, too, are their victims. By punishing them, we demonstrate that there are laws that bind men across generations as well as across (and within) nations, that we are not simply isolated individuals, each pursuing his selfish interests and connected with others by a mere contract to live and let live. To state it simply, Wiesenthal allows us to see that it is right, morally right, to be angry with criminals and to express that anger publicly, officially, and in an appropriate manner, which may require the worst of them to be executed.

Modern civil-libertarian opponents of capital punishment do not understand this. They say that to execute a criminal is to deny his human dignity; they also say that the death penalty is not useful, that nothing useful is accomplished by executing anyone. Being utilitarians, they are essentially selfish men, distrustful of passion, who do not understand the connection between anger and justice, and between anger and human dignity.

ANGER AS RESPONSE DUE

ANGER IS EXPRESSED or manifested on those occasions when someone has acted in a manner that is thought to be unjust, and one of its origins is the opinion that men are responsible, and should be held responsible, for what they do. Thus, as **Aristotle** teaches us, anger is accompanied not only by the pain caused by the one who is the object of anger, but by the pleasure arising from the expectation of inflicting revenge on someone who is thought to deserve it. We can become angry with an inanimate object (the door we run into and then kick in return) only by foolishly attributing responsibility to it, and we cannot do that for long, which is why we do not think of returning later to revenge ourselves on the door. For the same reason, we cannot be more than momentarily angry with any one creature other than man; only a fool or worse would dream of taking revenge on a dog. And, finally, we tend to pity rather than to be angry with men who—because they are insane, for example—are not responsible for their acts. Anger, then, is a very human passion not only because only a human being can be angry, but also because anger acknowledges the humanity of its objects: it holds them accountable for what they do. And in holding particular men responsible, it pays them the respect that is due them as men. Anger recognizes that only men have the capacity to be moral beings and, in so doing, acknowledges the dignity of human beings. Anger is somehow connected with *justice,* and it is this that modern penology has not understood; it tends, on the whole, to regard anger as a selfish indulgence.

Anger can, of course, be that; and if someone does not become angry with an insult or an injury suffered unjustly, we tend to think he does not think much of himself. But it need not be selfish, not in the sense of being provoked only by an injury suffered by oneself. There were many angry men in America when President Kennedy was killed; one of them—Jack Ruby—took it upon himself to exact the punishment that, if indeed deserved, ought to have been exacted by the law. There were perhaps even angrier men when Martin Luther King, Jr., was killed, for King, more than anyone else at the time, embodied a people's quest for justice; the anger—more, the "black rage"—expressed on that occasion was simply a manifestation of the great change that had occurred among black men in America, a change wrought in large part by King and his associates in the civil-rights movement: the servility and fear of the past had been replaced by pride and anger, and the treatment that had formerly been accepted as a matter of course or as if it were deserved was now seen for what it was, unjust and unacceptable. King preached love, but the movement he led depended on anger as well as love, and that anger was not despicable, being neither selfish nor unjustified. On the contrary, it was a reflection of what was called solidarity and may more accurately be called a profound caring for others, black for other blacks, white for blacks, and, in the world King was trying to build, American for other Americans. If men are not saddened when someone else suffers, or angry when someone else suffers unjustly, the implication is that they do not care for anyone other than themselves or that they lack some quality that befits a man. When we criticize them for this, we acknowledge that they ought to care for others. If men are not angry when a neighbor suffers at the hands of a criminal, the implication is that their moral faculties have been corrupted, that they are not good citizens.

Criminals are properly the objects of anger, and the perpetrators of terrible crimes—for example, Lee Harvey Oswald and James Earl Ray—are properly the objects of great anger. They have done more than inflict an injury on an isolated individual; they have violated the foundations of trust and friendship, the necessary elements of a moral community, the only community worth living in. A moral community, unlike a hive of bees or a hill of ants, is one whose members are expected freely to obey the laws and, unlike those in a tyranny, are trusted to obey the laws. The criminal has violated that trust, and in so doing has injured not merely his immediate victim but the community as such. He has called into question the very possibility of that community by suggesting that men cannot be trusted to respect freely the property, the person, and the dignity of those with whom they are associated. If, then, men are not angry when someone else is robbed, raped, or murdered, the implication is that no moral community exists, because those men do not care for anyone other than themselves. Anger is an expression of that caring, and society needs men who care for one another, who share their pleasures and their pains, and do so for the sake of the others. It is the passion that can cause us to act for reasons having nothing to do with selfish or mean calculation; indeed, when educated, it can become a generous passion, the passion that protects the community or country by demanding punishment for its enemies. It is the stuff from which heroes are made.

CAMUS VS. SHAKESPEARE

A MORAL COMMUNITY is not possible without anger and the moral indignation that accompanies it. Thus the most powerful attack on capital punishment was written by a man, Albert Camus, who denied the legitimacy of anger and moral indignation by denying the very possibility of a moral community in our time. The anger expressed in our world, he said, is nothing but hypocrisy. His novel *L'Etranger* (variously translated as *The Stranger* or *The Outsider*) is a brilliant portrayal of what Camus insisted is our world, a world deprived of God, as he put it. It is a world we would not choose to live in and one that Camus, the hero of the French Resistance, disdained. Nevertheless, the novel is a modern masterpiece, and Meursault, its antihero (for a world without anger can have no heroes), is a murderer.

He is a murderer whose crime is excused, even as his lack of hypocrisy is praised, because the universe, we are told, is "benignly indifferent" to how we live or what we do. Of course, the law is not indifferent; the law punished Meursault and it threatens to punish us if we do as he did. But Camus the novelist teaches us that the law is simply a collection of arbitrary conceits. The people around Meursault apparently were not indifferent; they expressed dismay at his lack of attachment to his mother and disapprobation of his crime. But Camus the novelist teaches us that other people are hypocrites. They pretend not to know what Camus the opponent of capital punishment tells us: namely, that "our civilization has lost the only values that, in a certain way, can justify that penalty ... [the existence of] a truth or a principle that is superior to man." There is no basis for friendship and no moral law; therefore, no one, not even a murderer, can violate the terms of friendship or break that law; and there is no basis for the anger that we express when someone breaks that law. The only thing we share as men, the only thing that connects us one to another, is a "solidarity against death," and a judgment of capital punishment "upsets" that solidarity. The purpose of human life is to stay alive.

Like Meursault, Macbeth was a murderer, and like *L'Etranger*, Shakespeare's *Macbeth* is the story of a murder; but there the similarity ends. As Lincoln said, "Nothing equals *Macbeth.*" He was comparing it with the other Shakespearean plays he knew, the plays he had "gone over perhaps as frequently as any unprofessional reader ...*Lear, Richard Third, Henry Eighth, Hamlet*"; but I think he meant to say more than that none of these equals *Macbeth.* I think he meant that no other literary work equals it. "It is wonderful," he said. Macbeth is wonderful because, to say nothing more here, it teaches us the awesomeness of the commandment "Thou shalt not kill."

What can a dramatic poet tell us about murder? More, probably, than anyone else, if he is a poet worthy of consideration, and yet nothing that does not inhere in the act itself. In *Macbeth*, Shakespeare shows us murders committed in a political world by a man so driven by ambition to rule that world that he becomes a tyrant. He shows us also the consequences, which were terrible, worse even than Macbeth feared. The cosmos rebelled, turned into chaos by his deeds. He shows a world that was not "benignly indifferent" to what we call crimes and especially to murder, a world constituted by laws divine as well as human, and Macbeth violated the most awful of those laws. Because the world was so constituted, Macbeth suffered the torments of the great and the damned, torments far beyond the "practice" of any physician. He had known glory and had deserved the respect and affection of king, countrymen, army, friends, and wife; and he lost it all. At the end he was reduced to saying that life "is a tale told by an idiot, full of sound and fury, signifying nothing"; yet, in spite of the horrors provoked in us by his acts, he excites no anger in us. We pity him; even so, we understand the anger of his countrymen and the dramatic necessity of his death. *Macbeth* is a play about ambition, murder, tyranny; about horror, anger, vengeance, and, perhaps more than any other of Shakespeare's plays, justice. Because of justice, Macbeth has to die, not by his own hand—he will not "play the Roman fool, and die on [his] own sword"—but at the hand of the avenging Macduff. The dramatic necessity of his death would appear to rest on its *moral* necessity. Is that right? Does this play conform to our sense of what a murder means? Lincoln thought it was "wonderful."

Surely Shakespeare's is a truer account of murder than the one provided by Camus, and by truer I mean truer to our moral sense of what a murder is and what the consequences that attend it must be. Shakespeare shows us vengeful men because there is something in the souls of men—then and now—that requires such crimes to be revenged. Can we imagine a world that does not take its revenge on the man who kills Macduff's wife and children? (Can we imagine the play in which Macbeth does not die?) Can we imagine a people that does not hate murderers? (Can we imagine a world where Meursault is an outsider only because he does not *pretend* to be outraged by murder?) Shakespeare's poetry could not have been written out of the moral sense that the death penalty's opponents insist we ought to have. Indeed, the issue of capital punishment can be said to turn on whether Shakespeare's or Camus' is the more telling account of murder.

Review Questions

1. According to Berns, what is the principle reason for punishing criminals?

2. Explain Bern's account of anger, including the connection between anger, justice, and humanity.

3. Why are criminals properly the objects of anger according to Berns?

4. What views of capital punishment does Berns find in Camus' *The Stranger?*

5. What view does he find in Shakespeare's *Macbeth?*

Discussion Questions

1. Do you agree that Shakespeare has given a better account of murder than Camus? Why or why not?

2. Are there any other reasons for punishing criminals besides paying them back? What are they?

3. Are there any criminals who do *not* deserve to be punished? Who are they?

Anthony G. Amsterdam
Capital Punishment

Anthony G. Amsterdam is a lawyer who has represented many clients who have received the death sentence.

Amsterdam begins by asserting that capital punishment is a great evil simply because it is intentionally killing a person. Furthermore, it is wrong because it results in killing people in error, and these errors cannot be corrected. Moreover, it is unfairly applied. The death sentence is disproportionately imposed on the poor and blacks.

Amsterdam concludes with a discussion of retribution and deterrence. He argues that neither the appeal to retribution nor the appeal to deterrence justifies capital punishment.

From the *Stanford Magazine,* Fall/Winter 1977. Copyright © Stanford Alumni Association. Reprinted with permission.

My discussion of capital punishment will proceed in three stages.

First, I would like to set forth certain basic factual realities about capital punishment, like the fact that capital punishment is a fancy phrase for legally killing people. Please forgive me for beginning with such obvious and ugly facts. Much of our political and philosophical debate about the death penalty is carried on in language calculated to conceal these realities and their implications. The implications, I will suggest, are that capital punishment is a great evil—surely the greatest evil except for war that our society can intentionally choose to commit.

This does not mean that we should do away with capital punishment. Some evils, like war, are occasionally necessary, and perhaps capital punishment is one of them. But the fact that it is a great evil means that we should not choose to do it without some very good and solid reason of which we are satisfactorily convinced upon sufficient evidence. The conclusion of my first point simply is that the burden of proof upon the question of capital punishment rightly rests on those who are asking us to use our laws to kill people with, and that this is a very heavy burden.

Second, I want to review the justifications that have been advanced to support capital punishment. I want to explore with you concepts such as retribution and deterrence, and some of the assumptions and evidence about them. The conclusion of my second point will be that none of these reasons which we like to give ourselves for executing criminals can begin to sustain the burden of proof that rightfully rests upon them.

Third, I would like to say a word about history—about the slow but absolutely certain progress of maturing civilization that will bring an inevitable end to punishment by death. That history does not give us the choice between perpetuating and abolishing capital punishment, because we could not perpetuate it if we wanted to. A generation or two within a single nation can retard but not reverse a long-term, worldwide evolution of this magnitude. Our choice is narrower although it is not unimportant: whether we shall be numbered among the last generations to put legal killing aside. I will end by asking you to cast your choice for life instead of death. But, first, let me begin with some basic facts about the death penalty.

I. The most basic fact, of course, is that capital punishment means taking, living, breathing men and women, stuffing them into a chair, strapping them down, pulling a lever, and exterminating them. We have almost forgotten this fact because there have been no executions in this country for more than ten years, except for Gary Gilmore whose combined suicide and circus were so wildly extravagant as to seem unreal. For many people, capital punishment has become a sanitized and symbolic issue: Do you or do you not support you local police? Do you or do you not care enough about crime to get tough with criminals? These abstractions were never what capital punishment was about,

although it was possible to think so during the ten-year moratorium on executions caused by constitutional challenges to the death penalty in the courts. That is no longer possible. The courts have now said that we can start up executions again, if we want to. Today, a vote for capital punishment is a vote to kill real, live people.

What this means is, first, that we bring men or women into court and put them through a trial for their lives. They are expected to sit back quietly and observe decent courtroom decorum throughout a proceeding whose purpose is systematically and deliberately to decide whether they should be killed. The jury hears evidence and votes; and you can always tell when a jury has voted for death because they come back into court and they will not look the defendant or defense counsel in the eyes. The judge pronounces sentence and the defendant is taken away to be held in a cell for two to six years, hoping that his appeals will succeed, not really knowing what they are all about, but knowing that if they fail, he will be taken out and cinched down and put to death. Most of the people in prison are reasonably nice to him, and even a little apologetic; but he realizes every day for that 700 or 2,100 days that they are holding him there helpless for the approaching slaughter; and that, once the final order is given, they will truss him up and kill him, and that nobody in that vast surrounding machinery of public officials and servants of the law will raise a finger to save him. This is why Camus once wrote that an execution

... is not simply death. It is just as different ... from the privation of life as a concentration camp is from prison.... It adds to death a rule, a public premeditation known to the future victim, an organization ... which is itself a source of moral sufferings more terrible than death ... [Capital punishment] is ... the most premeditated of murders, to which no criminal's deed, however calculated ... can be compared.... For there to be an equivalency, the death penalty would have to punish a criminal who had

warned his victim of the date at which he would inflict a horrible death on him and who, from that moment onward, had confined him at his mercy for months. Such a monster is not encountered in private life.

I will spare you descriptions of the execution itself. Apologists for capital punishment commonly excite their readers with descriptions of extremely gruesome, gory murders. All murders are horrible things, and executions are usually a lot cleaner physically—although, like Camus, I have never heard of a murderer who held his victim captive for two or more years waiting as the minutes and hours ticked away toward his preannounced death. The clinical details of an execution are as unimaginable to me as they are to most of you. We have not permitted public executions in this country for over 40 years. The law in every state forbids more than a few people to watch the deed done behind prison walls. In January of 1977, a federal judge in Texas ruled that executions could be photographed for television, but the attorneys general of 25 states asked the federal Court of Appeals to set aside that ruling, and it did. I can only leave to your imagination what they are trying so very hard to hide from us. Oh, of course, executions are too hideous to put on television; we all know that. But let us not forget that it is the same hideous thing, done in secret, which we are discussing under abstract labels like "capital punishment" that permit us to talk about the subject in after-dinner conversation instead of spitting up.

In any event, the advocates of capital punishment can and do accentuate their arguments with descriptions of the awful physical details of such hideous murders as that of poor Sharon Tate. All of us naturally and rightly respond to these atrocities with shock and horror. You can read descriptions of executions that would also horrify you (for example, in Byron Eshelman's 1962 book, *Death Row Chaplain*, particularly pages 160–61), but I prefer not to insult your intelligence by playing "can you top this" with issues of life and death. I ask you only to remember two things, if and when you are exposed to descriptions of terrifying murders.

First, the murders being described are not murders that are being done by us, or in our name, or with our approval; and our power to stop them is exceedingly limited even under the most exaggerated suppositions of deterrence, which I shall shortly return to question. Every execution, on the other hand, is done by our paid servants, in our collective name, and we can stop them all. Please do not be bamboozled into thinking that people who are against executions are in favor of murders. If we had the individual or the collective power to stop murders, we would stop them all—and for the same basic reason that we want to stop executions. Murders and executions are both ugly, vicious things, because they destroy the same sacred and mysterious gift of life which we do not understand and can never restore.

Second, please remember therefore that descriptions of murders are relevant to the subject of capital punishment only on the theory that two wrongs make a right, or that killing murderers can assuage their victims' sufferings or bring them back to life, or that capital punishment is the best deterrent to murder. The first two propositions are absurd, and the third is debatable—although, as I shall later show, the evidence is overwhelmingly against it. My present point is only that deterrence *is* debatable, whereas we *know* that persons whom we execute are dead beyond recall, no matter how the debate about deterrence comes out. That is a sufficient reason, I believe, why the burden of proof on the issue of deterrence should be placed squarely upon the executioners.

There are other reasons too. Let me try to state them briefly.

Capital punishment not merely kills people, it also kills some of them in error, and these are errors which we can never correct. When I speak about legal error, I do not mean only the question whether "they got the right man" or killed somebody who "didn't do it." Errors of that sort do occur: Timothy Evans, for example, an innocent man whose execution was among the reasons for the abolition of the death penalty in Great Britain. If you read Anthony Scaduto's recent book, *Scapegoat,* you will come away with unanswerable doubts whether Bruno Richard Hauptmann was really guilty of the kidnaping of the Lindbergh infant for which he was executed, or whether we killed Hauptmann, too, for a crime he did not commit.

In 1975, the Florida Cabinet pardoned two black men, Freddie Lee Pitts and Wilbert Lee, who were twice tried and sentenced to death and spent 12 years apiece on death row for a murder committed by somebody else. This one, I am usually glibly told, "does not count," because Pitts and Lee were never actually put to death. Take comfort if you will but I cannot, for I know that only the general constitutional attack which we were then mounting upon the death penalty in Florida kept Pitts and Lee alive long enough to permit discovery of the evidence of their innocence. Our constitutional attack is now dead, and so would Pitts and Lee be if they were tried tomorrow. Sure, we catch some errors. But we often catch them by extremely lucky breaks that could as easily not have happened. I represented a young man in North Carolina who came within a hair's breadth of being the Gary Gilmore of his day. Like Gilmore, he became so depressed under a death sentence that he tried to dismiss his appeal. He was barely talked out of it, his conviction was reversed, and on retrial a jury acquitted him in 11 minutes.

We do not know how many "wrong men" have been executed. We think and pray that they are rare—although we can't be sure because, after a man is dead, people seldom continue to investigate the possibility that he was innocent. But that is not the biggest source of error anyway.

What about *legal* error? In 1968, the Supreme Court of the United States held that it was unconstitutional to exclude citizens from capital trial juries simply because they had general conscientious or religious objections to the death penalty. That decision was held retroactive; and I represented 60 or 70 men whose death sentences were subsequently set aside for constitutional errors in jury selection. While researching their cases, I found the cases of at least as many more men who had already been executed on the basis of trials infected with identical errors. On June 29, 1977, we finally won a decision from the Supreme Court of the United States that the death penalty is excessively harsh and therefore unconstitutional for the crime of rape. Fine, but it comes too late for the 455 men executed for rape in this country since 1930—405 of them black.

In 1975, the Supreme Court held that the constitutional presumption of innocence forbids a trial judge to tell the jury that the burden of proof is on a homicide defendant to show provocation which reduces murder to manslaughter. On June 17, 1977, the Court held that this decision was also retroactive. Jury charges of precisely that kind were standard forms for more than a century in many American states that punished murder with death. Can we even begin to guess how many people were unconstitutionally executed under this so-called retroactive decision?

Now what about errors of fact that go to the degree of culpability of a crime? In almost every state, the difference between first- and second-degree murder—or between capital and noncapital murder—depends on whether the defendant acted with something called "premeditation" as distinguished from intent to kill. Premeditation means intent formed beforehand, but no particular amount of time is required. Courts tell juries that premeditation "may be as instantaneous as successive thoughts in the mind." Mr. Justice Cardozo wrote that *he* did not understand the concept of premeditation after several decades of studying and trying to apply it as a judge. Yet this is the kind of question to which a jury's answer spells out life or death in a capital trial—this, and the questions whether the defendant had "malice aforethought," or "provocation and passion," or "insanity," or the "reasonableness" necessary for killing in self-defense.

I think of another black client, Johnny Coleman, whose conviction and death sentence for killing a white truck driver named "Screwdriver" Johnson we twice got reversed by the Supreme Court of the United States. On retrial a jury acquitted him on the grounds of self-defense upon exactly the same evidence that an earlier jury had had when it sentenced him to die. When ungraspable legal standards are thus applied to intangible mental states, there is not merely the possibility but the actuarial certainty that juries deciding substantial volumes of cases are going to be wrong in an absolutely large number of them. If you accept capital punishment, you must accept the reality—not the risk, but the reality—that we shall kill people whom the law says that it is not proper to kill. No other outcome is possible when we presume to administer an infallible punishment through a fallible system.

You will notice that I have taken examples of black defendants as some of my cases of legal error. There is every reason to believe that discrimination on grounds of race and poverty fatally infect the administration of capital justice in this country. Since 1930, an almost equal number of white and black defendants has been executed for the crime of murder, although blacks constituted only about a tenth of the nation's population during this period. No sufficiently careful studies have been done of these cases, controlling variables other than race, so as to determine exactly what part race played in the outcome. But when that kind of systematic study *was* done in rape cases, it showed beyond the statistical possibility of a doubt that black men who raped white women were disproportionately sentenced to die on the basis of race alone. Are you prepared to believe that juries which succumbed to conscious or unconscious racial prejudices in rape cases were or are able to put those prejudices wholly aside where the crime charged is murder? Is it not much more plausible to believe that even the most conscientious juror—or judge, or pros-

ecuting attorney—will be slower to want to inflict the death penalty on a defendant with whom he can identify as a human being; and that the process of identification in our society is going to be very seriously affected by racial identity?

I should mention that there have been a couple of studies—one by the *Stanford Law Review* and the other by the Texas Judicial Council—which found no racial discrimination in capital sentencing in certain murder cases. But both of these studies had methodological problems and limitations; and both of them also found death-sentencing discrimination against the economically poor, who come disproportionately from racial minorities. The sum of the evidence still stands where the National Crime Commission found it ten years ago, when it described the following discriminatory patterns. "The death sentence," said the Commission, "is disproportionately imposed and carried out on the poor, the Negro, and members of unpopular groups."

Apart from discrimination, there is a haphazard, crazy-quilt character about the administration of capital punishment that every knowledgeable lawyer or observer can describe but none can rationally explain. Some juries are hanging juries, some counties are hanging counties, some years are hanging years; and men live or die depending on these flukes.

However atrocious the crime may have been for which a particular defendant is sentenced to die, "[e]xperienced wardens know many prisoners serving life or less whose crimes were equally, or more atrocious." That is a quotation, by the way, from former Attorney General Ramsey Clark's statement to a congressional subcommittee; and wardens Lewis Lawes, Clinton Duffy, and others have said the same thing.

With it I come to the end of my first point. I submit that the deliberate judicial extinction of human life is intrinsically so final and so terrible an act as to cast the burden of proof for its justification upon those who want us to do it. But certainly when the act is executed through a fallible system which assures that we kill some people wrongly, others because they are black or poor or personally unattractive or socially unacceptable, and all of them quite freakishly in the sense that whether a man lives or dies for any particular crime is a matter of luck and happenstance, *then,* at the least, the burden of justifying capital punishment lies fully and heavily on its proponents.

II. Let us consider those justifications. The first and the oldest is the concept of *retribution:* an eye for an eye, a life for a life. You may or may not believe in this kind of retribution, but I will not waste your time debating it because it cannot honestly be used to justify the only form of capital punishment that this country has accepted for the past half-century. Even before the judicial moratorium, executions in the United States had dwindled to an average of about 30 a year. Only a rare, sparse handful of convicted murderers was being sentenced to die or executed for the selfsame crimes for which many, many times as many murderers were sent away to prison. Obviously, as Professor Herbert Wechsler said a generation ago, the issue of capital punishment is no longer "whether it is fair or just that one who takes another person's life should lose his own.... [W]e do not and cannot act upon ... [that proposition] generally in the administration of the penal law. The problem rather is whether a small and highly random sample of people who commit murder.... ought to be despatched, while most of those convicted of ... [identical] crimes are dealt with by imprisonment."

Sometimes the concept of retribution is modernized a little with a notion called *moral reinforcement*—the ideal that we should punish very serious crimes very severely in order to demonstrate how much we abhor them. The trouble with *this* justification for capital punishment, of course, is that it completely begs the question, which is *how severely* we ought to punish any particular crime to show appropriate abhorrence for it. The answer can hardly be found in a literal application of the eye-for-an-eye formula. We do not burn down arsonists' houses or cheat back at bunco artists. But if we ought not punish all crimes exactly according to their kind, then what is the fit moral reinforcement for murder? You might as well say burning at the stake or boiling in oil as simple gassing or electrocution.

Or is it not more plausible—if what we really want to say is that the killing of a human being is wrong and ought to be condemned as clearly as we can—that we should choose the punishment of prison as the fitting means to make this point? So far as moral reinforcement goes, the difference between life imprisonment and capital punishment is precisely that imprisonment continues to respect the value of human life. The plain message of capital punishment, on the other hand, is that life ceases to be sacred whenever someone with the power to take it away decides that there is a sufficiently compelling pragmatic reason to do so.

But there is still another theory of a retributive sort which is often advanced to support the death penalty, particularly in recent years. This is the argument that *we*—that is, the person making the argument—we no longer believe in the outworn concept of retribution, but the *public*—they believe in retribution, and so we must let them have their prey or they will lose respect for law. Watch for this argument because it is the surest sign of demagogic depravity. It is disgusting in its patronizing attribution to "the public" of a primitive, uneducable bloodthirstiness which the speaker is unprepared to defend but is prepared to exploit as a means of sidestepping the rational and moral limitations of a *just* theory of retribution. It out-judases Judas in its abnegation of governmental responsibility to respond to popular misinformation with enlightenment, instead of seizing on it as a pretext for atrocity. This argument asserts that the proper way to deal with a lynch mob is to string its victim up before the mob does.

I don't think "the public" is a lynch mob or should be treated as one. People today are troubled and frightened by crime, and legitimately so. Much of the apparent increase of violent crime in our times is the product of intensified statistics keeping, massive and instantaneous and graphic news reporting, and manipulation of figures by law enforcement agencies which must compete with other sectors of the public economy for budget allocations. But part of the increase is also real, and very disturbing. Murders ought to disturb us all, whether or not they are increasing. Each and every murder is a terrible human tragedy. Nevertheless, it is irresponsible for public officials—particularly law enforcement officials whom the public views as experts—first to exacerbate and channel legitimate public concern about crime into public support for capital punishment by advertising unsupportable claims that capital punishment is an answer to the crime problem, and then to turn around and cite public support for capital punishment as justification when all other justifications are shown to be unsupportable. Politicians do this all the time, for excellent political reasons. It is much easier to advocate simplistic and illusory solutions to the crime problem than to find real and effective solutions. Most politicians are understandably afraid to admit that our society knows frighteningly little about the causes or cure of crime, and will have to spend large amounts of taxpayers' money even to begin to find out. The facile politics of crime do much to explain our national acceptance of capital punishment, but nothing to justify it.

Another supposed justification for capital punishment that deserves equally brief treatment is the notion of *isolation* or *specific deterrence*—the idea that we must kill a murderer to prevent him from murdering ever again. The usual forms that this argument takes are that a life sentence does not mean a life sentence—it means parole after 7, or 12, or 25

years; and that, within prisons themselves, guards and other prisoners are in constant jeopardy of death at the hands of convicted but unexecuted murderers.

It amazes me that these arguments can be made or taken seriously. Are we really going to kill a human being because we do not trust other people—the people whom we have chosen to serve on our own parole boards—to make a proper judgment in his case at some future time? We trust this same parole board to make far more numerous, difficult, and dangerous decisions: hardly a week passes when they do not consider the cases of armed robbers, for example, although armed robbers are much, much more likely statistically to commit future murders than any murderer is to repeat his crime. But if we really do distrust the public agencies of law—if we fear that they may make mistakes—then surely that is a powerful argument *against* capital punishment. Courts which hand out death sentences because they predict that a man will still be criminally dangerous 7 or 25 years in the future cannot conceivably make fewer mistakes than parole boards who release a prisoner after 7 or 25 years of close observation in prison have convinced them that he is reformed and no longer dangerous.

But pass this point. If we refuse to trust the parole system, then let us provide by law that the murderers whose release we fear shall be given sentences of life imprisonment without parole which *do* mean life imprisonment without parole. I myself would be against that, but it is far more humane than capital punishment, and equally safe.

As for killings inside prisons, if you examine them you will find that they are very rarely done by convicted murderers, but are almost always done by people imprisoned for crimes that no one would think of making punishable by death. Warden Lawes of Sing Sing and Governor Wallace of Alabama, among others, regularly employed murder convicts as house servants because they were among the very safest of prisoners. There are exceptions, of course; but these can be handled by adequate prison security. You cannot tell me or believe that a society which is capable of putting a man on the moon is incapable of putting a man in prison, keeping him there, and keeping him from killing while he is there. And if anyone says that this is costly, and that we should kill people in order to reduce government expenditures, I can only reply that the cost of housing a man for life in the most physically secure conditions imaginable is considerably less than the cost of putting the same man through all of the extraordinary legal proceedings necessary to kill him.

That brings me to the last supposed justification for the death penalty: *deterrence.* This is the subject that you most frequently hear debated, and many people who talk about capital punishment talk about nothing else. I have done otherwise here, partly for completeness, partly because it is vital to approach the subject of deterrence knowing precisely what question you want to ask and have answered. I have suggested that the proper question is *whether there is sufficiently convincing evidence that the death penalty deters murder better than does life imprisonment so that you are willing to accept responsibility for doing the known evil act of killing human beings—with all of the attending ugliness that I have described—on the faith of your conviction in the superior deterrent efficacy of capital punishment.*

If this is the question, then I submit that there is only one fair and reasonable answer. When the Supreme Court of the United States reviewed the evidence in 1976, it described that evidence as "inconclusive." Do not let anybody tell you—as death-penalty advocates are fond of doing—that the Supreme Court held the death penalty justifiable as a deterrent. What the Court's plurality opinion said, exactly, was that "there is no convincing evidence *either supporting or refuting* . . . [the] view" that "the death penalty may not function as a significantly greater deterrent than lesser penalties." *Because* the evidence was inconclusive, the Court held that the Constitution did not forbid judgment either way. But if the evidence is inconclusive, is it *your* judgment that we should conclusively kill people on a factual theory that the evidence does not conclusively sustain?

I hope not. But let us examine the evidence more carefully because—even though it is not conclusive—it is very, very substantial; and the overwhelming weight of it refutes the claims of those who say that capital punishment is a better deterrent than life imprisonment for murder.

For more than 40 years, criminologists have studied this question by a variety of means. They have compared homicide rates in countries and states that did and did not have capital punishment, or that actually executed people more and less frequently. Some of these studies compared large aggregates of abolitionist and retentionist states; others compared geographically adjacent pairs or triads of states, or states that were chosen because they were comparable in other socioeconomic factors that might affect homicide. Other studies compared homicide rates in the same country or state before and after the abolition or reinstatement of capital punishment, or they compared homicide rates for the same geographic area during periods preceding and following well publicized executions. Special comparative studies were done relating to police killings and prison killings. All in all, there were dozens of studies. Without a single exception, *none* of them found that the death penalty had any statistically significant effect upon the rate of homicide or murder. Often I have heard advocates of capital punishment explain away its failures by likening it to a great lighthouse: "We count the ships that crash," they say, "but we never know how many saw the light and were saved." What these studies show, however, is that coastlines of the same shape and depth and tidal structure, with and without lighthouses, invariably have the same number of shipwrecks per year. On that evidence, would you invest your money in a lighthouse, or would you buy a sonar if you really wanted to save lives?

In 1975, the first purportedly scientific study ever to find that capital punishment *did* deter homicides was published. This was done by Isaac Ehrlich of Chicago, who is not a criminologist but an economist. Using regression analysis involving an elaborate mathematical model, Ehrlich reported that every execution deterred something like eight murders. Naturally, supporters of capital punishment hurriedly clambered on the Ehrlich bandwagon.

Unhappily, for them, the wagon was a factory reject. Several distinguished econometricians—including a team headed by Lawrence Klein, president of the American Economic Association—reviewed Ehrlich's work and found it fatally flawed with numerous methodological errors. Some of these were technical: it appeared, for example, that Ehrlich had produced his results by the unjustified and unexplained use of a logarithmic form of regression equation instead of the more conventional linear form—which made his findings of deterrence vanish. Equally important, it was shown that Ehrlich's findings depended entirely on data from the post-1962 period, when executions declined and the homicide rate rose *as a part of a general rise, in the overall crime rate that Ehrlich incredibly failed to consider.*

Incidentally, the nonscientific proponents of capital punishment are also fond of suggesting that the rise in homicide rates in the 1960s and the 1970s, when executions were halted, proves that executions used to deter homicides. This is ridiculous when you consider that crime as a whole has increased during this period; that homicide rates have increased about *half* as much as the rates for all other FBI Index crimes; and that whatever factors are affecting the rise of most noncapital crimes (which *cannot* include cessation of executions) almost certainly affect the homicide-rate rise also.

In any event, Ehrlich's study was discredited and a second, methodologically inferior study by a fellow named Yunker is not even worth criticizing here. These are the only two

scientific studies in 40 years, I repeat, which have ever purported to find deterrence. On the other hand, several recent studies have been completed by researchers who adopted Ehrlich's basic regression-analysis approach but corrected its defects. Peter Passell did such a study finding no deterrence. Kenneth Avio did such a study finding no deterrence. Brian Forst did such a study finding no deterrence. If you want to review all of these studies yourselves, you may find them discussed and cited in an excellent article in the 1976 *Supreme Court Review* by Hans Zeisel, at page 317. The conclusion you will have to draw is that—during 40 years and today—the scientific community has looked and looked and looked for any reliable evidence that capital punishment deters homicide better than does life imprisonment, and it has found no such evidence at all.

Proponents of capital punishment frequently cite a different kind of study, one that was done by the Los Angeles Police Department. Police officers asked arrested robbers who did not carry guns, or did not use them, *why* they did not; and the answers, supposedly, were frequently that the robber "did not want to get the death penalty." It is noteworthy that the Los Angeles Police Department has consistently refused to furnish copies of this study and its underlying data to professional scholars, apparently for fear of criticism. I finally obtained a copy of the study from a legislative source, and I can tell you that it shows two things. First, an arrested person will tell a police officer anything that he thinks the officer wants to hear. Second, police officers, like all other human beings, hear what they want to hear. When a robber tries to say that he did not carry or use a gun because he did not wish to risk the penalties for homicide, he will describe those penalties in terms of whatever the law happens to be at the time and place. In Minnesota, which has no death penalty, he will say, "I didn't want to get life imprisonment." In Los Angeles, he will say, "I didn't want to get the death penalty." Both responses mean the same thing;

neither tells you that death is a superior deterrent to life imprisonment.

The real mainstay of deterrence thesis, however, is not evidence but intuition. You and I ask ourselves: Are we not afraid to die? Of course! Would the threat of death, then, not intimidate us to forbear from a criminal act? Certainly! *Therefore,* capital punishment must be a deterrent. The trouble with this intuition is that the people who are doing the reasoning and the people who are doing the murdering are not the same people. You and I do not commit murder for a lot of reasons other than the death penalty. The death penalty might perhaps also deter us from murdering—but altogether needlessly, since we would not murder with it or without it. Those who are sufficiently dissocialized to murder and are not responding to the world in the way that we are, and we simply cannot "intuit" their thinking processes from ours.

Consider, for example, the well-documented cases of persons who kill *because* there is a death penalty. One of these was Pamela Watkins, a babysitter in San Jose who had made several unsuccessful suicide attempts and was frightened to try again. She finally strangled two children so that the state of California would execute her. In various bizarre forms, this "suicide-murder" syndrome is reported by psychiatrists again and again. (Parenthetically, Gary Gilmore was probably such a case.) If you intuit that somewhere, sometime, the death penalty *does* deter some potential murders, are you also prepared to intuit that their numbers mathematically exceed the numbers of these wretched people who are actually induced to murder by the existence of capital punishment?

Here, I suggest, our intuition does—or should—fail, just as the evidence certainly does fail, to establish a deterrent justification for the death penalty. There is simply no credible evidence, and there is no rational way of reasoning about the real facts once you know them, which can sustain this or any other justification with the degree of confidence that should be demanded before a civilized society deliberately extinguishes human life.

III. I have only a little space for my final point, but it is sufficient because the point is perfectly plain. Capital punishment is a dying institution in this last quarter of the twentieth century. It has already been abandoned in law or in fact throughout most of the civilized world. England, Canada, the Scandinavian countries, virtually all of Western Europe except for France and Spain have abolished the death penalty. The vast majority of countries in the Western Hemisphere have abolished it. Its last strongholds in the world—apart from the United States—are in Asia and Africa, particularly South Africa. Even the countries which maintain capital punishment on the books have almost totally ceased to use it in fact. In the United States, considering only the last half century, executions have plummeted from 199 in 1935 to approximately 29 a year during the decade before 1967, when the ten-year judicial moratorium began.

Do you doubt that this development will continue? Do you doubt that it will continue because it is the path of civilization—the path up out of fear and terror and the barbarism that terror breeds, into self-confidence and decency in the administration of justice? The road, like any other built by men, has its detours, but over many generations it has run true, and will run true. And there will therefore come a time—perhaps in 20 years, perhaps in 50 or 100, but very surely and very shortly as the lifetime of nations is measured—when our children will look back at us in horror and unbelief because of what we did in their names and for their supposed safety, just as we look back in horror and unbelief at the thousands of crucifixions and beheadings and live disembowelments that our ancestors practiced for the supposed purpose of making our world safe from murderers and robbers, thieves, shoplifters, and pickpockets.

All of these kinds of criminals are still with us, and will be with our children—although we can certainly decrease their numbers and their damage, and protect ourselves from them a lot better, if we insist that our politicians stop pounding on the whipping boy of capital punishment and start coming up with some real solutions to the real problems of crime. Our children will cease to execute murderers for the same reason that we have ceased to string up pickpockets and shoplifters at the public crossroads, although there are still plenty of them around. Our children will cease to execute murderers because executions are a self-deluding, self-defeating, self-degrading, futile, and entirely stupid means of dealing with the crime of murder, and because our children will prefer to be something better than murderers themselves. Should we not—can we not—make the same choice now?

Review Questions

1. Why does Amsterdam think that capital punishment is a great evil?

2. What additional reasons does Amsterdam give for saying that capital punishment is wrong?

3. Why does Amsterdam reject the oldest concept of retribution, an eye for an eye, a life for a life?

4. What is the notion of moral reinforcement, and why doesn't Amsterdam accept it?

5. How does Amsterdam reply to the argument that the public's desire for retribution must be satisfied?

6. What is wrong with the notion of specific deterrence according to Amsterdam?

7. How does Amsterdam deal with the appeal to deterrence?

Discussion Questions

1. Do you agree with Amsterdam that capital punishment is a great evil? Why or why not?

2. Has Amsterdam successfully defeated the appeal to retribution?

3. Are you convinced that capital punishment is not a better deterrent than life imprisonment? Explain your answer.

Jonathan Glover

Execution and Assassination

Jonathan Glover is a Fellow and Tutor in Philosophy at New College, Oxford, and has written Responsibility, *and* Causing Death and Saving Lives, *from which our reading is taken.*

Glover begins with a discussion of Kant's retribu-

From Jonathan Glover: *Causing Death & Saving Lives* (Pelican Books 1977) pp. 228–245. Copyright © Jonathan Glover, 1977. Reprinted with permission of Penguin Books Ltd.

tive view and the absolutist rejection of capital punishment. He finds both of these to be unacceptable from a utilitarian point of view. The utilitarian approach is that the death penalty is justified if the number of lives saved exceeds the number of executions. But due to the bad side effects of execution on the person executed and on others, as well as other undesirable features, the death penalty is not justified unless it has a substantial deterrent effect. After considering arguments for this deterrent effect, Glover concludes that the case for capital punishment as a substantial deterrent fails.

The Penal Law is a Categorical Imperative; and woe to him who creeps through the serpent-windings of Utilitarianism to discover some advantage that may discharge him from the Justice of Punishment, or even from the due measure of it . . . For if Justice and Righteousness perish, human life would no longer have

any value in the world . . . Whoever has committed
murder must die.
                    Immanuel Kant, The Philosophy of Law

It is curious, but till that moment I had never realized
what it means to destroy a healthy, conscious man.
When I saw the prisoner step aside to avoid the puddle I
saw the mystery, the unspeakable wrongness, of cutting a
life short when it is in full tide. This man was not
dying, he was alive just as we are alive. All the organs
of his body were working—bowels digesting food, skin
renewing itself, nails growing, tissues forming—all
toiling away in solemn foolery. His nails would still be
growing when he stood on the drop, when he was falling
through the air with a tenth of a second to live. His eyes
saw the yellow gravel and the grey walls, and his brain
still remembered, foresaw, reasoned, even about puddles.
He and we were a party of men walking together, seeing,
hearing, feeling, understanding the same world; and in
two minutes, with a sudden snap, one of us would be
gone—one mind less, one world less.
            George Orwell, "A Hanging," Adelphi, 1931

The debate about capital punishment for murder is, emotionally at least, dominated by two absolutist views. On the retributive view, the murderer must be given the punishment he deserves, which is death. On the other view, analogous to pacifism about war, there is in principle no possibility of justifying capital punishment; in execution there is only "the unspeakable wrongness of cutting a life short when it is in full tide." Supporters of these two approaches agree only in rejecting the serpent-windings of utilitarianism.

Let us look first at the retributive view. According to retributivism in its purest form, the aim of punishment is quite independent of any beneficial social consequences it may have. To quote Kant again:

Even if a Civil Society resolved to dissolve itself with
the consent of all its members—as might be supposed
in the case of a people inhabiting an island resolving
to separate and scatter themselves throughout the whole
world—the last Murderer lying in the prison ought to
be executed before the resolution was carried out. This
ought to be done in order that everyone may realize the
desert of his deeds, and that blood-guiltiness may not
remain upon the people; for otherwise they might all be
regarded as participators in the murder as a public

violation of justice.

This view of punishment, according to which it has a value independent of its contribution to reducing the crime rate, is open to the objection that acting on it leads to what many consider to be pointless suffering. To impose suffering or deprivation on someone, or to take his life, is something that those of us who are not retributivists think needs very strong justification in terms of benefits, either to the person concerned or to other people. The retributivist has to say either that the claims of justice can make it right to harm someone where no one benefits, or else to cite the curiously **metaphysical** "benefits" of justice being done, such as Kant's concern that we should have "blood-guiltiness" removed. I have no way of refuting these positions, as they seem to involve no clear intellectual mistake. I do not expect to win the agreement of those who hold them, and I am simply presupposing the other view, that there is already enough misery in the world, and that adding to it requires a justification in terms of nonmetaphysical benefits to people.

This is not to rule out retributive moral principles perhaps playing a limiting role in a general theory of punishment. There is a lot to be said for the retributive restrictions that *only* those who deserve punishment should receive it and that they should never get more punishment than they deserve. (The case for this, which at least partly rests on utilitarian considerations, has been powerfully argued by H.L.A. Hart.[1]) But the approach to be adopted here rules out using retributive considerations to justify any punishment not already justifiable in terms of social benefits. In particular it rules out the argument that capital punishment can be justified, whether or not it reduces the crime rate, because the criminal deserves it.

This approach also has the effect of casting doubt on another way of defending capital punishment, which was forthrightly expressed by Lord Denning: "The ultimate justification of any punishment is not that it is a deterrent, but that it is the emphatic denunciation by the community of a crime: and from this point of view, there are some murders which, in the present state of public opinion, demand the most emphatic denunciation of all, namely the death penalty." [2] The question here is whether the point of the denunciation is to reduce the murder rate, in which case this turns out after all to be a utilitarian justification, or whether denunciation is an end in itself. If it is an end in itself, it starts to look like the retributive view in disguise, and should be rejected for the same reasons.

If we reject retribution for its own sake as a justification for capital punishment we are left with two alternative general approaches to the question. One is an absolute rejection in principle of any possibility of capital punishment being justified, in the spirit of Orwell's remarks. The other is the rather more messy approach, broadly utilitarian in character, of weighing up likely social costs and benefits.

THE ABSOLUTIST REJECTION OF CAPITAL PUNISHMENT

To some people, it is impossible to justify the act of killing a fellow human being. They are absolute pacifists about war and are likely to think of capital punishment as "judicial murder." They will sympathize with Beccaria's question: "Is it not absurd that the laws which detest and punish homicide, in order to prevent murder, publicly commit murder themselves?"

The test of whether an opponent of capital punishment adopts this absolutist position is whether he would still oppose it if it could be shown to save many more lives than it cost, if, say, every execution deterred a dozen potential murderers. The absolutist, unlike the utilitarian opponent of the death penalty, would be unmoved by any such evidence. This question brings out the links between the absolutist position and the **acts and omissions doctrine.** For those of us who reject the acts and omissions doctrine, the deaths we fail to prevent have to be given weight, as

well as the deaths we cause by execution. So those of us who do not accept the acts and omissions doctrine cannot be absolutist opponents of capital punishment.

There is a variant on the absolutist position that at first sight seems not to presuppose the acts and omissions doctrine. On this view, while saving a potential murder victim is in itself as important as not killing a murderer, there is something so cruel about the kind of death involved in capital punishment that this rules out the possibility of its being justified. Those of us who reject the acts and omissions doctrine have to allow that sometimes there can be side effects associated with an act of killing, but not with failure to save a life, which can be sufficiently bad to make a substantial moral difference between the two. When this view is taken of the cruelty of the death penalty, it is not usually the actual method of execution that is objected to, though this can seem important, as in the case where international pressure on General Franco led him to substitute shooting for the garrote. What seems pecularily cruel and horrible about capital punishment is that the condemned man has the period of waiting, knowing how and when he is to be killed. Many of us would rather die suddenly than linger for weeks or months knowing we were fatally ill, and the condemned man's position is several degrees worse than that of the person given a few months to live by doctors. He has the additional horror of knowing exactly when he will die, and of knowing that his death will be in a ritualized killing by other people, symbolizing his ultimate rejection by the members of his community. The whole of his life may seem to have a different and horrible meaning when he sees it leading up to this end.

For reasons of this kind, capital punishment can plausibly be claimed to fall under the United States Constitution's ban on "cruel and unusual punishments," so long as the word unusual is not interpreted too strictly. The same reasons make the death penalty a plausible candidate for falling under a rather similar ethical ban, which has been expressed by H.L.A. Hart: "There are many different ways in which we think it morally incumbent on us to *qualify* or *limit* the pursuit of the utilitarian goal by methods of punishment. Some punishments are ruled out as too barbarous to use *whatever their social utility*"[3] (final italics mine). Because of the extreme cruelty of capital punishment, many of us would, if forced to make a choice between two horrors, prefer to be suddenly murdered than be sentenced to death and executed. This is what makes it seem reasonable to say that the absolutist rejection of the death penalty need not rest on the acts and omissions doctrine.

But this appearance is illusory. The special awfulness of capital punishment may make an execution even more undesirable than a murder (though many would disagree on the grounds that this is outweighed by the desirability that the guilty rather than the innocent should die). Even if we accept that an execution is worse than an average murder, it does not follow from this that capital punishment is too barbarous to use *whatever its social utility*. For supposing a single execution deterred many murders? Or suppose that some of the murders deterred would themselves have been as cruel as an execution? When we think of the suffering imposed in a famous kidnapping case, where the mother received her son's ear through the post, we may feel uncertain even that capital punishment is more cruel than some "lesser" crimes than murder. The view that some kinds of suffering are too great to impose, whatever their social utility, rules out the possibility of justifying them, however much more suffering they would prevent. And this does presuppose the acts and omissions doctrine, and so excludes some of us even from this version of absolutism.

A UTILITARIAN APPROACH

It is often supposed that the utilitarian alternative to absolutism is simply one of adopting an unqualified maximizing policy. On such a view, the death penalty would be justified if, and only if, it was reasonable to think the number of lives saved exceeded the number of executions. (The question of what to do where the numbers exactly balance presupposes a fineness of measurement that is unattainable in these matters.) On any utilitarian view, numbers of lives saved must be a very important consideration. But there are various special features that justify the substantial qualification of a maximizing policy.

The special horror of the period of waiting for execution may not justify the absolutist rejection of the death penalty, but it is a powerful reason for thinking that an execution may normally cause more misery than a murder, and so for thinking that, if capital punishment is to be justified, it must do better than break even when lives saved through deterrence are compared with lives taken by the executioner.

This view is reinforced when we think of some of the other side effects of the death penalty. It must be appalling to be told that your husband, wife, or child has been murdered, but this is surely less bad than the experience of waiting a month or two for your husband, wife, or child to be executed. And those who think that the suffering of the murderer himself matters less than that of an innocent victim will perhaps not be prepared to extend this view to the suffering of the murderer's parents, wife, and children.

There is also the possibility of mistakenly executing an innocent man, something which it is very probable happened in the case of Timothy Evans. The German Federal Ministry of Justice is quoted in the Council of Europe's report on *The Death Penalty in European Countries* as saying that in the hundred years to 1953, there were twenty-seven death sentences "now established or presumed" to be miscarriages of justice. This point is often used as an argument against capital punishment, but what is often not noticed is that its force must depend on the special horrors of execution as compared with other forms of death, including being murdered. For the victim of murder is innocent too, and he also has no form of redress. It is only the (surely correct) assumption that an innocent man faces something much worse in execution than in murder that gives this argument its claim to prominence in this debate. For, otherwise, the rare cases of innocent men being executed would be completely overshadowed by the numbers of innocent men being murdered. (Unless, of course, the acts and omissions doctrine is again at work here, for execution is something that we, as a community, *do* while a higher murder rate is something, we at most *allow*.)

The death penalty also has harmful effects on people other than the condemned man and his family. For most normal people, to be professionally involved with executions, whether as judge, prison warden, chaplain, or executioner, must be highly disturbing. Arthur Koestler quotes the case of the executioner Ellis, who attempted suicide a few weeks after he executed a sick woman "whose insides fell out before she vanished through the trap." [4] (Though the chances must be very small of the experience of Mr. Pierrepoint, who describes in his autobiography how he had to execute a friend with whom he often sang duets in a pub. [5]) And there are wider effects on society at large. When there is capital punishment, we are all involved in the horrible business of a long-premeditated killing, and most of us will to some degree share in the emotional response George Orwell had so strongly when he had to be present. It cannot be good for children at school to know that there is an execution at the prison down the road. And there is another bad effect, drily stated in the *Report of the Royal Commission on Capital Punishment:* "No doubt the ambition that prompts an average of five applications a week for the post of hangman, and the craving that draws a crowd to the prison where a notorious murderer is being executed, reveal psychological qualities that no state would wish to foster in its citizens."

Capital punishment is also likely to operate erratically. Some murderers are likely to *go* free because the death penalty makes juries less likely to convict. (Charles Dickens, in a newspaper article quoted in the 1868 Commons debate, gave the example of a forgery case, where a jury found a £ 10 note to be worth thirty-nine shillings, in order to save the forger's life.) There are also great problems in operating a reprieve system without arbitrariness, say, in deciding whether being pregnant or having a young baby should qualify a woman for a reprieve.

Finally, there is the drawback that the retention or reintroduction of capital punishment contributes to a tradition of cruel and horrible punishment that we might hope would wither away. Nowadays we never think of disemboweling people or chopping off their hands as a punishment. Even if these punishments would be especially effective in deterring some very serious crimes, they are not regarded as a real possibility. To many of us, it seems that the utilitarian benefits from this situation outweigh the loss of any deterrent power they might have if reintroduced for some repulsive crime like kidnapping. And the longer we leave capital punishment in abeyance, the more its use will seem as out of the question as the no more cruel punishment of mutilation. (At this point, I come near to Hart's view that some punishments are too barbarous to use whatever their social utility. The difference is that I think that arguments for and against a punishment should be based on social utility, but that a widespread view that some things are unthinkable is itself of great social utility.)

For these reasons, a properly thought-out utilitarianism does not enjoin an unqualified policy of seeking the minimum loss of life, as the no trade-off view does. Capital punishment has its own special cruelties and horrors, which change the whole position. In order to be justified, it must be shown, with good evidence, that it has a deterrent effect not obtainable by less awful means, and one that is quite substantial rather than marginal.

DETERRENCE AND MURDER

The arguments over whether capital punishment deters murder more effectively than less drastic methods are of two kinds: statistical and intuitive. The statistical arguments are based on various kinds of comparisons of murder rates. Rates are compared before and after abolition in a country, and, where possible, further comparisons are made with rates after reintroduction of capital punishment. Rates are compared in neighboring countries, or neighboring states of the U.S.C.A., with and without the death penalty. I am not a statistician and have no special competence to discuss the issue, but will merely purvey the received opinion of those who have looked into the matter. Those who have studied the figures are agreed that there is no striking correlation between the absence of capital punishment and any alteration in the curve of the murder rate. Having agreed on this point, they then fall into two schools. On one view, we can conclude that capital punishment is not a greater deterrent to murder than the prison sentences that are substituted for it. On the other, more cautious, view, we can only conclude that we do not know that capital punishment is a deterrent. I shall not attempt to choose between these interpretations. For, given that capital punishment is justified only where there is good evidence that it is a substantial deterrent, either interpretation fails to support the case for it.

If the statistical evidence were conclusive that capital punishment did not deter more than milder punishments, this would leave no room for any further discussion. But, since the statistical evidence may be inconclusive, many people feel there is room left for intuitive arguments. Some of these deserve examination. The intuitive case was forcefully stated in 1864 by Sir James Fitzjames Stephen: [6]

No other punishment deters men so effectually from committing crimes as the punishment of death. This is one of those propositions which it is difficult to prove, simply because they are in themselves more obvious than any proof can make them. It is possible to display ingenuity in arguing against it, but that is all. The whole experience of mankind is in the other direction. The threat of instant death is the one to which resort has always been made when there was an absolute necessity for producing some result. . . . No one goes to certain inevitable death except by compulsion. Put the matter the other way. Was there ever yet a criminal who, when sentenced to death and brought out to die, would refuse the offer of a commutation of his sentence for the severest secondary punishment? Surely not. Why is this? It can only be because "All that a man has will he give for his life." In any secondary punishment, however terrible, there is hope; but death is death; its terrors cannot be described more forcibly.

These claims turn out when scrutinized to be much more speculative and doubtful than they at first sight appear.

The first doubt arises when Stephen talks of "certain inevitable death." The Royal Commission, in their *Report*, after quoting the passage from Stephen above, quote figures to show that, in the fifty years from 1900 to 1949, there was in England and Wales one execution for every twelve murders known to the police. In Scotland in the same period there was less than one execution for every twenty-five murders known to the police. Supporters of Stephen's view could supplement their case by advocating more death sentences and fewer reprieves, or by optimistic speculations about better police detection or greater willingness of juries to convict. But the reality of capital punishment as it was in these countries, unmodified by such recommendations and speculations, was not one where the potential murderer faced certain, inevitable death. This may incline us to modify Stephen's estimate of its deterrent effect, unless we buttress his view with the further speculation that a fair number of potential murderers falsely believed that what they would face was certain, inevitable death.

The second doubt concerns Stephen's talk of "the threat of instant death." The reality again does not quite fit this. By the time the police conclude their investigation, the case is brought to trial, and verdict and sentence are followed by appeal, petition for reprieve, and then execution, many months have probably elapsed, and when this time factor is added to the low probability of the murderers being executed, the picture looks very different. For we often have a time bias, being less affected by threats of future catastrophes than by threats of instant ones. The certainty of immediate death is one thing; it is another thing merely to increase one's chances of death in the future. Unless this were so, no one would smoke or take on such high-risk jobs as diving in the North Sea.

There is another doubt when Stephen very plausibly says that virtually all criminals would prefer life imprisonment to execution. The difficulty is over whether this entitles us to conclude that it is therefore a more effective deterrent. For there is the possibility that, compared with the long term of imprisonment that is the alternative, capital punishment is what may appropriately be called an "overkill." It may be that, for those who will be deterred by threat of punishment, a long prison sentence is sufficient deterrent. I am not suggesting that this is so, but simply that it is an open question whether a worse alternative here generates any additional deterrent effect. The answer is *not* intuitively obvious.

Stephen's case rests on the speculative psychological assumptions that capital punishment is not an overkill compared with a prison sentence, and that its additional deterrent effect is not obliterated by time bias, nor by the low probability of execution, nor by a combination of these factors. Or else it must be assumed that, where the additional deterrent effect would be obliterated by the low probability of death, either on its own or in combination with time bias, the potential murderer thinks the probability is higher than it is. Some of these assumptions may be true, but, when they are brought out into the open, it is by no means obvious that the required combination of them can be relied upon.

Supporters of the death penalty also sometimes use what David A. Conway, in his valuable discussion of this issue, calls "the best-bet argument." [7] On this view, since

there is no certainty whether or not capital punishment reduces the number of murders, either decision about it involves gambling with lives. It is suggested that it is better to gamble with the lives of murderers than with the lives of their innocent potential victims. This presupposes the attitude, rejected here, that a murder is a greater evil than the execution of a murderer. But, since this attitude probably has overwhelmingly widespread support, it is worth noting that, even if it is accepted, the best-bet argument is unconvincing. This is because, as Conway has pointed out, it overlooks the fact that we are not choosing between the chance of a murderer dying and the chance of a victim dying. In leaving the death penalty, we are opting for the certainty of the murderer dying that we hope will give us a chance of a potential victim being saved. This would look like a good bet only if we thought an execution substantially preferable to a murder and either the statistical evidence or the intuitive arguments made the effectiveness of the death penalty as a deterrent look reasonably likely.

Since the statistical studies do not give any clear indication that capital punishment makes any difference to the number of murders committed, the only chance of its supporters discharging the heavy burden of justification would be if the intuitive arguments were extremely powerful. We might then feel justified in supposing that other factors distorted the murder rate, masking the substantial deterrent effect of capital punishment. The intuitive arguments, presented as the merest platitudes, turn out to be speculative and unobvious. I conclude that the case for capital punishment as a substantial deterrent fails.

DETERRENCE AND POLITICAL CRIMES BY OPPOSITION GROUPS

It is sometimes suggested that the death penalty may be an effective deterrent in the case of a special class of "political" crimes. The "ordinary" murder (killing one's wife in a moment of rage, shooting a policeman in panic after a robbery, killing someone in a brawl) may not be particularly sensitive to different degrees of punishment. But some killings for political purposes have a degree of preparation and thought that may allow the severity of the penalty to affect the calculation. Two different kinds of killing come to mind here. There are killings as part of a political campaign, ranging from assassination through terrorist activities up to full-scale guerrilla war. And then there are policies carried out by repressive governments, varying from "liquidation" of individual opponents with or without "trial" to policies of wholesale extermination, sometimes, but not always, in wartime.

Let us look first at killings by groups opposed to governments. Would the various sectarian terrorist groups in Ireland stop their killings if those involved were executed? Would independence movements in countries like Algeria or Kenya have confined themselves to nonviolent means if more executions had taken place? Could the Nazis have deterred the French resistance by more executions? Could the Americans have deterred guerrillas war in Vietnam by more executions?

To ask these questions is to realize both the variety of different political situations in which the question of deterrent killing arises, and also to be reminded, if it is necessary, that moral right is not always on the side of the authorities trying to do the deterring. But let us, for the sake of argument, assume a decent government is trying to deal with terrorists or guerrillas whose cause has nothing to be said for it. People have always gone to war knowing they risk their lives, and those prepared to fight in a guerrilla war seem scarcely likely to change their mind because of the marginal extra risk of capital punishment if they are arrested. If the case is to be made, it must apply to lower levels of violence than full-scale guerrilla war.

Given the death penalty's drawbacks, is there any reason to think it would be suffi-

ciently effective in deterring a campaign of terrorist violence to be justified? The evidence is again inconclusive. In many countries there have been terrorist campaigns where the authorities have responded with executions without stopping the campaign. It is always open to someone to say that the level of terrorist activity might have been even higher but for the executions, but it is hard to see why this should be likely. Those who do the shooting or the planting of bombs are not usually the leaders and can be easily replaced by others willing to risk their lives. Danger to life does not deter people from fighting in wars, and a terrorist gunman may be just as committed to his cause as a soldier. And executions create martyrs, which helps the terrorist cause. They may even raise the level of violence by leading to reprisals.

But it may be that a sufficiently ruthless policy of executions would be effective enough to overcome these drawbacks. It has been claimed that the policy of the Irish government in 1922–3 is an instance of this. David R. Bates describes it as follows: [8]

In the turbulent period following the establishment of the Irish Free State, military courts with power to inflict the death penalty were set up to enable the Irregulars (opposing the Treaty) to be crushed. These powers were first used on 17 November 1922, when four young men were arrested in Dublin and, on being found to be armed, were executed. Shortly afterwards the Englishman, Erskine Childers, captured while carrying a revolver, was also executed. On 7 December two Deputies were shot (one fatally) by the Irregulars. The Minister for Defense, with the agreement of the Cabinet, selected four Irregular leaders who had been in prison since the fall of the Four Courts on 29 June. They were wakened, told to prepare themselves, and were executed by firing squad at dawn. During a six-month period, almost twice as many Irregular prisoners were executed as had been executed by the British from 1916 to 1921. At the end of April 1923, the Irregulars sought a cease fire to discuss terms. The Free State Government refused. In May 1924, the Irregulars conceded military defeat.

This is an impressive case, and it may be that this degree of ruthlessness by the government involved fewer deaths than would have taken place during a prolonged terrorist campaign. But against this must be set some doubts. What would have happened if the terrorists had been as ruthless in reprisal as the government, perhaps announcing that for every man executed there would be two murders? Is it clear that after a period of such counter-retaliation it would have been the Irregulars rather than the government who climbed down? Does not any net saving of lives by the government's ruthless policy depend on the terrorists refraining from counter-retaliation, and can this be relied on in other cases? And is there not something dangerous in the precedent set when a government has prisoners executed without their having been convicted and sentenced for a capital offence? And, in this case, is it even clear that the defeat of the Irregulars ended once and for all the violence associated with the issues they were campaigning about? I raise these questions, not to claim that the government policy was clearly wrong, but to show how even a case like this is ambiguous in the weight it lends to the argument for using the death penalty against terrorism.

I do not think that the chance of a net saving of lives will in general outweigh the combination of the general drawbacks of capital punishment combined with the danger of its merely leading to a higher level of violence in a terrorist situation. But this is a matter of judgment rather than proof, and I admit that it *may* be that the opposite view had better results than mine would have had in 1922.

DETERRENCE AND POLITICAL CRIMES BY THE AUTHORITIES

The other category of political crimes that sometimes seems so special as to justify the death penalty is atrocities committed by governments or their agents. The executions of leading Nazis after the Nuremberg trials and the execution of Eichmann after his trial in Jerusalem come to mind. The justification usually advanced for these executions is retributive, and it is hard to imagine any more deserving candidates for the death penalty. But, for those of us who do not consider retribution an acceptable aim of punishment, the question must be whether executing them made their kind of activity less likely to happen again in the future. For, if not, we have no answer to the question asked by Victor Gollancz at the time of the Eichmann trial: why should we think we improve the world by turning six million deaths into six million and one?

The chances of people who design or carry out governmental policies of murder being tried and sentenced must often be very small. Sometimes this happens as the result of revolution or defeat in war, but those in power stand a fairly good chance of being killed under these circumstances anyway, and the additional hazard of capital punishment may not have much deterrent effect. As with "ordinary" murderers, the hope of not being caught reduces the punishment's terrors. Some of those who murdered for Hitler were executed; their opposite numbers under Stalin paid no penalty. The torturers who worked for the Greek colonels were brought to trial, but those now at work in Chile, Brazil, and South Africa have every expectation of not being punished.

When considering isolated cases of governmental murder (perhaps the assassination of a troublesome foreign leader by a country's intelligence agency, or the single killing of a political opponent) there seems no reason to think capital punishment more of a deterrent than it is of "ordinary" nonpolitical murder. If anything, it is likely to be less of a deterrent because of the reduced chance of a murder charge ever being brought. So there seems no case for treating these crimes as other than ordinary murders. But when considering large-scale atrocities, on the scale of those of Hitler or Stalin, or even on the scale of Lyndon Johnson in Vietnam or General Gowon in Nigeria, a version of the best-bet argument comes into play. There are two possible advantages to the death penalty here. One is simply that of totally eliminating the chance of the same mass murderer occupying a position of leadership again. Suppose Hitler had been captured at the end of the Second World War and the question of executing him had arisen. If he had not been executed, it is overwhelmingly probable that he would have spent the rest of his life in Spandau prison, writing his memoirs and giving increasingly senile lectures on world history to visiting journalists. But there would always be the very slight risk of an escape and return to power in the style of Napoleon. This slight risk is removed by execution. The other advantage of the death penalty is the chance, which we have seen to be probably very slight, of deterring repetition of such policies by other leaders.

The best-bet argument in these cases can be used by someone who accepts that the dangers of a defeated leader returning to power are very small and that the chances of execution deterring future leaders from similar policies are also very small. The argument is simply that, where the prevention of such enormous atrocities is in question, even an extremely small probability of prevention is valuable. Consider a case in which numbers and probabilities are parallel, but in which act and omission are reversed. Suppose someone in the hospital can have his life saved only by the making of some organism that has previously been banned. The reason for the ban is that there is a danger, but only a very faint one, of the organism getting out of control. If it does this, the death rate will run into millions. Let us suppose that our intuitive estimate of the unquantifiable risk here is the same as our intuitive estimate of the unquantifiable reduction of risk caused by executing the murdering leader. Those who would rather let the hospital patient die than breach the ban on the dangerous organism must either rely on the acts and omissions doctrine, or else rely on some difference of side effects, if they are not prepared to support executing the murdering politician or official.

Part of the difficulty in interpreting comparisons of this sort arises from the fact that we are dealing with probabilities that cannot be measured. And, even if they could be measured, most of us are unclear what sacrifices are worth making for the reduction of some risk that is already very small. But if we make the highly artificial assumption that the alterations in probability of risk are the same in the medical case as in the execution case, the dilemma remains. Let us suppose that the risk is one that we would not take in the medical case to save a single life. Those of us who do not accept the acts and omissions doctrine must then either find some difference of side effects or else support the execution.

Side effects do go some way towards separating the two cases. For, to breach the ban on producing the organism, even if it does no harm itself, contributes by example to a less strict observance of that ban (and possibly others) in cases in which the risk may be much greater. In the case of the Nazi leaders, such bad side effects as exist follow from execution rather than from saving their lives. These side effects include the contribution made to a climate of opinion where the death penalty seems more acceptable in other contexts, and the precedent that may encourage politicians to have their overthrown rivals, at home or abroad, executed. This last effect could be mitigated by more effort than was made at Nuremberg to remove the impression of the defeated being tried by the victors. It would be possible to set up a court of a genuinely international kind, independent of governmental pressure, to which prosecutions for a large-scale murder could be brought. But the general effect on the public consciousness of having capital punishment as a serious possibility would remain. I am uncertain how to weigh this against the small chance of helping to avert a great evil. For this reason my own views on this question are undecided.

Endnotes

1. H.L.A. Hart, "Prolegomenon to the Principles of Punishment," *Proceedings of the Aristotelian Society,* 1959–60.

2. Quoted in the *Report of the Royal Commission on Capital Punishment,* 1953.

3. H.L.A. Hart, "Murder and the Principles of Punishment," *Northwestern Law Review,* 1958.

4. Arthur Koestler, *Reflections on Hanging,* London, 1956.

5. Albert Pierrepoint, *Executioner: Pierrepoint,* London, 1974.

6. James Fitzjames Stephen, "Capital Punishments," *Fraser's Magazine,* 1864.

7. David A. Conway, "Capital Punishment and Deterrence," *Philosophy and Public Affairs,* 1974.

8. Professor David R. Bates, Letter to *The Times,* 14 October 1975.

Review Questions

1. Why doesn't Glover accept Kant's view of capital punishment?

2. What is the other view that Glover is presupposing?

3. Why doesn't Glover accept the absolutist rejection of capital punishment?

4. Why does Glover think that capital punishment can plausibly be claimed to be a "cruel and unusual punishment?"

5. According to Glover, in what cases can capital

punishment be justified even if it is cruel?

6. State the maximizing policy, and the considerations that Glover introduces to qualify it.

7. According to Glover, how can capital punishment be justified?

8. Glover discusses three arguments (beginning with the statistical argument) that are used to defend capital punishment. What are these arguments, and why doesn't Glover accept them?

9. What is Glover's position on capital punishment for political crimes?

Discussion Questions

1. "Whoever has committed murder must *die.*" Do you agree with this statement? Explain your view.

2. Is the death penalty a cruel and unusual punishment? Explain your answer.

3. Glover concludes that the case for capital punishment as a substantial deterrent fails. Do you agree? Defend your position.

4. Can you think of any cases in which capital punishment would be justified? What are they?

Problem Cases

1. Death for Rape In the case of *Coker* v. *Georgia* (1977), the Supreme Court ruled that the death sentence could not be imposed for rape because such a punishment is grossly disproportionate to the injury caused the victim. Yet the following states allow the death penalty for the crime of rape in certain circumstances: Florida, Georgia, Louisiana, Mississippi, North Carolina, Oklahoma, and Tennessee. Is capital punishment justified for the crime of rape? If so, in what cases?

2. The Case of Troy Gregg (*Gregg* v. *Georgia,* 428 U.S. 153, 1976). Troy Gregg and Floyd Allen were hitchhiking when they were picked up by Fred Simmons and Bob Moore. Simmons and Moore left the car at a rest stop. According to the testimony of Allen, Gregg said that they were going to rob Simmons and Moore. He fired at them when they came back to the car, then shot

each of them in the head, robbed them, and finally drove away with Allen. Gregg first admitted that Allen's account was accurate, but later denied it. Gregg's story was that Simmons had attacked him and that he had killed the two men in self-defense. The jury found Gregg guilty of two counts of murder, and determined that the murders were committed for the purpose of robbery.

Should Gregg be given the death sentence or not? Defend your answer.

3. The Case of Paul Crump (See Ronald Bailey, "Facing Death: A New Life Perhaps Too Late," *Life,* July 27, 1962, pp. 28–29.) In the early 1950s, Paul Crump was convicted of a vicious murder, sentenced to death, and put in an Illinois prison. At his trial he was said to be full of hatred, animalistic and belligerent, and a danger to society. Yet under the influence of Warden Jack Johnson and his prison reforms, Crump became rehabilitated. Even though he had only a ninth-grade education, he took courses in reading and writing. Soon he was reading poetry, fiction, and philosophy, and writing stories, articles, and poems which were published in small magazines. He wrote an autobiographical novel, *Burn, Killer, Burn.* He also began to help his fellow prisoners. He was put in charge of caring for the sick and disabled in the convalescent section of the jail hospital. All this did not happen overnight, but took a period of seven years. At the end of this time, Warden Johnson claimed that Crump was completely rehabilitated, and on August 1, 1962, Illinois Governor Otto Kerner commuted Crump's death sentence to 199 years with the possibility of parole.

Do you think that Governor Kerner made the right decision or not? Explain your answer.

Would it have been morally right to free Crump? Why or why not?

Would it have been morally justifiable to execute Crump despite his rehabilitation? What do you think?

4. The Sacco–Vanzetti Case On April 15, 1920, a paymaster for a shoe company in South Braintree, Massachusetts, and his guard were shot and killed by two men who escaped with over $15,000. Witnesses thought the two men were Italians, and Nicola Sacco and Bartolomeo Vanzetti were arrested. Both men were anarchists and had evaded the army draft. Upon their arrest, they made false statements, and both carried firearms; but neither had a criminal record, nor was there any evidence that they had the money. In July 1921, they were found guilty and sentenced to death. The conduct of the trial by Judge Webster Thayer was criticized, and indeed much of the evidence against them was later discredited. The appeal for a new trial was denied, and Governor Alvan T. Fuller, after postponing the execution, allowed them to be executed on August 22, 1927. They were widely regarded as being innocent, and there were worldwide sympathy demonstrations. The case has been the subject of many books, most of which agree that Vanzetti was innocent, but that Sacco may have been guilty. The gun found on Sacco was tested with modern ballistics equipment in 1961, and these tests seem to show that the gun had been used to kill the guard.

Was it morally right to execute these two men or not? Why or not not?

5. William Alvin Smith (Reported in *Time*, July 19, 1989.) William Alvin Smith robbed and killed the owner of a grocery store in rural Georgia when he was twenty years old. Smith turned himself into the police and signed a confession. A local jury condemned Smith to death in the electric chair, but in July 1989 a federal judge ordered a new sentencing hearing for Smith on the grounds that he lacked the ability to understand the significance of waiving his rights to remain silent and to have an attorney present. Smith is mentally retarded with the mental capacity of a ten-year-old. Does he deserve the death sentence?

It is estimated that about 30 percent of the 2,200 convicts on death row are mentally retarded or mentally impaired. Should they be executed or not?

Suggested Readings

(1) Hugo Adam Bedau, "Capital Punishment," in Tom Regan, ed., *Matters of Life and Death,* 2d ed. (New York: Random House, 1986), pp. 175–212. Bedau is an abolitionist who argues that the appeal to neither retribution nor deterrence justifies the death penalty as opposed to the lesser penalty of life imprisonment. He claims that the verdict of scientists who have studied the issue is that the deterrence achieved by the death penalty is not measurably greater than the deterrence achieved by life imprisonment. As for preventing convicted murderers from killing again, Bedau asserts that there is little evidence that the death sentence does this. In fact, less than one convicted murderer in a hundred commits another murder.

(2) Hugo Adam Bedau, ed., *The Death Penalty in America,* 3d ed. (New York: Oxford University Press, 1982). This excellent anthology provides a number of useful articles on factual data relevant to the death penalty, and articles both for and against.

(3) Walter Berns, *For Capital Punishment* (New York: Basic Books, 1979). Berns develops his retributivist justification of capital punishment.

(4) Albert Camus, *Reflections on the Guillotine: An Essay on Capital Punishment,* trans. Richard Howard (Michigan City, IN: Fridtjof–Karla Press, 1959). Camus expresses his opposition to the death penalty.

(5) Gertrude Ezorsky, ed., *Philosophical Perspectives on Punishment* (Albany, NY: State University of New York Press, 1972). This anthology covers capital punishment and general philosophical questions about punishment.

(6) Robert S. Gerstein, "Capital Punishment—'Cruel and Unusual?': A Retributivist Response," *Ethics* 85, No. 1 (Jan. 1975), pp. 75–79. Gerstein argues that retributivism is not vengence, but rather the view that punishment restores the balance of advantages to a just community. The punishment must be proportionate to the offense, but also it must treat the offender with the respect due a member of a community founded on principles of justice.

(7) Steven Goldberg, "On Capital Punishment," *Ethics* 85 (October 1974), pp. 67–74. Goldberg examines the factual issue of whether or not the death penalty is a uniquely effective deterrent. A revised version entitled "Does Capital Punishment Deter?" appears in Richard A. Wasserstrom, ed., *Today's Moral Problems,* 2d ed. (New York: Macmillan, 1979), pp. 538–551).

(8) Ernest van den Haag, "In Defense of the Death Penalty: A Practical and Moral Analysis," in Hugo Adam Bedau, ed., *The Death Penalty in America,* 3d ed. (New York: Oxford University Press, 1982), pp. 323–333. Van den Haag offers a retentionist argument based on our uncertainty concerning the deterrent effect of the death penalty: Faced with this uncertainty, it is better to risk the lives of the convicted murderers than to risk the lives of innocent people. This "best-bet" argument is rejected by Glover and Bedau.

(9) _____, "The Ultimate Punishment: A Defense," *Harvard Law Review* 99 (1986), pp. 1662–1669. Van den Haag defends his position and responds to critics.

(10) Ernest van den Haag and John P. Conrad, *The Death Penalty: A Debate* (New York: Plenum, 1983). Conrad is against the death penalty and van den Haag is for it; each presents his case and critically responds to the other's arguments.

(11) Sidney Hook, "The Death Sentence," in Hugo Adam Bedau, ed. *The Death Penalty in America,* rev. ed. (Garden City, NY: Doubleday, 1967). Hook supports the retention of the death penalty in two cases: (1) defendants convicted of murder who choose the death sentence rather than life imprisonment, and (2) those who have been sentenced to prison for premeditated murder, and then commit murder again. Since the publication of the original essay, Professor Hook advises that he is now prepared to extend the scope of discretionary death sentences in cases of multiple and aggravated capital crimes.

(12) Immanuel Kant, *The Metaphysical Elements of Justice,* trans. John Ladd (Indianapolis, IN: Bobbs–Merrill, 1965). Kant's views on capital punishment are found on pp. 96–106.

(13) Thomas Long, "Capital Punishment—'Cruel and Unusual'?" *Ethics* 83 (April 1973), pp. 214–223. Long discusses various arguments for the view that capital punishment is cruel and unusual.

(14) Jeffrie G. Murphy, ed., *Punishment and Rehabilitation,* 2d ed. (Belmont, CA: Wadsworth, 1985). This anthology covers various philosophical aspects of punishment including capital punishment.

Chapter 5

Hunger and Welfare

Introduction

The World Health Organization conservatively estimates that there are ten million children under five in the world who are chronically malnourished. If these children survive at all, they will suffer lasting effects—stunted growth and brain damage from lack of protein. In addition, if we calculate from the ratio of children to adults in the world, we get a total of about seventy million chronically malnourished people in the world. This is a very conservative estimate; the Overseas Development Council says there are a billion malnourished people, or about one-fifth of the world's population.

Some of these needy people are in rich countries such as the United States. According to recent reports, the United States has about thirty million people living below the poverty level, including an increasing number of homeless people. According to the Coalition for the Homeless, in 1989 there were three to four million homeless people in the United States. What to do about these poor people is part of the welfare problem. The majority of needy people, however, are in other countries—countries on the subcontinent (India, Pakistan, and Bangladesh) and in poor nations of the Caribbean, Latin America, Southeast Asia, and Africa. What to do about starving people in other countries is the world hunger problem.

Before turning to these two related problems, we should briefly discuss two factual issues: (1) Can some countries provide welfare for their needy citizens, and (2) Is it possible to feed all the hungry people in the world?

The first question is easily answered: No doubt some poor countries cannot provide welfare for their citizens; that is one reason why we have the problem of world hunger. But rich countries like the United States can and do provide welfare for some of their poor citizens, and they could easily enough provide welfare for all their needy citizens if this was considered important, as important, say, as national defense. The main issue about welfare is not whether it is actually possible in rich countries—obviously it is. Rather, the moral question is whether or not citizens in rich countries have a right to welfare, and the governments a corresponding duty to provide it.

The second factual question is not so easy to answer. Is it even possible to feed all the hungry people in the world? To determine the amount of aid actually required to do this, we need to know how many people need food, what their nutritional requirements are, how distribution can be made, what population growth will be, and other facts relevant to the problem. If there are more than a billion people to be fed, as the Overseas Development Council claims, then the task is difficult but not impossible. Statistics on world grain production show that the world's farmers produce enough grain to provide every human being with 3,600 calories a day—more than enough for healthy men or women. Given some international cooperation, everyone could be fed, at least in principle. Furthermore, even more food could be produced by using available land. According to the Worldwatch Institute, less than 60 percent of the world's farmland is under cultivation, and in almost every country where there is widespread hunger and environmental destruction, much of the best agricultural land is used to raise export crops or livestock. These countries could produce more food by growing grain instead of raising livestock and growing export crops.

But if enough food is produced to feed everyone, then why do people starve to death? The standard answer is that the rich nations consume more than their fair share of the food; specifically, the rich nations (e.g., the United States, Russia, European countries, and Japan) consume seventy percent more protein than the rest of the world. They do this by consuming grain indirectly via feedstocks converted into animal protein rather than directly in the form of bread, noodles, rice, and so on. In other words, the problem is the result of unequal food distribution rather than inadequate food production.

The World Hunger Problem Let us assume that it is at least theoretically possible to feed all of the world's hungry people. Is there any moral obligation to do this? Do rich nations have any moral obligation to help prevent people from starving to death in poor countries?

One view of the problem, expressed by Foot (see her article "Euthanasia," cited in the Suggested Readings for Chapter 2) and others who distinguish between killing and letting die, is that we have a negative duty to not kill people, but not a positive duty to prevent people from dying of starvation. To be sure, it is a good thing to give to charity to prevent this, but this is optional—it is not required by morality.

The view that giving aid to needy people is morally optional charity and not a moral duty is attacked by Singer in our first reading for this chapter. He argues that the traditional distinction between duty and charity cannot be drawn, or at least not in the way that Foot and others draw it. He thinks that helping starving people in other countries should not be viewed as charity, but as a morally required duty. According to Singer, this duty can be derived from intuitively obvious moral principles.

At this point, the conservative will object that starving people do not have any right to be fed—they do not have any claim against us such that we must help them. At best, our duty to help them is merely optional; helping others is an act of charity that is morally praiseworthy, but not morally required.

This reply raises interesting questions about rights, and specifically the right to life: How are we to understand the right to life? Does this right imply that we have an obligation to help others or not? On the social contract conception of human rights developed by James P. Sterba in our readings, the right to life should be understood as noninterference with a person's attempts to acquire goods and resources for satisfying basic needs such as food and shelter. According to Sterba, the bearers of this right include not only people in our own society, but also people in other countries and even people in the future. If so, then it seems that we have a welfare obligation to people in our own society, a duty to help people in other countries, and an obligation to preserve the environment for future generations of people.

Garrett Hardin does not agree. He objects to welfare-style transfers from rich nations to poor ones. In his view, nations are lifeboats with limited carrying capacity; they cannot afford to feed poor nations. Besides, aid to poor nations just makes matters worse—the result is a vicious cycle of more overpopulation, more starvation, more aid, and so on until there is ecological disaster. The implication is that we should let people in poor nations die.

The Welfare Problem Even if we agree that rich nations should not help people in poor nations, there remains the question of what to do about the poor people in the rich nations themselves. As I said, it seems undeniable that welfare for these people is theoretically possible in rich countries such as the United States, particularly if welfare programs were considered as important as other matters, such as national defense. But does a rich nation such as the United States have a moral obligation to provide for the basic needs (food, clothing, shelter, and medical care) of its poor citizens?

Trudy Govier examines three different positions on the welfare problem: the individualist position which holds that no one has a right to welfare, the permissive view that everyone in a rich country has a right to welfare, and the more moderate puritan view that the right to welfare in an affluent society is conditional on one's willingness to work. She formulates these positions in terms of rights rather than obligations, but she agrees that rights imply obligations. If a person in a rich country has a legal or moral right to welfare, then the country has a moral obligation to provide welfare benefits. Which position does Govier accept? After a careful evaluation of the three positions with respect to social justice and consequences, Govier concludes that the permissive view is the most acceptable.

These views are not just hypothetical. It seems accurate enough to say that the United States follows a puritan type system of welfare, while Canada (where Govier lives) has a more permissive system. Which system works best? According to statistics cited in the *New York Times* (September 24, 1989), the Canadian system is more efficient when it comes to medical care. The United States spends about 12 percent of its gross national product on health care, but still there are thirty-one million Americans with no health insurance. By contrast, Canada spends less than 9 percent of its GNP to provide health care for all its citizens. On the Canadian system, the government is responsible for practically all health care expenses, paying hospitals at a negotiated rate and doctors according to a binding fee schedule.

In vivid contrast to Govier and Sterba, Hospers strongly believes that only individualism, or libertarianism (as he calls it), is acceptable. As Hospers explains it, libertarianism posits two positive principles: (1) a principle of liberty which says that individuals have a right to act as they choose unless their action interferes with the similar right of others to act as they choose, and (2) a principle of government which says that the only function of the government is to protect human rights. Hospers recognizes three human rights—the right to life, the right to liberty, and the right to property. But these rights are interpreted in terms of noninterference. One's life, liberty, or property should not be taken away, but these rights do not entitle one to anything such as food or shelter. In other words, these rights are **negative rights** rather than **positive rights.**

Peter Singer

Famine, Affluence, and Morality

For biographical information on Singer, see his reading in Chapter 3.

In this reading, Singer begins with two moral principles. The first is that suffering and death from lack of food, shelter, and medical care are bad. He expects us to accept this principle without argument. The second principle is more controversial, and is formulated in a strong and a weak version. The strong version is that if we can prevent something bad from happening "without thereby sacrificing anything of comparable moral importance," then we should do it. The weak version is that we ought to prevent something bad from happening "unless we have to sacrifice something morally significant." It follows from these two moral principles, Singer argues, that it is a moral duty, and not just a matter of charity, for affluent nations to help starving people in countries like East Bengal.

As I write this, in November 1971, people are dying in East Bengal from lack of food, shelter, and medical care. The suffering and death that are occurring there now are not

From Peter Singer, "Famine, Affluence, and Morality," *Philosophy & Public Affairs*, Vol. 1, No. 3 (Spring 1972), pp. 229–243. Copyright © 1972 Princeton University Press. Reprinted with permission of Princeton University Press.

inevitable, not unavoidable in any fatalistic sense of the term. Constant poverty, a cyclone, and a civil war have turned at least nine million people into destitute refugees; nevertheless, it is not beyond the capacity of the richer nations to give enough assistance to reduce any further suffering to very small proportions. The decisions and actions of human beings can prevent this kind of suffering. Unfortunately, human beings have not made the necessary decisions. At the individual level, people have, with very few exceptions, not responded to the situation in any significant way. Generally speaking, people have not given large sums to relief funds; they have not written to their parliamentary representatives demanding increased government assistance; they have not demonstrated in the streets, held symbolic fasts, or done anything else directed toward providing the refugees with the means to satisfy their essential needs. At the government level, no government has given the sort of massive aid that would enable the refugees to survive for more than a few days. Britain, for instance, has given rather more than most countries. It has, to date, given £14,750,000. For comparative purposes, Britain's share of the nonrecoverable development costs of the Anglo–French Concorde project is already in excess of £275,000,000, and on present estimates will reach £440,000,000. The implication is that the British government values a supersonic transport more than thirty times as highly as it values the lives of the nine million refugees. Australia is another country which, on a per capita basis, is well up in the "aid to Bengal" table. Australia's aid, however, amounts to less than one-twelfth of the cost of Sydney's new opera house. The total amount given, from all sources, now stands at about £65,000,000. The estimated cost of keeping the refugees alive for one year is £464,000,000. Most of the refugees have now been in the camps for more than six months. The World Bank has said that India needs a minimum of £300,000,000 in assistance from other countries before the end of the year. It seems obvious that assistance on this scale will not be forthcoming. India will be forced to choose between letting the refugees starve or diverting funds from her own development program, which will mean that more of her own people will starve in the future.[1]

These are the essential facts about the present situation in Bengal. So far as it concerns us here, there is nothing unique about this situation except its magnitude. The Bengal emergency is just the latest and most acute of a series of major emergencies in various parts of the world, arising both from natural and from man-made causes. There are also many parts of the world in which people die from malnutrition and lack of food independent of any special emergency. I take Bengal as my example only because it is the present concern, and because the size of the problem has ensured that it has been given adequate publicity. Neither individuals nor governments can claim to be unaware of what is happening there.

What are the moral implications of a situation like this? In what follows, I shall argue that the way people in relatively affluent countries react to a situation like that in Bengal cannot be justified; indeed, the whole way we look at moral issues—our moral conceptual scheme—needs to be altered, and with it, the way of life that has come to be taken for granted in our society.

In arguing for this conclusion I will not, of course, claim to be morally neutral. I shall, however, try to argue for the moral position that I take, so that anyone who accepts cer-

tain assumptions, to be made explicit, will, I hope, accept my conclusion.

I begin with the assumption that suffering and death from lack of food, shelter, and medical care are bad. I think most people will agree about this, although one may reach the same view by different routes. I shall not argue for this view. People can hold all sorts of eccentric positions, and perhaps from some of them it would not follow that death by starvation is in itself bad. It is difficult, perhaps impossible, to refute such positions, and so for brevity I will henceforth take this assumption as accepted. Those who disagree need read no further.

My next point is this: if it is in our power to prevent something bad from happening, without thereby sacrificing anything of comparable moral importance, we ought, morally, to do it. By "without sacrificing anything of comparable moral importance" I mean without causing anything else comparably bad to happen, or doing something that is wrong in itself, or failing to promote some moral good, comparable in significance to the bad thing that we can prevent. This principle seems almost as uncontroversial as the last one. It requires us only to prevent what is bad, and not to promote what is good, and it requires this of us only when we can do it without sacrificing anything that is, from the moral point of view, comparably important. I could even, as far as the application of my argument to the Bengal emergency is concerned, qualify the point so as to make it: if it is in our power to prevent something very bad from happening, without thereby sacrificing anything morally significant, we ought, morally, to do it. An application of this principle would be as follows: if I am walking past a shallow pond and see a child drowning in it, I ought to wade in and pull the child out. This will mean getting my clothes muddy, but this is insignificant, while the death of the child would presumably be a very bad thing.

The uncontroversial appearance of the principle just stated is deceptive. If it were acted upon, even in its qualified form, our lives, our society, and our world would be fundamentally changed. For the principle takes, firstly, no account of proximity or distance. It makes no moral difference whether the person I can help is a neighbor's child ten yards from me or a Bengali whose name I shall never know, ten thousand miles away. Secondly, the principle makes no distinction between cases in which I am the only person who could possibly do anything and cases in which I am just one among millions in the same position.

I do not think I need to say much in defense of the refusal to take proximity and distance into account. The fact that a person is physically near to us, so that we have personal contact with him, may make it more likely that we *shall* assist him, but this does not show that we *ought* to help him rather than another who happens to be further away. If we accept any principle of impartiality, universalizability, equality, or whatever, we cannot discriminate against someone merely because he is far away from us (or we are far away from him). Admittedly, it is possible that we are in a better position to judge what needs to be done to help a person near to us than one far away, and perhaps also to provide the assistance we judge to be necessary. If this were the case, it would be a reason for helping those near to us first. This may once have been a justification for being more concerned with the poor in one's own town than with famine victims in India. Unfortunately for those who like to keep their moral responsibilities limited, instant communication and swift transportation have changed the situation. From the moral point of view, the development of the world into a "global village" has made an important, though still unrecognized, difference to our moral situation. Expert observers and supervisors, sent out by famine relief organizations or permanently stationed in famine-prone areas, can direct our aid to a refugee in Bengal almost as effectively as we could get it to someone in our own block. There would seem, therefore, to be no possible justification for discriminating on geographical grounds.

There may be a greater need to defend the second implication of my principle—that the fact that there are millions of other people in the same position, in respect to the Bengali refugees, as I am, does not make the situation significantly different from a situation in which I am the only person who can prevent something very bad from occurring. Again, of course, I admit that there is a psychological difference between the cases; one feels less guilty about doing nothing if one can point to others, similarly placed, who have also done nothing. Yet this can make no real difference to our moral obligations.[2] Should I consider that I am less obliged to pull the drowning child out of the pond if on looking around I see other people, no further away than I am, who have also noticed the child but are doing nothing? One has only to ask this question to see the absurdity of the view that numbers lessen obligation. It is a view that is an ideal excuse for inactivity; unfortunately most of the major evils—poverty, overpopulation, pollution—are problems in which everyone is almost equally involved.

The view that numbers do make a difference can be made plausible if stated in this way: if everyone in circumstances like mine gave £5 to the Bengal Relief Fund, there would be enough to provide food, shelter, and medical care for the refugees; there is no reason why I should give more than anyone else in the same circumstances as I am; therefore I have no obligation to give more than £5. Each premise in this argument is true, and the argument looks sound. It may convince us, unless we notice that it is based on a hypothetical premise, although the conclusion is not stated hypothetically. The argument would be sound if the conclusion were: if everyone in circumstances like mine were to give £5, I would have no obligation to give more than £5. If the conclusion were so stated, however, it would be obvious that the argument has no bearing on a situation in which it is not the case that everyone else gives £5. This, of course, is the actual situation. It is more or less certain that not everyone in circumstances like mine will give £5. So there will not be enough to provide the needed food, shelter, and medical care. Therefore by giving more than £5 I will prevent more suffering than I would if I gave just £5.

It might be thought that this argument has an absurd consequence. Since the situation appears to be that very few people are likely to give substantial amounts, it follows that I and everyone else in similar circumstances ought to give as much as possible, that is, at least up to the point at which by giving more one would begin to cause serious suffering for oneself and one's dependents—perhaps even beyond this point to the point of marginal utility, at which by giving more one would cause oneself and one's dependents as much suffering as one would prevent in Bengal. If everyone does this, however, there will be more than can be used for the benefit of the refugees, and some of the sacrifice will have been unnecessary. Thus, if everyone does what he ought to do, the result will not be as good as it would be if everyone did a little less than he ought to do, or if only some do all that they ought to do.

The paradox here arises only if we assume that the actions in question—sending money to the relief funds—are performed more or less simultaneously, and are also unexpected. For if it is to be expected that everyone is going to contribute something, then clearly each is not obliged to give as much as he would have been obliged to had others not been giving too. And if everyone is not acting more or less simultaneously, then those giving later will know how much more is needed, and will have no obligation to give more than is necessary to reach this amount. To say this is not to deny the principle that people in the same circumstances have the same obligations, but to point out that the fact that others have given, or may be expected to give, is a relevant circumstance: those giving after it has become known that many others are giving and those giving before are not in the same circumstances. So the seemingly absurd consequence of the principle I have put forward can occur only if people are in error about the actual circumstances—that is, if they think they are giving when others are not, but in fact they are giving when others are. The result of everyone doing what he really ought to do cannot be worse than the result of everyone doing less than he ought to do, although the result of everyone doing what he reasonably believes he ought to do could be.

If my argument so far has been sound, neither our distance from a preventable evil nor the number of other people who, in respect to that evil, are in the same situation as we are, lessens our obligation to mitigate or prevent that evil. I shall therefore take as established the principle I asserted earlier. As I have already said, I need to assert it only in its qualified form: if it is in our power to prevent something very bad from happening, without thereby sacrificing anything else morally significant, we ought, morally, to do it.

The outcome of this argument is that our traditional moral categories are upset. The traditional distinction between duty and charity cannot be drawn, or at least, not in the place we normally draw it. Giving money to the Bengal Relief Fund is regarded as an act of charity in our society. The bodies which collect money are known as "charities." These organizations see themselves in this way—if you send them a check, you will be thanked for your "generosity." Because giving money is regarded as an act of charity, it is not thought that there is anything wrong with not giving. The charitable man may be praised, but the man who is not charitable is not condemned. People do not feel in any way ashamed or guilty about spending money on new clothes or a new car instead of giving it to famine relief. (Indeed, the alternative does not occur to them.) This way of looking at the matter cannot be justified. When we buy new clothes not to keep ourselves warm but to look "well-dressed" we are not providing for any important need. We would not be sacrificing anything significant if we were to continue to wear our old clothes, and give the money to famine relief. By doing so, we would be preventing another person from starving. It follows from what I have said earlier that we ought to give money away, rather than spend it on clothes which we do not need to keep us warm. To do so is not charitable, or generous. Nor is it the kind of act which philosophers and theologians have called "supererogatory"—an act which it would be good to do, but not wrong not to do. On the contrary, we ought to give the money away, and it is wrong not to do so.

I am not maintaining that there are no acts which are charitable, or that there are no acts which it would be good to do but not wrong not to do. It may be possible to redraw the distinction between duty and charity in some other place. All I am arguing here is that the present way of drawing the distinction, which makes it an act of charity for a man living at the level of affluence which most people in the "developed nations" enjoy to give money to save someone else from starvation, cannot be supported. It is beyond the scope of my argument to consider whether the distinction should be redrawn or abolished altogether. There would be many other possible ways of drawing the distinction—for instance, one might decide that it is good to make other people as happy as possible, but not wrong not to do so.

Despite the limited nature of the revision in our moral conceptual scheme which I am proposing, the revision would, given the extent of both affluence and famine in the world today, have radical implications. These implications may lead to further objections, distinct from those I have already considered. I shall discuss two of these.

One objection to the position I have taken might be simply that it is too drastic a revision of our moral scheme. People do not ordinarily judge in the way I have suggested they should. Most people reserve their moral condemnation for those who violate some moral norm, such as the norm against taking another person's property. They do not condemn those who indulge in luxury instead of giving to famine relief. But given that I did not set out to present a morally neutral description of the way people make moral judgments, the way people do in fact judge has nothing to do with the validity of my conclusion. My conclusion follows from the principle which I advanced earlier, and unless that principle is rejected, or the arguments shown to be unsound, I think the conclusion must stand, however strange it appears.

It might, nevertheless, be interesting to consider why our society, and most other societies, do judge differently from the way I have suggested they should. In a well-known article, J.O. Urmson suggests that the imperatives of duty, which tell us what we must do, as distinct from what it would be good to do but not wrong not to do, function so as to prohibit behavior that is intolerable if men are to live together in society.[3] This may explain the origin and continued existence of the present division between acts of duty and acts of charity. Moral attitudes are shaped by the needs of society, and no doubt society needs people who will observe the rules that make social existence tolerable. From the point of view of a particular society, it is essential to prevent violations of norms against killing, stealing, and so on. It is quite inessential, however, to help people outside one's own society.

If this is an explanation of our common distinction between duty and **supererogation,** however, it is not a justification of it. The moral point of view requires us to look beyond the interests of our own society. Previously, as I have already mentioned, this may hardly have been feasible, but it is quite feasible now. From the moral point of view, the prevention of the starvation of millions of people outside our society must be considered at least as pressing as the upholding of property norms within our society.

It has been argued by some writers, among

them Sidgwick and Urmson, that we need to have a basic moral code which is not too far beyond the capacities of the ordinary man, for otherwise there will be a general breakdown of compliance with the moral code. Crudely stated, this argument suggests that if we tell people that they ought to refrain from murder and give everything they do not really need to famine relief, they will do neither, whereas if we tell them that they ought to refrain from murder and that it is good to give to famine relief but not wrong not to do so, they will at least refrain from murder. The issue here is: Where should we drawn the line between conduct that is required and conduct that is good although not required, so as to get the best possible result? This would seem to be an empirical question, although a very difficult one. One objection to the Sidgwick–Urmson line of argument is that it takes insufficient account of the effect that moral standards can have on the decisions we make. Given a society in which a wealthy man who gives five percent of his income to famine relief is regarded as most generous, it is not surprising that a proposal that we all ought to give away half our incomes will be thought to be absurdly unrealistic. In a society which held that no man should have more than enough while others have less than they need, such a proposal might seem narrow-minded. What it is possible for a man to do and what he is likely to do are both, I think, very greatly influenced by what people around him are doing and expecting him to do. In any case, the possibility that by spreading the idea that we ought to be doing very much more than we are to relieve famine we shall bring about a general breakdown of moral behavior seems remote. If the stakes are an end to widespread starvation, it is worth the risk. Finally, it should be emphasized that these considerations are relevant only to the issue of what we should require from others, and not to what we ourselves ought to do.

The second objection to my attack on the present distinction between duty and charity is one which has from time to time been made against utilitarianism. It follows from some forms of utilitarian theory that we all ought, morally, to be working full time to increase the balance of happiness over misery. The position I have taken here would not lead to this conclusion in all circumstances, for if there were no bad occurrences that we could prevent without sacrificing something of comparable moral importance, my argument would have no application. Given the present conditions in many parts of the world, however, it does follow from my argument that we ought, morally, to be working full time to relieve great suffering of the sort that occurs as a result of famine or other disasters. Of course, mitigating circumstances can be adduced—for instance, that if we wear ourselves out through overwork, we shall be less effective than we would otherwise have been. Nevertheless, when all considerations of this sort have been taken into account, the conclusion remains: we ought to be preventing as much suffering as we can without sacrificing something else of comparable moral importance. This conclusion is one which we may be reluctant to face. I cannot see, though, why it should be regarded as a criticism of the position for which I have argued, rather than a criticism of our ordinary standards of behavior. Since most people are self-interested to some degree, very few of us are likely to do everything that we ought to do. It would, however, hardly be honest to take this as evidence that it is not the case that we ought to do it.

It may still be thought that my conclusions are so wildly out of line with what everyone else thinks and has always thought that there must be something wrong with the argument somewhere. In order to show that my conclusions, while certainly contrary to contemporary Western moral standards, would not have seemed so extraordinary at other times and in other places, I would like to quote a passage from a writer not normally thought of as a way-out radical, **Thomas Aquinas.**

Now, according to the natural order instituted by divine providence, material goods are provided for the satisfaction of human needs. Therefore the division and appropriation of property, which proceeds from human law, must not hinder the satisfaction of man's necessity from such goods. Equally, whatever a man has in superabundance is owed, of natural right, to the poor for their sustenance. So Ambrosius says, and it is also to be found in the Decretum Gratiani: *"The bread which you withhold belongs to the hungry; the clothing you shut away, to the naked; and the money you bury in the earth is the redemption and freedom of the penniless."* [4]

I now want to consider a number of points, more practical than philosophical, which are relevant to the application of the moral conclusion we have reached. These points challenge not the idea that we ought to be doing all we can to prevent starvation, but the idea that giving away a great deal of money is the best means to this end.

It is sometimes said that overseas aid should be a government responsibility, and that therefore one ought not to give to privately run charities. Giving privately, it is said, allows the government and the noncontributing members of society to escape their responsibilities.

This argument seems to assume that the more people there are who give to privately organized famine relief funds, the less likely it is that the government will take over full responsibility for such aid. This assumption is unsupported, and does not strike me as at all plausible. The opposite view—that if no one gives voluntarily, a government will assume that its citizens are uninterested in famine relief and would not wish to be forced into giving aid—seems more plausible. In any case, unless there were a definite probability that by refusing to give one would be helping to bring about massive government assistance, people who do refuse to make voluntary contributions are refusing to prevent a certain amount of suffering without being able to point to any tangible beneficial consequence of their refusal. So the onus of showing how their refusal will bring about government action is on those who refuse to give.

I do not, of course, want to dispute the contention that governments of affluent nations should be giving many times the amount of genuine, no-strings-attached aid that they are giving now. I agree, too, that giving privately is not enough, and that we ought to be campaigning actively for entirely new standards for both public and private contributions to famine relief. Indeed, I would sympathize with someone who thought that campaigning was more important than giving oneself, although I doubt whether preaching what one does not practice would be very effective. Unfortunately, for many people the idea that "it's the government's responsibility" is a reason for not giving which does not appear to entail any political action either.

Another, more serious reason for not giving to famine relief funds is that until there is effective population control, relieving famine merely postpones starvation. If we save the Bengal refugees now, others, perhaps the children of these refugees, will face starvation in a few years' time. In support of this, one may cite the now well-known facts about the population explosion and the relatively limited scope for expanded production.

This point, like the previous one, is an argument against relieving suffering that is happening now, because of a belief about what might happen in the future; it is unlike the previous point in that very good evidence can be adduced in support of this belief about the future. I will not go into the evidence here. I accept that the earth cannot support indefinitely a population rising at the present rate. This certainly poses a problem for anyone who thinks it important to prevent famine. Again, however, one could accept the argument without drawing the conclusion that it absolves one from any obligation to do anything to prevent famine. The conclusion that should be drawn is that the best means of preventing famine, in the long run, is population control. It would then follow from the position reached earlier that one ought to be doing all one can to promote population control (unless one held that all forms of population control were wrong in themselves, or would have significantly bad consequences).

Since there are organizations working specifically for population control, one would then support them rather than more orthodox methods of preventing famine.

A third point raised by the conclusion reached earlier relates to the question of just how much we all ought to be giving away. One possibility, which has already been mentioned, is that we ought to give until we reach the level of marginal utility—that is, the level at which, by giving more, I would cause as much suffering to myself or my dependents as I would relieve by my gift. This would mean, of course, that one would reduce oneself to very near the material circumstances of a Bengali refugee. It will be recalled that earlier I put forward both a strong and a moderate version of the principle of preventing bad occurrences. The strong version, which required us to prevent bad things from happening unless in doing so we would be sacrificing something of comparable moral significance, does seem to require reducing ourselves to the level of marginal utility. I should also say that the strong version seems to me to be the correct one. I proposed the more moderate version—that we should prevent bad occurrences unless, to do so, we had to sacrifice something morally significant—only in order to show that even on this surely undeniable principle a great change in our way of life is required. On the more moderate principle, it may not follow that we ought to reduce ourselves to the level of marginal utility, for one might hold that to reduce oneself and one's family to this level is to cause something significantly bad to happen. Whether this is so I shall not discuss, since, as I have said, I can see no good reason for holding the moderate version of the principle rather than the strong version. Even if we accepted the principle only in its moderate form, however, it should be clear that we would have to give away enough to ensure that the consumer society, dependent as it is on people spending on trivia rather than giving to famine relief, would slow down and perhaps disappear entirely. There are several reasons why this would be desirable in itself. The value and necessity of economic growth are now being questioned not only by conservationists, but by economists as well.[5] There is no doubt, too, that the consumer society has had a distorting effect on the goals and purposes of its members. Yet looking at the matter purely from the point of view of overseas aid, there must be a limit to the extent to which we should deliberately slow down our economy; for it might be the case that if we gave away, say, forty percent of our Gross National Product, we would slow down the economy so much that in absolute terms we would be giving less than if we gave twenty-five percent of the much larger GNP than we would have if we limited our contribution to this smaller percentage.

I mention this only as an indication of the sort of factor that one would have to take into account in working out an ideal. Since Western societies generally consider one percent of the GNP an acceptable level for overseas aid, the matter is entirely academic. Nor does it affect the question of how much an individual should give in a society in which very few are giving substantial amounts.

It is sometimes said, though less often now than it used to be, that philosophers have no special role to play in public affairs, since most public issues depend primarily on an assessment of facts. On questions of fact, it is said, philosophers as such have no special expertise, and so it has been possible to engage in philosophy without committing oneself to any position on major public issues. No doubt there are some issues of social policy and foreign policy about which it can truly be said that a really expert assessment of the facts is required before taking sides or acting, but the issue of famine is surely not one of these. The facts about the existence of suffering are beyond dispute. Nor, I think, is it disputed that we can do something about it, either through orthodox methods of famine relief or through population control or both. This is therefore an issue on which philosophers are competent to take a position. The issue is one which faces everyone who has more money than he needs to support himself and his dependents, or who is in a position to take some sort of political action. These categories must include practically every teacher and student of philosophy in the universities of the Western world. If philosophy is to deal with matters that are relevant to both teachers and students, this is an issue that philosophers should discuss.

Discussion, though, is not enough. What is the point of relating philosophy to public (and personal) affairs if we do not take our conclusions seriously? In this instance, taking our conclusion seriously means acting upon it. The philosopher will not find it any easier than anyone else to alter his attitudes and way of life to the extent that, if I am right, is involved in doing everything that we ought to be doing. At the very least, though, one can make a start. The philosopher who does so will have to sacrifice some of the benefits of the consumer society, but he can find compensation in the satisfaction of a way of life in which theory and practice, if not yet in harmony, are at least coming together.

Endnotes

1. There was also a third possibility: that India would go to war to enable the refugees to return to their lands. Since I wrote this paper, India has taken this way out. The situation is no longer that described above, but this does not affect my argument, as the next paragraph indicates.

2. In view of the special sense philosophers often give to the term, I should say that I use "obligation" simply as the abstract noun derived from "ought," so that "I have an obligation to" means no more, and no less, than "I ought to." This usage is in accordance with the definition of "ought" given by the *Shorter Oxford English Dictionary:* "the general verb to express duty or obligation." I do not think any issue of substance hangs on the way the term is used; sentences in which I use "obligation" could all be rewritten, although somewhat clumsily, as sentences in which a clause containing "ought" replaces the term "obligation."

3. J.O. Urmson, "Saints and Heroes," in *Essays in Moral Philosophy*, ed. Abraham I. Melden (Seattle and London, 1958), p. 214. For a related but significantly different view see also Henry Sidgwick, *The Methods of Ethics*, 7th edn. (London, 1907), pp. 220–221, 492–493.

4. *Summa Theologica*, II–II, Question 66, Article 7, in *Aquinas, Selected Political Writings*, ed. A.P. d'Entreves, trans. J.G. Dawson (Oxford, 1948), p. 171.

5. See, for instance, John Kenneth Galbraith, *The New Industrial State* (Boston, 1967); and E.J. Mishan, *The Costs of Economic Growth* (London, 1967).

Review Questions

1. According to Singer, what are the moral implications of the situation that occurred in East Bengal?

2. What is Singer's first moral principle?

3. What is the second principle? Distinguish between the two different versions of this principle.

4. Explain Singer's view of the distinction between duty and charity.

5. What is the Sidgwick–Urmson line of argument? How does Singer respond to it?

6. What is the criticism of utilitarianism? How does Singer reply?

7. What are Singer's conclusions?

Discussion Questions

1. Towards the end of his essay, Singer says that it would be desirable in itself if the consumer society would disappear. Do you agree? Why or why not?

2. What does the phrase morally significant in the weak version of the second principle mean? See if you can give a clear definition of this crucial phrase.

3. Singer grants that "until there is effective population control, relieving famine merely postpones starvation." Is this a good reason for not giving aid to countries that refuse to adopt any measures to control population? What is your view?

4. Singer attacks the traditional distinction between duty and charity. Is there any way to save this distinction? How?

5. Is Singer a utilitarian? Why or why not?

Garrett Hardin
Living on a Lifeboat

Garrett Hardin is Professor of Biology at the University of California at Santa Barbara. He is the author of many books, including The Limits of Altruism: An Ecologist's View of Survival *(1977).*

Hardin uses the metaphor of a lifeboat to argue that rich nations such as the United States do not have a moral obligation to help poor nations. In fact, he claims, aid in the form of food makes matters worse; it results in more population growth, and eventually the ruin of natural resources such as oceans.

Susanne Langer (1942) has shown that it is probably impossible to approach an unsolved problem save through the door of metaphor. Later, attempting to meet the demands of rigor, we may achieve some success in cleansing theory of metaphor, though our success is limited if we are unable to avoid using common language, which is shot through and through with fossil metaphors. (I count no less than five in the preceding two sentences.)

Since metaphorical thinking is inescapable it is pointless merely to weep about our human limitations. We must learn to live with them, to understand them, and to control them. "All of us," said George Eliot in *Middlemarch*, "get our thoughts entangled in metaphors, and act fatally on the strength of them." To avoid unconscious suicide we are well advised to pit one metaphor against another. From the interplay of competitive metaphors, thoroughly developed, we may come closer to metaphor-free solutions to our problems.

No generation has viewed the problem of the survival of the human species as seriously

as we have. Inevitably, we have entered this world of concern through the door of metaphor. Environmentalists have emphasized the image of the earth as a spaceship—Spaceship Earth. Kenneth Boulding (1966) is the principal architect of this metaphor. It is time, he says, that we replace the wasteful "cowboy economy" of the past with the frugal "spaceship economy" required for continued survival in the limited world we now see ours to be. The metaphor is notably useful in justifying pollution-control measures.

Unfortunately, the image of a spaceship is also used to promote measures that are suicidal. One of these is a generous immigration policy, which is only a particular instance of a class of policies that are in error because they lead to the tragedy of the commons (Hardin 1968). These suicidal policies are attractive because they mesh with what we unthinkingly take to be the ideals of "the best people." What is missing in the idealistic view is an insistence that rights and responsibilities must go together. The "generous" attitude of all too many people results in asserting inalienable rights while ignoring or denying matching responsibilities.

For the metaphor of a spaceship to be correct the aggregate of people on board would have to be under unitary sovereign control (Ophuls 1974). A true ship always has a captain. It is conceivable that a ship could be run by a committee. But it could not possibly survive if its course were determined by bickering tribes that claimed rights without responsibilities.

What about Spaceship Earth? It certainly has no captain, and no executive committee. The United Nations is a toothless tiger, because the signatories of its charter wanted it that way. The spaceship metaphor is used only to justify spaceship demands on common resources without acknowledging corresponding spaceship responsibilities.

An understandable fear of decisive action leads people to embrace "incrementalism"—moving toward reform by tiny stages. As we shall see, this strategy is counterproductive in the area discussed here if it means accepting rights before responsibilities. Where human survival is at stake, the acceptance of responsibilities is a precondition to the acceptance of rights, if the two cannot be introduced simultaneously.

LIFEBOAT ETHICS

Before taking up certain substantive issues let us look at an alternative metaphor, that of a lifeboat. In developing some relevant examples the following numerical values are assumed. Approximately two-thirds of the world is desperately poor, and only one-third is comparatively rich. The people in poor countries have an average per capita GNP (Gross National Product) of about $200 per year; the rich, of about $3,000. (For the United States it is nearly $5,000 per year.) Metaphorically, each rich nation amounts to a lifeboat full of comparatively rich people. The poor of the world are in other, much more crowded lifeboats. Continuously, so to speak, the poor fall out of their lifeboats and swim for a while in the water outside, hoping to be admitted to a rich lifeboat, or in some other way to benefit from the "goodies" on board. What should the passengers on a rich lifeboat do? This is the central problem of "the ethics of a lifeboat."

First we must acknowledge that each lifeboat is effectively limited in capacity. The land of every nation has a limited carrying capacity. The exact limit is a matter for argument, but the energy crunch is convincing more people every day that we have already exceeded the carrying capacity of the land. We have been living on "capital"—stored petroleum and coal—and soon we must live on income alone.

Let us look at only one lifeboat—ours. The ethical problem is the same for all, and is as follows. Here we sit, say fifty people in a lifeboat. To be generous, let us assume our boat has a capacity of ten more, making sixty. (This, however, is to violate the engineering principle of the "safety factor." A new plant disease or a bad change in the weather may decimate our population if we don't preserve some excess capacity as a safety factor.)

The fifty of us in the lifeboat see 100 others swimming in the water outside, asking for admission to the boat, or for handouts. How shall we respond to their calls? There are several possibilities.

One. We may be tempted to try to live by the Christian ideal of being "our brother's keeper," or by the Marxian ideal (Marx 1875) of "from each according to his abilities, to each according to his needs." Since the needs of all are the same, we take all the needy into our boat, making a total of 150 in a boat with a capacity of sixty. The boat is swamped, and everyone drowns. Complete justice, complete catastrophe.

Two. Since the boat has an unused excess capacity of ten, we admit just ten more to it. This has the disadvantage of getting rid of the safety factor, for which action we will sooner or later pay dearly. Moreover, *which* ten do we let in? "First come, first served?" The best ten? The neediest ten? How do we *discriminate?* And what do we say to the ninety who are excluded?

Three. Admit no more to the boat and preserve the small safety factor. Survival of the people in the lifeboat is then possible (though we shall have to be on our guard against boarding parties).

The last solution is abhorrent to many people. It is unjust, they say. Let us grant that it is.

"I feel guilty about my good luck," say some. The reply to this is simple: *Get out and yield your place to others.* Such a selfless action might satisfy the conscience of those who are addicted to guilt but it would not change the ethics of the lifeboat. The needy person to whom a guilt-addict yields his place will not himself feel guilty about his sudden good luck. (If he did he would not climb aboard.) The net result of conscience-stricken people relinquishing their unjustly held positions is the elimination of their kind of conscience from the lifeboat. The lifeboat, as it were, purifies itself of guilt. The ethics of the lifeboat persist, unchanged by such momentary aberrations.

This then is the basic metaphor within which we must work out our solutions. Let us enrich the image step by step with substantive additions from the real world.

REPRODUCTION

The harsh characteristics of lifeboat ethics are heightened by reproduction, particularly by reproductive differences. The people inside the lifeboats of the wealthy nations are doubling in numbers every eighty-seven years; those outside are doubling every thirty-five years, on the average. And the relative difference in prosperity is becoming greater.

Let us, for a while, think primarily of the U.S. lifeboat. As of 1973 the United States had a population of 210 million people, who were increasing by 0.8% per year, that is, doubling in number every eighty-seven years.

Although the citizens of rich nations are outnumbered two to one by the poor, let us imagine an equal number of poor people outside our lifeboat—a mere 210 million poor people reproducing at a quite different rate. If we imagine these to be the combined populations of Colombia, Venezuela, Ecuador, Morocco, Thailand, Pakistan, and the Philippines, the average rate of increase of the people "outside" is 3.3% per year. The doubling time of this population is twenty-one years.

Suppose that all these countries, and the United States, agreed to live by the Marxian ideal, "to each according to his needs," the ideal of most Christians as well. Needs, of course, are determined by population size, which is affected by reproduction. Every nation regards its rate of reproduction as a sovereign right. If our lifeboat were big enough in the beginning it might be possible to live *for a while* by Christian-Marxian ideals. *Might.*

Initially, in the model given, the ratio of non-Americans to Americans would be one to one. But consider what the ratio would be eighty-seven years later. By this time Americans would have doubled to a population of

420 million. The other group (doubling every twenty-one years) would now have swollen to 3,540 million. Each American would have more than eight people to share with. How could the lifeboat possibly keep afloat?

All this involves extrapolation of current trends into the future, and is consequently suspect. Trends may change. Granted: but the change will not necessarily be favorable. If—as seems likely—the rate of population increase falls faster in the ethnic group presently inside the lifeboat than it does among those now outside, the future will turn out to be even worse than mathematics predicts, and sharing will be even more suicidal.

RUIN IN THE COMMONS

The fundamental error of the sharing ethics is that it leads to the tragedy of the commons. Under a system of private property the man (or group of men) who own property recognize their responsibility to care for it, for if they don't they will eventually suffer. A farmer, for instance, if he is intelligent, will allow no more cattle in a pasture than its carrying capacity justifies. If he overloads the pasture, weeds take over, erosion sets in, and the owner loses in the long run.

But if a pasture is run as a commons open to all, the right of each to use it is not matched by an operational responsibility to take care of it. It is no use asking independent herdsmen in a commons to act responsibly, for they dare not. The considerate herdsman who refrains from overloading the commons suffers more than a selfish one who says his needs are greater. (As Leo Durocher says, "Nice guys finish last.") Christian-Marxian idealism is counterproductive. That it *sounds* nice is no excuse. With distribution systems, as with individual morality, good intentions are no substitute for good performance.

A social system is stable only if it is insensitive to errors. To the Christian-Marxian idealist a selfish person is a sort of "error." Prosperity in the system of the commons cannot survive errors. If *everyone* would only restrain himself, all would be well; but it takes *only one less than everyone* to ruin a system of voluntary restraint. In a crowded world of less than perfect human beings—and we will never know any other—mutual ruin is inevitable in the commons. This is the core of the tragedy of the commons.

One of the major tasks of education today is to create such an awareness of the dangers of the commons that people will be able to recognize its many varieties, however disguised. There is pollution of the air and water because these media are treated as commons. Further growth of population and growth in the per capita conversion of natural resources into pollutants require that the system of the commons be modified or abandoned in the disposal of "externalities."

The fish populations of the oceans are exploited as commons, and ruin lies ahead. No technological invention can prevent this fate; in fact, all improvements in the art of fishing merely hasten the day of complete ruin. Only the replacement of the system of the commons with a responsible system can save oceanic fisheries.

The management of western range lands, though nominally rational, is in fact (under the steady pressure of cattle ranchers) often merely a government-sanctioned system of the commons, drifting toward ultimate ruin for both the rangelands and the residual enterprisers.

WORLD FOOD BANKS

In the international arena we have recently heard a proposal to create a new commons, namely an international depository of food reserves to which nations will contribute according to their abilities, and from which nations may draw according to their needs. Nobel laureate Norman Borlaug has lent the prestige of his name to this proposal.

A world food bank appeals powerfully to our humanitarian impulses. We remember John Donne's celebrated line, "Any man's death diminishes me." But before we rush out to see for whom the bell tolls let us rec-

ognize where the greatest political push for international granaries comes from, lest we be disillusioned later. Our experience with Public Law 480 clearly reveals the answer. This was the law that moved billions of dollars worth of U.S. grain to food-short, population-long countries during the past two decades. When P.L. 480 first came into being, a headline in the business magazine *Forbes* (Paddock and Paddock 1970) revealed the power behind it: "Feeding the World's Hungry Millions: How it will mean billions for U.S. business."

And indeed it did. In the years 1960 to 1970 a total of $7.9 billion was spent on the "Food for Peace" program, as P.L. 480 was called. During the years 1948 to 1970 an additional $49.9 billion were extracted from American taxpayers to pay for other economic aid programs, some of which went for food and food-producing machinery. (This figure does *not* include military aid.) That P.L. 480 was a giveaway program was concealed. Recipient countries went through the motions of paying for P.L. 480 food—with IOUs. In December 1973 the charade was brought to an end as far as India was concerned when the United States "forgave" India's $3.2 billion debt (Anonymous 1974). Public announcement of the cancellation of the debt was delayed for two months; one wonders why.

"Famine—1974!" (Paddock and Paddock 1970) is one of the few publications that points out the commercial roots of this humanitarian attempt. Though all U.S. taxpayers lost by P.L. 480, special interest groups gained handsomely. Farmers benefited because they were not asked to contribute the grain—it was bought from them by the taxpayers. Besides the direct benefit there was the indirect effect of increasing demand and thus raising prices of farm products generally. The manufacturers of farm machinery, fertilizers, and pesticides benefited by the farmers' extra efforts to grow more food. Grain elevators profited from storing the grain for varying lengths of time. Railroads made money hauling it to port, and shipping lines by carrying it overseas. Moreover, once the machinery for P.L. 480 was established an immense bureaucracy had a vested interest in its continuance regardless of its merits.

Very little was ever heard of these selfish interests when P.L. 480 was defended in public. The emphasis was always on its humanitarian effects. The combination of multiple and relatively silent selfish interests with highly vocal humanitarian apologists constitutes a powerful lobby for extracting money from taxpayers. Foreign aid has become a habit that can apparently survive in the absence of any known justification. A news commentator in a weekly magazine (Lansner 1974), after exhaustively going over all the conventional arguments for foreign aid—self-interest, social justice, political advantage, and charity—and concluding that none of the known arguments really held water, concluded: "So the search continues for some logically compelling reasons for giving aid...." In other words, *Act now, justify later*—if ever. (Apparently a quarter of a century is too short a time to find the justification for expending several billion dollars yearly).

The search for a rational justification can be short-circuited by interjecting the word "emergency." Borlaug uses this word. We need to look sharply at it. What is an "emergency?" It is surely something like an accident, which is correctly defined as *an event that is certain to happen, though with a low frequency* (Hardin 1972a). A well-run organization prepares for everything that is certain, including accidents and emergencies. It budgets for them. It saves for them. It expects them—and mature decision-makers do not waste time complaining about accidents when they occur.

What happens if some organizations budget for emergencies and others do not? If each organization is solely responsible for its own well-being, poorly managed ones will suffer. But they should be able to learn from experience. They have a chance to mend their ways and learn to budget for infrequent

but certain emergencies. The weather, for instance, always varies and periodic crop failures are certain. A wise and competent government saves out of the production of the good years in anticipation of bad years that are sure to come. This is not a new idea. The Bible tells us that Joseph taught this policy to Pharaoh in Egypt more than 2,000 years ago. Yet it is literally true that the vast majority of the governments of the world today have no such policy. They lack either the wisdom or the competence, or both. Far more difficult than the transfer of wealth from one country to another is the transfer of wisdom between sovereign powers or between generations.

"But it isn't their fault! How can we blame the poor people who are caught in an emergency? Why must we punish them?" The concepts of blame and punishment are irrelevant. The question is, what are the operational consequences of establishing a world food bank? If it is open to every country every time a need develops, slovenly rulers will not be motivated to take Joseph's advice. Why should they? Others will bail them out whenever they are in trouble.

Some countries will make deposits in the world food bank and others will withdraw from it; there will be almost no overlap. Calling such a depository-transfer unit a "bank" is stretching the metaphor of *bank* beyond its elastic limits. The proposers, of course, never call attention to the metaphorical nature of the word they use.

THE RATCHET EFFECT

An "international food bank" is really, then, not a true bank but a disguised one-way transfer device for moving wealth from rich countries to poor. In the absence of such a bank, in a world inhabited by individually responsible sovereign nations, the population of each nation would repeatedly go through a cycle of the sort shown in Exhibit A. P_2 is greater than P_1, either in absolute numbers or because a deterioration of the food supply has removed the safety factor and produced a dangerously low ratio of resources to population. P_2 may be said to represent a state of overpopulation, which becomes obvious upon the appearance of an "accident," e.g., a crop failure. If the "emergency" is not met by outside help, the population drops back to the "normal" level—the "carrying capacity" of the environment—or even below. In the absence of population control by a sovereign, sooner or later the population grows to P_2 again and the cycle repeats. The long-term population curve (Hardin 1966) is an irregularly fluctuating one, equilibrating more or less about the carrying capacity.

A demographic cycle of this sort obviously involves great suffering in the restrictive phase, but such a cycle is normal to any independent country with inadequate population control. The third century theologian Tertullian (Hardin 1969a) expressed what must have been the recognition of many wise men when he wrote: "The scourges of pestilence, famine, wars, and earthquakes have come to be regarded as a blessing to overcrowded nations, since they serve to prune away the luxuriant growth of the human race."

Only under a strong and farsighted sovereign—which theoretically could be the people themselves, democratically organized—can a population equilibrate at some set point below the carrying capacity, thus avoiding the pains normally caused by periodic and unavoidable disasters. For this happy state to be achieved it is necessary that those in power be able to contemplate with equanimity the "waste" of surplus food in times of bountiful harvests. It is essential that those in power resist the temptation to convert extra food into extra babies. On the public relations level it is necessary that the phrase "surplus food" be replaced by "safety factor."

But wise sovereigns seem not to exist in the poor world today. The most anguishing problems are created by poor countries that are governed by rulers insufficiently wise and powerful. If such countries can draw on a world food bank in times of "emergency," the population *cycle* of Exhibit A will be replaced by the population *escalator* of Exhibit

B. The input of food from a food bank acts as the pawl of a ratchet, preventing the population from retracting its steps to a lower level. Reproduction pushes the population upward, inputs from the world bank prevent its moving downward. Population size escalates, as does the absolute magnitude of "accidents" and "emergencies." The process is brought to an end only by the total collapse of the whole system, producing a catastrophe of scarcely imaginable proportions.

Such are the implications of the well-meant sharing of food in a world of irresponsible reproduction.

I think we need a new word for systems like this. The adjective "melioristic" is applied to systems that produce continual improvement; the English word is derived from the Latin *meliorare,* to become or make better. Parallel with this it would be useful to bring in the word *pejoristic* (from the Latin *pejorare,* to become or make worse). This word can be applied to those systems that by their very nature, can be relied upon to make matters worse. A world food bank coupled with sovereign state irresponsibility in reproduction is an example of a pejoristic system.

This pejoristic system creates an unacknowledged commons. People have more

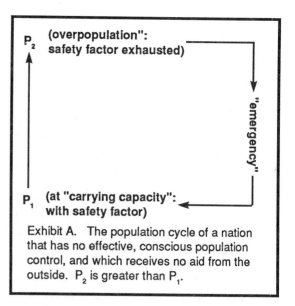

Exhibit A. The population cycle of a nation that has no effective, conscious population control, and which receives no aid from the outside. P_2 is greater than P_1.

motivation to draw from than to add to the common store. The license to make such withdrawals diminishes whatever motivation poor countries might otherwise have to control their populations. Under the guidance of this ratchet, wealth can be steadily moved in one direction only, from the slowly-breeding rich to the rapidly-breeding poor, the process finally coming to a halt only when all countries are equally and miserably poor.

All this is terribly obvious once we are acutely aware of the pervasiveness and danger of the commons. But many people still lack this awareness and the euphoria of the "benign demographic transition" (Hardin 1973) interferes with the realistic appraisal of pejoristic mechanisms. As concerns public policy, the deductions drawn from the benign demographic transition are these:

1. If the per capita GNP rises the birth rate will fall; hence, the rate of population increase will fall, ultimately producing ZPG (Zero Population Growth).

2. The long-term trend all over the world (including the poor countries) is of a rising per capita GNP (for which no limit is seen).

3. Therefore, all political interference in population matters is unnecessary; all we need to do is foster economic "development"—*note the metaphor*—and population problems will solve themselves.

Those who believe in the benign demographic transition dismiss the pejoristic mechanism of Exhibit B in the belief that each input of food from the world outside fosters development within a poor country thus resulting in a drop in the rate of population increase. Foreign aid has proceeded on this assumption for more than two decades. Unfortunately it has produced no indubitable instance of the asserted effect. It has, however, produced a library of excuses. The air is filled with plaintive calls for more massive foreign aid appropriations so that the hypothetical melioristic

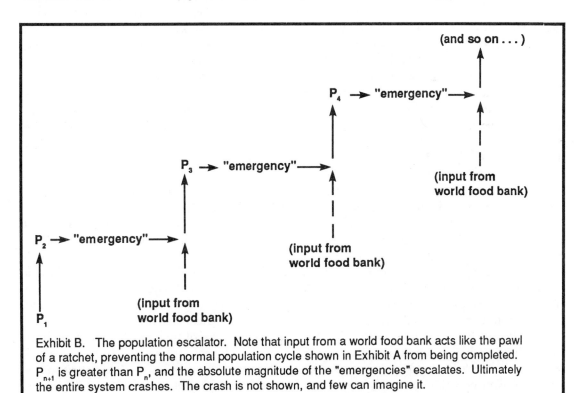

Exhibit B. The population escalator. Note that input from a world food bank acts like the pawl of a ratchet, preventing the normal population cycle shown in Exhibit A from being completed. P_{n+1} is greater than P_n, and the absolute magnitude of the "emergencies" escalates. Ultimately the entire system crashes. The crash is not shown, and few can imagine it.

process can get started.

The doctrine of demographic laissez-faire implicit in the hypothesis of the benign demographic transition is immensely attractive. Unfortunately there is more evidence against the melioristic system than there is for it (Davis 1963). On the historical side there are many counter-examples. The rise in per capita GNP in France and Ireland during the past century has been accompanied by a rise in population growth. In the twenty years following the Second World War the same positive correlation was noted almost everywhere in the world. Never in world history before 1950 did the worldwide population growth reach one percent per annum. Now the average population growth is over two percent and shows no signs of slackening.

On the theoretical side, the denial of the pejoristic scheme of Exhibit B probably springs from the hidden acceptance of the "cowboy economy" that Boulding castigated. Those who recognize the limitations of a spaceship, if they are unable to achieve population control at a safe and comfortable level, accept the necessity of the corrective feedback of the population cycle shown in Exhibit A. No one who knew in his bones that he was living on a true spaceship would countenance political support of the population escalator shown in Exhibit B.

ECO–DESTRUCTION VIA THE GREEN REVOLUTION

The demoralizing effect of charity on the recipient has long been known. "Give a man a fish and he will eat for a day; teach him how to fish and he will eat for the rest of his days." So runs an ancient Chinese proverb. Acting on this advice the Rockefeller and Ford Foundations have financed a multipronged program for improving agriculture in the hungry nations. The result, known as the "Green Revolution," has been quite remarkable. "Miracle wheat" and "miracle rice" are splendid technological achievements in the realm of plant genetics.

Whether or not the Green Revolution can increase food production is doubtful (Harris 1972, Paddock 1970, Wilkes 1972), but in any event not particularly important. What is missing in this great and well-meaning humanitarian effort is a firm grasp of fundamentals. Considering the importance of the Rockefeller Foundation in this effort it is ironic that the late Alan Gregg, a much-respected vice-president of the Foundation, strongly expressed his doubts of the wisdom of all attempts to increase food production some two decades ago. (This was before Borlaug's work—supported by Rockefeller—had resulted in the development of "miracle wheat.") Gregg (1955) likened the growth and spreading of humanity over the surface of the earth to the metastasis of cancer in the human body, wryly remarking that "Cancerous growths demand food; but, as far as I know, they have never been cured by getting it."

"Man does not live by bread alone"—the scriptural statement has a rich meaning even in the material realm. Every human being born constitutes a draft on all aspects of the environment—food, air, water, unspoiled scenery, occasional and optional solitude, beaches, contact with wild animals, fishing, hunting—the list is long and incompletely known. Food can, perhaps, be significantly increased, but what about clean beaches, unspoiled forests, and solitude? If we satisfy the need for food in a growing population we necessarily decrease the supply of other goods, and thereby increase the difficulty of equitably allocating scarce goods (Hardin 1969b, 1972b).

The present population of India is 600 million, and it is increasing by fifteen million per year. The environmental load of this population is already great. The forests of India are only a small fraction of what they were three centuries ago. Soil erosion, floods, and the psychological costs of crowding are serious. Every one of the net fifteen million lives added each year stresses the Indian environment more severely. *Every life saved this year in a poor country diminishes the quality of life for subsequent generations.*

Observant critics have shown how much harm we wealthy nations have already done to poor nations through our well-intentioned but misguided attempts to help them (Paddock and Paddock 1973). Particularly reprehensible is our failure to carry out post-audits of these attempts (Farvar and Milton 1972). Thus have we shielded our tender consciences from knowledge of the harm we have done. Must we Americans continue to fail to monitor the consequences of our external "do-gooding?" If, for instance, we thoughtlessly make it possible for the present 600 million Indians to swell to 1,200 million by the year 2001—as their present growth rate promises—will posterity in India thank *us* for facilitating an even greater destruction of *their* environment? Are good intentions ever a sufficient excuse for bad consequences?

IMMIGRATION CREATES A COMMONS

I come now to the final example of a commons in action, one for which the public is least prepared for rational discussion. The topic is at present enveloped by a great silence that reminds me of a comment made by Sherlock Holmes in A. Conan Doyle's story, "Silver Blaze." Inspector Gregory had asked, "Is there any point to which you wish to draw my attention?" To this Holmes responded:

"To the curious incident of the dog in the night-time."
"The dog did nothing in the night-time," said the Inspector.
"That was the curious incident," remarked Sherlock Holmes.

By asking himself what would repress the normal barking instinct of a watch dog Holmes realized that it must be the dog's recognition of his master as the criminal trespasser. In a similar way we should ask ourselves what repression keeps us from discussing something as important as immigration?

It cannot be that immigration is numerically of no consequence. Our government acknowledges a *net* inflow of 400,000 a year. Hard data are understandably lacking on the extent of illegal entries, but a not implausible figure is 600,000 per year. (Buchanan 1973). The natural increase of the resident population is now about 1.7 million per year. This means that the yearly gain from immigration is at least nineteen percent and may be thirty-seven percent, of the total increase. It is quite conceivable that educational campaigns like that of Zero Population Growth, Inc., coupled with adverse social and economic factors—inflation, housing shortage, depression, and loss of confidence in national leaders—may lower the fertility of American women to a point at which all of the yearly increase in population would be accounted for by immigration. Should we not at least ask if that is what we want? How curious it is that we so seldom discuss immigration these days!

Curious, but understandable—as one finds out the moment he publicly questions the wisdom of the status quo in immigration. He who does so is promptly charged with *isolationism, bigotry, prejudice, **ethnocentrism, chauvinism,** and selfishness.* These are hard accusations to bear. It is pleasanter to talk about other matters, leaving immigration policy to wallow in the crosscurrents of special interests that take no account of the good of the whole—*or of the interests of posterity.*

We Americans have a bad conscience because of things we said in the past about immigrants. Two generations ago the popular press was rife with references to *Dagos, Wops, Pollacks, Japs, Chinks,* and *Krauts*—all pejorative terms that failed to acknowledge our indebtedness to Goya, Leonardo, Copernicus, Hiroshige, Confucius, and Bach. Because the implied inferiority of foreigners was *then* the justification for keeping them out, it is *now* thoughtlessly assumed that restrictive policies can only be based on the assumption of immigrant inferiority. *This is not so.*

Existing immigration laws exclude idiots and known criminals; future laws will almost certainly continue this policy. But should we also consider the quality of the average immigrant, as compared with the quality of the average resident? Perhaps we should, perhaps we shouldn't. (What is "quality" anyway?) But the quality issue is not our concern here.

From this point on, *it will be assumed that immigrants and native-born citizens are of exactly equal quality,* however quality may be defined. The focus is only on quantity. The conclusions reached depend on nothing else, so all charges of ethnocentrism are irrelevant.

World food banks move food to the people, thus facilitating the exhaustion of the environment of the poor. By contrast, unrestricted immigration moves people to the food, thus speeding up the destruction of the environment in rich countries. Why poor people should want to make this transfer is no mystery, but why should rich hosts encourage it? This transfer, like the reverse one, is supported by both selfish interests and humanitarian impulses.

The principal selfish interest in unimpeded immigration is easy to identify: it is the interest of the employers of cheap labor, particularly that needed for degrading jobs. We have been deceived about the forces of history by the lines of Emma Lazarus inscribed on the Statue of Liberty:

Give me your tired, your poor,
Your huddled masses yearning to breathe free,
The wretched refuse of your teeming shore,
Send these, the homeless, tempest-tossed to me:
I lift my lamp beside the golden door.

The image is one of an infinitely generous earth-mother, passively opening her arms to hordes of immigrants who come here on their own initiative. Such an image may have been adequate for the early days of colonization, but by the time these lines were written (1886) the force for immigration was largely manufactured inside our own borders by factory and mine owners who sought cheap labor not to be found among laborers already here. One group of foreigners after another was thus enticed into the United States to work at wretched jobs for wretched wages.

At present, it is largely the Mexicans who

are being so exploited. It is particularly to the advantage of certain employers that there be many illegal immigrants. Illegal immigrant workers dare not complain about their working conditions for fear of being repatriated. Their presence reduces the bargaining power of all Mexican-American laborers. Cesar Chavez has repeatedly pleaded with congressional committees to close the doors to more Mexicans so that those here can negotiate effectively for higher wages and decent working conditions. Chavez understands the ethics of a lifeboat.

The interests of the employers of cheap labor are well served by the silence of the intelligentsia of the country. WASPS—White Anglo-Saxon Protestants—are particularly reluctant to call for a closing of the doors to immigration for fear of being called ethnocentric bigots. It was, therefore, an occasion of pure delight for this particular WASP to be present at a meeting when the points he would like to have made were made better by a non-WASP speaking to other non-WASPS. It was in Hawaii, and most of the people in the room were second-level Hawaiian officials of Japanese ancestry. All Hawaiians are keenly aware of the limits of their environment, and the speaker had asked how it might be practically and constitutionally possible to close the doors to more immigrants to the islands. (To Hawaiians, immigrants from the other forty-nine states are as much of a threat as those from other nations. There is only so much room in the islands, and the islanders know it. Sophistical arguments that imply otherwise do not impress them.)

Yet the Japanese-Americans of Hawaii have active ties with the land of their origin. This point was raised by a Japanese-American member of the audience who asked the Japanese-American speaker: "But how can we shut the doors now? We have many friends and relations in Japan that we'd like to bring to Hawaii some day so that they can enjoy this beautiful land."

The speaker smiled sympathetically and responded slowly, "Yes, but we have children now and someday we'll have grandchildren. We can bring more people here from Japan only by giving away some of the land that we hope to pass on to our grandchildren some day. What right do we have to do that?"

To be generous with one's own possessions is one thing; to be generous with posterity's is quite another. This, I think, is the point that must be gotten across to those who would, from a commendable love of **distributive justice,** institute a ruinous system of the commons, either in the form of a world food bank or that of unrestricted immigration. Since every speaker is a member of some ethnic group it is always possible to charge him with ethnocentrism. But even after purging an argument of ethnocentrism the rejection of the commons is still valid and necessary if we are to save at least some parts of the world from environmental ruin. Is it not desirable that at least some of the grandchildren of people now living should have a decent place in which to live?

THE ASYMMETRY OF DOOR–SHUTTING

We must now answer this telling point: "How can you justify slamming the door once you're inside? You say that immigrants should be kept out. But aren't we all immigrants, or the descendants of immigrants? Since we refuse to leave, must we not, as a matter of justice and symmetry, admit all others?"

It is literally true that we Americans of non-Indian ancestry are the descendants of thieves. Should we not, then, "give back" the land to the Indians, that is, give it to the now-living Americans of Indian ancestry? As an exercise in pure logic I see no way to reject this proposal. Yet I am unwilling to live by it, and I know no one who is. Our reluctance to embrace pure justice may spring from pure selfishness. On the other hand, it may arise from an unspoken recognition of consequences that have not yet been clearly spelled out.

Suppose, becoming intoxicated with pure justice, we "Anglos" should decide to turn our land over to the Indians. Since all our other wealth has also been derived from the land, we would have to give that to the Indians, too. Then what would we non-Indians do? Where would we go? There is no open land in the world on which men without capital can make their living (and not much unoccupied land on which men with capital can either). Where would 209 million putatively justice-loving, non-Indian Americans go? Most of them—in the persons of their ancestors—came from Europe, but they wouldn't be welcomed back there. Anyway, Europeans have no better title to their land than we to ours. They also would have to give up their homes. (But to whom? And where would *they* go?)

Clearly, the concept of pure justice produces an **infinite regress.** The law long ago invented statutes of limitations to justify the rejection of pure justice, in the interest of preventing massive disorder. The law zealously defends property rights—but only *recent* property rights. It is as though the physical principle of exponential decay applies to property rights. Drawing a line in time may be unjust, but any other action is practically worse.

We are all the descendants of thieves, and the world's resources are inequitably distributed, but we must begin the journey to tomorrow from the point where we are today. We cannot remake the past. We cannot, without violent disorder and suffering, give land and resources back to the "original" owners—who are dead anyway.

We cannot safely divide the wealth equitably among all present peoples, so long as people reproduce at different rates, because to do so would guarantee that our grandchildren—everyone's grandchildren—would have only a ruined world to inhabit.

MUST EXCLUSION BE ABSOLUTE?

To show the logical structure of the immigration problem I have ignored many factors that would enter into real decisions made in a real world. No matter how convincing the logic may be, it is probable that we would want, from time to time, to admit a few people from the outside to our lifeboat. Political refugees in particular are likely to cause us to make exceptions: We remember the Jewish refugees from Germany after 1933, and the Hungarian refugees after 1956. Moreover, the interests of national defense, broadly conceived, could justify admitting many men and women of unusual talents, whether refugees or not. (This raises the quality issue, which is not the subject of this essay.)

Such exceptions threaten to create runaway population growth inside the lifeboat, i.e., the receiving country. However, the threat can be neutralized by a population policy that includes immigration. An effective policy is one of flexible control.

Suppose, for example, that the nation has achieved a stable condition of ZPG, which (say) permits 1.5 million births yearly. We must suppose that an acceptable system of allocating birth-rights to potential parents is in effect. Now suppose that an inhumane regime in some other part of the world creates a horde of refugees, and that there is a widespread desire to admit some to our country. At the same time, we do not want to sabotage our population control system. Clearly, the rational path to pursue is the following. If we decide to admit 100,000 refugees this year we should compensate for this by reducing the allocation of birth-rights in the following year by a similar amount, that is, downward to a total of 1.4 million. In that way we could achieve both humanitarian and population control goals. (And the refugees would have to accept the population controls of the society that admits them. It is not inconceivable that they might be given proportionately fewer rights than the native population.)

In a democracy, the admission of immigrants should properly be voted on. But by whom? It is not obvious. The usual rule of a democracy is votes for all. But it can be questioned whether a universal franchise is the most just one in a case of this sort. Whatever

benefits there are in the admission of immigrants presumably accrue to everyone. But the costs would be seen as falling most heavily on potential parents, some of whom would have to postpone or forego having their (next) child because of the influx of immigrants. The double question *Who benefits? Who pays?* suggests that a restriction of the usual democratic franchise would be appropriate and just in this case. Would our particular quasi-democratic form of government be flexible enough to institute such a novelty? If not, the majority might, out of humanitarian motives, impose an unacceptable burden (the foregoing of parenthood) on a minority, thus producing political instability.

Plainly many new problems will arise when we consciously face the immigration question and seek rational answers. No workable answers can be found if we ignore population problems. And—if the argument of this essay is correct—so long as there is no true world government to control reproduction everywhere it is impossible to survive in dignity if we are to be guided by spaceship ethics. Without a world government that is sovereign in reproductive matters mankind lives, in fact, on a number of sovereign lifeboats. For the foreseeable future survival demands that we govern our actions by the ethics of a lifeboat. Posterity will be ill served if we do not.

References

Anonymous. 1974. *Wall Street Journal* 19 Feb.
Borlaug, N. 1973. Civilization's future: a call for international granaries. *Bull.At.Sci.* 29: 7–15.
Boulding, K. 1966. The economics of the coming Spaceship Earth. *In* H. Jarrett, ed. Environmental Quality in a Growing Economy. Baltimore: John Hopkins Press.
Buchanan, W. 1973. Immigration statistics. *Equilibrium* 1(3): 16–19.
Davis, K. 1963. Population. *Sci.Amer.* 209(3): 62–71.
Farvar, M.T., and J.P. Milton. 1972. The Careless Technology. Garden City, NY: Natural History Press.
Gregg, A. 1955. A medical aspect of the population problem. *Science* 121:681–682.
Hardin, G. 1966. Chap. 9 *in* Biology: Its Principles and Implications, 2nd ed. San Francisco: Freeman.
———. 1968. The tragedy of the commons. *Science* 162: 1243–1248.

_____. 1969a Page 18 *in* Population, Evolution, and Birth Control, 2nd ed. San Francisco: Freeman.

_____. 1969b. The economics of wilderness. *Nat. Hist.* 78(6): 20–27.

_____. 1972a. Pages 81–82 *in* Exploring New Ethics for Survival: The Voyage of the Spaceship *Beagle.* New York: Viking.

_____. 1972b. Preserving quality on Spaceship Earth. *In* J.B. Trefethen, ed. Transactions of the Thirty-Seventh North American Wildlife and Natural Resources Conference. Wildlife Management Institute, Washington, D.C.

_____. 1973. Chap. 23 *in* Stalking the Wild Taboo. Los Altos, CA: Kaufmann.

Harris, M. 1972. How green the revolution. *Nat. Hist.* 81(3): 28–30.

Langer, S.K. 1942. Philosophy in a New Key. Cambridge, MA: Harvard University Press.

Lansner, K. 1974. Should foreign aid begin at home? *Newsweek,* 11 Feb., p. 32.

Marx, K. 1875. Critique of the Gotha program. Page 388 *in* R.C. Tucker, ed. The Marx-Engels Reader. New York: Norton, 1972.

Ophuls, W. 1974. The scarcity society. *Harpers* 248(1487): 47–52.

Paddock, W.C. 1970. How green is the green revolution? *BioScience* 20: 897–902.

Paddock, W., and E. Paddock. 1973. We Don't Know How. Ames, IA: Iowa State University Press.

Paddock, W., and P. Paddock. 1967. Famine—1975! Boston: Little, Brown.

Wilkes, H.G. 1972. The green revolution. *Environment* 14(8): 32–39.

Review Questions

1. What is wrong with the spaceship metaphor according to Hardin?

2. Explain Hardin's lifeboat metaphor.

3. According to Hardin, why can't we live by the Christian or the Marxian ideal?

4. Explain what Hardin calls the tragedy of the commons. How is this supposed to apply to rich and poor nations?

5. Explain the ratchet effect and a pejoristic system.

6. Why isn't a benign demographic transition possible according to Hardin?

7. Why doesn't Hardin think that the Green Revolution will solve the problem of world hunger?

8. Explain Hardin's opposition to present immigration policies.

Discussion Questions

1. Are there any respects in which the United States is not a lifeboat?

2. Is there any solution to the problem of overpopulation in poor countries that does not involve letting people die? What is it?

3. Is there any way to avoid the tragedy of the commons that does not involve private ownership? Explain.

4. Is there any way to avoid the ratchet effect? Explain.

5. Should we allow more people to immigrate into the United States? Why or why not?

Trudy Govier

The Right to Eat and the Duty to Work

From Trudy Govier, "The Right to Eat and the Duty to Work," *Philosophy of the Social Sciences,* Vol. 5 (1975), pp. 125–143. Reprinted with permission of the author and *Philosophy of the Social Sciences.*

Trudy Govier has taught philosophy at Trent University in Ontario. She has written several articles on moral philosophy.

Govier discusses three different positions on the welfare question: Do needy people in an affluent society have a legal right to welfare benefits? First, there is the individualist position (called libertarianism by Hospers) that no one has a legal right to welfare benefits, not even in an affluent society. Second, there is the permissive position that in an affluent society, everyone has an unconditional legal right to welfare benefits. Third, there is the puritan position that everyone has a legal right to welfare, but this right ought to be conditional on one's willingness to work. *After evaluating these three positions in terms of their social consequences (the "teleological appraisal") and social justice, Govier concludes that the permissive position is superior.*

Although the topic of welfare is not one with which philosophers have often concerned themselves, it is a topic which gives rise to many complex and fascinating questions— some in the area of political philosophy, some in the area of ethics, and some of a more practical kind. The variety of issues related to the subject of welfare makes it particularly necessary to be clear just which issue one is examining in a discussion of welfare. In a recent book on the subject, Nicholas Rescher asks:

*In what respects and to what extent is society, working through the instrumentality of the state, responsible for the welfare of its members? What demands for the promotion of his welfare can an individual reasonably make upon his society? These are questions to which no answer can be given in terms of some **a priori** approach with reference to universal ultimates. Whatever answer can appropriately be given will depend, in the final analysis, on what the society decides it should be.*[1]

Rescher raises this question only to avoid it. His response to his own question is that a society has all and only those responsibilities for its members that it thinks it has. Although this claim is trivially true as regards legal responsibilities, it is inadequate from a moral perspective. If one imagines the case of an affluent society which leaves the blind, the disabled, and the needy to die of starvation, the incompleteness of Rescher's account becomes obvious. In this imagined case one is naturally led to raise the question as to whether those in power ought to supply those in need with the necessities of life. Though the needy have no legal right to welfare benefits of any kind, one might very well say that they ought to have such a right. It is this claim which I propose to discuss here.[2]

I shall approach this issue by examining three positions which may be adopted in response to it. These are:

1. The Individualist Position: Even in an affluent society, one ought not to have any legal right to state-supplied welfare benefits.
2. The Permissive Position: In a society with sufficient resources, one ought to have an unconditional legal right to receive state supplied welfare benefits. (That is, one's right to receive such benefits ought not to depend on one's behaviour; it should be guaranteed).
3. The Puritan Position: In a society with sufficient resources one ought to have a legal right to state-supplied welfare benefits; this right ought to be conditional, however, on one's willingness to work.

But before we examine these positions, some preliminary clarification must be attempted. . . .

Welfare systems are state-supported systems which supply benefits, usually in the form of cash income, to those who are in need. Welfare systems thus exist in the sort of social context where there is some private ownership of property. If no one owned anything individually (except possibly his own body), and all goods were considered to be the joint property of everyone, then this type of welfare system could not exist. A state might take on the responsibility for the welfare of its citizens, but it could not meet this responsibility by distributing a level of cash income which such citizens would spend to purchase the goods essential for life. The welfare systems which exist in the western world do exist against the background of extensive private ownership of property. It is in this context that I propose to discuss moral questions about having a right to welfare benefits. By setting out my questions in this way, I do not intend to endorse the institution of private property, but only to discuss questions which many people find real and difficult in the context of the social organization which they actually do experience. The present analysis of welfare is intended to apply to societies which (*a*) have the institution of private property, if not for means of production, at least for some basic good; and (*b*) possess sufficient resources so that it is at least possible for every member of the society to be supplied with the necessities of life.

The Individualist View

It might be maintained that a person in need has no legitimate moral claim on those around him and that the hypothetical inattentive society which left its blind citizens to beg or starve cannot rightly be censured for doing so. This view, which is dramatically at odds with most of contemporary social thinking, lives on in the writings of Ayn Rand and her followers.[3] The Individualist sets a high value on uncoerced personal choice. He sees each person as a responsible agent who is able to make his own decisions and to plan his own life. He insists that with the freedom to make decisions goes responsibility for the consequences of those decisions. A person has every right, for example, to spend ten years of his life studying Sanskrit—but if, as a result of this choice, he is unemployable, he ought not to expect others to labour on his behalf. No one has a proper claim on the labour of another, or on the income ensuing from that labour, unless he can repay the labourer in a way acceptable to that labourer himself. Government welfare schemes provide benefits from funds gained largely by taxing earned income. One cannot "opt out" of such schemes. To the Individualist, this means that a person is forced to work part of his time for others.

Suppose that a man works forty hours and earns two hundred dollars. Under modern-day taxation, it may well be that he can spend only two-thirds of that money as he chooses. The rest is taken by government and goes to support programmes which the working individual may not himself endorse. The beneficiaries of such programmes—those beneficiaries who do not work themselves—are as though they have slaves working for them. Backed by the force which government authorities can command, they are able to exist on the earnings of others. Those who support them do not do so voluntarily, out of charity; they do so on government command.

Someone across the street is unemployed. Should you be taxed extra to pay for his expenses? Not at all. You have not injured him, you are not responsible for the fact that he is unemployed (unless you are a senator or bureaucrat who agitated for further curtailing of business which legislation passed, with the result that your neighbour was laid off by the curtailed business). You may voluntarily wish to help him out, or better still, try to get him a job to put him on his feet again; but since you have initiated no aggressive act against him, and neither purposefully nor accidentally injured him in any way, you should not be legally penalized for the fact of his unemployment.[4]

The Individualist need not lack concern for those in need. He may give generously to charity; he might give more generously still, if his whole income were his to use, as he would like it to be. He may also believe that, as a matter of empirical fact, existing government programmes do not actually help the poor. They support a cumbersome bureaucracy and they use financial resources which, if untaxed, might be used by those with initiative to pursue job-creating endeavours. The thrust of the Individualist's position is that each person owns his own body and his own labour; thus each person is taken to have a virtually unconditional right to the income which that labour can earn him in a free market place.[5] For anyone to pre-empt part of a worker's earnings without that worker's voluntary consent is tantamount to robbery. And the fact that the government is the intermediary through which this deed is committed does not change its moral status one iota.

On an Individualist's view, those in need should be cared for by charities or through other schemes to which contributions are voluntary. Many people may wish to insure themselves against unforeseen calamities and they should be free to do so. But there is no justification for non-optional government schemes financed by taxpayers' money. . . .

The Permissive View

Directly contrary to the Individualist view of welfare is what I have termed the Permissive view. According to this view, in a society which has sufficient resources so that everyone could be supplied with the necessities of life, every individual ought to be given the legal right to social security, and this right ought not to be conditional in any way upon an individual's behavior. *Ex hypothesi* the society which we are discussing has sufficient goods to provide everyone with food, clothing, shelter and other necessities. Someone who does without these basic goods is scarcely living at all, and a society which takes no steps to change this state of affairs implies by its inaction that the life of such a person is without value. It does not execute him; but it may allow him to die. It does not put him in prison; but it may leave him with a life of lower quality than that of some prison inmates. A society which can rectify these circumstances and does not can justly be accused of imposing upon the needy either death or lifelong deprivation. And those characteristics which make a person needy—whether they be illness, old age, insanity, feeblemindedness, inability to find paid work, or even poor moral character—are insufficient to make him deserve the fate to which an inactive society would in effect condemn him. One would not be executed for inability or failure to find paid work; neither should one be allowed to die for this misfortune or failing.

A person who cannot or does not find his own means of social security does not thereby forfeit his status as a human being. If other human beings, with physical, mental and moral qualities different from his, are regarded as having the right to life and to the means of life, then so too should he be regarded. A society which does not accept the responsibility for supplying such a person with the basic necessities of life is, in effect, endorsing a difference between its members which is without moral justification....

The adoption of a Permissive view of wel-

fare would have significant practical implications. If there were a legal right, unconditional upon behaviour, to a specified level of state-supplied benefits, then state investigation of the prospective welfare recipient could be kept to a minimum. Why he is in need, whether he can work, whether he is willing to work, and what he does while receiving welfare benefits are on this view quite irrelevant to his right to receive those benefits. A welfare recipient is a person who claims from his society that to which he is legally entitled under a morally based welfare scheme. The fact that he makes this claim licenses no special state or societal interference with his behaviour. If the Permissive view of welfare were widely believed, then there would be no social stigma attached to being on welfare. There is such a stigma, and many long-term welfare recipients are considerably demoralized by their dependent status.[6] These facts suggest that the Permissive view of welfare is not widely held in our society.

The Puritan View

This view of welfare rather naturally emerges when we consider that no one can have a right to something without someone else's, or some group of other persons', having responsibilities correlative to this right. In the case in which the right in question is a legal right to social security, the correlative responsibilities may be rather extensive. They have been deemed responsibilities of "the state." The state will require resources and funds to meet these responsibilities, and these do not emerge from the sky miraculously, or zip into existence as a consequence of virtually effortless acts of will. They are taken by the state from its citizens, often in the form of taxation on earned income. The funds given to the welfare recipient and many of the goods which he purchases with these funds are produced by other members of society, many of whom give a considerable portion of their time and their energy to this end. If a state has the moral responsibility to ensure the social security of its citizens then all the citizens of that state have the responsibility to provide state agencies with the means to carry out their duties. This responsibility, in our present contingent circumstances, seems to generate an obligation to *work*.

A person who works helps to produce the goods which all use in daily living and, when paid, contributes through taxation to government endeavours. The person who does not work, even though able to work, does not make his contribution to social efforts towards obtaining the means of life. He is not entitled to a share of the goods produced by others if he chooses not to take part in their labours. Unless he can show that there is a moral justification for his not making the sacrifice of time and energy which others make, he has no legitimate claim to welfare benefits. If he is disabled or unable to obtain work, he cannot work; hence he has no need to justify his failure to work. But if he does choose not to work, he would have to justify his choice by saying "others should sacrifice their time and energy for me; I have no need to sacrifice time and energy for them." This principle, a version of what Rawls refers to as a **free-rider's principle**, simply will not stand up to criticism.[7] To deliberately avoid working and benefit from the labours of others is morally indefensible.

Within a welfare system erected on these principles, the right to welfare is conditional upon one's satisfactorily accounting for his failure to obtain the necessities of life by his own efforts. Someone who is severely disabled mentally or physically, or who for some other reason cannot work, is morally entitled to receive welfare benefits. Someone who chooses not to work is not. The Puritan view of welfare is a kind of compromise between the Individualist view and the Permissive view....

The Puritan view of welfare, based as it is on the inter-relation between welfare and work, provides a rationale for two connected principles which those establishing welfare schemes in Canada and in the United States seem to endorse. First of all, those on welfare should never receive a higher income than the working poor. Secondly, a welfare scheme should, in some way or other, incorporate incentives to work. These principles, which presuppose that it is better to work than not to work, emerge rather naturally from the contingency which is at the basis of the Puritan view: the goods essential for social security are products of the labour of some members of society. If we wish to have a continued supply of such goods, we must encourage those who work to produce them....

APPRAISAL OF POLICIES: SOCIAL CONSEQUENCES AND SOCIAL JUSTICE

In approaching the appraisal of prospective welfare policies under these two aspects I am, of course, making some assumptions about the moral appraisal of suggested social policies. Although these cannot possibly be justified here, it may be helpful to articulate them, at least in a rough way.

Appraisal of social policies is in part teleological. To the extent that a policy, P, increases the total human welfare more than does an alternative policy, P', P is a better social policy then P'. Or, if P leaves the total human welfare as it is, while P' diminishes it, then to that extent, P is a better social policy than P'. Even this skeletal formulation of the teleological aspect of appraisal reveals why appraisal cannot be entirely teleological. We consider total consequences—effects upon the total of "human well-being" in a society. But this total is a summation of consequences on different individuals. It includes no judgements as to how far we allow one individual's well-being to decrease while another's increases, under the same policy. Judgements relating to the latter problems are judgements about social justice.

In appraising social policies we have to weigh up considerations of total well-being against considerations of justice. Just how this is to be done, precisely, I would not pretend to know. However, the absence of precise methods does not mean that we should relinquish attempts at appraisal: some problems are already with us, and thought which is necessarily tentative and imprecise is still preferable to no thought at all.

Consequences of Welfare Schemes

First, let us consider the consequences of the non-scheme advocated by the Individualist. He would have us abolish all non-optional government programmes which have as their goal the improvement of anyone's personal welfare. This rejection extends to health schemes, pension plans and education, as well as to welfare and unemployment insurance. So following the Individualist would lead to very sweeping changes.

The Individualist will claim (as do Hospers and Ayn Rand) that on the whole his non-scheme will bring beneficial consequences. He will admit, as he must, that there are people who would suffer tremendously if welfare and other social security programmes were simply terminated. Some would even die as a result. We cannot assume that spontaneously developing charities would cover every case of dire need. Nevertheless the Individualist wants to point to benefits which would accrue to businessmen and to working people and their families if taxation were drastically cut. It is his claim that consumption would rise, hence production would rise, job opportunities would be extended, and there would be an economic boom, if people could only spend all their earned income as they wished. This boom would benefit both rich and poor.

There are significant omissions which are necessary in order to render the Individualist's optimism plausible. Either workers and businessmen would have insurance of various kinds, or they would be insecure in their prosperity. If they did have insurance to cover health problems, old age and possible job loss, then they would pay for it; hence they would not be spending their whole earned income on consumer goods. Those who run the insurance schemes could, of course, put this money back into the economy—but government schemes already do this. The economic boom under Individualism would not be as loud as originally expected. Furthermore the goal of increased consumption-increased productivity must be questioned from an ecological viewpoint: many necessary materials are available only in limited quantities.

Finally, a word about charity. It is not to be expected that those who are at the mercy of charities will benefit from this state, either materially or psychologically. Those who prosper will be able to choose between giving a great deal to charity and suffering from the very real insecurity and guilt which would accompany the existence of starvation and grim poverty outside their padlocked doors. It is to be hoped that they would opt for the first alternative. But, if they did, this might be every bit as expensive for them as government-supported benefit schemes are now. If they did not give generously to charity, violence might result. However one looks at it, the consequences of Individualism are unlikely to be good.

Welfare schemes operating in Canada today are almost without exception based upon the principles of the Puritan view. To see the consequences of that type of welfare scheme we have only to look at the results of our own welfare programmes. Taxation to support such schemes is high, though not so intolerably so as to have led to widescale resentment among taxpayers. Canadian welfare programmes are attended by complicated and often cumbersome bureaucracy, some of which results from the interlocking of municipal, provincial and federal governments in the administration and financing of welfare programmes. The cost of the programmes is no doubt increased by this bureaucracy; not all the tax money directed to welfare programmes goes to those in need. Puritan welfare schemes do not result in social catastrophe or in significant business stagnation—

this much we know, because we already live with such schemes. Their adverse consequences, if any, are felt primarily not by society generally nor by businessmen and the working segment of the public, but rather by recipients of welfare.

Both the Special Senate Committee Report on Poverty and the Real Poverty Report criticize our present system of welfare for its demoralization of recipients, who often must deal with several levels of government and are vulnerable to arbitrary interference on the part of administering officials. Welfare officials have the power to check on welfare recipients and cut off or limit their benefits under a large number of circumstances. The dangers to welfare recipients in terms of anxiety, threats to privacy and loss of dignity are obvious. According to the Senate Report, the single aspect shared by all Canada's welfare systems is "a record of failure and insufficiency, of bureaucratic rigidities that often result in the degradation, humiliation and alienation of recipients." [8] The writers of this report cite many instances of humiliation, leaving the impression that these are too easily found to be "incidental aberrations." [9] Concern that a welfare recipient either be unable to work or be willing to work (if unemployed) can easily turn into concern about how he spends the income supplied him, what his plans for the future are, where he lives, how many children he has. And the rationale underlying the Puritan scheme makes the degradation of welfare recipients a natural consequence of welfare institutions. Work is valued and only he who works is thought to contribute to society. Welfare recipients are regarded as parasites and spongers—so when they are treated as such, this is only what we should have expected. Being on welfare in a society which thinks and acts in this fashion can be psychologically debilitating. Welfare recipients who are demoralized by their downgraded status and relative lack of personal freedom can be expected to be made less capable of self-sufficiency. To the extent that this is so, welfare systems erected on Puritan principles may defeat their own purposes.

In fairness, it must be noted here that bureaucratic checks and controls are not a feature only of Puritan welfare systems. To a limited extent, Permissive systems would have to incorporate them too. Within those systems, welfare benefits would be given only to those whose income was inadequate to meet basic needs. However, there would be no checks on "willingness to work," and there would be no need for welfare workers to evaluate the merits of the daily activities of recipients. If a Permissive guaranteed income system were administered through income tax returns, everyone receiving the basic income and those not needing it paying it back in taxes, then the special status of welfare recipients would fade. They would no longer be singled out as a special group within the population. It is to be expected that living solely on government-supplied benefits would be psychologically easier in that type of situation.

Thus it can be argued that for the recipients of welfare, a Permissive scheme has more advantages than a Puritan one. This is not a very surprising conclusion. The Puritan scheme is relatively disadvantageous to recipients, and Puritans would acknowledge this point; they will argue that the overall consequences of Permissive schemes are negative in that these schemes benefit some at too great a cost to others. (Remember, we are not yet concerned with the *justice* of welfare policies, but solely with their consequences as regards *total* human well-being within the society in question.) The concern which most people have regarding the Permissive scheme relates to its costs and its dangers to the "work ethic." It is commonly thought that people work only because they have to work to survive in a tolerable style. If a guaranteed income scheme were adopted by the government, this incentive to work would disappear. No one would be faced with the choice between a nasty and boring job and starvation. Who would do the nasty and boring jobs then? Many of them are not eliminable and they have to be done somehow, by someone. Puritans fear that a great many people—even some with relatively pleasant jobs—might simply cease to work if they could receive non-stigmatized government money to live on. If this were to happen, the permissive society would simply grind to a halt.

In addressing these anxieties about the consequences of Permissive welfare schemes, we must recall that welfare benefits are set to ensure only that those who do not work have a bearable existence, with an income sufficient for basic needs, and that they have this income regardless of why they fail to work. Welfare benefits will not finance luxury living for a family of five! If jobs are adequately paid so that workers receive more than the minimum welfare income in an earned salary, then there will still be a financial incentive to take jobs. What guaranteed income schemes will do is to raise the salary floor. This change will benefit the many non-unionized workers in service and clerical occupations.

Furthermore it is unlikely that people work solely due to (i) the desire for money and the things it can buy and (ii) belief in the Puritan work ethic. There are many other reasons for working, some of which would persist in a society which had adopted a Permissive welfare system. Most people are happier when their time is structured in some way, when they are active outside their own homes, when they feel themselves part of an endeavour whose purposes transcend their particular egoistic ones. Women often choose to work outside the home for these reasons as much as for financial ones. With these and other factors operating I cannot see that the adoption of a Permissive welfare scheme would be followed by a level of slothfulness which would jeopardize human well-being.

Another worry about the Permissive scheme concerns cost. It is difficult to comment on this in a general way, since it would vary so much from case to case. Of Canada at the present it has been said that a guaranteed income scheme administered through income tax would cost less than social security payments administered through the present bureaucracies. It is thought that this saving would result from a drastic cut in administrative costs. The matter of the work ethic is also relevant to the question of costs. Within a Puritan framework it is very important to have a high level of employment and there is a tendency to resist any reorganization which results in there being fewer jobs available. Some of these proposed reorganizations would save money; strictly speaking we should count the cost of keeping jobs which are objectively unnecessary as part of the cost of Puritanism regarding welfare.

In summary, we can appraise Individualism, Puritanism and Permissivism with respect to their anticipated consequences, as follows: Individualism is unacceptable; Puritanism is tolerable, but has some undesirable consequences for welfare recipients; Permissivism appears to be the winner. Worries about bad effects which Permissive welfare schemes might have due to high costs and (alleged) reduced work-incentives appear to be without solid basis.

Social Justice Under Proposed Welfare Schemes

We must now try to consider the merits of Individualism, Puritanism and Permissivism with regard to their impact on the distribution of the goods necessary for well-being. [Robert] Nozick has argued against the whole conception of a distributive justice on the grounds that it presupposes that goods are like manna from heaven: we simply get them and then have a problem—to whom to give them. According to Nozick we know where things come from and we do not have the problem of to whom to give them. There is not really a problem of distributive justice, for there is no central distributor giving out manna from heaven! It is necessary to counter Nozick on this point since his reaction to the (purported) problems of distributive justice would undercut much of what follows.[10]

There is a level at which Nozick's point is obviously valid. If A discovers a cure for cancer, then it is A and not B or C who is responsible for this discovery. On Nozick's view this is taken to imply that A should reap any monetary profits which are forthcoming; other people will benefit from the cure itself. Now although it cannot be doubted that A is a bright and hardworking person, neither can it be denied that A and his circumstances are the product of many co-operative endeavours: schools and laboratories, for instance. Because this is so, I find Nozick's claim that "we know where things come from" unconvincing at a deeper level. Since achievements like A's presuppose extensive social co-operation, it is morally permissible to regard even the monetary profits accruing from them as shareable by the "owner" and society at large.

Laws support existing income levels in many ways. Governments specify taxation so as to further determine net income. Property ownership is a legal matter. In all these ways people's incomes and possibilities for obtaining income are affected by deliberate state action. It is always possible to raise questions about the moral desirability of actual conventional arrangements. Should university professors earn less than lawyers? More than waitresses? Why? Why not? Anyone who gives an account of distributive justice is trying to specify principles which will make it possible to answer questions such as these, and nothing in Nozick's argument suffices to show that the questions are meaningless or unimportant.

Any human distribution of anything is unjust insofar as differences exist for no good reason. If goods did come like manna from heaven and the Central Distributor gave A ten times more than B, we should want to know why. The skewed distribution might be deemed a just one if A's needs were objectively ten times greater than B's, or if B refused to accept more than his small portion of goods. But if no reason at all could be given for it, or if only an irrelevant reason could be given (e.g., A is blue-eyed and B is not), then it is an unjust distribution. All the views we have expounded concerning welfare permit differences in income level. Some philosophers would say that such differences are never just, although they may be necessary, for historical or utilitarian reasons. Whether or not this is so, it is admittedly very difficult to say just what would constitute a good reason for giving A a higher income than B. Level of need, degree of responsibility, amount of training, unpleasantness of work—all these have been proposed and all have some plausibility. We do not need to tackle all this larger problem in order to consider justice under proposed welfare systems. For we can deal here solely with the question of whether everyone should receive a floor level of income; decisions on this matter are independent of decisions on overall equality or principles of variation among incomes above the floor. The Permissivist contends that all should receive at least the floor income; the Individualist and the Puritan deny this. All would claim justice for their side.

The Individualist attempts to justify extreme variations in income, with some people below the level where they can fulfill their basic needs, with reference to the fact of people's actual accomplishments. This approach to the question is open to the same objections as those which have already been raised against Nozick's non-manna-from-heaven argument, and I shall not repeat them here. Let us move on to the Puritan account. It is because goods emerge from human efforts that the Puritan advances his view of welfare. He stresses the unfairness of a system which would permit some people to take advantage of others. A Permissive welfare system would do this, as it makes no attempt to distinguish between those who choose not to work and those who cannot work. No one should be able to take advantage of another under the auspices of a government institution. The Puritan scheme seeks to eliminate this possibility, and for that reason, Puritans would allege, it is a more just scheme than the Permissive one.

Permissivists can best reply to this contention by acknowledging that any instance of free-riding would be an instance where those working were done an injustice, but by showing that any justice which the Puritan preserves by eliminating free-riding is outweighted by *injustice* perpetrated elsewhere. Consider the children of the Puritan's free-riders. They will suffer greatly for the "sins" of their parents. Within the institution of the family, the Puritan cannot suitably hurt the guilty without cruelly depriving the innocent. There is a sense, too, in which Puritanism does injustice to the many people on welfare who are not free-riders. It perpetuates the opinion that they are non-contributors to society and this doctrine, which is over-simplified if not downright false, has a harmful effect upon welfare recipients.

Social justice is not simply a matter of the distribution of goods, or the income with which goods are to be purchased. It is also a matter of the protection of rights. Western societies claim to give their citizens equal rights in political and legal contexts; they also claim to endorse the larger conception of a right to life. Now it is possible to interpret these rights in a limited and formalistic way, so that the duties correlative to them are minimal. On the limited, or negative, interpretation, to say that A has a right to life is simply to say that others have a duty not to interfere with A's attempts to keep himself alive. This interpretation of the right to life is compatible with Individualism as well as with Puritanism. But it is an inadequate interpretation of the right to life and of other rights. A right to vote is meaningless if one is starving and unable to get to the polls; a right to equality before the law is meaningless if one cannot afford to hire a lawyer. And so on.

Even a Permissive welfare scheme will go only a very small way towards protecting people's rights. It will amount to a meaningful acknowledgement of a right to life, by ensuring income adequate to purchase food, clothing and shelter—at the very least. These minimum necessities are presupposed by all other rights a society may endorse in that their possession is a precondition of being able to exercise these other rights. Because it protects the rights of all within a society better than do Puritanism and Individualism, the Permissive view can rightly claim superiority over the others with regard to justice.

Endnotes

1. Nichols Rescher, *Welfare: Social Issues in Philosophical Perspective*, p. 114.

2. One might wish to discuss moral questions concerning welfare in the context of **natural rights** doctrines. Indeed, Article 22 of the United Nations Declaration of Human Rights states, "Everyone, as a member of society, has the right to social security and is entitled, through national effort and international cooperation and in accordance with the organization and resources of each State, to the economic, social and cultural rights indispensable for his dignity and the free development of his personality." I make no attempt to defend the right to welfare as a **natural right**. Granting that rights imply responsibilities or duties and that "ought" implies "can," it would only be intelligible to regard the right to social security as a natural right if all states were able to ensure the minimum well-being of their citizens. This is not the case. And a natural right is one which is by definition supposed to belong to all human beings simply in virtue of their status as human beings. The analysis given here in the permissive view is compatible with the claim that all human beings have a *prima facie* natural right to social security. It is not, however, compatible with the claim that all human beings have a natural right to social security if this right is regarded as one which is so absolute as to be inviolable under any and all conditions.

3. See, for example, Ayn Rand's *Atlas Shrugged, The Virtue of Selfishness,* and *Capitalism: the Unknown Ideal.*

4. John Hospers, *Libertarianism: A Political Philosophy for Tomorrow*, p. 67.

5. I say virtually unconditional, because an Individualist such as John Hospers sees a legitimate moral role for government in preventing the use of force by some citizens against others. Since this is the case, I presume that he would also regard as legitimate such taxation as was necessary to support this function. Presumably that taxation would be seen as consented to by all, on the grounds that all "really want" government protection.

6. Ian Adams, William Cameron, Brian Hill, and Peter Penz, *The Real Poverty Report*, pp. 167–187.

7. See *A Theory of Justice*, pp. 124, 136. Rawls defines the free-rider as one who relies on the principle "everyone is to act justly except for myself, if I choose not to," and says that his position is a version of egoism which is eliminated as a morally acceptable principle by formal constraints. This conclusion regarding the tenability of egoism is one which I accept and which is taken for granted in the present context.

8. *Senate Report on Poverty*, p. 73.

9. The Hamilton Public Welfare Department takes automobile licence plates from recipients, making them available again only to those whose needs meet with the Department's approval. (*Real Poverty Report*, p. 186.) The *Globe and Mail* for 12 January 1974 reported that welfare recipients in the city of Toronto are to be subjected to computerized budgeting. In the summer of 1973, the two young daughters of an Alabama man on welfare were sterilized against their own wishes and without their parents' informed consent. (See *Time*, 23 July 1973.)

10. Robert Nozick, "Distributive Justice," *Philosophy and Public Affairs*, Fall 1973.

Review Questions

1. Distinguish between the individualist view, the permissive view, and the puritan view (as Govier explains them).

2. State the free-rider principle. Why does Govier reject it?

3. Compare the consequences of the three views as Govier describes them.

4. What is Govier's conclusion with respect to the consequences of the three positions?

5. What is Govier's objection to the individualist's view with respect to justice?

6. How does Govier characterize social justice?

7. Which of the three positions is superior according to Govier and why?

Discussion Questions

1. Does everyone in a rich society such as the United States have a right to welfare? Explain your answer.

2. Does everyone in a society who is able to work have a right to work? Why or why not?

3. Is a person who is able to work, but who chooses not to work entitled to welfare? What is your position on this free-rider problem?

4. Some women with dependent children receive more money from welfare than they could make working at low-paying jobs. This gives them an incentive not to work. Is this acceptable? What is your view?

5. Is a guaranteed income administered through the income tax a good idea? What do you think of Govier's suggestion?

John Hospers
What Libertarianism Is

John Hospers is Professor of Philosophy at the University of Southern California. He is the author of Human Conduct: Problems of Ethics *(1972),* Libertarianism: A Political Philosophy for Tomorrow *(1971), and* Understanding the Arts *(1982). He was the Libertarian party's candidate for the president of the United States in a past presidential election.*

Hospers begins with several different statements of the libertarian thesis which says that every person

From John Hospers, "What Libertarianism Is," in Tibor R. Machan, ed., *The Libertarian Alternative* (Chicago: Nelson-Hall Co., 1974), pp. 3–20. Reprinted with permission.

is the owner of his or her life. This basic thesis entails a right to liberty and a right to act as you choose, unless your action infringes on the equal liberty of others to act as they choose. Hospers also recognizes a right to life and a right to property. These rights are interpreted negatively, that is, they imply only that no one, including the government, has a right to interfere with a person's liberty, life, or property, however, they do not require any positive actions. Since these rights are violated by an initial use of force, the only proper role of government is to prevent this use of force and to retaliate against those who do initiate the use of force. All other possible roles of government, including protecting individuals from themselves, or requiring people to help each other, are emphatically rejected by Hospers.

The political philosophy that is called libertarianism (from the Latin *libertas*, liberty) is the doctrine that every person is the owner of his own life, and that no one is the owner of anyone else's life; and that consequently every human being has the right to act in accordance with his own choices, unless those actions infringe on the equal liberty of other human beings to act in accordance with their choices.

There are several other ways of stating the same libertarian thesis:

1. No one is anyone else's master, and no one is anyone else's slave. Since I am the one to decide how my life is to be conducted just as you decide about yours, I have no right (even if I had the power) to make you my slave and be your master, nor have you the right to become the master by enslaving me. Slavery is *forced* servitude, and since no one owns the life of anyone else, no one has the right to enslave another. Political theories past and present have traditionally been concerned with who should be the master (usually the king, the dictator, or government bureaucracy) and who should be the slaves, and what the extent of the slavery should be. Libertarianism holds that no one has the right to use force to enslave the life of another, or any portion or aspect of that life.

2. Other men's lives are not yours to dispose of. I enjoy seeing operas; but operas are expensive to produce. Opera-lovers often say, "The state (or the city, etc.) should subsidize opera, so that we can all see it. Also it would be for people's betterment, cultural benefit, etc." But what they are advocating is nothing more or less than legalized plunder. They can't pay for the productions themselves, and yet they want to see opera, which involves a large number of people and their labor; so what they are saying in effect is, "Get the money through legalized force. Take a little bit more out of every worker's paycheck every week to pay for the operas we want to see." But I have no right to take by force from the workers' pockets to pay for what I want.

Perhaps it would be better if he *did* go to see opera—then I should try to convince him to go voluntarily. But to take the money from him forcibly, because in my opinion it would be good for *him,* is still seizure of his earnings, which is plunder.

Besides, if I have the right to force him to help pay for my pet projects, hasn't he equally the right to force me to help pay for his? Perhaps he in turn wants the government to subsidize rock-and-roll, or his new car, or a house in the country? If I have the right to milk him, why hasn't he the right to milk me? If I can be a moral cannibal, why can't he too?

We should beware of the inventors of utopias. They would remake the world according to their vision—with the lives and fruits of the labor of *other* human beings. Is it someone's utopian vision that others should build pyramids to beautify the landscape? Very well, then other men should provide the labor; and if he is in a position of political power, and he can't get men to do it voluntarily, then he must *compel* them to "cooperate"—i.e. he must enslave them.

A hundred men might gain great pleasure from beating up or killing just one insignificant human being; but other men's lives are not theirs to dispose of. "In order to achieve the worthy goals of the next five-year-plan, we must forcibly collectivize the peasants . . ."; but other men's lives are not theirs to dispose of. Do you want to occupy, rent-free, the mansion that another man has worked for twenty years to buy? But other men's lives are not yours to dispose of. Do you want operas so badly that everyone is forced to work harder to pay for their subsidization through taxes? But other men's lives are not yours to dispose of. Do you want to have free medical care at the expense of other people, whether they wish to provide it or not? But this would require them to work longer for you whether they want to or not, and other men's lives are not yours to dispose of. . . .

3. *No human being should be a nonvoluntary mortgage on the life of another.* I cannot claim your life, your work, or the products of your effort as mine. The fruit of one man's labor should not be fair game for every freeloader who comes along and demands it as his own. The orchard that has been carefully grown, nurtured, and harvested by its owner should not be ripe for the plucking for any bypasser who has a yen for the ripe fruit. The wealth that some men have produced should not be fair game for looting by government, to be used for whatever purposes its representatives determine, no matter what their motives in so doing may be. The theft of your money by a robber is not justified by the fact that he used it to help his injured mother.

It will already be evident that libertarian doctrine is embedded in a view of the rights of man. Each human being has the right to live his life as he chooses, compatibly with the equal right of all other human beings to live their lives as they choose.

All man's rights are implicit in the above statement. Each man has the right to life: any attempt by others to take it away from him, or even to injure him, violates this right, through the use of coercion against him. Each man has the right to liberty: to conduct his life in accordance with the alternatives open to him without coercive action by others. And every man has the right to property: to work to sustain his life (and the lives of whichever others he chooses to sustain, such as his family) and to retain the fruits of his labor.

People often defend the rights of life and liberty but denigrate property rights, and yet the right to property is as basic as the other two: indeed, without property rights no other rights are possible. Depriving you of property is depriving you of the means by which you live....

I have no right to decide how *you* should spend your time or your money. I can make that decision for myself, but not for you, my neighbor. I may deplore your choice of lifestyle, and I may talk with you about it provided you are willing to listen to me. But I have no right to use force to change it. Nor have I the right to decide how you should spend the money you have earned. I may appeal to you to give it to the Red Cross, and you may prefer to go to prize-fights. But that is your decision, and however much I may chafe about it I do not have the right to interfere forcibly with it, for example by robbing you in order to use the money in accordance with *my* choices. (If I have the right to rob you, have you also the right to rob me?)

When I claim a right, I carve out a niche, as it were, in my life, saying in effect, "This activity I must be able to perform without interference from others. For you and everyone else, this is off limits." And so I put up a "no trespassing" sign, which marks off the area of my right. Each individual's right is his "no trespassing" sign in relation to me and others. I may not encroach upon his domain any more than he upon mine, without my consent. Every right entails a duty, true—but the duty is only that of *forbearance* —that is, of *refraining* from violating the other person's right. If you have a right to life, I have no right to take your life; if you have a right to the products of your labor (property), I have no right to take it from you without your consent. The nonviolation of these rights will not guarantee you protection against natural catastrophes such as floods and earthquakes, but it will protect you against the aggressive activities *of other men.* And rights, after all, have to do with one's relations to other human beings, not with one's relations to physical nature.

Nor were these rights created by government; governments—some governments, obviously not all—*recognize* and *protect* the rights that individuals already have. Governments regularly forbid homicide and theft; and, at a more advanced stage, protect individuals against such things as libel and breach of contract....

The *right to property* is the most

misunderstood and unappreciated of human rights, and it is one most constantly violated by governments. "Property" of course does not mean only real estate; it includes anything you can call your own—your clothing, your car, your jewelry, your books and papers.

The right of property is not the right to just *take* it from others, for this would interfere with *their* property rights. It is rather the right to work for it, to obtain non-coercively, the money or services which you can present in voluntary exchange.

The right to property is consistently underplayed by intellectuals today, sometimes even frowned upon, as if we should feel guilty for upholding such a right in view of all the poverty in the world. But the right to property is absolutely basic. It is your hedge against the future. It is your assurance that what you have worked to earn will still be there and be yours, when you wish or need to use it, especially when you are too old to work any longer.

Government has always been the chief enemy of the right to property. The officials of government, wishing to increase their power, and finding an increase of wealth an effective way to bring this about seize some or all of what a person has earned—and since government has a monopoly of physical force within the geographical area of the nation, it has the power (but not the right) to do this. When this happens, of course, every citizen of that country is insecure: he knows that no matter how hard he works the government can swoop down on him at any time and confiscate his earnings and possessions. A person sees his life savings wiped out in a moment when the tax-collectors descend to deprive him of the fruits of his work; or, an industry which has been fifty years in the making and cost millions of dollars and millions of hours of time and planning, is nationalized overnight. Or the government, via inflation, cheapens the currency, so that hard-won dollars aren't worth anything any more. The effect of such actions, of course, is that people lose hope and incentive: if no matter how hard they work the government agents can take it all away, why bother to work at all, for more than today's needs? Depriving people of property is *depriving them of the means by which they live* —the freedom of the individual citizen to do what he wishes with his own life and to plan for the future. Indeed only if property rights are respected is there any point to planning for the future and working to achieve one's goals. *Property rights are what makes long-range planning possible* —the kind of planning which is a distinctively human endeavor, as opposed to the day-by-day activity of the lion who hunts, who depends on the supply of game tomorrow but has no real insurance against starvation in a day or a week. Without the right to property, the right to life itself amounts to little: how can you sustain your life if you cannot plan ahead? and how can you plan ahead if the fruits of your labor can at any moment be confiscated by government? ...

Indeed, the right to property may well be considered second only to the right to life. Even the freedom of speech is limited by considerations of property. If a person visiting in your home behaves in a way undesired by you, you have every right to evict him; he can scream or agitate elsewhere if he wishes, but not in your home without your consent. Does a person have a right to shout obscenities in a cathedral? No, for the owners of the cathedral (presumably the Church) have not allowed others on their property for that purpose; one may go there to worship or to visit, but not just for any purpose one wishes. Their property right is prior to your or my wish to scream or expectorate or write graffiti on their building. Or, to take the stock example, does a person have a right to shout "Fire!" falsely in a crowded theater? No, for the theater owner has permitted others to enter and use his property only for a specific purpose, that of seeing a film or watching a stage show. If a person heckles or otherwise disturbs other members of the audience, he can be thrown out. (In fact, he can be removed for any reason the owner chooses, provided his admission money is returned). And if he shouts "Fire!" when there is no fire, he may be endangering other lives by causing a panic or stampede. The right to free speech doesn't give one the right to say anything anywhere; it is circumscribed by property rights.

Again, some people seem to assume that the right to free speech (including written speech) means that they can go to a newspaper publisher and demand that he print in his newspaper some propaganda or policy statement for their political party (or other group). But of course they have no right to the use of his newspaper. Ownership of the newspaper is the product of his labor, and he has a right to put into his newspaper whatever he wants, for whatever reason. If he excludes material which many readers would like to have in, perhaps they can find it in another newspaper or persuade him to print it himself (if there are enough of them, they will usually do just that). Perhaps they can even cause his newspaper to fail. But as long as he owns it, he has the right to put in it what he wishes; what would a property right be if he could not do this? They have no right to place their material in his newspaper without his consent—not for free, nor even for a fee. Perhaps other newspapers will include it, or perhaps they can start their own newspaper (in which case they have a right to put in it what they like). If not, an option open to them would be to mimeograph and distribute some handbills.

In exactly the same way, no one has a right to "free television time" unless the owner of the television station consents to give it; it is his station, he has the property rights over it, and it is for him to decide how to dispose of his time. He may not decide wisely, but it is his right to decide as he wishes. If he makes enough unwise decisions, and courts enough unpopularity with the viewing public or the sponsors, he may have to go out of business; but as he is free to make his own decisions, so is he free to face their consequences. (If the government owns the television station, then government officials will make the decisions, and there is no guarantee of *their* superior wisdom. The difference is that when "the government" owns the station, you are forced to help pay for its upkeep through your taxes, whether the bureaucrat in charge decides to give you television time or not.)

"But why have *individual* property rights? Why not have lands and houses owned by everybody together?" Yes, this involves no violation of individual rights, as long as everybody consents to this arrangement and no one is forced to join it. The parties to it may enjoy the communal living enough (at least for a time) to overcome certain inevitable problems: that some will work and some not, that some will achieve more in an hour than others can do in a day, and still they will all get the same income. The few who do the most will in the end consider themselves "workhorses" who do the work of two or three or twelve, while the others will be "freeloaders" on the efforts of these few. But as long as they can get out of the arrangement if they no longer like it, no violation of rights is involved. They got in voluntarily, and they can get out voluntarily; no one has used force.

"But why not say that everybody owns everything? That we *all* own everything there is?"

To some this may have a pleasant ring— but let us try to analyze what it means. If everybody owns everything, then everyone has an equal right to go everywhere, do what he pleases, take what he likes, destroy if he wishes, grow crops or burn them, trample them under, and so on. Consider what it would be like in practice. Suppose you have saved money to buy a house for yourself and your family. Now suppose that the principle, "everybody owns everything," becomes adopted. Well then, why shouldn't every itinerant hippie just come in and take over, sleeping in your beds and eating in your kitchen and not bothering to replace the food supply or clean up the mess? After all, it belongs to all of us, doesn't it? So we have just as much right to it as you, the buyer, have. What happens if we *all* want to sleep in the bedroom and there's not room for all of us? Is it the strongest who wins?

What would be the result? Since no one would be responsible for anything, the property would soon be destroyed, the food used up, the facilities nonfunctional. Beginning as a house that *one* family could use, it would end up as a house that *no one* could use. And if the principle continued to be adopted, no one would build houses any more—or anything else. What for? They would only be occupied and used by others, without remuneration.

Suppose two men are cast ashore on an island, and they agree that each will cultivate half of it. The first man is industrious and grows crops and builds a shelter, making the most of the situation with which he is confronted. The second man, perhaps thinking that the warm days will last forever, lies in the sun, picks coconuts while they last, and does a minimum of work to sustain himself. At the time of harvest, the second man has nothing to harvest, nor does he assist the first man in his labors. But later when there is a dearth of food on the island, the second man comes to the first man and demands half of the harvest as his right. But of course he has no right to the product of the first man's labors. The first man may freely choose to give part of his harvest to the second out of charity rather than see him starve; but that is just what it is—charity, not the second man's right.

How can any of man's rights be violated? Ultimately, only by the use of force. I can make suggestions to you, I can reason with you, entreat you (if you are willing to listen), but I cannot *force* you without violating your rights; only by forcing you do I cut the cord between your free decisions and your actions. Voluntary relations between individuals involve no deprivation of rights, but murder, assault, and rape do, because in doing these things I make you the unwilling victim of my actions. A man's beating his wife involves no

violation of rights if she *wanted* to be beaten. *Force is behavior that requires the unwilling involvement of other persons.*

Thus the use of force need not involve the use of physical violence. If I trespass on your property or dump garbage on it, I am violating your property rights, as indeed I am when I steal your watch; although this is not force in the sense of violence, it *is* a case of your being an unwilling victim of my action. Similarly, if you shout at me so that I cannot be heard when I try to speak, or blow a siren in my ear, or start a factory next door which pollutes my land, you are again violating my rights (to free speech, to property); I am, again, an unwilling victim of your actions. Similarly, if you steal a manuscript of mine and publish it as your own, you are confiscating a piece of my property and thus violating my right to keep what is the product of my labor. Of course, if I give you the manuscript with permission to sign your name to it and keep the proceeds, no violation of rights is involved—any more than if I give you permission to dump garbage on my yard.

According to libertarianism, the role of government should be limited to the retaliatory use of force against those who have initiated its use. It should not enter into any other areas, such as religion, social organization, and economics.

GOVERNMENT

Government is the most dangerous institution known to man. Throughout history it has violated the rights of men more than any individual or group of individuals could do: it has killed people, enslaved them, sent them to forced labor and concentration camps, and regularly robbed and pillaged them of the fruits of their expended labor. Unlike individual criminals, government has the power to arrest and try; unlike individual criminals, it can surround and encompass a person totally, dominating every aspect of one's life, so that one has no recourse from it but to leave the country (and in totalitarian nations even that is prohibited). Government throughout history has a much sorrier record than any individual, even that of a ruthless mass murderer. The signs we see on bumper stickers are chillingly accurate: "Beware: the Government Is Armed and Dangerous."

The only proper role of government, according to libertarians, is that of the protector of the citizen against aggression by other individuals. The government, of course, should never initiate aggression; its proper role is as the embodiment of the *retaliatory* use of force against anyone who initiates its use.

If each individual had constantly to defend himself against possible aggressors, he would have to spend a considerable portion of his life in target practice, karate exercises, and other means of self-defenses, and even so he would probably be helpless against groups of individuals who might try to kill, maim, or rob him. He would have little time for cultivating those qualities which are essential to civilized life, nor would improvements in science, medicine, and the arts be likely to occur. The function of government is to take this responsibility off his shoulders: the government undertakes to defend him against aggressors and to punish them if they attack him. When the government is effective in doing this, it enables the citizen to go about his business unmolested and without constant fear for his life. To do this, of course, government must have physical power—the police, to protect the citizen from aggression within its borders, and the armed forces, to protect him from aggressors outside. Beyond that, the government should not intrude upon his life, either to run his business, or adjust his daily activities, or prescribe his personal moral code.

Government, then, undertakes to be the individual's protector; but historically governments have gone far beyond this function. Since they already have the physical power, they have not hesitated to use it for purposes far beyond that which was entrusted to them in the first place. Undertaking initially to protect its citizens against aggression, it has often itself become an aggressor—a far greater aggressor, indeed, than the criminals against whom it was supposed to protect its citizens. Governments have done what no private citizen can do: arrest and imprison individuals without a trial and send them to slave labor camps. Government must have power in order to be effective—and yet the very means by which alone it can be effective make it vulnerable to the abuse of power, leading to managing the lives of individuals and even inflicting terror upon them.

What then should be the function of government? In a word, the *protection of human rights.*

1. The right to life: libertarians support all such legislation as will protect human beings against the use of force by others, for example, laws against killing, attempted killing, maiming, beating, and all kinds of physical violence.
2. The right to liberty: there should be no laws compromising in any way freedom of speech, of the press, and of peaceable assembly. There should be no censorship of ideas, books, films, or of anything else by government.
3. The right to property: libertarians support legislation that protects the property rights of individuals against confiscation, nationalization, eminent domain, robbery, trespass, fraud and misrepresentation, patent and copyright, libel and slander.

Someone has violently assaulted you. Should he be legally liable? Of course. He has violated one of your rights. He has knowingly injured you, and since he has initiated aggression against you he should be made to expiate.

Someone has negligently left his bicycle on the sidewalk where you trip over it in the dark and injure yourself. He didn't do it intentionally; he didn't mean you any harm. Should he be legally liable? Of course; he has, however unwittingly, injured you, and since the injury is caused by him and you are the victim, he should pay.

Someone across the street is unemployed. Should you be taxed extra to pay for his expenses? Not at all. You have not injured him, you are not responsible for the fact that he is unemployed (unless you are a senator or bureaucrat who agitated for further curtailing of business, which legislation passed, with the result that your neighbor was laid off by the curtailed business). You may voluntarily wish to help him out, or better still, try to get him a job to put him on his feet again; but since you have initiated no aggressive act against him, and neither purposely nor accidentally injured him in any way, you should not be legally penalized for the fact of his unemployment. (Actually, it is just such penalties that increase unemployment.)

One man, A, works hard for years and finally earns a high salary as a professional man. A second man, B, prefers not to work at all, and to spend wastefully what money he has (through inheritance), so that after a year or two he has nothing left. At the end of this time he has a long siege of illness and lots of medical bills to pay. He demands that the bills be paid by the government—that is, by the taxpayers of the land, including Mr. A.

But of course B has no such right. He chose to lead his life in a certain way—that was his voluntary decision. One consequence of that choice is that he must depend on charity in case of later need. Mr. A chose not to live that way. (And if everyone lived like Mr. B, on whom would he depend in case of later need?) Each has a right to live in the way he pleases, but each must live with the consequences of his own decision (which, as always, fall primarily on himself). He cannot, in time of need, claim A's beneficence as his right. . . .

Laws may be classified into three types: (1) laws protecting individuals against themselves, such as laws against fornication and other sexual behavior, alcohol, and drugs; (2) laws protecting individuals against aggressions by other individuals, such as laws against murder, robbery, and fraud; (3) laws requiring people to help one another; for ex-

ample, all laws which rob Peter to pay Paul, such as welfare.

Libertarians reject the first class of laws totally. Behavior which harms no one else is strictly the individual's own affair. Thus, there should be no laws against becoming intoxicated, since whether or not to become intoxicated is the individual's own decision; but there should be laws against driving while intoxicated, since the drunken driver is a threat to every other motorist on the highway (drunken driving falls into type 2). Similarly, there should be no laws against drugs (except the prohibition of sale of drugs to minors) as long as the taking of these drugs poses no threat to anyone else. Drug addiction is a psychological problem to which no present solution exists. Most of the social harm caused by addicts, other than to themselves, is the result of thefts which they perform in order to continue their habit—and then the *legal* crime is the theft, not the addiction. The actual cost of heroin is about ten cents a shot; if it were legalized, the enormous traffic in illegal sale and purchase of it would stop, as well as the accompanying proselytization to get new addicts (to make more money for the pusher) and the thefts performed by addicts who often require eighty dollars a day just to keep up the habit. Addiction would not stop, but the crimes would: it is estimated that 75 percent of the burglaries in New York City today are performed by addicts, and all these crimes could be wiped out at one stroke through the legalization of drugs. (Only when the taking of drugs could be shown to constitute a threat to *others*, should it be prohibited by law. It is only laws protecting people against *themselves* that libertarians oppose.)

Laws should be limited to the second class only: aggression by individuals against other individuals. These are laws whose function is to protect human beings against encroachment by others; and this, as we have seen, is (according to libertarianism) the sole function of government.

Libertarians also reject the third class of laws totally: no one should be forced by law to help others, not even to tell them the time of day if requested, and certainly not to give them a portion of one's weekly paycheck. Governments, in the guise of humanitarianism, have given to some by taking from others (charging a "handling fee" in the process, which, because of the government's waste and inefficiency, sometimes is several hundred percent). And in so doing they have decreased incentive, violated the rights of individuals, and lowered the standard of living of almost everyone.

All such laws constitute what libertarians call *moral cannibalism.* A cannibal in the physical sense is a person who lives off the flesh of other human beings. A *moral* cannibal is one who believes he has a right to live off the "spirit" of other human beings—who believes that he has a moral claim on the productive capacity, time, and effort expended by others.

It has become fashionable to claim virtually everything that one needs or desires as one's *right.* Thus, many people claim that they have a right to a job, the right to free medical care, to free food and clothing, to a decent home, and so on. Now if one asks, apart from any specific context, whether it would be desirable if everyone had these things, one might well say yes. But there is a gimmick attached to each of them: *At whose expense?* Jobs, medical care, education, and so on, don't grow on trees. These are goods and services *produced only by men.* Who, then, is to provide them, and under what conditions?

If you have a right to a job, who is to supply it? Must an employer supply it even if he doesn't want to hire you? What if you are unemployable, or incurably lazy? (If you say "the government must supply it," does that mean that a job must be created for you which no employer needs done, and that you must be kept in it regardless of how much or little you work?) If the employer is forced to supply it at his expense even if he doesn't need you, then isn't *he* being enslaved to that extent? What ever happened to *his* right to conduct his life and his affairs in accordance

with his choices?

If you have a right to free medical care, then, since medical care doesn't exist in nature as wild apples do, some people will have to supply it to you for free: that is, they will have to spend their time and money and energy taking care of you whether they want to or not. What ever happened to *their* right to conduct their lives as they see fit? Or do you have a right to violate theirs? Can there be a right to violate rights?

All those who demand this or that as a "free service" are consciously or unconsciously evading the fact that there is in reality no such thing as free services. All man-made goods and services are the result of human expenditure of time and effort. There is no such thing as "something for nothing" in this world. If you demand something free, you are demanding that other men give their time and effort to you without compensation. If they voluntarily choose to do this, there is no problem; but if you demand that they be *forced* to do it, you are interfering with their right not to do it if they so choose. "Swimming in this pool ought to be free!" says the indignant passerby. What he means is that others should build a pool, others should provide the materials, and still others should run it and keep it in functioning order, so that *he* can use it without fee. But what right has he to the expenditure of *their* time and effort? To expect something "for free" is to expect it *to be paid for by others* whether they choose to or not.

Many questions, particularly about economic matters, will be generated by the libertarian account of human rights and the role of government. Should government have no role in assisting the needy, in providing social security, in legislating minimum wages, in fixing prices and putting a ceiling on rents, in curbing monopolies, in erecting tariffs, in guaranteeing jobs, in managing the money supply? To these and all similar questions the libertarian answers with an unequivocal no.

"But then you'd let people go hungry!" comes the rejoinder. This, the libertarian insists, is precisely what would not happen; with the restrictions removed, the economy would flourish as never before. With the controls taken off business, existing enterprises would expand and new ones would spring into existence satisfying more and more consumer needs; millions more people would be gainfully employed instead of subsisting on welfare, and all kinds of research and production, released from the stranglehold of government, would proliferate, fulfilling man's needs and desires as never before. It has always been so whenever government has permitted men to be free traders on a free market. But *why* this is so, and how the free market is the best solution to all problems relating to the material aspect of man's life, is another and far longer story....

Review Questions

1. How does Hospers explain libertarianism?

2. What are the three most basic human rights according to Hospers?

3. According to Hospers, why is the government "the chief enemy of the right to property?"

4. In Hospers' view, what is wrong with holding that everybody owns everything?

5. Hospers claims that human rights can be violated in only one way. How?

6. What is the only proper role of government according to libertarians?

7. How does Hospers propose to deal the problem of unemployment?

8. Which type of laws do libertarians accept? Which laws do they reject?

9. Why does Hospers think that people will not be hungry if libertarianism is followed?

Discussion Questions

1. Hospers thinks that the right to property is just as important as the right to life. Do you agree? Why or why not?

2. Compare Hospers' account of the right to life to that given by Rachels. Which account is more acceptable and why?

3. Hospers says, "I may deplore your choice of life-style, ... but I have no right to use force to change it." Can you think of any exceptions to this? What are they?

4. Hospers claims that human rights can be violated only by the use of force. Is this true? Explain your answer.

5. "A man's beating his wife involves no violation of rights if she *wanted* to be beaten." What is your view of voluntary wife-beating? Is this an acceptable practice?

6. Hospers says, "Libertarians support all such legislation as will protect human beings against the use of force by others." How would he apply this to abortion, euthanasia, and capital punishment?

7. Hospers rejects all laws which protect individuals from themselves, for example, laws prohibiting prostitution and drugs. Do you agree that all such laws should be abolished? Explain your view of these paternalistic laws.

8. Hospers is totally opposed to any welfare laws. Should all such laws be eliminated? What is your view?

9. Hospers denies that you have a right to a job, medical care, food, or anything free. Do you agree? Do you have any positive rights at all, as distinguished from the negative rights of noninterference?

James P. Sterba

Human Rights: A Social Contract Perspective

James P. Sterba teaches philosophy at the University of Notre Dame. He is the editor of Morality in Practice *(two editions),* The Ethics of War, Nuclear Deterrence, *and the author of several papers on topics in ethics.*

Sterba develops a conception of human rights based on Rawls' social contract theory. On this conception, the right to life has priority over the right to property. The right to life is interpreted to mean noninterference with a person's attempts to acquire the goods and resources necessary for satisfying basic needs. These basic needs include food, shelter, medical care, protection, companionship, and self-development. Sterba defends this social contract account of rights from attacks derived from libertarianism, socialism, and natural law theory.

There are many perspectives from which one might attempt to defend a conception of human rights. In this paper I argue that, from a social contract perspective, every human person possesses a right to life interpreted as a right to noninterference with that person's attempts to acquire the goods and resources necessary for satisfying his or her basic needs, and a right to property interpreted as a right to retain goods and resources acquired either by appropriation from nature or by voluntary agreement. I argue, moreover, that a person's right to life will generally have priority over other persons' rights to property. Finally, I defend this social contract justification of human rights against objections that arise from libertarian, socialist, and natural law perspectives.

James P. Sterba, "Human Rights: A Social Contract Perspective," American Catholic Philosophical Association Proceedings, Vol. 55 (1981), pp. 268–275. ©1981 The American Catholic Philosophical Association. Reprinted with permission.

The social contract perspective from which I defend this concept of human rights does not presuppose any actual agreement as the basis for a person's right to life or a person's right to property. Rather, with John Rawls, I contend that a suitably constrained hypothetical agreement suffices as the moral basis for such fundamental human rights. The main constraint I would place on such a hypothetical agreement is that the agreement be reached by persons who discount the knowledge of which particular interests happen to be their own. Persons who were so constrained obviously would know what their particular interests are; they would just not be taking that knowledge into account when agreeing to a conception of human rights. Rather, in agreeing to such a conception, they would be reasoning from their knowledge of all the particular interests of everyone affected by their agreement, but not from their knowledge of which particular interests happen to be their own. Persons who were so constrained would (like judges who discount prejudicial information in order to reach fair decisions) be able to give a fair hearing to everyone's particular interests. Assuming further that they were well-informed of the particular interests that would be affected by their agreement and were fully capable of rationally deliberating with respect to that information, then their deliberations would culminate in a unanimous agreement. This is because each of them would be deliberating in a rationally correct manner with respect to the same information and would be constrained so as to give a uniform evaluation of the alternatives; consequently, each of them would favor the same conception of human rights.

But what conception of human rights would result from such a constrained hypothetical agreement? Since in reaching such an agreement persons would not be using their knowledge of which particular interests happen to be their own, they would be quite concerned about the pattern according to which goods and resources happened to be distributed. They would be especially concerned that their particular interests might be either those of persons with the largest share of goods and resources or those of persons with the smallest share of goods and resources. On the one hand, if their interests were those of persons with the largest share of goods and resources then it would presumably be in their interest to favor a virtually unconditional right to property. On the other hand, if their interests were those of persons with the smallest share of goods and resources then it would presumably be in their interest to favor a virtually unconditional right to life. But it would not be reasonable for persons who have discounted their knowledge of which particular interests happen to be their own either to exclusively favor the interests of persons with the largest share of goods and resources by endorsing a virtually unconditional right to property or to favor exclusively the interests of persons with the smallest share of goods and resources by endorsing a virtually unconditional right of life. Rather it would be reasonable for them to compromise by endorsing a right to life interpreted as a right to noninterference with a person's attempts to acquire the goods and resources necessary for satisfying his or her basic needs and a right to property interpreted as a right to retain the goods and resources acquired by appropriation from nature or by free agreement provided that doing so does not violate anyone's right to life.

Now clearly the right to life that would be favored by persons constrained to discount the knowledge of which particular interests happen to be their own would not be as demanding as the right to life that would be most beneficial to those who have the smallest share of goods and resources. For the right to life that would be most beneficial to this group would be a virtually unconditional right to receive the highest possible minimum of goods and resources. By contrast, the right to life that would be favored by persons constrained to discount the knowledge

of which particular interests happen to be their own normally would only require that others not interfere with a person's attempts to take advantage of opportunities made available by others for meeting his or her basic needs by engaging in mutually beneficial work. Only when such opportunities are not available or when the person is unable to take advantage of them would this right to life also require that others not interfere with the person's attempts simply to appropriate from the surplus possessions of the more advantaged what is required to meet his or her basic needs. And even when a person's right to life would make this more demanding requirement, there would still be an obligation to return the equivalent of those surplus possessions once the person is able to do so and still satisfy his or her basic needs.

Moreover, just as the right to life that would be favored by persons constrained to discount the knowledge of which particular interests happen to be their own would not be as demanding as the right to life that would be most beneficial to those who have the smallest share of goods and resources, so likewise the right to property favored by persons so constrained would not be as demanding as the right to property that would be most beneficial to those who have the largest share of goods and resources. For the right to property that would be most beneficial to this group would be a right to property that is unrestricted by a right to life under almost any interpretation. By contrast, the right to property favored by persons constrained to discount the knowledge of which particular interests happen to be their own would be a right to property that is restricted by a right to life under the favored interpretation.

Obviously by agreeing to this conception of human rights persons constrained to discount the knowledge of which particular interests happen to be their own would be giving priority to the satisfaction of people's basic needs. Now a person's basic needs are simply those needs which must be satisfied in order not to endanger seriously the person's health and sanity. Thus the needs a person has for food, shelter, medical care, protection, companionship, and self-development are at least in part needs of this sort. Naturally, societies vary in their ability to satisfy a person's basic needs but the needs themselves would not seem to be similarly subject to variation unless there were a corresponding variation in what constitutes health and sanity in different societies. Consequently, even though the criterion of need would not be an acceptable standard for distributing all social goods because, among other things, of the difficulty of determining both what a person's nonbasic needs are and how they should be arranged according to priority, the criterion of need does appear to be an acceptable standard for determining when a right to life should have priority over a right to property.

In order to better assess the merits of this social contract conception of human rights, let us now consider how this conception might be defended against representative objections from libertarian, socialist, and natural law perspectives.

First of all, from a libertarian perspective this social contract conception of human rights would appear to be flawed in its foundation. Libertarians, like Robert Nozick and John Hospers, might grant that persons who were so constrained to discount the knowledge of which particular interests happen to be their own would agree to this conception of human rights, but they would surely deny that such a constrained hypothetical agreement shows that the conception of human rights is morally defensible. For libertarians would maintain that the ultimate moral foundation for a conception of human rights is not a constrained hypothetical agreement but rather an ideal of liberty. Taking liberty to be the absence of interference by other persons, libertarians would contend that an ideal of liberty justifies a conception of human rights that is quite different from the conception that would emerge from a constrained hypothetical agreement. More specifically, liber-

tarians would contend that an ideal of liberty justifies a conception of human rights which features a virtually unconditional right to property.

Suppose, however, for the sake of argument we accept a libertarian's contention that the ultimate moral foundation for a conception of human rights is an ideal of liberty and not a constrained hypothetical agreement. And suppose further that we also accept the libertarian's contention that liberty is to be understood as the absence of interference by other persons. From these assumptions it would follow that when the poor take what is necessary for meeting their basic needs from the surplus possessions of the rich (case 1), the poor would be restricting the liberty of the rich. But it also follows that when the rich interfere with the poor's taking what is necessary for meeting their basic needs from the surplus possessions of the rich (case 2), the rich would be restricting the liberty of the poor. For in both cases we have people performing actions that interfere with the actions of others. Thus given the practical impossibility of avoiding both of these competing restrictions of liberty, the key question is how to assess these restrictions from a moral point of view.

Libertarians, of course, would want to maintain that restricting the liberty of the poor as in case (2) is morally preferable to restricting the liberty of the rich as in case (1); but if we assume that, however else we specify the requirements of morality, they cannot be contrary to reason then it would seem that we cannot justify this preference. For while it would surely be contrary to reason to ask the poor to restrict their liberty as in case 2 and thus sacrifice the fulfillment of their basic needs, it would not at all seem contrary to reason to ask the rich to restrict their liberty as in case 1 and thus sacrifice the fulfillment of some of their nonbasic needs (e.g., their needs for exotic food, expensive wardrobes, and multiple dwellings). Surely restricting the liberty of the rich to satisfy their nonbasic needs is morally preferable to restricting the liberty of the poor to satisfy their basic needs.

Needless to say, this moral preference for restricting the liberty of the rich depends upon the willingness of the poor to take advantage of whatever opportunities are available to them for satisfying their basic needs by engaging in mutually beneficial work, so that failure of the poor to take advantage of such opportunities would normally either cancel or at least significantly reduce the obligation of the rich to restrict their own liberty for the benefit of the poor. In addition, the poor would be required to return the equivalent of any surplus possessions they have simply taken from the rich once they are able to do so and still satisfy their basic needs. Accordingly, a moral assessment of the competing liberties as determined by the libertarian's ideal of liberty leads to the same conception of human rights as would emerge from a constrained hypothetical agreement. It follows, then, that even if we accepted the libertarian's contention that an ideal of liberty is the ultimate moral foundation for a conception of human rights we should still endorse a social contract conception of human rights.

Turning now to a socialist perspective, we find a more practical objection to a social contract conception of human rights. For socialists would contend that while a social contract conception of human rights has considerable merit as an ideal, it fails to make clear that the proper implementation of such an ideal would require socialization of the means of production. For example, C.B. Macpherson claims

It is not difficult to show ... that a socialist system can meet the requirements of [a social contract conception of human rights]. But it can do so not as a "modification" of the capitalist market system, but by its rejection of exploitative property institutions.

Nevertheless, for persons who accept a social contract conception of human rights, the question of whether or not to socialize the means of production may not be as momentous as Macpherson takes it to be. The reason

for this is that in order for a system of private ownership of the means of production to satisfy the high minimum requirements of this conception, it would appear necessary to limit and redistribute private holdings to such a degree that the ownership of all the means of production would, as a result, be widely dispersed throughout the society. For example, in the United States where 5% of the population owns 83% of corporate stock and 63% of businesses and professions, the ownership of income-bearing investments would have to be significantly limited and redistributed in order to meet the requirements of this conception of human rights. As **Marx** pointed out, the widespread exploitation of laborers associated with early capitalism only began when large numbers "had been robbed of all their own means of production and of all the guarantees of existence afforded by the old feudal system" by persons and economic groups who already had considerable wealth and power. But the concentration of wealth and power necessary to carry out such exploitation is not likely to be found in a society which in accordance with a social contract conception of human rights provides for the basic needs of all its members as well as for the basic needs of distant peoples and future generations. Consequently, a shift from such restricted private ownership of the means of production to socialization of those means may in fact have little practical consequence.

Of course, socialists might respond that merely providing a minimum sufficient to satisfy the basic needs of each and every person does not go far enough in eliminating alienation and injustice from a society since these defects can manifest themselves in failure to satisfy nonbasic needs as well as basic needs. And it is just in this regard, so socialists might claim, that a socialist state would significantly differ from the welfare state usually endorsed by defenders of a social contract conception of human rights. For presumably in a welfare state after basic needs have been met, appropriation from nature and free agreement would determine the distribution of property, and hence, determine whose nonbasic needs would be satisfied whereas in a socialist state there would be a willingness to provide both for the basic and the nonbasic needs of each and every person.

But even granting that theoretically there may be this difference, practically speaking, in either a welfare state or a socialist state the scope for the satisfaction of nonbasic needs would be so drastically limited by the necessity of meeting not only the basic needs of the members of one's own society but also the basic needs of distant peoples and future generations as well that there would not appear to be any net benefit to be gained from enforcing some particular distribution of the relatively few social goods that could legitimately be used to satisfy nonbasic needs. Consequently, socialists would have little reason to object to a welfare state in which in accordance with a social contract conception of human rights people fulfill their obligation to provide a minimum for their fellow citizens as well as for distant peoples and future generations.

Finally, from a **natural law** perspective this social contract conception of human rights faces both a theoretical objection to its ultimate moral foundation and a practical objection to the completeness of its requirements.

The theoretical objection challenges the social contract theorist to show why the ultimate moral foundation for a conception of human rights should be a constrained hypothetical agreement rather than an adequate account of human nature. For at least some natural law theorists would surely maintain that grounding a conception of human rights on a constrained hypothetical agreement introduces an unwarranted element of conventionality into a conception of human rights. For such theorists, only by grounding a conception of human rights on an adequate account of human nature can we preserve the essential nonconventionality of a conception of human rights.

This theoretical objection to a social contract conception of human rights however, fails to take into account the fact that the constrained hypothetical agreement is itself made with a full appreciation of the morally relevant facts of human nature. Indeed, the only knowledge about human nature that is not taken into account in fashioning a social contract conception of human rights is the knowledge of which particular interests happen to belong to the persons making the constrained hypothetical agreement, and that knowledge, assuming that the social contract theorist is correct, is morally suspect and should be discounted. Thus, insofar as the knowledge of human nature can legitimately determine a conception of human rights, a social contract theorist can maintain that his conception of human rights would be determined by that knowledge. Accordingly, there is no reason to think that by employing a constrained hypothetical agreement, a social contract theorist cannot provide an essentially nonconventional moral foundation for a conception of human rights.

The second and more practical objection which natural law theorists would raise to this social contract conception of human rights concerns the completeness of the conception's practical requirements. For natural law theorists might grant that this social contract conception of human rights is correct as far as it goes. St. Thomas, for example, allowed that when there is no other remedy

... it is lawful for a man to satisfy his own need by means of another's property, by taking it either openly or secretly....

And obviously a claim of this sort is, practically speaking, quite close to the requirements of this social contract conception of human rights. But even granting that this social contract conception of human rights is correct as far as it goes, natural law theorists would still maintain that the conception is incomplete as a moral ideal, since, for example, it neither provides an account of self-regarding virtues nor an account of the requirements of supererogation.

Here, I think, it must be conceded that this objection is sound as an objection to the social contract theory so far elaborated. On the other hand, there does not seem to be any reason why this social contract theory could not be further elaborated to provide a relatively complete moral ideal. Particularly, once we recognize that a constrained hypothetical agreement can take into account all the morally relevant facts about human nature, there seems to be no reason to think that such an agreement could not be reached concerning a relatively complete moral ideal. Thus, while it is true that social contract theorists have generally directed their energies at determining basic human rights, there appears to be no reason why a social contract perspective might not also be used to determine a relatively complete moral ideal.

Summing up, I have argued that from a social contract perspective each human person possesses a right to life that places fairly strong demands on others to provide the means for meeting the person's basic needs and a right to property that is restricted by this right to life. I have also considered representative objections to this social contract conception of human rights arising from libertarian, socialist, and natural law perspectives. Of course, the fact that all of these objections proved ultimately unsuccessful does not suffice to show that some other objection might not yet succeed. However, given the representative character of the objections that have failed, there would seem to be a strong presumptive case in favor of this social contract conception of human rights.

Review Questions

1. How does Sterba explain the social contract perspective?

2. According to Sterba, how should we interpret the rights to life and property? Which right has priority?

3. What is the libertarian objection to the social contract view of rights? How does Sterba reply to this objection?

4. What criticism would the socialist make according to Sterba? How does Sterba answer this criticism?

5. What objections can be made from the natural law perspective? How does Sterba respond to these objections?

Discussion Questions

1. Sterba discusses four different views: social contract theory, libertarianism, socialism, and natural law theory. Which view is the most acceptable? Why? Which gives the best account of human rights? Why?

2. In replying to the libertarian objection, Sterba claims that restricting the liberty of the rich is morally preferable to restricting the liberty of the poor. Do you agree? Why or why not?

3. Sterba thinks we must consider not only the basic needs of the members of our own society, but also the basic needs of distant peoples and future generations. Is this acceptable? Why or why not?

Problem Cases

1. Eritrea (Reported in the *Star Tribune Newspaper of the Twin Cities,* October 29, 1989.) Eritrea is a province of Ethiopia that has been plagued by war, drought, and famine for many years. A rebel group, the Eritrean People Liberation Front, has been fighting for twenty-eight years to be- come independent of the Soviet-supported Ethiopian government. The land is rocky, mountainous, and subject to droughts. There has been a drought roughly every eleven years, and there have been crop failures in four of the last six years. In 1989 the rains failed again, and the harvest was poor. International agencies estimate that more than a million people in this area will need emergency food aid to avert starvation. Should any aid be given to these people? Why or why not?

2. The Poor in Brazil The population of Brazil is growing rapidly. If its present rate of growth of 2.8 percent continues, Brazil will soon become the most populous country in the Western Hemisphere. Although Brazil is rich in natural resources, and has significant economic growth, the majority of benefits have gone to the rich. Forty percent of the population is under fifteen years of age, and unemployment is high. Population growth in the cities has made it difficult for the government to provide education, health care, water, sanitation, food, and housing for the poor. What steps, if any, should be taken to provide for the poor and needy people in this country? Explain your proposals.

3. The Boarder Baby Scandal (As reported by Andrew Stein, president of the New York City Council in the *New York Times,* Saturday, January 17, 1987.) New York City is the most prosperous city in the world, with a 21 billion dollar budget and immense private and community wealth. Yet it has a very serious problem—abandoned and homeless children. At the end of 1986, the city officially counted 11,000 such children and babies living in municipal shelters, decrepit welfare hotels, and hospitals. Some have been living in such conditions for years. Some of the victims are called boarder babies because they were abandoned by their parents in hospitals; they will stay there because of the lack of certified foster parents, or qualified parents willing to adopt them. Others have been removed from their homes for their own protection; reports of child abuse and neglect (including a 250 percent increase in cases of drug-addicted babies) have risen so dramatically that welfare offices are overwhelmed with children, often keeping them overnight in the offices or placing them illegally in group foster homes.

What, if anything, should be done about these babies and children? Explain your recommendations carefully.

4. A Case of Unemployment John Smith and his wife Jane have three small children. Until recently, John had a good job in a factory in Dallas, Texas, and a good life: a house, car, T.V., new furniture, and so on. Unfortunately he lost his job when the factory closed, and he cannot find another one. He has sold all his possessions, and his unemployment compensation payments have run out. Married men and women do not qualify for Aid to Families with Dependent Children (AFDC), and, in fact, no welfare at all is available for John in Dallas. Jane has tried working as a waitress, leaving John to care for the children, but she did not make enough money to pay the bills. Now they are living on the street, and getting one free meal a day at the Salvation Army. The children are suffering from exposure and malnutrition, and John and Jane are tired, hungry, dirty, and depressed.

Should such a family receive welfare benefits or not? Explain your answer.

5. A Homeless Person (Reported in the *St. Cloud* [Minnesota] *Times,* October 6, 1989.) Sharon Lenger, forty-eight, has a bachelor's degree in psychology and an associate of arts degree in drug counseling. She worked as a residential counselor in a home for abused and molested adolescents in California until she was severely assaulted by one of the residents. As a result of the injuries sustained in the attack, she was unable to work in the home and moved out. She received worker's compensation, but this was not enough to live on in California since it was based on her low salary, and it did not take into account the fact that she had free room and board at the home where she worked. She moved to Minnesota to live near her sick and elderly parents. Then the state of California stopped her worker's compensation payments. She needed further surgery because of the assault injuries, so she applied for medical assistance and general assistance. Now she receives $203 a month in general assistance payments, but this is not enough to pay for food and a place to live. Currently she is staying at an emergency shelter run by Catholic Charities, and describes herself as one step away from the street. In other words, she is a homeless person.

Does Sharon Lenger have a right to adequate shelter? If so, how should this be provided?

Suggested Readings

(1) Peter G. Brown, Conrad Johnson, and Paul Vernier, eds., *Income Support: Conceptual and Policy Issues* (Totowa, NJ: Rowman and Littlefield, 1981). This anthology has articles on the moral and conceptual issues involved in the income support policies in the United States.

(2) Nick Eberstadt, "Myths of the Food Crisis," *The New York Review of Books* (February 19, 1976), pp. 32–37. Eberstadt argues that the cause of starvation today is not overpopulation, but inequalities in food distribution. But this inequality cannot be eliminated by welfare-style transfers of income; instead the productivity of the world's poor must be improved.

(3) Milton Friedman, *Capitalism and Freedom* (Chicago: University of Chicago Press, 1962). Friedman is an economist who thinks that the principle of distributing income in a free society should be that one gets what one produces or what the instruments one owns produce.

(4) Michael Harrington, *Socialism* (New York: Saturday Review Press, 1970). Harrington presents a version of socialism that is different from both communism and the welfare state.

(5) Frances Moore Lappe, *World Hunger: Twelve Myths* (New York: Grove Press, 1986). An informed look at various aspects of the problem of world hunger by a liberal who thinks that people in rich countries should change their diets.

(6) Robert Nozick, *Anarchy, State, and Utopia* (New York: Basic Books, 1974). Nozick defends a libertarian conception of justice. This book has produced a great deal of discussion among philosophers concerned with distributive justice, some of it very hostile.

(7) Ernest Patridge, ed., *Responsibilities to Future Generations* (Buffalo, NY: Prometheus Books, 1981). This is a collection of readings on whether or not we have any obligations to people who will live in the future.

(8) Onora O'Neill, "Lifeboat Earth," *Philosophy & Public Affairs* 4, No. 3 (Spring 1975), pp. 273–292. O'Neill assumes that people on the lifeboat Earth have a right not to be killed (except in cases of unavoidable killing and self-defense), and that there is a corollary duty not to kill others. It follows from this, she argues, that we ought to adopt policies that will prevent others from dying from starvation.

(9) ————, "The Moral Perplexities of Famine and World Hunger," in Tom Regan, ed., *Matters of Life and Death*, 2d ed. (New York: Random House, 1986), pp. 294–337. After covering some facts about famine, O'Neill compares the utilitarian and Kantian approaches to famine problems.

(10) James Rachels, "Killing and Starving to Death," *Philosophy* 54, No. 208 (April 1979), pp. 159–171. Rachels argues that our duty to not let people die of starvation is just as strong as our duty not to kill them. He defends this Equivalence Thesis against various attempts to show that there is a moral difference between killing and letting die.

(11) Henry Shue, *Basic Rights* (Princeton, NJ: Princeton University Press, 1980). Shue defends the view that everyone has a right to subsistence, and that this economic right is as important as political rights such as the right to liberty. An implication of this, Shue thinks, is that rich nations (those with a gross domestic product per capita of U.S. $400 or more) should make welfare-style transfers of food or money to poor nations. He claims that they could do this without impoverishing themselves or even causing a decline in their growth rate.

(12) Charles B. Shuman, "Food Aid and the Free Market," in Peter G. Brown and Henry Shue, eds., *Food Policy* (New York: The Free Press), pp. 145–163. In opposition to Shue, Shuman advocates a free-market approach to the problem of hunger and starvation.

(13) Julian L. Simon, *The Ultimate Resource* (Princeton, NJ: Princeton University Press, 1981). Simon argues for a position directly opposed to Hardin's.

(14) Peter Singer, *Practical Ethics* (Cambridge, MA: Cambridge University Press, 1979), pp. 158–181. Singer argues that rich nations have a moral obligation to help poor ones.

Chapter 6

Corporate Responsibility

Introduction

Businesses engage in a variety of practices that seem to be morally questionable: polluting the environment with toxic chemical wastes, producing unsafe or lethal products, discriminating against women and minorities, bribing government officials, lying and deceiving in advertising, buying and selling companies in order to plunder their assets, and giving executives excessive salaries and retirement benefits. Specific examples are not hard to find. There was the deadly chemical accident in Bhopal, India. The Rocky Flats Plant in Colorado has contaminated ground water and air with toxic and radioactive wastes from its production of plutonium triggers for nuclear weapons. There was the enormous oil spill from the Exxon ship, *Valdez.* Executives at Beech Nut tried to pass off flavored water as apple juice. Ivan Boesky and a ring of traders made huge profits by illegally trading on insider information. Takeovers and buyouts have ruined several airline companies while executives and investment bankers have made indecent profits. The list goes on and on; in fact, according to *Time* (July 3, 1989), two-thirds of the Fortune 500 companies were convicted of various crimes between 1975 and 1985.

Our readings begin with a detailed look at a case of pollution by a large corporation, the Hooker Chemical Company, the tenth largest chemical company in the United States, with thirty plants in eleven countries. Critics claim that this company is one of the worst polluters in the country. It has dumped kepone (a known carcinogen) into the James River in Virginia, and allowed mirex (another carcinogen) to run into Lake Ontario from improperly stored barrels. It has released a variety of dangerous gases (chlorine, phosphorous, mercury, and so on) into the air outside the company's Niagara Falls plant. From 1942 to 1953, it dumped over 21,000 tons of toxic chemical wastes into an abandoned canal digging called Love Canal. This site was sold, and an elementary school and a tract of houses were built adjacent to it. But the site eventually leaked its toxic chemicals into houses, causing a number of health problems: liver damage, miscarriages, birth defects, cancer, epilepsy, suicide, and rectal bleeding, to name a few.

A Philosophical Problem Critics of Hooker Chemical assume that this company has a moral responsibility to avoid immoral actions such as polluting the environment. But do corporations have moral responsibilities over and above the responsibility to make money? Should they adopt a moral point of view where they are concerned with the welfare of others, or should they act only in their own self-interest by pursuing profits? The latter view is accepted by Milton Friedman. He believes that the only responsibility of business is to increase its profits by open and free competition without deception or fraud. Friedman attacks what he calls the doctrine of social responsibility, the view that business has other social responsibilities besides making money, for example, the duty to reduce pollution or eliminate racial and sexual discrimination. To begin with, Friedman points out that only persons have responsibilities, and since business as a whole and corporations are not strictly speaking persons, they cannot be said to have responsibilities. Of course business executives are persons who have responsibilities, but their responsibility is to make money for the stockholders, and not to spend the money of the stockholders without their consent. If business executives do this in the pursuit of some socially responsible goal such as reducing pollution, then they are in effect imposing taxes on

the stockholders and the consumers, and this is taxation without representation. Furthermore, the doctrine of social responsibility has bad consequences: executives who follow it will be fired, and wage restraints justified by it will produce strikes and worker revolts. Finally, Friedman denounces the doctrine of social responsibility as a fundamentally subversive doctrine that is incompatible with the ideal of a free society.

Friedman's position has been attacked on a number of points. For example, Friedman contends that corporations cannot meaningfully be said to be persons who have responsibilities. But is this true? Ordinarily a person is an agent who makes decisions and acts, and is held morally responsible for these decisions and acts. But corporations are legally persons who make decisions and act, so why not hold them morally responsible too?

Christopher D. Stone states and criticizes some other points made by Friedman. The promissory argument (as Stone calls it) claims that the management of a corporation has promised the shareholders that it will maximize profits, so if it does not do this, management has broken its promise. Stone objects that management has made no such promise, and that even if it did, the promise is only to existent shareholders, and anyway a promise can always be overridden by more important moral concerns. The agency argument is another argument used by Friedman. According to this argument, the management is the agent of the individuals who own the corporation, and as such it has a duty to maximize profits. In reply, Stone points out that management often does not act like such an agent. Management not only ignores the wishes of the shareholders, it also actively opposes them in some cases.

Stone does not try to refute the so-called polestar argument, the argument that the single-minded pursuit of profits by corporations is a means of charting a straight course for what is best for society.

This argument seems to be a utilitarian one: the greatest good for the greatest number can be achieved only if corporations act solely in the pursuit of profits and ignore moral concerns. But is it really true that a selfish society in which everyone pursues their own self-interest will turn out to be better than a moral society in which people are regulated by moral concerns? This seems very doubtful.

In the final reading for the chapter, Bowie claims that business corporations have a social contract with society. In return for the permission to do business, society gives corporations certain obligations and duties. Corporations should accept these duties because it is in their self-interest to do so; if they don't act responsibly, then society will cancel the contract to do business. Furthermore, Bowie thinks that corporations have a social obligation to help solve social problems because they helped create them, and because they have the resources to resolve them.

Tom L. Beauchamp & Martha W. Elliott

Hooker Chemical and Love Canal

Tom L. Beauchamp is a member of the philosophy department at Georgetown University. He is the author of Philosophical Ethics, *and coauthor of* Hume and the Problem of Causation, Medical Ethics, *and* Principles of Biomedical Ethics.

Martha W. Elliott was a member of Beauchamp's research staff.

The authors describe the toxic chemical waste dumping by Hooker Chemical at the Love Canal site, and the consequences of the resulting pollution for the residents living near the site. Many other cases of pollution and exposure to dangerous chemicals involving Hooker Chemical are described. The efforts of the EPA to solve the problem of dangerous waste disposal are discussed. Finally, the defense of Hooker Chemical is presented.

From Martha W. Elliott and Tom L. Beauchamp, "Hooker Chemical and Love Canal," in Tom L. Beauchamp, *Case Studies in Business, Society, and Ethics* (Englewood Cliffs, NJ: Prentice Hall, Inc., 1983), pp. 107–115. Copyright © 1983 by Tom L. Beauchamp. Reprinted with permission.

Today the Love Canal area of Niagara Falls looks like a war zone. The 235 houses nearest the landfill are boarded up and empty, surrounded by an 8-foot-high cyclone fence that keeps tourists and looters away. Still other houses outside the fenced area are also boarded up and deserted, their owners having fled the unknown. Here and there throughout the neighborhood, newly erected green signs mark the pickup points for emergency evacuation in case there is a sudden release of toxins. An ambulance and a fire truck stand by in the area as workers struggle to seal off the flow of chemicals and render the area once again safe—if not exactly habitable.[1]

What is Love Canal? How did this desolation occur? Who, if anyone, is responsible?

Love Canal is named for William T. Love, a businessman and visionary who in the late nineteenth century attempted to create a model industrial city near Niagara Falls. Love proposed to build a canal that would figure in the generation and transmission of hydroelectric power from the falls to the city's industries. An economic recession that made financing difficult and the development of cheaper methods of transmitting electricity dampened Love's vision, and the partially dug canal in what is now the southeast corner of the city of Niagara Falls is the sole tangible legacy of the project.

However, industry was still drawn to the area, which provided easy access to transportation, cheap electricity, and abundant water for industrial processes. Several chemical companies were among those who took advantage of the natural resources. The Hooker Electrochemical Company, now Hooker Chemical and a major figure in the later events at Love Canal, built its first plant in the area in 1905. Presently a subsidiary of Occidental Petroleum, Hooker manufactures plastics, pesticides, chlorine, caustic soda, fertilizers, and a variety of other chemical products. With over 3,000 employees, Hooker is still one of the largest employers and an economic force in the Niagara Falls area.[2]

In the early 1940s, the abandoned section of Love Canal—for many years a summer swimming hole—became a dump for barrels of waste materials produced by the various chemical companies. Hooker received permission in 1942 to use the site for chemical dumping. It is estimated (though no accurate records were kept) that between the early dumping period and 1953, when this tract of land was sold, approximately 21,800 tons of many different kinds of chemical wastes— some extremely toxic—were put into the old canal. The chemicals were in drums, which were eventually covered with clay-like materials—a reasonable maneuver at the time, since the site was ideal for chemical dumping. It was in an undeveloped and largely unpopulated area and had highly impermeable clay walls that retained liquid chemical materials with virtually no penetration at all. Research indicated that the canal's walls permitted water penetration at the rate of $\frac{1}{3}$ of an inch over a 25–year period.

In 1947 Hooker purchased the Love Canal site from Niagara Power and Development Company. In 1953 the dump was closed and covered with an impermeable clay top. The land encompassing and surrounding the dump was acquired by the Niagara Falls School Board. This acquisition was against the advice of Hooker, which had warned of the toxic wastes. However, the Board persist-

ed and started condemnation proceedings to acquire land in the area. Subsequently an elementary school and a tract of houses were built adjacent to the site. Thousands of cubic yards of soil were removed from the top of the canal in the process. This series of developments set the stage for the desolate scene described in the opening quotation. Apparently, the construction damaged the integrity of the clay covering. Water from rains and heavy snows then seeped through the covering and entered the chemical-filled, clay-lined basin. Eventually the basin overflowed on the unfortunate residents, who were treated to the noxious smell and unwholesome sight of chemicals seeping into their basements and surfacing to the ground.

In April of 1978 evidence of toxic chemicals was found in the living area of several homes and the state health commissioner ordered an investigation. A number of health hazards came to light. Many of the adults examined showed incipient liver damage; young women in certain areas experienced three times the normal incidence of miscarriages; and the area had 3.5 times the normal incidence of birth defects. Epilepsy, suicide, rectal bleeding, hyperactivity, and a variety of other ills were also reported.

Upon review of these findings, the health commissioner recommended that the elementary school be temporarily closed and that pregnant women and children under the age of two be temporarily evacuated. Shortly thereafter the Governor of New York announced that the state would purchase the 235 houses nearest the canal and would assist in the relocation of dispossessed families. President Carter declared Love Canal a disaster area, qualifying the affected families for federal assistance.[3] However, families in the adjacent ring of houses were not able to move—although they firmly believed that their health was endangered. Early studies tended to confirm this view, but in mid-July, 1982, EPA released a study that concluded there was "no evidence that Love Canal has contributed to environmental contamination" in the outer ring of 400 homes. However, this report was on "health hazards" and did not address symptoms of stress that have been noted: For example, the divorce rate among remaining families increased as wives and children fled, while husbands tried to hold onto their investments: their houses and jobs.[4]

Since the investigation first began more than 100 different chemicals, some of them mutagens, teratogens, or carcinogens, have been identified. A number of unanswered questions are still being probed. One question has to do with the long range effects of chemical exposure. Cancer, for instance, often doesn't develop for 20 to 25 years after exposure to the cancer-producing agent. Chromosomal damage may appear only in subsequent generations. Other unanswered questions involve determining how to clean up the "mess" and who should be held responsible for it.

Hooker Chemical Company figures in both of these questions. In 1977 the city of Niagara Falls employed an engineering consulting firm to study Love Canal and make recommendations. Hooker supplied technical assistance, information, and personnel. The cost of a second study was shared equally by Hooker, the city, and the school board, which had originally purchased the land from Hooker. Hooker also offered to pay one-third of the estimated $850,000 cost of clean-up.[5]

In 1980 Hooker was faced with over $2 billion in lawsuits stemming from its activities at Love Canal and other locations. Thirteen-hundred private suits had been filed against Hooker by mid–1982. The additional complaints and suits stemmed from past and current activities in other states as well as from additional sites in New York. In addition, in 1976 suits of more than $100 million were filed by Virginia employees of Life Sciences who had been exposed to kepone, a highly toxic chemical known to cause trembling and sterility in humans. Hooker was named in the suit as a supplier of some of the raw materials used in the Virginia manufacturing process.

(This suit was ultimately settled out of court.) In 1977 Hooker was ordered to pay $176,000 for discharging HCCPD, a chemical used in the manufacture of Kepone and Mirex, which causes cancer in laboratory animals, into White Lake. In 1979 Michigan officials sued Hooker for a $200 million cleanup due to air, water, and land pollution around its White Lake plant. Hooker in 1978 acknowledged that it had buried an estimated 3,700 tons of trichlorophenol waste—which includes some quantities of the potent chemical dioxin—at various sites around Niagara Falls from 1942–1972.[6]

At the same time that Hooker was defending itself in Virginia and Michigan, the state of California was investigating the company and ultimately brought suit on charges that Hooker's Occidental Chemical Plant at Lathrop, California had for years violated state law by dumping toxic pesticides, thereby polluting nearby ground water. While Hooker officials denied the charges, a series of memos written by Robert Edson, Occidental's environmental engineer at Lathrop, suggests the company knew of the hazard as early as 1975 but chose to ignore it until pressured by the state investigation. In April 1975 Edson wrote, "Our laboratory records indicate that we are slowly contaminating all wells in our area, and two of our own wells are contaminated to the point of being toxic to animals or humans...." A year later he wrote, "To date, we have been discharging waste water ... containing about five tons of pesticide per year to the ground.... I believe we have fooled around long enough and already over-pressed our luck." Another year later, Edson reiterated his charges and added that "if anyone should complain, we could be the party named in an action by the Water Quality Control Board.... Do we correct the situation before we have a problem or do we hold off until action is taken against us?"[7]

Other complaints stemmed from the same general area as Love Canal. In 1976 the New York Department of Environmental Conservation banned consumption of seven species of fish taken from Lake Ontario claiming that they were contaminated with chemicals, including Mirex. It was alleged that Mirex had been discharged from the Hooker Niagara Falls plant. A Hooker-sponsored study of Lake Ontario fish disputed this allegation of Mirex contamination. While this study has not been accepted by the state, the ban has, for the most part, been lifted.

Hooker's Hyde Park chemical waste dump, located in the Niagara Falls area, has also been a source of continuing concern and dispute to residents and government officials. In 1972 the manager of a plant adjacent to the dump complained to Hooker about "an extremely dangerous condition affecting our plant and employees ... our midnight shift workers has [sic] complained of coughing and sore throats from the obnoxious and corrosive permeating fumes from the disposal site." [8] Apparently the "dangerous condition" was not adequately rectified, and in 1979 Hooker's Hyde Park landfill became the subject of a nearly $26 million suit filed by the town of Niagara. New York State filed a suit for more than $200 million for alleged damages at the Hyde Park site. A remedial program agreement, signed by the state, entailed an estimated $16 million in proposed work at this site.

In 1980 Hooker was also faced with four additional suits for $124.5 million in remedial work by the Environmental Protection Agency. Barbara Blum, EPA Deputy Administrator, explains the EPA concern and strategy as follows:

To help protect against toxic by-products, EPA has launched a major regulatory and enforcement drive, including suits using EPA's "imminent hazard" or "emergency" provisions to force the cleanup of the most dangerous hazardous waste problems. I anticipate that 50 such cases will be filed before the end of 1980.

The most widely recognized symbol of the hazardous waste crisis is Love Canal in Niagara Falls, where an entire neighborhood has been abandoned. There are, however, hundreds of other graphic examples scattered across the country.

The issue of how to deal with our legacy of

dangerous waste disposal sites and to prevent the development of new "Love Canals" may be the most difficult environmental challenge of the 1980's. EPA has launched four interrelated efforts to bring this problem under control. [9]

Two of these efforts are relevant to the actions against Hooker: (1) litigation under "imminent hazard" provisions of existing EPA laws and (2) the creation of programs, financed by government and industry, to clean up hazardous waste sites. The "imminent hazard" litigation is described as follows:

Primarily emphasizing injunctive relief, this program seeks to halt dangerous disposal practices and to force privately-funded clean-up. This approach gets results, of course, only where a responsible party can be identified and has adequate financial resources to carry some or all of the clean-up costs. [10]

Blum goes on to describe the specific statutes the EPA is acting under and the EPA's collaboration with the Justice Department in enforcing the statutes:

Sections of the Resource Conservation and Recovery Act, Safe Drinking Water Act, Toxic Substances Control Act, Clean Water Act, and Clean Air Act all authorize EPA to ask the court for injunctive relief in situations which pose threats to public health or the environment. Section 309 of the Clean Water Act levies a penalty of up to $10,000 a day for unpermitted discharges to navigable waters (a leaking dump can be considered a discharge). The 1899 "Refuse Act" provides additional penalties for unauthorized discharges or dumping. Available common law remedies include the common law of nuisance and trespass, restitution, and "strict liability" for damages caused by those who engaged in ultra-hazardous activities. We are aggressively using each of these legal tools to address the hazardous waste disposal problem.

The Agency—working with the Department of Justice—has launched a top-priority effort to pursue imminent hazard cases....

People are frightened by Love Canal and by the emergence of threatening hazardous waste sites in their local communities. They are demanding action—and they are getting it. [11]

The EPA currently estimates that only 10% of all hazardous wastes are disposed of in strict compliance with federal regulations. According to Thomas H. Maugh, II, writing in 1979 in *Science* magazine, "nearly 50 percent is disposed of by lagooning in unlined surface impoundments, 30 percent in non-secure landfills, and about 10 percent by dumping into sewers, spreading on roads, injection into deep wells, and incineration under uncontrolled conditions." [12] Maugh goes on to argue that "legal dumpsites gone awry" are actually a lesser problem than the growing problem of illegally dumped wastes in unsecured dumpsites, often in the middle of cities.[13] In October 1981 the EPA announced that "there are at least 29 toxic waste disposal sites around the country as dangerous or more so than Love Canal...." [14] This is partly because some clean-up has already been done at Love Canal and many of the endangered people have moved away.

Hooker Chemical believes that its role and defense have been misunderstood. While the company neither denies using the canal as a chemical dump nor denies that the dump has created a serious problem, officials of the company contend that (1) the company's efforts to prevent first the public and then the private development of the canal area are generally unrecognized; (2) the company has been an industry leader in safety; (3) Hooker is being unfairly blamed and singled out for waste disposal practices that were then almost universal throughout the chemical industry; and (4) a certain level of risk is an inevitable hazard in an industrial society.

Hooker has marshaled data to support its contentions. In the first place, Hooker believes that its efforts to warn the School Board and City against interfering with the waste disposal area are unappreciated. When the Niagara Falls School Board expressed an interest in selling a portion of the Love Canal tract to a developer, Hooker representatives argued against the plan in a public meeting and later reiterated to the Board its warnings of possible hazards. When the school board

persisted in its plans and began to obtain adjacent parcels of land through condemnation proceedings, Hooker, in the deed to the School Board, again referred to the past use of the property and stipulated that all future risks and liabilities be passed to the School Board. One part of the deed stipulated:

Prior to the delivery of this instrument of conveyance, the grantee herein has been advised by the grantor that the premises above described have been filled, in whole or in part, to the present grade level thereof with waste products resulting from the manufacturing of chemicals by the grantor at its plant in the City of Niagara Falls, New York, and the grantee assumes all risk and liability incident to the use thereof. It is, therefore, understood and agreed that, as a part of the consideration for this conveyance and as a condition thereof, no claim, suit, action or demand of any nature whatsoever shall ever be made by the grantee, its successors or assigns, against the grantor, its successors or assigns, for injury to a person or persons, including death resulting therefrom, or loss of or damage to property caused by, in connection with or by reason of the presence of said industrial wastes. [15]

When the school board later sold part of the land to a private developer who planned to build houses, Hooker officials protested the sale both verbally and in writing. Executives believe that the company is being unjustly blamed for the improvidence of others. Hooker also claims that it has no legal responsibility for the problem at Love Canal and that it has more than met its social and moral obligations in time and money spent on the clean-up effort. Through its experiences at Love Canal, Hooker environmental health and safety specialists have developed knowledge and skills that have enabled the company to take a leadership role in problems of underground pollution.

Hooker officials also argue that their past practices more than met then acceptable industry standards for waste disposal. During the period from 1942 to 1953 when Hooker was filling Love Canal with barrels of chemical wastes, the long-term environmental and personal hazzards of these industrial "left-overs" were not adequately recognized either by the industries involved or by the health and regulatory professions. Putting the chemical wastes into a clay canal was actually an improvement on common methods of disposal in unlined and unsecured landfills.

The company's defense of its behavior in the Love Canal situation parallels in some respects the reaction of certain Love Canal residents. They directed the major thrust of their antagonism not toward Hooker Chemical, but toward the New York State Health Department, which had failed to provide open access to the results of state-conducted health studies and left unexplained delays in admitting that a health problem existed. The Health Department attempted to discourage, and even actively harassed independent researchers whose reports indicated more widespread risks to the health of the community than the Department was willing to admit—or prepared to pay to rectify. Given these considerations, it was the Health Department, not Hooker Chemical, who did not meet its obligations to the community in the eyes of many residents.[16]

Hooker supports the common industry position that society will have to learn to accept a certain level of risk in order to enjoy the products of industrial society. Environmental hazards are just one more form of industrial "trade-offs." They cite such persons as Margery W. Shaw, an independent scientist who reviewed a chromosomal study of Love Canal residents. She points out that the level of acceptable risk is a general societal problem merely instanced in this case.

In our democratic society, perhaps we will decide that 500,000 deaths per year is an acceptable price for toxic chemicals in our environment, just as we have decided that 50,000 traffic deaths per year is an acceptable price for automobile travel. On the other hand, we may say that 5,000 deaths per year is an unacceptable price for toxic chemicals.[17]

Over the years Hooker has been among the most heavily criticized corporations for its environmental policies. Ralph Nader attacked Hooker as a "callous corporation" leaving toxic "cesspools." An ABC News documentary was highly critical of the company, concentrating on the increased incidence of disease at Love Canal. On the other hand, Hooker has picked up a number of defenders in recent years. In a July 27, 1981 editorial in *Fortune* magazine, the corporation was defended for having explicitly conformed to government standards of waste disposal, for resisting the construction at the canal, and for being the victim of exaggerated and irresponsible reports about the incidence of disease in the region.[18] An April 1981 editorial in *Discover* magazine laid the blame on the Niagara Falls board of education for Love Canal, but argued that Hooker did act irresponsibly in waste dumpage at a number of other sites.[19] The 1982 study released by the EPA had the effect of blunting some federal efforts and some law suits.

Endnotes

1. Thomas H. Maugh, II, "Toxic Waste Disposal a Gnawing Problem," *Science* 204 (May 1979), p. 820.

2. John F. Steiner, "Love can be Dangerous to your Health," in George A. Steiner and John F. Steiner, *Casebook for Business, Government and Society,* 2nd ed. (New York: Random House, Business Division, 1980), pp. 108–109.

3. Maugh, "Toxic Waste Disposal."

4. Constance Holden, "Love Canal Residents Under Stress," *Science* 208 (June 13, 1980), pp. 1242–1244. "Some Love Canal Areas Safe, A New EPA Study Concludes." *The Washington Post,* July 15, 1982. Sec. A, pp. 1, 9 (Byline: Sandra Sugawara). See also Beverly Paigen below on the earlier data.

5. Steiner, "Love can be Dangerous," p. 112.

6. Michael H. Brown, "Love Canal, U.S.A.," *New York Times Magazine* (January 21, 1979), p. 23, passim; and Gary Whitney, "Hooker Chemical and Plastics" (HBS Case Services, Harvard Business School, 1979), p. 3.

7. "The Hooker Memos," in Robert J. Baum, ed., *Ethical Problems in Engineering,* 2nd ed. (Troy, N.Y.: Center for the Study of the Human Dimensions of Science and Technology, Rensselaer Polytechnic Institute, 1980), Vol. 2: Cases, p. 38; and "An Occidental Unit Knowingly Polluted California Water, House Panel Charges," *The Wall Street Journal,* June 20, 1979, p. 14.

8. Whitney, "Hooker Chemical and Plastics."

9. Barbara Blum, "Hazardous Waste Action," *EPA Journal* (June 1980), p. 2.

10. Ibid.

11. Ibid., p. 8.

12. Maugh, "Toxic Waste Disposal," pp. 819, 821.

13. *Ibid.*, p. 110.

14. Joanne Omong, "EPA Names 115 Toxic Waste Dump Sites for Cleanup," *The Washington Post*, October 24, 1981, p. 4.

15. Steiner, "Love can be Dangerous," p. 110.

16. Beverly Paigen, "Controversy at Love Canal," *Hastings Center Report* 12 (June 1982), pp. 29–37.

17. Margery W. Shaw, "Love Canal Chromosome Study," *Science* 209 (August 15, 1980), p. 752.

18. *Fortune* (July 27, 1981), pp. 30–31.

19. *Discover* 2 (4) (April 1981), p. 8.

Review Questions

1. Describe the use of Love Canal as a site for chemical waste dumping by Hooker Chemical before 1953.

2. Why did the Love Canal site overflow with toxic chemicals? What effect did this have on the residents?

3. What did the government, the residents, and Hooker Chemical do about the pollution?

4. How does Hooker Chemical defend itself against the charge that it acted irresponsibly?

5. Why does Hooker Chemical claim that it has more than met its social and moral obligations?

6. Who do some residents blame?

Discussion Questions

1. Has Hooker Chemical adequately defended itself against the charge of acting irresponsibly? What do you think?

2. Has Hooker Chemical really met all of its social and moral obligations? If so, how have they done this? If not, where have they failed?

3. Is 500,000 deaths per year an acceptable price to pay for toxic chemicals in our environment, just as 50,000 traffic deaths per year is an acceptable price to pay for automobile travel?

Milton Friedman

The Social Responsibility of Business Is to Increase Its Profits

Milton Friedman is Professor of Economics at the University of Chicago, and the author of Capitalism and Freedom.

Friedman defends the conservative view that the only responsibility of business is to increase its profits by open and free competition without deception or fraud. He attacks the view that business has any other social responsibilities, such as eliminating discrimination or reducing pollution. He calls this view the doctrine of social responsibility. *Friedman*

thinks that the business executive who follows such doctrine will end up spending the money of the stockholders or the customers without their consent—in effect imposing taxes and spending tax money independent of the wishes of the public. He believes that this is wrong, it amounts to taxation without representation. Furthermore, the doctrine of social responsibility has bad consequences: business executives who try to follow it will be fired, and wage restraints justified by it will produce wildcat strikes and revolts by workers. Finally, Friedman condemns the doctrine of social responsibility as a fundamentally subversive doctrine that is incompatible with the ideal of a free society because if it is applied to every human activity, the result would be total conformity to general social interests and no freedom at all.

When I hear businessmen speak eloquently about the "social responsibilities of business in a free-enterprise system," I am reminded of the wonderful line about the Frenchman who discovered at the age of 70 that he had been speaking prose all his life. The businessmen believe that they are defending free enterprise when they declaim that business is not concerned "merely" with profit but also with promoting desirable "social" ends; that business has a "social conscience" and takes seriously its responsibilities for providing employment, eliminating discrimination, avoiding pollution and whatever else may be the catchwords of the contemporary crop of reformers. In fact they are—or would be if they or anyone else took them seriously—preaching pure and unadulterated socialism. Businessmen who talk this way are unwitting puppets of the intellectual forces that have been undermining the basis of a free society these past decades.

The discussion of the "social responsibilities of business" are notable for their analytical looseness and lack of rigor. What does it mean to say that "business" has responsibilities? Only people can have responsibilities. A corporation is an artificial person and in this sense may have artificial responsibilities, but "business" as a whole cannot be said to have responsibilities, even in this vague sense. The first step toward clarity to examining the doctrine of the social responsibility of business is to ask precisely what it implies for whom.

Presumably, the individuals who are to be responsible are businessmen, which means individual proprietors or corporate executives. Most of the discussion of social responsibility is directed at corporations, so in what follows I shall mostly neglect the individual proprietors and speak of corporate executives.

In a free-enterprise, private-property system, a corporate executive is an employee of the owners of the business. He has direct responsibility to his employers. That responsibility is to conduct the business in accordance with their desires, which generally will be to make as much money as possible while conforming to the basic rules of the society, both those embodied in law and those embodied in ethical custom. Of course, in some cases his employers may have a different objective. A group of persons might establish a corporation for an eleemosynary purpose—for ex-

ample, a hospital or a school. The manager of such a corporation will not have money profit as his objectives but the rendering of certain services.

In either case, the key point is that, in his capacity as a corporate executive, the manager is the agent of the individuals who own the corporation or establish the eleemosynary institution, and his primary responsibility is to them.

Needless to say, this does not mean that it is easy to judge how well he is performing his task. But at least the criterion of performance is straightforward, and the persons among whom a voluntary contractual arrangement exists are clearly defined.

Of course, the corporate executive is also a person in his own right. As a person, he may have many other responsibilities that he recognizes or assumes voluntarily—to his family, his conscience, his feelings of charity, his church, his clubs, his city, his country. He may feel impelled by these responsibilities to devote part of his income to causes he regards as worthy, to refuse to work for particular corporations, even to leave his job, for example, to join his country's armed forces. If we wish, we may refer to some of these responsibilities as "social responsibilities." But in these respects he is acting as a principal, not an agent; he is spending his own money or time or energy, not the money of his employers or the time or energy he has contracted to devote to their purposes. If these are "social responsibilities," they are the social responsibilities of individuals, not of business.

What does it mean to say that the corporate executive has a "social responsibility" in his capacity as businessman? If this statement is not pure rhetoric, it must mean that he is to act in some way that is not in the interest of his employers. For example, that he is to refrain from increasing the price of the product in order to contribute to the social objective of preventing inflation, even though a price increase would be in the best interests of the corporation. Or that he is to make expenditures on reducing pollution beyond the amount that is in the best interests of the corporation or that is required by law in order to contribute to the social objective of improving the environment. Or that, at the expense of corporate profits, he is to hire "hardcore" unemployed instead of better qualified available workmen to contribute to the social objective of reducing proverty.

In each of these cases, the corporate executive would be spending someone else's money for a general social interest. Insofar as his actions in accord with his "social responsibility" reduce returns to stockholders, he is spending their money. Insofar as his actions raise the price to customers, he is spending the customers' money. Insofar as his actions lower the wages of some employees, he is spending their money.

The stockholders or the customers or the employees could separately spend their own money on the particular action if they wished to do so. The executive is exercising a distinct "social responsibility," rather than serving as an agent of the stockholders or the customers or the employees, only if he spends the money in a different way than they would have spent it.

But if he does this, he is in effect imposing taxes, on the one hand, and deciding how the tax proceeds shall be spent, on the other.

This process raises political questions on two levels: principle and consequences. On the level of political principle, the imposition of taxes and the expenditure of tax proceeds are governmental functions. We have established elaborate constitutional, parliamentary and judicial provisions to control these functions, to assure that taxes are imposed so far as possible in accordance with the preferences and desires of the public—after all, "taxation without representation" was one of the battle cries of the American Revolution. We have a system of checks and balances to separate the legislative function of imposing taxes and enacting expenditures from the executive function of collecting taxes and administering expenditure programs and from

the judicial function of mediating disputes and interpreting the law.

Here the businessman—self-selected or appointed directly or indirectly by stockholders—is to be simultaneously legislator, executive and jurist. He is to decide whom to tax by how much and for what purpose, and he is to spend the proceeds—all this guided only by general exhortations from on high to restrain inflation, improve the environment, fight poverty and so on and on.

The whole justification for permitting the corporate executive to be selected by the stockholders is that the executive is an agent serving the interests of his principal. This justification disappears when the corporate executive imposes taxes and spends the proceeds for "social" purposes. He becomes in effect a public employee, a civil servant, even though he remains in name an employee of a private enterprise. On grounds of political principle, it is intolerable that such civil servants—insofar as their actions in the name of social responsibility are real and not just window-dressing—should be selected as they are now. If they are to be civil servants, then they must be elected through a political process. If they are to impose taxes and make expenditures to foster "social" objectives, then political machinery must be set up to make the assessment of taxes and to determine through a political process the objectives to be served.

This is the basic reason why the doctrine of "social responsibility" involves the acceptance of the socialist view that political mechanisms, not market mechanisms, are the appropriate way to determine the allocation of scarce resources to alternative uses.

On the grounds of consequences, can the corporate executive in fact discharge his alleged "social responsibilities"? On the one hand, suppose he could get away with spending the stockholders' or customers' or employees' money. How is he to know how to spend it? He is told that he must contribute to fighting inflation. How is he to know what action of his will contribute to that end? He is presumably an expert in running his company—in producing a product or selling it or financing it. But nothing about his selection makes him an expert on inflation. Will his holding down the price of his product reduce inflationary pressure? Or, by leaving more spending power in the hands of his customers, simply divert it elsewhere? Or, by forcing him to produce less because of the lower price, will it simply contribute to shortages? Even if he could answer these questions, how much cost is he justified in imposing on his stockholders, customers, and employees for this social purpose? What is his appropriate share and what is the appropriate share of others?

And, whether he wants to or not, can he get away with spending his stockholders', customers' or employees' money? Will not the stockholders fire him? (Either the present ones or those who take over when his actions in the name of social responsibility have reduced the corporation's profits and the price of its stock.) His customers and his employees can desert him for other producers and employers less scrupulous in exercising their social responsibilities.

This facet of "social responsibility" doctrine is brought into sharp relief when the doctrine is used to justify wage restraint by trade unions. The conflict of interest is naked and clear when union officials are asked to subordinate the interest of their members to some more general purpose. If the union officials try to enforce wage restraint, the consequence is likely to be wildcat strikes, rank-and-file revolts and the emergence of strong competitors for their jobs. We thus have the ironic phenomenon that union leaders—at least in the U.S.—have objected to Government interference with the market far more consistently and courageously than have business leaders.

The difficulty of exercising "social responsibility" illustrates, of course, the great virtue of private competitive enterprise—it forces people to be responsible for their own actions and makes it difficult for them to "ex-ploit" other people for either selfish or unselfish purposes. They can do good—but only at their own expense.

Many a reader who has followed the argument this far may be tempted to remonstrate that it is all well and good to speak of Government's having the responsibility to impose taxes and determine expenditures for such "social" purposes as controlling pollution or training the hard-core unemployed, but that the problems are too urgent to wait on the slow course of political processes, that the exercise of social responsibility by businessmen is a quicker and surer way to solve pressing current problems.

Aside from the question of fact—I share Adam Smith's skepticism about the benefits that can be expected from "those who affected to trade for the public good"—this argument must be rejected on grounds of principle. What it amounts to is an assertion that those who favor the taxes and expenditures in question have failed to persuade a majority of their fellow citizens to be of like mind and that they are seeking to attain by undemocratic procedures what they cannot attain by democratic procedures. In a free society, it is hard for "evil" people to do "evil," especially since one man's good is another's evil.

I have, for simplicity, concentrated on the special case of the corporate executive, except only for the brief digression on trade unions. But precisely the same argument applies to the newer phenomenon of calling upon stockholders to require corporations to exercise social responsibility (the recent G.M. crusade for example). In most of these cases, what is in effect involved is some stockholders trying to get other stockholders (or customers or employees) to contribute against their will to "social" causes favored by the activists. Insofar as they succeed, they are again imposing taxes and spending the proceeds.

The situation of the individual proprietor is somewhat different. If he acts to reduce the returns of his enterprise in order to exercise his "social responsibility," he is spending his own money, not someone else's. If he wishes to spend his money on such purposes, that is his right, and I cannot see that there is any objection to his doing so. In the process, he, too, may impose costs on employees and customers. However, because he is far less likely than a large corporation or union to have monopolistic power, any such side effects will tend to be minor.

Of course, in practice the doctrine of social responsibility is frequently a cloak for actions that are justified on other grounds rather than a reason for those actions.

To illustrate, it may well be in the long-run interest of a corporation that is a major employer in a small community to devote resources to providing amenities to that community or to improving its government. That may make it easier to attract desirable employees, it may reduce the wage bill or lessen losses from pilferage and sabotage or have other worthwhile effects. Or it may be that, given the laws about the deductibility of corporate charitable contributions, the stockholders can contribute more to charities they favor by having the corporation make the gift than by doing it themselves, since they can in that way contribute an amount that would otherwise have been paid as corporate taxes.

In each of these—and many similar—cases, there is a strong temptation to rationalize these actions as an exercise of "social responsibility." In the present climate of opinion, with its widespread aversion to "capitalism," "profits," and "soulless corporation" and so on, this is one way for a corporation to generate goodwill as a by-product of expenditures that are entirely justified in its own self-interest.

It would be inconsistent of me to call on corporate executives to refrain from this hypocritical window-dressing because it harms the foundations of a free society. That would be to call on them to exercise a "social responsibility"! If our institutions, and the attitudes of the public make it in their self-interest to cloak their actions in this way, I cannot summon much indignation to denounce them. At the same time, I can express admiration for those individual proprietors or owners of closely held corporations or stockholders of more broadly held corporations who disdain such tactics as approaching fraud.

Whether blameworthy or not, the use of the cloak of social responsibility, and the nonsense spoken in its name by influential and prestigious businessmen, does clearly harm the foundations of a free society. I have been impressed time and again by the schizophrenic character of many businessmen. They are capable of being extremely far-sighted and clear-headed in matters that are internal to their businesses. They are incredibly short-sighted and muddle-headed in matters that are outside their businesses but affect the possible survival of business in general. This short-sightedness is strikingly exemplified in the calls from many businessmen for wage and price guidelines or controls or income policies. There is nothing that could do more in a brief period to destroy a market system and replace it by a centrally controlled system than effective governmental control of prices and wages.

The short-sightedness is also exemplified in speeches by businessmen on social responsibility. This may gain them kudos in the short run. But it helps to strengthen the already too prevalent view that the pursuit of profits is wicked and immoral and must be curbed and controlled by external forces. Once this view is adopted, the external forces that curb the market will not be the social consciences, however highly developed, of the pontificating executives; it will be the iron fist of Government bureaucrats. Here, as with price and wage controls, businessmen seem to me to reveal a suicidal impulse.

The political principle that underlies the market mechanism is unanimity. In an ideal free market resting on private property, no individual can coerce any other, all cooperation is voluntary, all parties to such cooperation benefit or they need not participate. There are no values, no "social" responsibilities in any sense other than the shared values and responsibilities of individuals. Society is a collection of individuals and of the various groups they voluntarily form.

The political principle that underlies the political mechanism is conformity. The individual must serve a more general social interest—whether that be determined by a church or a dictator or a majority. The individual may have a vote and say in what is to be done, but if he is overruled, he must conform. It is appropriate for some to require others to contribute to a general social purpose whether they wish to or not.

Unfortunately, unanimity is not always feasible. There are some respects in which conformity appears unavoidable, so I do not see how one can avoid the use of the political mechanism altogether.

But the doctrine of "social responsibility" taken seriously would extend the scope of the political mechanism to every human activity. It does not differ in philosophy from the most explicitly collectivist doctrine. It differs only by professing to believe that collectivist ends can be attained without collectivist means. That is why, in my book *Capitalism and Freedom,* I have called it a "fundamentally subversive doctrine" in a free society, and have said that in such a society, "there is one and only one social responsibility of business—to use its resources and engage in activities designed to increase its profits so long as it stays within the rules of the game, which is to say, engages in open and free competition without deception or fraud."

Review Questions

1. According to Friedman, why doesn't it make sense to say that business itself has responsibilities?

2. In Friedman's view, who in business does have responsibilities, and what are they?

3. Explain Friedman's account of the corporate executive who acts out of social responsibility.

4. Why does Friedman think that a corporate executive should direct his or her actions by other considerations than social responsibility?

5. According to Friedman, why does the doctrine of social responsibility involve socialism?

6. How does Friedman reply to the objection that social activities such as pollution control should be left to the government?

7. Why does Friedman find the doctrine of social responsibility to be a fundamentally subversive doctrine?

8. What is the one and only social responsibility of business according to Friedman?

Discussion Questions

1. Can a business have responsibilities? Why or why not?

2. Is it possible for a business executive to follow the doctrine of social responsibility and not end up spending the money of consumers or stockholders? How?

3. If business ignores social problems such as discrimination in hiring and pay, pollution, unemployment, and so on, then how can these problems be solved? What is your view?

Christopher D. Stone

Why Shouldn't Corporations Be Socially Responsible?

Christopher D. Stone is a member of the department of law at the University of Southern California, and the author of Should Trees Have Standing?

Stone attacks four arguments used by conservatives such as Milton Friedman to defend the view that corporations have no responsibilities other than maximizing profits. The four arguments are the promissory argument, the agency argument, the role argument, and the polestar argument. He finds the first three to be defective; they rest on false assumptions and they are inconclusive. Stone says that the fourth argument, the so-called polestar argument, makes a number of assumptions, and that the arguments based on these assumptions have a germ of validity. Their essential failure is in not pursuing the alternatives to controlling corporations by market forces and by law. Such alternatives should be pursued because corporations need additional constraints.

The opposition to corporate social responsibility comprises at least four related though separable positions. I would like to challenge the fundamental assumption that underlies all four of them. Each assumes in its own degree that the managers of the corporation are to be steered almost wholly by profit, rather than by what they think proper for society on the whole. Why should this be so? So far as ordinary morals are concerned, we often expect human beings to act in a fashion that is calculated to benefit others, rather than themselves, and commend them for it. Why should the matter be different with corporations?

THE PROMISSORY ARGUMENT

The most widespread but least persuasive arguments advanced by the "antiresponsibility" forces take the form of a moral claim based upon the corporation's supposed obligations to its shareholders. In its baldest and least tenable form, it is presented as though management's obligation rested upon the keeping of a promise—that the management of the corporation "promised" the shareholders that it would maximize the shareholders' profits. But this simply isn't so.

Consider for contrast the case where a widow left a large fortune goes to a broker, asking him to invest and manage her money so as to maximize her return. The broker, let us suppose, accepts the money and the conditions. In such a case, there would be no disagreement that the broker had made a promise to the widow, and if he invested her money in some venture that struck his fancy for any reason other than that it would increase her fortune, we would be inclined to advance a moral (as well, perhaps, as a legal) claim against him. Generally, at least, we believe in the keeping of promises; the broker, we should say, had violated a promissory obligation to the widow.

But that simple model is hardly the one that obtains between the management of major corporations and their shareholders. Few if any American shareholders ever put their money into a corporation upon the express promise of management that the company would be operated so as to maximize their returns. Indeed, few American shareholders ever put their money directly *into* a corporation at all. Most of the shares outstanding today were issued years ago and found their way to their current shareholders only circuitously. In almost all cases, the current shareholder gave his money to some prior shareholder, who, in turn, had gotten it from B, who, in turn, had gotten it from A, and so on back to the purchaser of the original issue, who, many years before, had bought the shares through an underwriting syndicate. In the course of these transactions, one of the basic elements that exists in the broker case is missing: The manager of the corporation, unlike the broker, was never even offered a chance to refuse the shareholder's "terms" (if they were that) to maximize the shareholder's profits.

There are two other observations to be made about the moral argument based on a supposed promise running from the management to the shareholders. First, even if we do infer from all the circumstances a "promise" running from the management to the shareholders, but not one, or not one of comparable weight running elsewhere (to the company's employees, customers, neighbors, etc.), we ought to keep in mind that as a moral matter (which is what we are discussing here) sometimes it is deemed morally justified to break promises (even to break the law) in the furtherance of other social interests of higher concern. Promises can advance moral arguments, by way of creating presumptions, but few of us believe that promises, per se, can end them. My promise to appear in class on time would not ordinarily justify me from refusing to give aid to a drowning man. In other words, even if management *had* made an express promise to its shareholders to "maximize your profits," (a) I am not persuaded that the ordinary person would interpret it to mean "maximize *in every way you can possibly get away with,* even if that means polluting the environment, ignoring or breaking the law"; and (b) I am not persuaded that, even if it were interpreted as so blanket a promise, most people would not suppose it ought—morally—to be broken in some cases.

Finally, even if, in the face of all these considerations, one still believes that there is an overriding, unbreakable promise of some sort running from management to the shareholders, I do not think that it can be construed to be any stronger than one running to *existent* shareholders, arising from *their* expectations as measured by the price *they* paid. That is to say, there is nothing in the argument from promises that would wed us to a regime in which management was bound to maximize the income of shareholders. The argument might go so far as to support compensation for existent shareholders if the society chose to announce that henceforth management would have other specified obligations, thereby driving the price of shares to a lower adjustment level. All future shareholders would take with "warning" of, and a price that discounted for, the new "risks" of shareholding (i.e., the "risks" that management might put corporate resources to *pro bonum* ends).

THE AGENCY ARGUMENT

Related to the promissory argument but requiring less stretching of the facts is an argument from agency principles. Rather than trying to infer a promise by management to the shareholders, this argument is based on the idea that the shareholders designated the management their agents. This is the position advanced by Milton Friedman in his *New York Times* article. "The key point," he says, "is that ... the manager is the agent of the individuals who own the corporation...." [1]

Friedman, unfortunately, is wrong both as to the state of the law (the directors are *not* mere agents of the shareholders) [2] and on his assumption as to the facts of corporate life (surely it is closer to the truth that in major corporations the shareholders are *not,* in any meaningful sense, selecting the directors; management is more often using its control over the proxy machinery to designate who the directors shall be, rather than the other way around).

What Friedman's argument comes down to is that for some reason the directors ought morally to consider themselves more the agents for the shareholders than for the customers, creditors, the state, or the corporation's immediate neighbors. But why? And to what extent? Throwing in terms like "principal" and "agent" begs the fundamental questions.

What is more, the "agency" argument is not only morally inconclusive, it is embarrassingly at odds with the way in which supposed "agents" actually behave. If the managers truly considered themselves the agents of the shareholders, as agents they would be expected to show an interest in determining how their principals wanted them to act—and to act accordingly. In the controversy over Dow's production of napalm, for example, one would expect, on this model, that Dow's management would have been glad to have the napalm question put to the shareholders at a shareholders' meeting. In fact, like most major companies faced with shareholder requests to include "social action" measures on proxy statements, it fought the proposal tooth and claw.[3] It is a peculiar agency where the "agents" will go to such lengths (even spending tens of thousands of dollars of their "principals'" money in legal fees) to resist the determination of what their "principals" want.

THE ROLE ARGUMENT

An argument so closely related to the argument from promises and agency that it does not demand extensive additional remarks is a contention based upon supposed considerations of *role*. Sometimes in moral discourse, as well as in law, we assign obligations to people on the basis of their having assumed some role or status, independent of any specific verbal promise they made. Such obligations are assumed to run from a captain to a seaman (and vice versa), from a doctor to a patient, or from a parent to a child. The antiresponsibility forces are on somewhat stronger grounds resting their position on this basis, because the model more nearly accords with the facts—that is, management never actually promised the shareholders that they would maximize the shareholders' investment, nor did the shareholders designate the directors their agents for this express purpose. The directors and top management are, as lawyers would say, fiduciaries. But what does this leave us? So far as the directors are fiduciaries of the shareholders in a legal sense, of course they are subject to the legal limits on fiduciaries—that is to say, they

cannot engage in self-dealing, "waste" of corporate assets, and the like. But I do not understand any proresponsibility advocate to be demanding such corporate largesse as would expose the officers to legal liability; what we are talking about are expenditures on, for example, pollution control, above the amount the company is required to pay by law, but less than an amount so extravagant as to constitute a violation of these legal fiduciary duties. (Surely no court in America today would enjoin a corporation from spending more to reduce pollution than the law requires.) What is there about assuming the role of corporate officer that makes it immoral for a manager to involve a corporation in these expenditures? A father, one would think, would have stronger obligations to his children by virtue of his status than a corporate manager to the corporation's shareholders. Yet few would regard it as a compelling moral argument if a father were to distort facts about his child on a scholarship application form on the grounds that he had obligations to advance his child's career; nor would we consider it a strong moral argument if a father were to leave unsightly refuse piled on his lawn, spilling over into the street, on the plea that he had obligations to give every moment of his attention to his children, and was thus too busy to cart his refuse away.

Like the other supposed moral arguments, the one from role suffers from the problem that the strongest moral obligations one can discover have at most only prima facie force, and it is not apparent why those obligations should predominate over some contrary social obligations that could be advanced.

Then too, when one begins comparing and weighing the various moral obligations, those running back to the shareholder seem fairly weak by comparison to the claims of others. For one thing, there is the consideration of alternatives. If the shareholder is dissatisfied with the direction the corporation is taking, he can sell out, and if he does so quickly enough, his losses may be slight. On the other hand, as Ted Jacobs observes, "those most vitally affected by corporate decisions—people who work in the plants, buy the products, and consume the effluents—cannot remove themselves from the structure with a phone call." [4]

THE "POLESTAR" ARGUMENT

It seems to me that the strongest moral argument corporate executives can advance for looking solely to profits is not one that is based on a supposed express, or even implied promise to the shareholder. Rather, it is one that says, if the managers act in such fashion as to maximize profits—if they act *as though* they had promised the shareholders they would do so—then it will be best for all of us. This argument might be called the polestar argument, for its appeal to the interests of the shareholders is not justified on supposed obligations to the shareholders per se, but as a means of charting a straight course toward what is best for the society as a whole.

Underlying the polestar argument are a number of assumptions—some express and some implied. There is, I suspect, an implicit **positivism** among its supporters—a feeling (whether its proponents own up to it or not) that moral judgments are peculiar, arbitrary, or vague—perhaps even "meaningless" in the philosophic sense of not being amenable to rational discussion. To those who take this position, profits (or sales, or price-earnings ratios) at least provide some solid, tangible standard by which participants in the organization can measure their successes and failures, with some efficiency, in the narrow sense, resulting for the entire group. Sometimes the polestar position is based upon a related view—not that the moral issues that underlie social choices are meaningless, but that resolving them calls for special expertise. "I don't know any investment adviser whom I would care to act in my behalf in any matter except turning a profit.... The value of these specialists ... lies in their limitations; they ought not allow themselves to see so

much of the world that they become distracted." [5] A slightly modified point emphasizes not that the executives lack moral or social expertise per se, but that they lack the social authority to make policy choices. Thus, Friedman objects that if a corporate director took "social purposes" into account, he would become "in effect a public employee, a civil servant.... On grounds of political principle, it is intolerable that such civil servants ... should be selected as they are now." [6]

I do not want to get too deeply involved in each of these arguments. That the moral judgments underlying policy choices are vague, I do not doubt—although I am tempted to observe that when you get right down to it, a wide range of actions taken by businessmen every day, supposedly based on solid calculations of "profit," are probably as rooted in hunches and intuition as judgments of ethics. I do not disagree either that, ideally, we prefer those who have control over our lives to be politically accountable; although here, too, if we were to pursue the matter in detail we would want to inspect both the premise of this argument, that corporate managers are not *presently* custodians of discretionary power over us anyway, and also its logical implications: Friedman's point that "if they are to be civil servants, then they must be selected through a political process" [7] is not, as Friedman regards it, a *reductio ad absurdum*—not, at any rate, to Ralph Nader and others who want publicly elected directors.

The reason for not pursuing these counterarguments at length is that, whatever reservations one might have, we can agree that there is a germ of validity to what the "antis" are saying. But their essential failure is in not pursuing the alternatives. Certainly, *to the extent* that the forces of the market and the law can keep the corporation within desirable bounds, it may be better to trust them than to have corporate managers implementing their own vague and various notions of what is best for the rest of us. But are the "antis" blind to the fact that there are circumstances in which the law—and the forces of the market—are simply not competent to keep the corporation under control? The shortcomings of these traditional restraints on corporate conduct are critical to understand, not merely for the defects they point up in the "antis'" position. More important, identifying where the traditional forces are inadequate is the first step in the design of new and alternative measures of corporate control.

Endnotes

1. *New York Times*, September 12, 1962, sect. 6, p. 33, col. 2.

2. See, for example, *Automatic Self-Cleansing Filter Syndicate Co. Ltd. v. Cunninghame* (1906) 2 Ch. 34.

3. "Dow Shalt Not Kill," in S. Prakash Sethi, *Up Against the Corporate Wall*, (Englewood Cliffs, N.J.: Prentice-Hall, 1971), pp. 236–266, and the opinion of Judge Tamm in *Medical Committee for Human Rights v. S.E.C.*, 432 F.2d 659 (D.C.Cir.1970), and the dissent of Mr. Justice Douglas in the same case in the U.S. Supreme Court, 404 U.S. 403, 407–411 (1972).

4. Theodore J. Jacobs, "Pollution, Consumerism, Accountability," *Center Magazine* 5, 1 (January–February 1971): 47.

5. Walter Goodman, "Stocks Without Sin," *Harper's*, August 1971, p. 66.

6. *New York Times*, September 12, 1962, sec. 6, p. 122, col. 3.

7. Ibid., p. 122, cols. 3–4.

Review Questions

1. How does Stone attack the promissory argument?

2. What is wrong with Friedman's agency argument according to Stone?

3. How does Stone reply to the role argument?

4. State and explain the so-called polestar argument.

5. What assumptions does Stone find underlying this argument?

6. What is Stone's appraisal of the polestar argument and the assumptions underlying it?

Discussion Questions

1. Has Stone given a decisive refutation of Friedman's position? Why or why not?

2. Stone admits that there is a germ of validity in what his opposition is saying. What is this germ of validity? Can you clarify this?

Norman E. Bowie

Changing the Rules

Norman E. Bowie occupies the Elmer L. Andersen Chair in Corporate Responsibility, Curtis L. Carlson School of Management, University of Minnesota, Twin Cities.

Bowie suggests that a social contract is the basis for the moral responsibilities of business corporations.

From Norman E. Bowie, "Changing the Rules," in T. Beauchamp and N. Bowie, eds., *Ethical Theory and Business* (Englewood Cliffs, NJ: Prentice–Hall, 1983), pp. 147–150. © 1978 by Norman E. Bowie. Reprinted with the author's permission.

Even though society has been changing the rules of the contract by giving corporations more social responsibilities, corporations should accept the revised contract for three reasons: it is in their self-interest, they have contributed to social problems, and they have the resources to deal with social problems. In return they have the right to participate in redrafting the contract, and they have the right to ask other contributors to social problems to contribute to their solution.

It is not merely the introductory philosophy students who ask, "Why be moral?" An examination of much of the contemporary literature in business ethics indicates that the "Why be moral" question is very much on the mind of business persons as well.

One possibility for providing an answer to the "why be moral" question is to indicate the contractual basis on which business rests. The operation of a business, particularly when the business is a corporation, is not a matter of right. Rather the individuals enter into a contract with society. In turn for the permission to do business, the society places certain obligations and duties on the business. The corporation is created by society for a specific purpose or purposes. Robert A. Dahl has put the point this way:

Today it is absurd to regard the corporation simply as an enterprise established for the sole purpose of allowing profit making. We the citizens give them special rights, powers, and privileges, protection, and benefits on the understanding that their activities will fulfill purposes. Corporations exist only as they continue to benefit us . . . . Every corporation should be thought of as a social enterprise whose existence and decisions can be justified only insofar as they serve public or social purposes.[1]

Actually not only does Dahl's quotation indicate that the relation between business and society is contractual, but Dahl spells out the nature of that contract. The corporation must not only benefit those who create it, it must benefit those who permit it (namely society as a whole).

In many discussions of business ethics no one defines terms like "moral" or "corporate responsibility." This inadequacy can be corrected by adopting the perspective of the contract analysis. The morality of business or corporate responsibility is determined by the terms of the contract with society. The corporation has those obligations which the society imposes on it in its charter of incorporation. In accepting its charter, the corporation accepts those moral constraints. Failure to be moral is a violation of the principle of fairness. The corporation which violates the moral rules contained in or implied by its charter is in the position of agreeing to the rules and then violating them. It is in the position of one who makes a promise and then breaks it. Such unfairness is often con-

sidered a paradigm case of injustice and immorality. The corporation which finds itself in the position of breaking the agreements it has made is in a particularly vulnerable position, since the corporate enterprise depends for its survival on the integrity of contractual relations. Understanding business as a contractual relation between the corporation and the society as a whole provides a preliminary answer to our "why be moral" question. The corporation should be moral because it has agreed to be. However, what a corporation's moral obligations are is contained in the contract itself.

Although this analysis does provide the framework for showing that certain corporate activities are immoral and provides a moral *reason* for indicating why a corporation should not engage in them, many complicated questions remain to be answered.

The first focuses on the content of the contract. Many corporate executives could accept the contract analysis as outlined thus far and argue that current demands on corporations to be more socially responsible are themselves violations of the contract. After all, corporate charters do not contain an open-ended moral requirement that the corporation promote the public interest. Rather, corporations are founded primarily to promote the financial interests of the investors (the stockholders). Society had believed that by furthering the interests of the stockholders, society as a whole benefited. Now society has changed its mind, and frustrated corporation executives rightly argue that it is the corporate responsibility zealots and not the corporate executives who are changing the terms of the contract.

In several respects the corporate response is appropriate. Society is changing the rules of the game and it is appropriate to ask why corporations should acquiesce in these unilateral changes. Before considering these issues, however, I should like to point out one respect in which the corporate officials' charge that the rules are being changed is incorrect. In addition to the obligations spelled out in the contract itself, there are certain moral requirements, moral background conditions, if you will, which are assumed. Certain moral rules are rules that are required if contracts are to be made at all. These moral requirements are as obligatory as the obligations spelled out in the contract itself. After all, when I agree to pay my bills in order to get a Master Charge card, I do not also sign a meta-agreement that I keep my agreements. The whole market exchange mechanism rests on conditions of trust which can be embodied in moral principles. What is shocking about some of the current corporate scandals—bribery, falsification of records, theft, and corporate espionage—is that these acts violate the conditions for making contracts and market exchanges, conditions which are at the very heart of the free enterprise system. Such violations cannot be excused by saying that they do not appear in the contract. Such excuses are almost as absurd as someone defending the murder of a creditor by saying: I only promised to pay him back; I didn't promise not to murder him. Hence we can conclude that a company has moral obligations in the contract it makes with society and it has obligations to those moral rules which make contracts possible. Its agreement in the former is explicit; its agreement in the latter, implicit. Violation of either is a violation of fairness—a failure to keep one's promises.

We can now return to the charge that it is society which is changing the terms of the contract. Fortunately, not all the charges of immorality and irresponsibility leveled at corporations are directed at violations of contractual morality. Corporations are charged with neglecting to solve such social problems as pollution, racism, sexism, and urban blight. They are charged with sins of omission. At this point the corporation can argue that they have no obligation to resolve all of society's problems. Such a broad-based moral obligation is not a part of their contract with society. That corporations do not have such general contractual obligations is con-

ceded by most experts in the field.

We now face a more complicated form of the "why be moral" question. Why should the corporation agree to a rewriting of its contract with society—a rewriting which will impose greatly expanded social responsibilities on it?

One answer is prudential. It is in the interests of the corporation to do so. This idea has been expressed in the form of a law called the Iron Law of Responsibility: In the long run those who do not use power in a manner which society considers socially responsible will tend to lose it.[2] If society demands a rewriting of the contract, society has the *power* to rewrite it unilaterally. However, can we go beyond prudence to offer any moral reasons for business to revise its agreements? I believe there are several.

One might be called the principle of contribution: If one contributes to a social harm, then one has a proportional obligation to contribute to its alleviation. Since business clearly does contribute to social problems, it has at least some obligation to correct them. In saying that business has some responsibility, I do not wish to imply that it has the only responsibility. Government, labor, and all of us as consumers contribute our part to the problems and hence have some responsibility to work toward solutions. It is neither fair nor prudent to expect one segment of society to shoulder the entire burden. Hence only a *contribution* is required.

Another moral reason for business to accept a new contract might be based on the notion of power. Those constituents of society which have the most in the way of resources should contribute the most to resolving social ills. Since business is either the most powerful force or second only to the federal government, its superior resources impose special obligations upon it. There is an analogy here to arguments made on behalf of progressive taxation.

If the moral arguments are sound, there are moral reasons as well as a very strong prudential reason for corporations to revise their contractual relations with society. However, the corporation can reciprocally require certain agreements on the part of society. First, since a contract should be mutually acceptable, the contract cannot be rewritten unilaterally. Representatives from the corporate sector have a right to participate in the redrafting. Second, grounds of consistency require that other contributors to society's problems also contribute to their solution and that the requirements for the more powerful constituencies be stronger. So long as these conditions are met, corporations should agree to a revised contract and our original fairness arguments can be used to show why individual corporations should follow it.

Endnotes

1. Robert A. Dahl, "A Prelude to Corporate Reform." In *Corporate Social Policy,* ed. Robert L. Heilbroner and Paul London (Reading, Mass.: Addison–Wesley Publishing Company, 1975), pp. 18–19.

2. Keith Davis and Robert L. Blomstrom, *Business and Society: Environment and Responsibility,* 3rd ed. (New York: McGraw–Hill Book Company, 1975), p. 50.

Review Questions

1. Why should business corporations be socially responsible according to Bowie?

2. What rights do corporations have in Bowie's view?

Discussion Questions

1. Bowie claims that business clearly does contribute to social problems. Give some examples.

2. Bowie argues that corporations should be socially responsible because it is in their self-interest to do so. Is this true? Why or why not?

3. Does Friedman have a good reply to Bowie? What is it?

Problem Cases

1. Rockwell's Management of the Rocky Flats Plant (Reported extensively in *The New York Times,* September 20, 22, and 23, 1989.) Rockwell International Corporation is a defense contractor based in El Segundo, California, south of Los Angeles. It has been criticized for dumping toxic and radioactive wastes at its plants for more than a decade. The latest case involves Rockwell's management of the Rocky Flats nuclear weapons plant near Boulder, Colorado. The annual budget for the plant is nearly $500 million, and it employs about 5,200 people. The plant makes plutonium triggers for nuclear weapons under contract with the Department of Energy, and it produces radioactive waste products. It has been charged with dumping these poisons into a pond that empties into a drinking water reservoir and surreptitiously operating a hazardous waste incinerator that had been closed for safety reasons. These charges were investigated by more than seventy FBI agents, armed with a search warrant, in June 1989. Also, a grand jury is investigating. More-

over, in December 1988, the Energy Department identified the waste disposal site at the Rocky Flats Plant (which has 29,000 gallons of toxic chemicals stored in two large tanks and hundreds of barrels) as the most dangerous in the nuclear weapons industry because it threatens a source of drinking water for Denver's suburbs. The company denies the charges of polluting, but it admits to storing radioactive chemical wastes illegally. The company claims that there is no legal disposal method for these chemical wastes which are laced with radiation.

What should be done about this plant and its toxic and radioactive wastes? Should the plant be shut down and the toxic and radioactive wastes eliminated? Should Rockwell be fined? Why not put the executives of Rockwell on trial, and if they are found guilty, give them prison sentences?

2. Plutonium Hazard (Reported in *The New York Times,* October 7, 1989.) Besides the pollution problem, the Rocky Flats Plant has a problem with safety for its workers. Since 1962 the plant has had at least eight serious accidents involving radioactive plutonium, and thirteen deaths attributed to radiation poisoning. According to a study conducted by Scientech Inc., a company hired by the Department of Energy after it received anonymous tips from workers, the latest incident involved plutonium escaping unnoticed into an air duct. Apparently enough plutonium was released to create the danger of an accidental nuclear reaction. Such a chain reaction would not cause an explosion, but would generate large amounts of radiation and heat. In addition, it would scatter the highly toxic radioactive plutonium. It would probably not result in a release of plutonium outside the plant buildings. The study showed that the managers at the plant were not sufficiently concerned with the safety of the workers.

Should workers at this plant be provided with a safe environment? If so, how can this be done?

3. Antilock Brakes (Discussed by Lesley Hazleton in *The New York Times,* October 1, 1989.) Antilock braking is a computer-controlled system that prevents the wheels of a car from locking up in an emergency. Braking distances are reduced by up to 25 percent, and skidding or sliding is eliminated. The system is an obvious improvement, and no doubt it would save lives. (In the United States, about 50,000 people die every year in automobile accidents.) Currently antilock braking is available only on expensive top-of-the-line cars where profits are greatest. Why not put the system on all cars even if this reduces profits? Don't automobile companies have an obligation to produce safe cars?

4. Polygraph Tests Companies faced with thefts and dishonest employees have resorted to using polygraph tests, or lie detector tests, to screen employees. For example, the Adolph Coors Brewery in Golden, Colorado, has used these tests to screen job applicants.

Do companies have a right to do this? Why or why not?

5. Golden Parachutes Payments A large payment that an executive gets when leaving a company is called a golden parachute payment. Often it is a huge amount of money taken from the company's assets or from stock manipulations. For example, Steve Rothmeier took home $10 million when Northwest Airlines was bought. If the proposed buyout of United Airlines had worked, Steven M. Wolf would have received an incredible sum of $76 million after working only two years. After six months on the job, Philip Smith received $5.4 million when Grand Metropolitan bought Pillsbury. Nobert Berg, former deputy chairman of Control Data, quit with a generous retirement bonus of $4.7 million.

Are these golden parachute payments immoral? Why or why not?

Suggested Readings

(1) Robert L. Arrington, "Advertising and Behavior Control," *Journal of Business Ethics* 1 (1982), pp. 3–12. Arrington discusses questionable advertising techniques such as puffery, indirect information, and subliminal suggestion. He finds that advertising can control behavior, produce compulsive behavior, and create irrational desires.

(2) Tom L. Beauchamp, *Case Studies in Business, Society, and Ethics* (Englewood Cliffs, NJ: Prentice–Hall, 1983). This book is a collection of interesting case studies of business. Some examples are "The DC-10's Defective Doors," "Procter and Gamble's Rely Tampons," "Dow Chemical Company and Napalm–B," and "The Manufacture and Regulation of Laetrile."

(3) David Braybrooke, ed., *Ethics in the World of Business* (Totowa, NJ: Rowman & Allanheld, 1983). This anthology has twenty-three chapters covering a wide variety of topics including sexual harassment, the right to be promoted or retained, unionization, advertising, the arms business, sales tactics, and consumer concerns.

(4) Albert Carr, "Is Business Bluffing Ethical?" *Harvard Business Review* (January–February 1968), pp. 143–153. Carr defends the use of deception in business as an essential part of the legal pursuit of profits.

(5) Thomas Donaldson and Patricia H. Werhane, eds., *Ethical Issues in Business*, 3d ed. (Englewood Cliffs, NJ: Prentice–Hall, 1988). This collection of readings includes articles on the profit motive, business and employee rights and obligations, business responsibility and liability with respect to the consumer, and business and environmental issues.

(6) Milton Friedman, *Capitalism and Freedom* (Chicago: University of Chicago Press, 1981). Friedman explains his views about free markets, capitalism, and freedom from interference.

(7) John K. Galbraith, *The New Industrial State,* 4th ed. (Boston: Houghton Mifflin, 1985). Galbraith critiques conservative economists such as Friedman and offers his own views on economics and modern society.

(8) Alan H. Goldman, "Business Ethics: Profits, Utilities, and Moral Rights," *Philosophy & Public Affairs* 9, No. 3 (Spring 1980) pp. 260–286. Goldman argues that business executives ought to follow the same moral principles as everyone else and cannot defend their actions by claiming that the legal pursuit of profits is a moral end in itself.

(9) Kenneth E. Goodpaster and John B. Matthews, Jr., "Can a Corporation Have a Conscience?" *Harvard Business Review* (January–February, 1982) pp. 132–143. Goodpaster and Matthews argue that there is an analogy between the individual and the corporation such that corporations can be just as morally responsible as individuals.

(10) W. Michael Hoffman and Jennifer Mills Moore, eds., *Business Ethics* (New York: McGraw–Hill, 1984). This is an excellent anthology covering many different issues in business ethics. There are articles on the nature of the corporation, employee rights and duties, hiring practices such as preferential hiring and reverse discrimination, governmental regulation, the consumer, multinational business, deception, bribery, and anticompetitive behavior.

(11) John Hospers, *Libertarianism* (Los Angeles: Nash Publishing Co., 1971). Hospers defends the libertarian view that people should be free to pursue profits in a free market system and that taxation is a violation of a person's rights.

(12) Alex C. Michalos, "Advertising: Its Logic, Ethics, and Economics," in J.A. Blair and R.H. Johnson, eds., *Informal Logic: The First International Symposium* (Point Reyes, CA: Edgepress, 1980). Michalos discusses various types of deception in advertising.

(13) Tom Regan, ed., *Just Business* (New York: Random House, 1984). This is a collection of original essays on questions in business ethics. Included are articles on preferential hiring, advertising, corporate responsibility, business and the environment, and individual rights in business.

(14) Milton Snoeyenbos, Robert Almeder, and James Humber, eds., *Business Ethics* (Buffalo, NY: Prometheus Books, 1983). This collection has readings on business and social responsibility, employee obligations and rights, trade secrets and patents, ethics and the accounting profession, business and the consumer, business and the environment, and multinational corporations.

Chapter 7

Discrimination and Affirmative Action

Introduction

Facts About Discrimination   In the last century women were denied many of the legal rights they have today. They could not vote, own property, enter into contracts, serve on juries, or enter certain male-dominated professions. There was also blatant racial discrimination. Blacks were not allowed to vote in some states, they were excluded from union membership, they were denied access to nonmenial jobs, they could not marry whites, they had to sit in certain places on buses and in restaurants, and they received an inferior education.

In the late 1960s and early 1970s, two laws were passed that benefited women and minorities to some extent. The Equal Pay Act of 1963 asserted that men and women have to be given equal pay for equal work. Title VII of the Civil Rights Act of 1964 prohibited any discrimination on the basis of race, color, religion, sex, or national origin.

Despite these antidiscrimination laws, sexual and racial discrimination continue, although perhaps not as blatantly as before the laws were enacted. Consider some of the state laws that unfairly discriminate against women: there are laws which permit women to be imprisoned for three years for habitual drunkenness, while for males the penalty for the same offense is thirty days; there are laws which excuse all women from jury duty; laws which permit the withholding of credit from married women on the grounds that they are financially dependent on their husbands; laws which permit the plea of passion killing for wronged husbands but not wronged wives; laws which give the husband right of action in divorce cases of adultery but not the

249

wife; and so on. Why not eliminate these obviously sexist laws? That is one of the goals of the ERA, or Equal Rights Amendment, which simply states that "equality of rights under the law shall not be denied or abridged by the United States or by any state on account of sex." Yet even though this amendment was proposed by Alice Paul in 1923, and approved by Congress in 1971, it has not been ratified by three-fourths of the state legislatures, and it is now dead.

The evidence for discrimination against women and minorities in employment and admission is enormous and hard to summarize. Nevertheless, it seems clear that women and minorities are at a distinct disadvantage. Let us review a few statistics: (1) At all occupational levels, women make less money than men, even for the same work, and despite the Equal Pay Act of 1963. According to statistics from the U.S. Census Bureau in 1988, the median weekly income of male workers in 1986 was $419, while the comparable figure for women was $290. This is only a slight improvement over the figures in 1955, when women's earnings were 64 percent of men's. (2) The Census statistics from 1988 also indicate that the most desirable occupations (management and administration, professions and technical jobs, sales, and crafts) are dominated by whites, while the less desirable jobs (service and farm work) are dominated by blacks, Hispanics, and other ethnic minorities. Women predominate in the poorest-paying jobs: librarians, nurses, elementary teachers, sales clerks, secretaries, bank tellers, and waitresses. At the same time men dominate in the best-paying jobs: lawyers, doctors, sales representatives, insurance agents, and so on. (3) In the well-known AT & T case, this enormous company signed a settlement giving tens of millions of dollars to women and minority workers, thus admitting to massive discrimination against women and minorities. (4) Female college teachers with

identical credentials in terms of publications and experience are promoted at almost exactly one-half the rate of their male counterparts. (5) Eight thousand workers were employed in May 1967 in the construction of the Bay Area Rapid Transit system, but not one electrician, ironworker, or plumber was black. There is more evidence, but why go on? It seems clear that there is racial and sexual discrimination in employment and pay.

Why Is Discrimination Wrong? Discrimination on the basis of sex or race is not always wrong. It does not seem to matter much that rest rooms are segregated by sex, and it does not seem unjust to make a movie about black people in Harlem using only black actors. On the other hand, it does seem unfair to not hire a qualified person as a lawyer just because she is a woman, or to not admit a qualified student to medical school just because he is black.

What is it about racial and sexual discrimination that makes them wrong? As Singer points out in the first reading for the chapter, the standard view is that sexual and racial discrimination are wrong when race and sex are *irrelevant* to whether a person should be given a job, the vote, higher education, or some other benefit. Qualifications are relevant to getting these benefits, but not race or sex. If women or minority persons are not allowed to vote just because of their sex or race, then this is wrong—it is wrong because sex and race are irrelevant to voting. But sex is relevant when it comes to maternity leave, and race may be relevant when one is making a movie about black people and their culture.

A theory of justice is used to support this standard view. According to Aristotle, justice requires that equals be treated equally and unequals unequally. It must immediately be added that the equality or inequality should be relevant to the treatment in question. When we are concerned with employment, for example, the inequality of the job applicants with respect to qualifications is obviously relevant and justifies unequal treatment. In other words, it is not unjust to hire the most qualified candidate. But it is unjust to not hire a qualified person because of race or sex.

However, there are problems with the standard view. One difficulty is that it forbids us to take race or sex into account in employment and admission to school, since in most cases race or sex is irrelevant. But as we shall see, defenders of affirmative-actions programs which involve preferential treatment or reverse discrimination do want to take race or sex into account when it comes to employment and admission to school. Furthermore, the standard view allows sexual or racial discrimination when sex or race is relevant to the treatment in question, and this seems to allow objectionable racial or sexual discrimination. For example, landlords may refuse to rent apartments to black people because the white tenants will move out. Even though this racial discrimination is in the landlord's self-interest, and thus is not arbitrary, it does not seem to be morally justified. Or consider women in combat. It may be true that, on the average, women are not as strong and aggressive as men, and thus they are not as good in fighting as men. So sex does seem relevant when it comes to choosing people for combat duty. Does this mean that sexual discrimination is justified in this case? Again some people want to deny this, but the reason can't be that sex is irrelevant to the treatment in question.

Because of objections like these, Singer rejects the standard view that discrimination is wrong because it is arbitrary. In his view it is wrong when it violates a basic moral principle—the principle of equal consideration of interests. This principle says that in our treatment of people we must give equal consideration to equal interests. Let us apply this principle to the two problematic cases mentioned in the preceding paragraph. Suppose we have qualified women and men who have an equal interest in combat duty—they want to do this because it is easier to get a promotion in the army if one does combat duty. According to Singer's principle of equality, we must give equal consideration to the interests of both the men and the women; we are not justified in choosing the men and refusing the women. Or suppose we have both a black family and a white family who want to rent an apartment. Since their interest in renting is equal, we must give them equal consideration, and we cannot refuse the black family just because of its race.

How Can Unjust Discrimination Be Corrected?
If it is a fact that people have been wrongfully discriminated against in the past, and continue to be discriminated against in the present, then what should we do about it? Is there any way to correct this injustice? Two sorts of solutions have been proposed. Backward-looking solutions to the problem of unjust discrimination seek to compensate groups or individuals who have been unfairly discriminated against in the past. The compensation could take the form of payment, as when, for example, the claim is made that American Indians should be paid for the land and water rights that were taken from them, or it could be in the form of jobs given to women or minorities who could not get them in the past.

Forward-looking solutions try to realize a future society free of discrimination, or at least with reduced discrimination. For example, we might imagine a utopian society in the future where race and sex are no more significant than eye color is in our society. Or perhaps we could have a society where race and sex are at least less important than they are in our society.

Affirmative Action As amended by the Equal Employment Opportunity Act of

1972, the Civil Rights Act of 1964 requires businesses that have substantial dealings with the federal government to undertake so-called affirmative-action programs which are supposed to correct imbalances in employment that exist as a result of past discrimination. The programs that have been the focus of most debate are often called preferential treatment programs (by those who favor them) or reverse discrimination (by those who oppose them). Two sorts of preferential treatment programs are at issue. The first type involves quotas or specific numerical goals; a school or employer will specify some set number or proportion of women or minority applicants who must be accepted or hired. The second type involves no quota or numerical goal, but requires that women or minorities be given preferential treatment over white men who are equally or even better qualified.

The first type of program has resulted in some landmark lawsuits. One of these, *University of California* v. *Bakke* (1978), went to the Supreme Court, and is described in more detail in the Problem Cases for this chapter. In this case the Court ruled that the Medical School of the University of California at Davis acted illegally in using a specific quota approach, and in refusing to admit Alan Bakke while admitting less-qualified minority students. Another famous case is *DeFunis* v. *Odegaard* (1973). In that case, Marco DeFunis, a nonminority applicant, was denied admission to the University of Washington Law School's class of 1971. He filed a suit claiming that he had been treated unfairly insofar as he had been denied admission on the basis of race. Preferential treatment that year was accorded to blacks, American Indians, Chicanos, and Filipinos—thirty-seven of these minority applicants were accepted, and eighteen actually enrolled. The Law School Admission Test scores and Projected Grade Point Averages of almost all these minority students were lower than those of some of the rejected nonminority students.

The Supreme Court of the state of Washington ruled against DeFunis. The Court argued that racial classifications are not unconstitutional, that their use is acceptable if there is a compelling state interest, and that the shortage of minority attorneys constituted a compelling state interest. The case was appealed to the United States Supreme Court, but the Court did not hand down a ruling. DeFunis had been attending law school while the case was being appealed, and the case was declared moot.

As I noted above, the unequal treatment given Bakke and DeFunis is sometimes called reverse discrimination, usually by those who disapprove of it. This label describes actions or practices that discriminate against an individual or a group on the basis of some characteristic that is usually considered to be irrelevant, such as race. One common objection is that it is inconsistent. If discrimination is wrong, then reverse discrimination cannot be right. As Lisa Newton puts it, "All discrimination is wrong *prima facie* because it violates justice, and that goes for reverse discrimination too." In her view, discrimination is unjust if it involves unequal treatment when citizens ought to have equal treatment under the law, and this applies to reverse discrimination as well as ordinary discrimination. Besides the charge of inconsistency, Newton raises various practical problems for reverse discrimination. For example, how much reverse discrimination will compensate those who have been discriminated against?

Blackstone agrees with Newton that reverse discrimination is wrong, not only because it is unjust, but also because it will produce bad effects in our society. He predicts that majority group members will not cooperate with it, and the result will be social chaos. Furthermore, he thinks that even women and minorities will be harmed if the quality of instruction in higher education is lowered.

Those who defend reverse discrimination (or preferential treatment, as they call it) typically give either a forward-looking or a backward-looking defense. The forward-looking defense is that preferential treatment of women and minorities will help reduce unjust discrimination in the future. The backward-looking defense rests on the claim that women and minorities deserve to be compensated for past unjust discrimination. In our readings, Mary Ann Warren gives a backward-looking defense when she argues that preferential treatment of women in the form of numerical quotas for hiring and promotion is justified to compensate women for past and ongoing discriminatory practices that have put women at a disadvantage.

Peter Singer

Is Racial Discrimination Arbitrary?

For biographical information on Singer, see his reading in Chapter 3.

Singer uses the term racial discrimination *in a morally neutral, descriptive sense to refer to discrimination based on race. He claims that such discrimination is not always wrong, and when it is wrong, it is not wrong because it is arbitrary. In Singer's view, racial discrimination is wrong when it violates the basic moral principle of equal consideration of interests. As Singer formulates it, this principle says that we should give equal weight in our moral considerations to the like interests of all those affected by our actions.*

INTRODUCTION

There is nowadays wide agreement that racism is wrong. To describe a policy, law, movement or nation as 'racist' is to condemn it. It may be thought that since we all agree that racism is wrong, it is unnecessary to speculate on exactly what it is and why it is

Peter Singer; first published in *Philosophia*, Vol. 8, Nos. 2–3 (1978) pp. 185–203. Reprinted with author's and editor's permission.

wrong. This indifference to moral fundamentals could, however, prove dangerous. For one thing, the fact that most people agree today that racism is wrong does not mean that this attitude will always be so widely shared. Even if we had no fears for the future, though, we need to have some understanding of what it is about racism that is wrong if we are to handle satisfactorily all the problems we face today. For instance, there is the contentious issue of 'reverse discrimination' or discrimination in favor of members of oppressed minority groups. It must be granted that a university which admits members of minority groups who do not achieve the minimum standard that others must reach in order to be admitted is discriminating on racial lines. Is such discrimination therefore wrong?

Or, to take another issue, the efforts of Arab nations to have the United Nations declare Zionism a form of racism provoked an extremely hostile reaction in nations friendly to Israel, particularly the United States, but it led to virtually no discussion of whether Zionism is a form of racism. Yet the charge is not altogether without plausibility, for if Jews are a race, then Zionism promotes the idea of a state dominated by one race, and this has practical consequences in, for instance, Israel's immigration laws. Again, to consider whether this makes Zionism a form of racism we need to understand what it is that makes a policy racist and wrong.

First it is necessary to get our terms clear. 'Racism' is, as I have said, a word which now has an inescapable evaluative force, although it also has some descriptive content. Words with these dual functions can be confusing if their use is not specified. People sometimes try to argue: 'X is a case of racial discrimination, therefore X is racist; racism is wrong, therefore X is wrong'. This argument may depend on an equivocation in the meaning of 'racist', the term being used first in a morally neutral, descriptive sense, and secondly in its evaluative sense.

To avoid this kind of confusion, I shall accept the usual evaluative force of the term 'racist' and reserve it for practices that are judged to be wrong. Thus we cannot pronounce a policy, law etc. 'racist' unless we have decided that it is wrong. 'Racial discrimination' on the other hand I shall use in a descriptive, and morally neutral sense, so that to say that a policy or law discriminates racially is simply to point to the fact of discrimination based on race, leaving open the question of whether it can be justified. With this terminology it becomes possible to ask whether a given form of racial discrimination is racist; this is another way of asking whether it is justifiable.[1]

If we ask those who regard racial discrimination as wrong to say why it is wrong, it is commonly said that it is wrong to pick on race as a reason for treating one person differently from others, because race is irrelevant to whether a person should be given a job, the vote, higher education, or any benefits or burdens of this sort. The irrelevance of race, it is said, makes it quite arbitrary to give these things to people of one race while withholding them from those of another race. I shall refer to this account of what is wrong with racial discrimination as the "standard objection" to racial discrimination.

A sophisticated theory of justice can be invoked in support of this standard objection to racial discrimination. Justice requires, as Aristotle so plausibly said, that equals be treated equally and unequals be treated un-

equally. To this we must add the obvious proviso that the equalities or inequalities should be relevant to the treatment in question. Now when we consider things like employment, it becomes clear that the relevant inequalities between candidates for a vacant position are inequalities in their ability to carry out the duties of the position and, perhaps, inequalities in the extent to which they will benefit through being offered the position. Race does not seem to be relevant at all. Similarly with the vote, capacity for rational choice between candidates or policies might be held a relevant characteristic, but race should not be; and so on for other goods. It is hard to think of anything for which race in itself is a relevant characteristic, and hence to use race as a basis for discrimination is arbitrarily to single out an irrelevant factor, no doubt because of a bias or prejudice against those of a different race.[2]

As we shall see, this account of why racial discrimination is wrong is inadequate because there are many situations in which, from at least one point of view, the racial factor is by no means irrelevant, and therefore it can be denied that racial discrimination in these situations is arbitrary.

One type of situation in which race must be admitted to be relevant to the purposes of the person discriminating need not delay us at this stage; this is the situation in which those purposes themselves favor a particular race. Thus if the purpose of Hitler and the other Nazi leaders was, among other things, to produce a world in which there were no Jews, it was certainly not irrelevant to their purposes that those rounded up and murdered by the S.S. were Jews rather than so-called 'Aryans'. But the fundamental wrongness of the aims of the Nazis makes the 'relevance' of race to those aims totally inefficacious so far as justifying Nazi racial discrimination is concerned. While their type of racial discrimination may not have been arbitrary discrimination in the usual sense, it was no less wrong for that. *Why* it was wrong is something that I hope will become clearer later in this article. Meanwhile I shall look at some less cataclysmic forms of racial discrimination, for too much contemporary discussion of racial discrimination has focussed on the most blatant instances: Nazi Germany, South Africa, and the American 'Deep South' during the period of legally enforced racial segregation.[3] These forms of racism are not the type that face us now in our own societies (unless we live in South Africa) and to discuss racial discrimination in terms of these examples today is to present an over-simplified picture of the problem of racial discrimination. By looking at some of the reasons for racial discrimination that might actually be offered today in countries all over the world I hope to show that the real situation is usually much more complex than consideration of the more blatant instances of racial discrimination would lead us to believe.

EXAMPLES

I shall start by describing an example of racial discrimination which may at first glance seem to be an allowable exception to a general rule that racial discrimination is arbitrary and therefore wrong; and I shall then suggest that this case has parallels with other cases we may not be so willing to allow as exceptions.

Case 1.

A film director is making a film about the lives of blacks living in New York's Harlem. He advertises for black actors. A white actor turns up, but the director refuses to allow him to audition, saying that the film is about blacks and there are no roles for whites. The actor replies that, with the appropriate wig and make-up, he can look just like a black; moreover he can imitate the mannerisms, gestures, and speech of Harlem blacks. Nevertheless the director refuses to consider him for the role, because it is essential to the director's conception of the film that the black experience be authentically portrayed, and however good a white actor might be, the director would not be satisfied with the authenticity of the portrayal.

The film director is discriminating along racial lines, yet he cannot be said to be discriminating arbitrarily. His discrimination is apt for his purpose. Moreover his purpose is a legitimate one. So the standard objection to racial discrimination cannot be made in this instance.

Racial discrimination may be acceptable in an area like casting for films or the theatre, when the race of a character in the film or play is important, because this is one of the seemingly few areas in which a person's race is directly relevant to his capacity to perform a given task. As such, it may be thought, these areas can easily be distinguished from other areas of employment, as well as from areas like housing, education, the right to vote, and so on, where race has no relevance at all. Unfortunately there are many other situations in which race is not as totally irrelevant as this view assumes.

Case 2.

The owner of a cake shop with a largely white and racially prejudiced clientele wishes to hire an assistant. The owner has no prejudice against blacks himself, but is reluctant to employ one, for fear that his customers will go elsewhere. If his fears are well-founded (and this is not impossible) then the race of a candidate for the position is, again, relevant to the purpose of the employer, which in this case is to maintain the profitability of his business.

What can we say about this case? We cannot deny the connection between race and the owner's purposes, and so we must recognize that the owner's discrimination is not arbitrary, and does not necessarily indicate a bias or prejudice on his part. Nor can we say that the owner's purpose is an illegitimate one, for making a profit from the sale of cakes is not generally regarded as wrong, at least if the amount of profit made is modest.

We can, of course, look at other aspects of the matter. We can object to the racial discrimination shown by customers who will search out shops staffed by whites only—such people do discriminate arbitrarily, for race is irrelevant to the quality of the goods and the proficiency of service in a shop—but is this not simply a fact that the shop owner must live with, however much he may wish he could change it? We might argue that by pandering to the prejudices of his customers, the owner is allowing those prejudices to continue unchallenged; whereas if he and other shopkeepers took no notice of them, people would eventually become used to mixing with those of another race, and prejudices would be eroded. Yet it is surely too much to ask an individual shop owner to risk his livelihood in a lone and probably vain effort to break down prejudice. Few of the most dedicated opponents of racism do as much. If there were national legislation which distributed the burden more evenly, by a general prohibition of discrimination on racial grounds (with some recognized exceptions for cases like casting for a film or play) the situation would be different. Then we could reasonably ask every shop owner to play his part. Whether there should be such legislation is a different question from whether the shop owner may be blamed for discriminating in the absence of legislation. I shall discuss the issue of legislation shortly, after we consider a different kind of racial discrimination that, again, is not arbitrary.

Case 3.

A landlord discriminates against blacks in letting the accommodation he owns. Let us say that he is not so rigid as never to let an apartment to a black, but if a black person and a white person appear to be equally suitable as tenants, with equally good references and so on, the landlord invariably prefers the white. He defends his policy along the following lines:

If more than a very small proportion of my tenants get behind in their rent and then disappear without paying the arrears, I will be out of business. Over the years, I have found that more blacks do this than whites. I admit that there are many honest blacks (some of my best tenants have been black) and many dishonest whites, but, for some reason I do not claim to understand, the odds on a white tenant defaulting are longer than on a black doing so, even when their references and other credentials appear equally good. In this business you can't run a full-scale probe of every prospective tenant—and if I tried I would be abused for invading privacy—so you have to go by the average rather than the individual. That is why blacks have to have better indications of reliability than whites before I will let to them.

Now the landlord's impression of a higher rate of default among blacks than among comparable whites may itself be the result of prejudice on his part. Perhaps in most cases when landlords say this kind of thing, there is no real factual basis to their allegations. People have grown up with racial stereotypes, and these stereotypes are reinforced by a tendency to notice occurrences which conform to the stereotype and to disregard those which conflict with it. So if unreliability is part of the stereotype of blacks held by many whites, they may take more notice of blacks who abscond without paying the rent than of blacks who are reliable tenants; and conversely they will take less notice of absconding whites and more of those whites who conform to their ideas of normal white behaviour.

If it is prejudice that is responsible for the landlord's views about black and white tenants, and there is no factual basis for his claims, then the problem becomes one of eliminating this prejudice and getting the landlord to see his mistake. This is by no means an easy task, but it is not a task for philosophers, and it does not concern us here, for we are interested in attempts to justify racial discrimination, and an attempted justification based on an inaccurate description of a situation can be rejected without raising the deeper issue of justification.

On the other hand, the landlord's impression of a higher rate of default among black tenants *could* be entirely accurate. (It might be explicable in terms of the different cultural and economic circumstances in which blacks are brought up.) Whether or not we think this likely, we need to ask what its implications would be for the justifiability of the racial discrimination exercised by the landlord. To refuse even to consider this question would be to rest all one's objections to the landlord's practice on the falsity of his claims, and thereby to fail to examine the possibility that the landlord's practice could be open to objection even if his impressions on tenant reliability are accurate.

If the landlord's impressions were accurate, we would have to concede, once again, that racial discrimination in this situation is not arbitrary; that it is, instead, relevant to the purposes of the landlord. We must also admit that these purposes—making a living from letting property that one owns—are not themselves objectionable, provided the rents are reasonable, and so on. Nor can we, this time, locate the origin of the problem in the prejudices of others, except insofar as the problem has its origin in the prejudices of those responsible for the conditions of deprivation in which many of the present generation of blacks grew up—but it is too late to do anything to alter those prejudices anyway, since they belong to previous generations.

We have now looked at three examples of racial discrimination, and can begin to examine the parallels and differences between them. Many people, as I have already said, would make no objection to the discriminatory hiring practice of the film director in the first of these cases. But we can now see that if we try to justify the actions of the film director in this case on the grounds that his purpose is a legitimate one and the discrimination he uses is relevant for his purpose, we will have to accept the actions of the cake-shop owner and the landlord as well. I suspect that many of those ready to accept the discriminatory practice in the first case will be much more reluctant about the other two cases. But what morally significant difference is there between them?

It might be suggested that the difference between them lies in the nature of what blacks are being deprived of, and their title to it. The argument would run like this: No-one has a right to be selected to act in a film; the director must have absolute discretion to hire whomsoever he wishes to hire. After all, no-one can force the director to make the film at all, and if he didn't make it, no-one would be hired to play in it; if he does decide to make it, therefore, he must be allowed to make it on his own terms. Moreover, since so few people ever get the chance to appear in a film, it would be absurd to hold that the director violates someone's rights by not giving him something which most people will never have anyway. On the other hand, people do have a right to employment, and to housing. To discriminate against blacks in an ordinary employment situation, or in the letting of accommodation, threatens their basic rights and therefore should not be tolerated.

Plausible as it appears, this way of distinguishing the first case from the other two will not do. Consider the first and second cases: almost everything that we have said about the film director applies to the cake-shop owner as well. No-one can force the cake-shop owner to keep his shop open, and if he didn't, no one would be hired to work in it. If in the film director's case this was a reason for allowing him to make the film on his own terms, it must be a reason for allowing the shop owner to run his shop on his own terms. In fact, such reasoning, which would allow unlimited discrimination in restaurants, hotels and shops, is invalid. There are plenty of examples where we would not agree that the fact that someone did not have to make an offer or provide an opportunity at all means that if he does do it he must be allowed to make the offer or provide the opportunity on his own terms. The United States Civil Rights Act of 1965 certainly does not recognize this line of argument, for it prohibits those offering food and lodgings to the public from excluding customers on racial grounds. We may, as a society, decide that we shall not allow people to make certain offers, if the way in which the offers are made will cause hardship or offense to others. In so doing we are balancing people's freedom to do as they please against the harm this may do to others, and coming down on the side of preventing harm rather than enlarging freedom. This is a perfectly defensible position, if the harm is sufficiently serious and the restriction of freedom not grave.[4]

Nor does it seem possible to distinguish the first and second cases by the claim that since so few people ever get the chance to appear in a film, no-one's rights are violated if they are not given something that most people will never have anyway. For if the number of jobs in cake shops was small, and the demand for such jobs high, it would also be true that few people would ever have the chance to work in a cake shop. It would be odd if such an increase in competition for the job justified an otherwise unjustifiable policy of hiring whites only. Moreover, this argument would allow a film director to discriminate on racial lines even if race was irrelevant to the roles he was casting; and that is quite a different situation from the one we have been discussing.

The best way to distinguish the situations of the film director and the shop owner is by reference to the nature of the employment offered, and to the reasons why racial discrimination in these cases is not arbitrary. In casting for a film about blacks, the race of the actor auditioning is intrinsically significant, independently of the attitudes of those connected with the film. In the case of hiring a shop assistant, race is relevant only because of the attitudes of those connected (as customers) with the shop; it has nothing to do with the selling of cakes in itself, but only with the selling of cakes to racially prejudiced customers. This means that in the case of the shop assistant we could eliminate the relevance of race if we could eliminate the prejudices of the customers; by contrast there is no way in which we could eliminate the relevance of the race of an actor auditioning

for a role in a film about blacks, without altering the nature of the film. Moreover, in the case of the shop owner racial discrimination probably serves to perpetuate the very prejudices that make such discrimination relevant and (from the point of view of the owner seeking to maintain his profits) necessary. Thus people who can buy all their cakes and other necessities in shops staffed only by whites will never come into the kind of contact with comparable blacks which might break down their aversion to being served by blacks; whereas if shop owners were to hire more blacks, their customers would no doubt become used to it and in time might wonder why they ever opposed the idea. (Compare the change of attitudes toward racial integration in the American South since the 1956 United States Supreme Court decision against segregated schools and subsequent measures against segregation were put into effect.[5])

Hence if we are opposed to arbitrary discrimination we have reason to take steps against racial discrimination in situations like Case 2, because such discrimination, while not itself arbitrary, both feeds on and gives support to discrimination by others which is arbitrary. In prohibiting it we would, admittedly, be preventing the employer from discriminating in a way that is relevant to his purposes; but if the causal hypothesis suggested in the previous paragraph is correct, this situation would only be temporary, and after some time the circumstances inducing the employer to discriminate racially would have been eliminated.

The case of the landlord presents a more difficult problem. If the facts he alleges are true his non-arbitrary reasons for discrimination against blacks are real enough. They do not depend on present arbitrary discrimination by others, and they may persist beyond an interval in which there is no discrimination. Whatever the roots of hypothetical racial differences in reliability as tenants might be, they would probably go too deep to be eradicated solely by a short period in which there was no racial discrimination.

We should recognize, then, that if the facts are as alleged, to legislate against the landlord's racially discriminatory practice is to impose a long-term disadvantage upon him. At the very least, he will have to take greater care in ascertaining the suitability of prospective tenants. Perhaps he will turn to data-collecting agencies for assistance, thus contributing to the growth of institutions that are threats, potential or actual, to our privacy. Perhaps, if these methods are unavailable or unavailing, the landlord will have to take greater losses than he otherwise would have, and perhaps this will lead to increased rents or even to a reduction in the amount of rentable housing available.

None of this forces us to conclude that we should not legislate against the landlord's racial discrimination. There are good reasons why we should seek to eliminate racial discrimination even when such discrimination is neither arbitrary in itself, nor relevant only because of the arbitrary prejudices of others. These reasons may be so important as to make the disadvantage imposed on the landlord comparatively insignificant.

An obvious point that can be made against the landlord is that he is judging people, at least in part, as members of a race rather than as individuals. The landlord does not deny that some black prospective tenants he turns away would make better tenants than some white prospective tenants he accepts. Some highly eligible black prospective tenants are refused accommodation simply because they are black. If the landlord assessed every prospective tenant as an individual this would not happen.

A similar point is often made in the debate over alleged differences between blacks and whites in America in whatever is measured by IQ tests. Even if, as Jensen and others have suggested, there is a small inherited difference in IQ between blacks and whites, it is clear that this difference shows up only when we compare averages, and not when we compare individuals. Even if we ac-

cept the controversial estimates that the average IQ of American blacks is 15 points lower than the average IQ of American whites, there is still a tremendous amount of overlap between the IQs of blacks and whites, with many whites scoring lower than the majority of blacks. Hence the difference in averages between the races would be of limited significance. For any purpose for which IQ mattered—like entrance into higher levels of education—it would still be essential to consider each applicant individually, rather than as a member of a certain race.

There are plenty of reasons why in situations like admitting people to higher education or providing them with employment or other benefits we should regard people as individuals and not as members of some larger group. For one thing we will be able to make a selection better suited for our own purposes, for selecting or discarding whole groups of people will generally result in, at best, a crude approximation to the results we hope to achieve. This is certainly true in an area like education. On the other hand it must be admitted that in some situations a crude approximation is all that can be achieved anyway. The landlord claims that his situation is one of these, and that as he cannot reliably tell which individuals will make suitable tenants, he is justified in resorting to so crude a means of selection as race. Here we need to turn our attention from the landlord to the prospective black tenant.

To be judged merely as a member of a group when it is one's individual qualities on which the verdict should be given is to be treated as less than the unique individual that we see ourselves as. Even where our individual qualities would merit less than we receive as a member of a group—if we are promoted over better-qualified people because we went to the 'right' private school—the benefit is usually less welcome than it would be if it had been merited by our own attributes. Of course in this case qualms are easily stilled by the fact that a benefit has been received, never mind how. In the contrary case, however, when something of value has been lost, the sense of loss will be compounded by the feeling that one was not assessed on one's own merits, but merely as a member of a group.

To this general preference for individual as against group assessment must be added a consideration arising from the nature of the group. To be denied a benefit because one was, say, a member of the Communist Party would be unjust and a violation of basic principles of political liberty, but if one has chosen to join the Communist Party, then one is, after all, being assessed for what one has done, and one can choose between living with the consequences of continued party membership or leaving the party.[6] Race, of course, is not something that one chooses to adopt or that one can ever choose to give up. The person who is denied advantages because of his race is totally unable to alter this particular circumstance of his existence and so may feel with added sharpness that his life is clouded, not merely because he is not being judged as an individual, but because of something over which he has no control at all. This makes racial discrimination peculiarly invidious.

So we have the viewpoint of the victim of racial discrimination to offset against the landlord's argument in favor, and it seems that the victim has more at stake and hence should be given preference, even if the landlord's reason for discriminating is non-arbitrary and hence in a sense legitimate. The case against racial discrimination becomes stronger still when we consider the long-term social effects of discrimination.

When members of a racial minority are overwhelmingly among the poorest members of a society, living in a deprived area, holding jobs low in pay and status, or no jobs at all, and less well educated than the average member of the community, racial discrimination serves to perpetuate a divided society in which race becomes a badge of a much broader inferiority. It is the association of race with economic status and educa-

tional disadvantages which in turn gives rise to the situation in which there could be a coloring of truth to the claim that race is a relevant ground for discriminating between prospective tenants, applicants for employment, and so on. Thus there is, in the end, a parallel between the situation of the landlord and the cake-shop owner, for both, by their discrimination, contribute to the maintenance of the grounds for claiming that this discrimination is non-arbitrary. Hence prohibition of such discrimination can be justified as breaking this circle of deprivation and discrimination. The difference between the situations, as I have already said, is that in the case of the cake-shop owner it is only a prejudice against contact with blacks that needs to be broken down, and experience has shown that such prejudices do evaporate in a relatively short period of time. In the case of the landlord, however, it is the whole social and economic position of blacks that needs to be changed, and while overcoming discrimination would be an essential part of this process it may not be sufficient. That is why, if the facts are as the landlord alleges them to be, prohibition of racial discrimination is likely to impose more of a long-term disadvantage on the landlord than on the shop owner—a disadvantage which is, however, outweighed by the costs of continuing the circle of racial discrimination and deprivation for those discriminated against; and the costs of greater social inequality and racial divisiveness for the community as a whole.

A BASIC PRINCIPLE

If our discussion of the three examples has been sound, opposition to racial discrimination cannot rely on the standard objection that racial discrimination is arbitrary because race is irrelevant to employment, housing, and other things that matter. While this very often will be true, it will not always be true. The issue is more complicated than that appealing formula suggests, and has to do with the effect of racial discrimination on its victims, and on society as a whole. Behind all this, however, there is a more basic moral principle, and at this more basic level the irrelevance of race and the arbitrariness of racial discrimination reappear and help to explain why racism is wrong. This basic moral principle is the principle of equal consideration of interests.

The principle of equal consideration of interests is easy to state, though difficult to apply. Bentham's famous 'each to count for one and none for more than one' is one way of putting it, though not free from ambiguity; **Sidgwick's** formulation is more precise, if less memorable: 'The good of any one individual is of no more importance, from the point of view (if I may say so) of the Universe, than the good of any other.'[7] Perhaps the best way of explaining the effect of the principle is to follow **C.I. Lewis's** suggestion that we imagine ourselves living, one after the other, the lives of everyone affected by our actions; in this way we would experience all of their experiences as our own.[8] **R.M. Hare's** insistence that moral judgments must be universalizable comes to much the same thing, as he has pointed out.[9] The essence of the principle of equal consideration of interests is that we give equal weight in our moral deliberations to the like interests of all those affected by our actions. This means that if only X and Y would be affected by a possible act, and if X stands to lose more than Y stands to gain (for instance, X will lose his job and find it difficult to get another, whereas Y will merely get a small promotion) then it is better not to do the act. We cannot, if we accept the principle of equal consideration of interests, say that doing the act is better, despite the facts described, because we are more concerned about Y than we are about X. What the principle is really saying is that an interest is an interest, whoever's interest it may be.

We can make this more concrete by considering a particular interest, say the interest we have in the relief of pain. Then the principle says that the ultimate moral reason for relieving pain is simply the undesirability of pain as such, and not the undesirability of X's pain, which might be different from the undesirability of Y's pain. Of course, X's pain might be more undesirable than Y's pain because it is more painful, and then the principle of equal consideration would give greater weight to the relief of X's pain. Again, even where the pains are equal, other factors might be relevant, especially if others are affected. If there has been an earthquake we might give priority to the relief of a doctor's pain so that he can treat other victims. But the doctor's pain itself counts only once, and with no added weighting. The principle of equal consideration of interests acts like a pair of scales, weighing interests impartially. True scales favor the side where the interest is stronger, or where several interests combine to outweigh a smaller number of similar interests; but they take no account of whose interests they are weighing.

It is important to understand that the principle of equal consideration of interests is, to adopt Sidgwick's suggestive phrase, a 'point of view of the universe' principle. The phrase is, of course, a metaphor. It is not intended to suggest that the universe as a whole is alive, or conscious, or capable of having a point of view; but we can, without getting involved in any pantheist suppositions, imagine how matters would be judged by a being who was able to take in all of the universe, viewing all that was going on with an impartial benevolence.[10]

It is from this universal point of view that race is irrelevant to the consideration of interests; for all that counts are the interests themselves. To give less consideration to a specified amount of pain because that pain was experienced by a black would be to make an arbitrary distinction. Why pick on race? Why not on whether a person was born in a leap year? Or whether there is more than one vowel in his surname? All these characteristics are equally irrelevant to the undesirability of pain from the universal point of view. Hence the principle of equal consideration of interests shows straightforwardly why the most blatant forms of racism, like that of the Nazis, are wrong. For the Nazis were concerned only for the welfare of members of the 'Aryan' race, and the sufferings of Jews, Gypsies and Slavs were of no concern to them.

That the principle of equal consideration of interests is a 'point of view of the universe' principle allows us to account for the fact that it is a principle upon which it seems virtually impossible to act. Who of us can live as if our own welfare and that of our family and friends were of no more concern to us than the welfare of anonymous individuals in far away countries, of whom we know no more than the fact of their existence? Only a saint or a robot could live in this way; but this does not mean that only a saint or a robot can live in accordance with the principle of equal consideration of interests, for a principle which is valid from a universal point of view may yield subordinate principles to be acted upon by those who have limited resources and are involved in a particular segment of the world, rather than looking down upon the whole from a position of impartiality.

So subordinate principles giving members of families responsibility for the welfare of others in the family, or giving national governments responsibility for the welfare of their citizens, will be derivable from the principle of equal consideration, *if* everyone's interests are best promoted by such arrangements; and this is likely to be the case if, first, people are more knowledgeable about the interests of those close to them and more inclined to work to see that these interests are catered for, and, second, if the distribution of resources between families and between nations is not so unequally distributed that some families or nations are simply unable to provide for themselves the means to satisfying interests that could be satisfied with ease by other families or nations. In the world as it is presently constituted the first condition seems to hold, but not the second. For that reason I do not think that the subordinate principles mentioned correctly set out our present moral responsibilities, though they could do so if resources were more evenly distributed. Until then, we ought to strive to be more saint-like.[11]

Subordinate principles based on race, giving each race responsibility for the welfare of other members of that race are, I think, considerably less likely to be derivable from the principle of equal consideration than subordinate principles based on family or membership of a nation. For where they are not living together as a nation, races tend to be widely scattered; there is usually little knowledge of the circumstances of other members of one's race in different parts of the world, and there is nobody with the capacity to look after all members of a race as a national government can look after the interests of its citizens. There is, admittedly, often a degree of sentiment connecting members of a race, however widely they are separated. The contributions of American Jews to the support of members of their race in Israel is a well-known example of this, and there are many others. But the intermingling of races still makes it very doubtful that interests could be generally promoted by dividing responsibilities along racial lines.

The fundamental principle of equal consideration of interests, then, pays no regard to the race of those whose interests are under consideration; nor can we plausibly derive from the basic principle a subordinate principle enjoining us to consider the interests of members of our own race before we consider the interests of others; yet it cannot be said that the principle rules out racial discrimination in all circumstances. For the principle is an abstract one, and can only be applied in a concrete situation, in which the facts of the situation will be relevant. For instance, I have heard it said that somewhere in ancient Hindu writings members of the Brahmin or priestly caste are claimed to be so much more sensitive than members of the lower castes that their pleasures and pains are twenty times as intense as those of lesser human beings. We would, of course, do well to be suspicious of such a claim, particularly as the author of the document would no doubt have been a Brahmin himself. But let us assume that we somehow discovered that this extraordinary difference in sensitivity did in fact exist; it would follow that Brahmins have a greater interest in having access to a source of pleasure, and in avoiding a source of pain, than others. It would be as if when a Brahmin scratches his finger he feels a pain similar to that which others feel when they dislocate their shoulder. Then, consistently with the principle of equal consideration of interests, if a Brahmin and an ordinary person have both scratched their fingers, and we have only enough soothing ointment to cover one scratch, we should favor the Brahmin—just as, in the case of two normal people, if one had scratched a finger while the other had dislocated a shoulder we should favor the person with the more painful injury.

Needless to say, the example is a fanciful one, and intended to show only how, within the confines of the principle of equal consideration of interests, factual differences could be relevant to racial discrimination. In the absence of any real evidence of racial differences in sensitivity to pleasure and pain, the example has no practical relevance. Other differences between races—if they were differences between all members of races, and not differences which showed up only when averages were taken—could also justify forms of discrimination which ran parallel to the boundary of race. Examples would be substantial differences in intelligence, educability or the capacity to be self-governing. Strictly, if there were such differences then discrimination based on them would not be *racial* discrimination but rather discrimination on the ground of differences which happened to coincide with racial differences. But perhaps this is hair-splitting, since it would certainly be popularly known as racial discrimination. The kind of discrimination that such differences would justify would be only that

to which these differences were relevant. For instance, a respectable argument for benevolent colonialism could be mounted if it really were true that certain races were so incapable of self-government as to be obviously better off on the whole when ruled by people of a different race. I hasten to add that the historical record gives no support to such a hypothesis, but rather suggests the contrary. Again, this fictional example shows only that, given peculiar enough factual assumptions, any acceptable principle of equality can lead to racial discrimination.

On the other hand, the principle of equal consideration of interests does underpin the decisions we reached when considering the three more realistic examples of racial discrimination in the preceding section of this article. Although the principle is too general to allow the derivation of straightforward and indisputable conclusions from it in complex situations, it does seem that an impartial consideration of the interests of all involved would, for reasons already discussed, rule out discrimination by the shop owner and the landlord, though allowing that of the film director. Hence it is the arbitrariness of racial discrimination at the level of the principle of equal consideration of interests, rather than at the level of the particular decision of the person discriminating, that governs whether a given act of racial discrimination is justifiable.

This conclusion may be applied to other controversial cases. It suggests, for instance, that the problem of 'reverse discrimination' or 'compensatory discrimination' which arises when a university or employer gives preference to members of minority groups should be discussed by asking not whether racial discrimination is always and intrinsically wrong, but whether the proposal is, on balance, in the interests of all those affected by it. This is a difficult question, and not one that can be answered generally for all types of reverse discrimination. For instance, if white communities have a far better doctor-patient ratio than black communities because very few blacks are admitted to medical school and white doctors tend to work in white communities, there is a strong case for admitting some black candidates to medical school ahead of whites who are better qualified by the standard entry procedures, provided, of course, that the blacks admitted are not so poorly qualified as to be unable to become competent doctors. The case for separate and easier entry would be less strong in an area where there is no equivalent community need, for instance, in philosophy. Here much would depend on whether black students who would not otherwise have been admitted were able to make up ground and do as well as whites with higher ratings on standard entry procedures. If so, easier entry for blacks could be justified in terms of the conventional goal of admitting those students most likely to succeed in their course; taking into account a student's race would merely be a way of correcting for the failure of standard tests to allow for the disadvantages that face blacks in competing with whites on such tests. If, on the other hand, blacks admitted under easier entry in a field like philosophy did not do as well as the whites they displaced could have been expected to do, discrimination in their favor would be much harder to justify.

Immigration policy, too, is an area in which the principle of equal consideration of interests suggests the kinds of facts we should look for, instead of giving a definite answer. The relevant questions are the extent to which an immigrant will be benefited by admission, and the extent to which the admitting nation will be benefited. Race certainly does not provide an answer to the first of these questions. A country which chooses to give only those of a certain race the benefit of permanent residence fails to give equal consideration to those not of the favored race who may have a greater interest in leaving their present country than others who are accepted because of their race. While this kind of racial discrimination would in itself be unjustifiable, it has been defended on the grounds that the alternative would be disastrous for citizens of the admitting nation, and ultimately for those admitted too. An extreme version of this kind of defense is the line taken by the British politician Enoch Powell, who prophesied 'rivers of blood' if black immigration was not stopped and blacks who had already arrived were not encouraged to go back to where they had come from.[12] Here again, the facts are relevant. If Powell's claims had been soundly based, if it really were impossible for blacks and whites to live together without widespread bloodshed, then continued immigration would have been in the interests of neither blacks nor whites, and stopping immigration could not have been condemned as racist—though the epithet could have been applied to those Britons who were so hostile to blacks as to produce the situation Powell predicted. Despite occasional racial disturbances in Britain, however, there is no sign that Powell's predictions will come true. While a sudden influx of large numbers of immigrants of a different racial (or ethnic) group may cause problems, it is clear that people of different races can live together without serious strife. This being so, there is no justification for immigration policies that impose blanket prohibitions on people of a different race from that of the residents of the country. The most that can be defended in terms of the principle of equal consideration of interests is a quota system that leads to a gradual adjustment in the racial composition of a society.[13]

Endnotes

1. In popular usage, even the term 'discrimination' is often used to suggest that the practice referred to is wrong; this is, of course, an abuse of language, for to discriminate is merely to distinguish, or differentiate, and we could hardly get along without doing that.

2. For a brief and clear statement of this idea of justice, see H.L.A. Hart, *The Concept of Law* (Clarendon Press, Oxford, 1961) pp. 156–8; see also Joel Feinberg, *Social Philosophy* (Prentice–Hall, Englewood Cliffs, N.J. 1973) ch. 7.

3. See, for instance, R.M. Hare, *Freedom and Reason* (Clarendon Press, Oxford, 1963) chs. 9, 11; Richard

Wasserstrom, 'Rights, Human Rights, and Racial Discrimination' *Journal of Philosophy*, vol. 61 (1964) and reprinted in James Rachels, ed., *Moral Problems* (Harper and Row, New York, 1975).

4. See Feinberg, *op. cit.*, p. 78.

5. In most southern communities ... the adjustment to public desegregation following the enactment of the 1964 Civil Rights Act was amazing. Lewis M. Killian, *White Southerners* (New York: Random House, 1970). Similar comments have been made by many other observers; for a more recent report, see *Time*, September 27, 1976, especially the favorable comments of Northern blacks who have recently moved to the South (p. 44). That contact with those of another race helps to reduce racial prejudice had been demonstrated as early as 1949, when a study of U.S. soldiers showed that the more contact white soldiers had with black troops, the more favorable were their attitudes to integration. See Samuel Stouffer *et al.*, *The American Soldier: Adjustment During Army Life* (Princeton: Princeton University Press, 1949) p. 594. This finding was supported by a later study, 'Project Clear', reported by Charles Moskos, Jr., 'Racial Integration in the Armed Forces', *American Journal of Sociology*, vol. 72 (1966) pp. 132–48.

6. The situation is different if it is because of a past rather than a present political connection that one is subjected to disadvantages. Perhaps this is why the hounding of ex-communists in the McCarthy era was a particularly shameful episode in American history.

7. Henry Sidgwick, *The Methods of Ethics* (Macmillan, London, 7th Edition, 1907), p. 382.

8. C.I. Lewis, *Analysis of Knowledge and Valuation* (La Salle, 1946), p. 547; I owe this reference to R.M. Hare.

9. See Hare, 'Rules of War and Moral Reasoning' *Philosophy and Public Affairs*, vol. 1 (1972).

10. See the discussion of the Ideal Observer theory in Roderick Firth, 'Ethical Absolutism and the Ideal Observer', *Philosophy and Phenomenological Research*, vol. XII (1952) and the further discussion in the same journal by Richard Brandt, vol. XV (1955).

11. For a general discussion of this issue, see Sidgwick, *op. cit.* pp. 432–3; for considerations relevant to the present distribution of resources, see my 'Famine, Affluence and Morality', *Philosophy and Public Affairs*, vol. I (1972) and reprinted in James Rachels (ed.) *Understanding Moral Philosophy* (Dickenson, Encino, Calif. 1976) and Paula and Karsten Struhl (eds.) *Philosophy Now* (Random House, New York, 2nd Edition, 1975).

12. *The Times* (London) April 21, 1968.

13. I am grateful to Robert Young for comments and criticism on this paper.

Review Questions

1. Distinguish between the evaluative and descriptive senses of a term. How does Singer use the terms *racist* and *racial discrimination?*

2. What is the standard objection to racial discrimination according to Singer? Why doesn't he accept this objection?

3. State and explain the principle of equal consideration of interests accepted by Singer.

4. When is racial discrimination wrong according to Singer? Give examples.

5. What is Singer's view of reverse discrimination?

6. What is his position on immigration policies?

Discussion Questions

1. Can sexual discrimination be treated in the same way as Singer treats racial discrimination? Why or why not?

2. Can you think of any objections to the principle of equal consideration of interests? What are they?

3. Should we apply the principle of equal consideration of interests to children, nonhuman animals, other species, and the natural environment? What is your view? (In Chapter 9, we find Singer applying this principle to nonhuman animals.)

4. Singer is willing to allow reverse discrimination in some cases—for example, admitting a black candidate to medical school ahead of whites who are better qualified. Is such reverse discrimination acceptable?

Mary Anne Warren

Secondary Sexism and Quota Hiring

For biographical information on Mary Anne Warren, see her reading in Chapter 2.

Warren begins by distinguishing between primary and secondary sexism. Primary sexism is simply unfair discrimination on the basis of sex. Secondary sexism involves the use of sex-correlated criteria which are not valid measures of merit. One such criterion is: Does the candidate have an uninterrupted work record? This criterion discriminates against women who have interrupted their careers to have and raise children. To counteract primary and secondary sexist hiring practices which have put women at a disadvantage, Warren favors mandatory hiring quotas of a minimum sort based on the proportion of women among qualified and available candidates. Even though employers may have to use weak discrimination in favor of women to meet these quotas, Warren does not think that this is especially unfair to men. She feels that men have benefited in the past and will benefit in the future from sexist discrimination against women.

I want to call attention to a pervasive form of discrimination against women, one which helps to explain the continuing male monopoly of desirable jobs in the universities, as elsewhere. Discrimination of this sort is difficult to eliminate or even, in some cases, to recognize, because (1) it is not explicitly based on sex, and (2) it typically *appears* to be justified on the basis of plausible moral or practical considerations. The recognition of this form of discrimination gives rise to a new argument for the use of numerical goals or

From Mary Anne Warren, "Secondary Sexism and Quota Hiring," *Philosophy and Public Affairs,* Vol. 6, No. 3 (Spring 1977), pp. 240–261. Copyright © 1977 by Princeton University Press. Reprinted with permission of Princeton University Press. [Some of the footnotes have been renumbered.–Ed.]

quotas in the hiring of women for college and university teaching and administrative positions.

I shall argue that because of these de facto discriminatory hiring practices, minimum numerical quotas for the hiring and promotion of women are necessary, not (just) to compensate women for past discrimination or its results, or to provide women with role models, but to counteract this *ongoing* discrimination and thus make the competition for such jobs more nearly fair. Indeed, given the problems inherent in the compensatory justice and role-model arguments for reverse discrimination, this may well be the soundest argument for the use of such quotas.

I   PRIMARY AND SECONDARY SEXISM

Most of us try not to be sexists; that is, we try not to discriminate unfairly in our actions or attitudes toward either women or men. But it is not a simple matter to determine just which actions or attitudes discriminate unfairly, and a sincere effort to avoid unfair discrimination is often not enough. This is true of both of the forms of sexism that I wish to distinguish.

In its primary sense, "sexism" means *unfair discrimination on the basis of sex.* The unfairness may be unintentional; but the cause or reason for the discrimination must be the sex of the victim, not merely some factor such as size or strength that happens to be correlated with sex. Primary sexism may be due to dislike, distrust, or contempt for women, or, in less typical cases, for men or hermaphrodites. Or it may be due to sincerely held but objectively unjustified beliefs about women's properties or capacities. It may also be due to beliefs about the properties women *tend* to have, which are objectively justified but inappropriately applied to a particular case, in which the woman discriminated against does not have those properties.

For instance, if members of a philosophy department vote against hiring or promoting a woman logician because they dislike women (logicians), or because they think that women cannot excel in logic, or because they know that most women do not so excel and wrongly conclude that this one does not, then they are guilty of primary sexism. This much, I think, is noncontroversial.

But what should we say if they vote to hire or promote a man rather than a woman because he has a wife and children to support, while she has a husband who is (capable of) supporting her? Or because they believe that the woman has childcare responsibilities which will limit the time she can spend on the job? What if they hire a woman at a lower rank and salary than is standard for a man with comparable qualifications, for one of the above reasons? These actions are not sexist in the primary sense because there is no discrimination on the basis of sex itself. The criteria used *can* at least be applied in a sex-neutral manner. For instance, it might be asserted that if the woman candidate had had a spouse and children who depended upon her for support, this would have counted in her favor just as much as it would in the case of a man.

Of course, appeals to such intrinsically sex-neutral criteria may, in some cases, be mere rationalizations of what is actually done from primary sexist motives. In reality, the criteria cited may not be applied in a sex-neutral manner. But let us assume for the sake of argument that the application of these criteria *is* sex-neutral, not merely a smoke screen for primary sexism. On this assumption, the use of such criteria discriminates against women only because of certain contingent features of this society, such as the persistence of the traditional division of labor in marriage and childrearing.[1]

Many people see nothing morally objectionable in the use of such intrinsically sex-neutral yet de facto discriminatory criteria. For not only may employers who use such criteria be free of primary sexism, but their actions may appear to be justified on both moral and pragmatic grounds. It might, for instance, be quite clear that a department will really do more to alleviate economic hardship

by hiring or promoting a man with dependents rather than a woman with none, or that a particular woman's domestic responsibilities will indeed limit the time she can spend on the job. And it might seem perfectly appropriate for employers to take account of such factors.

Nevertheless, I shall argue that the use of such considerations is unfair. It is an example of secondary sexism, which I define as comprising all those actions, attitudes and policies which, while not using sex itself as a reason for discrimination, do involve sex-correlated factors or criteria and do result in an unfair impact upon (certain) women. In the case of university hiring policies, secondary sexism consists in the use of sex-correlated selection criteria which are not valid measures of academic merit, with the result that women tend to be passed over in favor of men who are not, in fact, better qualified. I call sexism of this sort *secondary,* not because it is any less widespread or harmful than primary sexism, but because (1) it is, in this way, indirect or covert, and (2) it is typically parasitic upon primary sexism, in that the injustices it perpetuates—for example, those apparent from the male monopoly of desirable jobs in the universities—are usually due in the first instance to primary sexism.

Two points need to be made with respect to this definition. First, it is worth noting that, although in the cases we will be considering the correlations between sex and the apparently independent but de facto discriminatory criteria are largely due to past and present injustices against women, this need not always be the case. The discriminatory impact of excluding pregnancy-related disabilities from coverage by employee health insurance policies, for example, probably makes this an instance of secondary sexism. Yet it is certainly not (human) injustice which is responsible for the fact that it is only women who become pregnant. The fact that the correlation is due to biology rather than prior injustice does not show that the exclusion is not sexist. Neither does the fact that pregnancy is often undertaken voluntarily. If such insurance programs fail to serve the needs of women employees as well as they serve those of men, then they can escape the charge of sexism only if—as seems unlikely—it can be shown that they cannot possibly be altered to include disabilities related to pregnancy without ceasing to serve their mutually agreed upon purposes, and/or producing an even greater injustice.

This brings us to the second point. It must be stressed that on the above definition the use of valid criteria of merit in hiring to university positions is not an instance of secondary sexism. Some might argue that merit criteria discriminate unfairly against women, because it is harder for women to earn the advanced degrees, to write the publications, and to obtain the professional experience that are the major traditional measures of academic merit. But it would be a mistake to suppose that merit criteria as such are therefore sexist. They are sexist only to the extent that they understate women's actual capacity to perform well in university positions; and to that extent, they are invalid as criteria of merit. To the extent that they are valid, that is, the most reliable available measurements of capacities which are indeed crucial for the performance of the job, they are not unjust, even though they may result in more men than women being hired.

If this seems less than obvious, the following analogy may help. It is surely not unjust to award first prize in a discus throwing contest to the contestant who actually makes the best throw (provided, of course, that none of the contestants have been unfairly prevented from performing up to their capacity on this particular occasion), even if some of the contestants have in the past been wrongly prevented from developing their skill to the fullest, say by sexist discrimination in school athletic programs. Such contestants may be entitled to other relevant forms of compensation, for example, special free training programs to help them make up for lost time, but they are not entitled to win this particular

contest. For the very *raison d'être* of an athletic contest dictates that prizes go to the best performers, not those who perhaps *could* have been the best, had past conditions been ideally fair.

So too, a university's central reasons for being dictate that positions within it be filled by candidates who are as well qualified as can be found. Choosing less qualified candidates deprives students of the best available instruction, colleagues of a more intellectually productive environment, and—in the case of state-funded universities—the public of the most efficient use of its resources.[2] To appoint inferior candidates defeats the primary purposes of the university, and is therefore wrong-headed, however laudable its motivations. It is also, as we shall see, a weapon of social change which is apt to backfire against those in whose interest it is advocated....

II SECONDARY SEXISM IN UNIVERSITY HIRING

Consider the following policies, which not infrequently influence hiring, retention, and promotion decisions in American colleges and universities:

1. Antinepotism rules, proscribing the employment of spouses of current employees.
2. Giving preference to candidates who (are thought to) have the greater financial need, where the latter is estimated by whether someone has, on the one hand, financial dependents, or, on the other hand, a spouse capable of providing financial support.
3. The "last hired-first fired" principle, used in determining who shall be fired or not rehired as a result of staffing cutbacks.
4. Refusing promotions, tenure, retention seniority, or pro-rata pay to persons employed less than full time, where some are so employed on a relatively long-term basis and where there is no evidence that such persons are (all) less well qualified than full time employees.
5. Hiring at a rank and salary determined

primarily by previous rank and salary rather than by more direct evidence of a candidate's competence, for example, degrees, publications, and student and peer evaluations.

6. Counting as a negative factor the fact that a candidate has or is thought to have, or to be more likely to have, childcare or other domestic responsibilities which may limit the time s/he can spend on the job.

7. Giving preference to candidates with more or less uninterrupted work records over those whose working careers have been interrupted (for example, by raising children) in the absence of more direct evidence of a present difference in competence.

8. Not hiring, especially to administrative or supervisory positions, persons thought apt to encounter disrespect or lack of cooperation from peers or subordinates, without regard for whether this presumed lack of respect may be itself unjustified, for example, as the result of primary sexism.

9. Discriminating against candidates on the grounds of probable mobility due to the mobility of a spouse, present or possible.

Each of these practices is an example of secondary sexism, in that while the criterion applied does not mention sex, its use nevertheless tends to result in the hiring and promotion of men in preference to women who are not otherwise demonstrably less well qualified. I suggest that in seeking to explain the continuing underrepresentation of women in desirable jobs in the universities, we need to look not only toward primary sexist attitudes within those institutions, and certainly not toward any intrinsic lack of merit on the part of women candidates,[3] but toward covertly, and often unintentionally, discriminatory practices such as these.

Of course, none of these practices operates to the detriment of women in every case; but each operates against women much more often than against men, and the cumulative effect is enormous. No doubt some of them

are more widespread than others and some (for example, the use of antinepotism rules) are already declining in response to pressures to remove barriers to the employment of women. Others, such as policies 3 and 4, are still fairly standard and have barely begun to be seriously challenged in most places. Some are publicly acknowledged and may have been written into law or administrative policy, for example, policies 1, 3, 4, and 5. Others are more apt to be private policies on the part of individual employers, to which they may not readily admit or of which they may not even be fully aware, for example, policies 2, 6, 7, and 8. It is obviously much more difficult to demonstrate the prevalence of practices of the latter sort. Nevertheless, I am certain that all of these practices occur, and I strongly suspect that none is uncommon, even now.

This list almost certainly does not include all of the secondary sexist practices which influence university hiring. But these examples are typical, and an examination of certain of their features will shed light on the way in which secondary sexism operates in the academic world and on the reasons why it is morally objectionable.

In each of these examples, a principle is used in choosing between candidates that in practice acts to discriminate against women who may even be better qualified intrinsically than their successful rivals, on any reliable and acceptable measure of merit.[4] Nevertheless, the practice may *seem* to be justified. Nepotism rules, for instance, act to exclude women far more often than men, since women are more apt to seek employment in academic and/or geographical areas in which their husbands are already employed than vice versa. Yet nepotism rules may appear to be necessary to ensure fairness to those candidates and appointees, both male and female, who are *not* spouses of current employees and who, it could be argued, would otherwise be unfairly disadvantaged. Similarly, giving jobs or promotions to those judged to have the greatest financial need may seem to be simple humanitarianism, and the seniority system may seem to be the only practical way of providing job security to *any* portion of the faculty. For policies 5 through 9, it could be argued that, although the criteria used are not entirely reliable, they may still have *some* use in predicting job performance.

Thus each practice, though discriminatory in its results, may be defended by reference to principles which are not intrinsically sex-biased. In the context of an otherwise sexually egalitarian society, these practices would probably not result in de facto discrimination against either sex. In such a society, for instance, men would not hold a huge majority of desirable jobs, and women would be under no more social or financial pressure than men to live where their spouses work rather than where they themselves work; thus they would not be hurt by nepotism rules any more often, on the average, than men.[5] The average earning power of men and women would be roughly equal, and no one could assume that women, any more than men, ought to be supported by their spouses, if possible. Thus the fact that a woman has an employed spouse would not be thought to reduce her need for a job any more—or any less—than in the case of a man. We could proceed down the list; in a genuinely nonsexist society, few or none of the conditions would exist which cause these practices to have a discriminatory impact upon women.

Of course, there may be other reasons for rejecting these practices, besides their discriminatory impact upon women. Nepotism rules might be unfair to married persons of both sexes, even in a context in which they were not *especially* unfair to women. My point is simply that these practices would not be instances of sexism in a society which was otherwise free of sexism and its results. Hence, those who believe that the test of the justice of a practice is whether or not it would unfairly disadvantage any group or individual *in the context of an otherwise just society* will see no sexual injustice whatever in these practices.

But surely the moral status of a practice, as it operates in a certain context, must be determined at least in part by its actual consequences, in that context. The fact is that each of these practices acts to help preserve the male monopoly of desirable jobs, in spite of the availability of women who are just as well qualified on any defensible measure of merit. This may or may not suffice to show that these practices are morally objectionable. It certainly shows that they are inconsistent with the "straight merit" principle, that is, that jobs should go to those best qualified for them on the more reliable measures of merit. Hence, it is ironic that attempts to counteract such de facto discriminatory practices are often interpreted as attacks on the "straight merit" principle.

III WHY SECONDARY SEXISM IS UNFAIR

Two additional points need to be stressed in order to show just why these practices are unfair. In the first place, the contingent social circumstances which explain the discriminatory impact of these practices are themselves morally objectionable, and/or due to morally objectionable practices. It is largely because men *are* more able to make good salaries, and because married women are still expected to remain financially dependent upon their husbands, if possible, that the fact that a woman has an employed husband can be seen as evidence that she doesn't "need" a job. It is because a disproportionate number of women must, because of family obligations and the geographical limitations these impose, accept part-time employment even when they would prefer full time, that the denial of tenure, promotion and pro-rata pay to part-time faculty has a discriminatory impact upon women. That women accept such obligations and limitations may seem to be their own free choice; but, of course, that choice is heavily conditioned by financial pressures—for example, the fact that the husband can usually make more money—and by sexually stereotyped social expectations.

Thus, the effect of these policies is to

compound and magnify prior social injustices against women. When a woman is passed over on such grounds, it is rather as if an athlete who had without her knowledge been administered a drug to hamper her performance were to be disqualified from the competition for failing the blood-sample test. In such circumstances, the very least that justice demands is that the unfairly imposed handicap not be used as a rationale for the imposition of further handicaps. If the unfair handicaps that society imposes upon women cause them to be passed over by employers because of a lack of straight merit, that is one thing, and it is unfortunate, but it is not obvious that it involves unfairness on the part of the employers. But if those handicaps are used as an excuse for excluding them from the competition regardless of their merit, as all too often happens, this is quite another thing, and it is patently unfair.

In the second place, practices such as these often tend to perpetuate the very (unjust) circumstances which underlie their discriminatory impact, thus creating a vicious circle. Consider the case of a woman who is passed over for a job or promotion because of her childcare responsibilities. Given a (better) job, she might be able to afford day care, or to hire someone to help her at home, or even to persuade her husband to assume more of the responsibilities. Denying her a job because of her domestic responsibilities may make it almost impossible for her to do anything to lessen those responsibilities. Similarly, denying her a job because she has a husband who supports her may force him to continue supporting her and her to continue to accept that support.

Both of these points may be illustrated by turning to a somewhat different sort of example. J.R. Lucas has argued that there are cases in which women may justifiably be discriminated against on grounds irrelevant to their merit. He claims, for example, that it is "not so evidently wrong to frustrate Miss Amazon's hopes of a military career in the Grenadier Guards on the grounds not that she would make a bad soldier, but that she would be a disturbing influence in the mess room."[6]

But this is a paradigm case of secondary, and perhaps also primary, sexism; it is also quite analogous to practice 8. To exclude women from certain jobs or certain branches of the military on the grounds that certain third parties are not apt to accept them, when that nonacceptance is itself unreasonable and perhaps based on sexual bigotry, is to compound the injustice of that bigotry. If it is inappropriate for soldiers to be disturbed or to make a disturbance because there are women in the mess room, then it is wrong to appeal to those soldiers' attitudes as grounds for denying women the opportunities available to comparably qualified men. It is also to help ensure the perpetuation of those attitudes, by preventing male soldiers from having an opportunity to make the sorts of observations which might lead to their eventually accepting women as comrades.

Thus, these practices are morally objectionable because they compound and perpetuate prior injustices against women, penalizing them for socially imposed disadvantages which cannot be reliably shown to detract from their actual present capacities. We may conclude that the hiring process will never be fair to women, nor will it be based on merit alone, so long as such practices persist on a wide scale. But it remains to be seen whether numerical hiring quotas for women are a morally acceptable means of counteracting the effects of sexist hiring practices.

IV WEAK QUOTAS

I shall discuss the case for mandatory hiring quotas of a certain very minimal sort: those based on the proportion of women, not in the population as a whole, but among qualified and available candidates in each academic field. Such a "weak" quota system would require that in each institution, and ideally within each department and each faculty and administrative rank and salary, women be hired and promoted at least in accordance with this proportion. If, for instance, a tenured or tenure-track position became available in a given department on an average of every other year, and if women were twenty percent of the qualified and available candidates in that field, then such a quota system would require that the department hire a woman to such a position at least once in ten years.[7]

Needless to say, this is not a formula for rapid change in the sexual composition of the universities. Suppose that the above department has twenty members, all male and all or almost all tenured, that it does not grow, and that it perhaps shrinks somewhat. Under these not atypical circumstances, it could easily take over forty years for the number of women in the department to become proportional to the number of qualified women available, even if the quota is strictly adhered to, and the proportion of qualified women does not increase in the meantime. Consequently, some would argue that such a quota system would be inadequate.[8]

Furthermore, it *could* be argued that if the job competition were actually based on merit, women would be hired and promoted at a *higher* rate than such a weak quota system would require, since the greater obstacles still encountered by women on the way to obtaining qualifications ensure that only very able women make it.[9] Or, it might be argued that women should be hired and promoted in more than such proportional numbers, in order to compensate for past discrimination or to provide other women with role models. Indeed, some existing affirmative action plans, so I am told, already require that women be hired in more than proportional numbers. Nevertheless, I will not defend quotas higher than these minimal ones. For, as will be argued in Section VIII, higher quotas at least give the appearance of being unfair to male candidates, and it is not clear that either the compensatory justice or the role-model argument is sufficient to dispel that appearance.

V QUOTAS OR GOALS?

Before turning to the case for such minimal hiring quotas, we need to comment on the "quotas vs. goals" controversy. Those who oppose the use of numerical guidelines in the hiring of women or racial minorities usually refer to such guidelines as *quotas,* while their defenders usually insist that they are not quotas but *goals.* What is at issue here? Those who use the term "quotas" pejoratively tend to assume that the numerical standards will be set so high or enforced so rigidly that strong reverse discrimination—that is, the deliberate hiring of demonstrably less well qualified candidates—will be necessary to implement them.[10] The term "goal," on the other hand, suggests that this will not be the case, and that good faith efforts to comply with the standards by means short of strong reverse discrimination will be acceptable.[11]

But whatever one calls such minimum numerical standards, and whether or not one suspects that strong reverse discrimination has in fact occurred in the name of affirmative action, it should be clear that it is not *necessary* for the implementation of a quota system such as I have described. Neither, for that matter, is weak reverse discrimination— that is, the deliberate hiring of women in preference to equally but not better qualified men.[12] For if hiring decisions were solely based on reliable measures of merit and wholly uncorrupted by primary or secondary sexist policies, then qualified women would *automatically* be hired and promoted at least in proportion to their numbers, except, of course, in statistically abnormal cases.[13] Consequently, reverse discrimination will *appear* to be necessary to meet proportional quotas only where the hiring process continues to be influenced by sexist practices—primary or secondary, public or private.

In effect, the implementation of a minimum quota system would place a price upon the continued use of sexist practices. Employers would be forced to choose between eliminating sexist practices, thus making it possible for quotas to be met without discriminating for or against anyone on the basis of sex, and practicing reverse discrimination on an ad hoc basis in order to meet quotas without eliminating sexist practices. Ideally, perhaps, they would all choose the first course, in which case the quota system would serve only to promote an ongoing check upon, and demonstration of, the non-sexist nature of the hiring process.

In reality, however, not all secondary sexist practices can be immediately eliminated. Some forms of secondary sexism have probably not yet been recognized, and given the nature of the interests involved it is likely that new forms will tend to spring up to replace those which have been discredited. More seriously, perhaps, some secondary sexist policies, such as the seniority system, cannot be eliminated without an apparent breach of contract (or of faith) with present employees. Others—for example, hiring on the basis of need—may survive because they are judged, rightly or wrongly, to be on the whole the lesser evil. A quota system, however, would require that the impact of such secondary sexist practices be counterbalanced by preferential treatment of women in other instances. Furthermore, it would hasten the elimination of all sexist policies by making it in the interest of all employees, men as well as women, that this be done, since until it is done both will run the risk of suffering from (sexist or reverse) discrimination. Certainly their elimination would be more probable than it is at present, when it is primarily women who have a reason based on self-interest for opposing them, yet primarily men who hold the power to eliminate or preserve them.

The most crucial point, however, is that under such a quota system, even if (some) employers do use weak discrimination in favor of women to meet their quota, this will not render the job competition especially unfair to men. For, as I will argue, unfairness would result only if the average male candidate's chances of success were reduced to below what they would be in an ongoing, just society, one in which men and women had complete equality of opportunity and the competition was based on merit alone; and I will argue that the use of weak reverse discrimination to meet proportional hiring quotas will not have this effect.

VI QUOTAS AND FAIRNESS

Now one way to support this claim would be to argue that in an ongoing, just society women would constitute a far higher proportion of the qualified candidates in most academic fields and that therefore the average male candidate's chances would, other things being equal, automatically be reduced considerably from what they are now. Unfortunately, however, the premise of this argument is overly speculative. It is possible that in a fully egalitarian society women would still tend to avoid certain academic fields and to prefer others, much as they do now, or even that they would fail to (attempt to) enter the academic profession as a whole in much greater numbers than at present.

But whatever the proportion of male and female candidates may be, it must at least be the case that in a just society the chances of success enjoyed by male candidates must be no greater, on the average, and no less than those enjoyed by comparably qualified women. Individual differences in achievement, due to luck or to differences in ability, are probably inevitable; but overall differences in the opportunities accorded to comparably qualified men and women, due to discrimination, would not be tolerated.

The question, then, is: Would the use of weak discrimination in favor of women, to a degree just sufficient to offset continuing sexist discrimination against women and thus to meet minimum quotas, result in lowering the average chances of male candidates to below those of comparably qualified women? The answer, surely, is that it would not, since by hypothesis men would be passed over, in order to fill a quota, in favor of women no better qualified only as often as women continue to be passed over, because of primary or secondary sexism, in favor of men no better qualified.

In this situation, individual departures from the "straight merit" principle might be no less frequent than at present; indeed, their frequency might even be doubled. But since it would no longer be predominantly women who were repeatedly disadvantaged by those departures, the overall fairness of the competition would be improved. The average long-term chances of success of *both* men and women candidates would more closely approximate those they would enjoy in an ongoing just society. If individual men's careers are temporarily set back because of weak reverse discrimination, the odds are good that these same men will have benefited in the past and/or will benefit in the future—not necessarily in the job competition, but in *some* ways—from sexist discrimination against women. Conversely, if individual women receive apparently unearned bonuses, it is highly likely that these same women will have suffered in the past and/or will suffer in the future from primary or secondary sexist attitudes. Yet, the primary purpose of a minimum quota system would not be to compensate the victims of discrimination or to penalize its beneficiaries, but rather to increase the overall fairness of the situation—to make it possible for the first time for women to enjoy the same opportunity to obtain desirable jobs in the universities as enjoyed by men with comparable qualifications.

It is obvious that a quota system implemented by weak reverse discrimination is not the ideal long-term solution to the problem of sexist discrimination in academic hiring. But it would be a great improvement over the present situation, in which the rate of unemployment among women Ph.D.'s who are actively seeking employment is still far higher than among men with Ph.D.'s, and in which women's starting salaries and chances of promotion are still considerably lower than those of men.[14] Strong reverse discrimination is clearly the least desirable method of implementing quotas. Not only is it unfair to the

men who are passed over, and to their potential students and colleagues, to hire demonstrably less well qualified women, but it is very apt to reinforce primary sexist attitudes on the part of all concerned, since it appears to presuppose that women cannot measure up on their merits. But to presume that proportional hiring quotas could not be met without strong reverse discrimination is also to make that discredited assumption. If, as all available evidence indicates, women in the academic world are on the average just as hard-working, productive, and meritorious as their male colleagues, then there can be no objection to hiring and promoting them at least in accordance with their numbers, and doing so will increase rather than decrease the extent to which success is based upon merit.

VII ARE QUOTAS NECESSARY?

I have argued that minimum proportional quotas such as I have described would not make the job competition (especially) unfair to men. But it might still be doubted that quotas are necessary to make the competition fair to women. Why not simply attack sexist practices wherever they exist and then let the chips fall as they may? Alan Goldman argues that quotas are not necessary, since, he says, other measures—for example, "active recruitment of minority candidates, the advertisement and application of nondiscriminatory hiring criteria . . . and the enforcement of these provisions by a neutral government agency"[15] would suffice to guarantee equal treatment for women. Goldman claims that if women candidates are as well qualified as men then, given these other measures, they will automatically be hired at least in proportion to their numbers. Indeed, he suggests that the only basis for doubting this claim is "an invidious suspicion of the real inferiority of women . . . even those with Ph.D.'s."[16] That discrimination against women might continue to occur in spite of such affirmative measures short of quotas, he regards as "an untested empirical hypothesis without much *prima facie* plausibility." [17]

In a similar vein, George Sher has argued that blacks, but not women, are entitled to reverse discrimination in hiring, since the former but not the latter have suffered from a poverty syndrome which has denied them the opportunity to obtain the qualifications necessary to compete on an equal basis with white men.[18] He views reverse discrimination—and presumably hiring quotas—as primarily a way of compensating those who suffer from present competitive disadvantages due to past discrimination, and claims that since women are not disadvantaged with respect to (the opportunity to obtain) qualifications, they are not entitled to reverse discrimination.

What both Goldman and Sher overlook, of course, is that women suffer from competitive disadvantages quite apart from any lack of qualifications. Even if primary sexism were to vanish utterly from the minds of all employers, secondary sexist practices such as those we have considered would in all likelihood suffice to perpetuate the male monopoly of desirable jobs well beyond our lifetimes. Such practices cannot be expected to vanish quickly or spontaneously; to insist that affirmative action measures stop short of the use of quotas is to invite their continuation and proliferation.

VIII THE COMPENSATORY JUSTICE AND ROLE–MODEL ARGUMENTS

Most of the philosophers who have recently defended the use of goals or quotas in the hiring of women and/or minority group members have assumed that this will necessarily involve at least weak and perhaps strong reverse discrimination, but have argued that it is nevertheless justified as a way of compensating individuals or groups for past injustices or for present disadvantages stemming from past injustices.[19] Others have argued that reverse discrimination is justified not (just) as a form of compensatory justice, but as a means of bringing about certain future goods—for example, raising the status of downtrodden groups,[20] or providing young women and blacks with role models and thus breaking the grip of self-fulfilling expectations which cause them to fail.[21]

If one is intent upon arguing for a policy which would give blacks or women "advantages in employment ... greater than these same blacks or women would receive in an ongoing just society," [22] then perhaps it is necessary to appeal to compensatory justice or to the role model or to other utilitarian arguments to justify the *prima facie* unfairness to white males which such a policy involves. But there is no need to use these arguments in justifying a weak quota system such as the one described here, and indeed, it is somewhat misleading to do so. For, as we have seen, such a system would not lower the average male candidate's overall chances of success to below what they would be if the selection were based on merit alone. It would simply raise women's chances, and lower men's, to a closer approximation of what they would be in an ongoing just society, in which the "straight merit" principle prevailed. This being the case, the fact that quotas may serve to compensate some women for past or present wrongs, or to provide others with role models, must be seen as a fortuitous side effect of their use and not their primary reasons for being. The primary reason for weak quotas is simply to increase the present fairness of the competition.

Furthermore, there are problems with the compensatory justice and role-model arguments which make their use hazardous. It is not clear that either suffices to justify any use of reverse discrimination beyond what may in practice (appear to) be necessary to implement weak quotas. For, granted that society as a whole has some obligation to provide compensation to the victims of past discrimination, and assuming that at least some women candidates for university positions are suitable beneficiaries of such compensation, it is by no means clear that male candidates should be forced to bear most of the burden for providing that compensation. It would be plausible to argue on the basis of compensatory justice for, say, tax-supported *extra* positions for women, since then the burden would be distributed relatively equitably. But compensatory justice provides no case for placing an extra, and seemingly punitive, burden on male candidates, who are no more responsible for past and present discrimination against women than the rest of us.

Similarly, however badly women may need role models, it is not clear that male candidates should be disproportionately penalized in order to provide them. It can be argued on the basis of simple fairness that male candidates' chances should not be allowed to remain *above* what they would be in a just society; but to justify reducing them to *below* that point requires a stronger argument than simply appealing to compensatory justice or the need for role models.

Nor does it help to argue that the real source of the injustice to male candidates, if and when preferential hiring of women results in lowering the former's chances to below what they would be in a just society, is not the preferential hiring policy itself, but something else. Thomas Nagel, for instance, argues that reverse discrimination is not seriously unjust, even if it means that it is harder for white men to get certain sorts of jobs than it is for women and blacks who are no better qualified, since, he suggests, the real source of the injustice is the entire system of providing differential rewards on the basis of differential abilities.[23] And Marlene Fried argues that the root of the injustice is not preferential hiring, but the failure of those with the power to do so to expand job opportunities so that blacks and women could be hired in increasing numbers without hiring fewer men.[24]

Unfortunately, we cannot, on the one hand, reject secondary sexist practices because of their contingent and perhaps unintended discriminatory effects, and, on the other hand, accept extenuations such as these for a policy which would, in practice, discrim-

inate unfairly against (white) men. These other sources of injustice are real enough; but this does not alter the fact that if reverse discrimination were practiced to the extent that certain men's chances of success were reduced to below those enjoyed, on the average, by comparably qualified women, then it would at least give every appearance of being unfair to those men. After all, the primary insight necessary for recognizing the injustice of secondary sexist policies is that a policy must be judged, at least in part, by its consequences in practice, regardless of whether or not these consequences are a stated or intended part of the policy. If a given policy results in serious and extensive injustice, then it is no excuse that this injustice has its roots in deeper social injustices which are not themselves easily amenable to change, at least not if there is any feasible way of altering the policy so as to lessen the resulting injustice.

I think we may conclude that while proportional quotas for the hiring of women are justified both on the basis of the merit principle and as a way of improving the overall fairness of the competition, it is considerably more difficult to justify the use of higher quotas. The distinction between such weak quotas and higher quotas is crucial, since although higher quotas have in practice rarely been implemented, the apparent injustice implied by what are typically *assumed* to be higher quotas has generated a backlash which threatens to undermine affirmative action entirely. If quotas are abandoned, or if they are nominally adopted but never enforced, then employers will be free to continue using secondary and even primary sexist hiring criteria, and it is probable that none of us will see the day when women enjoy job opportunities commensurate with their abilities and qualifications.

Endnotes

1. I mean, of course, the tradition that the proper husband earns (most of) the family's income, while the proper wife does (most of) the housekeeping and child-rearing.

2. It might be argued that the hiring process ought not to be based on merit alone, because there are cases in which being a woman, or being black, might itself be a crucial job qualification. As Michael Martin points out, this might well be the case in hiring for, say, a job teaching history in a previously all white-male department which badly needs to provide its students with a more balanced perspective. See "Pedagogical Arguments for Preferential Hiring and Tenuring of Women Teachers in the University." *The Philosophical Forum* 5, no. 2: 325–333. I think it is preferable, however, to describe such cases, not as instances requiring a departure from the merit principle, but as instances in which sex or race itself, or rather certain interests and abilities that are correlated with sex or race, constitutes a legitimate qualification for a certain job, and hence a measure of merit, vis-à-vis that job.

3. With respect to one such measure, books and articles published, married women Ph.D.'s published as much or slightly more than men, and unmarried women only slightly less. See "The Woman Ph.D.: A Recent Profile," by R.J. Simon, S.M. Clark, and K. Galway, in *Social Problems* 15, no. 2 (Fall 1967): 231.

4. I am assuming that whether a candidate is married to a current employee, or has dependents, or a spouse capable of supporting her, whether she is employed on a part-time or a full-time basis, her previous rank and salary, the continuity of her work record, and so on, are not in themselves reliable and acceptable measures of merit. As noted in example 5, more direct and pertinent measures of merit can be obtained. Such measures as degrees, publications, and peer and student evaluations have the moral as well as pragmatic advantage of being based on the candidate's actual past performance, rather than on unreliable and often biased conjectures of various sorts. Furthermore, even if there is or were *some* correlation (it would surely not be a *reliable* one) between certain secondary sexist criteria and job performance, it could still be argued that employers are not morally entitled to use such criteria, because of the unfair consequences of doing so. As Mary Vetterling has observed, there might well be some correlation between having "a healthy and active sex life" and "the patience and good humor required of a good teacher"; yet employers are surely not entitled to take into account the quality of a person's sex life in making hiring and promotion decisions. "Some Common Sense Notes on Preferential Hiring," *The Philosophical Forum* 5, no. 2: 321.

5. Unless, perhaps, a significant average age difference between wives and husbands continued to exist.

6. J.R. Lucas, "Because You Are a Woman," *Moral Problems*, ed. James Rachels (New York: Harper & Row, 1975), p. 139.

7. In practice problems of statistical significance will probably require that quotas be enforced on an institution-wide basis rather than an inflexible department-by-department basis. Individual departments, especially if they are small and if the proportion of qualified women in the field is low, may fail to meet hiring quotas, not because of primary or secondary sexism, but because the best qualified candidates happen in fact to be men. But if no real discrimination against women is occurring, then such statistical deviations should be canceled out on the institutional level, by deviations in the opposite direction.

8. See Virginia Held, "Reasonable Progress and Self-Respect," *The Monist* 57, no. 1: 19.

9. Gertrude Ezorsky cites in support of this point a study by L.R. Harmon of over 20,000 Ph.D.'s, which showed that "Women ... Ph.D.'s are superior to their male counterparts on all measures derived from high school records, in all ... specializations." *High School Ability Patterns: A Backward Look from the Doctorate,* Scientific Manpower [*sic*] Report No. 6, 1965, pp. 27–28; cited by Ezorsky in "The Fight Over University Women," *The New York Review of Books* 21, no. 8 (16 May 1974): 32.

10. See, for instance, Paul Seaburg, "HEW and the Universities," *Commentary* 53, no. 2 (February 1972): 38–44.

11. In practice, strong reverse discrimination is specifically prohibited by HEW affirmative action guidelines, and good faith efforts to implement affirmative action programs without resorting to strong reverse discrimination have been accepted as adequate. Nevertheless, though I would not wish to see *these* features of affirmative action policies changed, I prefer the term "quota" for what I am proposing, because this term suggests a standard which will be enforced, in one way or another, while the term "goal" suggests—and affirmative action is in great danger of becoming—a mere expression of good intentions, compliance with which is virtually unenforceable.

12. The distinction between strong and weak reverse discrimination is explored by Michael Bayles in "Compensatory Reverse Discrimination in Hiring," *Social Theory and Practice* 2, no. 3: 303–304, and by Vetterling, "Common Sense Notes," pp. 320–323.

13. This conclusion can be avoided only by assuming either that qualified women would not want better jobs if these were available, or that they are somehow less meritorious than comparably qualified men. The first assumption is absurd, since women who do not want desirable jobs are not apt to take the trouble to become qualified for them; and the second assumption is amply refuted by empirical data. See, for instance, the studies cited in fn. 9.

14. Elizabeth Scott tells me that her survey of 1974–1976 figures reveals that, in spite of affirmative action policies, unemployment among women Ph.D.'s who are actively seeking work is about twice as high as among men Ph.D.'s and that the starting salaries of women Ph.D.'s average $1,200 to $1,500 lower than those of men.

15. Alan H. Goldman, "Affirmative Action," *Philosophy & Public Affairs* 5, no. 2 (Winter 1976): 185.

16. Goldman, p. 186.

17. Goldman, p. 185.

18. Sher, p. 168.

19. See Bayles and Sher, respectively.

20. Irving Thalberg, "Reverse Discrimination and the Future," *The Philosophical Forum* 5, no. 2: 307.

21. See Marlene Gerber Fried, "In Defense of Preferential Hiring," *The Philosophical Forum* 5, no. 2: 316.

22. Charles King, "A Problem Concerning Discrimination," *Reason Papers*, no. 2 (Fall 1975), p. 92.

23. Thomas Nagel, "Equal Treatment and Compensatory Justice," *Philosophy & Public Affairs* 2, no. 4 (Summer 1973): 348–363, especially p. 353.

24. Fried, p. 318.

Review Questions

1. According to Warren, what is primary sexism?

2. What is secondary sexism, as it is explained by Warren?

3. Why does Warren think that secondary sexism is unfair?

4. What is the weak quota system recommended by Warren?

5. How does Warren characterize the quota vs. goals controversy?

6. According to Warren why isn't the use of weak reverse discrimination to meet proportional hiring quotas not unfair?

7. Why does Warren think that quotas are necessary to make competition for jobs fair for women?

8. What are the compensatory justice and role-model arguments?

9. Why doesn't Warren accept these arguments?

Discussion Questions

1. Is the sort of weak reverse discrimination advocated by Warren unfair to men? Explain your position.

2. Are the use of hiring quotas really necessary as Warren says? What do you think?

Lisa Newton

Reverse Discrimination as Unjustified

Lisa Newton is Professor of Philosophy at Fairfield University and adjunct professor of philosophy at Sacred Heart University.

Newton distinguishes between the moral ideal of equality which says that all humans should be citizens under the law, and justice in the political sense which says that those who are citizens should receive equal treatment under the law. Discrimination is unjust if it involves unequal treatment when citizens ought to have equal treatment under the law; for example, when the southern employer refuses to hire blacks for white-collar jobs. But reverse discrimination violates this political equality just as much as ordinary discrimination, and as such, it does not advance equality, but actually undermines it. Besides this theoretical objection to reverse discrimination, Newton also raises some practical problems. How do we determine which groups have been sufficiently discriminated against in the past to deserve preferred treatment in the present? How much reverse discrimination will compensate those who have been discriminated against? She conlcudes that reverse discrimination destroys justice, law, equality and citizenship itself.

I have heard it argued that "simple justice" requires that we favor women and blacks in employment and educational opportunities, since women and blacks were "unjustly" excluded from such opportunities for so many years in the not so distant past. It is a strange argument, an example of a possible implication of a true proposition advanced to dispute the proposition itself, like an octopus absentmindedly slicing off his head with a stray tentacle. A fatal confusion underlies this argument, a confusion fundamentally relevant to our understanding of the notion of the rule of law.

From Lisa Newton, "Reverse Discrimination as Unjustified," *Ethics*, Vol. 83, 1973, pp. 308–312, © University of Chicago Press.

Two senses of justice and equality are involved in this confusion. The root notion of justice, progenitor of the other, is the one that Aristotle (*Nicomachean Ethics* 5.6; *Politics* 1.2; 3.1) assumes to be the foundation and proper virtue of the political association. It is the conclusion which free men establish among themselves when they "share a common life in order that their association bring them self-sufficiency"—the regulation of their relationship by law, and the establishment, by law, of equality before the law. Rule of law is the name and pattern of this justice; its equality stands against the inequalities—of wealth, talent, etc.—otherwise obtaining among its participants, who by virtue of that equality are called "citizens." It is an achievement—complete, or, more frequently, partial—of certain people in certain concrete situations. It is fragile and easily disrupted by powerful individuals who discover that the blind equality of rule of law is inconvenient for their interests. Despite its obvious instability, Aristotle assumed that the establishment of justice in this sense, the creation of citizenship, was a permanent possibility for men and that the resultant association of citizens was the natural home of the species. At levels below the political association, this rule-governed equality is easily found; it is exemplified by any group of children agreeing together to play a game. At the level of the political association, the attainment of this justice is more difficult, simply because the stakes are so much higher for each participant. The equality of citizenship is not something that happens of its own accord, and without the expenditure of a fair amount of effort it will collapse into the rule of a powerful few over an apathetic many. But at least it has been achieved, at some times in some places; it is always worth trying to achieve, and eminently worth trying to maintain, wherever and to whatever degree it has been brought into being.

Aristotle's parochialism is notorious; he really did not imagine that persons other than Greeks could associate freely in justice, and the only form of association he had in mind was the Greek *polis*. With the decline of the *polis* and the shift in the center of political thought, his notion of justice underwent a sea change. To be exact, it ceased to represent a political type and became a moral ideal: the ideal of equality as we know it. This ideal demands that all men be included in citizenship—that one Law govern all equally, that all men regard all other men as fellow citizens, with the same guarantees, rights, and protections. Briefly, it demands that the circle of citizenship achieved by any group be extended to include the entire human race. Properly understood, its effect on our associations can be excellent: It congratulates us on our achievement of rule of law as a process of government but refuses to let us remain complacent until we have expanded the associations to include others within the ambit of the rules, as often and as far as possible. While one man is a slave, none of us may feel truly free. We are constantly prodded by this ideal to look for possible unjustifiable discrimination, for inequalities not absolutely required for the functioning of the society and advantageous to all. And after twenty centuries of pressure, not at all constant, from this ideal, it might be said that some progress has been made. To take the cases in point for this problem, we are now prepared to assert, as Aristotle would never have been, the equality of sexes and of persons of different colors. The ambit of American citizenship, once restricted to white males of property, has been extended to include all adult free men, then all adult males including ex-slaves, then all women. The process of acquisition of full citizenship was for these groups a sporadic trail of half-measures, even now not complete; the steps on the road to full equality are marked by legislation and judicial decisions which are only recently concluded and still often not enforced. But the fact that we can now discuss the possibility of favoring such groups in hiring shows that over the area that concerns us, at least, full equality is presupposed as a basis for discussion. To that extent, they are full citizens, fully protected by the law of the land.

It is important for my argument that the moral ideal of equality be recognized as logically distinct from the condition (or virtue) of justice in the political sense. Justice in this sense exists *among* a citizenry, irrespective of the number of the populace included in that citizenry. Further, the moral ideal is parasitic upon the political virtue, for "equality" is unspecified—it means nothing until we are told in what respect that equality is to be realized. In a political context, "equality" is specified as "equal rights"—equal access to the public realm, public goods and offices, equal treatment under the law—in brief, the equality of citizenship. If citizenship is not a possibility, political equality is unintelligible. The ideal emerges as a generalization of the real condition and refers back to that condition for its content.

Now, if justice (Aristotle's justice in the political sense) is equal treatment under law for all citizens, what is injustice? Clearly, injustice is the violation of that equality, discrimination for or against a group of citizens, favoring them with special immunities and privileges or depriving them of those guaranteed to the others. When the southern employer refuses to hire blacks in white-collar jobs, when Wall Street will only hire women as secretaries with new titles, when Mississippi high schools routinely flunk all the black boys above ninth grade, we have examples of injustice, and we work to restore the equality of the public realm by ensuring that equal opportunity will be provided in such cases in the future. But of course, when the employers and the schools *favor* women and blacks, the same injustice is done. Just as the previous discrimination did, this reverse discrimination violates the public equality which defines citizenship and destroys the rule of law for the areas in which these favors are granted. To the extent that we adopt a program of discrimination, reverse or otherwise, justice in the political sense is destroyed, and none of us, specifically affected or not, is a citizen, a bearer of rights—we are all petitioners for favors. And to the same extent, the ideal of equality is undermined, for it has content only where justice obtains, and by destroying justice we render the ideal meaningless. It is, then, an ironic paradox, if not a contradiction in terms, to assert that the ideal of equality justifies the violation of justice; it is as if one should argue, with William Buckley, that an ideal of humanity can justify the destruction of the human race.

Logically, the conclusion is simple enough: All discrimination is wrong *prima facie* because it violates justice, and that goes for reverse discrimination too. No violation of justice among the citizens may be justified (may overcome the *prima facie* objection) by appeal to the ideal of equality, for that ideal is logically dependent upon the notion of justice. Reverse discrimination, then, which attempts no other justification than an appeal to equality, is wrong. But let us try to make the conclusion more plausible by suggesting some of the implications of the suggested practice of reverse discrimination in employment and education. My argument will be that the problems raised there are insoluble, not only in practice but in principle.

We may argue, if we like, about what "discrimination" consists of. Do I discriminate against blacks if I admit none to my school when none of the black applicants are qualified by the tests I always give? How far must I go to root out cultural bias from my application forms and tests before I can say that I have not discriminated against those of different cultures? Can I assume that women are not strong enough to be roughnecks on my oil rigs, or must I test them individually? But this controversy, the most popular and well-argued aspect of the issue, is not as fatal as two others which cannot be avoided: If we are regarding the blacks as a "minority" victimized by discrimination, what is a "minority"? And for any group—blacks, women, whatever—that has been discriminated against, what amount of reverse discrimination wipes out the initial discrimination? Let us grant as true that women and blacks were discriminated against, even where laws forbade such discrimination, and grant for the sake of argument that a history of discrimination must be wiped out by reverse discrimination. What follows?

First, are there other groups which have been discriminated against? For they should have the same right of restitution. What about American Indians, Chicanos, Appalachian Mountain whites, Puerto Ricans, Jews, Cajuns, and Orientals? And if these are to be included, the principle according to which we specify a "minority" is simply the criterion of "ethnic (sub) group," and we're stuck with every hyphenated American in the lower middle class clamoring for special privileges for *his* group—and with equal justification. For be it noted, when we run down the Harvard roster, we find not only a scarcity of blacks (in comparison with the proportion in the population) but an even more striking scarcity of those second-, third-, and fourth-generation ethnics who make up the loudest voice of Middle America. Shouldn't they demand *their* share? And eventually, the WASPs will have to form their own lobby; for they too are a minority. The point is simply this: There is no "majority" in American who will not mind giving up just a bit of their rights to make room for a favored minority. There are only other minorities, each of which is discriminated against by the favoring. The initial injustice is then repeated dozens of times, and if each minority is granted the same right of restitution as the others, an entire area of rule governance is dissolved into a pushing and shoving match between self-interested groups. Each works to catch the public eye and political popularity by whatever means of advertising and power politics lend themselves to the effort, to capitalize as much as possible on temporary popularity until the restless mob picks another group to feel sorry for. Hardly an edifying spectacle, and in the long run no one can benefit: The pie is no larger—it's just that instead of setting up and enforcing rules for getting a piece, we've turned the contest into a free-for-all, requiring much more effort for no larger a reward. It would be in the interests of all the participants to reestablish an objective rule to govern the process, carefully enforced and the same for all.

Second, supposing that we do manage to agree in general that women and blacks (and all the others) have some right of restitution, some right to a privileged place in the structure of opportunities for a while, how will we know when that while is up? How much privilege is enough? When will the guilt be gone, the price paid, the balance restored? What recompense is right for centuries of exclusion? What criterion tells us when we are done? Our experience with the Civil Rights movement shows us that agreement on these terms cannot be presupposed: A process that appears to some to be going at a mad gallop into a black takeover appears to the rest of us to be at a standstill. Should a practice of reverse discrimination be adopted, we may safely predict that just as some of us begin to see "a satisfactory start toward righting the balance," others of us will see that we "have already gone too far in the other direction" and will suggest that the discrimination ought to be reversed again. And such disagreement is inevitable, for the point is that we could not *possibly* have any criteria for evaluating the kind of recompense we have in mind. The context presumed by any discussion of restitution is the context of the rule of law: Law sets the rights of men and simultaneously sets the method for remedying the violation of those rights. You may exact suffering from others and/or damage payments for yourself if and only if the others have violated your rights; the suffering you have endured is not sufficient reason for them to suffer. And remedial rights exist only where there is law: Primary human rights are useful guides to legislation but cannot stand as reasons for awarding remedies for injuries sustained. But then, the context presupposed by any discussion of restitution is the context of preexistent full citizenship. No remedial rights could exist for the excluded; neither in law nor in logic does there exist a right to *sue* for a standing to sue.

From these two considerations, then, the difficulties with reverse discrimination become evident. Restitution for a disadvantaged group whose rights under the law have been violated is possible by legal means, but restitution for a disadvantaged group whose grievance is that there was no law to protect them simply is not. First, outside of the area of justice defined by the law, no sense can be made of "the group's rights," for no law recognizes that group or the individuals in it, qua members, as bearers of rights (hence *any* group can constitute itself as a disadvantaged minority in some sense and demand similar restitution). Second, outside of the area of protection of law, no sense can be made of the violation of rights (hence the amount of the recompense cannot be decided by any objective criterion). For both reasons, the practice of reverse discrimination undermines the foundation of the very ideal in whose name it is advocated; it destroys justice, law, equality, and citizenship itself, and replaces them with power struggles and popularity contests.

Review Questions

1. What is the root notion of justice according to Newton?

2. What is the second sense of justice explained by Newton? What is the ideal of equality?

3. Newton claims that the ideal of equality is logically distinct from justice in the political sense. What is justice in the political sense, and how is it related to the ideal of equality?

4. What is injustice in Newton's account?

5. Why does Newton find reverse discrimination to be unjust?

6. In Newton's view, what is wrong with saying that the ideal of equality justifies the violation of justice?

7. What problems does Newton raise for reverse discrimination?

8. What is her conclusion?

Discussion Questions

1. Do you agree that the problems Newton raises for reverse discrimination are really insoluble? Why or why not?

2. Newton says that when an employer refuses to hire blacks for white-collar jobs an injustice is done, and that the *same* injustice is done when employers favor blacks. Is this true? Explain your answer.

William T. Blackstone

Reverse Discrimination and Compensatory Justice

From William T. Blackstone, "Reverse Discrimination and Compensatory Justice," *Social Theory and Practice* 3, No. 3 (Spring 1975), pp. 253–288. Reprinted by permission.

William T. Blackstone taught philosophy at the University of Georgia and wrote numerous articles on topics in ethics. He was the editor of Philosophy and Environmental Crisis *and, with Robert Heslep, the editor of* Social Justice and Preferential Treatment.

Blackstone argues on utilitarian grounds that reverse discrimination is morally improper. Even though it does have some good effects, the bad effects of reverse discrimination will outweigh these good effects, even for the women and minorities that it is supposed to help. Blackstone does approve of affirmative-action programs, however, provided they benefit the disadvantaged without regard to their race or sex.

Is reverse discrimination justified as a policy of compensation or of preferential treatment for women and racial minorities? That is, given the fact that women and racial minorities have been invidiously discriminated against in the past on the basis of the irrelevant characteristics of race and sex—are we now justified in discriminating in their favor on the basis of the same characteristics? This is a central ethical and legal question today, and it is one which is quite unresolved. Philosophers, jurists, legal scholars, and the man-in-the-street line up on both sides of this issue. These differences are plainly reflected (in the Supreme Court's majority opinion and Justice Douglas's dissent) in *DeFunis v. Odegaard*.[1] ...

I will argue that reverse discrimination is improper on both moral and constitutional grounds, though I focus more on moral grounds. However, I do this with considerable ambivalence, even "existential guilt." Several reasons lie behind that ambivalence. First, there are moral and constitutional arguments on both sides. The ethical waters are very muddy and I simply argue that the balance of the arguments are against a policy of reverse discrimination.[2] My ambivalence is further due not only to the fact that traditional racism is still a much larger problem than that of reverse discrimination but also because I am sympathetic to the *goals* of those who strongly believe that reverse discrimination as a policy is the means to overcome the debilitating effects of past injustice. Compensation and remedy are most definitely required both by the facts and by our value commitments. But I do not think that reverse discrimination is the proper means of remedy or compensation....

I

Let us now turn to the possibility of a utilitarian justification of reverse discrimination and to the possible conflict of justice-regarding reasons and those of social utility on this issue. The category of morally relevant reasons is broader, in my opinion, than reasons related to the norm of justice. It is broader than those related to the norm of utility. Also it seems to me that the norms of justice and utility are not reducible one to the other. We cannot argue these points of ethical theory here. But, if these assumptions are correct, then it is at least possible to morally justify injustice or invidious discrimination in some contexts. A case would have to be made that such injustice, though regrettable, will produce the best consequences for society and that this fact is an overriding or weightier moral reason than the temporary injustice. Some arguments for reverse discrimination have taken this line. Professor **Thomas Nagel** argues that such discrimination is justifiable as long as it is "clearly contributing to the eradication of great social evils."[3] ...

Another example of what I would call a utilitarian argument for reverse discrimination was recently set forth by Congressman Andrew Young of Georgia. Speaking specifically of reverse discrimination in the context of education, he stated: "While that may give minorities a little edge in some instances, and you may run into the danger of what we now commonly call reverse discrimination, I think the educational system needs this. Society needs this as much as the people we are trying to help ... a society working toward affirmative action and inclusiveness is going to be a stronger and more relevant society than one that accepts the limited concepts of objectivity. ... I would admit that it is perhaps an individual injustice. But it might be necessary in order to overcome an historic group injustice or series of group injustices."[4] Congressman Young's basic justifying grounds for reverse discrimination, which he recognizes as individual injustice, are the results which he thinks it will produce: a stronger and more relevant education system and society, and one which is more just overall. His argument may involve pitting some justice-regarding reasons (the right of women and racial minorities to be compensated for past injustices) against others (the right of the majority to the uniform application of the same standards of merit to all). But a major thrust of his argument also seems to be utilitarian.

Just as there are justice-regarding arguments on both sides of the issue of reverse discrimination, so also there are utilitarian arguments on both sides. In a nutshell, the utilitarian argument in favor runs like this: Our society contains large groups of persons who suffer from past institutionalized injustice. As a result, the possibilities of social discord and disorder are high indeed. If short-term reverse discrimination were to be effective in overcoming the effects of past institutionalized injustice and if this policy could alleviate the causes of disorder and bring a higher quality of life to millions of persons, then society as a whole would benefit.

There are moments in which I am nearly convinced by this argument, but the conclusion that such a policy would have negative utility on the whole wins out. For although reverse discrimination might appear to have the effect of getting more persons who have been disadvantaged by past inequities into the mainstream quicker, that is, into jobs, schools, and practices from which they have been excluded, the cost would be invidious discrimination against majority group members of society. I do not think that majority members of society would find this acceptable, i.e., the disadvantaging of themselves for past inequities which they did not control and for which they are not responsible. If such policies were put into effect by government, I would predict wholesale rejection or noncooperation, the result of which would be negative not only for those who have suffered past inequities but also for the justice-regarding institutions of society. Claims and counter-claims would obviously be raised by other ethnic or racial minorities—by Chinese, Chicanos, American Indians, Puerto Ricans— and by orphans, illegitimate children, ghetto residents, and so on. Literally thousands of types or groups could, on similar grounds as blacks or women, claim that reverse discrimination is justified on their behalf. What would happen if government attempted policies of reverse discrimination for all such

groups? It would mean the arbitrary exclusion or discrimination against all others relative to a given purpose and a given group. Such a policy would itself create an injustice for which those newly excluded persons could then, themselves, properly claim the need for reverse discrimination to offset the injustice to them. The circle is plainly a vicious one. Such policies are simply self-destructive. In place of the ideal of equality and distributive justice based on relevant criteria, we would be left with the special pleading of self-interested power groups, groups who gear criteria for the distribution of goods, services, and opportunities to their special needs and situations, primarily. Such policies would be those of special privilege, not the appeal to objective criteria which apply to all.[5] They would lead to social chaos, not social justice.

Furthermore, in cases in which reverse discrimination results in a lowering of quality, the consequences for society, indeed for minority victims of injustice for which reverse discrimination is designed to help, may be quite bad. It is no easy matter to calculate this, but the recent report sponsored by the Carnegie Commission on Higher Education points to such deleterious consequences.[6] If the quality of instruction in higher education, for example, is lowered through a policy of primary attention to race or sex as opposed to ability and training, everyone—including victims of past injustice—suffers. Even if such policies are clearly seen as temporary with quite definite deadlines for termination, I am skeptical about their utilitarian value....

II

The inappropriateness of reverse discrimination, both on utilitarian and justice-regarding grounds, in no way means that compensation for past injustices is inappropriate. It does not mean that those who have suffered past injustices and who have been disadvantaged by them are not entitled to compensation or that they have no moral right to remedy. It may be difficult in different contexts to translate that moral right to remedy into practice or into legislation. When has a disadvantaged person or group been compensated enough? What sort of allocation of resources will compensate without creating additional inequities or deleterious consequences? There is no easy answer to these questions. Decisions must be made in particular contexts. Furthermore, it may be the case that the effects of past injustices are so severe (poverty, malnutrition, and the denial of educational opportunities) that genuine compensation—the balancing of the scales—is impossible. The effects of malnutrition or the lack of education are often nonreversible (and would be so even under a policy of reverse discrimination). This is one of the tragedies of injustice. But if reverse discrimination is inappropriate as a means of compensation and if (as I have argued) it is unjust to make persons who are not responsible for the suffering and disadvantaging of others to suffer for those past injuries, then other means must be employed unless overriding moral considerations of another type (utilitarian) can be clearly demonstrated. That compensation must take a form which is consistent with our constitutional principles and with reasonable principles of justice. Now it seems to me that the Federal Government's Equal Opportunity and Affirmative Action programs are consistent with these principles, that they are not only not committed to reverse discrimination but rather absolutely forbid it.[7] However, it also seems to me that some officials authorized or required to implement these compensatory efforts have resorted to reverse discrimination and hence have violated the basic principles of justice embodied in these programs. I now want to argue both of these points: first, that these federal programs reject reverse discrimination in their basic principles; secondly, that some implementers of these programs have violated their own principles.

Obviously our country has not always been committed constitutionally to equality. We need no review of our social and political heritage to document this. But with the Four-

teenth Amendment, equality as a principle was given constitutional status. Subsequently, social, political, and legal practices changed radically and they will continue to do so. The Fourteenth Amendment declares that states are forbidden to deny any person life, liberty, or property without due process of law or to deny to any person the equal protection of the laws. In my opinion the principles of the Equal Opportunity and Affirmative Action Programs reflect faithfully this constitutional commitment. I am more familiar with those programs as reflected in universities. In this context they require that employers "recruit, hire, train, and promote persons in all job classifications without regard to race, color, religion, sex or national origin, except where sex is a bona fide occupational qualification."[8] They state explicitly that "goals may not be rigid and inflexible quotas which must be met, but must be targets reasonably attainable by means of good faith effort."[9] They require the active recruitment of women and racial minorities where they are "underutilized," this being defined as a context in which there are "fewer minorities or women in a particular job classification than would reasonably be expected by their availability."[10] This is sometimes difficult to determine; but some relevant facts do exist and hence the meaning of a "good faith" effort is not entirely fluid. In any event the Affirmative Action Program in universities requires that "goals, timetables and affirmative action commitment, must be designed to correct any identifiable deficiencies," with separate goals and timetables for minorities and women.[11] It recognizes that there has been blatant discrimination against women and racial minorities in universities and elsewhere, and it assumes that there are "identifiable deficiencies." But it does not require that blacks be employed because they are black or women employed because they are women; that is, it does not require reverse discrimination with rigid quotas to correct the past. It requires a good faith effort in the present based on data on the availability of qualified women and racial minorities in various disciplines and other relevant facts. (Similar requirements hold, of course, for non-academic employment at colleges and universities.) It does not mandate the hiring of the unqualified or a lowering of standards; it mandates only equality of opportunity for all which, given the history of discrimination against women and racial minorities, requires affirmative action in recruitment.

Now if this affirmative action in recruitment, which is not only consistent with but required by our commitment to equality and social justice, is translated into rigid quotas and reverse discrimination by those who implement equal opportunity and affirmative action programs in the effort to get results immediately—and there is no doubt in my mind that this has occurred—then such action violates the principles of these programs.

This violation—this inconsistency of principle and practice—occurs, it seems to me, when employers hire with *priority emphasis* on race, sex, or minority-group status. This move effectively eliminates others from the competition. It is like pretending that everyone is in the game from the beginning while all the while certain persons are systematically excluded. This is exactly what happened recently when a judge declared that a certain quota or number of women were to be employed by a given agency regardless of their qualifications for the job,[12] when some public school officials fired a white coach in order to hire a black one,[13] when a DeFunis is excluded from law school on racial grounds, and when colleges or universities announce that normal academic openings will give preference to female candidates or those from racial minorities.

If reverse discrimination is prohibited by our constitutional and ethical commitments, what means of remedy and compensation are available? Obviously, those means which are consistent with those commitments. Our commitments assure the right to remedy to those who have been treated unjustly, but our government has not done enough to bring this right to meaningful fruition in practice. Sound progress has been made in recent years, especially since the Equal Employment Opportunity Act of 1972 and the establishment of the Equal Employment Opportunities Commission. This Act and other laws have extended anti-discrimination protection to over 60% of the population.[14] The Commission is now authorized to enforce anti-discrimination orders in court and, according to one report, it has negotiated out-of-court settlements which brought 44,000 minority workers over 46 million dollars in back pay.[15] Undoubtedly this merely scratches the surface. But now the framework exists for translating the right to remedy into practice, not just for sloughing off race and sex as irrelevant criteria of differential treatment but other irrelevant criteria as well—age, religion, the size of hips (I am thinking of airline stewardesses), the length of nose, and so on.

Adequate remedy to overcome the sins of the past, not to speak of the present, would require the expenditure of vast sums for compensatory programs for those disadvantaged by past injustice in order to assure equal access. Such programs should be racially and sexually neutral, benefiting the disadvantaged of *whatever sex or race.* Such neutral compensatory programs would have a high proportion of blacks and other minorities as recipients, for they as members of these groups suffer more from the injustices of the past. But the basis of the compensation would be that fact, not sex or race. Neutral compensatory policies have definite theoretical and practical advantages in contrast to policies of reverse discrimination: Theoretical advantages, in that they are consistent with our basic constitutional and ethical commitments whereas reverse discrimination is not; practical advantages, in that their consistency, indeed their requirement by our constitutional and ethical commitments, means that they can marshal united support in overcoming inequalities whereas reverse discrimination, in my opinion, can not.

Endnotes

1. 94 S.Ct. 1704 (1974).

2. I hasten to add a qualification—more ambivalence!—resulting from discussion with Tom Beauchamp of Georgetown University. In cases of extreme recalcitrance to equal employment by certain institutions or businesses some quota requirements (reverse discrimination) may be justified. I regard this as distinct from a general policy of reverse discrimination.

3. "Equal Treatment and Compensatory Discrimination," *Philosophy and Public Affairs,* 2 (Summer 1974).

4. Atlanta Journal and Constitution, Sept. 22, 1974, p. 20–A.

5. For similar arguments see Lisa Newton, "Reverse Discrimination as Unjustified," *Ethics,* 83 (1973).

6. Richard A. Lester, *Antibias Regulation of Universities* (New York, 1974); discussed in *Newsweek,* July 15, 1974, p. 78.

7. See The Civil Rights Act of 1964, especially Title VII (which created the Equal Employment Opportunity Commission), amended by The Equal Employment Opportunity Act of 1972, found in *ABC's of The Equal Employment Opportunity Act,* prepared by the Editorial Staff of The Bureau of National Affairs, Inc., 1972. Affirmative Action Programs came into existence with Executive Order 11246. Requirements for affirmative action are found in the rules and regulations 41–CFR Part 60–2, Order # 4 (Affirmative Action Programs) generally known as Executive Order # 4 and Revised Order # 4 41–CFT 60–2 B. For discussion see Paul Brownstein, "Affirmative Action Programs," in *Equal Employment Opportunities Compliance,* Practising Law Institute, New York City (1972), pp. 73–111.

8. See Brownstein, "Affirmative Action Programs" and, for example, *The University of Georgia Affirmative Action Plan,* Athens, Ga., 1973–74, viii, pp. 133, 67.

9. Brownstein and *The University of Georgia Affirmative Action Plan,* Athens, Ga., 1973–74, p. 71.

10. Ibid., p. 69.

11. Ibid., p. 71.

12. See the *Atlanta Journal and Constitution,* June 9, 1974, p. 26–D.

13. See *Atlanta Constitution,* June 7, 1974, p. 13–B.

14. Newsweek, June 17, 1974, p. 75.

15. Ibid., p. 75.

Review Questions

1. According to Blackstone, what is the utilitarian argument for reverse discrimination? Why doesn't he accept this argument?

2. Why does Blackstone think that reverse discrimination is an inappropriate means of compensating for past injustices?

3. Why does Blackstone reject quotas?

Discussion Questions

1. Blackstone claims that the Equal Opportunity and Affirmative Action programs of the federal government forbid reverse discrimination. Is this true? Why or why not?

2. Blackstone says that affirmative-action programs should be racially and sexually neutral. Do you agree? Explain your position.

3. How would Warren reply to Blackstone?

Problem Cases

1. The University of California v. Bakke (1978)

In the years 1973 and 1974, Allan Bakke, a white male, applied for admission to the Medical School of the University of California at Davis. In both years, his application was rejected even though other applicants who had lower grade point averages and lower Medical College Admissions Test scores were admitted under a special program. After the second rejection in 1974, Bakke filed a lawsuit in the Superior Court of California. He alleged that the special program which admitted less-qualified minority students operated to exclude him from the school on the basis of race, in violation of his rights under Title VI of the Civil Rights Act of 1964 and the Equal Protection Clause of the Fourteenth Amendment. The trial court found that the special program operated as an unconstitutional racial quota because minority applicants were rated only against one another, and sixteen places in the class of one hundred were reserved for them. But the court refused to order Bakke's admission. Bakke appealed, and the case went to the Supreme Court of the United States. The justices of the Supreme Court were divided four-to-four on the issues in the case, with Justice Powell providing the decisive vote. Justice Powell sided with Chief Justice Warren Burger and three other justices in holding that the admissions program was unconstitutional, and that Bakke must be admitted to the school. But Justice Powell also sided with the other four justices in holding that colleges and universities can consider race as a factor in the admissions process.

Are quotas based on race or ethnic status unjust? What is your view?

Is it acceptable to consider race or sex as a factor in admissions? Why or why not?

2. A Case of Academic Hiring Suppose that the philosophy department of a state university has a tenure-track opening. The position is advertised and there are numerous applications, including one from a woman. It is not possible to determine the race of the applicants from the documents provided, and the department does not have the resources to interview the candidates. One of the male applicants has really outstanding credentials—a Ph.D. degree from Harvard with a dissertation on justice written under the direction of John Rawls (the dissertation is being published as a book by Harvard University Press), several articles published in leading journals, evidence of being an excellent teacher, and very flattering letters of recommendation. By comparison, the woman's credentials are good, but not really outstanding. She does not yet have a Ph.D. degree, although she says that her dissertation on feminism is almost done, and she has not published any articles. However, she does possess evidence of being a good teacher, and she has positive letters of recommendation.

Should the department hire the apparently less-qualified woman or not? Why or why not?

Suppose that it is discovered that one of the candidates is a black man; this fact is mentioned in one of the letters of recommendation. This man's credentials seem to be roughly equal to those of the woman. Should he be hired rather than the woman? What choice should be made in this case?

Suppose that the woman's credentials seem roughly equal to that of the leading man, that is, she has a Ph.D. degree from a good school, has publications and good letters of recommendation, and so on. Should the department hire her rather than the man? What do you think?

3. Women in Combat Jets The current policy of the air force is that women are not allowed to fly combat jets. But suppose that a qualified woman pilot demands to fly one of these jets. She has logged many hours of flight time; she holds the rank of major; she is in excellent physical condition; she is unmarried and has no children; and she is a black belt in karate. Are there any good reasons for refusing to let her fly? What are they?

4. Selling a House Suppose that Bob and Mary Smith have been trying to sell their three-bedroom house for two years. The house is only five years old and it is located in a pleasant middle-class neighborhood of Denver. The house has been appraised at $200,000, and the Smiths started out asking that much money for the house. But they have come down in price several times, and now they are asking for only $150,000. They feel that they cannot really go any lower in price because they have a $100,000 mortgage on the house, and they have spent at least $50,000 on various improvements. One day their real estate agent calls and says he has qualified buyers who are willing to pay $150,000 for the house. The only problem is that the buyers, Ralph and Sara Jones, are black. The real estate agent advises the Smiths to turn the offer down. He points out that the house is in an all-white neighborhood, and that if they sell to blacks, the property values in the area will go down dramatically. He has seen this happen in east Denver where houses that once sold for $500,000 are now selling for $50,000. Also, the real estate agent claims that the neighbors will be very angry if the Smiths sell their house to black people. On the other hand, the Smiths have a legal right to sell their house to qualified buyers, and the Joneses are definitely qualified. Ralph Jones is a successful lawyer, and his wife Sara is a grade-school teacher. They have three children, and they would be delighted to have the house.

Should the Smiths sell their house to the Joneses or not? Explain your position.

5. The Equal Rights Amendment The proposed Equal Rights Amendment reads as follows:

"Section 1. Equality of rights under the law shall not be denied or abridged by the United States or by any state on account of sex.

"Section 2. The Congress shall have the power to enforce, by appropriate legislation, the provisions of this article.

"Section 3. This amendment shall take effect two years after the date of ratification."

This Amendment was originally proposed by Alice Paul in 1923, just three years after women in the United States received the right to vote. It was approved by Congress in 1971, but it has not been ratified by the required three-fourths of the state legislatures and is now dead unless Congress revives it.

Should this amendment be ratified or not? Defend your position.

Suggested Readings

(1) Tom Beauchamp, "The Justification of Reverse Discrimination," in William T. Blackstone and Robert Heslep, eds., *Social Justice and Preferential Treatment* (Athens, GA: University of Georgia Press, 1976). Beauchamp argues that reverse discrimination in hiring is justified in order to eliminate present discriminatory practices. To prove that serious discrimination exists in our society, he presents an array of statistical and linguistic evidence.

(2) Bernard R. Boxill, "The Morality of Preferential Hiring," *Philosophy & Public Affairs* 7, No. 3 (Spring 1978), pp. 246–268. Boxill tries to refute two objections to preferential hiring: first, that preferential hiring benefits those who do not deserve compensation, and second, that it is unfair to young white men.

(3) _____, "Sexual Blindness and Sexual Equality," *Social Theory and Practice* 6, No. 3 (Fall 1980), pp. 281–298. Boxill attacks Wasserstrom's assimilationist ideal that a good and just society would be sex- and color-blind. His main objection is that this ideal has unacceptable costs. Not only does it require the elimination of sport and other important activities, it also removes opportunities to acquire self-esteem.

(4) Marshall Cohen, Thomas Nagel, and Thomas Scanlon, eds., *Equality and Preferential Treatment* (Princeton, NJ: Princeton University Press, 1977). With one exception, all of the articles in this book originally appeared in the journal *Philosophy & Public Affairs*. The exception is Ronald Dworkin's article on two important legal decisions, one dealing with a 1945 policy which denied a black man admittance to the University of Texas Law School, and the other on a 1971 policy which denied a white male (DeFunis) admittance to the University of Washington Law School.

(5) Ronald Dworkin, "Why Bakke Has No Case," *The New York Review of Books,* November 19, 1977. Dworkin argues that Bakke's rights were not violated by the University of California at Davis policy of having a quota of sixteen places out of a class of one hundred reserved for minority students. Soon after this article was published, the Supreme Court ruled five-to-four that the quota system at Davis was unconstitutional. See the Problem Cases.

(6) Ann Ferguson, "Androgyny As an Ideal for Human Development," in Mary Vetterling–Braggin, Frederick A. Elliston, and Jane English, eds., *Feminism and Philosophy* (Totowa, NJ: Littlefield, Adams and Co., 1977), pp. 45–69. Ferguson recommends androgyny as an ideal for human development rather than traditional sex roles. As she explains it, the ideal androgynous person would not be both masculine and feminine (the usual meaning of androgynous), but would transcend these categories.

(7) Steven Goldberg, *The Inevitability of Patriarchy* (New York: William Morrow, 1973). Goldberg defends the sexist view that the male hormone testosterone gives men an aggression advantage over women, making it impossible for women to successfully compete against men for high-status positions. Consequently women are better off if they accept male dominance and play traditional female roles involving helping and nurturing.

(8) Barry Gross, ed., *Reverse Discrimination* (Buffalo, NY: Prometheus Books, 1977). This anthology includes articles by Sidney Hook, Lisa Newton, Bernard Boxill, and Alan Goldman.

(9) Helen Remick, ed., *Comparable Worth and Wage Discrimination* (Philadelphia: Temple University Press, 1985). This is an anthology of readings on comparable worth—the controversial policy of equal pay for work of comparable value. Various issues are discussed: How are jobs to be evaluated? What should be the compensation for different jobs? How are wage differences to be justified?

(10) George Sher, "Justifying Reverse Discrimination in Employment," *Philosophy & Public Affairs*

4, no. 2 (Winter 1975) pp. 159–170. After examining and criticizing several arguments used to support reverse discrimination, Sher argues that a case can be made for reverse discrimination when it is compensation for lost ability to compete on equal terms due to inadequate education or factors such as an inadequate diet or lack of early intellectual stimulation.

(11) _____, "Reverse Discrimination, the Future, and the Past," *Ethics* 90 (October 1979), pp. 81–87. Sher distinguishes between backward-looking and forward-looking defenses of preferential treatment. The first makes the basic claim that in the past women and minorities were unfairly discriminated against, and so they deserve to be compensated for this past injustice. The second claims that preferential treatment at the present time will reduce or prevent discrimination in the future. Sher raises difficulties for both these types of defense.

(12) Irving Thalberg, "Justification of Institutional Racism," *Philosophical Forum* 3 (Winter 1972), pp. 243–264. Thalberg attacks the arguments of opponents of changes to equalize the economic and political status of blacks.

(13) Judith Jarvis Thomson, "Preferential Hiring," *Philosophy & Public Affairs* 2, no. 4 (Summer 1973), pp. 364–384. Thomson defends preferential hiring of women and minorities by universities in cases where their qualifications are equal to those of other applicants.

(14) Joyce Trebilcot, "Sex Roles: The Argument from Nature," *Ethics* 85, no. 3 (April 1975), pp. 249–255. Trebilcot critically examines three arguments used to support sexism, including Steven Goldberg's argument that alleged psychological differences between the sexes make sex roles and male dominance inevitable.

(15) Richard Wasserstrom, "A Defense of Programs of Preferential Treatment," *National Forum* (The Phi Kappa Phi Journal) 58, no. 1 (Winter 1978), pp. 15–18. Wasserstrom gives a limited defense of programs which have quotas for the admission of minority students.

(16) _____, "Racism and Sexism," in R.A. Wasserstrom, ed., *Today's Moral Problems*, 3d ed. (New York: Macmillan, 1985), pp. 1–29. After describing the social reality of racism and sexism, Wasserstrom proposes a forward-looking solution—the assimilationist ideal where race and sex in a future ideal society are no more important than eye color is in our present society.

Chapter 8

Sexual Issues

INTRODUCTION

Introduction

A Traditional View of Sex   The traditional Christian (and Jewish and Islamic) view of sex is that nonmarital sex is morally wrong. Nonmarital sex includes activities such as adultery, premarital sex, fornication, prostitution, masturbation, and homosexuality. An influential statement of the Christian view of sex is given in the Vatican Declaration on Sexual Ethics in our readings.

The Vatican position has been attacked by those both inside and outside the Church. One prominent Catholic critic has been Father Curren, professor of theology at the Catholic University of America. Despite this criticism, the Church seems unlikely to change its position. Father Curren has been suspended from his teaching duties, and the Vatican has recently issued a statement reaffirming its condemnation of homosexuality. Furthermore, it made a declaration condemning nonstandard methods of reproduction such as artificial insemination and surrogate parenting.

There is also a controversy about the use of contraceptives. The official teaching of the Roman Catholic Church, stated in the 1969 papal encyclical *Humane Vitae,* is that artificial birth control is immoral. But there are plenty of Catholics and non-Catholic Christians who think that there is nothing wrong with using artificial means of birth control.

Natural Law Theory   To understand the traditional Christian view of sex, it is helpful to know something about the natural law theory that is often used to support this view. The term *natural law* is used to mean a set of prescriptive rules of conduct that are

291

binding on all human beings simply because of human nature. In natural law theory, human action is naturally directed towards certain goals and purposes such as life and procreation. These natural goals and purposes are good, and the pursuit of them is morally right, while interfering with them is morally wrong. The natural goal or purpose of sexual activity is reproduction within the context of marriage. Interfering with this natural goal or purpose of sex is morally wrong.

This natural law theory is espoused in the Vatican Declaration. According to this declaration, homosexuality is seriously disordered because it contradicts its finality, that is, it opposes the natural end of sex, which is procreation. Masturbation is also a serious disorder for the same reason. Premarital sexual relations are condemned because they often exclude the prospect of children, and even if children are produced, they will be deprived of a proper and stable environment.

In our second reading, Richard Mohr attacks the natural law view of sex. He claims that human genitals can have other purposes besides reproduction, for example, achieving intimacy. He ridicules the idea that we should follow nature as it is found in humans or the nonhuman world. As for the appeal to a God-given design or purpose, Mohr objects that one of the basic principles of our society is that moral or legal decisions which are imposed on others should not be made on religious grounds. Although Mohr is concerned only with homosexuality, many of his arguments could be applied to masturbation and premarital sex.

Pornography   Pornography can be defined as any material with sexually explicit content that is intended to cause sexual arousal. There are several related issues about pornography: Is pornography obscene? Should it be censored or is it protected by the First Amendment? Is it morally objec-

tionable or not?

Let us start with the question about obscenity. In the cases of *Roth* v. *United States, Miller* v. *California,* and *Paris Adult Theatre I* v. *Slaton,* the Supreme Court ruled that laws banning obscenity are not unconstitutional, and in particular they do not violate the First Amendment protection of free speech and free press. In the case of *Miller* v. *California,* the Court formulated a threefold test for obscenity: A work is obscene if (1) the average person applying community standards finds that it appeals to prurient interest, (2) the work depicts or describes sexual conduct defined by the law in a patently offensive way, and (3) the work lacks serious literary, artistic, political, or scientific value. Given this definition, what is called hard-core pornography is obscene and may be banned.

In our readings, David A.J. Richards raises some objections to the Supreme Court ruling in *Miller:* It mistakenly permits censorship of any allegedly obscene work without serious value. It imposes on states banning obscenity an obligation to formulate standards, and these standards can vary from one state to another. The result is that what is counted as obscene in one state may not be considered obscene in another. Richards' own account of obscenity is quite different. He thinks that obscene communications involve the idea of the abuse of basic bodily functions, the improper use of which is an object of shame and disgust. Given this definition, pornography is not necessarily obscene, and obscene works are not necessarily pornographic. Furthermore, Richards thinks that the Supreme Court is wrong in allowing pornography to be banned. He believes that the First Amendment protects pornography because it tacitly expresses a Rawlsian principle of justice, namely, that there should be the greatest equal liberty of communication compatible with like liberty for all.

Ann Garry has a different view of the

matter. She finds pornography to be morally objectionable because it violates the Kantian principle of respect for people. More specifically, it humiliates and degrades women by treating them as passive and harmed sex objects. Garry does not wish to censor pornography, however; rather she suggests that it be changed into something having a nonsexist and nondegrading content.

AIDS In the 1980s AIDS (acquired immune deficiency syndrome) became the subject of widespread public attention and fear. Initially it was thought to be a disease found only in gay men, but as it spread to drug users and heterosexuals, it was perceived as a threat to everyone. It is known that AIDS is caused by a virus called HIV (or HTLV–III), and that the virus can be transmitted by sexual intercourse, sharing infected needles, transfusion with infected blood or blood products, or transmission to fetuses during pregnancy. It is possible that it can be transmitted in other ways such as accidents where one's blood comes in contact with an infected person's blood, but these incidents are very rare. Blood tests can detect antibodies, indicating exposure to the virus, but these tests are not conclusive, either positively or negatively. Individ-

uals can test positive and not have the virus, and the virus can apparently hide and reproduce in cells of the immune system in such a way that it is not detected by the blood tests currently used. In other words, there can be both false-positive and false-negative tests. Furthermore, it seems that not everyone exposed to the virus develops the full-blown syndrome that leads to illness and death; some develop the less serious symptoms—AIDS-related complex (ARC), and do not get AIDS itself. The picture is complicated by the fact that the time from exposure to the virus until the appearance of the symptoms can be unusually long (in some cases up to seven years), and no upper limit is known.

Various issues are raised by the AIDS epidemic: How should the spread of the disease be controlled? Should we have mandatory testing for AIDS? What are the obligations of those who have the disease or are at high risk of getting the disease? In our readings, Grant Gillett focuses on a question of medical confidentiality. Suppose a patient who tests positive for the AIDS virus refuses to inform his wife or allow her to be informed. Does the doctor have an obligation to inform the wife, or does he have a duty to the patient to keep this information confidential?

The Vatican

Declaration on Sexual Ethics

The Declaration on Sexual Ethics was issued in Rome by the Sacred Congregation for the Doctrine of the Faith on December 29, 1975.

The authors defend the Christian doctrine that "every genital act must be within the framework of

marriage." Premarital sex, masturbation, and homosexuality are specifically condemned, and chastity is recommended as a virtue.

1. According to contemporary scientific research, the human person is so profoundly affected by sexuality that it must be considered as one of the factors which give to each individual's life the principal traits that distinguish it. In fact it is from sex that the human person receives the characteristics which, on the biological, psychological and spiritual levels, make that person a man or a woman, and thereby largely condition his or her progress towards maturity and insertion into society. Hence sexual matters, as is obvious to everyone, today constitute a theme frequently and openly dealt with in books, reviews, magazines, and other means of social communication.

In the present period, the corruption of morals has increased, and one of the most serious indications of this corruption is the unbridled exaltation of sex. Moreover, through the means of social communication and through public entertainment this corruption has reached the point of invading the field of education and of infecting the general mentality.

In this context certain educators, teachers, and moralists have been able to contribute to a better understanding and integration into life of the values proper to each of the sexes; on the other hand there are those who have put forward concepts and modes of behavior which are contrary to the true moral exigencies of the human person. Some members of the latter group have even gone so far as to favor a licentious hedonism.

As a result, in the course of a few years, teachings, moral criteria, and modes of living hitherto faithfully preserved have been very much unsettled, even among Christians. There are many people today who, being confronted with so many widespread opinions opposed to the teachings which they received from the Church, have come to wonder what they must still hold as true.

2. The Church cannot remain indifferent to this confusion of minds and relaxation of morals. It is a question, in fact, of a matter which is of the utmost importance both for the personal lives of Christians and for the social life of our time.[1]

The Bishops are daily led to note the growing difficulties experienced by the faithful in obtaining knowledge of wholesome moral teaching, especially in sexual matters, and of the growing difficulties experienced by pastors in expounding this teaching effectively. The Bishops know that by their pastoral charge they are called upon to meet the needs of their faithful in this very serious matter, and important documents dealing with it have already been published by some of them or by Episcopal Conferences. Nevertheless, since the erroneous opinions and resulting deviations are continuing to spread everywhere, the Sacred Congregation for the Doctrine of the Faith, by virtue of its function in the universal Church [2] and by a mandate of the Supreme Pontiff, has judged it necessary to publish the present Declaration.

3. The people of our time are more and more convinced that the human person's dignity and vocation demand that they should discover, by the light of their own intelligence, the values innate in their nature, that they should ceaselessly develop these values and realize them in their lives, in order to achieve an ever greater development.

In moral matters man cannot make value judgments according to his personal whim: "In the depths of his conscience, man detects a law which he does not impose on himself, but which holds him to obedience.... For man has in his heart a law written by God. To obey it is the very dignity of man; according to it he will be judged." [3]

Moreover, through his revelation God has made known to us Christians his plan of salvation, and he has held up to us Christ, the Saviour and Sanctifier, in his teaching and example, as the supreme and immutable law of life: "I am the light of the world; anyone who follows me will not be walking in the dark, he will have the light of life." [4]

Therefore there can be no true promotion of man's dignity unless the essential order of his nature is respected. Of course, in the history of civilization many of the concrete conditions and needs of human life have changed and will continue to change. But all evolution of morals and every type of life must be kept within the limits imposed by the immutable principles based upon every human person's constitutive elements and essential relations—elements and relations which transcend historical contingency.

These fundamental principles, which can be grasped by reason, are contained in "the divine law—eternal, objective, and universal—whereby God orders, directs, and governs the entire universe and all the ways of the human community, by a plan conceived in wisdom and love. Man has been made by God to participate in this law, with the result that, under the gentle disposition of divine Providence, he can come to perceive ever increasingly the unchanging truth." [5] This divine law is accessible to our minds.

4. Hence, those many people are in error who today assert that one can find neither in human nature nor in the revealed law any absolute and immutable norm to serve for particular actions other than the one which expresses itself in the general law of charity and respect for human dignity. As a proof of their assertion they put forward the view that so-called norms of the natural law or precepts of Sacred Scripture are to be regarded only as given expressions of a form of particular culture at a certain moment of history.

But in fact, divine Revelation and, in its own proper order, philosophical wisdom, emphasize the authentic exigencies of human nature. They thereby necessarily manifest the existence of immutable laws inscribed in the constitutive elements of human nature and which are revealed to be identical in all beings endowed with reason.

Furthermore, Christ instituted his Church as "the pillar and bulwark of truth." [6] With the Holy Spirit's assistance, she ceaselessly preserves and transmits without error the truths of the moral order, and she authentically interprets not only the revealed positive law but "also . . . those principles of the moral order which have their origin in human nature itself" [7] and which concern man's full development and sanctification. Now in fact the Church throughout her history has always considered a certain number of precepts of the natural law as having an absolute and immutable value, and in their transgression she has seen a contradiction of the teaching and spirit of the Gospel.

5. Since sexual ethics concern certain fundamental values of human and Christian life, this general teaching equally applies to sexual ethics. In this domain there exist principles and norms which the Church has always unhesitatingly transmitted as part of her teaching, however much the opinions and morals of the world may have been opposed to them. These principles and norms in no way owe their origin to a certain type of culture, but rather to knowledge of the divine law and of human nature. They therefore cannot be considered as having become out of date or doubtful under the pretext that a new cultural situation has arisen.

It is these principles which inspired the exhortations and directives given by the Second Vatican Council for an education and an organization of social life taking account of the equal dignity of man and woman while respecting their difference. [8]

Speaking of "the sexual nature of man and the human faculty of procreation," the Council noted that they "wonderfully exceed the dispositions of lower forms of life." [9] It then took particular care to expound the principles and criteria which concern human sexuality in marriage, and which are based upon the finality of the specific function of sexuality.

In this regard the Council declares that the moral goodness of the acts proper to conjugal life, acts which are ordered according to true human dignity, "does not depend solely on sincere intentions or on an evaluation of motives. It must be determined by objective standards. These, based on the nature of the human person and his acts, preserve the full sense of mutual self-giving and human procreation in the context of true love." [10]

These final words briefly sum up the Council's teaching—more fully expounded in an earlier part of the same Constitution [11]—on the finality of the sexual act and on the principal criterion of its morality: it is respect for its finality that ensures the moral goodness of this act.

This same principle, which the Church holds from divine Revelation and from her authentic interpretation of the natural law, is also the basis of her traditional doctrine, which states that the use of the sexual function has its true meaning and moral rectitude only in true marriage. [12]

6. It is not the purpose of the present declaration to deal with all the abuses of the sexual faculty, nor with all the elements involved in the practice of chastity. Its object is rather to repeat the Church's doctrine on certain particular points, in view of the urgent need to oppose serious errors and widespread aberrant modes of behavior.

7. Today there are many who vindicate the right to sexual union before marriage, at least in those cases where a firm intention to marry and an affection which is already in some way conjugal in the psychology of the subjects require this completion, which they judge to be connatural. This is especially the case when the celebration of the marriage is impeded by circumstances or when this intimate relationship seems necessary in order for love to be preserved.

This opinion is contrary to Christian doctrine, which states that every genital act must be within the framework of marriage. However firm the intention of those who practice

such premature sexual relations may be, the fact remains that these relations cannot ensure, in sincerity and fidelity, the interpersonal relationship between a man and a woman, nor especially can they protect this relationship from whims and caprices. Now it is a stable union that Jesus willed, and he restored its original requirement, beginning with the sexual difference. "Have you not read that the creator from the beginning made them male and female and that he said: This is why a man must leave father and mother, and cling to his wife, and the two become one body? They are no longer two, therefore, but one body. So then, what God has united, man must not divide." [13] Saint Paul will be even more explicit when he shows that if unmarried people or widows cannot live chastely they have no other alternative than the stable union of marriage: ". . . it is better to marry than to be aflame with passion." [14] Through marriage, in fact, the love of married people is taken up into that love which Christ irrevocably has for the Church, [15] while dissolute sexual union [16] defiles the temple of the Holy Spirit which the Christian has become. Sexual union therefore is only legitimate if a definitive community of life has been established between the man and the woman.

This is what the Church has always understood and taught, [17] and she finds a profound agreement with her doctrine in men's reflection and in the lessons of history.

Experience teaches us that love must find its safeguard in the stability of marriage, if sexual intercourse is truly to respond to the requirements of its own finality and to those of human dignity. These requirements call for a conjugal contract sanctioned and guaranteed by society—a contract which establishes a state of life of capital importance both for the exclusive union of the man and the woman and for the good of their family and of the human community. Most often, in fact, premarital relations exclude the possibility of children. What is represented to be conjugal love is not able, as it absolutely should be, to develop into paternal and maternal love. Or, if it does happen to do so, this will be to the detriment of the children, who will be deprived of the stable environment in which they ought to develop in order to find in it the way and the means of their insertion into society as a whole.

The consent given by people who wish to be united in marriage must therefore be manifested externally and in a manner which makes it valid in the eyes of society. As far as the faithful are concerned, their consent to the setting up of a community of conjugal life must be expressed according to the laws of the Church. It is a consent which makes their marriage a Sacrament of Christ.

8. At the present time there are those who, basing themselves on observations in the psychological order, have begun to judge indulgently, and even to excuse completely, homosexual relations between certain people. This they do in opposition to the constant teaching of the Magisterium and to the moral sense of the Christian people.

A distinction is drawn, and it seems with some reason, between homosexuals whose tendency comes from a false education, from a lack of normal sexual development, from habit, from bad example, or from other similar causes, and is transitory or at least not incurable; and homosexuals who are definitively such because of some kind of innate instinct or a pathological constitution judged to be incurable.

In regard to this second category of subjects, some people conclude that their tendency is so natural that it justifies in their case homosexual relations within a sincere communion of life and love analogous to marriage insofar as such homosexuals feel incapable of enduring a solitary life.

In the pastoral field, these homosexuals must certainly be treated with understanding and sustained in the hope of overcoming their personal difficulties and their inability to fit into society. Their culpability will be judged with prudence. But no pastoral method can be employed which would give moral justification to these acts on the grounds that they would be consonant with the condition of such people. For according to the objective moral order, homosexual relations are acts which lack an essential and indispensable finality. In Sacred Scripture they are condemned as a serious depravity and even presented as the sad consequence of rejecting God.[18] This judgment of Scripture does not of course permit us to conclude that all those who suffer from this anomaly are personally responsible for it, but it does attest to the fact that homosexual acts are intrinsically disordered and can in no case be approved.

9. The traditional Catholic doctrine that masturbation constitutes a grave moral disorder is often called into doubt or expressly denied today. It is said that psychology and sociology show that it is a normal phenomenon of sexual development, especially among the young. It is stated that there is real and serious fault only in the measure that the subject deliberately indulges in solitary pleasure closed in on self ("ipsation"), because in this case the act would indeed be radically opposed to the loving communion between persons of different sex which some hold is what is principally sought in the use of the sexual faculty.

This opinion is contradictory to the teaching and pastoral practice of the Catholic Church. Whatever the force of certain arguments of a biological and philosophical nature, which have sometimes been used by theologians, in fact both the Magisterium of the Church—in the course of a constant tradition—and the moral sense of the faithful have declared without hesitation that masturbation is an intrinsically and seriously disordered act.[19] The main reason is that, whatever the motive for acting in this way, the deliberate use of the sexual faculty outside normal conjugal relations essentially contradicts the finality of the faculty. For it lacks the sexual relationship called for by the moral order, namely the relationship which realizes "the full sense of mutual self-giving and human procreation in the context of true love." [20] All deliberate exercise of sexuality must be reserved to this regular relationship. Even if it cannot be proved that Scripture condemns this sin by name, the tradition of the Church has rightly understood it to be condemned in the New Testament when the latter speaks of "impurity," "unchasteness," and other vices contrary to chastity and continence.

Sociological surveys are able to show the frequency of this disorder according to the places, populations, or circumstances studied. In this way facts are discovered, but facts do not constitute a criterion for judging the moral value of human acts.[21] The frequency of the phenomenon in question is certainly to be linked with man's innate weakness following original sin; but it is also to be linked with the loss of a sense of God, with the corruption of morals engendered by the commercialization of vice, with the unrestrained licentiousness of so many public entertainments and publications, as well as with the neglect of modesty, which is the guardian of chastity.

On the subject of masturbation modern psychology provides much valid and useful information for formulating a more equitable judgment on moral responsibility and for orienting pastoral action. Psychology helps one to see how the immaturity of adolescence (which can sometimes persist after that age), psychological imbalance, or habit can influence behavior, diminishing the deliberate character of the act and bringing about a situation whereby subjectively there may not always be serious fault. But in general, the absence of serious responsibility must not be presumed; this would be to misunderstand people's moral capacity.

In the pastoral ministry, in order to form an adequate judgment in concrete cases, the habitual behavior of people will be considered in its totality, not only with regard to the individual's practice of charity and of justice but also with regard to the individual's care in observing the particular precepts of chastity. In particular, one will have to examine whether the individual is using the necessary means, both natural and supernatural, which Christian asceticism from its long experience recommends for overcoming the passions and progressing in virtue. . . .

Endnotes

1. See Vatican II, *Pastoral Constitution on the Church in the World of Today*, no. 47: *Acta Apostolicae Sedis* 58 (1966) 1067 [*The Pope Speaks* XI, 289–290].

2. See the Apostolic Constitution *Regimini Ecclesiae universae* (August 15, 1967), no. 29: *AAS* 59 (1967) 897 [*TPS* XII, 401–402].

3. *Pastoral Constitution on the Church in the World of Today*, no. 16: *AAS* 58 (1966) 1037 [*TPS* XI, 268].

4. *Jn* 8, 12.

5. *Declaration on Religious Freedom*, no. 3: *AAS* 58 (1966) 931 [*TPS* XI, 86].

6. 1 *Tm* 3, 15.

7. *Declaration on Religious Freedom*, no. 14: *AAS* 58 (1966) 940 [*TPS* XI, 93]. See also Pius XI, Encyclical *Casti Connubii* (December 31, 1930): *AAS* 22 (1930) 579–580; Pius XII, Address of November 2, 1954 *AAS* 46 (1954) 671–672 [*TPS* I 380–381]; John XXIII, Encyclical *Mater et Magistra* (May 25, 1961), no. 239: *AAS* 53 (1961) 457 [*TPS* VII, 388]; Paul VI, Encyclical *Humanae Vitae* (July 25, 1968), no. 4: *AAS* 60 (1968) 483 [*TPS* XIII, 331–332].

8. See Vatican II, *Declaration on Christian Education*, nos. 1 and 8: *AAS* 58 (1966) 729–730, 734–736 [*TPS* XI, 201–202, 206–207]; *Pastoral Constitution on the Church in the World of Today*, nos. 29, 60, 67: *AAS* 58 (1966) 1048–1049, 1080–1081, 1088–1089 [*TPS* XI, 276–277, 299–300, 304–305].

9. *Pastoral Constitution on the Church in the World of Today*, no. 51: *AAS* 58 (1966) 1072 [*TPS* XI, 293].

10. *Loc. cit.;* see also no. 49: *AAS* 58 (1966) 1069–1070 [*TPS* XI, 291–292].

11. See *Pastoral Constitution on the Church in the World of Today*, nos. 49–50: *AAS* 58 (1966) 1069–1072 [*TPS* XI, 291–293].

12. The present Declaration does not review all the moral norms for the use of sex, since they have already been set forth in the encyclicals *Casti Connubii* and *Humanae Vitae.*

13. *Mt* 19, 4–6.

14. 1 *Cor* 7, 9.

15. See *Eph* 5, 25–32.

16. Extramarital intercourse is expressly condemned in *1 Cor* 5, 1; 6, 9; 7, 2; 10, 8; *Eph* 5, 5–7; *1 Tm* 1, 10; *Heb* 13, 4; there are explicit arguments given in *1 Cor* 6, 12–20.

17. See Innocent IV, Letter *Sub Catholicae professione* (March 6, 1254) (*DS* 835); Pius II, Letter *Cum sicut accepimus* (November 14, 1459) (*DS* 1367); Decrees of the Holy Office on September 24, 1665 (*DS* 2045) and March 2, 1679 (*DS* 2148); Pius XI, Encyclical *Casti Conubii* (December 31, 1930): *AAS* 22 (1930) 538–539.

18. *Rom* 1:24–27: "In consequence, God delivered them up in their lusts to unclean practices; they engaged in the mutual degradation of their bodies, these men who exchanged the truth of God for a lie and worshiped and served the creature rather than the Creator—blessed be he forever, amen! God therefore delivered them to disgraceful passions. Their women exchanged natural intercourse for unnatural, and the men gave up natural intercourse with women and burned with lust for one another. Men did shameful things with men, and thus received in their own persons the penalty for their perversity." See also what St. Paul says of sodomy in *1 Cor* 6, 9; *1 Tm* 1, 10.

19. See Leo IX, Letter *Ad splendidum nitentes* (1054) (*DS* 687–688); Decree of the Holy Office on March 2, 1679 (*DS* 2149); Pius XII, Addresses of October 8, 1953: *AAS* 45 (1953) 677–678, and May 19, 1956: *AAS* 48 (1956) 472–473.

20. *Pastoral Constitution on the Church in the World of Today*, no. 51: *AAS* 58 (1966) 1072 [*TPS* XI, 293].

21. See Paul VI, Apostolic Exhortation *Quinque iam anni* (December 8, 1970): *AAS* 63 (1971) 102 [*TPS* XV, 329]: "If sociological surveys are useful for better discovering the thought patterns of the people of a particular place, the anxieties and needs of those to whom we proclaim the word of God, and also the oppositions made to it by modern reasoning through the widespread notion that outside science there exists no legitimate form of knowledge, still the conclusions drawn from such surveys could not of themselves constitute a determining criterion of truth."

Review Questions

1. What is the traditional Christian doctrine about sex, according to the declaration?

2. Why does the declaration find premarital sexual relations to be immoral?

3. What is the declaration's objection to homosexuality?

4. What is wrong with masturbation, according to the declaration?

Discussion Questions

1. Is celibacy a violation of natural law? Explain your view.

2. Is contraception wrong too? Defend your answer.

3. Is procreation the only natural purpose of sex? Defend your position.

Richard D. Mohr

Gay Basics: Some Questions, Facts, and Values

Richard D. Mohr teaches philosophy at the University of Illinois. He is the author of Gays/Justice: A Study of Ethics, Society, and Law *and of several articles on gay rights.*

After examining some facts about gays including stereotypes and discrimination in our society, Mohr

replies to the charge that homosexuality is immoral. He argues that condemning homosexuality on religious grounds violates the Constitution, and that appeals to nature or natural law are unconvincing. He claims that our society would be improved if gays were given the rights and benefits of the heterosexual majority.

I. WHO ARE GAYS ANYWAY?

A recent Gallup poll found that only one in five Americans reports having a gay or lesbian acquaintance.[1] This finding is extraordinary given the number of practicing homosexuals in America. Alfred Kinsey's 1948 study of the sex lives of 12,000 white males shocked the nation: 37 percent had at least one homosexual experience to orgasm in their adult lives; an additional 13 percent had homosexual fantasies to orgasm; 4 percent were exclusively homosexual in their practices; another 5 percent had virtually no heterosexual experience; and nearly 20 percent had at least as many homosexual as heterosexual experiences.[2]

Two out of five men one passes on the street have had orgasmic sex with men. Every second family in the country has a member who is essentially homosexual and many more people regularly have homosexual experiences. Who are homosexuals? They are your friends, your minister, your teacher, your bank teller, your doctor, your mail carrier, your officemate, your roommate, your congressional representative, your sibling, parent, and spouse. They are everywhere, virtually all ordinary, virtually all unknown.

Several important consequences follow. First, the country is profoundly ignorant of the actual experience of gay people. Second, social attitudes and practices that are harmful to gays have a much greater overall harmful impact on society than is usually realized. Third, most gay people live in hiding—in the closet—making the "coming out" experience the central fixture of gay consciousness and invisibility the chief characteristic of the gay community.

II. IGNORANCE, STEREOTYPE, AND MORALITY

Ignorance about gays, however, has not stopped people from having strong opinions about them. The void which ignorance leaves has been filled with stereotypes. Society holds chiefly two groups of anti-gay stereotypes; the two are an oddly contradictory lot. One set of stereotypes revolves around alleged mistakes in an individual's gender identity: lesbians are women that want to be, or at least look and act like, men—bull dykes, diesel dykes; while gay men are those who want to be, or at least look and act like, women—queens, fairies, limp-wrists, nellies. These stereotypes of mismatched genders provide the materials through which gays and lesbians become the butts of ethniclike jokes. These stereotypes and jokes, though derisive,

basically view gays and lesbians as ridiculous.

Another set of stereotypes revolves around gays as a pervasive, sinister, conspiratorial threat. The core stereotype here is the gay person as child molester, and more generally as sex-crazed maniac. These stereotypes carry with them fears of the very destruction of family and civilization itself. Now, that which is essentially ridiculous can hardly have such a staggering effect. Something must be afoot in this incoherent amalgam.

Sense can be made of this incoherence if the nature of stereotypes is clarified. Stereotypes are not *simply* false generalizations from a skewed sample of cases examined. Admittedly, false generalizing plays some part in the stereotypes a society holds. If, for instance, one takes as one's sample homosexuals who are in psychiatric hospitals or prisons, as was done in nearly all early investigations, not surprisingly one will probably find homosexuals to be of a crazed and criminal cast. Such false generalizations, though, simply confirm beliefs already held on independent grounds, ones that likely led the investigator to the prison and psychiatric ward to begin with. Evelyn Hooker, who in the late fifties carried out the first rigorous studies to use nonclinical gays, found that psychiatrists, when presented with case files including all the standard diagnostic psychological profiles—but omitting indications of sexual orientation—were unable to distinguish files of gays from those of straights, even though they believed gays to be crazy and supposed themselves to be experts in detecting craziness.[3] These studies proved a profound embarrassment to the psychiatric establishment, the financial well-being of which has been substantially enhanced by "curing" allegedly insane gays. The studies led the way to the American Psychiatric Association finally in 1973 dropping homosexuality from its registry of mental illnesses.[4] Nevertheless, the stereotype of gays as sick continues apace in the mind of America.

False generalizations *help maintain* stereotypes; they do not *form* them. As the history of

Hooker's discoveries shows, stereotypes have a life beyond facts; their origin lies in a culture's ideology—the general system of beliefs by which it lives—and they are sustained across generations by diverse cultural transmissions, hardly any of which, including slang and jokes, even purport to have a scientific basis. Stereotypes, then, are not the products of bad science but are social constructions that perform central functions in maintaining society's conception of itself.

On this understanding, it is easy to see that the anti-gay stereotypes surrounding gender identification are chiefly means of reinforcing still powerful gender roles in society. If, as this stereotype presumes and condemns, one is free to choose one's social roles independently of gender, many guiding social divisions, both domestic and commercial, might be threatened. The socially gender-linked distinctions between breadwinner and homemaker, boss and secretary, doctor and nurse, protector and protected would blur. The accusations "dyke" and "fag" exist in significant part to keep women in their place and to prevent men from breaking ranks and ceding away theirs.

The stereotypes of gays as child molesters, sex-crazed maniacs, and civilization destroyers function to displace (socially irresolvable) problems from their actual source to a foreign (and so, it is thought, manageable) one. Thus the stereotype of child molester functions to give the family unit a false sheen of absolute innocence. It keeps the unit from being examined too closely for incest, child abuse, wife-battering, and the terrorism of constant threats. The stereotype teaches that the problems of the family are not internal to it, but external.[5]

One can see these cultural forces at work in society's and the media's treatment of current reports of violence, especially domestic violence. When a mother kills her child or a father rapes his daughter—regular Section B fare even in major urban papers—this is never taken by reporters, columnists, or pundits as evidence that there is something wrong

with heterosexuality or with traditional families. These issues are not even raised. But when a homosexual child molestation is reported it is taken as confirming evidence of the way homosexuals are. One never hears of heterosexual murders, but one regularly hears of "homosexual" ones. Compare the social treatment of Richard Speck's sexually motivated mass murder of Chicago nurses with that of John Wayne Gacy's murders of Chicago youths. Gacy was in the culture's mind taken as symbolic of gay men in general. To prevent the possibility that The Family was viewed as anything but an innocent victim in this affair, the mainstream press knowingly failed to mention that most of Gacy's adolescent victims were homeless hustlers. That knowledge would be too much for the six o'clock news and for cherished beliefs.

Because "the facts" largely don't matter when it comes to the generation and maintenance of stereotypes, the effects of scientific and academic research and of enlightenment generally will be, at best, slight and gradual in the changing fortunes of lesbians and gay men. If this account of stereotypes holds, society has been profoundly immoral. For its treatment of gays is a grand scale rationalization, a moral sleight-of-hand. The problem is not that society's usual standards of evidence and procedure in coming to judgments of social policy have been misapplied to gays; rather when it comes to gays, the standards themselves have simply been ruled out of court and disregarded in favor of mechanisms that encourage unexamined fear and hatred.

III. ARE GAYS DISCRIMINATED AGAINST? DOES IT MATTER?

Partly because lots of people suppose they don't know any gay people and partly through willful ignorance of its own workings, society at large is unaware of the many ways in which gays are subject to discrimination in consequence of widespread fear and hatred. Contributing to this social ignorance of discrimination is the difficulty for gay people, as an invisible minority, even to complain of discrimination. For if one is gay, to register a complaint would suddenly target one as a stigmatized person, and so in the absence of any protections against discrimination, would simply invite additional discrimination. Further, many people, especially those who are persistently downtrodden and so lack a firm sense of self to begin with, tend either to blame themselves for their troubles or to view injustice as a matter of bad luck rather than as indicating something wrong with society. The latter recognition would require doing something to rectify wrong and most people, especially the already beleaguered, simply aren't up to that. So for a number of reasons discrimination against gays, like rape, goes seriously underreported.

First, gays are subject to violence and harassment based simply on their perceived status rather than because of any actions they have performed. A recent extensive study by the National Gay Task Force found that over 90 percent of gays and lesbians had been victimized in some form on the basis of their sexual orientation.[6] Greater than one in five gay men and nearly one in ten lesbians had been punched, hit, or kicked; a quarter of all gays had had objects thrown at them; a third had been chased; a third had been sexually harassed; and 14 percent had been spit on—all just for being perceived as gay.

The most extreme form of anti-gay violence is "queerbashing"—where groups of young men target a person who they suppose is a gay man and beat and kick him unconscious and sometimes to death amid a torrent of taunts and slurs. Such seemingly random but in reality socially encouraged violence has the same social origin and function as lynchings of blacks—to keep a whole stigmatized group in line. As with lynchings in the recent past, the police and courts have routinely averted their eyes, giving their implicit approval to the practice.

Few such cases with gay victims reach the courts. Those that do are marked by inequitable procedures and results. Frequently judges will describe "queerbashers" as "just all-American boys." Recently a District of Columbia judge handed suspended sentences to queerbashers whose victim had been stalked, beaten, stripped at knife point, slashed, kicked, threatened with castration, and pissed on, because the judge thought the bashers were good boys at heart—after all, they went to a religious prep school.[7]

Police and juries will simply discount testimony from gays; they typically construe assaults on and murders of gays as "justified" self-defense—the killer need only claim his act was a panicked response to a sexual overture. Alternatively, when guilt seems patent, juries will accept highly implausible "diminished capacity" defenses, as in the case of Dan White's 1978 assassination of openly gay San Francisco city councilman Harvey Milk: Hostess Twinkies made him do it.[8]

These inequitable procedures and results collectively show that the life and liberty of gays, like those of blacks, simply count for less than the life and liberty of members of the dominant culture.

The equitable rule of law is the heart of an orderly society. The collapse of the rule of law for gays shows that society is willing to perpetrate the worst possible injustices against them. Conceptually there is only a difference in degree between the collapse of the rule of law and systematic extermination of members of a population simply for having some group status independent of any act an individual has performed. In the Nazi concentration camps, gays were forced to wear pink triangles as identifying badges, just as Jews were forced to wear yellow stars. In remembrance of that collapse of the rule of law, the pink triangle has become the chief symbol of the gay rights movement.[9]

Gays are subject to widespread discrimination in employment—the very means by which one puts bread on one's table and one of the chief means by which individuals identify themselves to themselves and achieve personal dignity. Governments are leading offenders here. They do a lot of discriminating themselves, require that others do it (e.g., government contractors), and set precedents favoring discrimination in the private sector. The federal government explicitly discriminates against gays in the armed forces, the CIA, FBI, National Security Agency, and the state department. The federal government refuses to give security clearances to gays and so forces the country's considerable private sector military and aerospace contractors to fire known gay employees. State and local governments regularly fire gay teachers, policemen, firemen, social workers, and anyone who has contact with the public. Further, through licensing laws states officially bar gays from a vast array of occupations and professions—everything from doctors, lawyers, accountants, and nurses to hairdressers, morticians, and used car dealers. The American Civil Liberties Union's handbook *The Rights of Gay People* lists 307 such prohibited occupations.[10]

Gays are subject to discrimination in a wide variety of other ways, including private-sector employment, public accommodations, housing, immigration and naturalization, insurance of all types, custody and adoption, and zoning regulations that bar "singles" or "nonrelated" couples. All of these discriminations affect central components of a meaningful life; some even reach to the means by which life itself is sustained. In half the states, where gay sex is illegal, the central role of sex to meaningful life is officially denied to gays.

All these sorts of discriminations also affect the ability of people to have significant intimate relations. It is difficult for people to live together as couples without having their sexual orientation perceived in the public realm and so becoming targets for discrimination. Illegality, discrimination, and the absorption by gays of society's hatred of them all interact to impede or block altogether the ability of gays and lesbians to create and maintain significant personal relations with loved ones. So every facet of life is affected by discrimination. Only the most compelling reasons could justify it.

IV. BUT AREN'T THEY IMMORAL?

Many people think society's treatment of gays is justified because they think gays are extremely immoral. To evaluate this claim, different senses of "moral" must be distinguished. Sometimes by "morality" is meant the overall beliefs affecting behavior in a society—its mores, norms, and customs. On this understanding, gays certainly are not moral: lots of people hate them and social customs are designed to register widespread disapproval of gays. The problem here is that this sense of morality is merely a *descriptive* one. On this understanding *every* society has a morality—even Nazi society, which had racism and mob rule as central features of its "morality," understood in this sense. What is needed in order to use the notion of morality to praise or condemn behavior is a sense of morality that is *prescriptive* or *normative*—a sense of morality whereby, for instance, the descriptive morality of the Nazis is found wanting.

As the Nazi example makes clear, that something is descriptively moral is nowhere near enough to make it normatively moral. A lot of people in a society saying something is good, even over eons, does not make it so. Our rejection of the long history of socially approved and state-enforced slavery is another good example of this principle at work. Slavery would be wrong even if nearly everyone liked it. So consistency and fairness require that we abandon the belief that gays are immoral simply because most people dislike or disapprove of gays or gay acts, or even because gay sex acts are illegal.

Furthermore, recent historical and anthropological research has shown that opinion about gays has been by no means universally negative. Historically, it has varied widely even within the larger part of the Christian era and even within the church itself.[11] There are even societies—current ones—where homosexuality is not only tolerated but a universal compulsory part of social maturation.[12] Within the last thirty years,

American society has undergone a grand turnabout from deeply ingrained, near total condemnation to near total acceptance on two emotionally charged "moral" or "family" issues: contraception and divorce. Society holds its current descriptive morality of gays not because it has to, but because it chooses to.

If popular opinion and custom are not enough to ground moral condemnation of homosexuality, perhaps religion can. Such argument proceeds along two lines. One claims that the condemnation is a direct revelation of God, usually through the Bible; the other claims to be able to detect condemnation in God's plan as manifested in nature.

One of the more remarkable discoveries of recent gay research is that the Bible may not be as univocal in its condemnation of homosexuality as has been usually believed.[13] Christ never mentions homosexuality. Recent interpreters of the Old Testament have pointed out that the story of Lot at Sodom is probably intended to condemn inhospitality rather than homosexuality. Further, some of the Old Testament condemnations of homosexuality seem simply to be ways of tarring those of the Israelites' opponents who happened to accept homosexual practices when the Israelites themselves did not. If so, the condemnation is merely a quirk of history and rhetoric rather than a moral precept.

What does seem clear is that those who regularly cite the Bible to condemn an activity like homosexuality do so by reading it selectively. Do ministers who cite what they take to be condemnations of homosexuality in Leviticus maintain in their lives all the hygienic and dietary laws of Leviticus? If they cite the story of Lot at Sodom to condemn homosexuality, do they also cite the story of Lot in the cave to praise incestuous rape? It seems then not that the Bible is being used to ground condemnations of homosexuality as much as society's dislike of homosexuality is being used to interpret the Bible.[14]

Even if a consistent portrait of condemnation could be gleaned from the Bible, what social significance should it be given? One of the guiding principles of society, enshrined in the Constitution as a check against the government, is that decisions affecting social policy are not made on religious grounds. If the real ground of the alleged immorality invoked by governments to discriminate against gays is religious (as it has explicitly been even in some recent court cases involving teachers and guardians), then one of the major commitments of our nation is violated.

V. BUT AREN'T THEY UNNATURAL?

The most noteworthy feature of the accusation of something being unnatural (where a moral rather than an advertising point is being made) is that the plaint is so infrequently made. One used to hear the charge leveled against abortion, but that has pretty much faded as anti-abortionists have come to lay all their chips on the hope that people will come to view abortion as murder. Incest used to be considered unnatural but discourse now usually assimilates it to the moral machinery of rape and violated trust. The charge comes up now in ordinary discourse only against homosexuality. This suggests that the charge is highly idiosyncratic and has little, if any, explanatory force. It fails to put homosexuality in a class with anything else so that one can learn by comparison with clear cases of the class just exactly what it is that is allegedly wrong with it.

Though the accusation of unnaturalness looks whimsical, in actual ordinary discourse when applied to homosexuality, it is usually delivered with venom aforethought. It carries a high emotional charge, usually expressing disgust and evincing queasiness. Probably it is nothing but an emotional charge. For people get equally disgusted and queasy at all sorts of things that are perfectly natural—to be expected in nature apart from artifice—and that could hardly be fit subjects for moral condemnation. Two typical examples in current American culture are some people's responses to mothers' suckling in public and to women who do not shave body hair. When people have strong emotional reactions, as they do in these cases, without being able to give good reasons for them, we think of them not as operating morally, but rather as being obsessed and manic. So the feelings of disgust that some people have to gays will hardly ground a charge of immorality. People fling the term "unnatural" against gays in the same breath and with the same force as when they call gays "sick" and "gross." When they do this, they give every appearance of being neurotically fearful and incapable of reasoned discourse.

When "nature" is taken in *technical* rather than ordinary usages, it looks like the notion also will not ground a charge of homosexual immorality. When unnatural means "by artifice" or "made by humans," it need only be pointed out that virtually everything that is good about life is unnatural in this sense, that the chief feature that distinguishes people from other animals is their very ability to make over the world to meet their needs and desires, and that their well-being depends upon these departures from nature. On this understanding of human nature and the natural, homosexuality is perfectly unobjectionable.

Another technical sense of natural is that something is natural and so, good, if it fulfills some function in nature. Homosexuality on this view is unnatural because it allegedly violates the function of genitals, which is to produce babies. One problem with this view is that lots of bodily parts have lots of functions and just because some one activity can be fulfilled by only one organ (say, the mouth for eating) this activity does not condemn other functions of the organ to immorality (say, the mouth for talking, licking stamps, blowing bubbles, or having sex). So the possible use of the genitals to produce children does not, without more, condemn the use of the genitals for other purposes, say, achieving ecstasy and intimacy.

The functional view of nature will only provide a morally condemnatory sense to the unnatural if a thing which might have many uses has but one proper function to the exclusion of other possible functions. But whether this is so cannot be established simply by looking at the thing. For what is seen is all its possible functions. The notion of function seemed like it might ground moral authority, but instead it turns out that moral authority is needed to define proper function. Some people try to fill in this moral authority by appeal to the "design" or "order" of an organ, saying, for instance, that the genitals are designed for the purpose of procreation. But these people cheat intellectually if they do not make explicit *who* the designer and orderer is. If it is God, we are back to square one—holding others accountable for religious beliefs.

Further, ordinary moral attitudes about childbearing will not provide the needed supplement which in conjunction with the natural function view of bodily parts would produce a positive obligation to use the genitals for procreation. Society's attitude toward a childless couple is that of pity not censure—even if the couple could have children. This pity may be an unsympathetic one, that is, not registering a course one would choose *for oneself,* but this does not make it a course one would *require* of others. The couple who discovers they cannot have children are viewed not as having thereby had a debt canceled, but rather as having to forgo some of the richness of life, just as a quadriplegic is viewed not as absolved from some moral obligation to hop, skip, and jump, but as missing some of the richness of life. Consistency requires then that, at most, gays who do not or cannot have children are to be pitied rather than condemned. What *is* immoral is the willful preventing of people from achieving the richness of life. Immorality in this regard lies with those social customs, regulations, and statutes that prevent lesbians and gay men from establishing blood or adoptive families, not with gays themselves.

Sometimes people attempt to establish authority for a moral obligation to use bodily parts in a certain fashion simply by claiming that moral laws are natural laws and vice versa. On this account, inanimate objects and plants are good in that they follow natural laws by necessity, animals by instinct, and persons by a rational will. People are special in that they must first discover the laws that govern them. Now, even if one believes the view—dubious in the post-Newtonian, post-Darwinian world—that natural laws in the usual sense ($E = mc^2$, for instance) have some moral content, it is not at all clear how one is to discover the laws in nature that apply to people.

On the one hand, if one looks to people themselves for a model—and looks hard enough—one finds amazing variety, including homosexuality as a social ideal (upper-class fifth-century Athens) and even as socially mandatory (Melanesia today). When one looks to people, one is simply unable to strip away the layers of social custom, history, and taboo in order to see what's really there to any degree more specific than that people are the creatures that make over their world and are capable of abstract thought. That this is so should raise doubts that neutral principles are to be found in human nature that will condemn homosexuality.

On the other hand, if one looks to nature apart from people for models, the possibilities are staggering. There are fish that change gender over their lifetimes: should we "follow nature" and be operative transsexuals? Orangutans, genetically our next of kin, live completely solitary lives without social organization of any kind: ought we to "follow nature" and be hermits? There are many species where only two members per generation reproduce: should we be bees? The search in nature for people's purpose, far from finding sure models for action, is likely to leave one morally rudderless.

VI. BUT AREN'T GAYS WILLFULLY THE WAY THEY ARE?

It is generally conceded that if sexual orientation is something over which an individual—for whatever reason—has virtually no control, then discrimination against gays is especially deplorable, as it is against racial and ethnic classes, because it holds people accountable without regard for anything they themselves have done. And to hold a person accountable for that over which the person has no control is a central form of prejudice.

Attempts to answer the question whether or not sexual orientation is something that is reasonably thought to be within one's own control usually appeal simply to various claims of the biological or "mental" sciences. But the ensuing debate over genes, hormones, twins, early childhood development, and the like, is as unnecessary as it is currently inconclusive.[15] All that is needed to answer the question is to look at the actual experience of gays in current society and it becomes fairly clear that sexual orientation is not likely a matter of choice. For coming to have a homosexual identity simply does not have the same sort of structure that decision making has.

On the one hand, the "choice" of the gender of a sexual partner does not seem to express a trivial desire that might be as easily well fulfilled by a simple substitution of the desired object. Picking the gender of a sex partner is decidedly dissimilar, that is, to such activities as picking a flavor of ice cream. If an ice-cream parlor is out of one's flavor, one simply picks another. And if people were persecuted, threatened with jail terms, shattered careers, loss of family and housing, and the like, for eating, say, rocky road ice cream, no one would ever eat it; everyone would pick another easily available flavor. That gay people abide in being gay even in the face of persecution shows that being gay is not a matter of easy choice.

On the other hand, even if establishing a sexual orientation is not like making a relatively trivial choice, perhaps it is nevertheless relevantly like making the central and serious life choices by which individuals try to establish themselves as being of some type. Again, if one examines gay experience, this seems not to be the case. For one never sees anyone setting out to become a homosexual, in the way one does see people setting out to become doctors, lawyers, and bricklayers. One does not find "gays-to-be" picking some end—"At some point in the future, I want to become a homosexual"—and then setting about planning and acquiring the ways and means to that end, in the way one does see people deciding that they want to become lawyers, and then sees them plan what courses to take and what sort of temperaments, habits, and skills to develop in order to become lawyers. Typically gays-to-be simply find themselves having homosexual encounters and yet at least initially resisting quite strongly the identification of being homosexual. Such a person even very likely resists having such encounters, but ends up having them anyway. Only with time, luck, and great personal effort, but sometimes never, does the person gradually come to accept her or his orientation, to view it as a given material condition of life, coming as materials do with certain capacities and limitations. The person begins to act in accordance with his or her orientation and its capacities, seeing its actualization as a requisite for an integrated personality and as a central component of personal well-being. As a result, the experience of coming out to oneself has for gays the basic structure of a discovery, not the structure of a choice. And far from signaling immorality, coming out to others affords one of the few remaining opportunities in ever more bureaucratic, mechanistic, and socialistic societies to manifest courage.

VII. HOW WOULD SOCIETY AT LARGE BE CHANGED IF GAYS WERE SOCIALLY ACCEPTED?

Suggestions to change social policy with regard to gays are invariably met with claims that to do so would invite the destruction of civilization itself: after all, isn't that what did Rome in? Actually Rome's decay paralleled not the flourishing of homosexuality but its repression under the later Christianized emperors.[16] Predictions of American civilization's imminent demise have been as premature as they have been frequent. Civilization has shown itself rather resilient here, in large part because of the country's traditional commitments to a respect for privacy, to individual liberties, and especially to people minding their own business. These all give society an open texture and the flexibility to try out things to see what works. And because of this one now need not speculate about what changes reforms in gay social policy might bring to society at large. For many reforms have already been tried.

Half the states have decriminalized homosexual acts. Can you guess which of the following states still have sodomy laws: Wisconsin, Minnesota; New Mexico, Arizona; Vermont, New Hampshire; Nebraska, Kansas. One from each pair does and one does not have sodomy laws. And yet one would be hard pressed to point out any substantial difference between the members of each pair. (If you're interested, it is the second of each pair with them.) Empirical studies have shown that there is no increase in other crimes in states that have decriminalized.[17] Further, sodomy laws are virtually never enforced. They remain on the books not to "protect society" but to insult gays, and for that reason need to be removed.

Neither has the passage of legislation barring discrimination against gays ushered in the end of civilization. Some 50 counties and municipalities, including some of the country's largest cities (like Los Angeles and Boston), have passed such statutes and among the states and colonies Wisconsin and the District of Columbia have model protective codes. Again, no more brimstone has fallen in these places than elsewhere. Staunchly anti-gay cities, like Miami and Houston, have not been spared the AIDS crisis.

Berkeley, California, has even passed domestic partner legislation giving gay couples the same rights to city benefits as married couples, and yet Berkeley has not become more weird than it already was.

Seemingly hysterical predictions that the American family would collapse if such reforms would pass proved false, just as the same dire predictions that the availability of divorce would lessen the ideal and desirability of marriage proved completely unfounded. Indeed if current discriminations, which drive gays into hiding and into anonymous relations, were lifted, far from seeing gays raze American families, one would see gays forming them.

Virtually all gays express a desire to have a permanent lover. Many would like to raise or foster children—perhaps those alarming numbers of gay kids who have been beaten up and thrown out of their "families" for being gay. But currently society makes gay coupling very difficult. A life of hiding is a pressure-cooker existence not easily shared with another. Members of non-gay couples are here asked to imagine what it would take to erase every trace of their own sexual orientation for even just a week.

Even against oppressive odds, gays have shown an amazing tendency to nest. And those gay couples who have survived the odds show that the structure of more usual couplings is not a matter of destiny but of personal responsibility. The so-called basic unit of society turns out not to be a unique immutable atom, but can adopt different parts, be adapted to different needs, and even be improved. Gays might even have a thing or two to teach others about division of labor, the relation of sensuality and intimacy, and stages of development in such relations.

If discrimination ceased, gay men and lesbians would enter the mainstream of the human community openly and with self-respect. The energies that the typical gay person wastes in the anxiety of leading a day-to-day existence of systematic disguise would be released for use in personal flourishing. From this release would be generated the many spinoff benefits that accrue to a society when its individual members thrive.

Society would be richer for acknowledging another aspect of human richness and diversity. Families with gay members would develop relations based on truth and trust rather than lies and fear. And the heterosexual majority would be better off for knowing that they are no longer trampling their gay friends and neighbors.

Finally and perhaps paradoxically, in extending to gays the rights and benefits it has reserved for its dominant culture, America would confirm its deeply held vision of itself as a morally progressing nation, a nation itself advancing and serving as a beacon for others—especially with regard to human rights. The words with which our national pledge ends—"with liberty and justice for all"—are not a description of the present but a call for the future. Ours is a nation given to a prophetic political rhetoric which acknowledges that morality is not arbitrary and that justice is not merely the expression of the current collective will. It is this vision that led the black civil rights movement to its successes. Those congressmen who opposed that movement and its centerpiece, the 1964 Civil Rights Act, on obscurantist grounds, but who lived long enough and were noble enough, came in time to express their heartfelt regret and shame at what they had done. It is to be hoped and someday to be expected that those who now grasp at anything to oppose the extension of that which is best about America to gays will one day feel the same.

Endnotes

1. "Public Fears—And Sympathies," *Newsweek*, August 12, 1985, p. 23.

2. Alfred C. Kinsey, *Sexual Behavior in the Human Male* (Philadelphia: Saunders, 1948), pp. 650–651. On the somewhat lower incidences of lesbianism, see Alfred C. Kinsey, *Sexual Behavior in the Human Female* (Philadelphia: Saunders, 1953), pp. 472–475.

3. Evelyn Hooker, "The Adjustment of the Male Overt Homosexual," *Journal of Projective Techniques* 21 (1957): 18–31, reprinted in Hendrik M. Ruitenbeek, ed., *The Problem of Homosexuality* (New York: Dutton, 1963), pp. 141–161.

4. See Ronald Bayer, *Homosexuality and American Psychiatry* (New York: Basic Books, 1981).

5. For studies showing that gay men are no more likely—indeed, are less likely—than heterosexuals to be child molesters and that the largest groups of sexual

abusers of children and the people most persistent in their molestation of children are the children's fathers or stepfathers or mother's boyfriends, see Vincent De Francis, *Protecting the Child Victim of Sex Crimes Committed by Adults* (Denver: The American Humane Association, 1969), pp. vii, 38, 69–70; A. Nicholas Groth, "Adult Sexual Orientation and Attraction to Underage Persons," *Archives of Sexual Behavior* 7 (1978): 175–181; Mary J. Spencer, "Sexual Abuse of Boys," *Pediatrics* 78, no. 1 (July 1986): 133–138.

6. See National Gay Task Force, *Anti–Gay/Lesbian Victimization* (New York: NGTF, 1984).

7. "2 St. John's Students Given Probation in Assault on Gay," *The Washington Post*, May 15, 1984, p. 1.

8. See Randy Shilts, *The Mayor of Castro Street: The Life and Times of Harvey Milk* (New York: St. Martin's, 1982), pp. 308–325.

9. See Richard Plant, *The Pink Triangle: The Nazi War Against Homosexuals* (New York: Holt, 1986).

10. E. Carrington Boggan, *The Rights of Gay People: The Basic ACLU Guide to a Gay Person's Rights* (New York: Avon, 1975), pp. 211–235.

11. John Boswell, *Christianity, Social Tolerance and Homosexuality: Gay People in Western Europe from the Beginning of the Christian Era to the Fourteenth Century* (Chicago: University of Chicago Press, 1980).

12. See Gilbert Herdt, *Guardians of the Flute: Idioms of Masculinity* (New York: McGraw–Hill, 1981), pp. 232–239, 284–288; and see generally Gilbert Herdt, ed., *Ritualized Homosexuality in Melanesia* (Berkeley: University of California Press, 1984). For another eye-opener, see Walter L. Williams, *The Spirit and the Flesh: Sexual Diversity in American Indian Culture* (Boston: Beacon, 1986).

13. See especially Boswell, *Christianity*, ch. 4.

14. For Old Testament condemnations of homosexual acts, see Leviticus 18:22, 21:3. For hygienic and dietary codes, see, for example, Leviticus 15:19–27 (on the uncleanliness of women) and Leviticus 11:1–47 (on not eating rabbits, pigs, bats, finless water creatures, legless creeping creatures, etc.). For Lot at Sodom, see Genesis 19:1–25. For Lot in the cave, see Genesis 19:30–38.

15. The preponderance of the scientific evidence supports the view that homosexuality is either genetically determined or a permanent result of early childhood development. See the Kinsey Institute's study by Alan Bell, Martin Weinberg, and Sue Hammersmith, *Sexual Preference: Its Development in Men and Women* (Bloomington: Indiana University Press, 1981); Frederick Whitam and Robin Mathy, *Male Homosexuality in Four Societies* (New York: Praeger, 1986), ch. 7.

16. See Boswell, *Christianity*, ch. 3.

17. See Gilbert Geis, "Reported Consequences of Decriminalization of Consensual Adult Homosexuality in Seven American States," *Journal of Homosexuality* 1, no. 4 (1976): 419–426; Ken Sinclair and Michael Ross, "Consequences of Decriminalization of Homosexuality: A Study of Two Australian States," *Journal of Homosexuality* 12, no. 1 (1985): 119–127.

Review Questions

1. How does Mohr explain the stereotypes about gays?

2. According to Mohr, how are gays discriminated against?

3. Does the Bible condemn homosexuality? What is Mohr's view?

4. How does Mohr respond to the charge that homosexuality is unnatural?

5. According to Mohr, why isn't homosexuality a matter of choice?

6. What would happen if gays were socially accepted in our society according to Mohr?

Discussion Questions

1. Does the Bible condemn homosexuality? If it does, is this a good reason for saying that it is immoral? Is this a good reason for making it illegal?

2. Is being gay a matter of choice? What is your view?

3. Is homosexuality immoral? Why or why not?

4. Should homosexuality be illegal? What is your position?

Ann Garry

Pornography and Respect for Women

Ann Garry is Professor of Philosophy at California State University at Los Angeles.

Garry argues that most pornography is morally objectionable because it degrades women by treating them as passive sex objects that are harmed. But it is possible, she claims, for pornography to have a non-sexist content that is not morally objectionable, and she gives some examples of how this could be done.

Pornography, like rape, is a male invention, designed to dehumanize women, to reduce the female to an object of sexual access, not to free sensuality from moralistic or parental inhibition. . . . Pornography is the undiluted essence of anti-female propaganda.
—Susan Brownmiller, Against Our Will: Men, Women and Rape[1]

It is often asserted that a distinguishing characteristic of sexually explicit material is the degrading and demeaning portrayal of the role and status of the human female. It has been argued that erotic materials describe the female as a mere sexual object to be exploited and manipulated sexually. . . . A recent survey shows that 41 percent of American males and 46 percent of the females believe that "sexual materials lead people to lose respect for women." . . . Recent experiments suggest that such fears are probably unwarranted.
—Presidential Commission on Obscenity and Pornography [2]

The kind of apparent conflict illustrated in these passages is easy to find in one's own thinking as well. For example, I have been inclined to think that pornography is innocuous and to dismiss "moral" arguments for censoring it because many such arguments rest on an assumption I do not share—that

This article first appeared in *Social Theory and Practice*, 4 (Summer 1978). It is reprinted here as it appears in Sharon Bishop and Marjorie Weinzweig, eds. *Philosophy and Women* (Wadsworth, 1979). Reprinted by permission of the author and *Social Theory and Practice*.

sex is an evil to be controlled. At the same time I believe that it is wrong to exploit or degrade human beings, particularly women and others who are especially susceptible. So if pornography degrades human beings, then even if I would oppose its censorship I surely cannot find it morally innocuous.

In an attempt to resolve this apparent conflict I discuss three questions: Does pornography degrade (or exploit or dehumanize) human beings? If so, does it degrade women in ways or to an extent that it does not degrade men? If so, must pornography degrade women, as Brownmiller thinks, or could genuinely innocuous, nonsexist pornography exist? Although much current pornography does degrade women, I will argue that it is possible to have nondegrading, non-sexist pornography. However, this possibility rests on our making certain fundamental changes in our conceptions of sex and sex roles. . . .

I

The argument I will consider . . . is that pornography is morally objectionable, not because it leads people to show disrespect for women, but because pornography itself exemplifies and recommends behavior that violates the moral principle to respect persons. The content of pornography is what one objects to. It treats women as mere sex objects "to be exploited and manipulated" and degrades the role and status of women. In order to evaluate this argument, I will first clarify what it would mean for pornography itself to treat someone as a sex object in a degrading manner. I will then deal with three issues central to the discussion of pornography and respect for women: how "losing respect" for a woman is connected with treating her as a sex object; what is wrong with treating someone as a sex object; and why it is worse to treat women rather than men as sex objects. I will argue that the current content of pornography sometimes violates the moral principle to respect persons. Then, in [the concluding part] of this paper, I will suggest that pornography need not violate this principle if certain fundamental changes were to occur in attitudes about sex.

To many people, including Brownmiller and some other feminists, it appears to be an obvious truth that pornography treats people, especially women, as sex objects in a degrading manner. And if we omit "in a degrading manner," the statement seems hard to dispute: How could pornography *not* treat people as sex objects?

First, is it permissible to say that either the content of pornography or pornography itself degrades people or treats people as sex objects? It is not difficult to find examples of degrading content in which women are treated as sex objects. Some pornographic films convey the message that all women really want to be raped, that their resisting struggle is not to be believed. By portraying women in this manner, the content of the movie degrades women. Degrading women is morally objectionable. While seeing the movie need not cause anyone to imitate the behavior shown, we can call the content degrading to women because of the character of the behavior and attitudes it recommends. The same kind of point can be made about films (or books or TV commercials) with other kinds of degrading, thus morally objectionable, content—for example, racist messages.

The next step in the argument is to infer that, because the content or message of pornography is morally objectionable, we can call pornography itself morally objectionable. Support for this step can be found in an analogy. If a person takes every opportunity to recommend that men rape women, we would think not only that his recommendation is immoral but that he is immoral too. In the case of pornography, the objection to making an inference from recommended behavior to the person who recommends is that we ascribe predicates such as "immoral" differently to people than to films or books. A film vehicle for an objectionable message is still an object independent of its message, its director, its producer, those who act in it, and those who respond to it. Hence one cannot make an unsupported inference from "the content of the film is morally objectionable" to "the film is morally objectionable." Because the central points in this paper do not depend on whether pornography itself (in addition to its content) is morally objectionable, I will not try to support this inference. (The question about the relation of content to the work itself is, of course, extremely interesting; but in part because I cannot decide which side of the argument is more persuasive, I will pass.[3]) Certainly one appropriate way to evaluate pornography is in terms of the moral features of its content. If a pornographic film exemplifies and recommends morally objectionable attitudes or behavior, then its content is morally objectionable.

Let us now turn to the first of our three questions about respect and sex objects: What is the connection between losing respect for a woman and treating her as a sex object? Some people who have lived through the era in which women were taught to worry about men "losing respect" for them if they engaged in sex in inappropriate circumstances find it troublesome (or at least amusing) that feminists—supposedly "liberated" women—are outraged at being treated as sex objects, either by pornography or in any other way. The apparent alignment between feminists and traditionally "proper" women need not surprise us when we look at it more closely.

The "respect" that men have traditionally believed they have for women—hence a respect they can lose—is not a general respect for persons as autonomous beings; nor is it respect that is earned because of one's personal merits or achievements. It is respect that is an outgrowth of the "double standard." Women are to be respected because they are more pure, delicate, and fragile than men, have more refined sensibilities, and so on. Because some women clearly do not have these qualities, thus do not deserve respect, women must be divided into two groups—the good ones on the pedestal and the bad ones who have fallen from it. One's mother, grandmother, Sunday School teacher, and usually one's wife are "good" women. The appropriate behavior by which to express respect for good women would be, for example, not swearing or telling dirty jokes in front of them, giving them seats on buses, and other "chivalrous" acts. This kind of "respect" for good women is the sort that adolescent boys in the back seats of cars used to "promise" not to lose. Note that men define, display, and lose this kind of respect. If women lose respect for women, it is not typically a loss of respect for (other) women as a class but a loss of self-respect.

It has now become commonplace to acknowledge that, although a place on the pedestal might have advantages over a place in the "gutter" beneath it, a place on the pedestal is not at all equal to the place occupied by other people (i.e., men). "Respect" for those on the pedestal was not respect for whole, full-fledged people but for a special class of inferior beings.

If a person makes two traditional assumptions—that (at least some) sex is dirty and that women fall into two classes, good and bad—it is easy to see how that person might think that pornography could lead people to lose respect for women or that pornography is itself disrespectful to women. Pornography describes or shows women engaging in activities inappropriate for good women to engage in—or at least inappropriate for them to be seen by strangers engaging in. If one sees these women as symbolic representatives of all women, then all women fall from grace with these women. This fall is possible, I believe, because the traditional "respect" that men have had for women is not genuine, wholehearted respect for full-fledged human beings but half-hearted respect for lesser beings, some of whom they feel the need to glorify and purify.[4] It is easy to fall from a pedestal. Can we imagine 41 percent of men and 46 percent of women answering "yes" to the question "Do movies showing men engaging in violent acts lead people to lose respect for men?"

Two interesting asymmetries appear. The first is that losing respect for men as a class (men with power, typically Anglo men) is more difficult than losing respect for women or ethnic minorities as a class. Anglo men whose behavior warrants disrespect are more likely to be seen as exceptional cases than are women or minorities (whose "transgressions" may be far less serious). Think of the following: women are temptresses; blacks cheat the welfare system; Italians are gangsters; but the men of the Nixon administration are exceptions—Anglo men as a class did not lose respect because of Watergate and related scandals.

The second asymmetry concerns the active and passive roles of the sexes. Men are seen in the active role. If men lose respect for women because of something "evil" done by women (such as appearing in pornography), the fear is that men will then do harm to women—not that women will do harm to men. Whereas if women lose respect for male politicians because of Watergate, the fear is still that male politicians will do harm, not that women will do harm to male politicians. This asymmetry might be a result of one way in which our society thinks of sex as bad—as harm that men do to women (or to the person playing a female role, as in a homosexual rape). Robert Baker calls attention to this point in "'Pricks' and 'Chicks': A Plea for 'Persons'." [5] Our slang words for sexual intercourse—'fuck', 'screw', or older words such as 'take' or 'have'—not only can mean harm but have traditionally taken a male subject and a female object. The active male screws (harms) the passive female. A "bad" woman only tempts men to hurt her further.

It is easy to understand why one's proper grandmother would not want men to see pornography or lose respect for women. But feminists reject these "proper" assumptions: good and bad classes of women do not exist; and sex is not dirty (though many people believe it is). Why then are feminists angry at the treatment of women as sex objects, and why are some feminists opposed to pornography?

The answer is that feminists as well as proper grandparents are concerned with respect. However, there are differences. A feminist's distinction between treating a woman as a full-fledged person and treating her as merely a sex object does not correspond to the good-bad woman distinction. In the latter distinction, "good" and "bad" are properties applicable to groups of women. In the feminist view, all women are full-fledged people—some, however, are treated as sex objects and perhaps think of themselves as sex objects. A further difference is that, although "bad" women correspond to those thought to deserve treatment as sex objects, good women have not corresponded to full-fledged people; only men have been full-fledged people. Given the feminist's distinction, she has no difficulty whatever in saying that pornography treats women as sex objects, not as full-fledged people. She can morally object to pornography or anything else that treats women as sex objects.

One might wonder whether any objection to treatment as a sex object implies that the person objecting still believes, deep down, that sex is dirty. I don't think so. Several other possibilities emerge. First, even if I believe intellectually and emotionally that sex is healthy, I might object to being treated *only* as a sex object. In the same spirit, I would object to being treated *only* as a maker of chocolate chip cookies or *only* as a tennis partner, because only one of my talents is being valued. Second, perhaps I feel that sex is healthy, but it is apparent to me that you think sex is dirty; so I don't want you to treat me as a sex object. Third, being treated as any kind of object, not just as a sex object, is unappealing. I would rather be a partner (sexual or otherwise) than an object. Fourth, and more plausible than the first three possibilities, is Robert Baker's view mentioned above. Both (1) our traditional double standard of sexual behavior for men and women and (2) the linguistic evidence that we con-

nect the concept of sex with the concept of harm point to what is wrong with treating women as sex objects. As I said earlier, 'fuck' and 'screw', in their traditional uses, have taken a male subject, a female object, and have had at least two meanings: harm and have sexual intercourse with. (In addition, a prick is a man who harms people ruthlessly; and a motherfucker is so low that he would do something very harmful to his own dear mother.) [6] Because in our culture we connect sex with harm that men do to women, and because we think of the female role in sex as that of harmed object, we can see that to treat a woman as a sex object is automatically to treat her as less than fully human. To say this does not imply that no healthy sexual relationships exist; nor does it say anything about individual men's conscious intentions to degrade women by desiring them sexually (though no doubt some men have these intentions). It is merely to make a point about the concepts embodied in our language.

Psychoanalytic support for the connection between sex and harm comes from Robert J. Stoller. Stoller thinks that sexual excitement is linked with a wish to harm someone (and with at least a whisper of hostility). The key process of sexual excitement can be seen as dehumanization (fetishization) in fantasy of the desired person. He speculates that this is true in some degree of everyone, both men and women, with "normal" or "perverted" activities and fantasies.[7]

Thinking of sex objects as harmed objects enables us to explain some of the first three reasons why one wouldn't want to be treated as a sex object: (1) I may object to being treated only as a tennis partner, but being a tennis partner is not connected in our culture with being a harmed object; and (2) I may not think that sex is dirty and that I would be a harmed object; I may not know what your view is; but what bothers me is that this is the view embodied in our language and culture.

Awareness of the connection between sex and harm helps explain other interesting points. Women are angry about being treated as sex objects in situations or roles in which they do not intend to be regarded in that manner—for example, while serving on a committee or attending a discussion. It is not merely that a sexual role is inappropriate for the circumstances; it is thought to be a less fully human role than the one in which they intended to function.

Finally, the sex-harm connection makes clear why it is worse to treat women as sex objects than to treat men as sex objects, and why some men have had difficulty understanding women's anger about the matter. It is more difficult for heterosexual men than for women to assume the role of "harmed object" in sex; for men have the self-concept of sexual agents, not of passive objects. This is also related to my earlier point concerning the difference in the solidity of respect for men and for women; respect for women is more fragile. Despite exceptions, it is generally harder for people to degrade men, either sexually or nonsexually, than to degrade women. Men and women have grown up with different patterns of self-respect and expectations regarding the extent to which they deserve and will receive respect or degradation. The man who doesn't understand why women do not want to be treated as sex objects (because he'd sure like to be) would not think of himself as being harmed by that treatment; a woman might.[8] Pornography, probably more than any other contemporary institution, succeeds in treating men as sex objects.

Having seen that the connection between sex and harm helps explain both what is wrong with treating someone as a sex object and why it is worse to treat a woman in this way, I want to use the sex-harm connection to try to resolve a dispute about pornography and women. Brownmiller's view, remember, was that pornography is "the undiluted essence of anti-female propaganda" whose purpose is to degrade women. Some people object to Brownmiller's view by saying that, since pornography treats both men and women as sex objects for the purpose of

arousing the viewer, it is neither sexist, antifemale, nor designed to degrade women; it just happens that degrading of women arouses some men. How can this dispute be resolved?

Suppose we were to rate the content of all pornography from most morally objectionable to least morally objectionable. Among the most objectionable would be the most degrading—for example, "snuff" films and movies which recommend that men rape women, molest children and puppies, and treat nonmasochists very sadistically.

Next we would find a large amount of material (probably most pornography) not quite so blatantly offensive. With this material it is relevant to use the analysis of sex objects given above. As long as sex is connected with harm done to women, it will be very difficult not to see pornography as degrading to women. We can agree with Brownmiller's opponent that pornography treats men as sex objects, too, but we maintain that this is only pseudoequality: such treatment is still more degrading to women.[9]

In addition, pornography often exemplifies the active/passive, harmer/harmed object roles in a very obvious way. Because pornography today is male-oriented and is supposed to make a profit, the content is designed to appeal to male fantasies. Judging from the content of the most popular legally available pornography, male fantasies still run along the lines of stereotypical sex roles—and, if Stoller is right, include elements of hostility. In much pornography the women's purpose is to cater to male desires, to service the man or men. Her own pleasure is rarely emphasized for its own sake; she is merely allowed a little heavy breathing, perhaps in order to show her dependence on the great male "lover" who produces her pleasure. In addition, women are clearly made into passive objects in still photographs showing only close-ups of their genitals. Even in movies marketed to appeal to heterosexual couples, such as *Behind the Green Door*, the woman is passive and undemanding (and in this case kidnapped and hypnotized as well). Although many kinds of specialty magazines and films are gauged for different sexual tastes, very little contemporary pornography goes against traditional sex roles. There is certainly no significant attempt to replace the harmer/harmed distinction with anything more positive and healthy. In some stag movies, of course, men are treated sadistically by women; but this is an attempt to turn the tables on degradation, not a positive improvement.

What would cases toward the least objectionable end of the spectrum be like? They would be increasingly less degrading and sexist. The genuinely nonobjectionable cases would be nonsexist and nondegrading; but commercial examples do not readily spring to mind.[10] The question is: Does or could any pornography have nonsexist, nondegrading content?

II

I want to start with the easier question: Is it possible for pornography to have nonsexist, morally acceptable content? Then I will consider whether any pornography of this sort currently exists.

Imagine the following situation, which exists only rarely today: Two fairly conventional people who love each other, enjoy playing tennis and bridge together, cooking good food together, and having sex together. In all these activities they are free from hang-ups, guilt, and tendencies to dominate or objectify each other. These two people like to watch tennis matches and old romantic movies on TV, like to watch Julia Child cook, like to read the bridge column in the newspaper, and like to watch pornographic movies. Imagine further that this couple is not at all uncommon in society and that nonsexist pornography is as common as this kind of nonsexist sexual relationship. This situation sounds fine and healthy to me. I see no reason to think that an interest in pornography would disappear in these circumstances. People seem to enjoy watching others experience or do (especially do well) what they enjoy experiencing, doing, or wish they could do themselves. We do not morally object to people watching tennis on TV; why would we object to these hypothetical people watching pornography?

Can we go from the situation today to the situation just imagined? In much current pornography, people are treated in morally objectionable ways. In the scene just imagined, however, pornography would be nonsexist, nondegrading, morally acceptable. The key to making the change is to break the connection between sex and harm. If Stoller is right, this task may be impossible without changing the scenarios of our sexual lives—scenarios that we have been writing since early childhood. (Stoller does not indicate whether he thinks it possible for adults to rewrite their scenarios or for social change to bring about the possibility of new scenarios in future generations.) But even if we believe that people can change their sexual scenarios, the sex-harm connection is deeply entrenched and has widespread implications. What is needed is a thorough change in people's deep-seated attitudes and feelings about sex roles in general, as well as about sex and roles in sex (sexual roles). Although I cannot even sketch a general outline of such changes here, changes in pornography should be part of a comprehensive program. Television, children's educational material, and nonpornographic movies and novels may be far better avenues for attempting to change attitudes; but one does not want to take the chance that pornography is working against one.

What can be done about pornography in particular? If one wanted to work within the current institutions, one's attempt to use pornography as a tool for the education of male pornography audiences would have to be fairly subtle at first; nonsexist pornography must become familiar enough to sell and be watched. One should realize too that any positive educational value that nonsexist pornography might have may well be as short-lived as most of the effects of pornography. But given these limitations, what could one do?

Two kinds of films must be considered. First is the short film with no plot or character development, just depicted sexual activity in which nonsexist pornography would treat men and women as equal sex partners.[11] The man would not control the circumstances in which the partners had sex or the choice of positions or acts; the woman's preference would be counted equally. There would be no suggestion of a power play or conquest on the man's part, no suggestion that "she likes it when I hurt her." Sexual intercourse would not be portrayed as primarily for the purpose of male ejaculation—his orgasm is not "the best part" of the movie. In addition, both the man and woman would express their enjoyment; the man need not be cool and detached.

The film with a plot provides even more opportunity for nonsexist education. Today's pornography often portrays the female characters as playthings even when not engaging in sexual activity. Nonsexist pornography could show women and men in roles equally valued by society, and sex equality would amount to more than possession of equally functional genitalia. Characters would customarily treat each other with respect and consideration, with no attempt to treat men or women brutally or thoughtlessly. The local Pussycat Theater showed a film written and directed by a woman (*The Passions of Carol*), which exhibited a few of the features just mentioned. The main female character in it was the editor of a magazine parody of *Viva*. The fact that some of the characters treated each other very nicely, warmly, and tenderly did not detract from the pornographic features of the movie. This did not surprise us, for even in traditional male-oriented films, lesbian scenes usually exhibit tenderness and kindness.

Plots for nonsexist films could include women in traditionally male jobs (e.g., long-distance truck-driver) or in positions usually held in respect by pornography audiences.

For example, a high-ranking female Army officer, treated with respect by men and women alike, could be shown not only in various sexual encounters with other people but also carrying out her job in a humane manner.[12] Or perhaps the main character could be a female urologist. She could interact with nurses and other medical personnel, diagnose illnesses brilliantly, and treat patients with great sympathy as well as have sex with them. When the Army officer or the urologist engages in sexual activities, she will treat her partners and be treated by them in some of the considerate ways described above.

In the circumstances we imagined at the beginning of [this part of the] paper, our nonsexist films could be appreciated in the proper spirit. Under these conditions the content of our new pornography would clearly be nonsexist and morally acceptable. But would the content of such a film be morally acceptable if shown to a typical pornography audience today? It might seem strange for us to change our moral evaluation of the content on the basis of a different audience, but an audience today is likely to see the "respected" urologist and Army officer as playthings or unusual prostitutes—even if our intention in showing the film is to counteract this view. The effect is that although the content of the film seems morally acceptable and our intention in showing it is morally flawless, women are still degraded.[13] The fact that audience attitude is so important makes one wary of giving wholehearted approval to any pornography seen today.

The fact that good intentions and content are insufficient does not imply that one's efforts toward change would be entirely in vain. Of course, I could not deny that anyone who tries to change an institution from within faces serious difficulties. This is particularly evident when one is trying to change both pornography and a whole set of related attitudes, feelings, and institutions concerning sex and sex roles. But in conjunction with other attempts to change this set of attitudes, it seems preferable to try to change pornography instead of closing one's eyes in the hope that it will go away. For I suspect that pornography is here to stay. . . .

Endnotes

1. (New York: Simon and Schuster, 1975), p. 394.

2. The Report of the Commission on Obscenity and Pornography (Washington, D.C., 1970), p. 201.

3. In order to help one determine which position one feels inclined to take, consider the following statement: It is morally objectionable to write, make, sell, act in, use, and enjoy pornography; in addition, the content of pornography is immoral; however, pornography itself is not morally objectionable. If this statement seems extremely problematic, then one might well be satisfied with the claim that pornography is degrading because its content is.

4. Many feminists point this out. One of the most accessible references is Shulamith Firestone, *The Dialectic of Sex: The Case for the Feminist Revolution* (New York: Bantam, 1970), especially pp. 128–32.

5. In Richard Wasserstrom, ed., *Today's Moral Problems* (New York: Macmillan, 1975), pp. 152–71. Also in Robert Baker and Frederick Elliston, eds., *Philosophy and Sex* (Buffalo, N.Y.: Prometheus Books, 1975).

6. Baker, in Wasserstrom, *Today's Moral Problems,* pp. 168–169.

7. "Sexual Excitement," *Archives of General Psychiatry* 33 (1976): 899–909, especially p. 903. The extent to which Stoller sees men and women in different positions with respect to harm and hostility is not clear. He often treats men and women alike, but in *Perversion: The Erotic Form of Hatred* (New York: Pantheon, 1975), pp. 89–91, he calls attention to differences between men and women especially regarding their responses to pornography and lack of understanding by men of women's sexuality. Given that Stoller finds hostility to be an essential element in male-oriented pornography, and given that women have not responded readily to such pornography, one can speculate about the possibilities for women's sexuality: their hostility might follow a different scenario; they might not be as hostile, and so on.

8. Men seem to be developing more sensitivity to being treated as sex objects. Many homosexual men have long understood the problem. As women become more sexually aggressive, some heterosexual men I know are beginning to feel treated as sex objects. A man can feel that he is not being taken seriously if a woman looks lustfully at him while he is holding forth about the French judicial system or the failure of liberal politics. Some of his most important talents are not being properly valued.

9. I don't agree with Brownmiller that the purpose of pornography is to dehumanize women, rather it is to arouse the audience. The differences between our views can be explained, in part, by the points from which we begin. She is writing about rape; her views about pornography grow out of her views about rape. I begin by thinking of pornography as merely depicted sexual activity, though I am well aware of the male hostility and contempt for women that it often expresses. That pornography degrades women and excites men is an illustration of this contempt.

10. Virginia Wright Wexman uses the film *Group Marriage* (Stephanie Rottman, 1973) as an example of "more enlightened erotica." Wexman also asks the following questions in an attempt to point out sexism in pornographic films:

> Does it [the film] portray rape as pleasurable to women? Does it consistently show females nude but present men fully clothed? Does it present women as childlike creatures whose sexual interests must be guided by knowing experienced men? Does it show sexually aggressive women as castrating viragos? Does it pretend that sex is exclusively the prerogative of women under twenty-five? Does it focus on the physical aspects of lovemaking rather than the emotional ones? Does it portray women as purely sexual beings? ("Sexism of X-rated Films." *Chicago Sun–Times,* 28 March 1976.)

11. If it is a lesbian or male homosexual film, no one would play a caricatured male or female role. The reader has probably noticed that I have limited my discussion to heterosexual pornography, but there are many interesting analogies to be drawn with male homosexual pornography. Very little lesbian pornography exists, though lesbian scenes are commonly found in male-oriented pornography.

12. One should note that behavior of this kind is still considered unacceptable by the military. A female officer resigned from the U.S. Navy recently rather than be court-martialed for having sex with several enlisted men whom she met in a class on interpersonal relations.

13. The content may seem morally acceptable only if one disregards such questions as, "Should a doctor have sex with her patients during office hours?" More important is the propriety of evaluating content wholly apart from the attitudes and reactions of the audience; one might not find it strange to say that one film has morally unacceptable content when shown tonight at the Pussycat Theater but acceptable content when shown tomorrow at a feminist conference.

Review Questions

1. What is Garry's account of the relation between respect for a person and treating a person as a sex object?

2. According to Garry, what is the connection between sex and harm? Why does this connection hold for women and not for men?

3. How is it possible for pornography to have a morally acceptable content according to Garry? Give some examples.

1. Is there a connection between sex and harm as Garry says? If so, then can a man be harmed by sex? Why or why not?

2. Can pornography be degrading for men? What do you think?

3. Do you agree that pornography can be morally acceptable?

David A.J. Richards

The Moral Theory of Free Speech and Obscenity Law

David Richards is Professor of Law at New York University. He is the author of Sex, Drugs, Death and the Law *and* The Moral Criticism of Law, *from which our reading is taken.*

Richards begins with a theory of the First Amendment based on Rawls' theory of justice. The First Amendment, Richards suggests, should be understood in terms of Rawls' first principle of justice so that it gives the greatest possible equal liberty of communication compatible with like liberty for all. After explicating the concepts of the obscene and pornography, Richards attacks the Supreme Court's opinions in Miller *and* Paris Adult Theatre. *Contrary to the Court, Richards thinks that laws banning obscenity violate the central moral purpose of the First Amendment, and thus are unconstitutional.*

In interpreting and enforcing the First Amendment, courts must determine the proper standards under which their responsibility is to be discharged. On the basis of our formulation of applicable principles of justice, the constitutional notions of free speech and free press should be understood in terms of certain relevant requirements of the first

From *The Moral Criticism of Law*, edited by David A.J. Richards © 1977 by Dickenson Publishing Company, Inc. Reprinted by permission of Wadsworth, Inc.

principle of justice, namely, the greatest equal liberty of communication compatible with a like liberty for all. Thus, all legal prohibitions and regulations which constrain liberty of communication in a manner incompatible with this idea should be constitutionally forbidden and invalid. But how are we to understand the concrete application of the equal liberty idea?[1]

One important point is that in applying the equal liberty principle, the basic liberties must be assessed as an interrelated system. The weights of each kind of liberty may depend on the specification of other kinds of liberty. The liberties of expression constitute both a right to communicate and a right to be the object of communication. Obviously, these liberties must be adjusted to one another in such a way as to best realize the underlying values of autonomous self-determination. The morally preferable adjustment is a liberty to communicate to any audience that is itself at liberty to choose to be or not to be an audience. Given this interpretation, the liberty to communicate and other liberties are to be assessed as a whole in the light of the principle requiring the greatest equal liberty compatible with a like liberty for all.

The crucial analytic question is whether institutions and practices governing human expression, assessed as a system,[2] violate or cohere with the idea of a system of greatest equal liberty compatible with a like liberty for all. For example, it is clear that procedural rules of order, time, and place, which regulate a reasonable pattern of communications, cohere with this idea, for they enlarge the equal liberty of communication compatible with a like liberty for all.[3] Without such rules of order, time, and place, the liberty of communication of one will be used to violate the liberty of communication of another so that the system of liberties is not the greatest *equal* liberty compatible with a like liberty for all.

Similarly, the punishment of communications that are an indispensable part of actions designed to and capable of overthrowing the constitutional order—for example, communicating military secrets to the enemy—does not violate this equal liberty of communications, for such communications would help to overthrow the system of equal liberties. The proof that such communications do advance the overthrow of the constitutional order must, however, appeal to general principles of empirical induction and inference. No special principles of inference, not admissible in deciding on the principles of justice, are admissible in the interpretation of those principles. Thus, special *a priori* views regarding the relation of certain communications to the decline and fall of the constitutional order, not justified on generally acceptable empirical grounds, are not morally tolerable as reasons for limiting such communications.

Attempts by the state to prohibit certain contents of communication per se are fundamentally incompatible with the moral and constitutional principle of equal liberty. Notwithstanding the outrage felt by the majority toward certain contents of communication, the equal liberty principle absolutely forbids the prohibition of such communications on the ground of such outrage alone. Otherwise, the liberty of expression, instead of the vigorous and potent defense of individual autonomy that it is, would be a pitifully meager permission allowing people to communicate only in ways to which no one has any serious objection. The interest of the few in free expression is not to be sacrificed on such grounds to the interest of the many. Conventional attitudes are not to be the procrustean measure of the exercise of human expressive and judgmental competence.

On this view, the constitutionally protected liberty of free expression is the legal embodiment of a moral principle which ensures to each person the maximum equal liberty of communication compatible with a like liberty for all. Importantly, if the First Amendment freedoms rest on a fundamental moral principle, they have no necessary justificatory relation to the liberty of equal voting rights. No doubt, both rights advance values of self-direction and autonomy, but a maximum equal liberty of self-expression is neither a necessary nor a sufficient condition of democratic voting rights or the competent exercise of those rights. Voting rights may exist and be competently exercised in a regime where expression is not in general free, but is limited to a small class of talented technicians who circulate relevant data on policy issues to the electorate. Similarly, free expression may exist in a political aristocracy or in a democracy where voting rights are not competently exercised because of illiteracy or political apathy.

The independent status of the value of free expression shows that its value is not intrinsically political but rests on deeper moral premises regarding the general exercise of autonomous expressive and judgmental capacity and the good that this affords in human life. It follows that the attempt to limit the constitutional protection of free expression to the political [4] must be rejected on moral and constitutional grounds.[5]

The foregoing account makes clear that strong moral ideas are implicit in the First Amendment and that moral analysis may clarify the proper constitutional interpretation and application of those ideas. It is significant in this connection that the account here proposed clarifies many concrete features of First Amendment adjudications,[6] for example, the propriety of reasonable regulations of time, place, and procedure,[7] the insistence that majority dislike of protected expression has no constitutional weight,[8] the basis of the clear and present danger test,[9] and the refusal to limit the First Amendment to the political.[10] It is equally clear that this account provides a framework from which the case law may be crucially assessed both as regards proper extensions of First Amendment rights, such as rights of access to the media,[11] and the criticism of anomalies in existing case law which depart from its deepest moral strains.

The Concept of the Obscene

A satisfying philosophical explication of the notion of the obscene would clarify the notion itself, its connections to related notions (such as the pornographic, the indecent, and the immoral), its uses in speech, and its relations to fundamental attitudes which explain how the notion comes to have moving appeal to conduct. Initially, we must describe some general marks of the obscene. Then, a constructive account of the notion will be proposed, and, finally, an attempt will be made to connect the account to related notions, especially the pornographic.

The Marks of the Obscene

The etymology of *obscene* is obscure. The *Oxford English Dictionary* notes that the etymology is "doubtful,"[12] while *Webster's* suggests a derivation from the Latin *ob*, meaning *to, before, against,* and the Latin *caenum,* meaning *filth.*[13] Other commentators suggest alternative derivations from the Latin *obscurus,* meaning *concealed,*[14] or a derivation as a corruption of the Latin *scena* meaning *what takes place off stage.*[15] In the latter sense, blinding Gloucester on stage in *King Lear* would have been an obscenity for a Greek playwright like Sophocles (thus, Oedipus is blinded offstage), but it was not for an Elizabethan playwright like Shakespeare, who was imbued with the bloodthirstiness of Senecan tragedy.

The standard dictionary definition of *obscene* turns on notions of what is disgusting, filthy, or offensive to decency.[16] While contemporary legal discussions emphasize the applicability of *obscene* to depictions, it is clearly significantly applied to acts themselves. Shakespeare, for example, speaks of an obscene deed,[17] and Sartre discusses obscene movements of the body.[18] In the law it

is notable that the earliest English obscenity conviction was for obscene acts.[19] Judicial decisions [20] and legal and general [21] commentary emphasize the connections of the obscene to the notion of shame. It is clear that in European thought the notion of the obscene has long been connected to the scatological [22] and the sexually lascivious,[23] a connection emphasized in Anglo–American legal history.[24] This history also makes clear the significant relation of the obscene to the notion of the morally corrupting. Many of these connections were summarized in the language of the Comstock Act, which, in forbidding the mailing of obscene material in interstate commerce in the United States, speaks of "obscene, lewd, or lascivious ... publication(s)" and included in its prohibitions contraceptives and abortifacients or anything else "for any indecent or immoral use." [25]

The most significant class of speech acts involving the notion of the obscene is that class of epithets, known as *obscenities,* which relate to excretory or sexual functions.[26] Such expressions are, at least in reasonably well-educated circles, conventionalized ways of expressing attitudes of disgust and contempt which depend for their sometimes shocking and bracing effect on the impropriety of their use.[27] In circles, like the army, where the verbal obscenities are constantly employed, their function seems quite different; [28] there they are used as a kind of manly, transgression-braving vocabulary whose use is a criterion of intimate membership in the group. Related to this is the use of obscenities among intimate friends and even as a language of love.

The verbal obscenities demonstrate the relation of the obscene not only to shock and offense, but to the anxiety-producing loss of control. On hearing or using such expressions in reasonably well-educated circles, one has the sense of a loss of control, a sudden frustration, or an explosion of pique, which may surprise the speaker as much as the listener.

In the light of these functions and marks of the verbal obscenities, one can better understand the functions of literature which employs obscene contents—for example, some works of Swift[29] and Pope.[30] By employing contents known to be offensive to the conventional proprieties, such literature can express complex communicative intentions of bitter satire and burlesque in ways related to the capacity of the verbal obscenities to express disgust and contempt.[31] Similarly, one can understand the use of the obscene in literary humor as well as in the smutty joke and obscene witticism.[32] Obviously, such effects of the obscene are in some important way tied to attitudes, the existence of which accounts for these effects.

An Explication of the Obscene

The concept of the obscene is identical with the concept of those actions, representations, works, or states which display an exercise of bodily or personal function which in certain circumstances constitutes an abuse of that function, as dictated by standards in which one has invested self-esteem, so that the supposed abuse of function is regarded as a demeaning object of self-contempt and self-disgust.[33]

On this view, the obscene is a subcategory of the objects of shame. Shame is, I believe, properly understood in terms of a fall from one's self-concept in the exercise of capacities which one desires to exercise competently. The objects of shame, thus, are explained by reference to the notions of personal competence and self-respect which are their bases. One feels ashamed because, for example, one has been cowardly, failing to exercise courageous self-control over fear when danger threatened. A characteristic mark of such failure is self-contempt or self-disgust.

The obscene identifies a special class of the possible objects of shame which are explained by reference to certain defined notions of competence in bodily or personal function. Thus, just as one explains to a child that it is an abuse and misuse of the function of a knife or fork to put either in the ear, so too one explains the proper exercise of bodi-

ly function. The use of the body is thought to have precise and sharply defined functions and ends. This idea, found widely among primitive peoples and the most ancient cultures,[34] including, significantly, ancient Judaism,[35] rigidly defines certain clear proprieties of bodily function as pure or clean. Failure to so exercise bodily function is unclean, polluting, an abomination, in short, obscene.[36]

The obscene, thus, is a conceptual residuum of very ancient ways of thinking about human conduct. Human beings are thought of as clusters of strengths or virtues and corresponding weaknesses or vices, where virtues and vices are not conceived in narrow moral terms.[37] Obscenity within this view is a kind of vice, a wasting and abuse of the natural employment of bodily or personal function. Hence, a culture's definition of the obscene will indicate those areas of bodily or personal function in which the culture centrally invests its self-esteem and in which deviance provokes the deepest anxieties. For example, incompetence with respect to excretory function typically defines the frailest members of society, infants and the senile. Where frailty and declining powers are a source of anxiety, excretory impropriety is likely to be regarded as obscene. Moreover, where the sexual function is regarded as akin to the excretory function, as it easily may be,[38] sexual behavior will come to share this condemnation.

This explication is intended to apply cross-culturally.[39] To the extent people in different cultures take different attitudes to certain bodily or personal functions, those cultures will take different views of those things that are obscene, though the cultures share the concept of the obscene as an abuse of bodily or personal function. A striking example is provided by the Tahitians, who do not take the Western view of the competent exercise of sexual function, but do take a rather stringent view of eating; thus for Tahitians, displays of coitus are not obscene, but displays of eating are.[40] For us, aside from contexts of satirical humor,[41] eating conventional food would be obscene only in extreme circumstances of gluttonous self-indulgence [42] or in circumstances where eating is associated with aphrodisiacal allure.[43]

Similarly, this explication is true over time as well. For example, English society in the eighteenth century was apparently very tolerant of obscene literature, despite the fact that obscene libel had become a common-law offense.[44] But in the nineteenth century, changing moral standards gave rise to groups like the Society for the Suppression of Vice and prosecutions for obscene libel increased rapidly.[45] Concern over the explosion of pornographic literature [46] finally received expression in English statutes.[47] In the same way, contemporary attitudes evince a shift in the application of the obscene; a growing modern usage applies the notion, for example, to violence and death and displays of violence and death (based on the idea, I believe, that these represent demeaning abuses of competences of the person),[48] but no longer applies the notion to sex or sexual displays.[49]

Significantly, this explication accounts for the application of *obscene* to acts as well as to depictions of acts. Both acts and depictions are obscene if they display certain exercises of bodily function; whether by the act itself or by depiction, our anxiety is aroused when we become aware of phenomena which threaten our self-esteem. It does not follow, of course, that obscene depictions are only of obscene acts. Normal heterosexual intercourse between a married couple is not typically viewed as obscene; but a public depiction of such intercourse would, by some people, be viewed as obscene. Nonetheless, there is little question that the obscenity of an act is a sufficient condition for the obscenity of a depiction of that act. Most cases of obscene depictions fall into this category. At one time obscenity convictions were granted for the mere sympathetic discussion of homosexuality or advocacy of birth control or abortion, apart from any pornographic representation of any kind.[50] The idea seems to have been that since homosexuality, birth control, and

abortion were obscene, any favorable discussion of them was obscene. Even today, it is clear that courts are quickest to make or affirm judgments of obscenity with respect to depictions of sexual acts such as cunnilingus, fellatio, sodomy, sadomasochism, and beastiality that are regarded as obscene in themselves.[51] The view that these acts are obscene is the basis for judging their depiction to be obscene.

The connection between the obscenity of acts and depictions of acts distinguishes the obscene from the indecent. The distinctive mark of the indecent is the public exhibition of that which, while unobjectionable in private, is offensive and embarrassing when done in public.[52] The obscene, by contrast, may be and often is condemned whether or not it involves a public display.

Finally, this linkage between the act and its depiction accounts for the use of obscenities to express contempt and disgust. Since the obscene identifies a disgusting abuse of bodily function, it is wholly natural that it should be used to express disgust. It follows that if one does not find certain communicative contents obscene, one may tendentiously advocate the abandonment of speech acts using those contents to express disgust.[53]

The Obscene and the Pornographic

Pornography etymologically derives from the Greek *pornographos,* meaning *writing of harlots,* literally, writing concerning or descriptive of prostitutes in their profession.[54] Thus, the depictions of various forms of sexual intercourse on the walls of a certain building in Pompeii, intended as aphrodisiacs for the orgiastic bacchanales housed there, were literally *pornographos.*[55] Pornography in this sense is identified by its sexually explicit content, its depiction of varied forms of sexual intercourse, turgid genitalia, and so on.[56]

Pornography is neither conceptually nor factually identical with the obscene. Conceptually, the notion of sexually explicit, aphrodisiacal depictions is not the same idea as that of the abuse of a bodily or personal function. Many cultures, though sharing the fundamental concept of the obscene, do not regard pornography as obscene.[57] Individuals within our culture may find coprophagy (eating feces) obscene,[58] but do not find pornography obscene,[59] because they fail to take a certain attitude toward "proper" sexual function although they do have ideas about "proper" excretory function. For such people, viewing sex or depictions of sex as obscene is an unfortunate blending of the sexual and the excremental.[60]

If there is no necessary connection between the pornographic and the obscene, how did the connection between them arise?

One account of the sexual morality behind this connection is that of Catholic canon law which

holds, as a basic and cardinal fact, that complete sexual activity and pleasure is licit and moral only in a naturally completed act in valid marriage. All acts which, of their psychological and physical nature, are designed to be preparatory to the complete act, take their licitness and their morality from the complete act. If, therefore, they are entirely divorced from the complete act, they are distorted, warped, meaningless, and hence immoral.[61]

This view of course derives from St. Augustine's classic conception that the only proper "genital commotion"[62] is one with the voluntary aim of reproduction of the species.[63] It follows from this view that only certain rigidly defined kinds of "natural" intercourse in conventional marriage are moral; "unnatural" forms of such intercourse are forbidden; extramarital and of course homosexual intercourse are forbidden. Further, all material that will induce to "genital commotion" not within marriage is forbidden. Pornography is obscene not only in itself, because it displays intercourse not within marriage, but also because it tempts to intercourse outside marriage or to masturbation, which are independently obscene acts because they are forms of sexual conduct that violate minimum standards of proper bodily function and thus cause disgust.

While this specific Catholic view is not the universal basis for the connection of the obscene and the pornographic, this general kind of view seems always present. Sexual function of certain rigidly defined kinds is alone the correct and competent exercise of sexual function. All other forms are marked by failure, weakness, and disgust. Masturbation in particular is a moral wrong.

Clearly this general notion, premised on supposed medical as well as theological facts, was behind the extraordinary explosion in obscenity legislation in England and the United States in the 1850s, 1860s, and 1870s. This legislation rested squarely on the remarkable Victorian medical view relating masturbation and sexual excess in general to insanity.[64] Pornography, being in part masturbation fantasy, was condemned on medical as well as theological grounds, so that Anthony Comstock, the father of the Comstock Act, could point with the support of medical authority to the fact that pornography's "most deadly effects are felt by the victims in the habit of secret vices."[65]

Significantly, Victorian medical literature and pornography[66] make transparent that sexual function was construed on the model of excretory function.[67] The proper exercise of sexual function was rigidly defined in terms of one mode, marital reproductive sexuality. Within that mode, the proper function was one of regularity and moderation. Thus, doctors condemned sexual excess within marriage[68] and deprecated infertile sexual activity within marriage as "conjugal onanism."[69] This rigid and narrow conception of sexual function was obviously profoundly opposed to pornography which would expose, in the words of one prominent Victorian court, "the minds of those hitherto pure . . . to the danger of contamination and pollution from the impurity it contains."[70]

Similar views regarding the evils of masturbation are echoed in contemporary writers who condemn pornography. Thus, D.H. Lawrence emphasized the corrosive effects of autoeroticism on the capacity for the central spiritual experience, for Lawrence, of sexual mutuality between partners.[71]

Whatever the form of theological, medical, or psychological belief underlying the association of the obscene and the pornographic, some such belief always prevails, so that there is a significant correlation between judgments of obscenity and the judgments that a certain work is both sexually arousing and quite unpleasant.[72]

THE CONSTITUTIONALITY OF OBSCENITY LAW

It should now be possible to apply the foregoing explication of the obscene and the moral analysis of the First Amendment to the issue raised in *Miller* v. *California* and *Paris Adult Theatre I* v. *Slaton*—the constitutionally permissible concept of the obscene.

Miller reaffirmed the holding of *Roth* v. *United States* that obscene expression is not protected by the First Amendment. In addition, the Court, speaking through the Chief Justice, formulated a constitutional test for obscenity. The test is threefold:

(a) whether "the average person, applying contemporary community standards" would find that the work, taken as a whole, appeals to the prurient interest . . .; (b) whether the work depicts or describes, in a patently offensive way, sexual conduct specifically defined by the applicable state law; and (c) whether the work, taken as a whole, lacks serious literary, artistic, political, or scientific value.[73]

This test imposes on states that wish to ban obscenity an obligation to formulate specific standards. Moreover, *Miller* limits the obscene to "representations or descriptions of ultimate sexual acts, normal or perverted, actual or simulated" or "of masturbation, excretory functions and lewd exhibition of the genitals." [74] In effect, only hard-core scatology and pornography may be banned.[75]

On the other hand, the *Miller* test permits censorship wherever the allegedly obscene work is without "serious" value.[76] Thus, a lighter burden is imposed on the prosecution than was imposed under the prior "utterly without redeeming social value" test.[77] Moreover, reliance on local standards,[78] within the bounds of the court's test, permits a variety of constitutionally permissible restrictions. Hence, a person's First Amendment rights may be restricted in one jurisdiction without appeal to a national standard.[79]

The *Miller* case involved a conviction for mailing unsolicited sexually explicit material, which is, of course, a problem of nonconsensual intrusion of offensive material. In *Paris Adult Theatre I* v. *Slaton,* however, a majority of the Court, again speaking through Chief Justice Burger, applied the *Miller* criteria for obscenity to an adult's fully informed and consensual access to obscene materials. The Court thus narrowly limited the holding of *Stanley* v. *Georgia* [80] to its facts. There the Court invalidated a state statute prohibiting the possession and private use in one's home of obscene (pornographic) materials on the grounds of infringing the constitutional right of privacy. In *Paris Adult Theatre,* and other cases decided concurrently, the Court made clear that the constitutional right of privacy as regards the use of obscene materials applies only to one's home, not to any theater, nor even to the transport of such materials in one's traveling bags for private use.[81]

Miller and *Paris Adult Theatre,* then, find obscenity, even for consenting adults, to be outside the protection of the First Amendment, but the analysis here presented suggests that the Court's decisions are wrong. An understanding of the moral function of the First Amendment compels a conclusion contrary to the Court's; there should be a presumption that obscenity, like other forms of expression, falls within the protection of the First Amendment.

To summarize, obscene communications, it has been proposed, implicate the idea of the abuse of basic bodily functions, the proper exercise of which is an object of basic self-esteem and the improper use of which is an object of shame and disgust. A sufficient, though not a necessary, condition of the obscenity of a communication is that the act depicted be obscene.

On this view, the precise application of the notion of the obscene crucially depends on beliefs and attitudes involving precise and rigid definitions of the proper exercise of bodily functions. Thus, different cultures, with different beliefs and attitudes, may regard dissimilar acts or objects as obscene. Similarly, within a culture, individuals may apply the label *obscene* to different phenomena. In the United States, for example, many people regard pornography as obscene because it reflects, for them, an improper exercise of sexual function. But others, not sharing their beliefs and attitudes, do not regard pornography as obscene,[82] though they may think that other things, like depictions of coprophagy or gratuitous violence, are obscene.

An obscenity law, then, must be understood as a political expression of broader popular attitudes toward the putative proper and improper use of the body. It is no accident that such laws have been used to forbid the transport of abortifacient and contraceptive information [83] and dissemination of sex manuals [84] and to prosecute advocacy of contraception and population control.[85] The moral attitudes behind such laws, directed against a supposed "abuse" of the body, were founded on a compound of religious, psychological, and medical beliefs basic to which was a deep fear of masturbation.[86] Masturbation, it was believed, led directly to physical debility and even death,[87] as well as crime and civil disorder.[88]

In judicial interpretation of the notion of the obscene, courts implicitly decide on and enforce popular attitudes about bodily function. Whatever may be the constitutional legitimacy of regulating obscene acts, it is impossible to see how regulating obscene communications can avoid raising the deepest First Amendment problems. Because judicial application of obscenity laws necessarily enforces a particular attitude, albeit presumably majoritarian, about the contents of communication, it seems to be obnoxious in principle to the central moral purpose of the First Amendment—to secure the greatest equal liberty of communication compatible with a like liberty for all.

Endnotes

1. For an interesting consideration of this general problem, see J. Feinberg, "Limits to the Free Expression of Opinion," J. Feinberg and H. Gross, *Philosophy of Law*, pp. 135–151.

2. I take the notion of a system of free expression from T. Emerson, *The System of Freedom of Expression* (1970).

3. See A. Meiklejohn, *Political Freedom* 21–28 (1960).

4. See A. Meiklejohn, *supra* note 3. Meiklejohn attempted to defend his view by interpreting the political quite broadly. A. Meiklejohn, "The First Amendment Is an Absolute," 1961 *Sup.Ct.Rev.* 245, 255–257, 262–263.

5. See Z. Chafee, Book Review, 62 *Harv.L.Rev.* 891, 896–898 (1949).

6. As an explication, this account seems to have more explanatory power than other comparable general theories of the First Amendment. Unlike Meiklejohn's theory, it accounts for the fact that free expression is not limited to politics. See Meiklejohn, *supra* note 3. It also accounts for the clear and present danger test, unlike the work of Thomas Emerson. See T. Emerson, *supra* note 2; T. Emerson, *Toward a General Theory of the First Amendment* (1966).

7. See, e.g., Cox v. Louisiana, 379 U.S. 536, 554–55 (1965); Poulos v. New Hampshire, 345 U.S. 395, 405 (1953); Kovacs v. Cooper, 336 U.S. 77 (1949).

8. See, e.g., A Book Named "John Cleland's Memoirs of a Woman of Pleasure" v. Attorney General, 383 U.S. 413, 427 (1966) (Douglas, J., concurring); Kingsley International Pictures Corp. v. Regents, 360 U.S. 684, 688–89 (1959); Roth v. United States, 354 U.S. 476, 484 (1957); Terminiello v. Chicago, 337 U.S. 1, 3–5 (1949).

9. See, e.g., Brandenburg v. Ohio, 395 U.S. 444 (1969); Dennis v. United States, 341 U.S. 494 (1951).

10. See, e.g., Roth v. United States, 354 U.S. 476, 484 (1957) (all ideas with the slightest redeeming social value have First Amendment protection); Joseph Burstyn, Inc. v. Wilson, 343 U.S. 495 (1952).

11. See J. Barron, "Access to the Press—a New First Amendment Right," 80 *Harv.L.Rev.* 1641 (1967).

12. See 7 *Oxford English Dictionary* 0.26 (1961).

13. See *Webster's Third New International Dictionary* 1557 (1965).

14. A. Kaplan, "Obscenity as an Esthetic Category," 20 *Law & Contemp. Prob.* 544, 550 (1955).

15. H. Ellis, *On Life and Sex* 175 (1962); G. Gorer, *The Danger of Equality* 218 (1966); W. Allen, "The Writer and the Frontiers of Tolerance," in *"To Deprave and Corrupt . . ."* 141, 147 (J. Chandos ed. 1962).

16. See notes 12 and 13 *supra*.

17. "O, forfend it, God, that, in a Christian climate,

souls refin'd should show so heinous, black, obscene a deed!" W. Shakespeare, *Richard II*, act 4, sc. 1. The deed in question is a subject's judging his king.

18. J.P. Sartre, *Being and Nothingness* 401–402 (H. Barnes trans. 1956): cf. the notion of "the jest obscene," as used in Nitocris's condemnation of her son in Handel, *Belshazzar*, act I, sc. 4 (1744).

19. *Sir Charles Sedley's Case*, 83 Eng.Rep. 1146 (K.B.1663). Sir Charles Sedley was here convicted "for shewing himself naked in a balcony, and throwing down bottles (pist in) vi & armis among the people in Covent Garden, contra pacem and to the scandal of the Government," *Id.* at 1146–1147. Sedley's conduct was condemned for its intrinsic obscenity as well as on the four additional grounds of indecent exposure, blasphemy, throwing missiles containing urine, and inciting to the small riot that ensued. See L. M. Alpert, "Judicial Censorship of Obscene Literature," 52 *Harv.L.Rev.* 40, 41–43 (1938). One commentary on these events states that Sedley also excreted in public. See A. Craig, *The Banned Books of England* 23–24 (1962); D. Thomas, *A Long Time Burning* 81 (1969).

20. Thus, the prurient interest test for obscenity, established in Roth v. United States, 354 U.S. 476, 487 (1957), and reaffirmed in Miller v. California, 413 U.S. 15, 24 (1973), and Paris Adult Theatre I v. Slaton, 413 U.S. 49 (1973), is defined in terms of "a shameful or morbid interest in nudity, sex, or excretion."

21. See *Model Penal Code* § 207.10, Comment at 1, 10, 29–31 (Tent.Draft No. 6 1957), and commentary thereon in L.B. Schwartz, "Morals Offenses and the Model Penal Code," 63 *Col.L.Rev.* 669 (1963), reprinted in Feinberg and Gross, *Philosophy of Law* 152–161. See also Kaplan, *supra* note 14, at 556.

22. For example, Alexander Pope in his remarkable denunciations of Curl in *The Dunciad* uses "obscene" in excretory contexts. See A. Pope, *The Dunciad* 299, 300 (J. Sutherland ed. 1963) (first published 1728, 1743).

23. For example, in Cavalli's characteristically lascivious opera *La Calisto* (ca. 1650), Calisto's amorous approach to the goddess Diana is rejected with "Taci, lascia, taci/Qual, qual delirio osceno/l'ingeno ti confonde?" meaning, "Silence, lascivious girl!/What, what obscene dilirium/has come over your reason?" Cavalli, *La Calisto*, act I, sc. 1.

24. For a useful general account, see Alpert, *supra* note 19. For accounts of English legal development, see D. Thomas, *supra* 19; N. St. John–Stevas, *Obscenity and the Law* (1956). For the best general account of earlier American developments, see W.B. Lockhart and R.C. McClure, "Literature, the Law of Obscenity, and the Constitution," 38 *Minn.L.Rev.* 295 (1954).

25. Comstock Act § 2, ch. 258, § 2, 17 Stat. 598, 599 (1873), as amended, 18 U.S.C. 1461 (1970).

26. See E. Sagarin, *The Anatomy of Dirty Words* (1962); Read, "An Obscenity Symbol," 9 *Am.Speech* 264 (1934).

27. For the force of such expressions in psychoanalysis, see S. Ferenczi, *Sex in Psychoanalysis* 132–153 (E. Jones trans. 1950); cf. Stone, "On the Principal Obscene Word of the English Language," 33 *Int'l J. Psycho–Anal.* 30 (1954).

28. See *Songs and Slang of the British Soldier* 1914–1918,

at 15 (3d ed. Brophy & Partridge eds. 1931).

29. See, e.g., J. Swift, *A Tale of a Tub, in Gulliver's Travels and Other Writings* 245, 327–329, 334–336 (L. Landa ed. 1960); J. Swift, *A Voyage to Lilliput, in id.* 3, 34–35.

30. See A. Pope, *supra* note 22, at 299–300, 303–304, 306, 308–314.

31. Cf. D. Thomas, *supra* note 19, at 273–274, 313–314 (1969); S. Sontag, *Styles of Radical Will* 35–73 (1969).

32. Cf. S. Freud, *Wit and Its Relation to the Unconscious*, in *The Basic Writings of Sigmund Freud* 631, 692–697 (A. Brill trans. & ed. 1938).

33. I am indebted, for this idea of the relevance of the demeaning to the obscene, to criticisms of John Kleining.

34. See M. Douglas, *Purity and Danger* (1966).

35. See *id.* 41–57.

36. See, e.g., *Leviticus* 11–15, 17–18.

37. See Aristotle *Nicomachean Ethics* 116–251 (M. Ostwald trans. 1962).

38. See notes 66 and 67 *infra* and accompanying text.

39. Cf. Honigman, "A Cultural Theory of Obscenity," in *Sexual Behavior and Personality Characteristics* 31 (M. DeMartino ed. 1963).

40. See W. LaBarre, "Obscenity: An Anthropological Appraisal," 20 *Law and Contemp. Prob.* 533, 541–542 (1955). Geoffrey Gorer cites the Trobriand Islanders as a people who finds public eating of solid food an obscenity; G. Gorer, *supra* note 15. For a discussion of the Indian idea that eating may be polluting, see M. Douglas, *supra* note 34, at 33–34.

41. The suggestion of the reversal of the roles of eating and excretion (namely, that eating would be obscene and excretion a social occasion) is the subject of one scene of hilarious social satire in L. Bunuel's movie *Le Fantôme de la Liberté* (1974).

42. E.g., the movie *La Grande Bouffe* (1974).

43. E.g., the famous eating scene in the movie *Tom Jones* (1963).

44. Rex v. Curl, 93 Eng.Rep. 849 (K.B.1727).

45. See N. St. John–Stevas, *supra* note 24, at 29–65.

46. For a literary analysis of some notable examples of Victorian pornography, see S. Marcus, *The Other Victorians* (1966).

47. E.g., the Customs Consolidating Act of 1853. 16 & 17 Vict., c. 107 (repealed by Customs Consolidating Act of 1876, 39 & 40 Vict., c. 36 paragraphs 42, 288); and Lord Campbell's Act of 1857, 20 & 21 Vict., c. 83 (repealed by Obscene Publications Act of 1959, 7 & 8 Eliz. 2, c. 66, paragraph 3(8)).

48. In 1948, the Supreme Court expressly declined to find that depictions of violence could be obscene, Winters v. New York, 333 U.S. 507 (1948), but this holding seems quite questionable today in view of growing modern usage. My views on the obscenity of violence and death gratefully acknowledge helpful criticisms of Joel Feinberg.

49. See note 59 *infra* and associated text.

50. See H.M. Hyde, *A History of Pornography* 3–8 (1964); N. St. John–Stevas, *supra* note 24, at 70–74, 98–103. See also notes 83, 84, and 85 *infra*.

51. Compare, e.g., Paris Adult Theatre I v. Slaton, 413 U.S. 49, 52 (Burger, C.J., emphasized the occurrence of "scenes of simulated fellatio, cunnilingus, and group sex intercourse") and Mishkin v. New York, 383 U.S. 502, 508 (1965) (depictions of flagellation, fetishism, and lesbianism held obscene), with Sunshine Book Co. v. Summerfield, 355 U.S. 372 (1958) (per curiam), rev'd 249 F.2d 114 (D.C.Cir.1957), aff'd 128 F.Supp. 564 (D.D.C.1955) (nudity per se not obscene). Cf. R. Kuh, *Foolish Figleaves?* 306–307 (1967) (suggesting that pictured bestiality and homosexuality are more obscene than comparable pictured heterosexuality).

52. See J. Feinberg, " 'Harmless Immoralities' and Offensive Nuisances," in *Issues in Law and Morality* 83, 87 (N. Care and T. Trelogan eds. 1973).

53. This proposal has been made with respect to sexual contents. See E. Sagarin, *supra* note 26, at 9–12, 160–174. Lenny Bruce, according to the show *The World of Lenny Bruce*, sc. 1 (1974), predicted the day when, pursuant to his view of the nonobscenity of sex, the erstwhile sexual obscenities would be used as forms of congratulation and good wishes.

54. See, e.g., *Webster's Third New International Dictionary* 1767 (1966).

55. See H.M. Hyde, *supra* note 50 at 1, 10.

56. See, e.g., M. Peckham *Art and Pornography* 46–47 (1969); A. Kinsey, *Sexual Behavior in the Human Female* 671–672 (1953); E. Kronhausen and P. Kronhausen, *Pornography and the Law* 262, 265 (1959).

57. See H.M. Hyde, *supra* note 50, at 30–58; D. Loth, *The Erotic in Literature* 41–68 (1961); M. Peckham, *supra* note 56, at 257–301: La Barre *supra* note 40, at 533–35.

58. The example of coprophagy occurs in M. de Sade, *120 Days of Sodom,* in 2 *The Complete Marquis de Sade* 215, 222 (P. Gillette trans. 1966). De Sade suggests other examples, such as eating vomit, which someone might find obscene, even if he would not find pornography obscene. *Id.* 215.

59. See R. Haney, *Comstockery in America* 58–59, 67–69, 75 (1960); D. Loth, *supra* note 57, at 208–233; L. Marcuse, *Obscene: The History of an Indignation* 307–327 (K. Gershon trans. 1965); M. Peckham, *supra* note 56, t 19–20; B. Russell, *Marriage and Morals* 93–117 (1929).

60. See H. Ellis, *supra* note 15, at 21–37; E. Kronhausen and P. Kronhausen, *supra* note 56, at 167; B. Russell, *supra* note 59, at 106–107.

61. H. Gardiner, "Moral Principles Toward a Definition of the Obscene," 20 *Law & Contemp. Prob.* 560, 564 (1955).

62. This quaint phrase appears in Gardiner, *id.* 567.

63. See Augustine, *The City of God* 470–472 (M. Dods trans. 1950). St. Thomas is in accord with Augustine's view. Of the emission of semen apart from generation in marriage, he wrote, "after the sin of homicide whereby a human nature already in existence is destroyed, this type of sin appears to take next place, for by it the generation of human nature is precluded." T. Aquinas, *On the Truth of the Catholic Faith: Summa Contra Gentiles* 146 (V. Bourke trans. 1946).

64. See A. Comfort, *The Anxiety Makers* (1970); J. Haller and R. Haller, *The Physician and Sexuality in Victorian*

America 199–234 (1974); S. Marcus, *supra* note 46; E.H. Hare, "Masturbational Insanity: The History of an Idea," 108 *J. Mental Science* 1, 6–9 (1962).

65. A. Comstock, *Traps for the Young* 136 (R. Bremner ed. 1967). See also *id.* 132–133, 139, 145, 169, 179, 205; A. Comstock, *Frauds Exposed* 388–389, 416, 437–438, 440–441 (1880; reprinted 1969).

66. See S. Marcus, *supra* note 46, at 24–25, 233, 243.

67. See H. Ellis, *supra* note 19, at 21–25. On the fundamental mistake involved in confusing sexual and excretory function, see W. Masters and V. Johnson, *Human Sexual Inadequacy* 10 (1970), who state: "Seemingly, many cultures and certainly many religions have risen and fallen on their interpretation and misinterpretation of one basic physiological fact. Sexual functioning is a natural physiological process, yet it has a unique facility that no other natural physiological process, such as respiratory, bladder, or bowel function, can imitate. *Sexual responsivity can be delayed indefinitely or functionally denied for a lifetime.* No other basic physiological process can claim such malleability of physical expression."

68. A. Comfort, *supra* note 64, at 57.

69. *Id.* 155, 161.

70. The Queen v. Hicklin, L.R. 3 Q.B. 359, 372 (1868).

71. See D.H. Lawrence, *Sex, Literature, and Censorship* 64–81 (1953). For similar sentiments, see M. Mead, "Sex and Censorship in Contemporary Society," in *New World Writing*, 7, 19–21 (1953).

72. See *United States Comm'n on Obscenity and Pornography, Report of the Comm'n on Obscenity and Pornography* 210–212 (GPO ed. 1979) [hereinafter *Report*] cf. J.W. Higgins & M.B. Katzman, "Determinants in the Judgment of Obscenity," 125 *Am.J.Psychiat.* 1733 (1969).

73. 413 U.S. at 24 (quoting Roth, 354 U.S. at 489).

74. *Id.* 25. In Jenkins v. Georgia, 418 U.S. 153 (1974), the Court made clear the force of these requirements; the movie *Carnal Knowledge* could not constitutionally be found obscene, for the depictions therein are not sexually explicit within the meaning of the *Miller* tests.

75. 413 U.S. at 27–28.

76. 413 U.S. at 24–25.

77. A Book Named "John Cleland's Memoirs of a Woman of Pleasure" v. Massachusetts, 383 U.S. 413, 419 (1966).

78. 413 U.S. at 30–34.

79. The Court thus rejected the previously urged view that the standards to be applied were national, not local. E.g., Jacobellis v. Ohio, 378 U.S. 184, 192–193 (1974) (Brennan, J.).

80. 394 U.S. 557 (1969).

81. United States v. Orito, 413 U.S. 139 (1973); United States v. 12 200–Ft. Reels of Film, 413 U.S. 123 (1973).

82. See notes 57 to 60 *supra.*

83. See note 25 *supra;* 18 U.S.C. paragraph 1461 (1964), as amended, 18 U.S.C. paragraph 1461 (1970) (mail); 18 U.S.C. paragraph 1462(c), as amended, 18 U.S.C. paragraph 1462(c) (1970) (interstate commerce).

84. See, e.g., United States v. Chesman, 19 F. 497 (E.D.Mo.1881).

85. See, e.g., United States v. Bennett, 24 F.Cas, 1093, No. 14, 571 (C.C.S.D.N.Y.1879); Regina v. Bradlaugh, 2 Q.B.D. 569 (1977), *rev'd on other grounds*, 3 A.B.D. 607 (1878).

86. See text accompanying notes 61 to 70, *supra.*

87. Comstock, for example. noted the case of a thirteen-year-old girl, in whose bureau he "found a quantity of the most debasing and foul-worded matter. The last heard from this child was she was in a dying condition, the result of habits induced by this foul reading." A. Comstock, *Traps for the Young* 139 (R. Bremner ed. 1967).

88. Comstock cited a number of instances where, in his view, access to obscene material led to robbery, burglary, and murder. A. Comstock, *Frauds Exposed* 437–39 (1880, reprinted 1969). See also A. Comstock, *supra* note 87, at 132–33, 169, 179).

Review Questions

1. How does Richards interpret the First Amendment?

2. Explain Richards' account of the obscene.

3. According to Richards, what is pornography and how is it related to the obscene?

4. Why doesn't Richards accept the Supreme Court's decisions in *Miller* and *Paris Adult Theatre?*

Discussion Questions

1. The First Amendment requires that Congress pass no law abriding freedom of speech and press. But the courts have held that certain expressions are not protected. Can you think of examples of these unprotected expressions?

2. Given the fact that there are various sorts of unprotected expressions, is Richards' interpretation of the First Amendment acceptable? Why or why not?

3. Can you think of any counterexamples to Richards' definition of the obscene? What are they?

4. All things considered, should pornography be censored? What is your position?

Grant Gillett

AIDS and Confidentiality

Dr. Grant Gillett is Senior Lecturer in Medical Ethics, University of Otago Medical School, New Zealand.

Gillett discusses a case in which a man infected with the AIDS virus insists that his condition be kept confidential, even from his wife. After considering a deontological and a rule-utilitarian defense of confidentiality, Gillett argues that the doctor's moral duty does not require that the patient's request for confidentiality be honored. The duty to do this is only a prima facie *duty that can be overridden by stronger moral duties such as the duty to not harm others.*

From Grant Gillett, "AIDS and Confidentiality," *Journal of Applied Philosophy*, Vol. 4, No. 1 (1987), pp. 15–20. Reprinted by permission of the editor and the author, Grant Gillett, University of Otago Medical School.

Does a doctor confronted by a patient with AIDS have a duty to maintain absolute confidentiality or could that doctor be considered to have some overriding duty to the sexual contacts of the AIDS sufferer? AIDS or Acquired Immune Deficiency Syndrome is a viral disease transmitted for the most part by sexual contact. It is fatal in the short or long term (i.e. nine months to six years) in those infected people who go on to develop the full-blown form of the disease.

Let us say that a 39-year-old man goes to his family doctor with a dry persistent cough which has lasted three or four weeks and a 10 day history of night sweats. He admits that he is bisexually active. He is tested and found to have antibodies to HIV virus (indicating that he is infected with the virus that causes AIDS). In the setting of this clinical picture he must be considered to have the disease. He is told of his condition and also, in the course of a prolonged interview, of the risk to his wife and of the distinct possibility of his children aged one and three years old being left without parents should she contract the disease. He refuses to allow her to be told of his condition. The doctor finally accedes to his demand for absolute confidentiality. After one or two initial illnesses which are successfully combatted he dies some 18 months later. Over the last few weeks of his life he relents on his former demands and allows his wife to be informed of his problem. She is tested and, though asymptomatic, is found to be antibody positive. A year later she goes to the doctor with fever, dry cough and loss of appetite. Distraught on behalf of her children, she bitterly accuses the doctor of having failed her and them by allowing her husband to infect her when steps could have been taken to diminish the risk had she only known the truth.

In this case there is a powerful inclination to say that the wife is justified in her grievance. It seems just plain wrong for her doctor to sit back and allow her to fall victim to a fatal disease because of the wish of her husband. Against this intuition we can mobilise two powerful arguments—one deontological and the other utilitarian (of a rule or restricted utilitarian type).[1]

(i) On a deontological view the practice of medicine will be guided by certain inviolate or absolute rules (not to harm, not to neglect the welfare of one's patients, etc.). Among these will be respect for confidentiality. Faced with this inviolable principle the deontologically inclined physician will not disclose what he has been told in confidence—he will regard the tacit agreement not to disclose his patient's affairs to others as tantamount to a substantive promise which he cannot break. Against this, in the present case, we might urge his *prima facie* duty not to neglect the welfare of his other patient, the young man's wife. His inaction has contributed to her death. In response to this he could both defend the absolute duty to respect confidentiality in general and urge some version of the doctrine of double effect,[2] claiming that his clear duty was to honour his implicit vow of confidentiality but it had the unfortunate effect, which he had foreseen as possible but not intended, that it caused the death of his other patient. One is inclined to offer an intuitive response such as 'No moral duty is so binding that you can hazard another person's life in this manner'. It is a notorious feature of deontological systems that they involve conflicts of duties for which there exists no principled method of resolution.

(ii) A rule-utilitarian doctor can mount a more convincing case. He can observe that confidentiality is a cornerstone of a successful AIDS practice. Lack of confidentiality can cause the irrational victimisation of sufferers by a poorly educated public who are prone to witch-hunts of all kinds. The detection and treatment of AIDS, and the consequent protection of that large group of people who have contacts with the patients being treated depends on the patients who seek medical advice believing that medical confidentiality is inviolate. If confidentiality were seen as a relative duty only, suspended or breached at the discretion of the doctor, then far fewer cases would present for detection and crucial guidance about diminishing risks of spread would not be obtained. This would lead to more people suffering and dying. It may be hard on a few, unfortunate enough to be involved with people like the recalcitrant young husband, but the general welfare can only be served by a compassionate but resolute refusal to abandon sound principles in the face of such cases. Many find this a convincing argument but I will argue that it is superficial in the understanding of moral issues that it espouses.

Imagine, in order to soften the way for a rather less neatly argued position, a doctor confronted by a young man who has a scratched face and blood on his shirt and who wants to be checked for VD. In the course of the doctor's taking his history it emerges that he has forcibly raped two women and is worried that the second was a prostitute. He says to the doctor "Of course, I am telling you this in confidence, doc, because I know that you won't rat on me". Producing a knife, he then says, "See, this is the blade that I get them going with". Rather troubled, the doctor takes samples and tells the young man that there is no evidence of VD. He tries to talk his patient into giving himself up for some kind of psychiatric treatment but the young man is adamant. It becomes clear that he has certain delusional and persecutional ideas. Two days later the doctor reads that his patient has been arrested because after leaving the surgery he raped and savagely mutilated a young woman who, as a result, required emergency surgery for multiple wounds and remains in a critical condition.

Here we might well feel that any principle which dictates that it is the moral duty of the doctor to keep silent is wrong—but as yet no principles conflicting with or supplementing those above have been introduced. A possible loophole is introduced by the rapist's sadomasochism and probable psychosis but we need to spell out why this is relevant. In such a case we suspend our normal moral obligations to respect the avowed interests of the patient and claim that he is incompetent to make a responsible and informed assessment of his own interests and so we assume the right to make certain decisions on his behalf. In this case it would probably mean arranging for him to be given psychiatric help and society to be protected from him in the meantime. Notice that he may have demonstrated a 'lucid' and 'intelligent' grasp of his predicament, vis-à-vis his own wish to avoid detection but we discern that his instrumental rationality is deployed in service of a deep or moral insanity. His lack of awareness of the enormity of what he is doing to others counts as a sufficient basis to diagnose madness even in the face of astute inferential thought. He is insane because a normal person would never begin from the moral position he occupies and so his rights, including

that to medical confidentiality, are suspended. He has moved outside the community of trust, mutual concern and non-malificence in which moral considerations for the preferences of others have their proper place. It is not that one 'contracts in' to such a community,[3] nor that one in any sense volunteers,[4] but rather one is a *de facto* member of it by virtue of possessing those human sensitivities and vulnerabilities which give moral predicates their meaning and importance.[5] Such weight as one claims for one's own personal privileges and moral principles—such as the demand for confidentiality—is derived from a 'form of life' where the interpersonal transactions which define trust, respect, harm, and so on, are in play (it is important that no particular ideological overlay has been grafted onto these). Of the insane rapist we can say that he has excluded himself from that moral community by the very fact of his violation of certain of its most basic tenets and assumptions. He has no right to demand a full place in that structure where morally significant human exchanges are operative because his behavior and attitudes do not fit the place to which he pretends. We are, of course, not released from a *prima facie* duty to try and help him in his odious predicament but we cannot be expected to accord him the full privileges of a member of the moral community as he persists, for whatever reason, in callously turning his back on the constraints normally operative there (albeit, perhaps, without reflective malevolence in its more usual forms). So, in this case, confidentiality can be suspended for legitimate moral reasons. The mad rapist has moved beyond the pale in terms of normal moral interactions and though we may have a duty to try and restore him to full participation within that order we are also entitled to protect ourselves in the interim at the expense of those considerations that would apply to a normal person. Notice again that the boundaries of our attitudes are not arbitrary or merely conventional but involve our most basic human feelings and reactions to one another.[6]

We can now move from a case where insanity weights the decision in a certain direction to a case where the issues are more purely moral. Imagine that a 45–year-old man goes to see his family doctor and is also worried about a sexually transmitted disease. On being questioned he admits, in confidence, not only to intercourse with a series of prostitutes but also to forced sexual intercourse with his daughter. He is confident that she will not tell anyone what is happening because she is too ashamed and scared. After counselling he gives no sign of a wish to change his ways but rather continues to justify himself because of his wife's behaviour. The doctor later hears from the school psychological service that the daughter is showing some potentially serious emotional problems.

Here, it seems to me, we have few compunctions about setting in motion that machinery to deal with child abuse, even though the sole source of our information is what was said, in medical confidence, by the father. The justification we might give for the doctor's actions is illuminating. We are concerned for the actual harm being done to the child, both physical and psychological, and we overturn the father's injunction to confidence in order to prevent further harm being done. In so doing we class the situation as one in which a *prima facie* moral claim can be suspended because of the actions and attitudes involved. I believe that we do so because we implicitly realise that here also the agent has acted in such a way as to put himself beyond the full play of moral consideration and to justify our withholding certain of his moral 'dues'. Confidentiality functions to allow the patient to be honest with the doctor and to put trust in him. Trust is (at least in part) a two-way thing and can only exist between morally sensitive human beings (this, of course, blurs a vast range of distinctions between degrees of sensitivity). A basic element of such moral attitudes is the responsiveness of the agents concerned to the moral features of human interactions. The legiti-

mate expectation that a doctor be trustworthy and faithful to his patient's wishes regardless of the behaviour of that patient is undermined when the patient abuses the relationship so formed in ways which show a lack of these basic human reactions because it is just these reactions which ground the importance of confidentiality in general. Therefore, if the father in this example refuses to accept the enormity of what he is doing to his daughter, he thereby casts doubt upon his standing as a moral agent. Stated baldly, that sounds like an open warrant for moralistic medical paternalism, but I do not think it need be. In asking that his affairs be concealed from others, a person is demanding *either* the right to preserve himself from the harms that might befall him if the facts about his life were generally known, *or* that his sensitivity as an individual be respected and protected. On either count it is inconsistent for him to claim some moral justification for that demand when it is made solely with the aim of allowing him to inflict comparable disregard or harm upon another. By his implicit intention to use a position, which only remains tenable with the collusion of the doctor, callously to harm another individual, the father undermines the moral force of his own appeal. His case is only worsened by the fact that from any moral perspective he would be considered to have a special and protective obligation toward his own offspring.

Implicit within what I have said is a reappraisal of the nature of medical confidentiality. I have argued that it is not to be treated as an absolute duty but is rather to rank among other *prima facie* duties and responsibilities of the doctor-patient relationship. Just as the performance of a life-saving procedure can be vetoed by the patient's choice to forego treatment, even though it is a doctor's duty to strive for his patient's life, so each of these duties can be negated by certain considerations. One generally attempts to prevent a fatal illness overtaking a patient but in the case of a deformed neonate or an elderly and demented patient often the attempt is not made. In the case of confidentiality, I have claimed that we recognise the right of a patient to preserve his own personal life as inviolate. We accept that patients can and should share with a doctor details which it would not be right to disclose to other people. But we must also recognise that implicit within this recognition is the assumption that the patient is one of us, morally speaking. Our attitude to him and his rights assumes that he is one of or a participant in a community of beings who matter (or are morally interacting individuals like himself to whom the same considerations apply). We could offer a superficial and rather gross systematisation of this assumption in the universalisability test.[7] The patient in the last two cases applies a standard to his own human concerns which he is not prepared to extend to others involved with him in relevant situations. We must therefore regard his moral demands as spurious; we are not at liberty to harm him but we are bound to see that his cynical abuse of the moral code within which he lives does not harm others. At this point it might be objected that we are on a 'slippery slope'. Will any moral transgression suffice to undermine the moral privileges of the patient? I do not think that this extreme conclusion can be supported from what I have said. Williams, remarking on the tendency to slide down 'slippery slopes', observes, "that requires that there should be some motive to move from one step to the next" and "Possible cases are not enough, and the situation must have some other feature which means that those cases have to be confronted."[8] Here we are not in such a position. Doctors in general have a strong tendency to protect their patients and keep their confidences. They require strong moral pressures to contemplate doing otherwise. All I have sought to do is to make explicit the moral justification upon which these exceptions can be seen to rest. I have not spelled out any formal decision-making procedure whereby the right answer will be yielded in each case. Indeed it is possible that whereas grounds and reasons recommending a certain course of action are the lifeblood of moral philosophy, such clearcut principles and derivations are a 'will o' the wisp'.

Now we can return to the AIDS patient. From what I have said it becomes clear that it is only the moral intransigent who forces us to breach confidentiality. In most cases it will be possible to guide the patient into telling those who need to know or allowing them to be told (and where it is possible to so guide him it will be mandatory to involve him in an informed way). In the face of an expressed disregard for the harm being caused to those others concerned, we will be morally correct in abandoning what would otherwise be a binding obligation. We should and do feel the need to preserve and protect the already affected life of the potential victim of his deception and in this feeling we exhibit a sensitivity to moral rectitude. Of course, it is only the active sexual partners of the patient who are at risk and thus it is only to them that we and the patient have a moral duty (in this respect talk of 'society at large' is just rhetoric). If it is the case that sexual activity, as Nagel claims, involves a mutual openness in those who have intercourse,[9] one could plausibly argue that the cynical moral and interpersonal attitudes here evinced undermined the patient's sexual rights (assuming that people have such). The sexual activity of this individual is aberrant or perverted in the important respect that it involves a harmful duplicity toward or deception of his sexual partner. Whereas people may have a right to sexual fulfilment in general, they can hardly be said to have a right to perverted sexual fulfilment; but both Nagel's contentions and this talk of rights are contentious and it is outside my present brief to discuss them.

The doctor's obligation to inform, in the face of an enjoinder to keep his confidence, can, even if I am right, be seen to be restricted to those in actual danger and would in no wise extend to employers, friends or non-sexually interacting relatives of the patient or any other person with an even more peripheral interest. His duty extends only so far as to avert the actual harm that he can reasonably expect to arise from his keeping confidence.

Given the intransigent case, one further desideratum presents itself. I believe that doctors should be open with their patients and that therefore the doctor is bound to share his moral dilemma with the patient and inform him of his intention to breach confidentiality. I think he can legitimately claim a pre-emptive duty to prevent harm befalling his patients and should do so in the case of the abuse of others which the patient intends. It may be the case, with the insane rapist for instance, that the doctor will need to deceive in order to carry out his prevailing duty but this will hardly ever be so, and should, I believe, be regarded as unacceptable in general.

One thorny problem remains—the possible deleterious effect on the detection and treatment of AIDS if confidentiality is seen as only a relative principle in medical practice. Clearly, if the attitude were ever to take root that the medical profession could not be trusted to 'keep their mouths shut' then the feared effect would occur. I believe that where agencies and informal groups were told of the *only* grounds on which confidentiality would be breached and the *only* people who would be informed then this effect would not occur.

It seems to me that the remarkable intensification of one's sensitivity to personal and ethical values that is produced by contact with life-threatening or 'abyss' situations means that the cynical abuse of confidentiality by the patient which I have sought to address is likely to be both rare and transient. The greatest resource available to any of us in 'the valley of the shadow' is the closeness of those who will walk alongside us, and for many that will be a close spiritual and sexual partner. Confidentiality within the mutuality of that relationship rather than interpersonal dishonesty would thus seem to be vital to the welfare not only of the co-respondent but also of the patient himself as he struggles to

cope with the disease that has him in its grip. To foster that welfare seems to me to be as close as a doctor can ever come to an absolute duty.

Endnotes

1. John Rawls, "Two Concepts of Rules," *Philosophical Review* 64 (1955): 3–32.
2. Jonathan Glover, *Causing Death and Saving Lives* (London: Penguin, 1977).
3. As is suggested by John Rawls in *A Theory of Justice* (Cambridge, Mass.: Harvard University Press, 1971).
4. Philippa Foot, "Morality As a System of Hypothetical Imperatives," in *Virtues and Vices* (Berkeley: University of California Press, 1978).
5. John McDowell suggests that one imbibes the capacities for such judgements as part of the rule-following in which one acquires language, in "Virtue and Reason," *Monist* 62 (1978): 331–350.
6. I stress this point in order to distance the considerations that are guiding our judgement in this case from those situations in which an ideological framework has been used to override these very natural human reactions and provide a 'justification' for an inhuman moral code.
7. R.M. Hare, *Freedom and Reason* (New York: Oxford University Press, 1965).
8. Bernard Williams, "Which Slopes are Slippery?" in M. Lockwood, ed., *Moral Dilemma in Modern Medicine* (Oxford: Oxford University Press, 1986).
9. Thomas Nagel, "Sexual Perversion," in *Mortal Questions* (London: Cambridge University Press, 1979).

Review Questions

1. What is the moral dilemma raised by the case of the man who tests positive for the AIDS virus?
2. Gillett discusses two arguments supporting confidentiality. What are they, and why doesn't Gillett accept them?
3. What is the point of the cases about the mad rapist and the child abuser?
4. How does Gillett view the nature of medical confidentiality?

Discussion Questions

1. Is the man who tests positive for the AIDS virus comparable to the mad rapist and the child abuser or not? Why or why not?
2. Suppose that certain people are, as Gillett says, beyond the pale of normal moral interaction. Does this mean that we have no moral

duties or obligations towards these people? What do you think?

3. Gillett admits that his position "sounds like an open warrant for moralistic medical paternalism." Does his view amount to this or not? Explain your answer.

4. Does a person with multiple sexual partners have a moral obligation to be routinely tested for the AIDS virus?

Problem Cases

1. Homosexuals in the Military (Reported in *The New York Times*, October 22, 1989.) The current policy of the Pentagon is to prohibit homosexuals from serving in the military. In 1982, the Pentagon issued a policy statement saying that men or women who engage in homosexual conduct undermine discipline, good order, and morale. The Pentagon has recently reaffirmed this statement, and added that it will exclude from military service those who have even a propensity to engage in homosexual activity.

Do you agree? Should homosexuals be barred from military service? If so, what is the reason?

2. Testing for AIDS We now have tests for the presence of the AIDS virus that are as reliable as any diagnostic test in medicine. An individual who tests positive can reasonably be presumed to carry the virus, whether or not he or she has symptoms of the disease. It should be noted, however, that false-positive and false-negative tests are possible.

Who should be tested? Some doctors recommend that everyone in the high-risk population (homosexual or bisexual men) should be tested for AIDS; otherwise the epidemic will get worse. Yet some people in the high-risk population refuse to be tested, claiming that they have a right not to be tested. They are afraid of being labeled, being quarantined, losing their jobs, or losing their health insurance. Are these people justified in refusing to be tested or not? What is your view?

One proposal is that there be some sort of mandatory testing for AIDS. For example, people who get marriage licenses could be required to get an AIDS test. What do you think? Should we have some kind of mandatory testing for AIDS or not? If so, how should it be carried out? And if not, why not?

3. The Gary Hart Case In the spring of 1987, Gary Hart was the front runner for the 1988 Democratic presidential nomination. Yet just twenty-five days after he had formally announced his candidacy, he suddenly withdrew from the race. His reason for this abrupt withdrawal was the scandal caused by a newspaper story in the *Miami Herald* which claimed that he had spent the night in his town house in Washington with a twenty-nine-year-old model named Donna Rice. Reporters for the newspaper had watched Hart's town house, and they asserted that they had observed Rice enter the house in the evening and leave the next morning. Although they had no proof of it, the reporters implied in their story that Hart and Rice had engaged in illicit sexual behavior during the night. Hart and Rice both denied that they had done anything immoral, and in his withdrawal speech, Hart accused the media of treating him unfairly. But when he was asked point-blank if he had ever committed adultery, Hart refused to answer. This was taken by the media as a tacit admission of adultery, at least at some time in the past.

This case raises some interesting questions:

a. Is the sexual behavior of a candidate for public office relevant in assessing the candidate's qualifications?

b. Should newspapers actively investigate the sexual behavior of public figures, or do these people have a right to privacy in this area?

c. Suppose, for the sake of discussion, that Hart was indeed guilty of committing adultery with his friend Rice. In your opinion, would this fact make him unqualified to hold public office? Why or why not?

4. Petit v. State Board of Education (1973) Mrs. Petit was a teacher of retarded, elementary-school children in the public-school system. She and her husband joined a private club in Los Angeles called The Swingers. An undercover policeman attended a private party during which Mrs. Petit was observed in several acts of oral copulation. She was arrested, charged with oral copulation under the California Penal Code, and pleaded guilty to the lesser charge of outraging public decency. After disciplinary proceedings, her teaching credentials were revoked on the grounds that her conduct involved moral turpitude. Although Mrs. Petit petitioned the courts to order the State Board of Education to restore her teaching credentials, the courts denied her request.

Was Mrs. Petit's conduct at the party morally wrong or not? Defend your view.

Should there be a law against private sex acts performed by consenting adults? Why, or why not?

5. Doe v. Commonwealth's Attorney for City of Richmond (1975) In this case, two anonymous homosexuals sought to have the Virginia sodomy statute making homosexual activity a crime declared unconstitutional. In a two-to-one decision, the District Court in Richmond, Virginia, upheld the constitutionality of the statute. The case was subsequently appealed to the United States Supreme Court, but in 1976, by a vote of six to three, the Court refused to hear arguments and affirmed the lower-court ruling.

Should there be a law making sodomy a crime? Defend your position.

Suggested Readings

(1) Robert Baker and Frederick Elliston, eds., *Philosophy and Sex,* new rev. ed. (Buffalo, NY: Prometheus Books, 1984). This anthology contains a number of useful articles relevant to sexual morality.

(2) Peter A. Bertocci, *Sex, Love, and the Person* (New York: Sheed & Ward, 1967). Bertocci defends conventional sexual morality.

(3) Paul Cameron, "A Case Against Homosexuality," *Human Life Review* 4 (Summer 1978), pp. 17–49. Cameron is a psychologist who provides us with facts about homosexuality. He maintains that it is an undesirable life-style.

(4) Joel Feinberg, *Offense to Others* (New York: Oxford University Press, 1985). Feinberg discusses pornography in Chapters 10–12.

(5) Burton Leiser, *Liberty, Justice and Morals,* 2d ed. (New York: Macmillan, 1979). In Chapter 2, Leiser discusses and attacks various arguments that are made for saying that homosexuality is morally wrong.

(6) Carol Levine and Joyce Bermel, eds., "AIDS: The Emerging Ethical Dilemmas," *Hastings Center Report, A Special Supplement* (August 1985), pp. 1–31. This report covers various issues arising from the AIDS epidemic.

(7) Donald Levy, "Perversion and the Unnatural as Moral Categories," in Alan Soble, ed., *The Phi-* losophy of Sex (Totowa, NJ: Littlefield, Adams and Co., 1980), pp. 169–189. Levy gives a survey of various definitions of sexual perversion, and then gives his own account.

(8) Gerald M. Oppenheimer and Robert A. Padgag, "AIDS: The Risks to Insurers, The Threat to Equity," *Hastings Center Report* (October 1986), pp. 18–22. The authors discuss the problems the AIDS crisis poses for the insurance industry.

(9) Christine Pierce and Donald VanDeVeer, eds., *AIDS: Ethics and Public Policy* (Belmont, CA: Wadsworth, 1987). This collection of readings includes David Mayo, "AIDS, Quarantines, and Non–Compliant Positives"; Donald Chambers, "AIDS Testing: An Insurer's Viewpoint"; Ronald Bayer and Gerald Oppenheimer, "AIDS in the Work Place: The Ethical Ramifications"; Kenneth R. Howe, "Why Mandatory Screening for AIDS Is a Very Bad Idea"; and many other interesting articles on AIDS and its implications.

(10) Vincent C. Punzo, *Reflective Naturalism* (New York: Macmillan, 1969). Punzo argues against premarital sexual intercourse. On his view, marriage is constituted by mutual and total commitment, and apart from this commitment, sexual unions are morally deficient.

(11) Richard Taylor, *Having Love Affairs* (Buffalo, NY: Prometheus Books, 1982.) Taylor claims that people have a right to love affairs even if they are married. He also thinks that there is nothing wrong or immoral with extralegal marriages, that is, people living together without being legally married.

(12) U.S. Department of Justice. *Attorney General's Commission on Pornography.* Final Report, July 1986. The commission surveyed and classified types of pornography. It found a causal relationship between violent pornography and sexual aggression, but there was disagreement about the harmfulness of nonviolent pornography.

(13) Russell Vannoy, *Sex Without Love* (Buffalo, NY: Prometheus Books, 1980). Vannoy defends sex for pleasure without love or marriage, and attacks the conservative view of sex.

(14) Carl Wellman, *Morals and Ethics* (Glenview, IL: Scott, Foresman, 1975). In Chapter 5, Wellman considers arguments given for and against the morality of premarital sex.

Chapter 9

Animals and the Environment

Introduction

Humans cause a great deal of animal suffering. Consider this example of animal experimentation taken from Peter Singer's book *Animal Liberation*. At the Lovelace Foundation in New Mexico, experimenters forced sixty-four beagles to inhale radioactive strontium 90. Twenty-five of the dogs died; initially most of them were feverish and anemic, and had hemorrhages and bloody diarrhea. One of the deaths occurred during an epileptic seizure, and another resulted from a brain hemorrhage. In a similar experiment, beagles were injected with enough strontium 90 to produce early death in 50 percent of the group. Are experiments such as these really necessary? It was already known that strontium 90 was unhealthy, and that the dogs would suffer and die. Furthermore, these experiments did not save any human lives or have any important benefits for humans. So why were they done?

Another common human practice that produces considerable animal suffering is factory farming. Take the treatment of veal calves, for example. In order to make their flesh pale and tender, these calves are given special treatment. They are put in narrow stalls and tethered with a chain so that they cannot turn around, lie down comfortably, or groom themselves. They are fed a totally liquid diet to promote rapid weight gain. This diet is deficient in iron, and, as a result, the calves lick the sides of the stall, which are impregnated with urine containing iron. They are given no water because thirsty animals eat more than those that drink water. Is this cruel treatment morally justified? Should we do this to animals just because we enjoy eating their flesh?

Speciesism In his book *Animal Liberation,* Singer introduces the term *speciesism.* As he defines it, speciesism is "a prejudice or attitude of bias toward the interests of members of one's own species and against those of members of other species." Singer goes on to argue that speciesism is analogous to racism and sexism. It is unjust to discriminate against blacks because of their color, or against women because of their sex. Their interests, e.g., their interest in voting, have to be considered equally to those of whites and men. Similarly, it is unjust to discriminate against nonhuman animals because of their species. Their interests, and particularly their interest in not suffering, have to be considered too.

But how do we go about reducing animal suffering? Does this mean that we should become vegetarians and eat no meat? Singer thinks so, but of course this is very controversial in our meat-eating society. In Singer's view we should stop eating meat in order to eliminate factory farming or at least to protest against it, and also because we should not treat animals as means to our end (to use Kant's phrase).

Singer's position is attacked by Bonnie Steinbock in our readings. Steinbock thinks that Singer's view has counterintuitive results. It implies, for example, that it is unfair to feed starving children before feeding starving dogs. But it seems intuitively obvious that the interests of humans are more important than those of animals. Why is this? According to Steinbock, humans have a higher moral status than animals because humans have certain morally relevant capacities that animals do not have, for example, the capacities to be morally responsible for actions, to have altruistic or moral reasons, and to desire self-respect.

Tom Regan takes a different position on the moral status of nonhuman animals. Unlike Singer, he does not want to appeal to any form of utilitarianism. According to Regan, utilitarianism is not an acceptable

moral theory because it incorrectly makes the morality of individual acts depend on how others behave. Nevertheless, Regan does think that we ought to be vegetarians and oppose commercial animal agriculture. The reason for doing this is not that there will be good consequences, but because some animals are persons who have moral rights, and commercial animal agriculture violates these rights.

Rights Theory In his defense of vegetarianism, Regan relies heavily on the concept of a moral right, but there is controversy about the meaning of the concept of a right and how it should be applied.

According to Joel Feinberg, to have a right is to have a claim *to* something and *against* someone. In his view, only beings who are capable of having interests are capable of having these claim-rights. But animals do have interests, and so they can have rights.

H. J. McCloskey has a different theory of rights. (His view is discussed in the Feinberg reading.) In McCloskey's analysis, a right is an entitlement to something and not a claim against someone. A person could have a right and not have a claim against someone else, for example, if he or she were the last person on earth. Nevertheless, McCloskey holds that being able to make a claim, either directly or through a representative, is essential to the possession of rights. Since animals cannot do this (or so McCloskey says), they cannot be possessors of rights.

Regan agrees with Feinberg that in order for an individual to have a right, there must be other people; it would not make sense to say that the last person on earth has any rights. In Regan's account, if an individual has a moral right, then there must be other moral agents who have a duty to respect it. But who possesses rights? Regan's answer is different from that of Feinberg or McCloskey. Regan's position is that only individuals who have inherent value have rights, where inherent value is a value that does not depend on utility. Those who have this inherent value are persons, and according to Regan, some animals are persons who have rights.

Sentientism   Singer assumes that only beings with mental states are a subject of moral concern. But isn't this sentientism (to put a label on it) just another kind of prejudice? He has escaped one prejudice, speciesism, only to embrace another, namely sentientism. Why not say that nonsentient things such as forests are of moral concern too? After all, human beings are rapidly destroying and polluting the natural environment. Isn't this morally wrong?

Holism   One way of defending environmental conservation and preservation is to argue that the environment has instrumental value for humans and animals. But William Godfrey–Smith thinks that instrumental justifications for environmental conservation— saving the wilderness because it is a cathedral, a laboratory, a silo, or a gymnasium— all fail to provide a satisfactory rationale. Not only are there conflicts between the activities justified, there is also the feeling that the wilderness has more than **instrumental value,** that it has an **intrinsic value.** Instead of sentientism or an anthropocentric view, Godfrey–Smith suggests that we adopt a holistic conception of nature where we think of humans and nature together forming a moral community, and where we must engage in cooperative behavior (and not exploitive behavior) for the sake of the health of the whole community. This means that we should have empathy for nature, and not think of ourselves as separate from it or superior to it.

Animal Liberation vs. Environmental Holism
We have two different views before us, the animal liberation view that nonhuman animals have rights, and the environmental holism view that the nonhuman environment

has intrinsic value. Are these two views compatible?

Some writers believe that they are not compatible; if you accept one, then you must reject the other. For example, Tom Regan, the animal liberationist, thinks that environmental holism amounts to environmental fascism because it implies that we are morally obligated to save wild grasses at the expense of the life and welfare of people. It is morally obvious, at least to Regan, that the interests of people are more important than the health and existence of wild grasses.

Some defenders of environmental holism, on the other hand, think that animal liberation is at odds with the goal of preserving the environment. As an example of the conflict between the environmental ethic and the ascription of rights to animals, we can take the situation on certain islands off the coast of New Zealand, where feral goats, pigs, and cats have had to be exterminated in order to protect indigenous species and habitats. This could not be justified on the animal rights view because it involves a violation of the rights of individual animals. This situation shows what is wrong with the animal rights view. Not only does it show no concern for the protection of the environment, it doesn't even recognize the importance of saving endangered species of plants and animals. Furthermore, animal liberationists are opposed to hunting, fishing, and rearing animals for food, but environmentalists have no objection to these practices provided they do not harm the environment. Indeed they believe hunting and fishing can help preserve natural habitats by preventing overpopulation.

Mary Ann Warren attempts to resolve the differences between these two rival positions. She argues that a harmonious marriage between the two is possible provided that each side makes some compromises. The animal liberationist must recognize that animal rights are not the same as human rights, and that animal rights can be overridden by environmental or utilitarian concerns more easily than can human rights. The environmentalist must realize that nonsentient natural entities do not have moral rights in the same way that sentient creatures with interests have rights, even though they do have an intrinsic value that makes them worth preserving. If it is stated in this way, the environmental view is fully compatible with animal liberation, and indeed supplements it, for it shows us why we should protect species of animals and plants, and not just individual animals.

Peter Singer

All Animals Are Equal

For biographical information on Singer, see his reading in Chapter 3.

Singer defines speciesism as a prejudice towards the interests of members of one's own species and against those of members of other species. He argues that speciesism is analogous to racism and sexism. If it is unjust to discriminate against women and blacks by not considering their interests, it is also unfair to ignore the interests of animals, particularly their interest in not suffering.

"Animal Liberation" may sound more like a parody of other liberation movements than a serious objective. The idea of "The Rights of Animals" actually was once used to parody the case for women's rights. When Mary Wollstonecraft, a forerunner of today's feminists, published her *Vindication of the Rights of Women* in 1792, her views were widely regarded as absurd, and before long an anonymous publication appeared entitled *A Vindication of the Rights of Brutes*. The author of this satirical work (now known to have been Thomas Taylor, a distinguished Cambridge philosopher)

From Peter Singer, *Animal Liberation* (The New York Review, 1975). Reprinted by permission of the author. Copyright © Peter Singer 1975. [One footnote has been deleted and the remaining ones renumbered.– Ed.]

tried to refute Mary Wollstonecraft's arguments by showing that they could be carried one stage further. If the argument for equality was sound when applied to women, why should it not be applied to dogs, cats, and horses? The reasoning seemed to hold for these "brutes" too, yet to hold that brutes had rights was manifestly absurd; therefore the reasoning by which this conclusion had been reached must be unsound, and if unsound when applied to brutes, it must also be unsound when applied to women, since the very same arguments had been used in each case.

In order to explain the basis of the case for the equality of animals, it will be helpful to start with an examination of the case for the equality of women. Let us assume that we wish to defend the case for women's rights against the attack by Thomas Taylor. How should we reply?

One way in which we might reply is by saying that the case for equality between men and women cannot validly be extended to nonhuman animals. Women have a right to vote, for instance, because they are just as capable of making rational decisions about the future as men are; dogs, on the other hand, are incapable of understanding the significance of voting, so they cannot have the right to vote. There are many other obvious ways in which men and women resemble each other closely, while humans and animals differ greatly. So, it might be said, men and women are similar beings and should have similar rights, while humans and nonhumans are different and should not have equal rights.

The reasoning behind this reply to Taylor's analogy is correct up to a point, but it does not go far enough. There *are* important differences between humans and other animals, and these differences must give rise to *some* differences in the rights that each have. Recognizing this obvious fact, however, is no barrier to the case for extending the basic principle of equality to nonhuman animals. The differences that exist between men and women are equally undeniable, and the supporters of Women's Liberation are aware that these differences may give rise to different rights. Many feminists hold that women have the right to an abortion on request. It does not follow that since these same feminists are campaigning for equality between men and women they must support the right of men to have abortions too. Since a man cannot have an abortion, it is meaningless to talk of his right to have one. Since a dog can't vote, it is meaningless to talk of its right to vote. There is no reason why either Women's Liberation or Animal Liberation should get involved in such nonsense. The extension of the basic principle of equality from one group to another does not imply that we must treat both groups in exactly the same way, or grant exactly the same rights to both groups. Whether we should do so will depend on the nature of the members of the two groups. The basic principle of equality does not require equal or identical *treatment;* it requires equal *consideration.* Equal consideration for different beings may lead to different treatment and different rights.

So there is a different way of replying to Taylor's attempt to parody the case for women's rights, a way that does not deny the obvious differences between humans and nonhumans but goes more deeply into the question of equality and concludes by finding nothing absurd in the idea that the basic principle of equality applies to so-called brutes. At this point such a conclusion may appear odd; but if we examine more deeply the basis on which our opposition to discrimination on grounds of race or sex ultimately rests, we will see that we would be on shaky ground if we were to demand equality for blacks, women, and other groups of oppressed humans while denying equal consideration to nonhumans. To make this clear we need to see first, exactly why racism and sexism are wrong.

When we say that all human beings, whatever their race, creed, or sex, are equal, what is it that we are asserting? Those who wish to defend hierarchical, inegalitarian societies have often pointed out that by whatever test we choose it simply is not true that all humans are equal. Like it or not we must face the fact that humans come in different shapes and sizes; they come with different moral capacities, different intellectual abilities, different amounts of benevolent feeling and sensitivity to the needs of others, different abilities to communicate effectively, and different capacities to experience pleasure and pain. In short, if the demand for equality were based on the actual equality of all human beings, we would have to stop demanding equality.

Still, one might cling to the view that the demand for equality among human beings is based on the actual equality of the different races and sexes. Although, it may be said, humans differ as individuals there are no differences between the races and sexes *as such.* From the mere fact that a person is black or a woman we cannot infer anything about that person's intellectual or moral capacities. This, it may be said, is why racism and sexism are wrong. The white racist claims that whites are superior to blacks, but this is false—although there are differences among individuals, some blacks are superior to some whites in all of the capacities and abilities that could conceivably be relevant. The opponent of sexism would say the same: a person's sex is no guide to his or her abilities, and this is why it is unjustifiable to discriminate on the basis of sex.

The existence of individual variations that cut across the lines of race or sex, however, provides us with no defense at all against a more sophisticated opponent of equality, one who proposes that, say, the interests of all those with IQ scores below 100 be given less consideration than the interests of those with ratings over 100. Perhaps those scoring below the mark, would, in this society, be made the slaves of those scoring higher. Would a hierarchical society of this sort really be so much better than one based on race or sex? I think not. But if we tie the moral principle of equality to the factual equality of the different races or sexes, taken as a whole, our opposition to racism and sexism does not provide us with any basis for objecting to this kind of inegalitarianism.

There is a second important reason why we ought not to base our opposition to racism and sexism on any kind of actual equality, even the limited kind that asserts that variations in capacities and abilities are spread evenly between the different races and sexes: we can have no absolute guarantee that these capacities and abilities really are distributed evenly, without regard to race or sex, among human beings. So far as actual abilities are concerned there do seem to be certain measurable differences between both races and sexes. These differences do not, of course, appear in each case, but only when averages are taken. More important still, we do not yet know how much of these differences is really due to the different genetic endowments of the different races and sexes, and how much is due to poor schools, poor housing, and other factors that are the result of past and continuing discrimination. Perhaps all the important differences will eventually prove to be environmental rather than genetic. Anyone opposed to racism and sexism will certainly hope that this will be so, for it will make the task of ending discrimination a lot easier; nevertheless it would be dangerous to rest the case against racism and sexism on the belief that all significant differences are environmental in origin. The opponent of, say, racism who takes this line will be unable to avoid conceding that *if* differences in ability

do after all prove to have some genetic connection with race, racism would in some way be defensible.

Fortunately there is no need to pin the case for equality to one particular outcome of a scientific investigation. The appropriate response to those who claim to have found evidence of genetically based differences in ability between the races or sexes is not to stick to the belief that the genetic explanation must be wrong, whatever evidence to the contrary may turn up: instead we should make it quite clear that the claim to equality does not depend on intelligence, moral capacity, physical strength, or similar matters of fact. Equality is a moral idea, not an assertion of fact. There is no logically compelling reason for assuming that a factual difference in ability between two people justifies any difference in the amount of consideration we give to their needs and interests. *The principle of the equality of human beings is not a description of an alleged actual equality among humans; it is a prescription of how we should treat humans.*

Jeremy Bentham, the founder of the reforming utilitarian school of moral philosophy, incorporated the essential basis of moral equality into his system of ethics by means of the formula: "Each to count for one and none for more than one." In other words, the interests of every being affected by an action are to be taken into account and given the same weight as the like interests of any other being. A later utilitarian, Henry Sidgwick, put the point in this way: "The good of any one individual is of no more importance, from the point of view (if I may say so) of the Universe, than the good of any other." More recently the leading figures in contemporary moral philosophy have shown a great deal of agreement in specifying as a fundamental presupposition of their moral theories some similar requirement that operates so as to give everyone's interests equal consideration—although these writers generally cannot agree on how this requirement is best formulated.[1]

It is an implication of this principle of equality that our concern for others and our readiness to consider their interests ought not to depend on what they are like or on what abilities they may possess. Precisely what this concern or consideration requires us to do may vary according to the characteristics of those affected by what we do: concern for the well-being of a child growing up in America would require that we teach him to read; concern for the well-being of a pig may require no more than that we leave him alone with other pigs in a place where there is adequate food and room to run freely. But the basic element—the taking into account of the interests of the being, whatever those interests may be—must, according to the principle of equality, be extended to all beings, black or white, masculine or feminine, human or nonhuman.

Thomas Jefferson, who was responsible for writing the principle of the equality of men into the American Declaration of Independence, saw this point. It led him to oppose slavery even though he was unable to free himself fully from his slaveholding background. He wrote in a letter to the author of a book that emphasized the notable intellectual achievements of Negroes in order to refute the then common view that they had limited intellectual capacities:

Be assured that no person living wishes more sincerely than I do, to see a complete refutation of the doubts I have myself entertained and expressed on the grade of understanding allotted to them by nature, and to find that they are on a par with ourselves . . . but whatever be their degree of talent it is no measure of their rights. Because Sir Isaac Newton was superior to others in understanding, he was not therefore lord of the property or person of others.[2]

Similarly when in the 1850s the call for women's rights was raised in the United States a remarkable black feminist named Sojourner Truth made the same point in more robust terms at a feminist convention:

. . . they talk about this thing in the head; what do they call it? ["Intellect," whispered someone near by.] That's it. What's that got to do with women's rights or

Negroes' rights? If my cup won't hold but a pint and yours holds a quart, wouldn't you be mean not to let me have my little half-measure full?[3]

It is on this basis that the case against racism and the case against sexism must both ultimately rest; and it is in accordance with this principle that the attitude that we may call "speciesism," by analogy with racism, must also be condemned. Speciesism—the word is not an attractive one, but I can think of no better term—is a prejudice or attitude of bias toward the interests of members of one's own species and against those of members of other species. It should be obvious that the fundamental objections to racism and sexism made by Thomas Jefferson and Sojourner Truth apply equally to speciesism. If possessing a higher degree of intelligence does not entitle one human to use another for his own ends, how can it entitle humans to exploit nonhumans for the same purpose?[4]

Many philosophers and other writers have proposed the principle of equal consideration of interests, in some form or other, as a basic moral principle, but not many of them have recognized that this principle applies to members of other species as well as to our own. Jeremy Bentham was one of the few who did realize this. In a forward-looking passage written at a time when black slaves had been freed by the French but the British dominions were still being treated in the way we now treat animals, Bentham wrote:

The day may come when the rest of the animal creation may acquire those rights which never could have been withholden from them but by the hand of tyranny. The French have already discovered that the blackness of the skin is no reason why a human being should be abandoned without redress to the caprice of a tormentor. It may one day come to be recognized that the number of the legs, the villosity of the skin, or the termination of the os sacrum are reasons equally insufficient for abandoning a sensitive being to the same fate. What else is it that should trace the insuperable line? Is it the faculty of reason, or perhaps the faculty of discourse? But a full-grown horse or dog is beyond comparison a more rational, as well as a more conversable animal,

than an infant of a day or a week or even a month old.
But suppose they were otherwise, what would it avail?
The question is not, Can they reason? nor Can they
talk? but, Can they suffer? [5]

In this passage Bentham points to the capacity for suffering as the vital characteristic that gives a being the right to equal consideration. The capacity for suffering—or more strictly, for suffering and/or enjoyment or happiness—is not just another characteristic like the capacity for language or higher mathematics. Bentham is not saying that those who try to mark "the insuperable line" that determines whether the interests of a being should be considered happen to have chosen the wrong characteristic. By saying that we must consider the interests of all beings with the capacity for suffering or enjoyment Bentham does not arbitrarily exclude from consideration any interests at all—as those who draw the line with reference to the possession of reason or language do. The capacity for suffering and enjoyment is *a prerequisite for having interests at all,* a condition that must be satisfied before we can speak of interests in a meaningful way. It would be nonsense to say that it was not in the interests of a stone to be kicked along the road by a schoolboy. A stone does not have interests because it cannot suffer. Nothing that we can do to it could possibly make any difference to its welfare. A mouse, on the other hand, does have an interest in not being kicked along the road, because it will suffer if it is.

If a being suffers there can be no moral justification for refusing to take that suffering into consideration. No matter what the nature of the being, the principle of equality requires that its suffering be counted equally with the like suffering—insofar as rough comparisons can be made—of any other being. If a being is not capable of suffering, or of experiencing enjoyment or happiness, there is nothing to be taken into account. So the limit of sentience (using the term as a convenient if not strictly accurate shorthand for the capacity to suffer and/or experience enjoyment) is the only defensible boundary of con-

cern for the interests of others. To mark this boundary by some other characteristic like intelligence or rationality would be to mark it in an arbitrary manner. Why not choose some other characteristic, like skin color?

The racist violates the principle of equality by giving greater weight to the interests of members of his own race when there is a clash between their interests and the interests of those of another race. The sexist violates the principle of equality by favoring the interests of his own sex. Similarly the speciesist allows the interests of his own species to override the greater interests of members of other species. The pattern is identical in each case.

Most human beings are speciesists. Ordinary human beings—not a few exceptionally cruel or heartless humans, but the overwhelming majority of humans—take an active part in, acquiesce in, and allow their taxes to pay for practices that require the sacrifice of the most important interests of members of other species in order to promote the most trivial interests of our own species....

Animals can feel pain. As we saw earlier, there can be no moral justification for regarding the pain (or pleasure) that animals feel as less important than the same amount of pain (or pleasure) felt by humans. But what exactly does this mean, in practical terms? To prevent misunderstanding I shall spell out what I mean a little more fully.

If I give a horse a hard slap across its rump with my open hand, the horse may start, but it presumably feels little pain. Its skin is thick enough to protect it against a mere slap. If I slap a baby in the same way, however, the baby will cry and presumably does feel pain, for its skin is more sensitive. So it is worse to slap a baby than a horse, if both slaps are administered with equal force. But there must be some kind of blow—I don't know exactly what it would be, but perhaps a blow with a heavy stick—that would cause the horse as much pain as we cause a baby by slapping it with our hand. That is what I mean by "the same amount of pain" and if we consider it wrong to inflict that much pain on a baby for no good reason then we must, unless we are speciesists, consider it equally wrong to inflict the same amount of pain on a horse for no good reason.

There are other differences between humans and animals that cause other complications. Normal adult human beings have mental capacities that will, in certain circumstances, lead them to suffer more than animals would in the same circumstances. If, for instance, we decided to perform extremely painful or lethal scientific experiments on normal adult humans, kidnapped at random from public parks for this purpose, every adult who entered a park would become fearful that he would be kidnapped. The resultant terror would be a form of suffering additional to the pain of the experiment. The same experiments performed on nonhuman animals would cause less suffering since the animals would not have the anticipatory dread of being kidnapped and experimented upon. This does not mean, of course, that it would be right to perform the experiment on animals, but only that there is a reason, which is *not* speciesist, for preferring to use animals rather than normal adult humans, if the experiment is to be done at all. It should be noted, however, that this same argument gives us a reason for preferring to use human infants—orphans perhaps—or retarded humans for experiments, rather than adults, since infants and retarded humans would also have no idea of what was going to happen to them. So far as this argument is concerned nonhuman animals and infants and retarded humans are in the same category; and if we use this argument to justify experiments on nonhuman animals we have to ask ourselves whether we are also prepared to allow experiments on human infants and retarded adults; and if we make a distinction between animals and these humans, on what basis can we do it, other than a barefaced—and morally indefensible—preference for members of our own species?

There are many areas in which the superior mental powers of normal adult humans make a difference: anticipation, more detailed memory, greater knowledge of what is happening, and so on. Yet these differences do not all point to greater suffering on the part of the normal human being. Sometimes an animal may suffer more because of his more limited understanding. If, for instance, we are taking prisoners in wartime we can explain to them that while they must submit to capture, search, and confinement they will not otherwise be harmed and will be set free at the conclusion of hostilities. If we capture a wild animal, however, we cannot explain that we are not threatening its life. A wild animal cannot distinguish an attempt to overpower and confine from an attempt to kill; the one causes as much terror as the other.

It may be objected that comparisons of the sufferings of different species are impossible to make, and that for this reason when the interests of animals and humans clash the principle of equality gives no guidance. It is probably true that comparisons of suffering between members of different species cannot be made precisely, but precision is not essential. Even if we were to prevent the infliction of suffering on animals only when it is quite certain that the interests of humans will not be affected to anything like the extent that animals are affected, we would be forced to make radical changes in our treatment of animals that would involve our diet, the farming methods we use, experimental procedures in many fields of science, our approach to wildlife and to hunting, trapping and the wearing of furs, and areas of entertainment like circuses, rodeos, and zoos. As a result, a vast amount of suffering would be avoided.

So far I have said a lot about the infliction of suffering on animals, but nothing about killing them. This omission has been deliberate. The application of the principle of equality to the infliction of suffering is, in theory at least, fairly straightforward. Pain and suffering are bad and should be prevented or minimized, irrespective of the race, sex, or species of the being that suffers. How bad a pain is depends on how intense it is and how long it lasts, but pains of the same intensity and duration are equally bad, whether felt by humans or animals.

The wrongness of killing a being is more complicated. I have kept, and shall continue to keep, the question of killing in the background because in the present state of human tyranny over other species the more simple, straightforward principle of equal consideration of pain or pleasure is a sufficient basis for identifying and protesting against all the major abuses of animals that humans practice. Nevertheless, it is necessary to say something about killing.

Just as most humans are speciesists in their readiness to cause pain to animals when they would not cause a similar pain to humans for the same reason, so most humans are speciesists in their readiness to kill other animals when they would not kill humans. We need to proceed more cautiously here, however, because people hold widely differing views about when it is legitimate to kill humans, as the continuing debates over abortion and euthanasia attest. Nor have moral philosophers been able to agree on exactly what it is that makes it wrong to kill humans, and under what circumstances killing a human being may be justifiable.

Let us consider first the view that it is always wrong to take an innocent human life. We may call this the "sanctity of life" view. People who take this view oppose abortion and euthanasia. They do not usually, however, oppose the killing of nonhumans—so perhaps it would be more accurate to describe this view as the "sanctity of *human* life" view.

The belief that human life, and only human life, is sacrosanct is a form of speciesism. To see this, consider the following example.

Assume that, as sometimes happens, an infant has been born with massive and irreparable brain damage. The damage is so severe that the infant can never be any more than a "human vegetable," unable to talk, recognize other people, act independently of others, or develop a sense of self-awareness. The parents of the infant, realizing that they cannot hope for any improvement in their child's condition and being in any case unwilling to spend, or ask the state to spend, the thousands of dollars that would be needed annually for proper care of the infant, ask the doctor to kill the infant painlessly.

Should the doctor do what the parents ask? Legally, he should not, and in this respect the law reflects the sanctity of life view. The life of every human being is sacred. Yet people who would say this about the infant do not object to the killing of nonhuman animals. How can they justify their different judgments? Adult chimpanzees, dogs, pigs, and may other species far surpass the brain-damaged infant in their ability to relate to others, act independently, be self-aware, and any other capacity that could reasonably be said to give value to life. With the most intensive care possible, there are retarded infants who can never achieve the intelligence level of a dog. Nor can we appeal to the concern of the infant's parents, since they themselves, in this imaginary example (and in some actual cases), do not want the infant kept alive.

The only thing that distinguishes the infant from the animal, in the eyes of those who claim it has a "right to life," is that it is, biologically, a member of the species Homo sapiens, whereas chimpanzees, dogs, and pigs are not. But to use *this* difference as the basis for granting a right to life to the infant and not to the other animals is, of course, pure speciesism.[6] It is exactly the kind of arbitrary difference that the most crude and overt kind of racist uses in attempting to justify racial discrimination.

This does not mean that to avoid speciesism we must hold that it is as wrong to kill a dog as it is to kill a normal human being. The only position that is irredeemably speciesist is the one that tries to make the boundary of the right to life run exactly parallel to the boundary of our own species. Those who hold the sanctity of life view do this because while distinguishing sharply between humans and other animals they allow no distinctions to be made within our own species, objecting to the killing of the severely retarded and the hopelessly senile as strongly as they object to the killing of normal adults.

To avoid speciesism we must allow that beings that are similar in all relevant respects have a similar right to life—and mere membership in our own biological species cannot be a morally relevant criterion for this right. Within these limits we could still hold that, for instance, it is worse to kill a normal adult human, with a capacity for self-awareness, and the ability to plan for the future and have meaningful relations with others, than it is to kill a mouse, which presumably does not share all of these characteristics; or we might appeal to the close family and other personal ties that humans have but mice do not have to the same degree; or we might think that it is the consequences for other humans, who will be put in fear of their own lives, that makes the crucial difference; or we might think it is some combination of these factors, or other factors altogether.

Whatever criteria we choose, however, we will have to admit that they do not follow precisely the boundary of our own species. We may legitimately hold that there are some features of certain beings which make their lives more valuable than those of other beings; but there will surely be some nonhuman animals whose lives, by any standards, are more valuable than the lives of some humans. A chimpanzee, dog, or pig, for instance, will have a higher degree of self-awareness and a greater capacity for meaningful relations with others than a severely retarded infant or someone in a state of advanced senility. So if we base the right to life on these characteristics we must grant these animals a right to life as good as, or better than, such retarded or senile humans.

Now this argument cuts both ways. It could be taken as showing that chimpanzees, dogs, and pigs, along with some other species, have a right to life and we commit a grave moral offense whenever we kill them, even when they are old and suffering and our intention is to put them out of their misery. Alternatively one could take the argument as showing that the severely retarded and hopelessly senile have no right to life and may be killed for quite trivial reasons, as we now kill animals.

Since the focus here is on ethical questions concerning animals and not on the morality of euthanasia I shall not attempt to settle this issue finally. I think it is reasonably clear, though, that while both of the positions just described avoid speciesism, neither is entirely satisfactory. What we need is some middle position that would avoid speciesism but would not make the lives of the retarded and senile as cheap as the lives of pigs and dogs now are, nor make the lives of pigs and dogs so sacrosanct that we think it wrong to put them out of hopeless misery. What we must do is bring nonhuman animals within our sphere of moral concern and cease to treat their lives as expendable for whatever trivial purposes we may have. At the same time, once we realize that the fact that a being is a member of our own species is not in itself enough to make it always wrong to kill that being, we may come to reconsider our policy of preserving human lives at all costs, even when there is no prospect of a meaningful life or of existence without terrible pain.

I conclude, then, that a rejection of speciesism does not imply that all lives are of equal worth. While self-awareness, intelligence, the capacity for meaningful relations with others, and so on are not relevant to the question of inflicting pain—since pain is pain, whatever other capacities, beyond the capacity to feel pain, the being may have—these capacities may be relevant to the question of taking life. It is not arbitrary to hold that the life of a self-aware being, capable of abstract thought, of planning for the future, of complex acts of communication, and so on, is more valuable than the life of a being without these capacities. To see the difference between the issues of inflicting pain and taking life, consider how we would choose within our own species. If we had to choose to save the life of a normal human or a mentally defective human, we would probably choose to save the life of the normal human; but if we had to choose between preventing pain in the normal human or the mental defective—imagine that both have received painful but superficial injuries, and we only have enough painkiller for one of them—it is not nearly so clear how we ought to choose. The same is true when we consider other species. The evil of pain is, in itself, unaffected by the other characteristics of the being that feels the pain; the value of life is affected by these other characteristics.

Normally this will mean that if we have to choose between the life of a human being and the life of another animal we should choose to save the life of the human, but there may be special cases in which the reverse holds true, because the human being in question does not have the capacities of a normal human being. So this view is not speciesist, although it may appear to be at first glance. The preference, in normal cases, for saving a human life over the life of an animal when a choice *has* to be made is a preference based on the characteristics that normal humans have, and not on the mere fact that they are members of our own species. This is why when we consider members of our own species who lack the characteristics of normal humans we can no longer say that their lives are always to be preferred to those of other animals. In general, the question of when it is wrong to kill (painlessly) an animal is one to which we need give no precise answer. As long as we remember that we should give the same respect to the lives of animals as we give to the lives of those humans at a similar mental level, we shall not go far wrong.

In any case, the conclusions that are argued for here flow from the principle of minimizing suffering alone. The idea that it is also wrong to kill animals painlessly gives some of these conclusions additional support that is welcome, but strictly unnecessary. Interestingly enough, this is true even of the conclusion that we ought to become vegetarians, a conclusion that in the popular mind is generally based on some kind of absolute prohibition on killing.

Endnotes

1. For Bentham's moral philosophy, see his *Introduction to the Principles of Morals and Legislation,* and for Sidgwick's see *The Methods of Ethics* (the passage quoted is from the seventh edition, p. 382). As examples of leading contemporary moral philosophers who incorporate a requirement of equal consideration of interests, see R.M. Hare, *Freedom and Reason* (New York, Oxford University Press, 1963) and John Rawls, *A Theory of Justice* (Cambridge: Harvard University Press, Belknap Press, 1972). For a brief account of the essential agreement on this issue between these and other positions, see R.M. Hare, "Rules of War and Moral Reasoning," *Philosophy and Public Affairs* 1 (1972).

2. Letter to Henri Gregoire, February 25, 1809.

3. Reminiscences by Francis D. Gage, from Susan B. Anthony, *The History of Woman Suffrage,* vol. 1; the passage is to be found in the extract in Leslie Tanner, ed., *Voices from Women's Liberation* (New York: Signet, 1970).

4. I owe the term "speciesism" to Richard Ryder.

5. *Introduction to the Principles of Morals and Legislation,* chapter 17.

6. I am here putting aside religious views, for example the doctrine that all and only humans have immortal souls, or are made in the image of God. Historically these views have been very important, and no doubt are partly responsible for the idea that human life has a special sanctity. Logically, however, these religious views are unsatisfactory, since a reasoned explanation of why it should be that all humans and no nonhumans have immortal souls is not offered. This belief too, therefore, comes under suspicion as a form of speciesism. In any case, defenders of the "sanctity of life" view are generally reluctant to base their position on purely religious doctrines, since these doctrines are no longer as widely accepted as they once were.

Review Questions

1. Explain the principle of equality that Singer adopts.

2. How does Singer define speciesism?

3. What is the sanctity of life view? Why does Singer reject this view?

Discussion Questions

1. Is speciesism analogous to racism and sexism? Why, or why not?

2. Is there anything wrong with killing animals painlessly? Defend your view.

3. Do human interests outweigh animal interests? Explain your position.

Tom Regan

Ethical Vegetarianism and Commercial Animal Farming

Tom Regan teaches philosophy at North Carolina State University. He has written numerous books and articles, and he has edited many textbooks. His most recent books on the subject of animal rights are All That Dwell Therein: Essays on Animal Rights and Environmental Ethics *(1982) and* The Case for Animal Rights *(1983).*

*Regan begins with a discussion of moral **anthropocentrism**, the view of Kant and others that only human interest should be morally considered. This view is rejected by utilitarianism and by some proponents of moral rights including Regan. Regan does not find the utilitarianism of Bentham and Singer to be morally acceptable. Instead he defends a rights theory. On this theory, moral rights imply a duty to respect the rights. Persons with "inherent value" possess rights, and some animals are persons. So we have a duty to respect animal rights by abolishing commercial animal farming and becoming vegetarians.*

INTRODUCTION

Time was when a few words in passing usually were enough to exhaust the philosophical interest in the moral status of animals other than human beings. "Lawless beasts," writes Plato. "Of the order of sticks and stones," opines the nineteenth-century Jesuit W.D. Ritchie. True, there are notable exceptions, at least as far back as Pythagoras, who advocated vegetarianism on ethical grounds—Cicero, Epicurus, Herodotus, Horace, Ovid, Plutarch, Seneca, Virgil: hardly a group of "animal crazies"! By and large, however, a few words would do nicely, thank you, or, when one's corpus took on grave proportions, a few paragraphs or pages. Thus we find Kant, for example, by all accounts one of the most influential philosophers in the history of ideas, devoting almost two full pages to the question of our duties to animals, while St. Thomas Aquinas, easily the most important philosopher-theologian in the Catholic tradition, bequeaths perhaps ten pages to the topic at hand.

Times change. Today an even modest bibliography listing titles of the past decade's work on the moral status of animals would easily equal the length of Kant's and Aquinas' treatments combined, a quantitative symbol of the changes that have taken place, and continue to take place, in philosophy's attempts to rouse slumbering prejudices lodged in the anthropocentrism of western thought.

With relatively few speaking to the contrary (St. Francis always comes to mind in this context), theists and humanists, rowdy bedfellows in most quarters, have gotten along amicably when questions were raised about the moral center of the terrestrial universe: *Human* interests form the center of that universe. Let the theist look hopefully beyond the harsh edge of bodily death, let the humanist denounce, in Freud's terms, this "infantile view of the world," at least the two could agree that the moral universe revolves around us humans—our desires, our needs, our goals, our preferences, our love for one another. The intense dialectic now characterizing philosophy's assaults on the traditions of humanism and theism, assaults aimed not only at the traditional account of the moral status of animals but at the foundation of our moral dealings with the natural environment, with Nature generally—these assaults should not be viewed as local skirmishes between obscure academicians each bent on occupying a deserted fortress. At issue are the validity of alternative visions of the scheme of things and our place in it. The growing philosophical debate over our treatment of animals and the environment is both a symptom and a cause of a culture's attempt to come to critical terms with its past as it attempts to shape its future.

At present there are three major challenges being raised against moral anthropocentrism. The first is the one issued by *utilitarians;* the second, by proponents of *moral rights;* and the third emanates from the camp of those who advocate what we shall term a *holistic ethic.* This essay offers brief summaries of each position with special reference to how their advocates answer two questions: (a) Is vegetarianism required on ethical grounds? and (b) Judged ethically, what should we say, and what should we do, about commercial animal agriculture? To ask whether vegetarianism is required on ethical grounds is to ask whether there are reasons other than those that relate to one's own welfare (for example, other than those that relate to one's own health or financial well-being) that call for leading a vegetarian way of life. As for the expression "commercial animal agriculture," that should be taken to apply to the practice of raising animals to be sold for food. The ethics of other practices that involve killing animals (for example, hunting, the use of animals in science, "the family farm" where the animals raised are killed and eaten by the people who raise them, etc.) will not be considered, except in passing, not because the ethics of these practices should not demand our close attention but because space and time preclude our giving them this attention here. Time and space also preclude anything approaching "complete" assessments of the three views to be discussed. None can be proven right or wrong in a few swift strokes. Even so, it will be clear where my own sympathies lie.

TRADITIONAL MORAL ANTHROPOCENTRISM

Aquinas and Kant speak for the anthropocentric tradition. That tradition does not issue a blank check when it comes to the treatment of animals. Morally, we are enjoined to be kind to animals and, on the other side of the coin, not to be cruel to them. But we are not enjoined to be the one and prohibited from being the other because we owe such treatment to *animals themselves*—not, that is, because we have any duties *directly* to nonhumans; rather, it is because of *human* interests that we have these duties regarding animals. "So far as animals are concerned," writes Kant, "we have no direct duties.... Our duties to animals are merely indirect duties to mankind." In the case of cruelty, we are not to be cruel to animals because treating them cruelly will develop a habit of cruelty, and a habit of cruelty, once it has taken up lodging in our breast, will in time include human beings among its victims. "(H)e who is cruel to animals becomes hard also in his dealings with men." And *that* is why cruelty to animals is wrong. As for kindness, "(t)ender feelings towards dumb animals develop humane feelings toward mankind." [1] And *that* is why we have a duty to be kind to animals.

So reasons Kant. Aquinas, predictably, adds theistic considerations, but the main storyline is the same, as witness the following passage from his *Summa Contra Gentiles.*

Hereby is refuted the error of those who said it is sinful for a man to kill dumb animals: for by divine providence they are intended for man's use in the natural order. Hence it is no wrong for man to make use of them, either by killing, or in any other way whatever.... And if any passages of Holy Writ seem to forbid us to be cruel to dumb animals, for instance to kill a bird with its young: this is either to remove men's thoughts from being cruel to other men, and lest through being cruel to animals one becomes cruel to human beings: or because injury to an animal leads to the temporal hurt of man, either of the doer of the deed, or of another: or on account of some (religious) signification: thus the Apostle expounds the prohibition against muzzling the ox that treadeth the corn.[2]

To borrow a phrase from the twentieth-century English philosopher Sir W.D. Ross, our treatment of animals, both for Kant and Aquinas, is "a practice ground for moral virtue." The *moral game* is played between human players or, on the theistic view, human players plus God. The way we treat animals is a sort of moral warmup, character calisthenics, as it were, for the moral game in which animals themselves play no part.

THE UTILITARIAN CHALLENGE

The first fairly recent spark of revolt against moral anthropocentrism comes, as do other recent protests against institutionalized prejudice, from the pens of the nineteenth-century utilitarians, most notably Jeremy Bentham and John Stuart Mill. These utilitarians—who count the balance of pleasure over pain for all sentient creatures as the yardstick of moral right and wrong, and who reject out of hand Descartes' famous teaching that animals are "nature's machines," lacking any trace of conscious awareness—recognize the direct moral significance of the pleasures and pains of animals. In an oft-quoted passage, Bentham enfranchises animals within the utilitarian moral community by declaring that "(t)he question is not, Can they talk?, or Can they reason?, but, Can they suffer?"[3] And Mill stakes the credibility of utilitarianism itself on its implications for the moral status and treatment of animals, writing that "(w)e (that is, those who subscribe to utilitarianism) are perfectly willing to stake the whole question on this one issue. Granted that any practice causes more pain to animals than it gives pleasure to man: is that practice moral or immoral? And if, exactly in proportion as human beings raise their heads out of the slough of selfishness, they do not with one voice answer 'immoral' let the morality of the principle of utility be forever condemned."[4] The duties we have regarding animals, then, are duties we have *directly to them*, not indirect duties to humanity. For utilitarians, animals are themselves involved in the moral game.

Viewed against this historical backdrop, the position of the contemporary Australian moral philosopher Peter Singer can be seen to be an extension of the attack on the tradition of moral anthropocentrism initiated by his utilitarian forebears. For though this sometimes goes unnoticed by friend and foe alike, Singer, whose book *Animal Liberation* is unquestionably the most influential work published in the 1970s on the topic of the ethics of our treatment of animals, is a utilitarian.[5] That view requires, he believes, observance of the equality of interests principle. This principle requires that, before we decide what to do, we consider the interests (that is, the preferences) of all those who are likely to be affected by what we do *and* weigh equal interests equally. We must not, that is, refuse to consider the interests of some of those who will be affected by what we do because, say, they are Catholic, or female, or black. *Everyone's* interests must be considered. And we must not discount the importance of comparable interests because they are the interests of, say, a Catholic, woman, or black. Everyone's interests must be weighed *equitably*. Of course, to ignore or discount the importance of a woman's interests *because she is a woman* is the very **paradigm** of the moral prejudice we call sexism, just as to ignore or discount the importance of the interests of blacks (or Native Americans, Chicanos, etc.) are paradigmatic forms of racism. It remained for Singer to argue, which he does with great vigor, passion, and skill, that a similar moral prejudice lies at the heart of moral anthropocentrism, a prejudice that Singer, borrowing a term first coined by the English author and animal activist Richard Ryder, denominates *speciesism.* [6] *Like Bentham and Mill before him, Singer, the utilitarian, denies* that we are to treat animals well in the name of the betterment of humanity, *denies* that we are to do this because this will help us discharge our duties to our fellow humans, *denies* that acting dutifully toward animals is a moral warmup for the real moral game played between humans, or, as theists would add, between humans-and-humans-and-God. *We owe it to those animals who have interests to take their interests into account, just as we also owe it to them to count their interests equitably.* Our duties regarding animals are, in these respects, *direct* duties we have to them, not indirect duties to humanity. To think otherwise is to give sorry testimony to the prejudice of speciesism Singer is intent upon unmasking.

FARMING TODAY

Singer believes that the utilitarian case for ethical vegetarianism is strengthened when we inform ourselves of the changes taking place in commercial animal farming today. In increasing numbers, animals are being brought in off the land and raised indoors, in unnatural, crowded conditions—raised "intensively," to use the jargon of the animal industry, in structures that look for all the world like factories. Indeed, it is now common practice to refer to such commercial ventures as *factory farms.* The inhabitants of these "farms" are kept in cages, or stalls, or pens, or closely-confined in other ways, living out their abbreviated lives in a technologically created and sustained environment: automated feeding, automated watering, automated light cycles, automated waste removal, automated what-not. And the crowding: as many as nine hens in cages that measure eighteen by twenty-four inches; veal calves confined to twenty-two inch wide stalls; hogs similarly confined, sometimes in tiers of cages—two, three, four rows high. Could any

impartial, morally sensitive person view what goes on in a factory farm with benign approval? Certainly many of the basic interests of the animals are simply ignored or undervalued, Singer claims, because they do not compute economically. Their interest in physical freedom or in associating with members of their own species, these interests routinely go by the board. And for what? So that we humans can dine on steaks and chops, drumsticks and roasts, food that is simply inessential for our own physical well-being. Add to this sorry tale of speciesism on today's farm the enormous waste that characterizes animal industry, waste to the tune of six or seven pounds of vegetable protein to produce a pound of animal protein in the case of beef cattle, for example, and add to the accumulated waste of nutritious food the chronic need for just such food throughout the countries of the Third World, whose populations characteristically are malnourished at best and literally starving to death at worst—add all these factors together and we have, Singer believes, the basis for the utilitarian's answers to our two questions. In response to the question, "Is vegetarianism required on ethical grounds?" the Singer-type utilitarian replies affirmatively. For it is not for self-interested reasons that Singer calls us to vegetarianism (though such reasons, including a concern for one's health, are not irrelevant). It is for ethical reasons that we are to take up a vegetarian way of life. And as for our second question, the one that asks what we should think and do about commercial animal farming, Singer's utilitarian argument prescribes, he thinks, that we should think ill of today's factory farms and act to bring about significant humane improvements by refusing to purchase their products. Ethically considered, we ought to become vegetarians.

THE CHALLENGE TO UTILITARIANISM

Singer, then, is the leading contemporary representative of the utilitarian critique of the anthropocentric heritage bequeathed to us by humanism and theism. How should we assess his critique? Our answer requires answering two related questions. First, How adequate is the general utilitarian position Singer advocates? Second, How adequate is Singer's application of this general position to the particular case of commercial animal agriculture and, allied with this, the case for ethical vegetarianism? A brief response to each question, beginning with the second, will have to suffice. Consider Singer's claim that each of us has a duty to become a vegetarian. How can this alleged duty be defended on *utilitarian* grounds? Well, on this view, we know, the act I *ought* to perform, the act I have a *duty* to do, is the one that will bring about the best consequences for all those affected by the outcome, which, for Singer, means the act that will bring about the optimal balance of preference satisfaction over preference frustration. But it is naive in the extreme to suppose that, were I individually henceforth to abstain from eating meat and assiduously lead a vegetarian existence, this will improve the lot of a single animal. Commercial animal farming simply does not work in this way. It does not, that is, fine-tune its production to such a high degree that it responds to the decisions of each individual consumer. So, no, the individual's abstention from meat will not make the slightest dent, will not effect the smallest change, in commercial animal agriculture. No one, therefore, Singer included, can ground *the individual's* ethical obligation to be vegetarian on the effects *the individual's* acts will have on the welfare of animals.

Similar remarks apply to the other presumed beneficiaries of the individual's conversion to vegetarianism. The starving, malnourished masses of the Third World will not receive the food they need if I would but stop eating animals. For it is, again, naive in the extreme to suppose that the dietary decisions and acts of any given *individual* will make the slightest difference to the quality of life for any inhabitant in the Third World. Even were it true, which it is not (and it is not true because commercial animal agriculture

is not so fine-tuned in this respect either), that a given amount of protein-rich grain *would not be fed to animals* if I abstained from eating meat, it simply would not follow that this grain *would find its way to any needy human being.* To suppose otherwise is to credit one's individual acts and decisions with a kind of godlike omnipotence a robust sense of reality cannot tolerate. Thus, since the type of utilitarianism Singer advocates prescribes that we decide what our ethical duties are by asking what will be the consequences of our acts, and since there is no realistic reason to believe that the consequences of my abstaining from meat will make any difference whatever to the quality of life of commercially raised farm animals or the needy people of the Third World, the alleged duties to become a vegetarian and to oppose commercial animal agriculture lack the kind of backing a utilitarian like Singer requires.

Here one might attempt to defend Singer by arguing that it is the total or sum of the consequences of *many* people becoming vegetarians, not just the results of each individual's decisions, that will spare some animals the rigors of factory farms and save some humans from malnutrition or starvation. Two replies to this attempted defense may be briefly noted. First, this defense at most gives *a sketch of a possible* reply; it does not give a finished one. As a utilitarian, Singer must show that the consequences for everyone involved would be better if a number of people became vegetarians than if they did not. But to show this, Singer must provide a thorough rundown of what the consequences would be, or would be in all probability, if we abstained from eating meat, *or ate less of it, or ate none at all.* And this is no easy task. Would the grains not fed to animals even be grown if the animal industry's requirements for them were reduced or eliminated? Would there be an economically viable market for corn, oats, and other grains if we became vegetarians? Would farmers have the necessary economic incentive to produce enough grain to feed the world's hungry human beings? Who knows? In particular, does Singer know? One looks in vain to find the necessary empirical backing for an answer here. Or consider: Suppose the grain is available. From a utilitarian point of view, would it be best (that is, would we be acting to produce the best consequences) if we made this grain available to the present generation of the world's malnourished? Or would it be better in the long run to refuse to aid these people at this point in time? After all, if we assist them now, will they not simply reproduce? And won't their additional numbers make the problem of famine for the next generation even more tragic? Who knows what the correct answers to these questions are? Who knows what is even "most likely" to be true? It is not unfair to a utilitarian such as Singer to mark the depths of our ignorance in these matters. And neither is it unfair to emphasize how our ignorance stands in the way of his attempt to ground the obligatoriness of vegetarianism on utilitarian considerations. If we simply do not know what the consequences of our becoming vegetarians would be, or are most likely to be, and if we simply do not know whether the consequences that would result would be, or are most likely to be, better than those that would obtain if we did not become vegetarians, then we simply lack any semblance of a utilitarian justification for the obligation to become vegetarians or for amounting a frontal assault on commercial animal agriculture. The decision to lead a vegetarian way of life and, by doing so, to lodge a moral complaint against commercial animal agriculture, viewed from the perspective of Singer's utilitarianism, must be diagnosed as at best symbolic gestures.

Aside from these matters, what can be said about the adequacy of utilitarianism in general? That is a question raised earlier to which we must now direct our attention. There is a vast literature critical of utilitarian theory, and it will obviously not be possible to survey it here. Here let us note just one difficulty. Utilitarianism, at least as understood by Singer, implies that whether *I* am doing what I ought to do is crucially dependent on what *other* people do. For example, although the consequences of *my* abstaining from eating meat are too modest to make any difference to how animals are raised or whether grains are made available to needy people, if enough *other* people join me in a vegetarian way of life we could collectively bring about changes in the number of animals raised, how they are raised, what use is made of grain, etc. The situation, in other words, is as follows: If enough people join me so that the consequences of what we do *collectively* makes some impact, then what I do might be right, whereas if too few people join me, with the result that the consequences of what we do fails to make any difference to how animals are raised, etc., then I am *not* doing what is right.

To make the morality of an individual's acts depend on how others behave is a highly unsatisfactory consequence for any moral theory. When people refuse to support racist or sexist practices (for example, in employment or education), they do what is right, but their doing what is right does not depend on how many *other* people join them. The number of people who join them determines how many people do or support what is right, *not* what is right in the first place. Utilitarianism, because it makes *what is right* dependent in many cases on how many people act in a certain way, puts the moral cart before the horse. What we want is a theory that illuminates moral right and wrong independently of how many people act in this or that way. And that is precisely what utilitarianism, at least in the form advocated by Singer, fails to give us. For all its promise as an attack on the anthropocentric traditions of humanism and theism, for all its insistence on the direct relevance of the interests of animals, and despite the radical sounding claims made by utilitarians in criticism of current practices on the farm and in the laboratory, utilitarianism proves to be more ethical shadow than substance. If we look beyond the rhetoric and examine the arguments, utilitarianism might not change these practices as much as it would fortify them.[7]

THE RIGHTS VIEW

An alternative to the utilitarian attack on anthropocentrism is what we shall call "the rights view."[8] Those who accept this view hold that (1) certain individuals have certain moral rights, (2) these individuals have these rights independently of considerations about the value of the consequences of treating them in one way or another, and (3) the duty the individual has to respect the rights of others does not depend on how many other people act in ways that respect these rights. The first point distinguishes proponents of the rights view from, among others, those utilitarians like Bentham and Singer who deny that individuals have moral rights; the second distinguishes advocates of the rights view from, among others, those utilitarians such as Mill who hold that individuals have moral rights if, and only if, the general welfare would be promoted by saying and acting as if they do; and the third point distinguishes those who champion the rights view from, among others, any advocate of utilitarianism who holds that my duty to act in certain ways depends on how many other people act in these ways. According to the rights view, certain individuals have moral rights, and my duty to act in ways that respect such an individual's (A's) rights is a duty I have directly to A, a duty I have to A that is not grounded in considerations about the value of consequences for all those affected by the outcome, and a duty I have to A whatever else others might do to A. *Those who advocate animal rights, understanding this idea after the fashion of the rights view, believe that some of those individuals who have moral rights, and thus some of those to whom we have duties of the type just described, are animals.*

GROUNDS FOR THE RIGHTS VIEW

To proclaim "the moral rights of Man" sounds good but is notoriously difficult to defend. Bentham, who writes more forcefully

to support what he rejects than to establish what he accepts, dismisses rights other than legal rights as "nonsense upon stilts." So we will not settle the thorny question about human rights of an essay's reading or writing. And, it goes without saying, the moral rights of animals must remain even less established. Were Bentham in his grave (in fact he remains above ground, encased in glass in an anteroom in University College, London, where he is dutifully brought to dinner each year on the occasion of his birthday) he would most certainly roll over at the mere mention of *animal* rights! Still, something needs to be said about the rational grounds for the rights view.

An important (but not the only possible) argument in this regard takes the following form: Unless we recognize that certain individuals have moral rights, we will be left holding moral principles that sanction morally reprehensible conduct. Thus, in order to avoid holding principles that allow such conduct, we must recognize that certain individuals have moral rights. The following discussion of utilitarianism is an example of this general line of argument.

Utilitarians cut from the same cloth as Bentham would have us judge moral right and wrong by appeal to the consequences of what we do. Well, suppose aged Aunt Bertha's heirs could have a lot more pleasure than she is likely to have in her declining years if she were to die. But suppose that neither nature nor Aunt Bertha will cooperate: She simply refuses to die as expeditiously as, gauged by the interest of her heirs, is desirable. Why not speed up the tempo of her demise? The reply given by Bentham-type utilitarians shows how far they are willing to twist our moral intuitions to save their theory. If we were to kill Aunt Bertha, especially if we took care to do so painlessly, then, these utilitarians submit, we would do no wrong to Aunt Bertha. However, if *other* people found out about what we did, they would quite naturally grow more anxious, more insecure about their own safety and mortality, and these mental states (anxiety, insecurity, and the like) are painful. Thus, so we are told, killing Aunt Bertha is wrong (if it is) because of the painful consequences for others!

Except for those already committed to a Bentham-style utilitarianism, few are likely to find this account satisfactory. Its shortcomings are all the more evident when we note that *if* others did not find out about our dastardly deed (and so were not made more anxious and insecure by their knowledge of what we did), and *if* we have a sufficiently undeveloped conscience not to be terribly troubled by what we did, and *if* we do not get caught, and *if* we have a jolly good time with Aunt Bertha's inheritance, a much better time, in fact, than we would have had if we had waited for nature to run its course, then Bentham-style utilitarianism implies that we did nothing wrong in killing Aunt Bertha and, indeed, acted as we morally ought to have acted. People who, in the face of this kind of objection, remain Bentham-type utilitarians, may hold a consistent position. But one pays a price for a "foolish consistency." The spectacle of people "defending their theory to the last" in spite of its grave implications must, to put it mildly, take one's moral breath away.

There are, of course, many ethical theories in addition to utilitarianism, and many versions of utilitarianism in addition to the one associated with Bentham. So even if the sketch of an argument against Bentham's utilitarianism proves successful, the rights view would not thereby "win" in its competition with other theories. But the foregoing does succeed in giving a representative sample of one argument deployed by those who accept the rights view: If you deny moral rights, as Bentham does, then the principles you put in their place, which, in Bentham's case, is the principle of utility, will sanction morally reprehensible conduct (for example, the murder of Aunt Bertha). If those who affirm and defend the rights view could show this given *any* initially plausible theory that denies moral rights, and if they could crystalize and defend the methodology on which this argument depends, then they would have a powerful reason for their position.

THE VALUE OF THE INDIVIDUAL

The rights view aspires to satisfy our intellect, not merely our appetite for rhetoric, and so it is obliged to provide a theoretical home for moral rights. Part, but by no means not the whole, of this home is furnished by the rights views' theory of value. Unlike utilitarian theories (for example, value hedonism), the rights view recognizes *the value of individuals*, not just the value of their mental states (for example, their pleasures). Following custom, let us call these latter sorts of value "intrinsic values" and let us introduce the term "inherent value" for the type of value attributed to individuals. Then the notion of inherent value can be explained as follows. First, the inherent value of an individual who has such value is not the same as, is not reducible to, and is incommensurate with the intrinsic value of that individual's, or of any combination of individuals', mental states. The inherent value of an individual, in other words, is not equal to any sum of intrinsic values (for example, any sum of pleasures). Second, all individuals who have inherent value have it equally. Inherent value, that is, does not come in degrees; some who have it do not have it more or less than others. One either has it or one does not, and all who have it have it to the same extent. It is, one might say, a categorical concept. Third, the possession of inherent value by individuals does not depend on their utility relative to the interests of others, which, if it were true, would imply that some individuals have such value to a greater degree than do others, because some (for example, surgeons) have greater utility than do others (for example, bank thieves). Fourth, and relatedly, individuals cannot acquire or lose such value by anything they do. And fifth, and finally, the inherent value of individuals does not depend on what or how others think or feel about them. The loved and admired are neither more nor less inherently valuable than the despised and forsaken.

Now, the rights view claims that any individual who has inherent value is due treatment that respects this value (has, that is, a *moral right* to such treatment), and though not everything can be said here about what such respect comes to, at least this much should be clear: We fail to treat individuals with the respect they are due whenever we assume that how we treat them can be defended *merely* by asking about the value of the mental states such treatment produces for those affected by the outcome. This must fail to show appropriate respect since it is tantamount to treating these individuals as if they lacked inherent value—as if, that is, we treat them as we ought whenever we can justify our treatment of them *merely* on the grounds that it promotes the interests other individuals have in obtaining preferred mental states (for example, pleasure). Since individuals who have inherent value have a kind of value that is not reducible to their utility relative to the interests of others, we are not to treat them merely as a means to bringing about the best consequences. We ought not, then, kill Aunt Bertha, given the rights view, even if doing so brought about "the best" consequences. That would be to treat her with a lack of appropriate respect, something she has a moral right to. To kill her for these reasons would be to violate her rights.

WHICH INDIVIDUALS HAVE INHERENT VALUE?

Even assuming the rights view could succeed in providing a coherent, rationally persuasive theoretical framework for "the rights of Man," further argument would be necessary to illuminate and justify the rights of animals. That argument, not surprisingly, will be long and torturous. At least we can be certain of two things, however. First, it must include considerations about the criteria of right possession; and, second, it will have to include an explanation and defense of how animals meet these criteria. A few remarks about each of these two points will have to suffice.

Persons [9] are the possessors of moral rights, and though most human beings are persons, not all are. And some persons are not human beings. Persons are individuals who have a cluster of actual (not merely potential or former) abilities. These include awareness of their environment, desires and preferences, goals and purposes, feelings and emotions, beliefs and memories, a sense of the future and of their own identity. Most adult humans have these abilities and so are persons. But some (the irreversibly comatose, for example) lack them and so are not persons. Human fetuses and infants also are not persons, given this analysis, and so have no moral rights (which is not to say that we may therefore do anything to them that we have a mind to; there are moral constraints on what we may do in addition to those constraints that involve respect for the moral rights of others—but this is a long story ...!).

As for nonhumans who are persons, the most famous candidate is God as conceived, for example, by Christians. When believers speak of "the blessed Trinity, three persons in one," they don't mean "three human beings in one." Extraterrestrials are another obvious candidate, at least as they crop up in standard science fiction. The extraterrestrials in Ray Bradbury's *Martian Chronicles,* for example, are persons, in the sense explained, but they assuredly are not human beings. But, of course, the most important candidates for our purposes are animals. And they are successful candidates if they perceive and remember, believe and desire, have feelings and emotions, and, in general, actually possess the other abilities mentioned earlier.

Those who affirm and defend the rights of animals believe that some animals actually possess these abilities. Of course, there are some who will deny this. All animals, they will say, lack all, or most, or at least some of the abilities that make an individual a person. In a fuller discussion of the rights view, these worries would receive the respectful airing they deserve. It must suffice here to say that the case for animal rights involves the two matters mentioned and explained—first, con-

siderations about the criteria of right possession (or, alternatively, personhood), and, second, considerations that show that some
animals satisfy these criteria. Those who
would squelch the undertaking before it gets
started by claiming that "it's *obvious* that animals cannot be persons!" offer no serious
objection; instead, they give sorry expression
to the very speciesist prejudice those who affirm and defend the rights of animals seek to
overcome.

LINE DRAWING

To concede that some animals are persons
and so have moral rights is not to settle the
question, *Which* animals are persons? "Where
do we draw the line?" it will be asked; indeed,
it must be asked. The correct answer seems
to be: We do not know with certainty. Perhaps there is no exact line to be drawn in this
case, any more than there is an exact line to
be drawn in other cases (for example, "Exactly how tall do you have to be to be tall?"
"Exactly how old must you be before you are
old?"). What we must ask is where in the
animal kingdom we find individuals who are
most like paradigmatic persons—that is, most
like us, both behaviorally and physiologically.
The greater the similarity in these respects,
the stronger the case for believing that these
animals have *a mental life similar to our own*
(including memory and emotion, for example), a case that is strengthened given the
major thrust of evolutionary theory. So, while
it remains a matter of uncertainty *exactly*
where we are to draw this line, it is implausible to deny that adult mammalian animals
have the abilities in question (just as, analo-
gously, it would be implausible to deny that
eighty-eight-year-old Aunt Bertha is old because we don't know exactly how old someone must be before they are old). To get this
far in the argument for animal rights is not to
finish the story, but it is to give a rough outline of a major chapter in it.

THE INHERENT VALUE
OF ANIMALS

Moral rights, as explained earlier, need a theoretical home, and the rights view provides
this by its use of the notion of inherent value.
Not surprisingly, therefore, the rights view
affirms this value in the case of those animals
who are persons; not to do so would be to
slide back into the prejudice of speciesism.
Moreover, because all who possess this value
possess it equally, the rights view makes no
distinction between the inherent value
human persons possess as distinct from that
possessed by those persons who are animals.
And just as *our* inherent value, as persons,
does not depend on our utility relative to the
interests of others, or on how much we are
liked or admired, or on anything we do or fail
to do, the same must be true in the case of
animals who, as persons, have the same inherent value we do.

To regard animals in the way advocated
by the rights view makes a truly profound
difference to our understanding of what,
morally speaking, we may do to them, as well
as how, morally speaking, we can defend
what we do. Those animals who have inherent value have a moral right to respectful
treatment, a right we fail to respect whenever
we attempt to justify what we do to them by
appeal to "the best consequences." What
these animals are due, in other words, is the
same respectful treatment we are. We must
never treat them in this or that way merely
because, we claim, doing so is necessary to
bring about "the best consequences" for all
affected by the outcome.

The rights view therefore calls for the total dissolution of commercial animal agriculture as we know it. Not merely "modern"
intensive rearing methods must cease. For
though the harm visited upon animals raised
in these circumstances is real enough and is
morally to be condemned, its removal would
not eliminate the basic wrong its presence
compounds. The *basic* wrong is that animals
raised for commercial profit are viewed and
treated in ways that fail to show respect for

their moral right to respectful treatment. *They are not* (though of course they may be treated as if they are) "commodities," "economic units," "investments," "a renewable resource," etc. They are, like us, persons and so, like us, are owed treatment that accords with their right to be treated with respect, a respect we fail to show when we end their life before doing so can be defended on the grounds of mercy. Since animals are routinely killed on grounds other than mercy in the course of commercial animal agriculture, that human enterprise violates the rights of animals.

Unlike the utilitarian approach to ethical vegetarianism, the rights view basis does not require that we know what the consequences of our individual or collective abstention from meat will be. The moral imperatives to treat farm animals with respect and to refuse to support those who fail to do so do not rest on calculations about consequences. And unlike a Singer-type utilitarianism, the rights view does not imply that the individual's duty to become a vegetarian depends on how many other people join the ranks. *Each individual* has the duty to treat others with the respect they are due independently of how many others do so, and each has a similar duty to refrain in principle from supporting practices that fail to show proper respect. Of course, anyone who accepts the rights view must profoundly wish that others *will* act similarly, with the result that commercial animal agriculture, from vast agribusiness operations to the traditional family farm, will go the way of the slave trade—will, that is, cease to exist. But the *individual's* duty to cease to support those who violate the rights of animals does not depend on humanity in general doing so as well.

The rights view is, one might say, a "radical" position, calling, as it does, for the total abolition of a culturally accepted institution to wit, commercial animal farming. The way to "clean up" this institution is not by giving animals bigger cages, cleaner stalls, a place to roost, thus and so much hay, etc. When an institution is grounded in injustice, because it fails to respect the rights of those involved, there is no room for internal house cleaning. Morality will not be satisfied with anything less than its total abolition. And that, for the reasons given, is the rights view's verdict regarding commercial animal agriculture.

HOLISM

The "radical" implications of the rights view suggest how far some philosophers have moved from the anthropocentric traditions of theism and humanism. But, like the utilitarian attacks on this tradition, one should note that the rights view seeks to make its case by working within the major ethical categories of this tradition. For example, hedonistic utilitarians do not deny the moral relevance of human pleasures and pain, so important to our humanist forebears; rather, they accept this and seek to extend our moral horizons to include the moral relevance of the pleasures and pains of animals. And the rights view does not deny the distinctive moral importance of the individual, a central article of belief in theistic thought; rather, it accepts this moral datum and seeks to widen the class of individuals who are to be thought of in this way to include many animals.

Because both the positions discussed in the preceding work with major ethical categories handed down to us by our predecessors, some influential thinkers argue that these positions are, despite all appearances, in the hip pocket, so to speak, of the *Weltanschauung* they aspire to overturn. What is needed, these thinkers contend or imply, is not a broader interpretation of traditional categories (for example, the category of "the rights of the individual"); rather, what is required is the overthrow of these categories. Only then will we have a new vision, one that liberates us from the last vestiges of anthropocentrism.

"THE LAND ETHIC"

Among those whose thought moves in this direction, none is more influential than Aldo Leopold.[10] *Very* roughly, Leopold can be seen as rejecting the "atomism" dear to the hearts of those who build their moral thinking on "the value (or rights) of the individual." What has ultimate value is not the individual but the collective, not the "part" but the "whole," whereby "the whole" is meant the entire biosphere: the *totality* of the things and systems in the natural order. Acts are right, Leopold claims, if they tend to promote the integrity, beauty, diversity, and harmony of the biosphere; they are wrong if they tend contrariwise. As for individuals, be they humans or animals, they are merely "members of the biotic team," having neither more nor less value in themselves than any other member—having, that is, *no* value "in themselves." What good individuals have, so far as this is computable at all, is instrumental only: They are good to the extent that they promote the "welfare," so to speak, of the biosphere. For a Leopoldian, the rights view rests on the fictional view that individuals have a kind of value they in fact lack.

Traditional utilitarianism, not just the rights view, goes by the board, given Leopold's vision. To extend our moral concern to the experiences of animals (for example, their pleasures and pains) is not to overcome the prejudices indigenous to anthropocentrism. One who does this is still in the grip of these prejudices, supposing that mental states that matter to humans must be the yardstick of what matters morally. Utilitarians are people who escape from one prejudice (speciesism) only to embrace another (what we might call "sentientism," the view that mental states allied with or reducible to pleasure and pain are what matter morally). "Animal liberation" is not "nature liberation." In order to forge an ethic that liberates us from our anthropocentric tradition, we must develop a holistic understanding of things, a molecular, rather than an atomistic, vision of the scheme of things and our place in it. "The land" must be viewed as meriting or moral concern. Water, soil, plants, rocks—inanimate, not just animate, existence must be seen to be morally considerable. All are "members" of the same team—the "biotic team."

HOLISM AND ETHICAL VEGETARIANISM

The holism Leopold advocates has interesting implications regarding how we should approach the issue of ethical vegetarianism. Appeals to the rights of animals, of course, are ruled out from the start. Based, as they are, on ideas about the independent value of the individual, such appeals are the voice of anthropocentrism past. That ghost can be exorcised once and for all only if we see the illusoriness of the atomistic view of the individual, *any* individual, as having an independent value, dignity, sanctity, etc. Standard versions of utilitarianism, restricted, as they are, to sentient creation, are similarly out of place. The "moral community" is comprised of all that inhabits the biosphere, not just some select portion of it, and there is no guarantee that what optimizes the balance of, say, pleasure over pain for sentient creation would be the right thing to do, when gauged by what promotes the "welfare" of the biosphere as a whole. If we are to approach the question of ethical vegetarianism with a clear head, therefore, we should refuse the guidance of both the rights view and utilitarianism.

Holism implies that the case for or against ethical vegetarianism must be decided by asking how certain practices involving animals promote or diminish the integrity, diversity, beauty, and harmony of the biosphere. This will be no easy task. Utilitarianism, as was noted earlier, encounters a very serious problem, when it faces the difficulty of saying what the consequences will be, or are most likely to be, if we do one thing rather than another. And this problem arises for utilitarians despite the fact that they restrict their calculations just to the effects on sentient creation. How much more difficult it must be, then, to calculate the consequences for *the biosphere!* There is some danger that "the Land Ethic" will not be able to get off the ground.

Let us assume, however, that this challenge could be met. Then it seems quite likely that the land ethic might judge some practices involving animals morally right, others wrong. For example, raising cattle on nonarable pastures might promote the biosphere's "welfare," whereas destroying a delicately balanced ecosystem in order to construct a factory farm, or allowing chemicals used in animal agriculture to pollute a stream or pond, might be roundly condemned as "unhealthy" for the biosphere. Holism, in short, presumably would decide the ethics of animal agriculture on a case by case basis. When a given commercial undertaking meets the principles of the land ethic, it is right, and we are free to support it by purchasing its wares. When a given commercial undertaking fails to meet the appropriate principles, it is wrong, and we ought not to help it along by buying its products. So far as the matter of the pain, stress, and deprivations that might be caused farm animals in a commercial endeavor that promotes the "welfare" of the biosphere, these "mental states" simply do not compute, and to be morally troubled by such concerns is unwittingly to slip back into the misplaced atomistic concern for the individual holism aspires to redirect.

HOLISM AS ENVIRONMENTAL FASCISM

Few will be easily won over to this "new vision" of things. Like political fascism, where "the good of the State" supercedes "the good of the individual," what holism gives us is a fascist understanding of the environment. Rare species of wild grasses doubtless contribute more to the diversity of the biosphere than do the citizens of Cleveland. But are we therefore morally obliged to "save the wild grasses" at the expense of the life or welfare of these people? If holism is to hold its ground, it must acknowledge that it has this implication, and, in acknowledging this it must acknowledge further that its theoretical boat will come to grief on the shoals of our considered moral beliefs. Of course, those who are determined to awaken us to holism's

virtues may be expected to reply that they are out to *reform* our moral vision, to *change* it, and so should not be expected to provide us with a theory that conforms with our "moral intuitions"—intuitions that, they are likely to add, are but another layer of our uncritical acceptance of our anthropocentric traditions and the ethnocentrism with which they are so intimately allied.

Well, perhaps this is so. Everything depends on the arguments given to support these bold pronouncements. What those arguments come to, or even if they come, must be considered elsewhere.[11] Here it must suffice to note that people who remain sympathetic to notions like "the rights of Man" and "the value of the individual" will not find environmental fascism congenial. And that is a crucial point, given the debate over ethical vegetarianism and commercial animal agriculture. For one cannot consistently defend meat-eating or commercial animal agriculture by appeal to the principles of "the Land Ethic," on the one hand, and, on the other, appeal to principles involving human rights and the value of the individual to defend one's convictions about how human beings should be treated. Environmental fascism and *any* form of a rights theory are like oil and water; they don't mix.

SUMMARY

Two related questions have occupied our attention throughout: (1) Is vegetarianism required on moral grounds? and (2) Judged ethically, what should we say, and what should we do, about commercial animal agriculture? Three different ways to approach these questions have been characterized: utilitarianism, the rights view, and holism. Of the three, the rights view is the most "radical"; it calls for the total abolition of commercial animal agriculture and argues that, as individuals, we have an obligation to cease eating meat, including the meat produced by the animal industry, independently of how many other people do so and independently of the actual consequences our individual abstention have on this industry. Since this industry routinely violates the rights of farm animals, those who support it, not just those who run and profit from it, have "dirty hands."

Some utilitarians evidently seek the same answers offered by the rights view, but their arguments are radically different. Since what we ought to do depends on the consequences, and since our individual abstention from meat eating would not make a whit of difference to any individual animal, it seems we cannot have an obligation to be vegetarians, judged on utilitarian grounds. If, in reply, we are told that it is the consequences of *many* people becoming vegetarians, not just those that flow from the individual's abstention, that grounds the obligation to be vegetarian, utilitarians are, so to speak, out of the frying pan but into the fire. First, we do not know what the consequences will be (for example, for the economy, the starving masses of the Third World, or even farm animals) if many people became vegetarians, and, second, it distorts our very notion of the duties of the individual to suppose that these duties depend on how many other people act in similar ways. So, no, these utilitarians do not succeed in showing *either* that we have an obligation to be vegetarians *or* that commercial animal agriculture is morally to be condemned. These utilitarians may want the conclusions the rights view reaches, but, paradoxically, their utilitarianism stands in the way of getting them.

Holism (the kind of theory we find in Aldo Leopold's work, for example) was the third view considered. So long as we have reason to believe that this or that commercial endeavor in farm animals is not contrary to the beauty, harmony, diversity, and integrity of the biosphere, we have no reason to condemn its operation nor any reason to refuse to consume its products. If, however, particular commercial ventures are destructive of these qualities of the biosphere, we ought to bring them to a halt, and one way of helping to do this is to cease to buy their products.

Holism, in short, answers our two questions, one might say, with an unequivocal "Yes and no." Very serious questions remain, however, concerning how we can know what, according to holism, we must know, before we can say that a given act or practice is right or wrong. Can we really presume to know the consequences of our acts "for the biosphere?" Moreover, holism implies that individuals are of no consequence apart from their role as "members of the biotic team," a fascist view of the individual that would in principle allow mass destruction of the members of a plentiful species (for example, Homo sapiens) in order to preserve the last remaining members of another (for example, a rare wild flower), all in the name of preserving "the diversity" of the biosphere. Few will find holism intuitively congenial, and none can rely on it to answer our two questions and, in mid-stride, invoke "the rights of man" to defend a privileged moral status for human beings. At least none can consistently do this.

Despite their noteworthy differences, the three views we have examined speak with one voice on the matter of the tradition of anthropocentrism bequeathed to us by humanism and theism. That tradition is morally bankrupt. On that the three are agreed. And on this, it seems, we may all agree as well. That being so, and while conceding that the foregoing does not "prove" its merits, it can be no objection to the rights view's answers to our two questions to protest that they are at odds with our moral traditions. To be at odds with these traditions is devoutly to be wished.

Nor is it an objection to the rights view to claim that because it proclaims the rights of animals, it must be unmindful of "the rights of Man" or insensitive to the beauty or integrity of the environment. The rights view does not deny "the rights of Man"; it only refuses to be species-bound in its vision of inherent value and moral rights. No principle it upholds opposes making grains not fed to animals available to needy humans, as commercial animal agriculture winds down. It simply insists that *these* (real or imaginary) consequences of the dissolution of commercial animal agriculture are not the reason why we ought to seek to dissolve it. As for the natural environment, one can only wonder what more one could do to ensure that its integrity and beauty are promoted or retained, than to act in ways that show respect to animals, including wild animals. In respecting the rights of this "part" of the biosphere, will not the "welfare of the whole" be promoted?

CONCLUSION

Theories are one thing; our practice quite another. And so it may seem that all this talk about rights and duties, utility and preferences, the biosphere and anthropocentrism comes to naught. People are people, and they will do what they are used to doing, what they like to do. History gives the lie to this lazy acquiescence in the face of custom and convenience. Were it true, whites would still own blacks, women would still lack the vote, and people could still be put to death for sodomy. Times and customs change, and one (but by no means not the only) force for change are the ideas that trickle down over time into the language and thought of a culture. The language of "animal rights" is in the air, and the thought behind those words is taking root. What not too long ago could be laughed out of court now elicits serious concern. Mill says it well: "All great movements go through three stages: ridicule, discussion, adoption." The movement for animal rights is beyond the stage of ridicule. For those persuaded of its truth, it is an irresistible force. Commercial animal agriculture is the movable object.

Endnotes

1. Immanuel Kant, "Duties to Animals and Spirits," *Lectures on Ethics*, trans. Louis Infield (New York: Harper and Row, 1963), pp. 239–41. Collected in *Animal Rights and Human Obligations*, Tom Regan and Peter Singer, eds. (Englewood Cliffs, NJ: Prentice-Hall Inc., 1976), pp. 122–23.

2. St. Thomas Aquinas, *Summa Contra Gentiles*, literally translated by the English Dominican Fathers (Benzinger Books, 1928), Third Book, Part II, Chap. C XII. Collected in *Animal Rights and Human Obligations*, op. cit., pp. 58–59.

3. Jeremy Bentham, *The Principles of Morals and Legislation* (1789: many editions), Chapter XVII, Section 1. Collected in *Animal Rights and Human Obligations*, op. cit., pp. 129–30.

4. John Stuart Mill, "Whewell on Moral Philosophy," *Collected Works*, Vol. X, pp. 185–87. Collected in *Animal Rights and Human Obligations*, op. cit., pp. 131–32.

5. Peter Singer, *Animal Liberation* (New York: Avon Books, 1975). By far the best factual account of factory farming is J. Mason and Peter Singer, *Animal Factories* (New York: Collier Books, 1982).

6. Richard Ryder, "Experiments on Animals," in *Animals, Men and Morals*, ed. S. and R. Godlovitch and J. Harris (New York: Taplinger, 1972). Collected in *Animal Rights and Human Obligations*, op. cit., pp. 33–47.

7. These criticisms of utilitarianism are developed at greater length in my *The Case For Animal Rights* (Berkeley: University of California Press. London: Routledge and Kegan Paul, 1983).

8. The rights view is developed at length in *The Case For Animal Rights*, ibid.

9. I use the familiar idea of "person" here because it is helpful. I do not use it in *The Case For Animal Rights*. I do not believe anything of substance turns on its use or nonuse.

10. Aldo Leopold, *A Sand County Almanac* (New York: Oxford University Press, 1949). For additional criticism and suggested readings, see William Aiken, "Ethical Issues in Agriculture," in Tom Regan, ed., *Earthbound: New Introductory Essays in Environmental Ethics* (New York: Random House (paper); Philadelphia: Temple University Press (cloth), 1983), pp. 268–70.

11. See *The Case For Animal Rights*, op. cit., ch. 5.

Review Questions

1. Explain Regan's account of traditional moral anthropocentrism.

2. What is the utilitarian objection to this view according to Regan?

3. What objections does Regan make to Singer's position?

4. What is the rights view as Regan expounds it?

5. What is inherent value in Regan's view?

6. Who has rights according to Regan?

7. Why does Regan think that commercial animal agriculture violates the rights of animals?

8. What is the holistic view advocated by Leopold (according to Regan)?

9. Why doesn't Regan accept this view?

Discussion Questions

1. Does Regan refute utilitarianism or not? Explain your answer.

2. Is Regan's notion of inherent value coherent?

3. Do you agree that some animals are persons? Defend your answer.

4. Do you eat meat? If so, do you think that there is anything morally wrong with this practice? Defend your position.

Bonnie Steinbock

Speciesism and the Idea of Equality

Bonnie Steinbock teaches philosophy at the State University of New York at Albany.

Steinbock presents a defense of speciesism, the practice of weighing human interests more heavily than those of animals. While she agrees with Singer that nonhuman pain and suffering deserve some moral consideration, she denies that this consideration should be equal to that given to humans. She claims that humans have morally relevant capacities that nonhuman animals do not have, and this entitles humans to greater moral consideration. These capacities include the ability to be morally responsible, to reciprocate in ways that animals cannot, and to desire self-respect.

Most of us believe that we are entitled to treat members of other species in ways which would be considered wrong if inflicted on members of our own species. We kill them for food, keep them confined, use them in painful experiments. The moral philosopher has to ask what relevant difference justifies this difference in treatment. A look at this question will lead us to re-examine the distinctions which we have assumed make a moral difference.

It has been suggested by Peter Singer [1] that our current attitudes are 'speciesist', a

From Bonnie Steinbock, "Speciesism and the Idea of Equality," *Philosophy* 53, No. 204 (April 1978), pp. 247–256. 1978 © Cambridge University Press. Reprinted with the permission of Cambridge University Press.

word intended to make one think of 'racist' or 'sexist'. The idea is that membership in a species is in itself not relevant to moral treatment, and that much of our behaviour and attitudes towards non-human animals is based simply on this irrelevant fact.

There is, however, an important difference between racism or sexism and 'speciesism'. We do not subject animals to different moral treatment simply because they have fur and feathers, but because they are in fact different from human beings in ways that could be morally relevant. It is false that women are incapable of being benefited by education, and therefore that claim cannot serve to justify preventing them from attending school. But this is not false of cows and dogs, even chimpanzees. Intelligence is thought to be a morally relevant capacity because of its relation to the capacity for moral responsibility.

What is Singer's response? He agrees that non-human animals lack certain capacities that human animals possess, and that this may justify different *treatment*. But it does not justify giving less consideration to their needs and interests. According to Singer, the moral mistake which the racist or sexist makes is not essentially the factual error of thinking that blacks or women are inferior to white men. For even if there were no factual error, even if it were true that blacks and women are less intelligent and responsible than whites and men, this would not justify giving less consideration to their needs and interests. It is important to note that the term 'speciesism' is in one way like, and in another way unlike, the terms 'racism' and 'sexism'. What the term 'speciesism' has in common with these terms is the reference to focusing on a characteristic which is, in itself, irrelevant to moral treatment. And it is worth reminding us of this. But Singer's real aim is to bring us to a new understanding of the idea of equality. The question is, on what do claims to equality rest? The demand for *human* equality is a demand that the interests of all human beings be considered equally, unless there is a moral justification for not doing so. But why should the interests of all human beings be considered equally? In order to answer this question, we have to give some sense to the phrase, 'All men (human beings) are created equal'. Human beings are manifestly *not* equal, differing greatly in intelligence, virtue and capacities. In virtue of what can the claim to equality be made?

It is Singer's contention that claims to equality do not rest on factual equality. Not only do human beings differ in their capacities, but it might even turn out that intelligence, the capacity for virtue, etc., are not distributed evenly among the races and sexes:

The appropriate response to those who claim to have found evidence of genetically based differences in ability between the races or sexes is not to stick to the belief that the genetic explanation must be wrong, whatever evidence to the contrary may turn up; instead we should make it quite clear that the claim to equality does not depend on intelligence, moral capacity, physical strength, or similar matters of fact. Equality is a moral ideal, not a simple assertion of fact. There is no logically compelling reason for assuming that a factual difference in ability between two people justifies any difference in the amount of consideration we give to satisfying their needs and interests. The principle of equality of human beings is not a description of an alleged actual equality among humans: it is a prescription of how we should treat humans.[2]

In so far as the subject is human equality, Singer's view is supported by other philosophers. Bernard Williams, for example, is concerned to show that demands for equality cannot rest on factual equality among people, for no such equality exists.[3] The only respect in which all men are equal, according to Williams, is that they are all equally men. This seems to be a platitude, but Williams denies that it is trivial. Membership in the species *homo sapiens* in itself has no special moral significance, but rather the fact that all men are human serves as a *reminder* that being human involves the possession of characteristics that are morally relevant. But on what characteristics does Williams focus? Aside from the desire for self-respect (which I will discuss later), Williams is not concerned with uniquely human capacities. Rather, he focuses on the capacity to feel pain and the capacity to feel affection. It is in virtue of these capacities, it seems, that the idea of equality is to be justified.

Apparently Richard Wasserstrom has the same idea as he sets out the racist's 'logical and moral mistakes' in 'Rights, Human Rights and Racial Discrimination'.[4] The racist fails to acknowledge that the black person is as capable of suffering as the white person. According to Wasserstrom, the reason why a person is said to have a right not to be made to suffer acute physical pain is that we all do in fact value freedom from such pain. Therefore, if anyone has a right to be free from suffering acute physical pain, *everyone* has this right, for there is no possible basis of discrimination. Wasserstrom says, 'For, if all persons do have equal capacities of these sorts and if the existence of these capacities is the reason for ascribing these rights to anyone, then all persons ought to have the right to claim equality of treatment in respect to the possession and exercise of these rights'.[5] The basis of equality, for Wasserstrom as for Williams, lies not in some uniquely human capacity, but rather in the fact that all human beings are alike in their capacity to suffer. Writers on equality have focused on this capacity, I think, because it functions as some sort of lowest common denominator, so that whatever the other capacities of a human being, he is entitled to equal consideration because, like everyone else, he is capable of suffering.

If the capacity to suffer is the reason for ascribing a right to freedom from acute pain, or a right to well being, then it certainly looks as though these rights must be extended to animals as well. This is the conclusion Singer arrives at. The demand for human equality rests on the equal capacity of all human beings to suffer and to enjoy well being. But if this is the basis of the demand for equality, then this demand must include all beings which have an equal capacity to suffer and enjoy well being. That is why Singer places at the basis of the demand for equality, not intelligence or reason, but sentience. And equality will mean, not equality of treatment, but 'equal consideration of interests'. The equal consideration of interests will often mean quite different treatment, depending on the nature of the entity being considered. (It would be as absurd to talk of a dog's right to vote, Singer says, as to talk of a man's right to have an abortion.)

It might be thought that the issue of equality depends on a discussion of rights. According to this line of thought, animals do not merit equal consideration of interests because, unlike human beings, they do not, or cannot, have rights. But I am not going to discuss rights, important as the issue is. The fact that an entity does not have rights does not necessarily imply that its interests are going to count for less than the interests of entities which are right-bearers. According to the view of rights held by H.L.A. Hart and S.I. Benn, infants do not have rights, nor do the mentally defective, nor do the insane, in so far as they all lack certain minimal conceptual capabilities for having rights.[6] Yet it certainly does not seem that either Hart or Benn would agree that *therefore* their interests are to be counted for less, or that it is morally permissible to treat them in ways in which it would not be permissible to treat right-bearers. It seems to mean only that we must give different sorts of reasons for our obligations to take into consideration the interests of those who do not have rights.

We have reasons concerning the treatment of other people which are clearly independent of the notion of rights. We would say that it is wrong to punch someone because doing that infringes his rights. But we could also say that it is wrong because doing that hurts him, and that is, ordinarily, enough of a reason not to do it. Now this particular reason extends not only to human beings, but to all sentient creatures. One has a *prima facie* reason not to pull the cat's tail (whether or not the cat has rights) because it hurts the cat. And this is the only thing, normally, which is relevant in this case. The fact that the cat is not a 'rational being', that it is not capable of moral responsibility, that it cannot make free choices or shape its life—all of these differences from us have nothing to do with the justifiability of pulling its tail. Does this show that rationality and the rest of it are irrelevant to moral treatment?

I hope to show that this is not the case. But first I want to point out that the issue is not one of cruelty to animals. We all agree that cruelty is wrong, whether perpetrated on a moral or non-moral, rational or non-rational agent. Cruelty is defined as the infliction of unnecessary pain or suffering. What is to count as necessary or unnecessary is determined, in part, by the nature of the end pursued. Torturing an animal is cruel, because although the pain is logically necessary for the action to be torture, the end (deriving enjoyment from seeing the animal suffer) is monstrous. Allowing animals to suffer from neglect or for the sake of large profits may also be thought to be unnecessary and therefore cruel. But there may be some ends, which are very good (such as the advancement of medical knowledge), which can be accomplished by subjecting animals to pain in experiments. Although most people would agree that the pain inflicted on animals used in medical research ought to be kept to a minimum, they would consider pain that cannot be eliminated 'necessary' and therefore not cruel. It would probably not be so regarded if the subjects were non-voluntary human beings. Necessity, then, is defined in terms of human benefit, but this is just what is being called into question. The topic of cruelty to animals, while important from a practical viewpoint, because much of our present treatment of animals involves the infliction of suffering for no good reason, is not very interesting philosophically. What is philosophically interesting is whether we are justified in having different standards of necessity for human suffering and for animal suffering.

Singer says, quite rightly I think, 'If a being suffers, there can be no moral justification for refusing to take that suffering into consideration'.[7] But he thinks that the principle of equality requires that, no matter what the nature of the being, its suffering be counted equally with the like suffering of any other being. In other words sentience does not simply provide us with reasons for acting; it is the *only* relevant consideration for equal consideration of interests. It is this view that I wish to challenge.

I want to challenge it partly because it has such counter-intuitive results. It means, for example, that feeding starving children before feeding starving dogs is just like a Catholic charity's feeding hungry Catholics before feeding hungry non-Catholics. It is simply a matter of taking care of one's own, something which is usually morally permissible. But whereas we would admire the Catholic agency which did not discriminate, but fed all children, first come, first served, we would feel quite differently about someone who had this policy for dogs and children. Nor is this, it seems to me, simply a matter of a sentimental preference for our own species. I might feel much more love for my dog than for a strange child—and yet I might feel morally obliged to feed the child before I fed my dog. If I gave in to the feelings of love and fed my dog and let the child go hungry, I would probably feel guilty. This is not to say that we can simply rely on such feelings. Huck Finn felt guilty at helping Jim escape, which he viewed as stealing from a woman who had never done him any harm. But while the existence of such feelings does not settle the morality of an issue, it is not clear to me that they can be explained away. In any event, their existence can serve as a motivation for trying to find a rational justification for considering human interests above non-human ones.

However, it does seem to me that this *requires* a justification. Until now, common sense (and academic philosophy) have seen no such need. Benn says, 'No one claims equal consideration for all mammals—human beings count, mice do not, though it would not be easy to say *why* not. . . . Although we hesitate to inflict unnecessary pain on sentient creatures, such as mice or dogs, we are quite sure that we do not need to show good reasons for putting human interests before theirs.'[8]

I think we do have to justify counting our interests more heavily than those of animals. But how? Singer is right, I think, to point out that it will not do to refer vaguely to the greater value of human life, to human worth and dignity:

Faced with a situation in which they see a need for some basis for the moral gulf that is commonly thought to separate humans and animals, but can find no concrete difference that will do this without undermining the equality of humans, philosophers tend to waffle. They resort to high-sounding phrases like 'the intrinsic dignity of the human individual'. They talk of 'the intrinsic worth of all men' as if men had some worth that other beings do not have or they say that human beings, and only human beings, are 'ends in themselves', while 'everything other than a person can only have value for a person'. . . . Why should we not attribute 'intrinsic dignity' or 'intrinsic worth' to ourselves? Why should we not say that we are the only things in the universe that have intrinsic value? Our fellow human beings are unlikely to reject the accolades we so generously bestow upon them, and those to whom we deny the honour are unable to object.[9]

Singer is right to be sceptical of terms like 'intrinsic dignity' and 'intrinsic worth'. These phrases are no substitute for a moral argument. But they may point to one. In trying to understand what is meant by these phrases, we may find a difference or differences between human beings and non-human animals that will justify different treatment while not undermining claims for human equality. While we are not compelled to discriminate among people because of different capacities, if we can find a significant difference in capacities between human and non-human animals, this could serve to justify regarding human interests as primary. It is not arbitrary or smug, I think, to maintain that human beings have a different moral status from members of other species because of certain capacities which are characteristic of being human. We may not all be equal in these capacities, but all human beings possess them to some measure, and non-human animals do not. For example, human beings are normally held to be responsible for what they do. In recognizing that someone is responsible for his or her actions, you accord that person a respect which is reserved for those possessed of moral autonomy, or capable of achieving such autonomy. Secondly, human beings can be expected to reciprocate in a way that non-human animals cannot. Non-human animals cannot be motivated by altruistic or moral reasons; they cannot treat you fairly or unfairly. This does not rule out the possibility of an animal being motivated by sympathy or pity. It does rule out altruistic motivation in the sense of motivation due to the recognition that the needs and interests of others provide one with certain reasons for acting.[10] Human beings are capable of altruistic motivation in this sense. We are sometimes motivated simply by the recognition that someone else is in pain, and that pain is a bad thing, no matter who suffers it. It is this sort of reason that I claim cannot motivate an animal or any entity not possessed of fairly abstract concepts. (If some non-human animals do possess the requisite concepts—perhaps chimpanzees who have learned a language—they might well be capable of altruistic motivation.) This means that our moral dealings with animals are necessarily much more limited than our dealings with other human beings. If rats invade our houses, carrying disease and biting our children, we cannot reason with them, hoping to persuade them of the injustice they do us. We can only attempt to get rid of them. And it is this that

makes it reasonable for us to accord them a separate and not equal moral status, even though their capacity to suffer provides us with some reason to kill them painlessly, if this can be done without too much sacrifice of human interests. Thirdly, as Williams points out, there is the 'desire for self-respect': 'a certain human desire to be identified with what one is doing, to be able to realize purposes of one's own, and not to be the instrument of another's will unless one has willingly accepted such a role'.[11] Some animals may have some form of this desire, and to the extent that they do, we ought to consider their interest in freedom and self-determination. (Such considerations might affect our attitudes toward zoos and circuses.) But the desire for self-respect *per se* requires the intellectual capacities of human beings, and this desire provides us with special reasons not to treat human beings in certain ways. It is an affront to the dignity of a human being to be a slave (even if a well-treated one); this cannot be true for a horse or a cow. To point this out is of course only to say that the justification for the treatment of an entity will depend on the sort of entity in question. In our treatment of other entities, we must consider the desire for autonomy, dignity and respect, but only where such a desire exists. Recognition of different desires and interests will often require different treatment, a point Singer himself makes.

But is the issue simply one of different desires and interests justifying and requiring different treatment? I would like to make a stronger claim, namely, that certain capacities, which seem to be unique to human beings, entitle their possessors to a privileged position in the moral community. Both rats and human beings dislike pain, and so we have a *prima facie* reason not to inflict pain on either. But if we can free human beings from crippling diseases, pain and death through experimentation which involves making animals suffer, and if this is the only way to achieve such results, then I think that such experimentation is justified because human lives are more valuable than animal lives. And this is because of certain capacities and abilities that normal human beings have which animals apparently do not, and which human beings cannot exercise if they are devastated by pain or disease.

My point is not that the lack of the sorts of capacities I have been discussing gives us a justification for treating animals just as we like, but rather that it is these differences between human beings and non-human animals which provide a rational basis for different moral treatment and consideration. Singer focuses on sentience alone as the basis of equality, but we can justify the belief that human beings have a moral worth that non-human animals do not, in virtue of specific capacities, and without resorting to 'high-sounding phrases'.

Singer thinks that intelligence, the capacity for moral responsibility, for virtue, etc., are irrelevant to equality, because we would not accept a hierarchy based on intelligence any more than one based on race. We do not think that those with greater capacities ought to have their interests weighed more heavily than those with lesser capacities, and this, he thinks, shows that differences in such capacities are irrelevant to equality. But it does not show this at all. Kevin Donaghy argues (rightly, I think) that what entitles us human beings to a privileged position in the moral community is a certain minimal level of intelligence, which is a prerequisite for morally relevant capacities.[12] The fact that we would reject a hierarchical society based on degree of intelligence does not show that a minimal level of intelligence cannot be used as a cut-off point, justifying giving greater consideration to the interests of those entities which meet this standard.

Interestingly enough, Singer concedes the rationality of valuing the lives of normal human beings over the lives of non-human animals.[13] We are not required to value equally the life of a normal human being and the life of an animal, he thinks, but only their suffering. But I doubt that the value of an entity's life can be separated from the value of its suffering in this way. If we value the lives of human beings more than the lives of animals, this is because we value certain capacities that human beings have and animals do not. But freedom from suffering is, in general, a minimal condition for exercising these capacities, for living a fully human life. So, valuing human life more involves regarding human interests as counting for more. That is why we regard human suffering as more deplorable than comparable animal suffering.

But there is one point of Singer's which I have not yet met. Some human beings (if only a very few) are less intelligent than some non-human animals. Some have less capacity for moral choice and responsibility. What status in the moral community are these members of our species to occupy? Are their interests to be considered equally with ours? Is experimenting on them permissible where such experiments are painful or injurious, but somehow necessary for human well being? If it is certain of our capacities which entitle us to a privileged position, it looks as if those lacking those capacities are not entitled to a privileged position. To think it is justifiable to experiment on an adult chimpanzee but not on a severely mentally incapacitated human being seems to be focusing on membership in a species where that has no moral relevance. (It is being 'speciesist' in a perfectly reasonable use of the word.) How are we to meet this challenge?

Donaghy is untroubled by this objection. He says that it is fully in accord with his intuitions, that he regards the killing of a normally intelligent human being as far more serious than the killing of a person so severely limited that he lacked the intellectual capacities of an adult pig. But this parry really misses the point. The question is whether Donaghy thinks that the killing of a human being so severely limited that he lacked the intellectual capacities of an adult pig would be less serious than the killing of that pig. If superior intelligence is what justifies privileged status in the moral community, then the pig who is smarter than a human being ought to have superior moral status. And I doubt that this is fully in accord with Donaghy's intuitions.

I doubt that anyone will be able to come up with a concrete and morally relevant difference that would justify, say, using a chimpanzee in an experiment rather than a human being with less capacity for reasoning, moral responsibility, etc. Should we then experiment on the severely retarded? Utilitarian considerations aside (the difficulty of comparing intelligence between species, for example), we feel a special obligation to care for the handicapped members of our own species, who cannot survive in this world without such care. Non-human animals manage very well, despite their 'lower intelligence' and lesser capacities; most of them do not require special care from us. This does not, of course, justify experimenting on them. However, to subject to experimentation those people who depend on us seems even worse than subjecting members of other species to it. In addition, when we consider the severely retarded, we think, 'That could be me'. It makes sense to think that one might have been born retarded, but not to think that one might have been born a monkey. And so, although one can imagine oneself in the monkey's place, one feels a closer identification with the severely retarded human being. Here we are getting away from such things as 'morally relevant differences' and are talking about something much more difficult to articulate, namely, the role of feeling and sentiment in moral thinking. We would be *horrified* by the use of the retarded in medical research. But what are we to make of this horror? Has it moral significance or is it 'mere' sentiment, of no more import than the sentiment of whites against blacks? It is terribly difficult to know how to evaluate such feelings.[14] I am not going to say more about this, because I think that the treatment of severely incapacitated human beings does not pose an insurmountable objection to the privileged status principle. I am willing to admit that my horror at the thought of experi-

ments being performed on severely mentally incapacitated human beings in cases in which I would find it justifiable and preferable to perform the same experiments on non-human animals (capable of similar suffering) may not be a moral emotion. But it is certainly not wrong of us to extend special care to members of our own species, motivated by feelings of sympathy, protectiveness, etc. If this is speciesism, it is stripped of its tone of moral condemnation. It is not racist to provide special care to members of your own race; it is racist to fall below your moral obligation to a person because of his or her race. I have been arguing that we are morally obliged to consider the interests of all sentient creatures, but not to consider those interests equally with human interests. Nevertheless, even this recognition will mean some radical changes in our attitude toward and treatment of other species.[15]

Endnotes

1. Peter Singer, *Animal Liberation* (A New York Review Book, 1975).

2. Singer, 5.

3. Bernard Williams, 'The Idea of Equality', *Philosophy, Politics and Society* (Second Series), Laslett and Runciman (eds.) (Blackwell, 1962), 110–131, reprinted in *Moral Concepts*, Feinberg (ed.) (Oxford, 1970), 153–171.

4. Richard Wasserstrom, 'Rights, Human Rights, and Racial Discrimination', *Journal of Philosophy* 61, No. 20 (1964), reprinted in *Human Rights*, A.I. Melden (ed.) (Wadsworth, 1970), 96–110.

5. Ibid., 106.

6. H.L.A. Hart, 'Are There Any Natural Rights?', *Philosophical Review* 64 (1955), and S.I. Benn, 'Abortion, Infanticide, and Respect for Persons', *The Problem of Abortion*, Feinberg (ed.) (Wadsworth, 1973), 92–104.

7. Singer, 9.

8. Benn, 'Equality, Moral and Social', *The Encyclopedia of Philosophy* 3, 40.

9. Singer, 266–267.

10. This conception of altruistic motivation comes from Thomas Nagel's *The Possibility of Altruism* (Oxford, 1970).

11. Williams, op. cit., 157.

12. Kevin Donaghy, 'Singer on Speciesism', *Philosophic Exchange* (Summer 1974).

13. Singer, 22.

14. We run into the same problem when discussing abortion. Of what significance are our feelings toward the unborn when discussing its status? Is it relevant or irrelevant that it looks like a human being?

15. I would like to acknowledge the help of, and offer thanks to, Professor Richard Arneson of the University of California, San Diego; Professor Sidney Gendin of Eastern Michigan University; and Professor Peter Singer of Monash University, all of whom read and commented on earlier drafts of this paper.

Review Questions

1. According to Steinbock, what is the important difference between racism or sexism and speciesism?

2. What is the basis for equality according to Singer, Williams, Wasserstrom, and Steinbock?

3. Steinbock claims that Singer's view has counterintuitive results. What are they?

4. According to Steinbock, why are we justified in counting human interests more heavily than those of animals?

Discussion Questions

1. Steinbock maintains that we should give greater moral consideration to severely mentally incapacitated humans than to animals who may have a greater mental capacity. Does she give good reasons for this? How would Singer reply?

2. Do Steinbock's criticisms of Singer also apply to Regan? Explain your answer.

3. Suppose that alien beings settle on the earth. They are superior to humans in intelligence, moral virtue, desire for self-respect, and so on. What is their moral status? Are they equal to humans? Do they have a higher moral status, just as humans have a higher moral status than animals? What would Steinbock say? What do you think?

Joel Feinberg

The Rights of Animals and Unborn Generations

Joel Feinberg is Professor of Philosophy at the University of Arizona. He is the author of Doing and Deserving, Social Philosophy, and The Moral Limits of the Criminal Law (in four volumes), and editor of Reason and Responsibility and Moral Concepts.

Feinberg begins with an analysis of the concept of a right: To have a right is to have a claim to something against someone. But who has rights? Feinberg's answer is that any being who can have an interest can have a right. This interest principle (as

From Philosophy and Environmental Crisis, ed. William T. Blackstone (Athens, GA: University of Georgia Press), pp. 43–68. Copyright © 1974 by the University of Georgia Press. Reprinted by permission of the author and publisher.

Feinberg calls it) implies that humans and animals can have rights, but rocks, vegetables, and whole species cannot have rights. Future generations of people do have rights, but only contingent on their coming into existence; they do not have a right to existence.

Every philosophical paper must begin with an unproved assumption. Mine is the assumption that there will still be a world five hundred years from now, and that it will contain human beings who are very much like us. We have it within our power now, clearly, to affect the lives of these creatures for better or worse by contributing to the conservation or corruption of the environment in which they must live. I shall assume furthermore that it is psychologically possible for us to care about our remote descendants, that many of us in fact do care, and indeed that we ought to care. My main concern then will be to show that it makes sense to speak of the rights of unborn generations against us, and that given the moral judgment that we ought to conserve our environmental inheritance for them, and its grounds, we might well say that future generations *do* have rights correlative to our present duties toward them. Protecting our environment now is also a matter of elementary prudence, and insofar as we do it for the next generation already here in the persons of our children, it is a matter of love. But from the perspective of our remote descendants it is basically a matter of justice, of respect for their rights. My main concern here will be to examine the concept of a right to better understand how that can be.

THE PROBLEM

To have a right is to have a claim [1] *to* something and *against* someone, the recognition of which is called for by legal rules or, in the case of moral rights, by the principles of an enlightened conscience. In the familiar cases of rights, the claimant is a competent adult human being, and the claimee is an office-holder in an institution or else a private individual, in either case, another competent adult human being. Normal adult human beings, then, are obviously the sorts of beings of whom rights can meaningfully be predicated. Everyone would agree to that, even extreme misanthropes who deny that anyone in fact has rights. On the other hand, it is absurd to say that rocks can have rights, not because rocks are morally inferior things unworthy of rights (that statement makes no sense either), but because rocks belong to a category of entities of whom rights cannot be meaningfully predicated. That is not to say that there are no circumstances in which we ought to treat rocks carefully, but only that the rocks themselves cannot validly claim good treatment from us. In between the clear cases of rocks and normal human beings, however, is a spectrum of less obvious cases, including some bewildering borderline ones. Is it meaningful or conceptually possible to ascribe rights to our dead ancestors? to individual animals? to whole species of animals? to plants? to idiots and madmen? to fetuses? to generations yet unborn? Until we know how to settle these puzzling cases, we cannot

claim fully to grasp the concept of a right, or to know the shape of its logical boundaries.

One way to approach these riddles is to turn one's attention first to the most familiar and unproblematic instances of rights, note their most salient characteristics, and then compare the borderline cases with them, measuring as closely as possible the points of similarity and difference. In the end, the way we classify the borderline cases may depend on whether we are more impressed with the similarities or the differences between them and the cases in which we have the most confidence.

It will be useful to consider the problem of individual animals first because their case is the one that has already been debated with the most thoroughness by philosophers so that the dialectic of claim and rejoinder has now unfolded to the point where disputants can get to the end game quickly and isolate the crucial point at issue. When we understand precisely what *is* at issue in the debate over animal rights, I think we will have the key to the solution of all the other riddles about rights.

INDIVIDUAL ANIMALS

Almost all modern writers agree that we ought to be kind to animals, but that is quite another thing from holding that animals can claim kind treatment from us as their due. Statutes making cruelty to animals a crime are now very common, and these, of course, impose legal duties on people not to mistreat animals; but that still leaves open the question whether the animals, as beneficiaries of those duties, possess rights correlative to them. We may very well have duties *regarding* animals that are not at the same time duties *to* animals, just as we may have duties regarding rocks, or buildings, or lawns, that are not duties *to* the rocks, buildings, or lawns. Some legal writers have taken the still more extreme position that animals themselves are not even the directly intended beneficiaries of statutes prohibiting cruelty to animals. During the nineteenth century, for example, it was commonly said that such statutes were designed to protect human beings by preventing the growth of cruel habits that could later threaten human beings with harm too. Prof. Louis B. Schwartz finds the rationale of the cruelty-to-animals prohibition in its protection of animal lovers from affronts to their sensibilities. "It is not the mistreated dog who is the ultimate object of concern," he writes. "Our concern is for the feelings of other human beings, a large proportion of whom, although accustomed to the slaughter of animals for food, readily identify themselves with a tortured dog or horse and respond with great sensitivity to its sufferings." [2] This seems to me to be factitious. How much more natural it is to say with John Chipman Gray that the true purpose of cruelty-to-animals statutes is "to preserve the dumb brutes from suffering." [3] The very people whose sensibilities are invoked in the alternative explanation, a group that no doubt now includes most of us, are precisely those who would insist that the protection belongs primarily to the animals themselves, not merely to their own tender feelings. Indeed, it would be difficult even to account for the existence of such feelings in the absence of a belief that the animals deserve the protection in their own right and for their own sakes.

Even if we allow, as I think we must, that animals are the intended direct beneficiaries of legislation forbidding cruelty to animals, it does not follow directly that animals have legal rights, and Gray himself, for one,[4] refused to draw this further inference. Animals cannot have rights, he thought, for the same reason they cannot have duties, namely, that they are not genuine "moral agents." Now, it is relatively easy to see why animals cannot have duties, and this matter is largely beyond controversy. Animals cannot be "reasoned with" or instructed in their responsibilities; they are inflexible and unadaptable to future contingencies; they are subject to fits of instinctive passion which they are incapable of repressing or controlling, postponing or sublimating. Hence, they cannot enter into contractual agreements, or make promises; they cannot be trusted; and they cannot (except within very narrow limits and for purposes of conditioning) be blamed for what would be called "moral failures" in a human being. They are therefore incapable of being moral subjects, of acting rightly or wrongly in the moral sense, of having, discharging, or breaching duties and obligations.

But what is there about the intellectual incompetence of animals (which admittedly disqualifies them for duties) that makes them logically unsuitable for rights? The most common reply to this question is that animals are incapable of *claiming* rights on their own. They cannot make motion, on their own, to courts to have their claims recognized or enforced; they cannot initiate, on their own, any kind of legal proceedings; nor are they capable of even understanding when their rights are being violated, of distinguishing harm from wrongful injury, and responding with indignation and an outraged sense of justice instead of mere anger or fear.

No one can deny any of these allegations, but to the claim that they are the grounds for disqualification of rights of animals, philosophers on the other side of this controversy have made convincing rejoinders. It is simply not true, says W.D. Lamont,[5] that the ability to understand what a right is and the ability to set legal machinery in motion by one's own initiative are necessary for the possession of rights. If that were the case, then neither human idiots nor wee babies would have any legal rights at all. Yet it is manifest that both of these classes of intellectual incompetents have legal rights recognized and easily enforced by the courts. Children and idiots start legal proceedings, not on their own direct initiative, but rather through the actions of proxies or attorneys who are empowered to speak in their names. If there is no conceptual absurdity in this situation, why should there be in the case where a proxy makes a claim on behalf of an animal? People commonly enough make wills leaving money to trustees for the care of animals. Is it not natural to speak of the animal's right to his inheritance in cases of this kind? If a trustee embezzles money from the animal's account,[6] and a proxy speaking in the dumb brute's behalf presses the animal's claim, can he not be described as asserting the animal's *rights?* More exactly, the animal itself claims its rights through the vicarious actions of a human proxy speaking in its name and in its behalf. There appears to be no reason why we should require the animal to understand what is going on (so the argument concludes) as a condition for regarding it as a possessor of rights.

Some writers protest at this point that the legal relation between a principal and an agent cannot hold between animals and human beings. Between humans, the relation of agency can take two very different forms, depending upon the degree of discretion granted to the agent, and there is a continuum of combinations between the extremes. On the one hand, there is the agent who is the mere "mouthpiece" of this principal. He is a "tool" in much the same sense as is a typewriter or telephone; he simply transmits the instructions of his principal. Human beings could hardly be the agents or representatives of animals in this sense, since the dumb brutes could no more use human "tools" than mechanical ones. On the other hand, an agent may be some sort of expert hired to exercise his professional judgment on behalf of, and in the name of, the principal. He may be given, within some limited area of expertise, complete independence to act as he deems best, binding his principal to all the beneficial or detrimental consequences. This is the role played by trustees, lawyers, and ghost-writers. This type of representation requires that the agent have great skill, but makes little or no demand upon the principal, who may leave everything to the judgment of his agent. Hence, there appears, at first, to be no reason why an animal cannot be a totally passive principal in this second kind of agency relationship.

There are still some important dissimilarities, however. In the typical instance of representation by an agent, even of the second, highly discretionary kind, the agent is hired by a principal who enters into an agreement or contract with him; the principal tells his agent that within certain carefully specified boundaries "You may speak for me," subject always to the principal's approval, his right to give new directions, or to cancel the whole arrangement. No dog or cat could possibly do any of those things. Moreover, if it is the assigned task of the agent to defend the principal's rights, the principal may often decide to release his claimee, or to waive his own rights, and instruct his agent accordingly. Again, no mute cow or horse can do that. But although the possibility of hiring, agreeing, contracting, approving, directing, canceling, releasing, waiving, and instructing is present in the typical (all-human) case of agency representation, there appears to be no reason of a logical or conceptual kind why that *must* be so, and indeed there are some special examples involving human principals where it is not in fact so. I have in mind legal rules, for example, that require that a defendant be represented at his trial by an attorney, and impose a state-appointed attorney upon reluctant defendants, or upon those tried *in absentia,* whether they like it or not. Moreover, small children and mentally deficient and deranged adults are commonly represented by trustees and attorneys, even though they are incapable of granting their own consent to the representation, or of entering into contracts, of giving directions, or waiving their rights. It may be that it is unwise to permit agents to represent principals without the latters' knowledge or consent. If so, then no one should ever be permitted to speak for an animal, at least in a legally binding way. But that is quite another thing than saying that such representation is logically incoherent or conceptually incongruous—the contention that is at issue.

H.J. McCloskey,[7] I believe, accepts the argument up to this point, but he presents a new and different reason for denying that animals can have legal rights. The ability to make claims, whether directly or through a representative, he implies, is essential to the possession of rights. Animals obviously cannot press their claims on their own, and so if they have rights, these rights must be assertable by agents. Animals, however, cannot be represented, McCloskey contends, and not for any of the reasons already discussed, but rather because representation, in the requisite sense, is always of interests, and animals (he says) are incapable of having interests.

Now, there is a very important insight expressed in the requirement that a being have interests if he is to be a logically proper subject of rights. This can be appreciated if we consider just why it is that mere things cannot have rights. Consider a very precious "mere thing"—a beautiful natural wilderness, or a complex and ornamental artifact, like the Taj Mahal. Such things ought to be cared for, because they would sink into decay if neglected, depriving some human beings, or perhaps even all human beings, of something of great value. Certain persons may even have as their own special job the care and protection of these valuable objects. But we are not tempted in these cases to speak of "thing-rights" correlative to custodial duties, because, try as we might, we cannot think of mere things as possessing interests of their own. Some people may have a duty to preserve, maintain, or improve the Taj Mahal, but they can hardly have a duty to help or hurt it, benefit or aid it, succor or relieve it. Custodians may protect it for the sake of a nation's pride and art lovers' fancy; but they don't keep it in good repair for "its own sake," or for "its own true welfare," or "well-being." A mere thing, however valuable to others, has no good of its own. The explanation of that fact, I suspect, consists in the fact that mere things have no conative life: no conscious wishes, desires, and hopes; or urges and impulses; or unconscious drives, aims, and goals; or latent tendencies, direction of growth, and natural fulfillments. Interests must be compounded somehow out of

conations; hence mere things have no interests. *A fortiori*, they have no interests to be protected by legal or moral rules. Without interests a creature can have no "good" of its own, the achievement of which can be its due. Mere things are not loci of value in their own right, but rather their value consists entirely in their being objects of other beings' interests.

So far McCloskey is on solid ground, but one can quarrel with his denial that any animals but humans have interests. I should think that the trustee of funds willed to a dog or cat is more than a mere custodian of the animal he protects. Rather his job is to look out for the interests of the animal and make sure no one denies it its due. The animal itself is the beneficiary of his dutiful services. Many of the higher animals at least have appetites, conative urges, and rudimentary purposes, the integrated satisfaction of which constitutes their welfare or good. We can, of course, with consistency treat animals as mere pests and deny that they have any rights; for most animals, especially those of the lower orders, we have no choice but to do so. But it seems to me, nevertheless, that in general, animals *are* among the sorts of beings of whom rights can meaningfully be predicated and denied.

Now, if a person agrees with the conclusion of the argument thus far, that animals are the sorts of beings that *can* have rights, and further, if he accepts the moral judgment that we ought to be kind to animals, only one further premise is needed to yield the conclusion that some animals do in fact have rights. We must now ask ourselves for whose sake ought we to treat (some) animals with consideration and humaneness? If we conceive our duty to be one of obedience to authority, or to one's own conscience merely, or one of consideration for tender human sensibilities only, then we might still deny that animals have rights, even though we admit that they are the kinds of beings that *can* have rights. But if we hold not only that we ought to treat animals humanely but also that we should do so for the animals' own sake, that such treatment is something we owe animals as their due, something that can be claimed for them, something the withholding of which would be an injustice and a wrong, and not merely a harm, then it follows that we do ascribe rights to animals. I suspect that the moral judgments most of us make about animals do pass these phenomenological tests, so that most of us do believe that animals have rights, but are reluctant to say so because of the conceptual confusions about the notion of a right that I have attempted to dispel above.

Now we can extract from our discussion of animal rights a crucial principle for tentative use in the resolution of the other riddles about the applicability of the concept of a right, namely, that the sorts of beings who *can* have rights are precisely those who have (or can have) interests. I have come to this tentative conclusion for two reasons: (1) because a right holder must be capable of being represented and it is impossible to represent a being that has no interests, and (2) because a right holder must be capable of being a beneficiary in his own person, and a being without interests is a being that is incapable of being harmed or benefitted, having no good or "sake" of its own. Thus, a being without interests has no "behalf" to act in, and no "sake" to act for. My strategy now will be to apply the "interest principle," as we can call it, to the other puzzles about rights, while being prepared to modify it where necessary (but as little as possible), in the hope of separating in a consistent and intuitively satisfactory fashion the beings who can have rights from those which cannot.

VEGETABLES

It is clear that we ought not to mistreat certain plants, and indeed there are rules and regulations imposing duties on persons not to misbehave in respect to certain members of the vegetable kingdom. It is forbidden, for example, to pick wildflowers in the mountainous tundra areas of national parks, or to endanger trees by starting fires in dry forest areas. Members of Congress introduce bills designed, as they say, to "protect" rare redwood trees from commercial pillage. Given this background, it is surprising that no one [8] speaks of plants as having rights. Plants, after all, are not "mere things"; they are vital objects with inherited biological propensities determining their natural growth. Moreover, we do say that certain conditions are "good" or "bad" for plants, thereby suggesting that plants, unlike rocks, are capable of having a "good." (This is a case, however, where "what we say" should not be taken seriously: we also say that certain kinds of paint are good or bad for the internal walls of a house, and this does not commit us to a conception of walls as being possessed of a good or welfare of their own.) Finally, we are capable of feeling a kind of affection for particular plants, though we rarely personalize them, as we do in the case of animals, by giving them proper names.

Still, all are agreed that plants are not the kinds of beings that can have rights. Plants are never plausibly understood to be the direct intended beneficiaries of rules designed to "protect" them. We wish to keep redwood groves in existence for the sake of human beings who can enjoy their serene beauty, and for the sake of generations of human beings yet unborn. Trees are not the sorts of beings who have their "own sakes," despite the fact that they have biological propensities. Having no conscious wants or goals of their own, trees cannot know satisfaction or frustration, pleasure or pain. Hence, there is no possibility of kind or cruel treatment of trees. In these morally crucial respects, trees differ from the higher species of animals.

Yet trees are not mere things like rocks. They grow and develop according to the laws of their own nature. Aristotle and Aquinas both took trees to have their own "natural ends." Why then do I deny them the status of beings with interests of their own? The reason is that an interest, however the concept is finally to be analyzed, presupposes at least rudimentary cognitive equipment. Interests are compounded out of *desires* and *aims,* both of which presuppose something like *belief,* or cognitive awareness. . . .

WHOLE SPECIES

The topic of whole species, whether of plants or animals, can be treated in much the same way as that of individual plants. A whole collection, as such, cannot have beliefs, expectations, wants, or desires, and can flourish or languish only in the human interest-related sense in which individual plants thrive and decay. Individual elephants can have interests, but the species elephant cannot. Even where individual elephants are not granted rights, human beings may have an interest—economic, scientific, or sentimental—in keeping the species from dying out, and *that* interest may be protected in various ways by law. But that is quite another matter from recognizing a right to survival belonging to the species itself. Still, the preservation of a whole species may quite properly seem to be a morally more important matter than the preservation of an individual animal. Individual animals can have rights but it is implausible to ascribe to them a right to life on the human model. Nor do we normally have duties to keep individual animals alive or even to abstain from killing them provided we do it humanely and nonwantonly in the promotion of legitimate human interests. On the other hand, we do have duties to protect threatened species, not duties to the species themselves as such, but rather duties to future human beings, duties derived from our housekeeping role as temporary inhabitants of this planet.

We commonly and very naturally speak of corporate entities, such as institutions, churches, and national states as having rights and duties, and an adequate analysis of the conditions for ownership of rights should account for that fact. A corporate entity, of course, is more than a mere collection of things that have some important traits in common. Unlike a biological species, an insti-

tution has a charter, or constitution, or by-laws, with rules defining offices and procedures, and it has human beings whose function it is to administer the rules and apply the procedures. When the institution has a duty to an outsider, there is always some determinant human being whose duty it is to do something for the outsider, and when the state, for example, has a right to collect taxes, there are always certain definite flesh and blood persons who have rights to demand tax money from other citizens. We have no reluctance to use the language of corporate rights and duties because we know that in the last analysis these are rights or duties of individual persons, acting in their "official capacities." And when individuals act in their official roles in accordance with valid empowering rules, their acts are imputable to the organization itself and become "acts of state." Thus, there is no need to posit any individual superperson named by the expression "the State" (or for that matter, "the company," "the club," or "the church.") Nor is there any reason to take the rights of corporate entities to be exceptions to the interest principle. The United States is not a superperson with wants and beliefs of its own, but it is a corporate entity with corporate interests that are, in turn, analyzable into the interests of its numerous flesh and blood members.

DEAD PERSONS

So far we have refined the interest principle but we have not had occasion to modify it. Applied to dead persons, however, it will have to be stretched to near the breaking point if it is to explain how our duty to honor commitments to the dead can be thought to be linked to the rights of the dead against us. The case against ascribing rights to dead men can be made very simply: a dead man is a mere corpse, a piece of decaying organic matter. Mere inanimate things can have no interests, and what is incapable of having interests is incapable of having rights. If, nevertheless, we grant dead men rights against us, we would seem to be treating the interests they had while alive as somehow surviving their deaths. There is the sound of paradox in this way of talking, but it may be the least paradoxical way of describing our moral relations to our predecessors. And if the idea of an interest's surviving its possessor's death is a kind of fiction, it is a fiction that most living men have a real interest in preserving.

Most persons while still alive have certain desires about what is to happen to their bodies, their property, or their reputations after they are dead. For that reason, our legal system has developed procedures to enable persons while still alive to determine whether their bodies will be used for purposes of medical research or organic transplantation, and to whom their wealth (after taxes) is to be transferred. Living men also take out life insurance policies guaranteeing that the accumulated benefits be conferred upon beneficiaries of their own choice. They also make private agreements, both contractual and informal, in which they receive promises that certain things will be done after their deaths in exchange for some present service or consideration. In all these cases promises are made to living persons that their wishes will be honored after they are dead. Like all other valid promises, they impose duties on the promisor and confer correlative rights on the promisee.

How does the situation change after the promisee has died? Surely the duties of the promisor do not suddenly become null and void. If that were the case, and known to be the case, there could be no confidence in promises regarding posthumous arrangements; no one would bother with wills or life insurance companies to pay benefits to survivors, which are, in a sense, only conditional duties before a man dies. They come into existence as categorical demands for immediate action only upon the promisee's death. So the view that death renders them null and void has the truth exactly upside down.

The survival of the promisor's duty after the promisee's death does not prove that the promisee retains a right even after death, for we might prefer to conclude that there is one class of cases where duties to keep promises are not logically correlated with a promisee's right, namely, cases where the promisee has died. Still, a morally sensitive promisor is likely to think of his promised performance not only as a duty (i.e., a morally required action) but also as something owed to the deceased promisee as his due. Honoring such promises is a way of keeping faith with the dead. To be sure, the promisor will not think of his duty as something to be done for the promisee's "good," since the promisee, being dead, has no "good" of his own. We can think of certain of the deceased's interests, however, (including especially those enshrined in wills and protected by contracts and promises) as surviving their owner's death, and constituting claims against us that persist beyond the life of the claimant. Such claims can be represented by proxies just like the claims of animals. This way of speaking, I believe, reflects more accurately than any other an important fact about the human condition: we have an interest while alive that other interests of ours will continue to be recognized and served after we are dead. The whole practice of honoring wills and testaments, and the like, is thus for the sake of the living, just as a particular instance of it may be thought to be for the sake of one who is dead.

Conceptual sense, then, can be made of talk about dead men's rights; but it is still a wide open moral question whether dead men in fact have rights, and if so, what those rights are. In particular, commentators have disagreed over whether a man's interest in his reputation deserves to be protected from defamation even after his death. With only a few prominent exceptions, legal systems punish a libel on a dead man "only when its publication is in truth an attack upon the interests of living persons." [9] A widow or a son may be wounded, or embarrassed, or even injured economically, by a defamatory attack on the memory of their dead husband or father. In Utah defamation of the dead is a misdemeanor, and in Sweden a cause of action in tort. The law rarely presumes, however, that a dead man himself has any interests, representable by proxy, that can be injured by defamation, apparently because of the maxim that what a dead man doesn't know can't hurt him.

This presupposes, however, that the whole point of guarding the reputations even of living men, is to protect them from hurt feelings, or to protect some other interests, for example, economic ones, that do not survive death. A moment's thought, I think, will show that our interests are more complicated than that. If someone spreads a libelous description of me, without my knowledge, among hundreds of persons in a remote part of the country, so that I am, still without my knowledge, an object of general scorn and mockery in that group, I have been injured, even though I never learn what has happened. That is because I have an interest, so I believe, in having a good reputation *simpliciter*, in addition to my interest in avoiding hurt feelings, embarrassment, and economic injury. In the example, I do not know what is being said and believed about me, so my feelings are not hurt; but clearly if I did know, I would be enormously distressed. The distress would be the natural consequence of my belief that an interest other than my interest in avoiding distress had been damaged. How else can I account for the distress? If I had no interest in a good reputation as such, I would respond to news of harm to my reputation with indifference.

While it is true that a dead man cannot have his feelings hurt, it does not follow, therefore, that his claim to be thought of no worse than he deserves cannot survive his death. Almost every living person, I should think, would wish to have this interest protected after his death, at least during the lifetimes of those persons who were his contemporaries. We can hardly expect the law to protect Julius Caesar from defamation in the history books. This might hamper historical research and restrict socially valuable forms of expression. Even interests that survive their owner's death are not immortal. Anyone should be permitted to say anything he wishes about George Washington or Abraham Lincoln, though perhaps not everything is morally permissible. Everyone ought to refrain from malicious lies even about Nero or King Tut, though not so much for those ancients' own sakes as for the sake of those who would now know the truth about the past. We owe it to the brothers Kennedy, however, as their due, not to tell damaging lies about them to those who were once their contemporaries. If the reader would deny that judgment, I can only urge him to ask himself whether he now wishes his own interest in reputation to be respected, along with his interest in determining the distribution of his wealth, after his death.

HUMAN VEGETABLES

Mentally deficient and deranged human beings are hardly ever so handicapped intellectually that they do not compare favorably with even the highest of the lower animals, though they are commonly so incompetent that they cannot be assigned duties or be held responsible for what they do. Since animals can have rights, then, it follows that human idiots and madmen can too. It would make good sense, for example, to ascribe to them a right to be cured whenever effective therapy is available at reasonable cost, and even those incurables who have been consigned to a sanatorium for permanent "warehousing" can claim (through a proxy) their right to decent treatment.

Human beings suffering extreme cases of mental illness, however, may be so utterly disoriented or insensitive as to compare quite unfavorably with the brightest cats and dogs. Those suffering from catatonic schizophrenia may be barely distinguishable in respect to those traits presupposed by the possession of interests from the lowliest vegetables. So long as we regard these patients as potentially curable, we may think of them as human beings with interests in their own restoration and treat them as possessors of rights. We may think of the patient as a genuine human person inside the vegetable casing struggling to get out, just as in the old fairy tales a pumpkin could be thought of as a beautiful maiden under a magic spell waiting only the proper words to be restored to her true self. Perhaps it is reasonable never to lose hope that a patient can be cured, and therefore to regard him always as a person "under a spell" with a permanent interest in his own recovery that is entitled to recognition and protection.

What if, nevertheless, we think of the catatonic schizophrenic and the vegetating patient with irreversible brain damage as absolutely incurable? Can we think of them at the same time as possessed of interests and rights too, or is this combination of traits a conceptual impossibility? Shocking as it may at first seem, I am driven unavoidably to the latter view. If redwood trees and rosebushes cannot have rights, neither can incorrigible human vegetables.[10] The trustees who are designated to administer funds for the care of these unfortunates are better understood as mere custodians than as representatives of their interests since these patients no longer have interests. It does not follow that they should not be kept alive as long as possible: that is an open moral question not foreclosed by conceptual analysis. Even if we have duties to keep human vegetables alive, however, they cannot be duties *to* them. We may be obliged to keep them alive to protect the sensibilities of others, or to foster humanitarian tendencies in ourselves, but we cannot keep them alive for their own good, for they are no longer capable of having a "good" of their own. Without awareness, expectation, belief, desire, aim, and purpose, a being can have no interests; without interests, he cannot be benefited; without the capacity to be a beneficiary, he can have no rights. But there may nevertheless be a dozen other reasons to treat him as if he did.

FETUSES

If the interest principle is to permit us to ascribe rights to infants, fetuses, and generations yet unborn, it can only be on the grounds that interests can exert a claim upon us even before their possessors actually come into being, just the reverse of the situation respecting dead men where interests are respected even after their possessors have ceased to be. Newly born infants are surely noisier than mere vegetables, but they are just barely brighter. They come into existence, as Aristotle said, with the capacity to acquire concepts and dispositions, but in the beginning we suppose that their consciousness of the world is a "blooming, buzzing confusion." They do have a capacity, no doubt from the very beginning, to feel pain, and this alone may be sufficient ground for ascribing both an interest and a right to them. Apart from that, however, during the first few hours of their lives, at least, they may well lack even the rudimentary intellectual equipment necessary to the possession of interests. Of course, this induces no moral reservations whatever in adults. Children grow and mature almost visibly in the first few months so that those future interests that are so rapidly emerging from the unformed chaos of their earliest days seem unquestionably to be the basis of their present rights. Thus, we say of a newborn infant that he has a right now to live and grow into his adulthood, even though he lacks the conceptual equipment at this very moment to have this or any other desire. A new infant, in short, lacks the traits necessary for the possession of interests, but he has the capacity to acquire those traits, and his inherited potentialities are moving quickly toward actualization even as we watch him. Those proxies who make claims in behalf of infants, then, are more than mere custodians: they are (or can be) genuine representatives of the child's emerging interests, which may need protection even now if they are to be allowed to come into existence at all.

The same principle may be extended to

"unborn persons." After all, the situation of fetuses one day before birth is not strikingly different from that a few hours after birth. The rights our law confers on the unborn child, both proprietary and personal, are for the most part, placeholders or reservations for the rights he shall inherit when he becomes a full-fledged interested being. The law protects a potential interest in these cases before it has even grown into actuality, as a garden fence protects newly seeded flower beds long before blooming flowers have emerged from them. The unborn child's present right to property, for example, is a legal protection offered now to his future interest, contingent upon his birth, and instantly voidable if he dies before birth. As Coke put it: "The law in many cases hath consideration of him in respect of the apparent expectation of his birth"; [11] but this is quite another thing than recognizing a right actually to be born. Assuming that the child will be born, the law seems to say, various interests that he will come to have after birth must be protected from damage that they can incur even before birth. Thus prenatal injuries of a negligently inflicted kind can give the newly born child a right to sue for damages which he can exercise through a proxy-attorney and in his own name any time *after* he is born.

There are numerous other places, however, where our law seems to imply an unconditional right to be born, and surprisingly no one seems ever to have found that idea conceptually absurd. One interesting example comes from an article given the following headline by the *New York Times:* "Unborn Child's Right Upheld Over Religion." [12] A hospital patient in her eighth month of pregnancy refused to take a blood transfusion even though warned by her physician that "she might die at any minute and take the life of her child as well." The ground of her refusal was that blood transfusions are repugnant to the principles of her religion (Jehovah's Witnesses). The Supreme Court of New Jersey expressed uncertainty over the constitutional question of whether a non-pregnant

adult might refuse on religious grounds a blood transfusion pronounced necessary to her own survival, but the court nevertheless ordered the patient in the present case to receive the transfusion on the grounds that "the unborn child is entitled to the law's protection."

It is important to reemphasize here that the questions of whether fetuses do or ought to have rights are substantive questions of law and morals open to argument and decision. The prior question of whether fetuses are the kind of beings that can have rights, however, is a conceptual, not a moral, question, amenable only to what is called "logical analysis," and irrelevant to moral judgment. The correct answer to the conceptual question, I believe, is that unborn children are among the sorts of beings of whom possession of rights can meaningfully be predicated, even though they are (temporarily) incapable of having interests, because their future interests can be protected now, and it does make sense to protect a potential interest even before it has grown into actuality. The interest principle, however, makes perplexing, at best, talk of a noncontingent fetal right to be born; for fetuses, lacking actual wants and beliefs, have no actual interest in being born, and it is difficult to think of any other reason for ascribing any rights to them other than on the assumption that they will in fact be born. [13]

FUTURE GENERATIONS

We have it in our power now to make the world a much less pleasant place for our descendants than the world we inherited from our ancestors. We can continue to proliferate in ever greater numbers, using up fertile soil at an even greater rate, dumping our wastes into rivers, lakes, and oceans, cutting down our forests, and polluting the atmosphere with noxious gases. All thoughtful people agree that we ought not to do these things. Most would say that we have a duty not to do these things, meaning not merely that conservation is morally required (as opposed to merely desirable) but also that it is something due our descendants, something to be done for their sakes. Surely we owe it to future generations to pass on a world that is not a used up garbage heap. Our remote descendants are not yet present to claim a livable world as their right, but there are plenty of proxies to speak now in their behalf. These spokesmen, far from being mere custodians, are genuine representatives of future interests.

Why then deny that the human beings of the future have rights which can be claimed against us now in their behalf? Some are inclined to deny them present rights out of a fear of falling into obscure metaphysics, by granting rights to remote and unidentifiable beings who are not yet even in existence. Our unborn great-great-grandchildren are in some sense "potential" persons, but they are far more remotely potential, it may seem, than fetuses. This, however, is not the real difficulty. Unborn generations are more remotely potential than fetuses in one sense, but not in another. A much greater period of time with a far greater number of causally necessary and important events must pass before their potentiality can be actualized, it is true; but our collective posterity is just as certain to come into existence "in the normal course of events" as is any given fetus now in its mother's womb. In that sense the existence of the distant human future is no more remotely potential than that of a particular child already on its way.

The real difficulty is not that we doubt whether our descendants will ever be actual, but rather that we don't know who they will be. It is not their temporal remoteness that troubles us so much as their indeterminacy—their present facelessness and namelessness. Five centuries from now men and women will be living where we live now. Any given one of them will have an interest in living space, fertile soil, fresh air, and the like, but that arbitrarily selected one has no other qualities we can presently envision very clearly. We don't even know who his parents, grandparents, or great-grandparents are, or even whether he is related to us. Still, whoever these human beings may turn out to be, and whatever they might reasonably be expected to be like, they will have interests that we can affect, for better or worse, right now. That much we can and do know about them. The identity of the owners of these interests is now necessarily obscure, but the fact of their interest-ownership is crystal clear, and that is all that is necessary to certify the coherence of present talk about their rights. We can tell, sometimes, that shadowy forms in the spatial distance belong to human beings, though we know not who or how many they are; and this imposes a duty on us not to throw bombs, for example, in their direction. In like manner, the vagueness of the human future does not weaken its claim on us in light of the nearly certain knowledge that it will, after all, be human.

Doubts about the existence of a right to be born transfer neatly to the question of a similar right to come into existence ascribed to future generations. The rights that future generations certainly have against us are contingent rights: the interests they are sure to have when they come into being (assuming of course that they will come into being) cry out for protection from invasions that can take place now. Yet there are no actual interests, presently existent, that future generations, presently nonexistent, have now. Hence, there is no actual interest that they have in simply coming into being, and I am at a loss to think of any other reason for claiming that they have a right to come into existence (though there may well be such a reason). Suppose then that all human beings at a given time voluntarily form a compact never again to produce children, thus leading within a few decades to the end of our species. This of course is a wildly improbable hypothetical example but a rather crucial one for the position I have been tentatively considering. And we can imagine, say, that the whole world is converted to a strange ascetic religion which absolutely requires sexual abstinence for everyone. Would this arrangement violate the rights of anyone? No one can complain on behalf of presently nonexistent future generations that their future interests which give them a contingent right of protection have been violated since they will never come into existence to be wronged. My inclination then is to conclude that the suicide of our species would be deplorable, lamentable, and a deeply moving tragedy, but that it would violate no one's rights. Indeed if, contrary to fact, all human beings could ever agree to such a thing, that very agreement would be a symptom of our species' biological unsuitability for survival anyway.

CONCLUSION

For several centuries now human beings have run roughshod over the lands of our planet, just as if the animals who do live there and the generations of humans who will live there had no claims on them whatever. Philosophers have not helped matters by arguing that animals and future generations are not the kinds of beings who can have rights now, that they don't presently qualify for membership, even "auxiliary membership," in our moral community. I have tried in this essay to dispel the conceptual confusions that make such conclusions possible. To acknowledge their rights is the very least we can do for members of endangered species (including our own). But that is something.

APPENDIX

The Paradoxes of Potentiality

Having conceded that rights can belong to beings in virtue of their merely potential interests, we find ourselves on a slippery slope; for it may seem at first sight that anything at all can have potential interests, or much more generally, that anything at all can be potentially almost anything else at all! Dehydrated orange powder is potentially orange juice, since if we add water to it, it will be orange juice. More remotely, however, it is also potentially lemonade, since it will become lem-

onade if we add a large quantity of lemon juice, sugar, and water. It is also a potentially poisonous brew (add water and arsenic), a potential orange cake (add flour, etc., and bake), a potential orange-colored building block (add cement and harden), and so on, *ad infinitum.* Similarly a two-celled embryo, too small to be seen by the unaided eye, is a potential human being; and so is an unfertilized ovum; and so is even an "uncapacitated" spermatozoan. Add the proper nutrition to an implanted embryo (under certain other necessary conditions) and it becomes a fetus and then a child. Looked at another way, however, the implanted embryo has been combined (under the same conditions) with the nutritive elements, which themselves are converted into a growing fetus and child. Is it then just as proper to say that food is a "potential child" as that an embryo is a potential child? If so, then what isn't a "potential child?" (Organic elements in the air and soil are "potentially food," and hence potentially people!)

Clearly, some sort of line will have to be drawn between direct or proximate potentialities and indirect or remote ones; and however we draw this line, there will be borderline cases whose classification will seem uncertain or even arbitrary. Even though any X can become a Y provided only that it is combined with the necessary additional elements, $a, b, c, d,$ and so forth, we cannot say of any given X that it is a "potential Y" unless certain further—rather strict—conditions are met. (Otherwise the concept of potentiality, being universally and promiscuously applicable, will have no utility.) A number of possible criteria of proximate potentiality suggest themselves. The first is the criterion of causal importance. Orange powder is not properly called a potential building block because of those elements needed to transform it into a building block, the cement (as opposed to any of the qualities of the orange powder) is the causally crucial one. Similarly, any pauper might (misleadingly) be called a "potential millionaire" in the sense that all that need be added to any man to transform him into a millionaire is a great amount of money. The absolutely crucial element in the change, of course, is no quality of the man himself but rather the million dollars "added" to him.

What is causally "important" depends upon our purposes and interests and is therefore to some degree a relativistic matter. If we seek a standard, in turn, of "importance," we may posit such a criterion, for example, as that of the ease or difficulty (to some persons or other) of providing those missing elements which, when combined with the thing at hand, convert it into something else. It does seem quite natural, for example, to say that the orange powder is potentially orange juice, and that is because the missing element is merely common tap water, a substance conveniently near at hand to everyone; whereas it is less plausible to characterize the powder as potential cake since a variety of further elements, and not just one, are required, and some of these are not conveniently near at hand to many. Moreover, the process of combining the missing elements into a cake is rather more complicated than mere "addition." It is less plausible still to call orange powder a potential curbstone for the same kind of reason. The criterion of ease or difficulty of the acquisition and combination of additional elements explains all these variations.

Still another criterion of proximate potentiality closely related to the others is that of degree of deviation required from "the normal course of events." Given the intentions of its producers, distributors, sellers, and consumers, dehydrated orange juice will, in the normal course of events, become orange juice. Similarly, a human embryo securely imbedded in the wall of its mother's uterus will in the normal course of events become a human child. That is to say that if no one deliberately intervenes to prevent it happening, it will, in the vast majority of cases, happen. On the other hand, an unfertilized ovum will not become an embryo unless someone intervenes deliberately to make it happen.

Without such intervention in the "normal" course of events, an ovum is a mere bit of protoplasm of very brief life expectancy. If we lived in a world in which virtually every biologically capable human female became pregnant once a year throughout her entire fertile period of life, then we would regard fertilization as something that happens to every ovum in "the natural course of events." Perhaps we would regard every unfertilized ovum, in such a world, as a potential person even possessed of rights corresponding to its future interests. It would perhaps make conceptual if not moral sense in such a world to regard deliberate nonfertilization as a kind of homicide.

It is important to notice, in summary, that words like *important, easy,* and *normal* have sense only in relation to human experiences, purposes, and techniques. As the latter change, so will our notions of what is important, difficult, and usual, and so will the concept of potentiality, or our application of it. If our purposes, understanding, and techniques continue to change in indicated directions, we may even one day come to think of inanimate things as possessed of "potential interests." In any case, we can expect the concept of a right to shift its logical boundaries with changes in our practical experience.

Endnotes

1. I shall leave the concept of a claim unanalyzed here, but for a detailed discussion, see my "The Nature and Value of Rights," *Journal of Value Inquiry* 4 (Winter 1971): 263–277.

2. Louis B. Schwartz, "Morals, Offenses and the Model Penal Code," *Columbia Law Review* 63 (1963): 673.

3. John Chipman Gray, *The Nature and Sources of the Law,* 2d ed. (Boston: Beacon Press, 1963), p. 43.

4. And W.D. Ross for another. See *The Right and the Good* (Oxford: Clarendon Press, 1930), app. I, pp. 48–56.

5. W.D. Lamont, *Principles of Moral Judgment* (Oxford: Clarendon Press, 1946), pp. 83–85.

6. Cf. H.J. McCloskey, "Rights," *Philosophical Quarterly* 15 (1965): 121, 124.

7. Ibid.

8. Outside of Samuel Butler's *Erewhon.*

9. William Salmond, *Jurisprudence*, 12th ed., ed. P.J. Fitzgerald (London: Sweet and Maxwell, 1966), p. 304.

10. Unless, of course, the person in question, before he became a "vegetable," left testamentary directions about what was to be done with his body just in case he should ever become an incurable vegetable. He may have directed either that he be preserved alive as long as possible, or else that he be destroyed, whichever he preferred. There may, of course, be sound reasons of public policy why we should not honor such directions, but if we did promise to give legal effect to such wishes, we would have an example of a man's earlier interest in what is to happen to his body surviving his very competence as a person, in quite the same manner as that in which the express interest of a man now dead may continue to exert a claim on us.

11. As quoted by Salmond, *Jurisprudence*, p. 303. Simply as a matter of policy the potentiality of some future interests may be so remote as to make them seem unworthy of present support. A testator may leave property to his unborn child, for example, but not to his unborn grandchildren. To say of the potential person presently in his mother's womb that he owns property now is to say that certain property must be held for him until he is "real" or "mature" enough to possess it. "Yet the law is careful lest property should be too long withdrawn in this way from the uses of living men in favor of generations yet to come; and various restrictive rules have been established to this end. No testator could now direct his fortune to be accumulated for a hundred years and then distributed among his descendants"—Salmond, ibid.

12. *The New York Times*, 17 June 1966, p. I.

13. In an essay entitled "Is There a Right to be Born?" I defend a negative answer to the question posed, but I allow that under certain very special conditions, there can be a "right *not* to be born." See *Abortion*, ed. J. Feinberg (Belmont, Calif.: Wadsworth, 1973).

Review Questions

1. Explain Feinberg's analysis of the concept of a right.

2. Do animals have rights? What is Gray's view? What is McCloskey's view? What position does Feinberg take?

3. According to Feinberg, what sorts of beings can have rights? Give examples of beings that do and do not have rights according to Feinberg.

4. On Feinberg's view, what sorts of rights do future generations have?

Discussion Questions

1. Suppose we grant that animals have rights. Exactly what rights do they have? For example, do they have a right to life?

2. Do dead people have rights? What would Feinberg say? What do you think?

3. Do human vegetables (as Feinberg calls them) have rights? What is Feinberg's answer? Do you agree or not?

4. What is Feinberg's position on fetuses and infants? Is it acceptable to you or not? Why or why not?

5. At the end of his article, Feinberg claims that the suicide of our species would violate no one's rights. Do you agree? Why or why not?

William Godfrey-Smith

The Value of Wilderness

William Godfrey-Smith teaches philosophy at Australian National University (Canberra, Australia). Godfrey-Smith explores two kinds of justification

From William Godfrey-Smith, "The Value of Wilderness," *Environmental Ethics* (1979), pp. 309–310. Reprinted with permission of *Environmental Ethics* and the author.

for wilderness preservation, an instrumental justification and a holistic one based on the intrinsic value of the wilderness. He finds that the instrumental justifications for conservation—saving the wilderness because it is a cathedral, a laboratory, a silo, or a gymnasium—all fail to provide a satisfactory rationale. Instead he suggests a holistic conception of nature where we think of humans and nature together forming a moral community, and where we must engage in cooperative behavior for the sake of the whole community.

Wilderness is the raw material out of which man has hammered the artifact called civilization.[1]

Aldo Leopold

The framework that I examine is the framework of *Western* attitudes toward our natural environment, and wilderness in particular. The philosophical task to which I shall address myself is an exploration of attitudes toward wilderness, especially the sorts of justification to which we might legitimately appeal for the preservation of wilderness: what grounds can we advance in support of the claim that wilderness is something that we should *value?*

There are two different ways of appraising something as valuable. It may be that the thing in question is good or valuable *for the sake* of something that we hold to be valuable. In this case the thing is not considered to be good in itself; value in this sense is ascribed in virtue of the thing's being a *means* to some valued end, and not as an *end in itself.* Such values are standardly designated *instrumental* values. Not everything that we hold to be good or valuable can be good for the sake of something else; our values must ultimately be *grounded* in something that is held to be good or valuable in itself. Such things are said to be *intrinsically* valuable. As a matter of historical fact, those things that have been held to be intrinsically valuable, within our Western traditions of thought, have nearly always been taken to be states or conditions of *persons*, e.g., happiness, pleasure, knowledge, or self-realization, to name but a few.

It follows from this that a very central assumption of Western moral thought is that value can be ascribed to the nonhuman world only insofar as it is good for the sake of the well-being of human beings.[2] Our entire attitude toward the natural environment, therefore, has a decidedly anthropocentric bias, and this fact is reflected in the sorts of justification that are standardly provided for the preservation of the natural environment.

A number of thinkers, however, are becoming increasingly persuaded that our anthropocentric morality is in fact inadequate to provide a satisfactory basis for a moral philosophy of ecological obligation. It is for this reason that we hear not infrequently the claim that we need a "new morality." A new moral framework—that is, a network of recognized obligations and duties—is not, however, something that can be casually conjured up in order to satisfy some vaguely felt need. The task of developing a sound biologically based moral philosophy, a philosophy that is not anthropocentrically based, and that provides a satisfactory justification for ecological obligation and concern, is, I think, one of the most urgent tasks confronting moral philosophers at the present. It will entail a radical reworking of accepted attitudes—attitudes that we currently accept as "self-evident"— and this is not something that can emerge suddenly. Indeed, I think the seminal work remains largely to be done, though I suggest below the broad outline that an environmentally sound moral philosophy is likely to take.

In the absence of a comprehensive and convincing ecologically based morality we naturally fall back on *instrumental* justifications for concern for our natural surroundings, and for preserving wilderness areas and animal species. We can, I think, detect at least four main lines of instrumental justification for the preservation of wilderness. By *wilderness* I understand any reasonably large tract of the earth, together with its plant and animal communities, which is substantially unmodified by humans and in particular by human technology. The natural contrast to *wilderness* and *nature* is an *artificial* or *domesticated* environment. The fact that there are borderline cases that are difficult to classify does not, of course, vitiate this distinction.

The first attitude toward wilderness espoused by conservationists to which I wish to draw attention is what I shall call the "cathedral" view. This is the view that wilderness areas provide a vital opportunity for spiritual revival, moral regeneration, and aesthetic delight. The enjoyment of wilderness is often compared in this respect with religious or mystical experience. Preservation of magnificent wilderness areas for those who subscribe to this view is essential for human well-being, and its destruction is conceived as something akin to an act of vandalism, perhaps comparable to—some may regard it as more serious than [3]—the destruction of a magnificent and moving human edifice, such as the Parthenon, the Taj Mahal, or the Palace of Versailles.

Insofar as the "cathedral" view holds that value derives solely from human satisfactions gained from its contemplation it is clearly an instrumentalist attitude. It does, however, frequently approach an *intrinsic value* attitude, insofar as the feeling arises that there is importance in the fact that it is there to be contemplated, whether or not anyone actually takes advantage of this fact. Suppose for example, that some wilderness was so precariously balanced that *any* human intervention or contact would inevitably bring about its destruction. Those who maintained that the area should, nevertheless, be preserved, unexperienced and unenjoyed, would certainly be ascribing to it an intrinsic value.

The "cathedral" view with respect to wilderness in fact is a fairly recent innovation in Western thought. The predominant Greco-Christian attitude, which generally speaking was the predominant Western attitude prior to eighteenth- and nineteenth-century romanticism, had been to view wilderness as threatening or alarming, an attitude still reflected in the figurative uses of the expression *wilderness,* clearly connoting a degenerate state to be avoided. Christianity, in general, has enjoined "the transformation of wilderness, those dreaded haunts of demons, the ancient nature-gods, into farm and pasture," [4] that is, to a domesticated environment.

The second instrumental justification of the value of wilderness is what we might call the "laboratory" argument. This is the argument that wilderness areas provide vital subject matter for scientific inquiry that provides us with an understanding of the intricate interdependencies of biological systems, their modes of change and development, their energy cycles, and the source of their stabilities. If we are to understand our own biological dependencies, we require natural systems as a norm, to inform us of the biological laws that we transgress at our peril.

The third instrumentalist justification is the "silo" argument, which points out that one excellent reason for preserving reasonable areas of the natural environment intact is that we thereby preserve a stockpile of genetic diversity, which it is certainly prudent to maintain as a backup in case something should suddenly go wrong with the simplified biological systems that, in general, constitute agriculture. Further, there is the related point that there is no way of anticipating our future needs, or the undiscovered applications of apparently useless plants, which might turn out to be, for example, the source of some pharmacologically valuable drug—a cure, say, for leukemia. This might be called, perhaps, the "rare herb" argument, and it provides another persuasive instrumental justification for the preservation of wilderness.

The final instrumental justification that I think should be mentioned is the "gymnasium" argument, which regards the preservation of wilderness as important for athletic or recreational activities.

An obvious problem that arises from these instrumental arguments is that the various activities that they seek to justify are not always possible to reconcile with one another. The interests of the wilderness lover who subscribes to the "cathedral" view are not always reconcilable with those of the ordinary vacationist. Still more obvious is the conflict between the recreational use of wilderness and the interests of the miner, the farmer, and the timber merchant.

The conflict of interest that we encounter here is one that it is natural to try and settle through the economic calculus of cost-benefit considerations. So long as the worth of natural systems is believed to depend entirely on instrumental values, it is natural to suppose that we can sort out the conflict of interests within an objective frame of reference, by estimating the human satisfactions to be gained from the preservation of wilderness, and by weighing these against the satisfactions that are to be gained from those activities that may lead to its substantial modification, domestication, and possibly even destruction.

Many thinkers are liable to encounter here a feeling of resistance to the suggestion that we can apply purely economic considerations to settle such conflicts of interest. The assumption behind economic patterns of thought, which underline policy formulation and planning, is that the values that we attach to natural systems and to productive activities are commensurable; this is an assumption that may be called into question. It is not simply a question of the difficulty of quantifying what value should be attached to the preservation of the natural environment. The feeling is more that economic considerations are simply out of place. This feeling is one that is often too lightly dismissed by tough-minded economists as being obscurely mystical or superstitious; but it is a view worth examining. What it amounts to, I suggest, is the belief that there is something *morally* objectionable in the destruction of natural systems, or at least in their wholesale elimination, and this is precisely the belief that natural systems, or economically "useless" species do possess an *intrinsic* value. That is, it is an attempt to articulate the rejection of the anthropocentric view that all value, ultimately, resides in *human* interests and concerns. But it is a difficult matter to try to provide justification for such attitudes, and this is, for reasons that are deeply bound up with the problems of resolving basic value conflict, a problem that I have discussed elsewhere.[5]

The belief that all values are commensurable, so that there is no problem *in principle* in providing a satisfactory resolution of value conflict, involves the assumption that the quantitative social sciences, in particular economics, can provide an *objective* frame of reference within which all conflicts of interest can be satisfactorily resolved. We should, however, note that in the application of cost-benefit analyses there is an inevitable bias in the sorts of values that figure in the calcula-tion, to wit, a bias toward those considerations that are readily quantifiable, and toward those interests that will be staunchly defended. This is a fairly trivial point, but it is one that has substantial consequences, for there are at least three categories of values and interests that are liable to be inadequately considered, or discounted altogether.[6] First, there are the interests of those who are too widely distributed spatially, or too incrementally affected over time, to be strongly supported by any single advocate. Second, there are the interests of persons not yet existing, to wit, future generations, who are clearly liable to be affected by present policy, but who are clearly not in a position to press any claims. Third, there are interests not associated with humans at all, such as the "rights" of wild animals.[7]

This last consideration, in particular, is apt to impress many as ludicrous, as quite simply "unthinkable." It is an unquestioned axiom of our present code of ethics that the class of individuals to which we have obligations is the class of humans. The whole apparatus of rights and duties is in fact based on an ideal of reciprocal contractual obligations, and in terms of this model the class of individuals to whom we may stand in moral relations—i.e., those with whom we recognize a network of rights, duties, and obligations—is the class of humans. A major aspect of a satisfactory ethic of ecological obligation and concern will be to challenge this central anthropocentric assumption. I return to this point below.

Even restricting our attention to the class of human preference havers, however, we should be wary of dismissing as simply inadmissible the interests of future generations. The claims of posterity tend to be excluded from our policy deliberations not, I suspect, because we believe that future generations will be unaffected by our policies, but because we lack any clear idea as to how to set about attaching weight to their interests. This is an instance of the familiar problem of "the dwarfing of soft variables." In settling conflicts of interest, any consideration that cannot be precisely quantified tends to be given little weight or, more likely, left out of the equation altogether: "If you can't measure it, it doesn't exist." [8] The result of ignoring soft variables is a spurious appearance of completeness and precision, but in eliminating all soft variables from our cost-benefit calculations, the conclusion is decidedly biased. If, as seems plausible, it is *in principle* impossible to do justice to soft variables, such as the interests of posterity, it may be that we have to abandon the idea that the economic models employed in cost-benefit calculations are universally applicable for sorting out all conflicts of interest. It may be necessary to abandon the economic calculus as the universal model for rational deliberation.[9]

Another category of soft variable that tends to be discounted from policy deliberations is that which concerns economically unimportant species of animals or plants. A familiar subterfuge that we frequently encounter is the attempt to invest such species with spurious economic value, as illustrated in the rare herb argument. A typical example of this, cited by Leopold, is the reaction of ornithologists to the threatened disappearance of certain species of songbirds: they at once came forward with some distinctly shaky evidence that they played an essential role in the control of insects.[10] The dominance of economic modes of thinking is again obvious: the evidence has to be economic in order to be acceptable. This exemplifies the way in which we turn to instrumentalist justifications for the maintenance of biotic diversity.

The alternative to such instrumentalist justifications, the alternative that Leopold advocated with great insight and eloquence, is to widen the boundary of the moral community to include animals, plants, the soil, or collectively *the land*.[11] This involves a radical shift in our conception of nature, so that land is recognized not simply as property, to be dealt with or disposed of as a matter of expediency; land in Leopold's view is not a commodity that belongs to us, but a community to which we belong. This change in conception is far-reaching and profound. It involves a shift in our metaphysical conception of nature—that is, a change in what sort of thing we take our natural surroundings to *be*. This is a point that I would like to elaborate, albeit sketchily.

The predominant Western conception of nature is exemplified in—and to no small extent is a consequence of—the philosophy of Descartes, in which nature is viewed as something separate and apart, to be transformed and controlled at will. Descartes divided the world into conscious thinking substances—minds—and extended, mechanically arranged substances—the rest of nature. It is true that we find in Western thought alternatives to the Cartesian metaphysical conception of nature—the views of Spinoza and Hegel might be mentioned in particular [12]—but the predominant spirit, especially among scientists, has been Cartesian. These metaphysical views have become deeply embedded in Western thought, which has induced us to view the world through Cartesian spectacles. One of the triumphs of Descartes' mechanistic view of nature has been the elimination of occult qualities and forces from the explanation of natural events. The natural world is to be understood, in the Cartesian model, in purely mechanistic terms. An unfortunate consequence of the triumph, nevertheless, has been a persistent fear among some thinkers that the rejection of Cartesian metaphysics may lead to the reinstatement of occult and mystical views of nature.

An important result of Descartes' sharp ontological division of the world into active mental substances and inert material substances, has been the alienation of man from the natural world. Although protests have been raised against Cartesian metaphysics ever since its inception, it has exercised a deep influence on our attitudes toward nature. Descartes' mechanistic conception of nature naturally leads to the view that it is possible in principle to obtain complete mastery and technical control over the natural world. It is significant to recall that for Descartes the paradigm instance of a natural object was a lump of wax, the perfect exemplification of malleability. This conception of natural objects as wholly pliable and passive is clearly one that leaves no room for anything like a network of obligations.

A natural corollary of the mechanistic conception of nature, and integral to the Cartesian method of inquiry, is the role played by reductive thinking. In order to understand a complex system one should, on this view, break it into its component parts and examine them. The Cartesian method of inquiry is a natural correlate of Cartesian metaphysics, and is a leitmotif of our science-based technology.

It should be stressed that a rejection of the Cartesian attitude and its method of inquiry need *not* involve a regression to occult and mystical views about the "sacredness" of the natural world, and the abandoning of systematic rational inquiry. It must be conceded, however, that the rejection of the view that nature is an exploitable commodity has, unfortunately, frequently taken this form. This sort of romantic nature mysticism *does* provide a powerful exhortation for exercising restraint in our behavior to the natural world, but it carries with it a very clear danger. This is that while prohibiting destructive acts toward the natural world, it equally prohibits constructive acts; we surely cannot rationally adopt a complete "hands off" policy with respect to nature, on the basis of what looks like the extremely implausible—and highly cynical—a priori assumption that *any* attempt to modify our surroundings is bound to be for the worse.

It may, however, be that advocates of the "sacredness" of nature are attempting to do no more than articulate the idea that natural systems have their own intrinsic value, and adopt this manner of speaking as a convenient way of rejecting the dominant anthropocentric morality. If *this* is all that is being claimed, then I have no quarrel with it. And it

may be inevitable that this mode of expression is adopted in the absence of a developed ecologically sound alternative morality. But I think we should be wary of this style of justification; what is needed, as Passmore has nicely expressed it, is not the spiritualizing of nature, but the naturalizing of man.[13] This involves a shift from the piecemeal reductive conception of natural items to a *holistic* or systemic view in which we come to appreciate the symbiotic interdependencies of the natural world. On the holistic or total-field view, organisms—including man—are conceived as nodes in a biotic web of intrinsically related parts.[14] That is, our understanding of biological organisms requires more than just an understanding of their structure and properties; we also have to attend seriously to their interrelations. Holistic or systemic thinking does not deny that organisms are complex physicochemical systems, but it affirms that the methods employed in establishing the high-level functional relationships expressed by physical laws are often of very limited importance in understanding the nature of biological systems. We may now be facing, in the terminology of Thomas Kuhn,[15] a shift from a physical to a biological paradigm in our understanding of nature. This seems to me to be an important aspect of the rejection of Cartesian metaphysics.

The limitations of the physical paradigm have long been accepted in the study of human society, but the tendency has been to treat social behavior and human action as quite distinct from the operations of our natural surroundings. The inappropriateness of the physical paradigm for understanding *human* society seems to me to be quite correct; what is comparatively new is the post-Cartesian realization that the physical paradigm is of more limited application for our understanding of *nature* than was previously supposed.

The holistic conception of the natural world contains, in my view, the possibility of extending the idea of community beyond human society. And in this way biological wisdom does, I think, carry implications for ethics. Just as Copernicus showed us that man does not occupy the physical center of the universe, Darwin and his successors have shown us that man occupies no *biologically* privileged position. We still have to assimilate the implications that this biological knowledge has for morality.

Can we regard man and the natural environment as constituting a community in any morally significant sense? Passmore, in particular, has claimed that this extended sense of community is entirely spurious.[16] Leopold, on the other hand, found the biological extension of community entirely natural.[17] If we regard a community as a collection of individuals who engage in cooperative behavior, Leopold's extension seems to me entirely legitimate. An ethic is no more than a code of conduct designed to ensure cooperative behavior among the members of a community. Such cooperative behavior is required to underpin the health of the community, in this biologically extended sense, *health* being understood as the biological capacity for self-renewal,[18] and *ill-health* as the degeneration or loss of this capacity.

Man, of course, cannot be placed on "all fours" with his biologically fellow creatures in all respects. In particular, man is the only creature who can act as a full-fledged moral agent, i.e., an individual capable of exercising reflective rational choice on the basis of principles. What distinguishes man from his fellow creatures is not the capacity to *act*, but the fact that his actions are, to a great extent, free from programming. This capacity to modify our own behavior is closely bound up with the capacity to acquire knowledge of the natural world, a capacity that has enabled us, to an unprecedented extent, to manipulate the environment, and—especially in the recent past—to alter it rapidly, violently, and globally. Our hope must be that the capacity for knowledge, which has made ecologically hazardous activities possible, will lead to a more profound understanding of the delicate biological interdependencies that some of these actions now threaten, and thereby generate the wisdom for restraint.

To those who are skeptical of the possibility of extending moral principles in the manner of Leopold, to include items treated heretofore as matters of expediency, it can be pointed out that extensions have, to a limited extent, already taken place. One clear—if partial—instance, is in the treatment of animals. It is now generally accepted, and this is a comparatively recent innovation,[19] that we have at least a *prima facie* obligation not to treat animals cruelly or sadistically. And this certainly constitutes a shift in moral attitudes. If—as seems to be the case—cruelty to animals is accepted as intrinsically wrong, then there *is* at least one instance in which it is *not* a matter of moral indifference how we behave toward the nonhuman world.

More familiar perhaps are the moral revolutions that have occurred within the specific domain of human society—witness the progressive elimination of the "right" to racial, class, and sex exploitation. Each of these shifts involves the acceptance, on the part of some individuals, of new obligations, rights, and values that, to a previous generation, would have been considered unthinkable.[20] The essential step in recognizing an enlarged community involves coming to see, feel, and understand what was previously perceived as alien and apart: it is the evolution of the capacity of *empathy.*

I have digressed a little into the history of ideas, stressing in particular the importance of the influence of Descartes.[21] My justification for this excursion is that our present attitudes toward nature, and toward wilderness, are very largely the result of Descartes' metaphysical conception of what nature is, and the concomitant conception that man has of himself. Our metaphysical assumptions are frequently extremely influential invisible persuaders; they determine the boundaries of what is thinkable. In rejecting the Cartesian conception the following related shifts in attitudes can, I think, be discerned.

1. A change from reductive convergent patterns of thought to divergent holistic patterns.

2. A shift from man's conception of himself as the center of the biological world, to one in which he is conceived of as a component in a network of biological relations, a shift comparable to the Copernican discovery that man does not occupy the *physical* center of the universe.

3. An appreciation of the fact that in modifying biological systems we do not simply modify the properties of a substance, but alter a network of relations. This rejection of the Cartesian conception of nature as a collection of independent physical parts is summed up in the popular ecological maxim "it is impossible to do only one thing."

4. A recognition that the processes of nature are independent and indifferent to human interests and concerns.

5. A recognition that biological systems are items that possess intrinsic value, in Kant's terminology, that they are "ends in themselves."

We can, however, provide—and it is important that we can provide—an answer to the question: "What is the *use* of wilderness?" We certainly ought to preserve and protect wilderness areas as gymnasiums, as laboratories, as stockpiles of genetic diversity, and as cathedrals. Each of these reasons provides a powerful and sufficient instrumental justification for their preservation. But note how the very posing of this question about the *utility* of wilderness reflects an anthropocentric system of values. From a genuinely ecocentric point of view the question "What is the *use* of wilderness?" would be as absurd as the question "What is the *use* of happiness?"

The philosophical task is to try to provide adequate justification, or at least clear the way for a scheme of values according to which concern and sympathy for our environment is immediate and natural, and the desirability of protecting and preserving wilder-

ness self-evident. When once controversial propositions become platitudes, the philosophical task will have been successful.

I will conclude, nevertheless, on a deflationary note. It seems to me (at least much of the time) that the shift in attitudes that I think is required for promoting genuinely harmonious relations with nature is too drastic, too "unthinkable," to be very persuasive for most people. If this is so, then it will be more expedient to justify the preservation of wilderness in terms of instrumentalist considerations, and I have argued that there *are* powerful arguments for preservation that can be derived from the purely anthropocentric considerations of human self-interest. I hope, however, that there will be some who feel that such anthropocentric considerations are not wholly satisfying, i.e., that they do not really do justice to our intuitions. But at a time when *human* rights are being treated in some quarters with a great deal of skepticism it is perhaps unrealistic to expect the rights of nonhumans to receive sympathetic attention. Perhaps, though, we should not be too abashed by this; extensions in ethics have seldom followed the path of political expediency.

Endnotes

1. Aldo Leopold, *A Sand County Almanac* (New York: Oxford University Press, 1949), p. 188.

2. Other cultures have certainly included the idea that nature should be valued for its own sake in their moral codes, e.g., the American Indians (cf. Chief Seattle's letter to President Franklin Pierce of 1854, reprinted in *The Canberra Times*, 5 July 1966, p. 9), the Chinese (cf. Joseph Needham, "History and Human Values," in H. and S. Rose, eds. *The Radicalisation of Science* [London: Macmillan, 1976], pp. 90–117), and the Australian Aborigines (cf. W.E.H. Stanner, *Aboriginal Man in Australia* [Sydney: Angus and Robertson, 1965], pp. 207–237).

3. We can after all *replace* human artifacts such as buildings with something closely similar, but the destruction of a wilderness or a biological species is irreversible.

4. John Passmore, *Man's Responsibility for Nature* (London: Duckworth, 1974; New York: Charles Scribner's Sons, 1974), p. 17; cf. ch. 5.

5. In "The Rights of Non-humans and Intrinsic Values," in M.A. McRobbie, D. Mannison, and R. Routley, eds. *Environmental Philosophy* (Canberra: Australian National University Research School of Social Sciences, forthcoming).

6. Cf. Laurence H. Tribe, "Policy Science: Analysis or Ideology?" *Philosophy and Public Affairs* 2 (1972–3): 66–110.

7. I should mention that I am a skeptic about "rights"; it seems to me that talk about rights is always eliminable in favor of talk about legitimate claims for considerations, and obligations to respect those claims. Rights-talk does, however, have useful rhetorical effect in exhorting people to recognize claims. The reason for this is that claims pressed in these terms perform the crucial trick of shifting the onus of proof. This is accomplished by the fact that a *denial* of a right appears to be a more positive and deliberate act than merely refusing to acknowledge an obligation.

8. Laurence H. Tribe, "Trial by Mathematics: Precision and Ritual in Legal Process," *Harvard Law Review* 84 (1971): 1361.

9. Of course, in practice cost-benefit considerations *do* operate within deontic constraints, and we do *not* accept economics unrestrictedly as providing the model for rational deliberation. We would not accept exploitative child labor, for example, as a legitimate mode of production, no matter how favorable the economics. This is not just because we attach too high a cost to this form of labor; it is just unthinkable.

10. Aldo Leopold, "The Land Ethic," in *A Sand County Almanac*, p. 210.

11. Cf. Aldo Leopold, "The Conservation Ethic," *Journal of Forestry* 31 (1933): 634–43, and "The Land Ethic," *Sand County Almanac*.

12. Cf. John Passmore, "Attitudes to Nature," in R.S. Peters, ed., *Nature and Conduct* (London: Macmillan, 1975), pp. 251–64.

13. Ibid., p. 260.

14. Cf. Arne Naess, "The Shallow and the Deep, Long-Range Ecology Movement," *Inquiry* 16 (1973): 95–100.

15. T.S. Kuhn, *The Structure of Scientific Revolutions* (Chicago: University of Chicago Press, 1962).

16. Passmore, *Man's Responsibility for Nature*, ch. 6; "Attitudes to Nature," p. 262.

17. Leopold, "The Land Ethic."

18. Ibid., p. 221.

19. Cf. Passmore, "The Treatment of Animals," *Journal of the History of Ideas* 36 (1975): 195–218.

20. Cf. Christopher D. Stone, "Should Trees Have Standing? Toward Legal Rights for Natural Objects," *Southern California Law Review* 45 (1972): 450–501.

21. Here I differ from the well-known claim of Lynn White ("The Historical Roots of Our Ecological Crisis," *Science* 155 [1967]: 1203–7) that the Judeo-Christian tradition is predominantly responsible for the development of Western attitudes toward nature.

Review Questions

1. Distinguish between instrumental value and intrinsic value.

2. How does Godfrey-Smith define wilderness?

3. What is the cathedral view?

4. Explain the laboratory argument.

5. What is the silo argument?

6. What is the gymnasium argument?

7. What problems arise for these instrumental justifications for preserving wilderness areas?

8. What is the dominant Western conception of nature?

9. Explain the holistic conception of the natural world.

Discussion Questions

1. Is the holistic conception of the natural world acceptable? Defend your position.

2. Should human beings frustrate important interests in order to preserve the natural environment? Defend your answer.

Mary Anne Warren

The Rights of the Nonhuman World

For biographical information on Mary Anne Warren, see her reading in Chapter 2.

Warren wants to propose a "harmonious marriage" between the animal liberation view and Leopold's land ethic. Despite apparent conflicts between the two views, she thinks that a compromise can be reached provided certain concessions are made by each side. Briefly, the animal liberationist must allow that animal rights are different from human rights in both strength and content, and that animal rights can be easily overridden by environmental and utilitarian reasons, reasons that would not suffice to override stronger human rights. The environmentalists, for their part, should grant that mountains, oceans, and other natural objects do not have moral rights. But we should still preserve them because they have not only instrumental value to us and future generations, but also instrinsic value. The result of this compromise, Warren contends, is a more complete nonhomocentric moral theory. It explains why we ought to protect not only individual animals, but also species of plants and animals, and the natural environment.

Western philosophers have typically held that human beings are the only proper objects of human moral concern. Those who speak of *duties* generally hold that we have duties only to human beings (or perhaps to God), and that our apparent duties towards animals, plants and other nonhuman entities in nature are in fact indirect duties to human beings.[1] Those who speak of moral *rights* generally

From Mary Anne Warren, "The Rights of the Nonhuman World," Robert Elliot and Arran Gare, eds., *Environmental Philosophy* (Queensland: The University of Queensland Press, 1983), pp. 109–134, Reprinted by permission of Dr. Mary Anne Warren, San Francisco State University and the University of Queensland Press.

ascribe such rights only to human beings.

This strictly homocentric (human-centered) view of morality is currently challenged from two seemingly disparate directions. On the one hand, environmentalists argue that because humanity is only one part of the natural world, an organic species in the total, interdependent, planetary biosystem, it is necessary for consistency to view all of the elements of that system, and not just its human elements, as worthy of moral concern in themselves, and not only because of their usefulness to us. The ecologist Aldo Leopold was one of the first and most influential exponents of the view that not only human beings, but plants, animals and natural habitats, have moral rights. We need, Leopold argued, a new ethical system that will deal with our relationships not only with other human individuals and with human society, but also with the land, and its nonhuman inhabitants. Such a "land ethic" would seek to change "the role of *Homo sapiens* from conqueror of the land community to plain member and citizen of it".[2] It would judge our interaction with the nonhuman world as "right when it tends to preserve the integrity, stability, and beauty of the biotic community", and "wrong when it tends otherwise".[3]

On the other hand, homocentric morality is attacked by the so-called animal liberationists, who have argued, at least as early as the eighteenth century (in the Western tradition), that insofar as (some) nonhuman animals are sentient beings, capable of experiencing pleasure and pain,[4] they are worthy in their own right of our moral concern.[5] On the surface at least, the animal liberationist ethic appears to be quite different from that of ecologists such as Leopold. The land ethic is *wholistic* in its emphasis: it treats the good of the biotic *community* as the ultimate measure of the value of individual organisms or species, and of the rightness or wrongness of human actions. In contrast, the animal-liberationist ethic is largely inspired by the utilitarianism of Jeremy Bentham and John Stuart Mill.[6] The latter tradition is individualist in its moral focus, in that it treats the needs and interests of individual sentient beings as the ultimate basis for conclusions about right and wrong.

These differences in moral perspective predictably result in differences in the emphasis given to specific moral issues. Thus, environmentalists treat the protection of endangered species and habitats as matters for utmost concern, while, unlike many of the animal liberationists,[7] they generally do not object to hunting, fishing or rearing animals for food, so long as these practices do not endanger the survival of certain species or otherwise damage the natural environment. Animal liberationists, on the other hand, regard the inhumane treatment or killing of animals which are raised for meat, used in scientific experimentation and the like, as just as objectionable as the killing or mistreatment of "wild" animals.[8] They oppose such practices not only because they may sometimes lead to environmental damage, but because they cause suffering or death to sentient beings.

Contrasts such as these have led some philosophers to conclude that the theoretical foundations of the Leopoldian land ethic and those of the animal-liberationist movement are fundamentally incompatible,[9] or that there are "intractable practical differences" between them.[10] I shall argue on the contrary, that a harmonious marriage between these two approaches is possible, provided that each side is prepared to make certain compromises. In brief, the animal liberationists must recognize that although animals do have significant moral rights, these rights are not precisely the same as those of human beings; and that part of the difference is that the rights of animals may sometimes be overridden, for example, for environmental or utilitarian reasons, in situations where it would not be morally acceptable to override human rights for similar reasons. For their part, the environmentalists must recognize that while it may be acceptable, as a legal or rhetorical tactic, to speak of the rights of trees or mountains,[11] the logical foundations of such rights are quite different from those of the rights of human and other sentient beings. The issue is of enormous importance for moral philosophy, for it centres upon the theoretical basis for the the ascription of moral rights, and hence bears directly upon such disputed cases as the rights of (human) foetuses, children, the comatose, the insane, etc. Another interesting feature is the way in which utilitarians and **deontologists** often seem to exchange sides in the battle—the former insist upon the universal application of the principle that to cause unnecessary pain is wrong, while the latter refuse to apply that principle to other than human beings, unless there are utilitarian reasons for doing so.

In section I, I will examine the primary line of argument presented by the contemporary animal-rights advocates, and suggest that their conclusions must be amended in the way mentioned above. In section II, I will present two arguments for distinguishing between the rights of human beings and those of (most) nonhuman animals. In section III, I will consider the animal liberationists' objection that any such distinction will endanger the rights of certain "nonparadigm" human beings, for example, infants and the mentally incapacitated. In section IV, I will reply to several current objections to the attempt to found basic moral rights upon the sentience, or other psychological capacities, of the entity involved. Finally, in section V, I will examine the moral theory implicit in the land ethic, and argue that it may be formulated and put into practice in a manner which is consistent with the concerns of the animal liberationists.

I WHY (SOME) ANIMALS HAVE (SOME) MORAL RIGHTS

Peter Singer is the best known contemporary proponent of animal liberation. Singer maintains that all sentient animals, human or otherwise, should be regarded as morally equal; that is, that their interests should be given equal consideration. He argues that sentience, the capacity to have conscious experiences such as pain or pleasure, is "the only defensible boundary of concern for the interests of others".[12] In Bentham's often-quoted words, "the question is not, Can they reason? nor, Can they talk? but Can they suffer?"[13] To suppose that the interests of animals are outside the scope of moral concern is to commit a moral fallacy analogous to sexism or racism, a fallacy which Singer calls *speciesism*. True, women and members of "minority" races are more *intelligent* than (most) animals—and almost certainly no less so than white males—but that is not the point. The point does not concern these complex capabilities at all. For, Singer says, "The claim to equality does not depend on intelligence, moral capacity, physical strength, or similar matters of fact."[14]

As a utilitarian, Singer prefers to avoid speaking of moral *rights*, at least insofar as these are construed as claims which may sometimes override purely utilitarian considerations.[15] There are, however, many other advocates of animal liberation who do maintain that animals have moral rights, rights which place limitations upon the use of utilitarian justifications for killing animals or causing them to suffer.[16] Tom Regan, for example, argues that if all or most human beings have a right to life, then so do at least some animals.[17] Regan points out that unless we hold that animals have a right to life, we may not be able to adequately support many of the conclusions that most animal liberationists think are important, for example, that it is wrong to kill animals painlessly to provide human beings with relatively trivial forms of pleasure.[18]

This disagreement between Singer and Regan demonstrates that there is no single well-defined theory of the moral status of animals which can be identified as *the* animal liberationist position. It is clear, however, that neither philosopher is committed to the claim that the moral status of animals is completely identical to that of humans. Singer points out that his basic principle of equal *consideration* does not imply identical *treat-

ment*.[19] Regan holds only that animals have *some* of the same moral rights as do human beings, not that *all* of their rights are necessarily the same.[20]

Nevertheless, none of the animal liberationists have thus far provided a clear explanation of how and why the moral status of (most) animals differs from that of (most) human beings; and this is a point which must be clarified if their position is to be made fully persuasive. That there is such a difference seems to follow from some very strong moral intuitions which most of us share. A man who shoots squirrels for sport may or may not be acting reprehensibly; but it is difficult to believe that his actions should be placed in *exactly* the same moral category as those of a man who shoots women, or black children, for sport. So too it is doubtful that the Japanese fishermen who slaughtered dolphins because the latter were thought to be depleting the local fish populations were acting quite *as* wrongly as if they had slaughtered an equal number of their human neighbours for the same reason.

Can anything persuasive be said in support of these intuitive judgments? Or are they merely evidence of unreconstructed speciesism? To answer these questions we must consider both certain similarities and certain differences between ourselves and other animals, and then decide which of these are relevant to the assignment of moral rights. To do this we must first ask just what it means to say than an entity possesses a certain moral right.

There are two elements of the concept of a moral right which are crucial for our present purposes. To say that an entity, X, has a moral right to Y (some activity, benefit or satisfaction) is to imply at least the following:

1. that it would be morally wrong for any moral agent to intentionally deprive X or Y without some sufficient justification;
2. that this would be wrong, at least in part, *because of the (actual or potential) harm which it would do to the interests of X.*

On this (partial) definition of a moral right, to ask whether animals have such rights is to ask whether there are some ways of treating them which are morally objectionable because of the harm done to the animals themselves, and not merely because of some *other* undesirable results, such as damaging the environment or undermining the moral character of human beings. As Regan and other animal liberationists have pointed out, the arguments for ascribing at least some moral rights to sentient nonhuman animals are very similar to the arguments for ascribing those same rights to sentient human beings.[21] If we argue that human beings have rights not to be tortured, starved or confined under inhumane conditions, it is usually by appealing to our knowledge that they will suffer in much the same ways that we would under like circumstances. A child must learn that other persons (and animals) can experience, for example, pain, fear or anger, on the one hand; pleasure or satisfaction, on the other, in order to even begin to comprehend why some ways of behaving towards them are morally preferable to others.

If these facts are morally significant in the case of human beings, it is attractive to suppose that they should have similar significance in the case of animals. Everything that we know about the behaviour, biology and neurophysiology of, for instance, nonhuman mammals, indicates that they are capable of experiencing the same basic types of physical suffering and discomfort as we are, and it is reasonable to suppose that their pleasures are equally real and approximately as various. Doubts about the sentience of other animals are no more plausible than doubts about that of other human beings. True, most animals cannot use human language to *report* that they are in pain, but the vocalizatons and "body language" through which they *express* pain, and many other psychological states, are similar enough to our own that their significance is generally clear.

But to say this is not yet to establish that animals have moral rights. We need a con-necting link between the premise that certain ways of treating animals cause them to suffer, and the conclusion that such actions are *prima facie* morally wrong, that is, wrong unless proven otherwise. One way to make this con-nection is to hold that it is a *self-evident truth* that the unnecessary infliction of suffering upon any sentient being is wrong. Those who doubt this claim may be accused (perhaps with some justice) of lacking empathy, the ability to "feel with" other sentient beings, to comprehend the reality of their experience. It may be held that it is possible to regard the suffering of animals as morally insignificant only to the extent that one suffers from blind-ness to "the **ontology** of animal reality",[22] that is, from a failure to grasp the fact that they are centres of conscious experience, as we are.

This argument is inadequate, however, since there may be those who fully compre-hend the fact that animals are sentient be-ings, but who still deny that their pains and pleasures have any direct moral significance. For them, a more persuasive consideration may be that our moral reasoning will gain in clarity and coherence if we recognize that the suffering of a nonhuman being is an evil of the same general sort as that of a human be-ing. For if we do not recognize that suffering is an intrinsic evil, something which ought not to be inflicted deliberately without just cause, then we will not be able to fully under-stand why treating *human beings* in certain ways is immoral.

Torturing human beings, for example, is not wrong merely because it is illegal (where it is illegal), or merely because it violates some implicit agreement amongst human be-ings (though it may). Such legalistic or con-tractualistic reasons leave us in the dark as to why we *ought* to have, and enforce, laws and agreements against torture. The essential reason for regarding torture as wrong is that it *hurts*, and that people greatly prefer to avoid such pain—as do animals. I am not ar-guing, as does Kant, that cruelty to animals is wrong because it causes cruelty to human beings, a position which consequentialists often endorse. The point, rather, is that unless we view the deliberate infliction of needless pain as inherently wrong we will not be able to understand the moral objection to cruelty of *either* kind.

It seems we must conclude, therefore, that sentient nonhuman animals have certain basic moral rights, rights which they share with all beings that are psychologically organized around the pleasure/pain axis. Their capacity for pain gives them the right that pain not be intentionally and needlessly inflicted upon them. Their capacity for pleasure gives them the right not to be prevented from pursuing whatever pleasures and fulfillments are natural to creatures of their kind. Like human rights, the rights of animals may be overriden if there is a morally sufficient reason for doing so. What *counts* as a morally significant reason, however, may be different in the two cases.

II HUMAN AND ANIMAL RIGHTS COMPARED

There are two dimensions in which we may find differences between the rights of human beings and those of animals. The first involves the *content* of those rights, while the second involves their strength; that is, the strength of the reasons which are required to override them.

Consider, for instance, the right to liberty. The *human* right to liberty precludes imprisonment without due process of law, even if the prison is spacious and the conditions of confinement cause no obvious physical suffering. But it is not so obviously wrong to imprison animals, especially when the area to which they are confined provides a fair approximation of the conditions of their natural habitat, and a reasonable opportunity to pursue the satisfactions natural to their kind. Such conditions, which often result in an increased lifespan, and which may exist in wildlife sanctuaries or even well-designed zoos, need not frustrate the needs or interests of animals in any significant way, and thus do

not clearly violate their rights. Similarly treated human beings, on the other hand (e.g., native peoples confined to prison-like reservations), do tend to suffer from their loss of freedom. Human dignity and the fulfillment of the sorts of plans, hopes and desires which appear (thus far) to be uniquely human, require a more extensive freedom of movement than is the case with at least many nonhuman animals. Furthermore, there are aspects of human freedom, such as freedom of thought, freedom of speech and freedom of political association, which simply do not apply in the case of animals.

Thus, it seems that the human right to freedom is more extensive; that is, it precludes a wider range of specific ways of treating human beings than does the corresponding right on the part of animals. The argument cuts both ways, of course. *Some* animals, for example, great whales and migratory birds, may require at least as much physical freedom as do human beings if they are to pursue the satisfactions natural to their kind, and this fact provides a moral argument against keeping such creatures imprisoned.[23] And even chickens may suffer from the extreme and unnatural confinement to which they are subjected on modern "factory farms". Yet it seems unnecessary to claim for *most* animals a right to a freedom quite as broad as that which we claim for ourselves.

Similar points may be made with respect to the right to life. Animals, it may be argued, lack the cognitive equipment to value their lives in the way that human beings do. Ruth Cigman argues that animals have *no* right to life because death is no misfortune for them.[24] In her view, the death of an animal is not a misfortune, because animals have no desires which are *categorical;* that is which do not "merely presuppose being alive (like the desire to eat when one is hungry), but rather answer the question whether one wants to remain alive".[25] In other words, animals appear to lack the sorts of long-range hopes, plans, ambitions and the like, which give human beings such a powerful interest in continued life. Animals, it seems, take life as it comes and do not specifically desire that it go on. True, squirrels store nuts for the winter and deer run from wolves; but these may be seen as instinctive or conditioned responses to present circumstances, rather than evidence that they value life as such.

These reflections probably help to explain why the death of a sparrow seems less tragic than that of a human being. Human lives, one might say, have greater intrinsic value, because they are worth more *to their possessors.* But this does not demonstrate that no nonhuman animal has *any* right to life. Premature death may be a less *severe* misfortune for sentient nonhuman animals than for human beings, but it is a misfortune nevertheless. In the first place, it is a misfortune in that it deprives them of whatever pleasures the future might have held for them, regardless of whether or not they ever *consciously anticipated* those pleasures. The fact that they are not here afterwards, to *experience* their loss, no more shows that they have not lost anything than it does in the case of humans. In the second place, it is (possibly) a misfortune in that it frustrates whatever future-oriented desires animals *may* have, unbeknownst to us. Even now, in an age in which apes have been taught to use simplified human languages and attempts have been made to communicate with dolphins and whales, we still know very little about the operation of nonhuman minds. We know much too little to assume that nonhuman animals never consciously pursue relatively distant future goals. To the extent that they do, the question of whether such desires provide them with *reasons for living* or merely *presuppose* continued life, has no satisfactory answer, since they cannot contemplate these alternatives—or, if they can, we have no way of knowing what their conclusions are. All we know is that the more intelligent and psychologically complex an animal is, the more *likely* it is that it possesses specifically future-oriented desires, which would be frustrated even by *painless* death.

For these reasons, it is premature to conclude from the apparent intellectual inferiority of nonhuman animals that they have no right to life. A more plausible conclusion is that animals do have a right to life but that it is generally somewhat weaker than that of human beings. It is, perhaps, weak enough to enable us to justify killing animals when we have no other ways of achieving such vital goals as feeding or clothing ourselves, or obtaining knowledge which is necessary to save human lives. Weakening their right to life in this way does not render meaningless the assertion that they have such a right. For the point remains that *some* serious justification for the killing of sentient nonhuman animals is always necessary; they may not be killed merely to provide amusement or minor gains in convenience.

If animals' rights to liberty and life are somewhat weaker than those of human beings, may we say the same about their right to *happiness;* that is, their right not to be made to suffer needlessly or to be deprived of the pleasures natural to their kind? If so, it is not immediately clear why. There is little reason to suppose that pain or suffering are any less unpleasant for the higher animals (at least) than they are for us. Our large brains *may* cause us to experience pain more intensely than do most animals, and *probably* cause us to suffer more from the anticipation or remembrance of pain. These facts might tend to suggest that pain is, on the whole, a worse experience for us than for them. But it may also be argued that pain may be *worse* in some respects for nonhuman animals, who are presumably less able to distract themselves from it by thinking of something else, or to comfort themselves with the knowledge that it is temporary. Brigid Brophy points out that "pain is likely to fill the sheep's whole capacity for experience in a way it seldom does in us, whose intellect and imagination can create breaks for us in the immediacy of our sensations".[26]

The net result of such contrasting considerations is that we cannot possibly claim to know whether pain is, on the whole, worse for us than for animals, or whether their pleasures are any more or any less intense than ours. Thus, while we may justify assigning them a somewhat weaker right to life or liberty, on the grounds that they desire these goods less intensely than we do, we cannot discount their rights to freedom from needlessly inflicted pain or unnatural frustration on the same basis. There may, however, be *other* reasons for regarding all of the moral rights of animals as somewhat less stringent than the corresponding human rights.

A number of philosophers who deny that animals have moral rights point to the fact that nonhuman animals evidently lack the capacity for moral autonomy. Moral autonomy is the ability to act as a moral agent; that is, to act on the basis of an understanding of, and adherence to, moral rules or principles. H.J. McCloskey, for example, holds that "it is the capacity for moral autonomy . . . that is basic to the possibility of possessing a right".[27] McCloskey argues that it is inappropriate to ascribe moral rights to any entity which is not a moral agent, or *potentially* a moral agent, because a right is essentially an entitlement granted to a moral agent, licensing him or her to *act* in certain ways and to *demand* that other moral agents refrain from interference. For this reason, he says, "Where there is no possibility of [morally autonomous] action, potentially or actually . . . and where the being is not a member of a kind which is normally capable of [such] action, we withhold talk of rights." [28]

If moral autonomy—or being *potentially* autonomous, or a member of a kind which is *normally* capable of autonomy—is a necessary condition for having moral rights, then probably no nonhuman animal can qualify. For moral autonomy requires such probably uniquely human traits as "the capacity to be critically self-aware, manipulate concepts, use a sophisticated language, reflect, plan, deliberate, choose, and accept responsibility for acting".[29]

But why, we must ask, should the capacity for autonomy be regarded as a precondition for possessing moral rights? Autonomy is clearly crucial for the *exercise* of many human moral or legal rights, such as the right to vote or to run for public office. It is less clearly relevant, however, to the more basic human rights, such as the right to life or to freedom from unnecessary suffering. The fact that animals, like many human beings, cannot *demand* their moral rights (at least not in the words of any conventional human language) seems irrelevant. For, as Joel Feinberg points out, the interests of non-morally autonomous human beings may be defended by others, for example, in legal proceedings; and it is not clear why the interests of animals might not be represented in a similar fashion.[30]

It is implausible, therefore, to conclude that because animals lack moral autonomy they should be accorded *no moral rights whatsoever*. Nevertheless, it may be argued that the moral autonomy of (most) human beings provides a second reason, in addition to their more extensive interests and desires, for according somewhat *stronger* moral rights to human beings. The fundamental insight behind contractualist theories of morality [31] is that, for morally autonomous beings such as ourselves, there is enormous mutual advantage in the adoption of a moral system designed to protect each of us from the harms that might otherwise be visited upon us by others. Each of us ought to accept and promote such a system because, to the extent that others also accept it, we will all be safer from attack by our fellows, more likely to receive assistance when we need it, and freer to engage in individual as well as cooperative endeavours of all kinds.

Thus, it is the possibility of *reciprocity* which motivates moral agents to extend *full and equal* moral rights, in the first instance, only to other moral agents. I respect your rights to life, liberty and the pursuit of happiness in part because you are a sentient being, whose interests have intrinsic moral significance. But I respect them as *fully equal to my own* because I hope and expect that you will do the same for me. Animals, insofar as they lack the degree of rationality necessary for moral autonomy, cannot agree to respect our interests as equal in moral importance to their own, and neither do they expect or demand such respect from us. Of course, domestic animals may expect to be fed, etc. But they do not, and cannot, expect to be treated as moral equals, for they do not understand that moral concept or what it implies. Consequently, it is neither pragmatically feasible nor morally obligatory to extend to them the same *full and equal* rights which we extend to human beings.

Is this a speciesist conclusion? Defenders of a more extreme animal-rights position may point out that this argument, from the lack of moral autonomy, has exactly the same form as that which has been used for thousands of years to rationalize denying equal moral rights to women and members of "inferior" races. Aristotle, for example, argued that women and slaves are naturally subordinate beings, because they lack the capacity for moral autonomy and self-direction;[32] and contemporary versions of this argument, used to support racist or sexist conclusions, are easy to find. Are we simply repeating Aristotle's mistake, in a different context?

The reply to this objection is very simple: animals, unlike women and slaves, really *are* incapable of moral autonomy, at least to the best of our knowledge. Aristotle certainly *ought* to have known that women and slaves are capable of morally autonomous action; their capacity to use moral language alone ought to have alerted him to this likelihood. If comparable evidence exists that (some) nonhuman animals are moral agents we have not yet found it. The fact that some apes (and, possibly, some cetaceans) are capable of learning radically simplified human languages, the terms of which refer primarily to objects and events in their immediate environment, in no way demonstrates that they can understand abstract moral concepts, rules or principles, or use this understanding to regulate their own behaviour.

On the other hand, this argument implies that if we *do* discover that certain nonhuman animals are capable of moral autonomy (which is certainly not impossible), then we ought to extend full and equal moral rights to those animals. Furthermore, if we someday encounter extraterrestrial beings, or build robots, androids or supercomputers which function as self-aware moral agents, then we must extend full and equal moral rights to these as well. Being a member of the human species is not a necessary condition for the possession of full "human" rights. Whether it is nevertheless a *sufficient* condition is the question to which we now turn.

III THE MORAL RIGHTS OF NONPARADIGM HUMANS

If we are justified in ascribing somewhat different, and also somewhat stronger, moral rights to human beings than to sentient but non-morally autonomous animals, then what are we to say of the rights of human beings who happen not to be capable of moral autonomy, perhaps not even potentially? Both Singer and Regan have argued that if any of the superior intellectual capacities of normal and mature human beings are used to support a distinction between the moral status of *typical*, or paradigm, human beings, and that of animals, then consistency will require us to place certain "nonparadigm" humans, such as infants, small children and the severely retarded or incurably brain damaged, in the same inferior moral category.[33] Such a result is, of course, highly counterintuitive.

Fortunately, no such conclusion follows from the autonomy argument. There are many reasons for extending strong moral rights to nonparadigm humans; reasons which do not apply to most nonhuman animals. Infants and small children are granted strong moral rights in part because of their *potential* autonomy. But *potential* autonomy, as I have argued elsewhere,[34] is not in itself a sufficient reason for the ascription of full moral rights; if it were, then not only human foetuses (from conception onwards) but even ununited human sperm-egg pairs would have to be regarded as entities with a right to life the equivalent of our own—thus making not only abortion, but any intentional failure to procreate, the moral equivalent of murder. Those who do not find this extreme conclusion acceptable must appeal to reasons other than the *potential* moral autonomy of infants and small children to explain the strength of the latter's moral rights.

One reason for assigning strong moral rights to infants and children is that they possess not just *potential* but *partial* autonomy, and it is not clear how much of it they have at any given moment. The fact that, unlike baby chimpanzees, they are already learning the things which will enable them to *become* morally autonomous, makes it likely that their minds have more subtleties than their speech (or the lack of it) proclaims. Another reason is simply that most of us tend to place a very high value on the lives and well-being of infants. Perhaps we are to some degree "programmed" by nature to love and protect them; perhaps our reasons are somewhat egocentric; or perhaps we value them for their potential. Whatever the explanation, the fact that we do feel this way about them is in itself a valid reason for extending to them stronger moral and legal protections than we extend to nonhuman animals, even those which may have just as well or better-developed psychological capacities.[35] A third, and perhaps the most important, reason is that if we did *not* extend strong moral rights to infants, far too few of them would ever *become* responsible, morally autonomous adults; too many would be treated "like animals" (i.e., in ways that it is generally wrong to treat even animals), and would consequently become socially crippled, antisocial or just very unhappy people. If any part of our moral code is to remain intact, it seems that infants and small children *must* be protected and cared for.[36]

Analogous arguments explain why strong moral rights should also be accorded to other nonparadigm humans. The severely retarded or incurably senile, for instance, may have no potential for moral autonomy, but there are apt to be friends, relatives or other people who care what happens to them. Like children, such individuals may have more mental capacities than are readily apparent. Like children, they are more apt to achieve, or return to moral autonomy if they are valued and well cared for. Furthermore, any one of us may someday become mentally incapacitated to one degree or another, and we would all have reason to be anxious about our own futures if such incapacitation were made the basis for denying strong moral rights.[37]

There are, then, sound reasons for assigning strong moral rights even to human beings who lack the mental capacities which justify the general distinction between human and animal rights. Their rights are based not only on the value which they themselves place upon their lives and well-being, but also on the value which other human beings place upon them.

But is this a valid basis for the assignment of moral rights? Is it consistent with the definition presented earlier, according to which X may be said to have a moral right to Y only if depriving X of Y is *prima facie* wrong *because of the harm done to the interests of X,* and not merely because of any further consequences? Regan argues that we cannot justify the ascription of stronger rights to nonparadigm humans than to nonhuman animals in the way suggested, because "what underlies the ascription of rights to any given X is that X has value independently of anyone's valuing X".[38] After all, we do not speak of expensive paintings or gemstones as having rights, although many people value them and have good reasons for wanting them protected.

There is, however, a crucial difference between a rare painting and a severely retarded or senile human being; the latter not only has (or may have) value for other human beings but *also* has his or her own needs and interests. It may be this which leads us to say that such individuals have intrinsic value. The sentience of nonparadigm humans, like that of sentient nonhuman animals, gives them a place in the sphere of rights holders. So long as the moral rights of all sentient beings are given due recognition, there should be no objection to providing some of them with *additional* protections, on the basis of our interests as well as their own. Some philosophers speak of such additional protections, which are accorded to X on the basis of interests other than X's own, as *conferred* rights, in contrast to *natural* rights, which are entirely based upon the properties of X itself.[39] But such "conferred" rights are not necessarily any weaker or less binding upon moral agents than are "natural" rights. Infants, and most other nonparadigm humans have the *same* basic moral rights that the rest of us do, even though the reasons for ascribing those rights are somewhat different in the two cases.

IV OTHER OBJECTIONS TO ANIMAL RIGHTS

We have already dealt with the primary objection to assigning *any* moral rights to non-human animals; that is, that they lack moral autonomy, and various other psychological capacities which paradigm humans possess. We have also answered the animal liberationists' primary objection to assigning somewhat *weaker,* or less-extensive rights to animals; that is, that this will force us to assign similarly inferior rights to nonparadigm humans. There are two other objections to animal rights which need to be considered. The first is that the claim that animals have a right to life, or other moral rights, has absurd consequences with respect to the natural relationships *among* animals. The second is that to accord rights to animals on the basis of their (differing degrees of) sentience will introduce intolerable difficulties and complexities into our moral reasoning.

Opponents of animal rights often accuse the animal liberationists of ignoring the realities of nature, in which many animals survive only by killing others. Callicott, for example, maintains that, whereas environmentally aware persons realize that natural predators are a vital part of the biotic community, those who believe that animals have a right to life are forced to regard all predators as "merciless, wanton, and incorrigible murderers of their fellow creatures".[40] Similarly, Ritchie asks whether, if animals have rights, we are not morally obligated to "protect the weak among them against the strong? Must we not put to death blackbirds and thrushes because they feed on worms, or (if capital punishment offends our humanitarianism) starve them slowly by permanent captivity and vegetarian diet?"[41]

Such a conclusion would of course be ridiculous, as well as wholly inconsistent with the environmental ethic. However, nothing of the sort follows from the claim that animals have moral rights. There are two independently sufficient reasons why it does not. In the first place, nonhuman predators are not moral agents, so it is absurd to think of them as wicked, or as *murdering* their prey. But this is not the most important point. Even if wolves and the like *were* moral agents, their predation would still be morally acceptable, given that they generally kill only to feed themselves, and generally do so without inflicting prolonged or unnecessary suffering. If we have the right to eat animals, in order to avoid starvation, then why shouldn't animals have the right to eat one another, for the same reason?

This conclusion is fully consistent with the lesson taught by the ecologists, that natural predation is essential to the stability of biological communities. Deer need wolves, or other predators, as much as the latter need them; without predation they become too numerous and fall victim to hunger and disease, while their overgrazing damages the entire ecosystem.[42] Too often we have learned (or failed to learn) this lesson the hard way, as when the killing of hawks and other predators produces exploding rodent populations—which must be controlled, often in ways which cause further ecological damage. The control of natural predators may *sometimes* be necessary, for example, when human pressures upon the populations of certain species become so intense that the latter cannot endure continued *natural* predation. (The controversial case of the wolves and caribou in Alaska and Canada may or may not be one of this sort.) But even in such cases it is preferable, from an environmentalist perspective, to reduce human predation enough to leave room for natural predators as well.

Another objection to assigning moral rights to sentient nonhuman animals is that it will not only complicate our own moral system, but introduce seemingly insoluble dilemmas. As Ritchie points out, "Very difficult questions of casuistry will ... arise because of the difference in grades of sentience."[43] For instance, is it morally worse to kill and eat a dozen oysters (which are at most minimally sentient) or one (much more highly sentient) rabbit? Questions of this kind, considered in isolation from any of the practical circumstances in which they might arise, are virtually unanswerable. But this ought not to surprise us, since similarly abstract questions about the treatment of human beings are often equally unanswerable. (For instance, would it be worse to kill one child or to cause a hundred to suffer from severe malnutrition?)

The reason such questions are so difficult to answer is not just that we lack the skill and knowledge to make such precise comparisons of interpersonal or interspecies utility, but also that these questions are posed in entirely unrealistic terms. Real moral choices rarely depend entirely upon the comparison of two abstract quantities of pain or pleasure deprivation. In deciding whether to eat molluscs or mammals (or neither or both) a human society must consider *all* of the predictable consequences of each option, for example, their respective impacts on the ecology or the economy, and not merely the individual interests of the animals involved.

Of course, other things being equal, it would be morally preferable to refrain from killing *any* sentient animal. But other things are never equal. Questions about human diet involve not only the rights of individual animals, but also vital environmental and human concerns. On the one hand, as Singer points out, more people could be better fed if food suitable for human consumption were not fed to meat-producing animals.[44] On the other hand, a mass conversion of humanity to vegetarianism would represent "an increase in the efficiency of the conversion of solar energy from plant to human biomass",[45] with the likely result that the human population would continue to expand and, in the process, to cause greater environmental destruction than might occur otherwise. The issue is an enormously complex one, and cannot be solved by any simple appeal to the claim that animals have (or lack) certain moral rights.

In short, the ascription of moral rights to animals does not have the absurd or environmentally damaging consequences that some philosophers have feared. It does not require us to exterminate predatory species, or to lose ourselves in abstruse speculations about the relative degrees of sentience of different sorts of animals. It merely requires us to recognize the interests of animals as having intrinsic moral significance; as demanding some consideration, regardless of whether or not human or environmental concerns are also involved. We must now consider the question of how well the animal rights theory meshes with the environmental ethic, which treats not only animals but plants, rivers and other nonsentient elements of nature as entities which may demand moral consideration.

V ANIMAL LIBERATION AND THE LAND ETHIC

The fundamental message of Leopold's land ethic, and of the environmentalist movement in general, is that the terrestrial biosphere is an integrated whole, and that humanity is a part of that natural order, wholly dependent upon it and morally responsible for maintaining its integrity.[46] Because of the wholistic nature of biotic systems, it is impossible to determine the value of an organism simply by considering its individual moral rights: we must also consider its relationship to other parts of the system. For this reason, some philosophers have concluded that the theoretical foundations of the environmentalist and animal liberation movements are mutually contradictory.[47] Alastair Gunn states: "Environmentalism seems incompatible with the Western obsession with individualism, which leads us to resolve questions about our treatment of animals by appealing to the essentially atomistic, competitive notion of rights." [48]

As an example of the apparent clash between the land ethic and the ascription of rights to animals, Gunn points to the situation on certain islands off the coast of New Zealand, where feral goats, pigs and cats have had to be exterminated in order to protect indigenous species and habitats, which were threatened by the introduced species. "Considered purely in terms of rights," he says, "it is hard to see how this could be justified. [For,] if the goats, etc. are held to have rights, then we are violating these rights in order perhaps to save or increase a rare species." [49]

I maintain, on the contrary, that the appearance of fundamental contradiction between the land ethic and the claim that sentient nonhuman animals have moral rights is illusory. If we were to hold that the rights of animals are *identical to those of human beings*, then we would indeed be forced to conclude that it is wrong to eliminate harmful introduced species for the good of the indigenous ones or of the ecosystem as a whole—just as wrong as it would be to exterminate all of the human inhabitants of North America who are immigrants, however greatly this might benefit the native Americans and the natural ecology. There is no inconsistency, however, in the view that animals have a significant right to life, but one which is somewhat more easily overridden by certain kinds of utilitarian or environmental considerations than is the human right to life. On this view, it is wrong to kill animals for trivial reasons, but not wrong to do so when there is no other way of achieving a vital goal, such as the preservation of threatened species.

Another apparent point of inconsistency between the land ethic and the animal liberation movement involves the issue of whether sentience is a *necessary*, as well as *sufficient*, condition for the possession of moral rights. Animal liberationists sometimes maintain that it is, and that consequently plants, rivers, mountains and other elements of nature which are not themselves sentient (though they may *contain* sentient life forms) cannot have moral rights.[50] Environmentalists, on the other hand, sometimes argue for the ascription of moral rights to even the nonsentient elements of the biosphere.[51] Does this difference represent a genuine contradiction between the two approaches?

One argument that it does not is that the fact that a particular entity is not accorded moral rights does not imply that there are no sound reasons for protecting it from harm. Human health and survival alone requires that we place a high value on clean air, unpolluted land, water and crops, and on the maintenance of stable and diverse natural ecosystems. Furthermore, there are vital scientific, spiritual, aesthetic and recreational values associated with the conservation of the natural world, values which cannot be dismissed as luxuries which benefit only the affluent portion of humanity.[52] Once we realize how *valuable* nature is, it may seem immaterial whether or not we also wish to speak of its nonsentient elements as possessing moral *rights*.

But there is a deeper issue here than the precise definition of the term "moral rights". The issue is whether trees, rivers and the like ought to be protected *only* because of their value to us (and to other sentient animals), or whether they also have *intrinsic* value. That is, are they to be valued and protected because of what they are, or only because of what they are good for? Most environmentalists think that the natural world is intrinsically valuable, and that it is therefore wrong to wantonly destroy forests, streams, marshes and so on, even where doing so is not *obviously* inconsistent with the welfare of human beings. It is this conviction which finds expression in the claim that even nonsentient elements of nature have moral rights. Critics of the environmental movement, on the other hand, often insist that the value of the nonhuman world is purely instrumental, and that it is only sentimentalists who hold otherwise.

John Passmore, for instance, deplores "the cry ... for a new morality, a new religion, which would transform man's attitude to nature, which would lead us to believe that it is *intrinsically* wrong to destroy a species, cut down a tree, clear a wilderness." [53] Passmore refers to such a call for a nonhomocentric morality as "mystical rubbish".[54] In his view, nothing in the nonhuman world has *either* intrinsic value or moral rights. He would evidently agree with William F. Baxter, who says that "damage to penguins, or to sugar pines, or geological marvels is, without more, simply irrelevant.... Penguins are important [only] because people enjoy seeing them walk about the rocks." [55]

This strictly instrumentalist view of the value of the nonhuman world is rejected by animal liberationists and environmentalists alike. The animal liberationists maintain that the sentience of many nonhuman animals constitutes a sufficient reason for regarding their needs and interests as worthy of our moral concern, and for assigning them certain moral rights. Sentience is, in this sense, a sufficient condition for the possession of intrinsic value. It does not follow from this that it is also a *necessary* condition for having intrinsic value. It may be a necessary condition for having individual moral *rights;* certainly it is necessary for *some* rights, such as the right not to be subjected to unnecessary pain. But there is room to argue that even though mountains and trees are not subject to pleasure or pain, and hence do not have rights of the sort we ascribe to sentient beings, nevertheless they have intrinsic value of another sort, or for another reason.

What sort of intrinsic value might they have? The environmentalists' answer is that they are valuable as organic parts of the natural whole. But this answer is incomplete, in that it does not explain why we ought to value the natural world *as a whole,* except insofar as it serves our own interests to do so. No clear and persuasive answer to this more basic question has yet been given. Perhaps, as Thomas Auxter has suggested, the answer is to be found in a teleological ethic of the same general sort of that of Plato or Aristotle, an ethic which urges us "to seek the highest good, which is generally understood as the most perfect or complete state of affairs possible".[56] This most perfect or complete state of affairs would include "a natural order which encompasses the most developed and diverse types of beings",[57] one in which "every species finds a place ... and ... the existence and functioning of any one species is not a threat to the existence and functioning of any other species".[58]

It is not my purpose to endorse this or any other philosophical explanation of why even the nonsentient elements of nature should be regarded as having intrinsic value. I want only to suggest that better answers to this question can and should be developed, and that there is no reason to presume that these answers will consist entirely of "mystical rubbish". Furthermore, I would suggest that the claim that mountains and forests have intrinsic value of *some* sort is intuitively much more plausible than its denial.

One way to test your own intuitions, or unformulated convictions, about this claim is to consider a hypothetical case of the following sort. Suppose that a virulent virus, developed by some unwise researcher, has escaped into the environment and will inevitably extinguish all animal life (ourselves included) within a few weeks. Suppose further that this or some other scientist has developed another virus which, if released, would destroy all plant life as well, but more slowly, such that the effects of the second virus would not be felt until after the last animal was gone. If the second virus were released *secretly,* its release would do no further damage to the well-being of any sentient creature; no one would suffer, even from the knowledge that the plant kingdom is as doomed as we are. Finally, suppose that it is known with certainty that sentient life forms would never re-evolve on the earth (this time from plants), and that no sentient aliens will ever visit the planet. The question is would it be morally preferable, in such a case, *not* to release the second virus, even secretly? If we tend to think that it would be, that it would certainly be better to allow the plants to survive us than to render the earth utterly lifeless (except perhaps for the viruses), then we do not really believe that it is only sentient—let alone only human—beings which have intrinsic value.

This being the case, it is relatively unimportant whether we say that even nonsentient natural entities may have moral *rights,* or whether we say only that, because of their intrinsic value, they ought to be protected, even at some cost to certain human interests. Nevertheless, there is an argument for preferring the latter way of speaking. It is that nonsentient entities, not being subject to pleasure or pain, and lacking any preferences with respect to what happens to them, cannot sensibly be said to have *interests.* The Gulf Stream or the south wind may have value because of their role in the natural order, but if they were to be somehow altered or destroyed, *they* would not experience suffering, or lose anything which it is in *their* interest to have. Thus, "harming" them would not be wrong *in and of itself,* but rather because of the kinds of environmental efforts which the land ethic stresses. In contrast, harm done to a sentient being has moral significance even if it has no further consequences whatsoever.

The position at which we have arrived represents a compromise between those animal liberationists who hold that only sentient beings have *either* intrinsic value or moral rights, and those environmentalists who ascribe *both* intrinsic value and moral rights to even the nonsentient elements of nature. Mountains and trees should be protected not because they have moral rights, but because they are intrinsically—as well as instrumentally—valuable.

So stated, the land ethic is fully compatible with the claim that individual sentient animals have moral rights. Indeed, the two positions are complementary; each helps to remedy some of the apparent defects of the other. The animal liberation theory, for instance, does not in itself explain why we ought to protect not only *individual* animals, but also threatened *species* of plants as well as animals. The land ethic, on the other hand, fails to explain why it is wrong to inflict needless suffering or death even upon domestic animals, which may play little or no role in the maintenance of natural ecosystems, or only a negative role. Practices such as rearing animals in conditions of severe confinement and discomfort, or subjecting them to painful experiments which have no *significant* scientific purpose, are wrong primarily because of the suffering inflicted upon individual sentient beings, and only secondarily because of any social or environmental damage they may incidentally cause.

Thus, it is clear that as we learn to extend our moral concern beyond the boundaries of our own species we shall have to take account of both the rights of individual animals *and* the value of those elements of the natural world which are not themselves sentient. Respecting the interests of creatures who, like ourselves, are subject to pleasure and pain is in no way inconsistent with valuing and protecting the richness, diversity and stability of natural ecosystems. In many cases, such as the commercial slaughter of whales, there are both environmental and humane reasons for altering current practices. In other cases, in which humane and environmental considerations appear to point in opposite directions e.g., the case of the feral goats on the New Zealand islands) these factors must be weighed against each other, much as the rights of individual human beings must often be weighed against larger social needs. In no case does a concern for the environment preclude *also* considering the rights of individual animals; it may, for instance, be possible to trap and deport the goats alive, rather than killing them.

VI SUMMARY AND CONCLUSION

I have argued that the environmentalist and animal liberationist perspectives are complementary, rather than essentially competitive or mutually inconsistent approaches towards a nonhomocentric moral theory. The claim that animals have certain moral rights, by virtue of their sentience, does not negate the fact that ecosystems are complexly unified wholes, in which one element generally cannot be damaged without causing repercussions elsewhere in the system. If sentience is a necessary, as well as sufficient, condition for having moral rights, then we cannot ascribe such rights to oceans, mountains and the like; yet we have a moral obligation to protect such natural resources from excessive damage at human hands, both because of their value to us and to future generations, and because they are intrinsically valuable, as elements of the planetary biosystem. It is not necessary to choose between regarding biological communities as unified systems, analogous to organisms, and regarding them as containing many individual sentient creatures, each with its own separate needs and interests; for it is clearly both of these things at once. Only by *combining* the environmentalist and animal rights perspectives can we take account of the full range of moral considerations which ought to guide our interactions with the nonhuman world.

Endnotes

1. See, for instance, Immanuel Kant, "Duties to Animals and Spirits", in *Lectures on Ethics,* trans. Louis Infield (New York: Harper and Row, 1964), excerpted in *Animal Rights and Human Obligations* ed. Tom Regan and Peter Singer (Englewood Cliffs, N.J.: Prentice-Hall, 1976), pp. 122–23.

2. Aldo Leopold, *A Sand County Almanac* (New York: Oxford University Press, 1949), p. 204.

3. Ibid., p. 225.

4. Here, as elsewhere in this paper, the terms "pleasure" and "pain" should not be understood in the narrow sense in which they refer only to particular sorts of *sensation,* but rather as an abbreviated way of referring

to the fulfillment or frustration, respectively, of the needs, interests and desires of sentient beings.

5. See, for example, the selections by Jeremy Bentham, "A Utilitarian View"; John Stuart Mill, "A Defence of Bentham"; and Henry S. Salt, "The Humanities of Diet", "Animal Rights", and "The Logic of the Larder", in *Animal Rights,* ed. Regan and Singer.

6. Ibid.

7. See, Maureen Duffy, "Beasts for Pleasure", in *Animals, Men and Morals,* ed. Stanley and Rosalind Godlovitch (New York: Taplinger Publishing Co. 1972), pp. 111–24.

8. See, Stephen R.L. Clark, *The Moral Status of Animals* (Oxford: Clarendon Press, 1977); Tom Regan, "Animal Rights, Human Wrongs", *Environmental Ethics* 2, no. 2 (Summer 1980): 99–120; Richard Ryder, "Experiments on Animals", in *Animal Rights,* ed. Regan and Singer, pp. 33–47; and Peter Singer, *Animal Liberation: A New Ethics for Our Treatment of Animals* (New York: Avon, 1975), especially chaps. 2 and 3.

9. J. Baird Callicott, "Animal Liberation: A Triangular Affair", *Environmental Ethics* 2, no. 4 (Winter 1980): 315.

10. Ibid., p. 337.

11. See Christopher D. Stone, *Should Trees Have Standing? Toward Legal Rights for Natural Objects* (Los Altos, Calif.: William Kaufman, 1974).

12. Singer, *Animal Liberation,* p. 9.

13. Jeremy Bentham, *The Principles of Morals and Legislation* (1789), chap. 18, sec. 1; cited by Singer, *Animal Liberation,* p. 8.

14. Singer, *Animal Liberation,* p. 5.

15. Peter Singer, "The Fable of the Fox", *Ethics* 88, no. 2 (January 1978): 122.

16. See, for instance, Brigid Brophy, "In Pursuit of a Fantasy", in *Animals, Men and Morals,* pp. 125–45; Joel Feinberg, "The Rights of Animals and Unborn Generations", in *Philosophy and Environmental Crisis,* ed. William T. Blackstone (Athens, Ga. University of Georgia Press, 1974), pp. 43–68; Rosalind Godlovitch, "Animals and Morals", in *Animals, Men and Morals,* pp. 156–71; Lawrence Haworth, "Rights, Wrongs and Animals", *Ethics* 88, no. 2 (January 1978): 95–105; Anthony J. Povilitis, "On Assigning Rights to Animals and Nature", *Environmental Ethics* 2 (Spring 1980): 67–71; and Tom Regan, "Do Animals Have a Right to Life?", in *Animal Rights,* ed. Regan and Singer, pp. 197–204.

17. Regan, "Right to Life?"

18. Ibid., p. 203.

19. Singer, *Animal Liberation,* p. 3.

20. Regan, "Right to Life?"; see also, idem, "An Examination and Defence of One Argument Concerning Animal Rights", *Inquiry* 22, nos. 1–2 (1979): 189–217.

21. Regan, "Right to Life?", p. 197.

22. T.L.S. Sprigge, "Metaphysics, Physicalism, and Animal Rights", *Inquiry* 22, nos. 1–2 (1979): 101.

23. See John C. Lilly, *Lilly on Dolphins* (New York: Anchor Books, Garden City, 1975), p. 210. Lilly, after years of experimenting with dolphins and attempting to communicate with them, concluded that keeping them captive was wrong because they, like us, suffer from such confinement.

24. Ruth Cigman, "Death, Misfortune, and Species Inequality", *Philosophy and Public Affairs* 10, no. 1 (Winter 1981): p. 48.

25. Ibid., pp. 57–58. The concept of a categorical desire is introduced by Bernard Williams, "The Makropoulous Case", in his *Problems of the Self* (Cambridge: Cambridge University Press), 1973.

26. Brophy, "Pursuit of Fantasy", p. 129.

27. H.J. McCloskey, "Moral Rights and Animals", *Inquiry* 22, nos. 1–2 (1979): 31.

28. Ibid., p. 29.

29. Michael Fox, "Animal Liberation: A Critique", *Ethics* 88, no. 2 (January 1978): 111.

30. Feinberg, "Rights", pp. 46–47.

31. Such as that presented by John Rawls, *A Theory of Justice* (Oxford: Oxford University Press, 1972).

32. Aristotle *Politics* 1. 1254, 1260, and 1264.

33. Singer, *Animal Liberation*, pp. 75–76; Regan, "One Argument Concerning Animal Rights".

34. Mary Anne Warren, "Do Potential People Have Moral Rights?", *Canadian Journal of Philosophy* 7, no. 2 (June 1977): 275–89.

35. This argument does not, as one might suppose, justify placing restrictions upon (early) abortions which are as severe as the restrictions upon infanticide or murder, although there are certainly many people who place a high value upon the lives of foetuses. The reason it does not is that such restrictions, unlike restrictions upon infanticide (given the possibility of adoption), violate all of the most basic moral rights of women, who are not morally obligated to waive their own rights to life, liberty and happiness, in order to protect the sensibilities of human observers who are not directly affected.

36. Anthropological evidence for this claim may be found in Margaret Mead's study of the Mundugumor, a Papuan tribe in New Guinea which placed little value on infants and abused them casually; adult Mundugumors, men and women alike, appear to be hostile, aggressive and generally amoral, to a degree barely compatible with social existence (Margaret Mead, *Sex and Temperament in Three Primitive Societies* [New York: William Morrow, 1963]).

37. One exception to the rule that mental incapacitation does not justify the denial of basic human rights is *total and permanent* incapacitation, such that there is no possibility of any future return to sentience. Once a person has entered a state of terminal coma, he or she has nothing to gain from continued biological life, and nothing to lose by dying. Where there is any doubt about the possibility of full or partial recovery, every benefit of the doubt should be given; but where there is clearly no such possibility, the best course is usually to allow death to occur naturally, provided that this is consistent with the wishes of the individual's family or friends. (To sanction *active* euthanasia, i.e., the deliberate *killing* of such terminally comatose persons might be unwise, in that it might lead all of us to fear [somewhat more] for our lives when we are forced to place them in the hands of medical personnel; but that is an issue which we need not settle here.)

38. Regan, "One Argument Concerning Animal Rights", p. 189.

39. See, for example, Edward A. Langerak, "Abortion, Potentiality, and Conferred Claims", (Paper delivered at the Eastern Division of the American Philosophical Association, December 1979).

40. Callicott, "Animal Liberation", p. 320.

41. D.G. Ritchie, "Why Animals Do Not Have Rights", in *Animal Rights,* ed. Regan and Singer, p. 183.

42. See Aldo Leopold, *Sand County Almanac,* pp. 129–33.

43. Ritchie, "Why Animals Do Not Have Rights".

44. Singer, *Animal Liberation* pp. 169–74.

45. Callicott, "Animal Liberation", p. 335.

46. For exposition of this holistic message, see, William T. Blackstone, "Ethics and Ecology", in *Philosophy and Environmental Crisis*, pp. 16–42; Thomas Auxter, "The Right Not To Be Eaten", *Inquiry* 22, nos. 1–2 (Spring 1979): 221–30; Robert Cahn, *Footprints on the Planet: The Search for an Environmental Ethic* (New York: Universe Books, 1978); Albert A. Fritsch, *Environmental Ethics* (New York: Anchor Press, Doubleday, 1980), p. 3; Alastair S. Gunn, "Why Should We Care About Rare Species?", *Environmental Ethics* 2, no. 1 (Spring 1980): 17–37, Eugene P. Odum, "Environmental Ethics and the Attitude Revolution", in *Philosophy and Environmental Crisis*, pp. 10–15; and, of course, Leopold, *Sand County Almanac.*

47. See Callicott, "Animal Liberation", p. 315.

48. Gunn, "Rare Species", p. 36.

49. Ibid., p. 37.

50. See Feinberg, "Rights", pp. 52–53.

51. See Stone, *Should Trees Have Standing?*

52. For example, Baxter maintains that "environmental amenities . . . fall in the category of a luxury good" (William F. Baxter, *People or Penguins: The Case for Optimal Pollution* [New York and London: Columbia University Press, 1974], p. 105).

53. John Passmore, *Man's Responsibility for Nature* (London: Duckworth, 1974), p. 111.

54. Ibid., p. 173.

55. Baxter, *People or Penguins*, p. 5.

56. Thomas Auxter, "The Right Not To Be Eaten", *Inquiry* 22, nos. 1–2 (1979): 222.

57. Ibid., p. 225.

58. Ibid., p. 226.

Review Questions

1. Distinguish between the land ethic and the animal liberation view, as Warren explains them.

2. How does Warren think that the two views can be made compatible?

3. What problem does Warren find in the animal rights view?

4. How does Warren analyze the concept of a moral right?

5. According to Warren, why do animals have some rights? What are these rights?

6. In Warren's view, what are the differences in content and strength between animal and human rights?

7. According to Warren, what is the fundamental message of Leopold's land ethic?

8. Why does there appear to be a fundamental contradiction between the land ethic and the animal rights view, and how does Warren propose to resolve it?

Discussion Questions

1. Warren says, "If we someday encounter extra-terrestrial beings, or build robots, androids or supercomputers which function as self-aware moral agents, then we must extend full and equal moral rights to these as well." Do you agree? Why or why not?

2. Reread the example about the virulent virus. Do you agree that it would be morally preferable not to release the second virus? Explain your view.

Problem Cases

1. *Killing Chickens* Suppose a farmer raises chickens on his farm. They are well fed, they have plenty of room, they have a comfortable place to sleep, and they are well cared for. Each year the farmer kills some of the chickens quickly and with little pain. Then he eats them with great relish. He replaces the chickens killed with other chickens so that the chicken population remains stable. Does this farmer do anything that is morally wrong or not? Explain your position.

2. *The Draize Test* The Draize eye test is used by cosmetic companies such as Revlon and Procter and Gamble to test the eye irritancy of their products—cosmetics, hair shampoos, and so on. The substance to be tested is injected into the eyes of rabbits; more specifically, 0.1 milligrams (a large volume dose) is injected into the conjuctival sac of one eye of each of six rabbits, with the other eye serving as a control. The lids are held together for one second, and then the animal is released. The eyes are examined at twenty-four, forty-eight, and seventy-two hours to see if there is corneal damage. Although the test is very painful, as you can imagine, anesthetics are not used. The eyes are not washed. Very large doses are used (often resulting in permanent eye damage) to provide a large margin of safety in extrapolating to the human response. Should companies continue to test their new products in this way or not? What is your view?

3. *Mechanical Mothers* (These experiments were mentioned in *Newsweek*, December 26, 1988.) Researchers at the Primate Research Center in Madison, Wisconsin, have been conducting experiments to gauge the effects of child abuse on monkeys. One experiment involves putting baby monkeys with mechanical surrogate mothers who eject sharp brass spikes when the babies try to hug them. Another experiment consists of impregnating females who have been driven insane by social isolation. When given their babies, the mothers crush their skulls with their teeth. Are these experiments justified or not?

4. *Guerilla Warfare in Cathedral Forest* (Reported in *Esquire*, February 1987.) Cathedral Forest in Oregon is one of the last large stands of virgin forest remaining on the North American continent. The forest is called old growth because the trees (Douglas firs) are among the oldest and biggest on the planet. Old growth constitutes an almost infinitesimal percentage of forested lands in the United States. Even though there is no commercial demand for the timber, the U.S. Forest Service has made the harvesting of the last of the old trees a priority. The Forest Service has sold Cathedral Forest to Willamette Industries, a large wood-products company.

To prevent the forest from being cut down, radical environmentalist Mike Roselle has resorted to an illegal guerrilla action called tree spiking. He has driven long nails into trees in a spiral pattern. Chain saws and saw blades will shatter when they hit the buried nails. Mike hopes that the spiked trees will prevent Willamette from cutting down the forest. Is this tree spiking morally justified or not? What is your view?

5. The Burning of Amazon Rain Forests (See the cover story in *Time,* September 18, 1989.) Farmers and cattle ranchers in Brazil are burning the rain forests of the Amazon River. They are doing this to clear the land for crops and livestock. According to the article in *Time,* an estimated 12,350 square miles have been destroyed so far, and the burning continues. Conservationists and leaders of rich industrial nations have asked Brazil to stop the destruction. They claim that if the Amazon rain forests are destroyed, more than one million species will vanish. This would be a significant loss of the earth's genetic and biological heritage. Furthermore, they are worried about changes in the climate. The Amazon system of forests plays an important role in the way the sun's heat is distributed around the earth because it stores more than 75 billion tons of carbon in its trees. If the trees are burned, then there will be a dramatic increase in the amount of carbon dioxide in the atmosphere, and this will magnify the greenhouse effect—the trapping of heat by atmospheric carbon dioxide. In other words, the destruction of the Amazon forests will significantly increase the global warming trend.

Brazilians reply that they have a sovereign right to use their land as they see fit. They complain that the rich industrial nations are just trying to maintain their economic supremacy. Brazilian President José Sarney argues that the burning is necessary for Brazilian economic development, particularly when Brazil is struggling under an $111–billion foreign debt load.

Should Brazil continue burning the Amazon rain forests or not? If not, then what should rich industrial nations do to help Brazil?

Suggested Readings

(1) *Environmental Ethics.* This journal is edited by Eugene C. Hargrove and is dedicated to the philosophical aspects of environmental problems.

(2) Leslie Pickering Francis and Richard Norman, "Some Animals Are More Equal Than Others," *Philosophy* 53 (October 1978), pp. 507–527. Francis and Norman agree with Singer and others that it is wrong to cause animal suffering, other things being equal, but unlike Singer they do not think that this requires us to adopt vegetarianism or abandon animal experimentation.

(3) R.G. Frey, *Interests and Rights: The Case Against Animals* (Oxford: Clarendon Press, 1980.) Frey argues that animals have neither interests nor moral rights.

(4) William K. Frankena, "Ethics and the Environment." In Kenneth Goodpaster and K.M. Sayre, eds., *Ethics and Problems of the 21st Century* (Notre Dame, IN: University of Notre Dame Press, 1979), pp. 3–19. Frankena distinguishes between eight types of ethics: (1) ethical egoism, (2) humanism, (3) sentientism, or the view that the class of moral patients includes only sentient beings, (4) the ethics of "reverence for life," (5) the view that everything should be morally considered, (6) theistic ethics, (7) combination ethics, where different types of ethics are combined, and (8) naturalistic ethics. He finds ethical egoism and humanism to be morally inadequate, and he has doubts about theistic ethics and combination ethics. He concludes that sentientism provides an adequate basis for environmental ethics. His view is rejected both by Frey and by those who adopt a holistic environmental ethic.

(5) Alastair S. Gunn, "Why Should We Care About Rare Species?" *Environmental Ethics,* 2, no. 1 (Spring 1989), pp. 17–37. Gunn analyzes the concept of rarity and its relation to value. He argues that the extermination of a rare species is wrong because each species, and also ecological wholes, have intrinsic value.

(6) Aldo Leopold, "The Land Ethic," in *A Sand County Almanac* (New York: Oxford University Press, 1966), pp. 217–241. This is the classic presentation of Leopold's Land Ethic. As he puts it, "The land ethic simply enlarges the boundaries of the community to include soils, waters, plants, and animals, or collectively, the land."

(7) H.J. McCloskey, "Moral Rights and Animals," *Inquiry* 22 (Spring–Summer 1979), pp. 25–54. McCloskey attacks Feinberg's analysis of the concept of a right and presents his own account. According to McCloskey, a right is an entitlement to something and not a claim against someone. Beings who are able to make a claim, either directly or through a representative, can possess rights. But since animals cannot do this, they cannot be said to possess rights.

(8) John Passmore, *Man's Responsibility for Nature* (New York: Scribner's, 1974). Passmore thinks that we should not waste natural resources, but we should not sacrifice art, science, or other human interests for the sake of conservation.

(9) Tom Regan, ed., *Earthbound: New Introductory Essays in Environmental Ethics* (New York: Random House, 1984). This is a collection of original essays on a variety of topics related to the environment, including Alastair S. Gunn, "Preserving Rare Species;" Annette Baier, "For the Sake of Future Generations;" and Mark Sagoff, "Ethics and Economics in Environmental Law."

(10) _____, *The Case for Animal Rights* (Berkeley: University of California Press, 1983). Regan argues that animals are not thoughtless brutes, but persons who have beliefs and desires, memories and expectations, and who feel pleasure and pain. As such they have a basic moral right to be treated with respect. To do this we must eliminate commercial animal agriculture, hunting and trapping, and animal experimentation.

(11) Mark Sagoff, "On Preserving the Natural Environment," *Yale Law Journal* 84 (December 1974), pp. 205–267. Sagoff proposes a nonutilitarian rationale for preserving the natural environment.

(12) Donald Scherer and Thomas Attig, eds., *Ethics and the Environment* (Englewood Cliffs, NJ: Prentice–Hall, 1983). This is a collection of readings on specific environmental problems and the general question of defining an environmental ethic.

(13) Christopher Stone, *Should Trees Have Standing?* (Los Altos, CA: Kaufman, 1974). In this short book, Stone argues that trees and other objects in the environment should be granted legal standing so that it is possible for them to sue for their own protection.

(14) Paul W. Taylor, *Respect for Nature: A Theory of Environment Ethics* (Princeton, NJ: Princeton University Press, 1986). Taylor develops a theory of respect for nature that is similar to the ethical theory based on respect for persons. It requires us to see other living things as having an inherent worth that is equal to our own, and a denial that humans have a higher worth or value.

Chapter 10

Nuclear Deterrence

Introduction

War Scenarios   Discussions of nuclear deterrence usually include war scenarios, possible ways in which nuclear weapons might be used. Of course these are hypothetical, but they could become actual very quickly with present-day missiles.

There are two main scenarios: MAD (mutual assured destruction) and limited or tactical war. The MAD scenario dates back to the Eisenhower–Dulles era, and it still dominates popular thinking about nuclear war (for example, in the 1980s ABC broadcast "The Day After," a dramatization of a nuclear holocaust). In such a war, there would be massive first strikes (called preemptive first strikes) and massive retaliations against civilian populations. There might be more flexible responses against lesser strikes, but these would very likely escalate into massive strikes; there would be no way to limit the exchange. In such an exchange, both sides would use thousands of nuclear warheads—together the United States and the Soviet Union have around 50,000 warheads. (This figure does not include the warheads stockpiled by Great Britain, France, China, India, Israel, and South Africa. If those warheads are counted, then there are more than 60,000 nuclear weapons in the world's arsenals according to a U.S. Department of Defense study cited by Richard Halloran in *The New York Times,* June 18, 1984.) It is generally agreed that nobody could really be said to win a global nuclear holocaust, although during the Reagan administration there was talk of prevailing in such a war. It seems safe to say that no rational leader or group would intentionally start a global nuclear war, but there is still the possibility of threatening a nuclear attack for political or military gain. For example, when President Kennedy ordered a naval blockade of Cuba in 1962 in order to halt the Soviet deployment of intermediate-range missiles, he was tacitly threatening to use nuclear weapons if the Soviets did not withdraw.

Current military thinking places more emphasis on the limited use of nuclear weapons to counter setbacks in conventional military battles, and thereby win the conflict. A possible conflict that was widely discussed in the 1980s was a Soviet invasion of West Germany. Given the dramatic downfall of Communist rule in East Germany and other Eastern European countries, and the reunification of Germany, now such a conflict seems out of the question. It appears that both the Soviets and the United States will begin withdrawing their troops from Eastern Europe. Indeed some political commentators claim that the cold war has ended, and the Soviet Union with Gorbachev as its leader no longer threatens the United States. Even so, some conservatives worry that the political climate may change if, for example, Gorbachev falls from power or resigns, and they believe that the Soviet Union is still an evil empire that threatens the United States. (Recall that in 1983 President Ronald Reagan told an evangelical group that the Soviet Union is "the focus of evil in the modern world" and "an evil empire.") Furthermore, even if Russia really is no longer a threat, there is always the possibility that some other unfriendly country might start a war that requires the tactical use of nuclear weapons.

The Effects of Nuclear War

In his book *The Fate of the Earth,* Jonathan Schell vividly describes the effects of an air burst of a one-megaton bomb—a bomb equal in explosive yield to a million tons of TNT. There is initial radiation, an electromagnetic pulse, a thermal pulse, a blast wave, initial radioactive fallout, and mass fires. The electromagnetic pulse would produce widespread damage to solid-state electrical circuits; this means, for one thing, that unshielded defense communications would be disrupted and electronic guidance systems on missiles would not work properly. Schell also describes some global effects of nuclear bombs: delayed or worldwide radioactive fallout lasting millions of years, dust in the stratosphere cooling the earth's surface producing a nuclear winter, and destruction of the layer of ozone that shields the earth from ultraviolet radiation. He emphasizes that a nuclear holocaust in which ten thousand megatons are detonated would probably make life on earth impossible except in the ocean. The United States would become a republic of insects and grass (to use his memorable phrase).

Moral Issues

There are two important moral issues raised by nuclear weapons: Is nuclear war ever morally justified? Is it morally justifiable to threaten to use nuclear weapons?

Jonathan Schell gives good reasons for holding that a global nuclear war is never morally justified. Not only would millions of innocent people be killed, but the environment would be harmed to such an extent that human beings might become extinct.

It is not so clear, however, that a strictly limited or tactical nuclear war is never justified. In fact, a plausible justification of some such war can be given by the traditional just-war theory. According to this theory, there are two principles that a just war must follow. First, there is the principle of discrimination which prohibits direct intentional attacks on innocent noncombatants. Second, there is the principle of proportionality which requires that the good achieved by the war must be proportionate to the evil resulting from the war. It is possible to imagine a nuclear war that satisfies these principles, e.g., one fought in outer space using space stations (as in the movie *Star Wars*), or one in the ocean. Let us consider the real possibility of an ocean battle. Suppose that a single U.S. battleship is suddenly and unexpectedly confronted by a fleet of small ships from Iraq. The ships are clearly hostile, and even announce their intention to attack. Before Iraq's ships can get close enough to begin effective firing, the U.S. ship defensively launches one short-range tactical nuclear missile which completely destroys the attacking fleet. Only combatants are killed, the radioactive fallout is fairly limited, and Iraq has no nuclear weapons to use in retaliation. Wouldn't this very limited use of nuclear weapons be morally justified?

Nuclear Deterrence Strategy   Assuming that global nuclear war is never morally justified, and that only a very few tactical uses of nuclear weapons are justifiable, there is still the question about nuclear deterrence strategy. Is it morally acceptable to have a nuclear deterrence strategy which involves the threat of global nuclear war? The United States seems to have just such a strategy— we have over 24,000 nuclear weapons, and the official policy of the United States, announced when Casper Weinberger was Secretary of Defense, is that we will be the first to use nuclear weapons in the case of a conventional war. The Soviet Union has announced that it would retaliate with nuclear weapons in self-defense, but the USSR has insisted that it would not be the first to use them. The result is a balance of power or a balance of terror where each side is threatening the other with annihilation.

The position of President Mikhail S. Gorbachev of the Soviet Union seems to be that such a deterrence strategy is not morally acceptable. He believes that it would be better to eliminate nuclear weapons completely. To achieve this, he proposes a three-step program of nuclear disarmament that ends with no nuclear weapons or delivery vehicles left on the earth by 1999. One of Gorbachev's proposals has been accepted by the United States. In 1987 President Ronald Reagan and President Gorbachev signed a treaty, the Intermediate Nuclear Forces Treaty (INF), which eliminated the superpowers' medium-range intermediate nuclear forces in Europe.

But President Reagan did not accept Gorbachev's demand that the United States stop the development, testing, and deployment of space-based nuclear weapons. In a famous speech on March 23, 1983, President Reagan proposed that the United States begin a Strategic Defense Initiative which involves the development of a space-based missile defense system. This proposed defense system is popularly called a Star Wars system because it calls for the development and deployment of the sorts of high-tech weapons seen in the science-fiction movie *Star Wars.* Just exactly what weapons or systems would or could be deployed in space is a matter of speculation. One proposal is for Brilliant Pebbles, sophisticated computer-driven missiles that track and destroy enemy missiles. Other speculations have been about conventional optical lasers, particle-beam devices, and X-ray lasers powered by nuclear explosions. Some of the technology for these weapons is known, but most scientists agree that much work needs to be done, and that it will be very expensive. Leon Sloss says that some systems will cost hundreds of billions of dollars. The best estimates available indicate that the cost of developing a laser battle station in space (as in the *Star Wars* movie) would be about ten times as much as that of other roughly similar modern high-technology systems, that is, it would be tens of billions of dollars.

In our readings, Leon Sloss argues in favor of Reagan's Strategic Defense Initiative. He claims that a nuclear strategy including both offensive and defensive forces increases stability and security for both the United States and the Soviet

Union. Sloss does not discuss the possibility of disarmament; he asserts that the main alternative to Strategic Defense is the Finite Deterrence or MAD strategy in which deterrence is entirely based on offensive forces and the threat to retaliate if attacked. He quickly dismisses this view as unacceptable to both the United States and the Soviet Union.

Douglas P. Lackey presents some of the main criticisms of Strategic Defense. It cannot be totally effective even if it works perfectly and stops all incoming ICBMs. The enemy could deliver bombs in other ways, on low-flying cruise missiles or small boats. Worse still, it makes nuclear war more likely because Soviet insecurity will be increased by the threat of U.S. first-strike capability. Finally, it would probably increase American threats of nuclear war.

What are the alternatives to Strategic Defense? According to Lackey, there are at least three: Countervailing Strategy, Finite Deterrence, and Multilateral Disarmament (as in Gorbachev's proposal). The Countervailing Strategy (which Lackey says is the current weapons policy of the United States) is for the United States to survive any Soviet nuclear attack, and to inflict unacceptable damage in retaliation, and thus prevail or dominate no matter what. Lackey notes that there are problems with this strategy. It ignores the right to self-defense, it leaves the United States vulnerable to attack by an enemy not deterred by the threat of destruction, it commits the United States to the first use of nuclear weapons in the face of a Soviet conventional attack, and it provokes a very expensive strategic arms race with the Russians. The result is that we waste all our resources on arms and neglect more important things such as social services and education.

The Finite Deterrence view is that the only legitimate use of nuclear weapons is to deter nuclear wars. To do this, only a small number of nuclear weapons is needed. It is not necessary to have the over 24,000 weapons that the United States currently has stockpiled, or any short- or medium-range nuclear missiles. Critics of this view complain that it would drastically weaken U.S. defense and thus increase the chances of conventional war. Also, it would make the United States vulnerable to a decapitating first strike or a preemptive first strike.

The Multilateral Disarmament proposal is that the United States and the Soviet Union should agree to a step-by-step elimination of all nuclear weapons and delivery vehicles. This is what Gorbachev proposes, except that he includes all weapons in all countries. On the face of it, it seems like a good idea. Surely, 50,000 nuclear weapons (or 60,000 if they are all counted) are too many. Why not eliminate some of them? That seems reasonable enough, but should the superpowers reduce their nuclear arsenals to zero? There are problems with this. What about the other countries that have nuclear weapons? They would have to be eliminated too. And even if all the weapons were eliminated, they could be quickly rebuilt in a crisis. Lackey's reply to these objections is that the United States and other countries should rely on a strong nonnuclear defense. But his final appeal is moral. Speaking for the nuclear disarmer, he says, "Nuclear weapons are as wicked as slavery, and . . . if slavery could be abolished, so can nuclear weapons."

Jonathan Schell

The Effects of Nuclear Bombs

Jonathan Schell is a writer. His book The Fate of
the Earth *originally appeared in* The New Yorker.

   *Schell describes the effects of an air burst of a
one-megaton bomb (initial radiation, electromagnetic
pulse, thermal pulse, blast wave, radioactive fallout,
and destruction of the ozone layer), and he speculates
about the effects of a nuclear holocaust on individual
life, human society, and the earth as a whole.*

Whereas most conventional bombs produce
only one destructive effect—the shock
wave—nuclear weapons produce many destructive effects. At the moment of the explosion, when the temperature of the weapon
material instantly gasified, is at the superstel-
lar level, the pressure is millions of times the
normal atmospheric pressure. Immediately,
radiation, consisting mainly of gamma rays,
which are a very high-energy form of electromagnetic radiation, begins to stream outward
into the environment. This is called the "initial nuclear radiation," and is the first of the
destructive effects of a nuclear explosion. In
an air burst of a one-megaton bomb—a bomb
with the explosive yield of a million tons of
TNT, which is a medium-sized weapon in
present-day nuclear arsenals—the initial nuclear radiation can kill unprotected human
beings in an area of some six square miles.
Virtually simultaneously with the initial nuclear radiation, in a second destructive effect
of the explosion, an electromagnetic pulse is
generated by the intense gamma radiation
acting on the air. In a high-altitude detona-
tion, the pulse can knock out electrical equip-

ment over a wide area by inducing a powerful
surge of voltage through various conductors,
such as antennas, overhead power lines,
pipes, and railroad tracks. The Defense Department's Civil Preparedness Agency reported in 1977 that a single multi-kiloton nuclear weapon detonated one hundred and
twenty-five miles over Omaha, Nebraska,
could generate an electromagnetic pulse
strong enough to damage solid-state electrical circuits throughout the entire continental
United States and in parts of Canada and
Mexico, and thus threaten to bring the econ-
omies of these countries to a halt. When the
fusion and fission reactions have blown themselves out, a fireball takes shape. As it expands, energy is absorbed in the form of X-
rays by the surrounding air, and then the air
re-radiates a portion of that energy into the
environment in the form of the thermal
pulse—a wave of blinding light and intense
heat—which is the third of the destructive
effects of a nuclear explosion. (If the burst is
low enough, the fireball touches the ground,
vaporizing or incinerating almost everything
within it.) The thermal pulse of a one-megaton bomb lasts for about ten seconds and can
cause second-degree burns in exposed
human beings at a distance of nine and a half
miles, or in an area of more than two hundred and eighty square miles, and that of a
twenty-megaton bomb (a large weapon by
modern standards) lasts for about twenty
seconds and can produce the same consequences at a distance of twenty-eight miles,
or in an area of 2,460 square miles. As the
fireball expands, it also sends out a blast
wave in all directions, and this is the fourth
destructive effect of the explosion. The blast
wave of an air-burst one-megaton bomb can
flatten or severely damage all but the strongest buildings within a radius of four and a half
miles, and that of a twenty-megaton bomb
can do the same within a radius of twelve
miles. As the fireball burns, it rises, con-
densing water from the surrounding atmosphere to form the characteristic mushroom
cloud. If the bomb has been set off on the

ground or close enough to it so that the fire-ball touches the surface, in a so-called ground burst, a crater will be formed, and tons of dust and debris will be fused with the intensely radioactive fission products and sucked up into the mushroom cloud. This mixture will return to earth as radioactive fallout, most of it in the form of fine ash, in the fifth destructive effect of the explosion. Depending upon the composition of the surface, from forty to seventy percent of this fallout—often called the "early" or "local" fallout—descends to earth within about a day of the explosion, in the vicinity of the blast and downwind from it, exposing human beings to radiation disease, an illness that is fatal when exposure is intense. Air bursts may also produce local fallout, but in much smaller quantities. The lethal range of the local fallout depends on a number of circumstances, including the weather, but under average conditions a one-megaton ground burst would, according to the report by the Office of Technology Assessment, lethally contaminate over a thousand square miles. (A lethal dose, by convention, is considered to be the amount of radiation that, if delivered over a short period of time, would kill half the able-bodied young adult population.)

The initial nuclear radiation, the electromagnetic pulse, the thermal pulse, the blast wave, and the local fallout may be described as the local primary effects of nuclear weapons. Naturally, when many bombs are exploded the scope of these effects is increased accordingly. But in addition these primary effects produce innumerable secondary effects on societies and natural environments, some of which may be even more harmful than the primary ones. To give just one example, nuclear weapons, by flattening and setting fire to huge, heavily built-up areas, generate mass fires, and in some cases these may kill more people than the original thermal pulses and blast waves. Moreover, there are—quite distinct from both the local primary effects of individual bombs and their secondary effects—global primary effects, which do not become significant unless thousands of bombs are detonated all around the earth. And these global primary effects produce innumerable secondary effects of their own throughout the ecosystem of the earth as a whole. For a full-scale holocaust is more than the sum of its local parts; it is also a powerful direct blow to the ecosphere. In that sense, a holocaust is to the earth what a single bomb is to a city. Three grave direct global effects have been discovered so far. The first is the "delayed," or "worldwide," fallout. In detonations greater than one hundred kilotons, part of the fallout does not fall to the ground in the vicinity of the explosion, but rises high into the troposphere and into the stratosphere, circulates around the earth, and then, over months or years, descends, contaminating the whole surface of the globe—although with doses of radiation far weaker than those delivered by the local fallout. Nuclear-fission products comprise some three hundred radioactive isotopes, and though some of them decay to relatively harmless levels of radioactivity within a few hours, minutes, or even seconds, others persist to emit radiation for up to millions of years. The short-lived isotopes are the ones most responsible for the lethal effects of the local fallout, and the long-lived ones are responsible for the contamination of the earth by stratospheric fallout. The energy released by all fallout from a thermonuclear explosion is about five percent of the total. By convention, this energy is not calculated in the stated yield of a weapon, yet in a ten-thousand-megaton attack the equivalent of five hundred megatons of explosive energy, or forty thousand times the yield of the Hiroshima bomb, would be released in the form of radioactivity. This release may be considered a protracted afterburst, which is dispersed into the land, air, and sea, and into the tissues, bones, roots, stems, and leaves of living things, and goes on detonating there almost indefinitely after the explosion. The second of the global effects that have been discovered so far is the lofting, from ground bursts, of millions of tons of dust into the stratosphere; this is likely to produce general cooling of the earth's surface. The third of the global effects is a predicted partial destruction of the layer of ozone that surrounds the entire earth in the stratosphere. A nuclear fireball, by burning nitrogen in the air, produces large quantities of oxides of nitrogen. These are carried by the heat of the blast into the stratosphere, where, through a series of chemical reactions, they bring about a depletion of the ozone layer. Such a depletion may persist for years. The 1975 N.A.S. report has estimated that in a holocaust in which ten thousand megatons were detonated in the Northern Hemisphere the reduction of ozone in this hemisphere could be as high as seventy percent and in the Southern Hemisphere as high as forty percent, and that it could take as long as thirty years for the ozone level to return to normal. The ozone layer is crucial to life on earth, because it shields the surface of the earth from lethal levels of ultraviolet radiation, which is present in sunlight. Glasstone remarks simply, "If it were not for the absorption of much of the solar ultraviolet radiation by the ozone, life as currently known could not exist except possibly in the ocean." Without the ozone shield, sunlight, the life-giver, would become a life-extinguisher. In judging the global effects of a holocaust, therefore, the primary question is not how many people would be irradiated, burned or crushed to death by the immediate effects of the bombs but how well the ecosphere, regarded as a single living entity, on which all forms of life depend for their continued existence, would hold up. The issue is the habitability of the earth, and it is in this context, not in the context of the direct slaughter of hundreds of millions of people by the local effects, that the question of human survival arises.

Usually, people wait for things to occur before trying to describe them. (Futurology has never been a very respectable field of inquiry.) But since we cannot afford under any circumstances to let a holocaust occur, we are forced in this one case to become the historians of the future—to chronicle and commit to memory an event that we have never experienced and must never experience. This unique endeavor, in which foresight is asked to perform a task usually reserved for hindsight, raises a host of special difficulties. There is a categorical difference, often overlooked, between trying to describe an event that has already happened (whether it is Napoleon's invasion of Russia or the pollution of the environment by acid rain) and trying to describe one that has yet to happen—and one, in addition, for which there is no precedent, or even near-precedent, in history. Lacking experience to guide our thoughts and impress itself on our feelings, we resort to speculation. But speculation, however brilliantly it may be carried out, is at best only a poor substitute for experience. Experience gives us facts, whereas in pure speculation we are thrown back on theory, which has never been a very reliable guide to future events. Moreover, experience engraves its lessons in our hearts through suffering and the other consequences that it has for our lives; but speculation leaves our lives untouched, and so gives us leeway to reject its conclusions, no matter how well argued they may be. (In the world of strategic theory, in particular, where strategists labor to simulate actual situations on the far side of the nuclear abyss, so that generals and statemen can prepare to make their decisions in case the worst happens, there is sometimes an unfortunate tendency to mistake pure ratiocination for reality, and to pretend to a knowledge of the future that it is not given to human beings to have.) Our knowledge of the local primary effects of the bombs, which is based both on the physical principles that made their construction possible and on experience gathered from the bombings of Hiroshima and Nagasaki and from testing, is quite solid. And our knowledge of the extent of the local primary effects of many weapons used together, which is obtained simply by using the multiplication table, is also solid: knowing that the thermal pulse of a twenty-megaton bomb can give people at least second-degree burns in an area of 2,460 square miles, we can easily figure out that the pulses of a hundred twenty-megaton bombs can give people at least second-degree burns in an area of 246,000 square miles. Nevertheless, it may be that our knowledge even of the primary effects is still incomplete, for during our test program new ones kept being discovered. One example is the electromagnetic pulse, whose importance was not recognized until around 1960, when, after more than a decade of tests, scientists realized that this effect accounted for unexpected electrical failures that had been occurring all along in equipment around the test sites. And it is only in recent years that the Defense Department has been trying to take account strategically of this startling capacity of just one bomb to put the technical equipment of a whole continent out of action.

When we proceed from the local effects of single explosions to the effects of thousands of them on societies and environments, the picture clouds considerably, because then we go beyond both the certainties of physics and our slender base of experience, and speculatively encounter the full complexity of human affairs and of the biosphere. Looked at in its entirety, a nuclear holocaust can be said to assail human life at three levels: the level of individual life, the level of human society, and the level of the natural environment—including the environment of the earth as a whole. At none of these levels can the destructiveness of nuclear weapons be measured in terms of firepower alone. At each level, life has both considerable recuperative powers, which might restore it even after devastating injury, and points of exceptional vulnerability, which leave it open to sudden, wholesale, and permanent collapse, even when comparatively little violence has been applied. Just as a machine may break down if one small part is removed, and a person may die if a single artery or vein is blocked, a modern technological society may come to a standstill if its fuel supply is cut off, and an ecosystem may collapse if its ozone shield is depleted. Nuclear weapons thus do not only kill directly, with their tremendous violence, but also kill indirectly, by breaking down the man-made and the natural systems on which individual lives collectively depend. Human beings require constant provision and care, supplied both by their societies and by the natural environment, and if these are suddenly removed people will die just as surely as if they had been struck by a bullet. Nuclear weapons are unique in that they attack the support systems of life at every level. And these systems, of course, are not isolated from each other but are parts of a single whole: ecological collapse, if it goes far enough, will bring about social collapse, and social collapse will bring about individual deaths. Furthermore, the destructive consequences of a nuclear attack are immeasurably compounded by the likelihood that all or most of the bombs will be detonated within the space of a few hours, in a single huge concussion. Normally, a locality devastated by a catastrophe, whether natural or man-made, will sooner or later receive help from untouched outside areas, as Hiroshima and Nagasaki did after they were bombed; but a nuclear holocaust would devastate the "outside" areas as well, leaving the victims to fend for themselves in a shattered society and natural environment. And what is true for each city is also true for the earth as a whole: a devastated earth can hardly expect "outside" help. The earth is the largest of the support systems for life, and the impairment of the earth is the largest of the perils posed by nuclear weapons.

The incredible complexity of all these effects, acting, interacting, and interacting again, precludes confident detailed representation of the events in a holocaust. We deal inevitably with approximations, probabilities, even guesses. However, it is important to point out that our uncertainty pertains not to *whether* the effects will interact, multiplying their destructive power as they do so, but only to *how*. It follows that our almost built-in bias, determined by the limitations of the human mind in judging future events, is to underestimate the harm. To fear interactive consequences that we cannot predict, or even imagine, may not be impossible, but it is very difficult. Let us consider, for example, some of the possible ways in which a person in a targeted country might die. He might be incinerated by the fireball or the thermal pulse. He might be lethally irradiated by the initial nuclear radiation. He might be crushed to death or hurled to his death by the blast wave or its debris. He might be lethally irradiated by the local fallout. He might be burned to death in a firestorm. He might be injured by one or another of these effects and then die of his wounds before he was able to make his way out of the devastated zone in which he found himself. He might die of starvation, because the economy had collapsed and no food was being grown or delivered, or because existing local crops had been killed by radiation, or because the local ecosystem had been ruined, or because the ecosphere of the earth as a whole was collapsing. He might die of cold, for lack of heat and clothing, or of exposure, for lack of shelter. He might be killed by people seeking food or shelter that he had obtained. He might die of an illness spread in an epidemic. He might be killed by exposure to the sun if he stayed outside too long following serious ozone depletion. Or he might be killed by any combination of these perils. But while there is almost no end to the ways to die in and after a holocaust, each person has only one life to lose; someone who has been killed by the thermal pulse can't be killed again in an epidemic. Therefore, anyone who wishes to describe a holocaust is always at risk of depicting scenes of devastation that in reality would never take place, because the people in them would already have been killed off in some earlier scene of devastation. The task is made all the more confusing by the fact that causes of death and destruction do not exist side by side in the world but often encompass one another, in widening rings. Thus, if it turned

out that a holocaust rendered the earth uninhabitable by human beings, then all the more immediate forms of death would be nothing more than redundant preliminaries, leading up to the extinction of the whole species by a hostile environment. Or if a continental ecosystem was so thoroughly destroyed by a direct attack that it could no longer sustain a significant human population, the more immediate causes of death would again decline in importance. In much the same way, if an airplane is hit by gunfire, and thereby caused to crash, dooming all the passengers, it makes little difference whether the shots also killed a few of the passengers in advance of the crash. On the other hand, if the larger consequences, which are less predictable than the local ones, failed to occur, then the local ones would have their full importance again.

Faced with uncertainties of this kind, some analysts of nuclear destruction have resorted to fiction, assigning to the imagination the work that investigation is unable to do. But then the results are just what one would expect: fiction. An approach more appropriate to our intellectual circumstances would be to acknowledge a high degree of uncertainty as an intrinsic and extremely important part of dealing with a possible holocaust. A nuclear holocaust is an event that is obscure because it is future, and uncertainty, while it has to be recognized in all calculations of future events, has a special place in calculations of a nuclear holocaust, because a holocaust is something that we aspire to keep in the future forever, and never to permit into the present. You might say that uncertainty, like the thermal pulses or the blast waves, is one of the features of a holocaust. Our procedure, then, should be not to insist on a precision that is beyond our grasp, but to inquire into the rough probabilities of various results insofar as we can judge them, and then to ask ourselves what our political responsibilities are in the light of these probabilities. This embrace of investigative modesty—this acceptance of our limited ability to predict the consequences of a holocaust—would itself be a token of our reluctance to extinguish ourselves.

There are two further aspects of a holocaust that, though they do not further obscure the factual picture, nevertheless vex our understanding of this event. The first is that although in imagination we can try to survey the whole prospective scene of destruction, inquiring into how many would live and how many would die and how far the collapse of the environment would go under attacks of different sizes, and piling up statistics on how many square miles would be lethally contaminated, or what percentage of the population would receive first-, second-, or third-degree burns, or be trapped in the rubble of its burning houses, or be irradiated to death, no one actually experiencing a holocaust would have any such overview. The news of other parts necessary to put together that picture would be one of the things that were immediately lost, and each surviving person, his vision drastically foreshortened by the collapse of his world, and his impressions clouded by his pain, shock, bewilderment, and grief, would see only as far as whatever scene of chaos and agony happened to lie at hand. For it would not be only such abstractions as "industry" and "society" and "the environment" that would be destroyed in a nuclear holocaust; it would also be, over and over again, the small collections of cherished things, known landscapes, and beloved people that made up the immediate contents of individual lives.

The other obstacle to our understanding is that when we strain to picture what the scene would be like after a holocaust we tend to forget that for most people, and perhaps for all, it wouldn't be *like* anything, because they would be dead. To depict the scene as it would appear to the living is to that extent a falsification, and the greater the number killed, the greater the falsification. The right vantage point from which to view a holocaust is that of a corpse, but from that vantage point, of course, there is nothing to report.

Review Questions

1. Describe the effects of an air burst of a one-megaton bomb.

2. What would happen in a nuclear holocaust?

Discussion Questions

1. Can you think of any circumstances in which a nuclear holocaust would be morally justified?

2. The United States presently has about 9,000 H-bombs with more being made every day, and about 20,000 smaller A-bombs like the one dropped on Hiroshima. The Soviet Union has about 240 medium-sized cities and perhaps a few hundred military targets such as air bases and missile sites. Why do we need so many bombs? Why are we building more and more?

Mikhail S. Gorbachev

A Proposal for Nuclear Disarmament

Before he became the leader of the USSR in 1985, Mikhail S. Gorbachev was an agricultural specialist with no experience in foreign affairs. As the father of the doctrines of glasnost *and* perestroika, *he helped bring about dramatic changes in Russia, including open discussion and criticism (*glasnost*) and economic reform in the direction of capitalism (*perestroika*). He is credited with allowing the incredible democratic revolution in Eastern Europe, and ending the cold war with the United States. Because of his achievements, he was honored by* Time *as the Man of the Decade at the end of 1989 (previously he had been* Time's *Man of the Year).*

The Soviet Union proposes that a step-by-step, consistent process of ridding the earth of nuclear weapons be implemented and completed within the next 15 years, before the end of this century....

How does the Soviet Union envisage today in practical terms the process of reducing nuclear weapons, both delivery vehicles and warheads, up to their complete elimination? Our proposals on this subject can be summarized as follows.

Stage One. Within the next 5 to 8 years the USSR and the USA will reduce by one half the nuclear weapons that can reach each other's territory. As for the remaining delivery vehicles of this kind, each side will retain no more than 6,000 warheads.

It stands to reason that such a reduction is possible only if both the USSR and the USA renounce the development, testing and deployment of space-strike weapons. As the Soviet Union has repeatedly warned, the develop-

Reprinted by permission from "Statement by Mikhail Gorbachev, General Secretary of the CPSU Central Committee, January 15, 1986." Copyright © Novosti Press Agency Publishing House, 1986.

opment of space-strike weapons will dash the hopes for a reduction of nuclear armaments on earth.

The first stage will include the adoption and implementation of a decision on the complete elimination of medium-range missiles of the USSR and the USA in the European zone—both ballistic and cruise missiles—as a first step towards ridding the European continent of nuclear weapons.

At the same time the United States should undertake not to transfer its strategic and medium-range missiles to other countries, while Britain and France should pledge not to build up their respective nuclear arsenals.

The USSR and the USA should from the very beginning agree to stop all nuclear explosions and call upon other states to join in such a moratorium as soon as possible.

The reason why the first stage of nuclear disarmament should concern the Soviet Union and the United States is that it is they who should set an example for the other nuclear powers. We said that very frankly to President Reagan of the United States during our meeting in Geneva.

Stage Two. At this stage, which should start no later than 1990 and last for 5 to 7 years, the other nuclear powers will begin to join the process of nuclear disarmament. To start with, they would pledge to freeze all their nuclear arms and not to have them on the territories of other countries.

In this period the USSR and the USA will continue to carry out the reductions agreed upon during the first stage and also implement further measures aimed at eliminating their medium-range nuclear weapons and freezing their tactical nuclear systems.

Following the completion by the USSR and the USA of a 50–per–cent reduction of their respective armaments at the second stage, another radical step will be taken: all nuclear powers will eliminate their tactical nuclear weapons, i.e. weapons having a range (or radius of action) of up to 1,000 kilometers.

At this stage the Soviet–US accord on the prohibition of space-strike weapons would become multilateral, with the mandatory participation in it of major industrial powers.

All nuclear powers would stop nuclear weapon tests.

There would be a ban on the development of non-nuclear weapons based on new physical principles, whose destructive power is close to that of nuclear arms or other weapons of mass destruction.

Stage Three will begin no later than 1995. At this stage the elimination of all remaining nuclear weapons will be completed. By the end of 1999 there will be no nuclear weapons on earth. A universal accord will be drawn up that such weapons should never again come into being.

We envisage that special procedures will be worked out for the destruction of nuclear weapons as well as for the dismantling, re-equipment or scrapping of delivery vehicles. In the process, agreement will be reached on the number of weapons to be scrapped at each stage, the sites of their destruction and so on.

Verification of the destruction or limitation of arms should be carried out both by national technical means and through on-site inspections. The USSR is ready to reach agreement on any other additional verification measures.

Adoption of the nuclear disarmament programme that we are proposing would unquestionably have a favourable impact on the negotiations conducted at bilateral and multilateral forums. The programme would envisage clearly-defined routes and reference points, establish a specific time-table for achieving agreements and implementing them and would make the negotiations purposeful and task-oriented. This would stop the dangerous trend whereby the momentum of the arms race is greater than the progress of negotiations.

Thus, we propose that we should enter the third millennium without nuclear weapons, on the basis of mutually acceptable and strictly verifiable agreements. If the United States Administration is indeed committed to the goal of the complete elimination of nuclear weapons everywhere, as it has repeatedly stated, it now has a practical opportunity to carry it out in practice. Instead of spending the next 10 to 15 years in developing new space weapons, which are extremely dangerous for mankind, weapons, allegedly designed to make nuclear arms unnecessary, would it not be more sensible to start eliminating those weapons and finally doing away with them altogether? The Soviet Union, I repeat, proposes precisely that.

The Soviet Union calls upon all peoples and states, and, naturally, above all nuclear states, to support the programme of eliminating nuclear weapons before the year 2000. It is absolutely clear to any unbiased person that if such a programme is implemented, nobody would lose and all stand to gain. This is a problem common to all mankind and it can and must be solved only through joint efforts. And the sooner this programme is translated into practical deeds, the safer life on our planet will be....

Review Questions

1. Describe stage one of Gorbachev's proposal.

2. Describe stage two.

3. What happens in stage three?

Discussion Questions

1. Gorbachev insists that arms reduction is possible only if the United States renounces the space-based weapons it is developing under the Strategic Defense Initiative, that is, the so-called Star Wars weapons. Should the United States abandon the Star Wars program? Why or why not?

2. Gorbachev wants all nuclear powers to eliminate their tactical nuclear weapons. Is this a good idea or not?

3. Gorbachev proposes that by the end of 1999 there be no nuclear weapons on earth. Is this desirable? Is it possible? How would this be enforced and verified?

Leon Sloss

The Case for Deploying Strategic Defenses

Leon Sloss is a consultant on defense strategy and foreign affairs, based in Washington. He has served in the Department of State, the Department of Defense, the Arms Control and Disarmament Agency, and other governmental agencies.

Sloss argues in favor of deploying strategic defenses including an intermediate Strategic Defense Initiative. The basic reason for doing this is that a strategy involving a mixture of offensive and defensive forces is better than one relying on just offensive forces and the threat of retaliation. We have more security and stability, Sloss thinks, if we can at least partially defend against a nuclear attack. Sloss discusses and replies to a number of objections: It will be too expensive, it will not work perfectly, and it will produce a new arms race.

INTRODUCTION

In a landmark speech on March 23, 1983, President Reagan called for a major national effort aimed at exploring the feasibility and effectiveness of active defenses against ballistic missiles. The speech has been hailed by some and condemned by others as signaling a revolutionary change in U.S. strategy. This characterization is greatly exaggerated. However, the speech did reopen a major debate over the role of defense in the U.S. strategic posture—a subject that had been neglected for more than a decade.

The first concrete outcome of Reagan's address was the launching of the Strategic Defense Initiative as a well-funded, comprehensive research program. SDI has become

From Leon Sloss, "The Case for Deploying Strategic Defenses," in Henry Shue, ed., *Nuclear Deterrence and Moral Restraint* (Cambridge: Cambridge University Press, 1989), pp. 343–379. © 1989, Cambridge University Press. Reprinted with permission of Cambridge University Press.

highly controversial, for it appears to challenge conventional wisdom about nuclear strategy while at the same time introducing new complications in NATO relations and arms control negotiations. It also promises to be extremely expensive.

The purpose of this chapter is to provide a strategic—not a moral or ethical—rationale for strategic defenses. It makes the case for a U.S. strategy that includes such defenses, but not for replacing offense with defense. Nor does it suggest that a deterrent that seeks to deny an aggressor confidence in achieving his military objectives can wholly supplant the threat of retaliation. Thus, the approach advocated here differs in emphasis from the long-range goals that were advanced by President Reagan.

To provide some context for the discussion, I first review current U.S. national security policy and strategy.... I conclude by detailing the case for deploying strategic defenses.

U.S. NATIONAL SECURITY POLICY AND STRATEGY

Goals of Policy

Throughout its history, the United States has sought to achieve the traditional national security goals of protecting its territory, its citizens, and its way of life. The fundamental national interests we have sought to defend and to promote have been "peace, freedom, and prosperity for ourselves and for others around the world ... [and] an international order that encourages self-determination, democratic institutions, economic development, and human rights." [1]

Since the end of World War II, the principal challenge to U.S. security has come from the Soviet Union. To meet this challenge the United States has attempted to balance Soviet power in Eurasia by maintaining a globally deployed peace-time defense establishment. Alliances with nations located near the borders of the Soviet bloc have become an integral part of this effort. Such alliances, notably NATO, are needed because neither the United States nor its allies wants to shoulder the burdens of defense individually, and because a common effort is more effective than individual national efforts in discouraging aggression. At the same time, the United States and its allies have sought to settle disputes with the Soviet Union peaceably and to control and reduce arms through negotiation.

Challenges and Threats to U.S. Security

While a hostile Soviet Union presents the principal threat to U.S. security, there are two closely related challenges: the existence and potential use of nuclear weapons, and local conflicts that could draw the United States into war. Both of these sources of danger to U.S. security have existed since World War II and are likely to persist in the future—although they may eventually take different forms and present new challenges.

The United States and the Soviet Union have been hostile rivals since the founding of the Soviet state, save for the brief interlude of World War II. This rivalry is due primarily to a fundamental opposition between their respective national objectives and value systems, which in turn creates competing global interests. This competition does not appear reconcilable in the foreseeable future. However, the two superpowers do share at least one common security interest. Both recognize the destructiveness of modern warfare and therefore have a shared interest in avoiding conflict, particularly nuclear conflict. They also have acted in consort to curb the spread of nuclear weapons.[2] Yet even cooperative actions are conducted in a manner reflective of the enduring competitive nature of the relationship.

The existence of nuclear weapons is a by-product of political hostilities. These armaments do not cause wars, but they can make war enormously destructive. Pressure for their use could come from two sources: the potential for escalation inherent in any super-power conflict, and the instabilities created by local conflicts made potentially more dangerous by the nuclear capabilities of certain regional actors.

There are several developments—above and beyond U.S.–Soviet political competition—that threaten to destabilize the strategic nuclear balance. Most important are improvements in the range, accuracy, targeting flexibility, and payload of nuclear weapons systems, which have brought small fixed targets, such as missile silos, within intercontinental attacking range. In addition to these offensive capabilities, the deployment of active and passive defenses could be a means of limiting the damage to forces and leadership. These developments are creating conditions that many perceive as unstable because they could lead to increasing pressure to strike first in a crisis, in the hope of gaining an advantage or out of fear that the opponent will be the first to do so.

It is important, however, not to exaggerate the risks, for nuclear war remains unlikely. The potential consequences for a large nuclear war and the uncertainties of controlling any war create strong disincentives for initiating one. Even if nuclear weapons are used, escalation is by no means automatic. Most experts agree that a full-scale preemptive strike with no warning is most unlikely. If nuclear weapons were ever used on a more limited scale the parties might well recoil in fear after only a few weapons were employed, for neither the United States nor the Soviet Union has a strong impulse toward suicide.

The other danger of nuclear weapons use comes from regional powers. New nuclear states may simply not be careful or technically sophisticated in controlling their weapons. Inadequate security precautions could allow the weapons of new nuclear states to fall into the hands of terrorists. In addition, these states may not have safety devices sophisticated enough to prevent unauthorized use. Proliferation, moreover, raises uncertainties for U.S. decision makers because new nuclear states represent additional decision centers that if involved in a conflict may not be susceptible to superpower control.

A direct superpower conflict is not likely to become a reality unless activated by some type of political dispute arising from a local crisis or conflict. The United States and the Soviet Union have a variety of competing interests in many areas of the world where tensions already exist. Great-power commitments range from security treaties to military assistance relationships to general political interests. Both major powers could find themselves using their respective military forces in the same local conflict. While it is impossible to predict the consequences, it is questionable whether such a situation could remain "limited" for any extended period of time, particularly if one side achieved significant advantages on the local battlefield....

THE ROLE OF NUCLEAR WEAPONS

Current Strategy

U.S. strategy, as reflected in official statements and documents, assumes that nuclear weapons must and do contribute to deterrence across a wide spectrum of threats.[3] These include, as Secretary Weinberger pointed out in his FY 1986 report to Congress, deterring nuclear attack on the United States, deterring nuclear attack on U.S. allies ("extended deterrence"), contributing to the deterrence of nonnuclear attack against the United States and its allies, and contributing to deterrence of the threat of political coercion with military force.[4]

To implement this strategy, the United States has developed plans and capabilities for the use of nuclear weapons in a controlled fashion. The necessity for a variety of nuclear options flows from the belief that we need other choices besides inaction or automatic escalation to general war. Flexible strategic capabilities, including plans for a proportionate response to an enemy attack, are viewed as a means to reinforce deterrence and limit escalation if deterrence fails.

However, we cannot be sure that once nuclear weapons are used (especially in large numbers) escalation will be controlled and the fighting limited. U.S. officials recognize this. President Reagan remarked on many occasions that "a nuclear war cannot be won." Secretary of Defense Harold Brown, who played a major role in crafting an important refinement of U.S. nuclear policy (PD–59), aimed at enhancing the flexibility of U.S. nuclear strategy, remained skeptical of escalation control, stating that he had "very serious doubts" that a nuclear exchange could remain limited. Nonetheless, the need for flexible plans and capabilities remains, because having flexibility seems preferable to having none, and it is held by many strategists to strengthen the credibility of deterrence. In Secretary Brown's words, these measures are intended to "prevent the Soviets from being able to win [a limited nuclear] war and to convince them that they could not win such a war."[5]

Among the components seen as necessary to achieve the objectives of this strategy are: a range of targeting options, with enemy military forces and command and control centers as the principal targets;[6] a durable command, control, communications, and intelligence (C I) apparatus that could provide the means to control escalation and lessen the temptation for a "decapitating attack" designed to eliminate command and control; survivable counterforce capabilities sufficiently accurate to destroy enemy military forces and reduce unwanted collateral damage; and a diverse and secure reserve force that would endure beyond the initial attack. The reserve force is designed primarily to protect the United States and its allies from post-attack nuclear blackmail and enable the United States to be in a position to protect its interests and facilitate the termination of hostilities on "favorable" terms.

"Favorable," according to the 1986 formulation of U.S. strategy,

means that if war is forced upon us, we must win—we cannot allow aggression to benefit the aggressor. It does not mean more territory or other elements of power for the United States. . . . In seeking the earliest termination of conflict, the United States not only would act to defeat the aggression but also try to convince the attacker to halt his advance because his continued aggression would entail grave risks to his own interests.[7]

The plans and capabilities for the use of nuclear forces in a discriminate and flexible manner are intended to facilitate escalation control and also provide a potential means for limiting damage. Damage could also be limited by the use of active defenses. However, except for certain early warning systems and a limited air defense capability, the United States, which once had extensive air defenses and the start of an anti-ballistic-missile (ABM) system, has in the last fifteen years eschewed active defenses (even those permitted by the ABM Treaty of 1972).

This strategy of "flexible response" has many ambiguities and shortcomings. As Soviet nuclear capabilities have grown, the efficacy of escalation control has been widely questioned. Many efforts have been made to reduce reliance on nuclear weapons. Nevertheless, flexible response has persisted as U.S. strategy over two decades and through four administrations—Republican and Democratic—for two primary reasons. First, this strategy has been fashioned to assure or reassure our allies of the United States' commitment to protect them through extended deterrence. Second, flexible response, with all its limitations, is seen by many as the best means to deter Soviet aggression. . . .

STRATEGIC DEFENSE

Role, Objectives, Benefits

Since the late 1960s, the Soviets have markedly improved their strategic and theater offensive capabilities, both nuclear and conventional. They have deployed extensive passive defenses and air defenses and have also actively pursued research in ballistic missile defense systems.[8] The Soviets have therefore moved effectively to reduce the United States' ability to achieve its strategic objectives—deterrence of a range of threats, reassurance of allies, escalation control, damage limitation, and war termination.

In addition, Soviet strategy places emphasis on the value of preemptive attack and surprise, with strikes aimed at military targets rather than retaliatory strikes aimed at industry and cities. Soviet forces reflect the pursuit of damage-limiting objectives as these were defined by the United States in the 1960s. This was accomplished by heavy investment in prompt counterforce and defense capabilities rather than through a strategy of escalation control as now envisioned in the U.S. posture. Soviet defensive activities seek to protect governmental and societal assets, with particular emphasis on continuity of government.

Given these developments, the requirements necessary to maintain deterrence have changed, as President Reagan stated in his 1983 address. Our present posture still serves as a powerful deterrent. However, when one considers the current Soviet posture along with likely future developments, U.S. capabilities to counter this buildup need to be augmented in some important way. It is not clear that reliance on offensive forces alone will suffice to meet U.S. security objectives.

The incremental incorporation of intermediate, less-than-perfect defenses in U.S. strategy would work to offset Soviet gains. The principal rationale for deployment of some level of active defenses against ballistic missiles is that they will reinforce deterrence. Intercepting some portion of the attacking force makes the enemy's calculations of the attack outcome more complicated. He could not be certain how many warheads would reach their targets and thus which targets his attack would destroy. High uncertainty about the outcome of an attack will act as a deterrent for the enemy. Moreover, defenses will raise the cost of attacking, thereby placing the onus for escalation on the Soviet Union.

I am not arguing that defenses should supplant offensive forces or that the mechanism of denial should replace the threat of retaliation as a deterrent. Defenses of this sort would supplement offenses as a deterrent. The problem with relying on offenses only is that the implementation of the retaliatory threat is not cost-free—far from it—and this is well known to everyone: adversaries, allies, and our own public. Thus, such a threat is not credible unless the nation's most vital interests are at stake. Specifically, it is becoming less and less credible in extending deterrence to third parties.

Limited defenses help extended deterrence in two ways. First, they reduce the confidence that the Soviets would have of achieving calculable results from a first strike, and thus they make such a strike less likely. Second, they could make it at least somewhat more credible to the Soviets (who will assume the defense works better than it probably will) that the United States would initiate the use of nuclear weapons in support of an ally, because we would have some protection against Soviet retaliation. With partial defenses, we might not have very much confidence in our ability to limit damage; but one has to ask how it looks to the Soviets—who, after all, are the ones we are trying to deter. With no defenses at all, extended deterrence does not look very credible any more. With some defenses it at least looks more credible, and as our defenses grow in capability so should the credibility of extended deterrence.

A nuclear war remains most unlikely, but calculations about war outcomes affect perceptions and the actions of states in peacetime. As things now stand, if the Soviet Union decided to strike U.S. forces—and, again, Soviet doctrine emphasizes the value of preemptive surprise attacks—they would meet with virtually no resistance and should have little uncertainty about the results of the attack save for failures in their own systems (for which they can compensate). After a Soviet countermilitary strike the United States, having lost a significant portion of its force, would face a serious dilemma. On the one

hand it could choose to try to respond in kind with an attack that would cause heavy collateral damage and might have little military effect, since Soviet high-value military forces would either have been used or would be, in the aftermath of attack, unlocatable. This result would be due to degradation of U.S. C I and the likely mobility of Soviet residual forces. In addition, even the limited present-day Soviet ABM capability could serve to blunt if not deter the—probably "ragged"—U.S. retaliation. On the other hand, the United States could choose not to respond, conceding victory to the aggressor.

The deployment of limited active defenses would make such an attack less likely in the first place. Furthermore, such deployment is perfectly consistent with our traditional nuclear strategy, enhancing the denial component of deterrence while working to preserve retaliatory forces. A carefully blended mix of offensive and defensive forces will reinforce deterrence rather than replace it. Intermediate defenses can also support U.S. damage-limiting objectives, even if in an imperfect manner. If a war does occur, some defenses are better than none. If the capability exists to limit damage, would it be a responsible policy for the U.S. government not to deploy it?

At this juncture it is not possible to define a future offense/defense mix precisely; one can give only an impressionistic view. The future mix will depend on how SDI technologies develop, how the Soviets respond to SDI, and what progress, if any, can be made in arms control. However, we envision defenses that are less than perfect and offenses that are reduced from today's levels, either through negotiated arms control or through unilateral action in response to the rising cost of penetrating defenses. The process of moving toward a more balanced offense/defense mix will take many years, if not decades, to accomplish. Thus, a decade from now offensive forces are still likely to predominate in the mix. Two decades hence, defenses could begin to play a dominant role; if so, offenses may well be reduced further.

The current emphasis in SDI research is to design nonnuclear kill mechanisms to destroy incoming missiles at some point during their trajectory, which is usually divided into boost-phase, post-boost, midcourse, and terminal stages of flight. Each layer of defense poses a different problem to the attacker. From the standpoint of the defender, the earlier the missile is destroyed the better, to preclude the release of penetration aids designed to confuse the defender with decoys that mask the location of the armed warhead. Early interception, however, is the most demanding phase of defense. The ABM systems of the 1960s were unable to limit damage or even complicate an attack, owing to technical limitations, which meant that they could be relatively easily overwhelmed by the attacker. Today's technology offers opportunities in the next ten to fifteen years for creating limited layered defenses.[9] Such defenses should be seen not as defending specific targets but rather as providing several layers of protection, simultaneously defending several military targets or military targets and collocated population.[10]

The most recent research also suggests that boost and post-boost interception would depend heavily on the development of space-based sensors and weapons possessing the ability to track, assess, and destroy warheads quickly. These are the elements that the supporters of the Reagan vision are counting on to provide a "near-perfect" defense.

Intermediate defenses can add to the complexity and cost of the attacker's plans without reaching nearly this level of capability. Deterrence can be enhanced by the creation of one or more layers of defense (even if that defense is "leaky") and by the possibility of preferential, ambiguously arrayed defenses that leave the attacker unsure as to what is defended and to what level. He will get some warheads through these defenses, but he cannot have in advance any confidence in being able to neutralize most of the targets high on his priority list. Thus, he is more likely to be deterred from an attack even in a serious crisis. The destruction of a few targets will not meet Soviet objectives. And if the Soviets choose to limit themselves to a restricted target set, defenses might, as the Hoffman Panel analysis suggests, "require a level of force inconsistent with limiting the level of violence, while depleting the attacker's inventory for other tasks."[11] This prospect could serve as a powerful deterrent to the contemplation of an initial attack....

Problems and Costs

The incorporation of intermediate defenses is bound to raise strategic, political, technical, and financial questions. This section addresses the most prominent criticisms of an intermediate SDI.[12]

One of the most frequent criticisms of SDI has to do with the cost, particularly the opportunity cost, of an SDI program. At a time when the defense budget is declining, budgetary aspects are an important consideration. There are several points to be made. First, no one knows today what the outlays for SDI will be. This will depend a great deal on what kind of SDI is deployed and over what period of time.[13] But under any circumstances SDI deployment will be very expensive—at least tens and in some cases hundreds of billions of dollars. However, deployment will occur over a period of many years, which will attenuate (though by no means eliminate) the fiscal impact of the program. Finally, it is likely that other defense programs will be affected by SDI deployment, but it is impossible at this point to predict which programs will be affected or how. Whether an SDI program is "worth the cost" depends precisely on what the program consists of, how well it works, how expensive it is, and the extent to which it impacts on other programs. None of these factors can be determined with any precision now. They should and undoubtedly will be important determinants of future decisions on SDI.

Another frequent criticism relates to arms control. Critics charge that SDI will inevitably lead to a breakdown of the ABM Treaty, which is viewed as a major constraint on a new arms race in defensive weapons and as the centerpiece of an arms control regime devoted to the preservation of mutual deterrence. While there is some question as to how much the ABM Treaty constrains the Soviets, the critics are correct in asserting that the treaty would have to be modified, unilaterally or by negotiation, to allow for the testing and eventually the deployment of advanced defenses. But would SDI lead to a new arms race? Not necessarily. Defenses may lead to new forms of arms competition, but it is not clear what form this competition will take or whether it will replicate the dangerous trends of the current race, which sees the Soviets consolidating advantages, particularly in hard-target kill capabilities and in the sort of defenses—those at the tactical ballistic level—that are not prohibited by the ABM Treaty.

Furthermore, if defenses become truly cost-effective for the role they are intended to play, then at some point it will cease to make sense to try to overwhelm the defenses. If they do not become cost-effective, we should not deploy them. It may take some time to find out whether or not defenses will provide positive cost-benefit ratios. In the meantime we could have some competition, but it appears that we have that already. The question is whether the competition that may be stimulated by defenses is going to be more or less harmful to stability and U.S. interests than the competition we would have without defenses. The answer is not apparent but is not clearly in the negative. If the Soviets are forced to deploy penetration aids or to design fast-burn boosters, they will not be creating more destructive power but, rather, utilizing some of their throw-weight to overcome defenses. If they simply try to increase the number of warheads (which they could do with their large missiles), they are probably choosing the wrong solution if the defense has a boost-phase capability, for that will make more warheads vulnerable to each suc-

cessful intercept in the boost phase. However, both sides will be limited on what they can spend on armaments, so a major effort to build defenses and to respond to the other side's defenses will likely come at the expense of something else. What is the "something else"? Unless we know what the alternatives facing the United States and the Soviet Union are, it is hard to evaluate this issue. In sum, new forms of arms competition are not necessarily bad. If one assumes that competition is inherent in the U.S.–Soviet relationship, then it becomes necessary to contemplate what new forms might emerge and whether they are really worse than what we have now.

Another criticism of defenses relates to their impact on extended deterrence. Initially, the United States' allies reacted adversely to SDI.[14] But by late 1985 and early 1986 some changes had occurred, especially when the British formally agreed to participate in the SDI research program. This agreement has been followed by similar ones with Germany, Italy, Japan, and Israel. Despite these official commitments, legitimate questions remain: Would SDI lead to a strategic environment where the United States is so secure that it no longer feels compelled to extend deterrence, thereby "decoupling" the U.S. guarantee to our allies? If SDI renders ballistic missiles "impotent and obsolete," what are the implications for the investments that the French and British governments have made and will continue to make in order to upgrade their nuclear deterrent forces? Will SDI lead to a new arms race with the Soviet Union that creates greater international tensions, reduces Western security, and jeopardizes European relations with the Soviet bloc? If a theater-based SDI is pursued by the Europeans, how much will it cost, and would the United States agree to share sensitive technologies with its allies? Will the SDI program exacerbate antidefense and antinuclear sentiments that could create dangerous political divisions within European countries? How great will be the resources that SDI would divert from other defense programs, such as conventional forces? Finally, how credible is SDI, given past U.S. initiatives that have either failed or increased intra-NATO tensions, such as the Multilateral Force, the Enhanced Radiation Warhead, and Intermediate Nuclear Force plans?

These are serious questions. Yet what is remarkably evident from these questions is that a very wide spectrum of defensive systems is under discussion, including tactical, intermediate, and population defense. This suggests that the United States does not have and therefore has not been able to present to its allies a clear rationale for the purposes and ultimate direction of the SDI program. Before the United States can demonstrate to its allies the benefits of an intermediate SDI, it must establish objectives and coherence for the SDI research and development program, which has yet to focus on specific systems....

In any event, there are no easy answers to the above questions. The SDI program, as currently envisioned, will have a fundamental impact on the strategic relationship between the superpowers and therefore on the U.S. relationship with NATO. The United States has attempted to reassure its allies that defenses will neither decouple the U.S. guarantee nor cut off the Europeans from the benefits (strategic and technological) that SDI might yield. The Reagan Administration rightly protested the notion that SDI could lead the United States to a "Fortress America" posture. Indeed, it emphasized that defenses will be used to strengthen extended deterrence. This goal is consistent with the objectives of an intermediate defense and must be further stressed.

Another point that has to be emphasized is that the Soviets have been conducting SDI-type research for some time; they are not just responding to the U.S. SDI program. Thus, we should not assume that U.S. restraint will bring about similar Soviet restraint. The continuation of Soviet activities (both defensive and offensive) is moving us toward a point where NATO's capacity to execute limited options or a flexible response will be critically eroded.

Yet another area of concern is that the development of defenses could be destabilizing, especially in the transition period. Intermediate defenses, it is argued, "work much better if an adversary's force has previously been damaged in a counterforce strike, intensifying incentives for preemption in a crisis." [15] But assessments of stability often proceed from different assumptions about national defense and nuclear strategy. In a Finite Deterrence or MAD view, defenses are deemed inherently destabilizing because they threaten to reduce the opponent's ability to destroy cities—the central feature of the assured destruction retaliatory strike. If one rejects this view, as the U.S. government has for over twenty years, defenses can be viewed in a more positive light. Intermediate defenses could improve crisis stability by reducing the Soviets' confidence in their ability to strike U.S. forces—strategic or conventional. Defenses could reduce the growing Soviet advantages in strategic offensive and defensive forces; and, from the standpoint of political perceptions and resolve, defenses can increase Western confidence in our deterrent and enhance our ability to resist Soviet political pressures and intimidation.

With regard to transition to a U.S.–Soviet strategic regime embodying intermediate defenses, two general possibilities exist. One is that if the United States is seen as determined to proceed with an SDI program that appears to be making progress, the Soviets could engage in even more strenuous efforts to try to disrupt the program. This would of course place additional strain on superpower relations. On the other hand, as has been previously noted, the Soviets already have a strong commitment to defenses. They may come to accept the need to adjust to a world in which both sides will have defensive systems.[16]

Finally, a strategy including both offensive and defensive forces (or defenses in combination with other measures) can enhance stability by reducing the pre-launch vulnerability of offensive forces. Stability will be further increased if, to quote from the Hoffman Panel, "defenses avoid high vulnerability, [are] robust in the face of enemy technical or tactical countermeasures, and ... compete favorably in cost terms with expansion of the Soviet offensive force." [17] The Reagan Administration, as evidenced by the statements of Ambassador Paul Nitze, supported these important and demanding criteria, which SDI will have to respond to in order to be viable: Defenses will have to be survivable and cost-effective at the margin. If overwhelming them through increased offenses is cheaper than adding to the defense, then the whole exercise may prove to be futile. It should be noted that Nitze made this argument in relation to the ultimate goal of a "near-perfect" defensive system. If the objective is instead to strengthen deterrence by a mix of offensive and defensive forces, the criteria could become more flexible.

This last point raises another criticism of SDI touched on above: its financial cost. The Reagan Administration originally requested $26 billion for Fiscal 1985–89 for research to investigate a future decision whether to develop and deploy defenses.[18] However, Congress has substantially cut the administration's requests for funding. In an era of budgetary restrictions, economic considerations must be closely monitored. Yet, while we know the research and development of strategic defenses will be costly, even the advocates of SDI admit that we cannot accurately calculate how much money would be spent. The cost will depend heavily on the program's objectives. Moreover, as already pointed out, the expenditures will be spread out over many years.

Congressional oversight will be an important check on ensuring procurement of cost-efficient defenses. To date, Congress has reduced every SDI budget request while allowing the Strategic Defense Initiative Organization (SDIO) to distribute the cuts as it sees fit. Finally, costs have to be related to benefits. If strategic defenses do enhance de-

terrence in the future while simultaneously lowering the level of nuclear risk, they could prove to be well worth the expense in terms of our strategic and security objectives.

CONCLUSION: THE CASE FOR DEPLOYING STRATEGIC DEFENSES

One theme has been emphasized throughout this essay: A strategy that incorporates defenses is not a panacea, but neither is a strategy without defenses. Given Soviet strategic preferences and existing programs, a world without any defenses is illusory. There remain many uncertainties and lingering concerns about the impact of defenses. However, a strategy that carefully incorporates a mix of offensive and defensive forces is better than what we have at present, and also better than the other more or less plausible options outlined above. I do not intend to repeat the shortcomings encountered with each alternative. Suffice it to say there are no panaceas. Extreme solutions—be they Finite Deterrence or a population defense—do not present realistic options to those responsible for national security, given the state of today's technical or strategic environment.

The strategy advocated above would be achieved through an evolutionary process, permitting the effects of defenses on deterrence and stability to be examined and evaluated on a step-by-step basis as we proceed. The ultimate test of these defenses is whether they are able to stabilize deterrence and reduce the risks of war by making the prospect of attack less likely. These are goals that we all can share.

Endnotes

1. These goals are reiterated in Caspar W. Weinberger, *Annual Report to the Congress for Fiscal 1986* (Washington: U.S. Government Printing Office, 1985), pp. 13, 25.
2. On this subject, see William C. Potter, "Nuclear Proliferation: U.S.–Soviet Cooperation," *Washington Quarterly* 8 (Winter 1985), 141–54.
3. For a history of the evolution of current strategy, see Leon Sloss and Marc Dean Millot, "U.S. Nuclear

Strategy in Evolution," *Strategic Review* 12, no. 1 (Winter 1984), 19–28; Colin S. Gray, *Nuclear Strategy and Strategic Planning* (Philadelphia: Foreign Policy Research Institute, 1984), esp. ch. 3; and Henry S. Rowen, "The Evolution of Strategic Doctrine," in Laurence Martin, ed., *Strategic Thought in the Nuclear Age* (Baltimore: Johns Hopkins University Press, 1979), pp. 136–41.

4. Weinberger, *Annual Report 1986*, pp. 25–32.

5. See Senate Foreign Relations Committee, *Nuclear War Strategy* (Washington: U.S. Government Printing Office, 1981) (proceedings of Top Secret hearing on PD–59, held September 16, 1980), pp. 8–9.

6. While command and control is a primary target, it may not be attacked in a limited strike in order to leave open the possibility of negotiating a cease-fire. Industry, of course, remains a target but is thought of more as a target of last resort.

7. Weinberger, *Annual Report 1986*, p. 27.

8. See Future Security Strategy Study, Fred S. Hoffman, study director, *Ballistic Missile Defense and U.S. National Security: Summary Report* (October 1983); reprinted in Steven E. Miller and Stephen Van Evera, ed., *The Star Wars Controversy: An "International Security" Reader* (Princeton: Princeton University Press, 1986); and Albert Carnesale, "Special Supplement: The Strategic Defense Initiative," in George Hudson and Joseph Kruzel, ed., *American Defense Annual*, 1985–86 (Lexington, MA: Lexington Books, 1985).

9. See Hoffman Panel Report, passim; and the technical discussion in another report prepared for the U.S. government by the "Fletcher Panel": Defense Technologies Study (James C. Fletcher, director), *Defense Against Ballistic Missiles: An Assessment of Technologies and Policy Implications* (April 1983); reprinted in Miller and Van Evera, *The Star Wars Controversy*.

10. Fred S. Hoffman, "The SDI in U.S. Nuclear Strategy," *International Security* 10, no. 1 (Summer 1985), 13–24, at 20; rpt. in Miller and Van Evera, *The Star Wars Controversy*, 3–14.

11. Hoffman Panel *Report*, p. 10.

12. For a balanced discussion that highlights the problems and costs of SDI (and provides useful citations), consult Carnesale. Also see the more critical discussion in the July–August 1984 issue of *Arms Control Today* 14, no. 6, and in Charles L. Glaser, "Do We Want the Missile Defenses We Can Build?" *International Security* 10, no. 1 (Summer 1985), 25–57; rpt. in Miller and Van Evera, *The Star Wars Controversy*, pp. 98–130.

13. The most comprehensive public study of SDI costs so far is Barry M. Blechman and Victor A. Utgoff, "The Fiscal and Economic Implications of Strategic Defenses," SAIS Papers in International Affairs No. 12

(Boulder, Colo.: Westview, September 1986). In this paper the authors postulate several SDI programs, each of which would have different fiscal and economic implications.

14. See John Newhouse, "The Diplomatic Round," *The New Yorker*, July 22, 1985, pp. 37–45.

15. Hoffman, "SDI in U.S. Nuclear Strategy," p. 21.

16. For a discussion of possible Soviet countermeasures, see Thomas Krebs, "Moscow's Many Problems in Countering a U.S. Strategic Defense System," *Heritage Foundation Backgrounder No. 454*, September 17, 1985.

17. Hoffman Panel *Report*, p. 12.

18. See Department of Defense, *Report to the Congress on the Strategic Defense Initiative 1985*, p. C–24.

Review Questions

1. According to Sloss, what are the threats to U.S. security?

2. What is the role of nuclear weapons in Sloss' view?

3. Why have the requirements for maintaining nuclear deterrence changed?

4. Why should the United States develop a limited defense against nuclear attack according to Sloss?

5. Sloss discusses several objections to SDI. What are these objections, and how does Sloss respond to them?

Discussion Questions

1. One objection frequently made to SDI is that it gives the United States a dangerous first-strike capability, the ability to attack and destroy the Soviet Union and escape retaliation. Does Sloss have a good reply to this objection?

2. Sloss admits that SDI will be very expensive to deploy. Is it really worth it? Why or why not?

3. Some political analysts claim that the Soviet Union is no longer a threat to the United States, and indeed never was a threat. Is this true or not?

Douglas P. Lackey
Nuclear Deterrence Strategy

Douglas P. Lackey teaches philosophy at Baruch College and the Graduate Center, City University of New York. He is the author of numerous articles on nuclear war and deterrence and The Ethics of War, *from which our reading is taken.*

Lackey carefully discusses and evaluates four different nuclear weapons strategies: Countervailing Strategy, Strategic Defense, Finite Deterrence, and Multilateral Disarmament. The Countervailing Strategy is for the United States to prevail or dominate in any nuclear exchange. Strategic Defense calls for systems capable of intercepting and destroying Soviet missiles before they hit. Finite Deterrence requires the United States to have only a small number of nuclear weapons to deter a Soviet attack, only enough to cause severe damage in retaliation. Multilateral Disarmament proposes a step-by-step reduction and eventual elimination of nuclear weapons. Lackey objectively and fairly considers criticisms of these strategies from both the right and the left and possible replies.

THE COUNTERVAILING STRATEGY DEFENDED

The current nuclear weapons policy of the United States, adopted by Gerald Ford in 1974 and revised by Jimmy Carter in 1980, has come to be called "The Countervailing Strategy." The basic goals of the Countervailing Strategy are to deter military aggression by the Soviet Union (a) against the United States, (b) against American allies, (c) in the area around the Persian Gulf. According to the strategy's supporters, the aggressive character of the Soviet regime is manifest in

From Douglas P. Lackey, *The Ethics of War and Peace* (Englewood Cliffs, NJ: Prentice-Hall, Inc., © 1989), pp. 99–111, 113–118, 124–126, 129–131. Reprinted by permission of Prentice-Hall, Inc., Englewood Cliffs, New Jersey.

its ideology of revolution; its vast military expenditures; its absorption of reluctant minorities—Ukrainians, Latvians, Estonians, and others—into the Soviet state; its political and military domination of eastern Europe; its invasions of Hungary, Czechoslovakia, and Afghanistan; and its military meddlings in several African states. The technique of the Countervailing Strategy is to demonstrate to the Soviets that whatever gains they might obtain from a military attack on the United States or its allies or in the Persian Gulf will be more than offset by losses they will sustain from American retaliation. In military terms, if there is war between the superpowers, the Countervailing Strategy seeks to guarantee that the United States will win.

To achieve these goals, the United States must have forces that can ride out a Soviet nuclear attack, and still enable the United States to retaliate and inflict unacceptable damage on the Soviet Union. Thus American forces must be hidden and dispersed, and dispersal is achieved by distributing nuclear weapons among bombers, land missiles, and submarines. To prevail in nuclear war, however, requires more than inflicting "unacceptable" retaliatory damage. The United States must plan to retaliate in ways that will impose military defeat on the Soviets, without blowing ourselves up in the process and without encouraging the Soviets to blow us up in return.

Since the Soviets are capable of many different types of aggression, diverse counterattack plans must be developed, each tailored to a specific Soviet act: not so small as to appear weak, not so big as to provoke further conflict. If the Soviets respond to an American response by moving to a higher level of military force, the United States must be prepared to meet and prevail at that higher level, in a measured manner that makes the Soviets regret their escalation, without provoking them to further and more intense attacks. Thus the Countervailing Strategy requires what strategists call escalation dominance, and escalation dominance requires nuclear weapons of all sizes, from the very small to the very big: battlefield nuclear weapons like the Lance missile, "theater" nuclear weapons like the Pershing II, and the big intercontinental missiles like the MX to dominate the highest levels of escalation.

Finally, if the United States is to prevail in a nuclear war with the Soviet Union, the United States needs weapons that can destroy as many Soviet weapons as possible, before they are used against the United States. The United States also needs weapons that can destroy the communications systems that the Soviets need in order to wage war. These "damage limitation" missions require powerful and precise missiles like the MX land missile and the D–5 submarine-based missile, and special space weapons to attack Soviet satellites as well.

The Countervailing Strategy is a grim business. Given Soviet superiority in conventional forces, the Countervailing Strategy calls for the use of American nuclear weapons against the Soviets, *even if the Soviets have not used them first.* By endorsing "first use," it practically guarantees that any war between the two superpowers will be a nuclear war. In many military circumstances, it calls for massive uses of American nuclear weapons, uses that will have widespread destructive side effects. But the main aim of the Countervailing Strategy of "peace through nuclear strength" is not to win a nuclear war but to prevent Soviet aggression, and if Soviet aggression is prevented, there will be no nuclear war.

According to its supporters, history shows that the strategy works. The Soviet Union has not attacked the United States or any ally of the United States, and no nuclear weapon has been used in war since 1945. True, not all the features of the Countervailing Strategy have been part of American planning since 1945. But the basic idea of preventing Soviet expansion through the threat to wage nuclear war has guided American policy at least since Truman broke the Soviet blockade of Berlin in 1948. Given the immense peril of nuclear war, any change in a policy that has produced

40 years of nuclear peace should be viewed with suspicion.

The arguments for the Countervailing Strategy are not all military. Since a nuclear war would be very bad for the human race, whatever prevents a nuclear attack on the United States serves the common interest of mankind, not just American national interests.

Furthermore, nations have a right to defend themselves against aggression. Since nuclear missiles cannot be intercepted once they are launched, this right to self-defense implies a right to threaten counterattacks, which are the only way to prevent those missiles from being launched in the first place.

The United States concedes the same right of nuclear self-defense to the Soviet Union. The United States made no attempt to stop the development of Soviet nuclear weapons and nuclear bombers, and in 1972 the United States agreed not to construct a national antiballistic missile (ABM) system. In effect the ABM agreement permits the Soviets to destroy the United States, should the Americans attack them first. This is an irrefutable guarantee to the Soviets that the United States will not be the first to attack.

If the Countervailing Strategy looks morally suspicious because of its essential reliance on nuclear threats, its supporters argue that the principal alternatives—Strategic Defense, Finite Deterrence, and Nuclear Disarmament—are morally far worse.

According to supports of the status quo, while the Countervailing Strategy respects the right of the Soviets to nuclear self-defense, Strategic Defense—the so-called Star Wars system—will prevent the Soviets from exercising that right. It will permit the United States to inflict nuclear risks on others while refusing to accept those risks itself.

In the eyes of the Countervailing Strategy, Finite Deterrence—the retention of just a few American nuclear weapons to be used as a last resort in the face of Soviet nuclear attack—provides no protection against Soviet *non*nuclear aggression. In the face of nuclear aggression, its only recourse (assuming a small American nuclear stockpile) is an attack on Soviet cities. Unlike the Countervailing Strategy, Finite Deterrence makes Soviet citizens hostages to American nuclear weapons: in effect, it commits kidnapping before the war starts and follows with murder after war breaks out.

Unilateral Nuclear Disarmament—giving up nuclear weapons while the Soviets retain theirs—is not only unfair to the United States, but it would permit the Soviet aggressors to blackmail the United States into submission on any point in dispute—so the argument goes. If the United States threatened to use nonnuclear weapons, the Soviets could always respond with nuclear threats and, given the power of nuclear weapons, these threats would always succeed. Instead of collapsing before threats, the Countervailing Strategy responds with measured, believable counterthreats.

The Countervailing Strategy is a tough strategy, but nuclear weapons have created a tough world, and they cannot be disinvented. The result of 40 years of adjustments, the Countervailing Strategy is, according to its defenders, the only morally appropriate response to the post-Hiroshima world.

Criticisms have been launched at the Countervailing Strategy from the political right and left. Critics on the left worry principally about the risks the strategy inflicts on innocent parties around the world. Critics on the right worry mainly about the risks it inflicts on Americans.

CRITICISMS OF THE COUNTERVAILING STRATEGY FROM THE RIGHT

(a) Critics on the right focus on the disturbing fact that the Countervailing Strategy leaves the United States defenseless against Soviet attack. Should the Soviets choose to launch a nuclear strike against the United States, under the Countervailing Strategy the United States would be destroyed. The Countervailing Strategy operates via threats of counterattack—in other words, through nuclear deterrence. But deterrence is not the same thing as a physical defense that the enemy cannot penetrate no matter what he thinks or does. Deterrence depends for its success on the psychological intimidation of Soviet leaders, and these leaders might choose not to be intimidated. Deterrence, even nuclear deterrence, places the safety of the American people in the hands of the Soviets. If there is a right to self-defense, deterrence does not satisfy that right.

(b) The current vulnerability of the United States to nuclear attack implies that the Countervailing Strategy does not provide escalation dominance against an opponent that wants to destroy the United States even at the cost of its own destruction. Lack of escalation dominance makes it impossible for the United States to make credible nuclear threats, and lack of credible nuclear threats allows the Soviets to use their superior conventional military strength to defend their interests and spread their influence around the world. Lack of ability to dominate in nuclear war may cause the United States to lose the cold war without a shot being fired. This is not only bad for the United States; it is bad for nations falling under Soviet influence. American influence in the world is not invariably benign. But when measured by moral values, it is morally superior to Soviet influence.

(c) Military leaders note that the Countervailing Strategy is essentially a strategy of retaliation, and a strict strategy of retaliation leaves the military initiative in the hands of the enemy. From the military point of view, if there is going to be war, it is far better to seize the initiative and strike first, especially in a nuclear age, when striking first may be the only way to save the United States from annihilation. Given the aggressive tendencies of the Soviet Union and the deep ideological differences between the Soviets and the Americans, deterrence will not last forever. When deterrence breaks down, all Americans, even those who are presently doves, will grasp the logic of striking first.

(d) The Countervailing Strategy attempts to provide deterrence, not defense, but there is some reason to think that it cannot even provide deterrence. Through the 1970s, the Soviets developed powerful and accurate missiles with multiple warheads. These weapons put American land-based missiles and other locatable assets at increased risk from Soviet attack. With advances in air defense, antisubmarine warfare, and ballistic missile defense, the Soviets have put all American strategic weapons at risk, and may have deprived the United States of the ability to retaliate against nuclear attack.

(e) The Countervailing Strategy commits the United States to the use of tactical and theater nuclear weapons in the event of a Soviet attack against western Europe. The use—or anticipated use—of American theater nuclear weapons, presumably against the Soviet homeland, would substantially increase the chances of a Soviet strike against the United States. But it is irresponsible of Western leaders to risk the survival of the United States on behalf of nations that are capable of conducting their own defense. It is unfair to the American people to put them at risk to assist Germany and Japan, which have—to say the least—no history of service that puts the United States in their debt.

THE CASE FOR STRATEGIC DEFENSE

The criticisms from the right against the Countervailing Strategy lead naturally to proposals for replacing deterrence with Strategic Defense. Strategic defenses are systems for intercepting and destroying Soviet nuclear weapons before they land on the United States. Proposals for strategic defense date back to the 1950s, when antibomber surface-to-air missiles were deployed around the United States and when work on anti-ballistic missile (ABM) systems was begun. By the late 1960s, both the Soviet Union and the United States had developed partially effective antimissile systems, designed to shoot down missiles as they approached the ground. But

a "partially effective" strategic defense provides little safety in an age when a single bomb can kill 20 million people, and both sides agreed by treaty to stop the race in ABM systems in 1972.

In the late 1970s, the increasing vulnerability of land ICBMs, combined with technological innovations in computers, new remote sensing and tracking devices, and new ways of attacking missiles, revived interest in strategic defense. In 1983, a major research effort in this direction was inaugurated by President Reagan. The system of strategic defense projected by the Reagan administration for the late 1990s involves laser attacks on Soviet missiles in the boost phase as they come up, various types of attacks in the midcourse phase, and further attacks in the terminal (descent) phase, perhaps with solid projectiles that crash into enemy missiles.

The difficulties of knocking down 1,000 or 2,000 missiles and perhaps 10,000 separable warheads, mixed in among thousands of decoys, in less than 30 minutes, are formidable. Since the system could never be tested under wartime conditions, one could never be confident that it would knock down all or nearly all incoming enemy missiles. But supporters of strategic defenses argue that we could be reasonably confident that the system would work, and certainly the Soviets could never be confident that it wouldn't.

Furthermore, suppose that the system "failed," and shot down only 50 percent of incoming enemy missiles in a large attack. With half the enemy missiles gone, the United States would surely retain enough of its strategic forces and communications systems to launch a devastating counterstrike: strategic defenses, in short, would deny to any adversary the chance to launch a "decapitating" nuclear first strike against the United States. If 50 percent of enemy missiles were shot down before they reached the United States, 50 million rather than 100 million Americans might die from the attack. Any ABM system that lets 50 million Americans die has failed. But even in failure the system will have saved

50 million lives.

This argument assumes a large attack on the United States. But suppose that only a small attack is launched, or a single missile heads toward the United States by accident, or a single missile is launched at us by terrorists. Currently, such events might kill millions of Americans. But even a small system of strategic defense could shoot down one or two missiles, and everyone would be saved.

Strategic defenses do not threaten people; they threaten only nuclear weapons. They constitute a system of true defense, not a system of deterrence, and are justified by the right of self-defense. People of all political persuasions must agree that anything which destroys nuclear weapons on their way to targets cannot be morally bad.

THE CASE AGAINST STRATEGIC DEFENSE

(a) The argument that strategic defenses might save 50 million American lives starts by positing a Soviet attack and then imagines that 50 percent of the attack will be wiped out by defenses that are 50 percent effective. But it is a mistake to assume that the presence of American strategic defenses will not affect the size of the incoming Soviet attack. If the Americans construct defenses that are 50 percent effective, then the Soviets can achieve the same level of destruction as before by shooting off twice as many missiles. No strategic defense can prevent them from doing this. True, it will cost the Soviets money to fire twice as many missiles, but it will cost us even more to try and stop them. Unless a shield is 100 percent effective, it cannot protect the United States from total destruction by ballistic missiles.

No one believes that a 100 percent effective defense against ballistic missiles can be constructed. But suppose that one could be. Would the United States cease to be vulnerable to nuclear attack? Not at all, since nuclear weapons can be delivered not just on missiles but also on bombers or cruise missiles or small boats. They can be put on mines in harbors, or even delivered in luggage. Of all nuclear weapons policies, admittedly only Strategic Defense attempts to rescue the United States from the condition of nuclear vulnerability. But there is little point in making an attempt that is bound to fail on its own terms.

(b) The publicized purpose of Strategic Defense is to blunt a nuclear sneak attack—or "first strike"—by the Soviet Union. But any system that can stop a Soviet first strike will be even more effective in stopping a Soviet *second* strike—the missiles that the Soviets would direct back against the United States should they suffer an American first strike.

Consider the military position of the Soviet Union should American defenses be constructed and should the United States choose to attack. The war begins as American anti-satellite weapons, launched from F–15 fighters, destroy Soviet warning systems and communications satellites. With Soviet satellites blinded, the United States launches its fleet of highly accurate MX and Trident D–5 missiles, pulverizing Soviet ICBM fields, while superaccurate cruise missiles seek out and destroy Soviet command and control centers. Meanwhile, American ships, subs, helicopters, and planes hunt down Soviet strategic submarines, tracked continuously from their "choke points" as they exit the Baltic Sea, the Black Sea, and the Sea of Japan, and destroy them with nuclear depth charges. The few surviving Soviet missiles remain unfired or are picked off by the American Star Wars defenses.

All the weaponry in this American first strike plan currently exists—except the strategic defenses. Thus, effective strategic defenses would deprive the Soviets of their ability to deter American attacks with threats of retaliation. This loss of deterrent capability will increase Russian insecurity, a sense of insecurity well buttressed by recollections of previous "first strikes" by the Mongols (1238), the French (1812), the British and Americans (1918), the Poles (1920), and the Germans (1941). Deprived of their ability to launch an effective second strike, the Soviets in a crisis might feel that they must use their nuclear weapons in the only effective way left open to them—a first strike against the United States. Instead of decreasing the Soviet threat, a Star Wars system actually increases it.

(c) If the United States succeeds in constructing partially effective strategic defenses, the Soviet Union will follow suit. Then each side will have deprived the other of the capacity to retaliate in a second strike. Each side will know that if it strikes first, it can will a nuclear war; if it waits, it will surely lose. Each side will suspect the other of trying to strike first, and each side will feel forced to strike as quickly as possible. Strategic defenses on both sides virtually guarantee that every crisis between the superpowers will develop into nuclear war.

(d) Since 1945, the main function of nuclear weapons has not been to fight wars but to make threats. The United States directed nuclear threats at the Soviet Union during the Iran crisis in 1946, the Berlin blockade in 1948, the Cuban missile crisis in 1962, the Vietnam War in 1969, and the Yom Kippur War in 1973. In general these threats have been less efficacious than one might expect, mainly because the opposing side did not believe that they would be carried out. Confronted, for example, with Nixon's threat (conveyed through Kissinger) to use nuclear weapons against North Vietnam and perhaps against Russia in 1969, the Soviets correctly surmised that the Americans would not attack North Vietnam with nuclear weapons for fear of suffering nuclear retaliation. The American bluff was called.

Since the Soviets achieved nuclear parity with the United States in the early 1970s, the frequency of American nuclear threats has diminished. The construction of strategic defenses, which might give the United States the ability to win a nuclear war, would restore credibility to American nuclear threats, and the practice of nuclear threats might revive. This would give the United States some ability to control Soviet behavior. But it would also increase the probability of nuclear war, a risk not worth taking for small gains obtainable in safer ways.

(e) The supporters of strategic defense argue that strategic defenses—true defenses—are grounded in the right to self-defense in a way that the Countervailing Strategy is not. If they are justified by self-defense, it follows, on this view, that we are obliged to build them. But suppose it is true that the United States has the *right* to build strategic defenses. It does not follow from this that the United States is obliged to build them, since no one is obliged to do everything that he has a right to do. We have at all times a right to express our ideas. It does not follow that we are obliged to express them, and that we would be wicked if we kept silent. Likewise, no right to self-defense can make strategic defense morally obligatory. It is part of the logic of rights that we always have a right not to do what we have a right to do.

CRITICISMS OF THE COUNTERVAILING STRATEGY FROM THE LEFT

(a) The Countervailing Strategy makes assumptions about history, especially recent history, for which there is less evidence than most Americans think.

The Countervailing Strategy assumes that American readiness to use nuclear weapons has produced 40 years of peace in Europe. This presumes there would have been war in Europe if the United States had not had nuclear weapons. But it is impossible to guess what might have happened in Europe if the United States had deployed only conventional weapons, and impossible to show that fear of nuclear war has produced 40 years of European peace. Europe had 40 years of peace after the Franco–Prussian War of 1871, in days when there were no nuclear weapons and when governments in general were more militaristic than they are now. Both world wars were disasters in Europe, and those terrible lessons help to prevent war, nuclear weapons or no nuclear weapons. Besides, since 1945 the industrialized nations have realized that, given technological innovation, internal development does not require external conquest. Fear of conventional war, the division of Germany, the decline in militaristic political movements, and general prosperity have all contributed as much to peace in Europe as has fear of nuclear war.

The Countervailing Strategy appropriates the popular view of the Soviets as aggressors. But though Soviet propaganda is revolutionary, the Soviet leaders are old and conservative, especially in military matters. In the historical record, the Russians are rarely aggressors, and when they are, as in the Crimean War, they invariably lose. Since 1945, the main thrust of Soviet military action has been not to support aggressive change but to restore and preserve the status quo. The incorporation of the Baltic states, for example, restores those countries to the condition they were in 1917. The Warsaw Pact (i.e. Soviet) invasions of Hungary, Czechoslovakia, and Afghanistan were in each case undertaken to restore a pro-Soviet regime to power. Soviet domination in eastern Europe, which includes domination of former allies of Nazi Germany, is a result of the unique circumstances that ended World War II, and provides no proof of plans for further conquest. There is little indication that the Soviets, at present or at any time since 1945, planned the military invasion of any western European nation. It is absurd to suggest that the Soviets, who spent millions constructing a pipeline to sell natural gas in West Germany, would set about blowing up their customers the minute the United States stopped issuing nuclear threats.

(b) The Countervailing Strategy calls for the use of tactical and theater nuclear weapons in the face of Soviet conventional attack. The Soviets would probably respond in kind, and even if they did not, the use of these weapons on the crowded plains of Europe would kill millions of citizens in nations the tactical nuclear weapons are supposed to protect. Indeed, the destruction caused by nuclear weapons on the battlefield is so great that it is problematic whether permission for their use would ever be granted. The threat to use these weapons is incredible, and their actual use is suicidal.

The standard argument for deploying tactical nuclear weapons is "superior Soviet conventional strength." But the nonnuclear military resources of the NATO states outclass the Soviet Union, and the Soviets cannot muster anything like the 3:1 ratio of forces military experts claim is needed for successful invasion. The Soviets cannot depend on the loyalty of eastern European troops and must maintain a military presence along the long Chinese border as well. Furthermore, current military trends—precision antitank weapons, for example—generally favor defense over offense. All these factors show that the Countervailing Strategy's reliance on tactical and theater nuclear weapons is outdated and dangerous.

(c) If there is any consolation the student can draw from military history since 1945, it is that the political leaders of nuclear nations have been exceedingly reluctant to use nuclear weapons. The French refused an American offer of nuclear weapons during the Indochina war in 1954, the same year in which Eisenhower tabled a recommendation from a subcommittee of the Joint Chiefs of Staff calling for a nuclear attack on Russia before the Soviets could develop intercontinental strategic bombers. The Soviets considered and backed off from a preemptive, presumably nuclear, strike against China in 1969. The nonuse of nuclear weapons for over 40 years has generated a nuclear taboo that is one of the world's best safeguards against nuclear holocaust. In military planning, safety demands that the nuclear threshold—the point at which a military conflict moves from the conventional stage to the nuclear stage—be set as high as possible. By calling for a first use of nuclear weapons in the early stages of superpower conflict, the Countervailing Strategy ignores the nuclear taboo and lowers the nuclear threshold.

(d) The key idea of the Countervailing Strategy is to issue a measured "countervailing" response to every Soviet initiative. The execution of these measured responses assumes that the president and his generals will be able to control the course of an ongoing nuclear war, using strategic weapons with restraint and precision. Many experts doubt that this can be done. It is not merely that Soviet submarine-based missiles can destroy Washington seven minutes after launch, probably killing the president and all his potential successors. The problem is that each large nuclear explosion produces an electromagnetic pulse that will destroy computers and communications systems for hundreds—perhaps thousands—of miles around.

The Countervailing Strategy also assumes that strategic weapons, once launched, will strike their targets precisely, and that the Soviets, suffering these strikes, will be forced to realize that further responses are futile. But it is dubious that in such circumstances rational Soviet heads will prevail. Suppose the Soviets launched a measured and precise attack against American strategic installations, wiping out most American strategic weapons, but incidentally killing several million American citizens. Could the Soviets expect that American leaders would decide that response is futile and that no counterattack should be launched to avenge these deaths? Would they not be fools to expect American surrender? Isn't the Countervailing Strategy equally foolish in expecting surrender from Soviet leaders in similar circumstances?

Many liberal critics of the Countervailing Strategy believe that the most likely result of any use of strategic weapons by either superpower is escalation to a massive nuclear exchange that would destroy both countries.

(e) One crucial element in the Countervailing Strategy is "damage limitation," designed, as Caspar Weinberger put it, "to end the war on favorable terms." "Damage limitation" in nuclear war consists mainly in preemptive strikes against the nuclear weapons of the opponent. Such strikes against the

hardest of targets require nuclear missiles of great accuracy and great explosive force, firing multiple warheads to assure that if one warhead misses, the others will destroy the target. Such highly accurate multiple-warhead missiles, like the land-based MX and the sea-based D–5, introduce an element of instability in relations between the superpowers. The Soviets, worrying about the MX and its 10 warheads, might think that their missiles are in peril, and might be prompted to fire their weapons for fear of losing them in an American attack. Firing their missiles, they will necessarily consider American MXs choice targets, since a Soviet warhead striking an MX will destroy 10 American warheads: a 10 to 1 exchange. The Americans, thinking that the Soviets are thinking this, will feel pressured to use the MX before losing it to Soviet attack. In general, precise "counterforce" weapons like the MX connote "damage limitation" to those who possess them but "preemptive strike" to those at whom they are aimed.

(f) The Countervailing Strategy requires that American weapons be better than Soviet weapons, not merely equal to them. The Soviets, for their part, want American weapons to be no better than their own. Thus the Countervailing Strategy provokes a strategic arms race, in which the Americans innovate and the Soviets respond, or the Soviets innovate and the Americans respond. For example, the Soviet ABM of 1967 provoked the American MIRV of 1969, which provoked the Soviet MIRV of 1974, which provoked new interest in an American ABM and the Star Wars proposal of 1983.

Though it consumes only a fraction of the overall defense budget, American spending on strategic arms under the Countervailing Strategy is exceedingly expensive compared with discretionary spending on social welfare and education. Furthermore, spending on complex strategic weapons diverts scientific talent from basic research and from the development of consumer products and services. But the most negative feature of the strategic arms race is that the development of ever more complex strategic systems raises the risk of accidental nuclear war.

The *Challenger* and Chernobyl disasters of 1986 show that the most carefully supervised technology of both superpowers is subject to catastrophic failure. Most specialists agree that the chance of accidental nuclear war resulting from either a mechanical or a human failure is quite small, and that the chance of a deliberate or accidental launch of nuclear weapons is also quite small—in normal circumstances. But the chance of accidental nuclear war will increase substantially in the case of a crisis between the superpowers, and the chances of accident are proportionately greater when the technology is new than when it is tried and true.

Some experts doubt that the strategic systems of the superpowers could maintain a state of peace during an extended, full-fledged nuclear alert. The systems might go off by accident, or commanders in the field or at central posts might be prompted to fire off weapons before the system breaks down. At least in times of international crisis, the two strategic systems of the superpowers, summed together, might become a single self-detonating doomsday machine.

(g) The main moral argument for the Countervailing Strategy is that it is sustained by the right to self-defense. Most people subscribe to the right to self-defense, and when they do so, they have a clear idea in mind of the sort of situation in which this right applies. The paradigm case, perhaps, is the person threatened by a mugger with a gun who shoots the mugger with a gun of his own. To the degree that a situation differs from this paradigm case, the applicability of the "right to self-defense" becomes more and more questionable.

Obviously there are many differences between a street mugging and the present confrontation between the superpowers.

(i) The paradigm case assigns the right to self-defense to an individual person; defenders of the Countervailing Strategy assign it to a nation-state. But to speak of the rights of nonindividuals leads into muddy waters: do business corporations, for example, have a right to life and a right to self-defense.

(ii) In the paradigm case, force is used to stop the mugging in progress; in the nuclear case, force is to be used not to stop a nuclear attack but to make the Soviets regret what they have already done. This is more like punishment than self-defense.

(iii) In the paradigm case, force is directed at the attacker and injures only the attacker. In the Countervailing Strategy, force is directed at the attacker but injures many innocent bystanders. Moral philosophers disagree on the extent to which it is permissible to injure bystanders in the course of self-defense. Suppose that one could shoot back at the mugger, but only by shooting through the body of a bystander the mugger has seized as a shield. Would it be permissible to shoot? Would it be morally permissible to shoot through *ten* bystanders? Studies show that many limited nuclear attack patterns under the Countervailing Strategy, though directed at military targets, will kill millions of noncombatant bystanders, both in the Soviet Union and in countries not allied with either superpower.

Though nuclear attacks under the Countervailing Strategy are not, to use Elliot Richardson's phrase, aimed at "cities as such," the side effects of American nuclear attacks will probably destroy cities and will certainly kill many civilians. The threat of such collateral destruction, according to the strategy, is one of the things that deters the Soviets from attacking us. Thus the collateral damage serves our purposes; it is one of the means by which we achieve the ends of deterrence. But actions that are means to an end are always intended actions. Thus, although American missiles are not aimed at cities, the mass killing of civilians and the destruction of cities is an intended part of the Countervailing Strategy.

Thus, the Countervailing Strategy is like telling a mugger that if he does not break off his attack, you will surely kill not only him but his daughter as well. Such a threat, if executed, is hardly justifiable on grounds of self-defense, and if the daughter dies, most juries would call it murder.

In sum, then, the critics of the left view the Countervailing Strategy as unnecessary, dangerous, technically unimplementable, expensive, risky, unstable, and immoral. It lowers the nuclear threshold and provokes an arms race....

FINITE DETERRENCE

According to Finite Deterrence, nuclear devices are not genuine weapons and they have no military function. They do, however, have one and only one legitimate use, which is to prevent the use of nuclear weapons by the other side. Thus the United States should keep a small stock of nuclear weapons for use as a last resort, after the other side has used them first.

From the principles of Finite Deterrence, it follows—contrary to Eisenhower's directive—that nuclear devices should *not* be "available for use" by the armed services. The battlefield nuclear weapons now in possession of the Army should be decommissioned, as should the Army's short- and medium-range nuclear missiles: the Lance, the Nike–Hercules, the Pershing I, and the Pershing II. (This process is already underway as a result of the Reagan–Gorbachev summit in 1987.) The Navy should remove nuclear weapons from its attack submarines, aircraft carriers, cruisers, destroyers, and frigates, and should not release nuclear weapons to the Marines—as current arrangements provide. The Air Force should remove nuclear weapons from all nuclear equipped tactical aircraft, such as the Phantom, the Eagle, and the Falcon. Any systems that the Army or Navy or Air Force deploys that are "dual capable" (capable of using either conventional or nuclear weapons) such as ground- and sea-launched cruise missiles—should be decommissioned or redesigned so they cannot carry nuclear weapons. Officers and staff involved in strategy and tactics should be instructed by the president not to expect to use nuclear weapons in military encounters, no matter how hard pressed. Finite Deterrence strategists make parallel recommendations for NATO forces in Europe not already covered by these suggestions.

Would the defense of the United States and Europe be jeopardized by such sweeping denuclearization of fighting forces? Consider the *current* military situation. American and NATO forces are instructed to stock all kinds of nuclear weapons and to plan on using them. Yet the authorization for the use of these weapons can come only from the president or his specific delegates. The president may be reluctant to issue the authorization—for fear of nuclear reprisals, for psychological or moral reasons, or because use of the weapons would injure allies more than the enemy. Since 1945 the presidents have made occasional nuclear threats, but no president has come near to authorizing the use of nuclear weapons. So the military services are required to plan on using weapons they may never be allowed to use.

One does not have to be a military expert to see that current arrangements are a battlefield disaster waiting to happen. The addiction of American military forces to nuclear weapons planning may be part of the reason for the services' current ineffectiveness in conventional military operations, as the botched Son Tay, *Mayagüez,* and Tehran rescue attempts, the Beirut barracks catastrophe, the Grenada invasion mix-ups, and the U.S.S. *Stark* debacle all testify. All Finite Deterrence asks is that the military plan on using weapons they actually will use. Once the break from nuclear dependency is accomplished, all the time spent on training personnel to protect and use nuclear weapons could be spent on improving the skills of conventional fighting forces. This will make the armed services more, rather than less, effective....

This leaves the large-scale strategic nuclear weapons. For Finite Deterrence, the guiding principle for strategic weapons is "No first use—no early second use." The United States must never be the first to use nuclear weapons, and should nuclear weapons be used against the United States, the president or his successor must not feel that a second strike need be launched immediately if it is going to be launched at all. The nuclear weapons systems of the United States must be able to ride out a nuclear first strike and be ready for use days and perhaps even weeks after war has commenced.

This should be American policy, and what is more, the United States should demonstrate the existence of the policy with actions and not just with words. It must design strategic systems that cannot rationally be used for a first strike but that can survive to launch a delayed second strike.

It follows that the United States must abandon its antisatellite weapons program, since shooting down satellites is a first step toward a first strike. To assure opponents that their strategic weapons are not targets of an American first strike, American missiles should lack "hard target kill capacity," that is, the ability to strike enemy missile silos and command bunkers accurately enough to destroy them. The United States should abandon all attempts at constructing strategic defenses, since the only feasible use of strategic defenses is to pick off enemy missiles retaliating against an American first strike.

Most important of all, the United States should replace all multiple-warhead missiles with single-warhead missiles, scrapping or retooling the Minuteman III, Poseidon 3-A, MX, and D-5 missiles. The reason for this is evident with a little mathematics. Suppose that two nations have 100 missiles apiece and that each warhead on each missile has a 90 percent chance of destroying an enemy missile if it catches it on the ground. If each nation places one warhead on top of each missile, then if nation A launches all of its missiles at B in a first strike, there is a 99 percent chance that at least one missile from B will survive with the capacity to kill millions

of citizens of A in a second strike. On the other hand, suppose that each nation puts ten independently targeted missiles on top of each missile. Then if A attacks B, it is 99 percent probable that A will wipe out *all* of B's missiles, and B will have no power to retaliate. Without multiple warheads, each nation is deterred by the thought of sure retaliation. With multiple warheads, each nation is strongly tempted to destroy all the missiles of the other, before the other destroys its missiles first. This is what Finite Deterrence theorists have in mind when they say that MIRVs (multiple independently targeted reentry vehicles) are "destabilizing" and must be eliminated.

Would all these reductions weaken American defense? If "American defense" means "attacking and destroying the Soviet Union," then these reductions will weaken defense. But for Finite Deterrence, plans to destroy the Soviet Union are immoral and dangerous, and have nothing to do with genuine national defense. If national defense means "increasing the chances of American survival," then these reductions will enhance defense. Large multiple-warhead missiles facilitate American first strikes, and this makes them so threatening that, in a crisis, they might provoke an opponent into a "damage limiting" first strike on the United States. Giving them up will decrease the chance of such Soviet attack, so sacrificing MIRVs actually increases national security.

Once the first-strike-facilitating nuclear devices are removed from the strategic arsenal, Finite Deterrence demands that all the rest should be as invulnerable as possible. Strategic submarines at sea are hidden and dispersed, and the fleet as a whole is invulnerable for the foreseeable future. Thus, the core of the nuclear deterrent should be submarine-based. Two features of current submarine basing, however, need to be changed. The current trend toward fewer and larger submarines should be reversed, as a larger fleet of smaller subs would be more secure. And the current "fail deadly" arrangement, which permits submarine commanders to launch missiles in the absence of certain countervailing commands, should be abandoned and replaced by locked weapons and secure communications, whatever the cost.

Strategic bombers are vulnerable on the ground but less vulnerable in the air. When armed with cruise missiles, they have a better chance of delivering nuclear devices on target, but they also become MIRVed missiles with wings, usable for first strike options if a crisis has brought them close to the enemy border. If strategic bombers are to be retained at all, they should combine advanced penetration technology with a return to shorter-range attack missiles. One argument in favor of retaining at least some strategic bombers is that strategic bombers can be recalled but missiles cannot. (Recallability is consistent with the Finite Deterrence principle of "no early second use.")

Fixed land-based ICBMs are the most vulnerable strategic weapons, and Finite Deterrence theorists generally feel that invulnerability requires that all fixed ICBMs be replaced by smaller, more dispersed, mobile ICBMs, if the United States is to retain ICBMs at all. To guard against accidental, unauthorized, or otherwise regrettable launches, a radio-controlled self-destruct device should be placed on each missile.

It is clear from this outline that Finite Deterrence increases the role of the Navy in nuclear deterrence, while decreasing the roles of the Air Force and the Army. Traditionally such changes arouse fierce resistance, and an uncomfortably large fraction of American strategic planning has been more the result of interservice rivalries than of strict calculation of national needs. To put an end to this irrational competition, Finite Deterrence recommends that all delivery systems for nuclear weapons should be concentrated in a separate military service, under the direct control of the president and the secretary of defense, and disconnected from the Joint Chiefs of Staff. Such an administrative system for nu-

clear devices is a necessary expression of the concept that nuclear devices are not weapons and should not be available for military use. Only such a system will convince the military that they must learn to rely on conventional weapons, and that nuclear devices are not weapons at all but harbingers of Armageddon.

In sum, Finite Deterrence proposes that the entire stock of deployed nuclear weapons be placed on a fleet of small strategic submarines, mobile ICBMs, and strategic bombers. All missiles will have single warheads, and will remain at all times under the positive control of the president and secretary of defense or their designated successors. These weapons are to be used only in the event of a nuclear attack on the United States, but not necessarily even then.

Should the president choose to launch a second strike, he must choose appropriate responses to nuclear attacks of various kinds. It is sometimes alleged that under Finite Deterrence the president will have so few weapons available that they must be targeted on cities to maximize the destructive efficiency of the reduced nuclear arsenal. But with all nuclear weapons concealed and dispersed, it is highly probable that the president would have several hundred warheads available for a second strike. Directed at enemy military forces, isolated industrial establishments, power stations, dams, and so forth, these warheads could cause enough damage to offset by a large margin anything a potential enemy might hope to gain from an attack on the United States. Furthermore, these forces *could* be directed against enemy cities, and no enemy could be sure that its cities would not be destroyed if it attacked the United States. This capacity, by itself, provides a strong deterrent against nuclear attacks on American cities. Though Finite Deterrence permits the possibility of future Hiroshimas, it does not commit the president in advance to city-destroying second strikes.

CRITICISMS OF FINITE DETERRENCE FROM THE RIGHT

(a) Deterrence is an attempt to influence the mind of an opponent, so what is crucial to deterrence is not what you intend but how what you intend to do appears to your opponent. Nuclear weapons are greatly feared, and the removal of nuclear weapons makes military forces less intimidating, regardless of how effective they actually are. Removal of nuclear weapons from NATO and American military forces will increase the chances that those forces will be challenged. If the Soviet challenge begins with conventional weapons, and the Soviets find themselves losing they will escalate the conflict to the nuclear level. If Finite Deterrence decreases the chances of outright nuclear attacks, it increases the chance of conventional war, and conventional wars between superpowers will turn into nuclear wars.

(b) Finite Deterrence insists on strong command and control links between the president and all strategic forces. Admittedly, communications links between simplified strategic forces are easier to maintain than links between the complex strategic forces of the Countervailing Strategy. But this concentration of authority provides a military opening for opponents. If an opponent can succeed in killing the president and secretary of defense before they delegate their authority, then commanders in the field will have neither the authority nor the physical ability to release strategic weapons. In its own way, Finite Deterrence may collapse before a decapitating first strike.

(c) Finite Deterrence is designed to give the president time to think about what to do after the United States suffers a first strike. The president will know the condition of the country; he will know whether American cities are largely unscathed or destroyed. If they are unscathed, he will not order a second strike, for fear of provoking a third strike that will indeed destroy American cities. If they are already destroyed, he will not order a second strike because there is nothing left to save. Thus, no matter what happens, under Finite Deterrence it is irrational to launch a second strike.

If we adopt Finite Deterrence, the president will have thought these things through in advance. His potential opponents will also have thought things through, and will realize that if the American president is rational, there are no conditions in which he will launch a second strike, which means they can issue a first strike without fear of retaliation. Under Finite Deterrence, nuclear deterrence becomes incredible and fails to deter. It is no remedy to this problem to suggest that the president should become manifestly irrational. Visible irrationality in the American president will cause anxiety, and anxiety will tempt the opponent toward a preemptive first strike. . . .

ARMS CONTROL AND MULTILATERAL DISARMAMENT

Most Americans believe that the United States should not give up its nuclear weapons if the Soviets keep theirs. But the majority of Americans believe that the United States should give up some nuclear weapons if the Soviets also give up some. At the Reykjavik summit meeting in 1986, leaders of both superpowers toyed with the idea of a step-by-step elimination of American and Soviet ballistic missiles. Many Americans supported this initiative, and many Americans think that it would be a good idea for the United States to give up all its nuclear weapons if the other nuclear powers gave up all of theirs.

The attraction of such bilateral and multilateral reductions is obvious. Each superpower has had the experience of investing heavily in a weapons system that was supposed to provide increased security, only to find its security decreased when the other side constructed the same system. In such cases, it would have been far better for both sides to agree not to build the systems in the first place. MIRV provides perhaps the best example of a system built and then regretted; the ABM treaty provides the best example of an agreement not to build.

The two superpowers have a common interest in agreements not to build parallel strategic systems. Yet in 30 years of arms control negotiations the two superpowers have succeeded only in constructing a hot line, banning nuclear tests in the atmosphere, limiting ABM systems, eliminating strategically superfluous medium range missiles, and setting modest and temporary limits on totals of strategic missiles. Each side has a military-industrial complex with a vested interest in military spending, regardless of long-term negative effects. Each side distrusts the other, and fears that the other side will use the agreement to gain some special advantage. But perhaps the greatest obstacle to mutual agreements is that each side shares the assumption of the Countervailing Strategy that a nuclear weapons system can provide a military advantage—at least until your opponent builds one of his own.

If nuclear weapons systems convey military advantages, then each side has an irresistible argument for building weapons systems. Call a weapons system W. Either my opponent will build W or he won't. If he doesn't and I do, I will have an advantage. If he does and I don't, I will be at a disadvantage. Thus, I should build W no matter what my opponent does. The argument works for both sides, so both build W, even though both realize they would be better off if they chose not to build. (Game theorists call such situations "prisoner's dilemmas.")

The prisoner's dilemma argument fails, however, on the assumptions of Finite Deterrence. Provided we retain the ability to launch a second strike, we gain no advantage by adding on nuclear weapons systems, nor do we stand at a disadvantage if the Soviets build nuclear weapons systems we do not have. If we have superfluous nuclear weapons systems, we have an incentive to negotiate their removal in return for similar reductions on the other side. If we do not succeed, we should scrap them anyway. For the countervailing strategy, arms control is a sacrifice at best and a swindle at worst. For Finite Deterrence, it is a liquidation sale.

Finite Deterrence and mutual nuclear disarmament go hand in hand—up to a point. That stopping point is the point at which each side has reduced its nuclear arsenal to the small set of nuclear weapons prescribed by Finite Deterrence. Beyond that point, each superpower fears that if it gives up its nuclear weapons, the other side might gain a tremendous advantage by hiding a few nuclear missiles in caves. Furthermore, even if two nuclear powers wanted to give up their nuclear weapons, each side might fear that the other has the ability to *rebuild* nuclear weapons faster than it can rebuild them. Can two nuclear powers with small arsenals find a way to make a final and permanent reduction to zero nuclear weapons on each side?

Each side fears that the other may conceal its last few nuclear weapons. One way to allay this fear would be for some third power—a world government, perhaps—to assure the United States and the Soviet Union that if either makes a military move using nuclear weapons, *it* will take reprisals against the offender. The United States and the Soviet Union might even agree to turn their nuclear weapons over to this third power. But supporters of nuclear disarmament are unlikely to be happy with this idea. Not only are world governments dreams for the distant future, but the idea of a world government that goes around making nuclear threats looks to nuclear disarmers like a continuation of the present reign of nuclear terror.

Nuclear disarmers will propose only remedies that do not themselves require nuclear weapons. Rather than a world government armed with nuclear bombs, nuclear disarmers would prefer the creation of an international authority with the power to control the fissionable material from which nuclear weapons are made. Such a proposal was developed by the United States in 1946 and placed before the United Nations, where it was rejected by the Soviet Union, that is, by Stalin. But Stalin is long dead, and the Soviets, chastened by their experiences with the Chernobyl disaster, seem increasingly to share the view that nuclear weapons provide more insecurity than security. They proposed and unilaterally maintained a moratorium on nuclear weapons testing from 1985 to 1987, and have even gone so far as to invite on-site inspection of Soviet nuclear weapons tests by Western scientific observers. In this new context, nuclear disarmers argue that the time is ripe for the United States to press once again for the international supervision of the materials needed to produce nuclear weapons....

LAST WORDS ABOUT NUCLEAR DISARMAMENT

Supporters of nuclear disarmament are often portrayed as irresponsible fanatics who care only for the sacred cause of nuclear disarmament and pay no attention to other values, such as political freedom. They are accused of feeling that somehow the world would be better off if the United States were weak and the Soviet Union were strong. Their proposals—it is alleged—would allow the Soviet Union to blackmail the United States at will.

Supporters of nuclear disarmament protest that these arguments confuse nuclear disarmament with pacifism. Nuclear disarmament does not imply general and complete disarmament. Nuclear disarmers believe that nuclear devices are not weapons and that reliance on nuclear devices is a sign of national weakness, not military strength. Nuclear devices cannot be integrated into usable, effective fighting plans. And if they are reserved for purposes of retaliation only, when the time comes to use them, it will be too late.

Most nuclear disarmers believe in a strong defense. But they believe that the only strong defense is a nonnuclear defense. They want the Army, Navy, Air Force, and Marines to be trained in the use of weapons that will win military objectives, not blow up everything in sight. Many nuclear disarmers also believe that the civilian populations of nation-states,

especially the states of western Europe, should be trained in the techniques of political resistance, which could create such difficulties for occupying forces as to make the conquest of these nations manifestly not worth the trouble. Sweden, Switzerland, and Yugoslavia have already taken serious steps in this direction. Nuclear disarmers, then, are not demanding sacrifices in American strength, or forcing the president to violate his oath.

Opponents of nuclear disarmament claim that nonnuclear forces, however strong, cannot withstand nuclear attack and cannot repel nuclear blackmail. But nuclear weapons provide no magic remedy against nuclear blackmail. A blackmailer with nuclear weapons can effectively threaten any nuclear power by making it appear that he does not care about dying. Blackmail is essentially a contest of wills, and the problem is solved by willpower, not by missiles and nuclear bombs.

A nonnuclear nation with confidence in the fighting effectiveness of its armed forces is unlikely to collapse before nuclear blackmail. From 1945 to 1949 the United States had nuclear weapons and the Soviet Union had none. This did not stop the Soviet Union from blocking elections in Poland, subverting Czechoslovakia, and consolidating control of eastern Europe. In those years Stalin knew that any use of nuclear weapons against Russia could be countered by moving the Red Army into Western Europe. There is no reason why a nonnuclear United States, confronted by a nuclear opponent, could not exhibit similar strength of will in the service of democratic causes.

If the United States "transarmed," substituting effective conventional weaponry for its present blind reliance on nuclear devices, other states would have scant motive to develop or increase nuclear forces. The British, French, and Chinese have in deed, if not in word, endorsed Finite Deterrence: they retain small arsenals as a last-resort deterrent against Soviet attack. They will retain exactly the same deterrent—no more, no less—

regardless of whether the United States arms or disarms.

Likewise, whether West Germany acquires nuclear weapons does not depend on American strategic decisions: it depends on internal politics in West Germany and on the perceived threat of Soviet invasion. Since the Berlin Wall was built in 1961, this threat of invasion has been considered minimal, and the volume of trade between West Germany and the Soviet bloc is now so great that the real chance of Soviet invasion is less than ever. Unlike their critics, nuclear disarmers are not so blind as to think that everything that happens in the world depends on what the United States does first.

In a world in which some sovereign states possess nuclear weapons and in which even "conventional" wars can claim millions of lives, it is crucial to prevent all wars, not just nuclear wars. The new conventional forces that nuclear disarmament will substitute for nuclear weapons must provide a secure defense, without increasing the insecurity of nearby countries. They must provide defense without offense, security without threats. The design of such forces is a delicate matter. Fixed emplacements provide defense without offense, but trust in fixed emplacements died with the Maginot Line. On the other hand, too much emphasis on penetration toward the invader's homeland—along the lines of NATO's current "deep strike" strategy— sends the wrong signal to the opponent and tempts military leaders toward maneuvers as catastrophic as MacArthur's plunge toward the Yalu River in Korea. What must be stressed are mobile antitank weapons and other antiarmor devices that cancel high technology with low cost, and the development of tactics using dispersed but highly mobile forces.

Such forces may appear light relative to invading heavy armor, but to be safe from conquest, a country need not shatter the invading army or destroy the invader's country; it need prove only that the cost of conquest far outweighs any expectable gains. Low-tech nonnuclear forces are best suited to the task of defense without offense. Nuclear weapons are eminently unsuitable, since nuclear weapons in any configuration will always be perceived as a threat.

Since nuclear disarmers want military forces used only to forestall conquest, they reject the view that American forces should be used to intervene around the world in defense of American interests. If such interventions do moral good, then this is a moral good that nuclear disarmament must forgo. But in the court of world opinion, American interventions in the nuclear era—in Iran, in Guatemala, in Vietnam, in Chile, for example—have in general been viewed as moral evils. If nuclear disarmament produces a new isolationism, and prevents us from doing good, it also prevents us from doing harm.

Defense without offense does not require that the United States give up all influence— only influence based on the threat of force. Obviously one can influence people not only by threatening them with some harm but also by promising them some good. In the future, if there is one, it is not clear that the most influential countries will remain the ones that can threaten world destruction. In the 1940s, the Japanese tried to control East Asia by building bigger battleships. Fortunately and predictably, they failed. Forty years later they have gained worldwide influence by building better cameras. The moral gap between the two methods is plain to the Japanese, but the ethical message does not seem to have penetrated the nuclear powers, East or West.

Nuclear disarmament is derided as utopian. But it was utopian in the early nineteenth century to call for abolition of slavery. Yet slavery was abolished, and it is difficult to imagine now how it was tolerated at all. Nuclear disarmers feel that nuclear weapons are as wicked as slavery, and they argue that if slavery could be abolished, so can nuclear weapons. They pray that abolition will not require a global Civil War.

Review Questions

1. What is the Countervailing Strategy? What are the criticisms of this strategy?

2. What is Strategic Defense, and how is it criticized?

3. Explain Finite Deterrence and its problems.

4. What is the Multilateral Disarmament proposal? What objections are made to it?

Discussion Questions

1. Which strategy, if any, do you find the most acceptable and why?

2. Lackey does not explicitly commit himself, but which strategy do you think he favors and why?

3. How would Sloss reply to the criticisms of Strategic Defense?

Problem Cases

1. The Nuclear Freeze Resolution (Senate Joint Resolution 163 and House Joint Resolution 434, 1982) introduced by Senators Edward M. Kennedy and Mark O. Hatfield: Resolved by the Senate and the House of Representatives of the United States of America in Congress assembled,

i. As an immediate strategic arms control objective, the United States and the Soviet Union should:

a. pursue a complete halt to the nuclear arms race;

b. decide when and how to achieve a mutual and verifiable freeze on the testing, production, and future deployment of nuclear warheads, missiles, and other delivery systems; and

c. give special attention to destabilizing weapons whose deployment would make such a freeze more difficult to achieve.

ii. Proceeding from this freeze, the United States and the Soviet Union should pursue major, mutual, and verifiable reductions in nuclear warheads, missiles, and other delivery systems, through annual percentages or equally effective means, in a manner that enhances stability.

Referendums in support of the freeze proposal have won in several states, and opinion polls show that the majority of people in the United States support it. Should the freeze proposal be passed by Congress or not? Explain your position.

2. An Extended Nuclear War The Reagan administration developed plans for prevailing or winning an extended global nuclear war. These plans included building long tunnels deep underground that would be stocked with food, weapons, and supplies. The plans called for mili-

tary personnel to inhabit these tunnels for years while fighting continues on the surface of the Earth. No doubt the surface of the Earth would become uninhabitable, except perhaps by ants.

Are these plans a good idea or not? What do you think?

Civilians could build their own underground shelters and stock them. Should we be doing this or not?

3. The Decapitation Scenario Suppose that we have evidence of a Soviet nuclear attack on Washington, D.C., at 1 A.M. on Easter Sunday. The evidence is a radar warning coming from a station on the coast of the Atlantic Ocean. We know that there is a Soviet submarine off the coast of Washington because we have been tracking it. The radar seems to indicate that this submarine has launched two missiles, and since subs of that type are known to be carrying nuclear warheads, it is possible that these are short-range missiles armed with nuclear bombs. Or perhaps it is some kind of Soviet test or trick, to see how we will respond. Maybe it is just a false radar warning; false radar warnings have happened more than once. One time it turned out to be an unusual flock of birds; another time the computer mistook a war game for the real thing. Given the cloud cover, it is impossible to get a visual confirmation. But fighter jets have been scrambled, and are in the air with orders to hit the sub with air-to-surface missiles. We can justify the attack by saying that the sub was spying, and that it violated our territorial waters (although actually they are international waters). The main worry is whether it is really a nuclear attack or not, and given the speed of the missiles or apparent missiles, we have only ten minutes to decide. If it is a real attack, then there will be damage to the unprotected command and control systems of the United States, and we will lose a lot of our capacity to carry out a retaliatory response. (In strategy books, an attack on Washington or Moscow is called the "decapitation scenario.") Also, there will be massive loss of life including the president, who is asleep at the White House. Should we launch our missiles in retaliation now, before we are hit and lose much of our command and control ability, or should we wait for ten minutes and make sure that the attack is genuine? What should we do in this crisis situation?

Suppose we wait and Washington is hit with two hydrogen bombs, resulting in a communications blackout except for the shielded connection to the hollow mountain communications center near Colorado Springs. Now what? Should a response be ordered? Given the communications difficulties, it will be hard, if not impossible, to control a limited response. It looks like it is either an all-out, massive response or nothing at all. Which should it be in your opinion? And given this possibility, what should our policy be? Think about it.

Suggested Readings

(1) Nigel Blake and Kay Pole, eds., *Objections to Nuclear Defense: Philosophers on Deterrence* (London: Routledge & Kegan Paul, 1984). This is a collection of articles on the morality of nuclear deterrence, including an interesting article by Anthony Kenny on the slogan "Better dead than red."

(2) *Ethics* 95 (April 1985). This issue has papers given at a conference on ethics and nuclear deterrence in Aspen in 1984. The authors include philosophers and strategists; they are seen to have different approaches to the problems.

(3) Russell Hardin, "Unilateral Versus Mutual Disarmament," *Philosophy & Public Affairs* 12, No. 5 (1983), pp. 236–254. Hardin rejects Lackey's argument (in "Missiles and Morals"—see the citation below) that utilitarianism recommends unilateral nuclear disarmament by the United States, and gives arguments for mutual disarmament.

(4) Harvard Nuclear Study Group, *Living with Nuclear Weapons* (Cambridge, MA: Harvard University Press, 1983). The group claims that disarmament is inherently unstable and not in the nation's best interests. They accept the common view that nuclear arms are necessary to deter aggression and to protect political influence. Still they grant that some kind of arms control might contribute to deterrence, arms-race stability, and crisis stability.

(5) Gregory S. Kavka, "Doubts About Unilateral Nuclear Disarmament," *Philosophy & Public Affairs* (Summer 1983), pp. 255–260. Kavka also replies to Lackey's article; Kavka is opposed to unilateral nuclear disarmament by the United States.

(6) ———, "Some Paradoxes of Deterrence," *The Journal of Philosophy* 75, No. 6 (June 1978), pp. 285–302. In this classic article, Kavka argues that the standard view of deterrence results in serious moral paradoxes that challenge three widely accepted moral principles: the Wrongful Intention Principle, the Right–Good Principle, and the Virtue Preservation Principle.

(7) George P. Kennan, *The Nuclear Delusion* (New York: Viking Press, 1982. Kennan is a former ambassador to the Soviet Union. In this book, he argues that Soviet foreign policy is conservative and that the Soviets do not want war with the United States. Kennan is opposed to nuclear war and threatening nuclear war.

(8) Douglas P. Lackey, "Missiles and Morals: A Utilitarian Look at Nuclear Deterrence," *Philosophy & Public Affairs* 11, No. 4, (Summer 1982), pp. 189–231. Lackey gives utilitarian arguments in favor of unilateral nuclear disarmament by the United States.

(9) ———, "Moral Principles and Strategic Defense," *The Philosophical Forum* 18, No. 1, (Fall 1986), pp. 1–7. Lackey attacks former President Reagan's Star Wars proposal. He argues that a system of deterrence with defenses is not, as Reagan and his supporters claim, morally superior to the current system of deterrence without defenses.

(10) Douglas P. Lackey, ed., *Ethics and Strategic*

Defense (Belmont, CA: Wadsworth, 1988). This collection of readings presents the moral arguments both for and against strategic defense.

(11) Douglas Maclean, ed., *The Security Gamble: Deterrence Dilemmas in the Nuclear Age* (Totowa, NJ: Rowman & Allanheld, 1984). This is a collection of papers and responses written for a conference held at the University of Maryland in 1983. Two are on the U.S. Catholic Bishops' position.

(12) The National Conference of Catholic Bishops, *The Challenge of Peace: God's Promise and Our Response* (Office of Publishing Services, United States Catholic Conference, 1312 Massachusetts Ave., N.W., Washington, DC 20005). The bishops condemn any use of nuclear weapons, even in retaliation. They also evaluate current strategies of deterrence and make specific recommendations for arms control.

(13) Ronald Reagan, "Speech on Military Spending and a New Defense," *The New York Times*, March 24, 1983. This is the famous Star Wars speech.

(14) Jonathan Schell, *The Abolition* (New York: Knopf, 1984). In this book, Schell continues his attack on nuclear weapons and deterrence. He contends that there is no defense against nuclear weapons. Deterrence strategy recognizes this superiority of the offense and seeks to prevent a first strike, which can't be defended against, by threatening a retaliatory second strike, which also can't be defended against. To restore the superiority of defense, Schell recommends that we abolish nuclear weapons, hence the title *The Abolition*.

(15) Henry Shue, ed., *Nuclear Deterrence and Moral Restraint* (New York: Cambridge University Press, 1989). This is a collection of original articles by academics and defense experts on nuclear deterrence strategy and the moral problems it raises. It includes interesting articles on finite deterrence by David Lewis and Harold Feiveson.

(16) James P. Sterba, ed., *The Ethics of War and Nuclear Deterrence* (Belmont, CA: Wadsworth, 1985). This excellent anthology includes articles about the morality of war in general, articles about nuclear war in particular, and discussions of deterrence strategies and arms negotiations. Different points of view are represented.

(17) _____, "How to Achieve Nuclear Deterrence Without Threatening Nuclear Destruction," in *Sterba, op. cit.*, pp. 155–174. Sterba grants that nuclear deterrence is morally justified, and also accepts the view that it is immoral to threaten nuclear destruction. As a result, he tries to combine both views by contending that we can achieve nuclear deterrence without threatening nuclear destruction.

Philosophical Glossary

Acts and omissions doctrine The doctrine that there is an important moral difference between acts and omissions (or failures to act) such that an act can be wrong but an omission with the same effect not wrong. As it is applied to killing and letting die, the doctrine says that killing an innocent person is wrong, but letting him or her die may not be wrong, or is less wrong. The application of the doctrine to euthanasia is attacked by Rachels in the reading in Chapter 3. Glover (who has a reading in Chapter 4) discusses and rejects the doctrine and its application to euthanasia in Chapter 7 of his book *Causing Death and Saving Lives*. A limited defense of the doctrine as it is applied to killing and letting die can be found in Foot's "Euthanasia" and Ladd's "Positive and Negative Euthanasia" (see the Suggested Readings for Chapter 3).

Anthropocentrism The belief that human beings, rather than animals or the nonhuman world, are central or most important in the universe. Contrasted with ecocentrism, the view that the environment, not human beings, is central or important.

A priori Known prior to experience, as distinguished from a posteriori, known after experience. The statement "No statement can be both true and false" is known a priori, while the statement "Some crows are black" is known a posteriori.

St. Thomas Aquinas (1225–1274) An Italian Catholic who was one of the greatest medieval philosophers. He is usually referred to as St. Thomas. As an Angelic Doctor of the Roman Catholic Church, his teachings have special authority for members of the Church, but this does not mean that all Catholic thinkers agree with him on every point of doctrine. His best-known works are *Summa contra Gentiles* (*Against the Errors of the Infidels*) and *Summa Theologiae*. These are comprehensive syntheses of philosophy and theology which combine, among other things, Aristotle's philosophy and Christian theology. Aquinas' most famous contribution to philosophy and theology is his Five Ways of proving the existence of God. Most commentators think that they all commit some fallacy or other, but some have tried to defend them or reformulate them so that they are free of error. Aquinas is also known for his careful discussion of the traditional attributes of God such as omnipotence, omniscience, benevolence, and eternity, and his attempt to solve the various philosophical puzzles which they raise. One of the most difficult of these puzzles is the problem of evil: Why does an omnipotent and benevolent God allow evil to exist in the world?

Aristotle (384–322 B.C.) The Greek philosopher who was the student of Plato. He is recognized as one of the greatest philosophers of all time. He made important contributions to all areas of philosophy, including the formulation of traditional logic. His most important work in ethics is the *Nicomachean Ethics*. In this book, Aristotle claims that happiness is the highest practical good, but he denies that happiness is to be identified with pleasure. Instead he argues that happiness consists of virtuous activity, where this includes both moral and intellectual virtues.

Jeremy Bentham (1748–1832) An English philosopher who was one of the founders of utilitarianism along with Mill. He was also a hedonist who believed that only pleasure is intrinsically good, and only pain is intrinsically bad. Unlike Epicurus, Mill, and other hedonists, he did not distinguish between different types of pleasure, e.g., so-called higher and lower pleasures. According to Bentham, all pleasures are equal as far as quality is concerned—as put in his famous aphorism, "Quantity of pleasure being equal, pushpin is as good as poetry." Bentham did think one could compare pleasures with respect to their quantity or amount; he invented a hedonic calculus (as he called it) to do this. Using the calculus, one was supposed to be able to determine which of two actions would likely produce the greatest quantity of pleasure or the greatest number of units of pleasure. Critics have complained that there are no such things as units of pleasure, that it doesn't make any sense to say, for example, that eating candy produces ten units of pleasure while reading a philosophy book causes thirty units of pleasure.

Claim right A right that is a claim to something from somebody. Welfare rights, for example, are usually said to assert a claim to basic necessities from the state. In his reading in Chapter 9, Joel Feinberg explains rights in terms of claims.

Criterion (pl. criteria) Something that provides a conclusive way of knowing whether something exists, or whether a word is used correctly. In the abortion controversy, writers have tried to find criteria for the fetus being a person, that is, features that provide logically conclusive evidence that fetuses are persons. Sometimes criteria are formulated in terms of necessary and sufficient conditions. See *necessary and sufficient conditions*.

Cultural relativism A theory of moral values which holds that values are relative to society. If a society approves of a certain action, then it is right; if it disapproves of an action, then it is wrong. This theory should not be confused with anthropological relativism, the factual thesis that different societies have different moral codes—for example, some societies have considered slavery to be morally acceptable, and others have not. If cultural relativism is true, then it follows, supposedly, that there are no universal moral values that hold in all societies at all times and there are no objective moral values that hold independent of society. Both cultural and anthropological relativism have been popular with sociologists and anthropologists, but very few philosophers have accepted these views. Philosophers insist with some support from anthropologists that there are universal moral values, e.g., caring for children is morally approved in all known societies. Philosophers also want to criticize societies and reform them; this means that societies have made moral mistakes in the past and the present. If so, then acts approved by a society could be wrong (e.g., slavery was approved by some societies, but it is objectively wrong), and acts disapproved by a society may be right (e.g., allowing women to vote was disapproved by Western society until the 1920s, but nevertheless this is objectively right).

Deontologists Those who hold a deontological ethical theory. Such a theory holds that the rightness or wrongness of an act is determined by something other than its consequences—for example, by God's commands or moral intuition. Contrasted with teleological ethical theories, including utilitarianism and egoism, which hold that the rightness or wrongness of an act is determined by its consequences.

Distributive justice The problem or theory of how to allocate or distribute goods and services in a society. Should there be an equal distribution, or should some people be allowed to have more goods and services than others?

Divine command theory In its standard form, the divine command theory says that an act is right if it is commanded by God, and wrong if it is forbidden by God. This theory has been defended by a few philosophers, but it faces a host of difficulties. First, it assumes that God exists and issues commands, and this is very difficult to prove. The history of philosophy contains numerous attempts to prove that a personal God exists, but it is safe to say that each of these so-called proofs is controversial. Second, even assuming that God exists, there is the problem of finding out what God's commands are. Do we accept Jesus, Moses, or Muhammad as the prophet of God? Do we read the Old Testament, the New Testament, or the Koran? Third, if we decide, say, that the New Testament is the word of God, we still have the problem of interpreting it. Different people interpret the Bible in different ways. For example, how are we to understand the basic commandment "Thou shalt not kill"? Fourth, why should we obey God in the first place? Surely, threats of reward or punishment are not good moral reasons for obeying. Don't we have a right and a duty to decide for ourselves what is right or wrong? Finally, there is the famous question found in Plato's dialogue the *Euthyphro*, namely, Is an act right because God commands it, or does God command it because it is right? It seems that no satisfactory answer can be given. If an act is right just because God commands it, then its being right is arbitrary. God could arbitrarily command you to murder your beloved son (as in the Biblical story of Abraham and his son Isaac), and that would supposedly make it right. But would it? On the other hand, if God commands an act because it is right, then a standard of rightness exists independent of God's commands. It might be, say, Mill's Principle of Utility. If so, then we could discover this principle without knowing God's commands, and God's commands are unnecessary for morality.

Doctrine of demographic laissez-faire   The doctrine that people should be free to have as many children as they wish.

Doctrine of double effect   A traditional doctrine that makes a distinction between two effects of an action, an unintended but foreseen consequence and an intended consequence. According to the doctrine in its basic form, a foreseen evil consequence of an action is allowable provided it is unintended, and provided that the intended consequence is good. Different philosophers give different accounts of the doctrine. According to Philippa Foot, in her classical article "The Problem of Abortion and the Doctrine of Double Effect" (*Oxford Review* No. 5, pp. 5–15), the doctrine is that it is permissible to bring about by oblique intention (that is, to foresee as a consequence of action, but to not directly intend) what is wrong to directly intend. Appealing to this doctrine, conservatives like Noonan and Finnis (in our readings) hold that it is permissible to perform an abortion to save the mother's life if the death of the fetus is only indirectly or obliquely intended. The doctrine is used to justify euthanasia, too. See the reading by Gay–Williams in Chapter 3. The doctrine is controversial; critics contend that no clear distinction can be made between intended and unintended consequences, and assuming the distinction can be made out, the doctrine can be used to justify obviously immoral but supposedly unintended acts, e.g., the terrorist who kills people with the good intention of making a political protest.

Doctrine of ensoulment   Generally speaking, the medieval doctrine that God puts an immortal soul into a body at some time, say at birth. The special theory of instantaneous ensoulment that Noonan refers to holds that God puts the soul into the zygote at the very instant of conception and not afterwards. This is a common Roman Catholic belief that is sometimes used to defend the conservative prohibition of abortion.

Epicureanism   See *Epicurus.*

Epicurus   (341–270 B.C.) The Greek philosopher who founded Epicureanism, which combined hedonism with the view that all things are really just atoms in the void. Hedonism is usually explained in terms of a distinction between intrinsic and instrumental goodness. Something is intrinsically good if it is good in itself, considered apart from anything else, while something is instrumentally good if it is good as a means of getting something else. According to hedonism, only pleasure is intrinsically good, but other things such as possessions can be instrumentally good. Epicurus (like Mill) distinguished between different types of pleasures. He held that mental pleasure (e.g., the pleasure one gets from conversation) is better than physical pleasure (e.g., the pleasure one gets from eating). But the most complete pleasure according to Epicurus is the total elimination of pain. To achieve this, Epicurus recommended a simple, tranquil life devoted to philosophical activity.

Equivocation   Using a word in two different senses. The fallacy of equivocation is committed by an argument that gives one word different meanings. The example given by Jane English is this: A fetus is a being that is living and human, so a fetus is a human being (the word *being* is used equivocally).

Ethical Egoism   The standard formulation of the theory is that everyone ought to act in his or her own self-interest. My act is right if it is in my self-interest, and wrong if it is not. Your act is right if it is in your self-interest, and wrong if it is not. This version of the theory is called universal ethical egoism since it is supposed to apply to everyone equally. The standard criticism of universal ethical egoism is that it involves some sort of contradiction—but it is not so easy to find this alleged contradiction. Suppose John and Mary are in a fight. As a practicing universal ethical egoist, I tell John to win (since that is in John's self-interest), but then I tell Mary that she should win (since that is in Mary's self-interest). But they both can't win, so there is something odd about this advice. Nevertheless, it is not formally self-contradictory to tell them both to try to win.

Another possible version of egoism is personal ethical egoism, where I say that I ought to do those actions that most benefit me, but I have nothing to say about your actions. This is not really an ethical theory, but more like a personal philosophy of life. Still another version is individual ethical egoism, where I say that you and I both ought to do what is in my self-interest. This view involves a strange asymmetry: You ought to always help me, but I should never help you, unless that benefits me.

None of these views should be confused with psychological egoism, the theory that everyone in fact does what is in their self-interest. Obviously this is not an ethical theory, but a factual claim about how people act.

Ethnocentrism   The belief that one's own race or ethnic group is superior to other races or ethnic groups.

Fallacy of affirming the consequence   A fallacy of reasoning committed by arguments having the logical form P implies Q; Q; therefore P, where P and Q are statements that are true or false. In the conditional statement P implies Q, Q is called the consequent and P the antecedent. For example, consider this argument: If the fetus is a person, then the fetus is conscious. The fetus is conscious after the eighth week. So the fetus is a person after the eighth week. Here is an argument with the same logical form, only it is about Fido the dog: If Fido is a person, then Fido is conscious. Fido is conscious when barking. So Fido is a person when barking.

Free rider's principle   A free rider is one who gets or tries to benefit without paying, for example, a worker who gets the benefits of a union contract without being a member of the union. The free rider's principle is that one should be allowed to do this.

Richard Mervyn Hare   A British moral philosopher and White's Professor of Moral Philosophy at Oxford University. He is the author of numerous books, including *The Language of Morals, Freedom and Reason,* and *Moral Thinking,* and many articles. He is best known for his prescriptive theory of moral language. On this theory, moral statements are not descriptive but prescriptive in the sense of implying an imperative. For example, on Hare's analysis, the statement "Murder is wrong" implies the imperative "Don't commit murder."

Hedonism   See *Epicurus.*

Thomas Hobbes   See *social contract theory.*

Infinite regress   A series of events that continues without end—usually with the implication that this is impossible. A vicious infinite regress is one that is impossible, while a benign infinite regress is not impossible.

Instrumental value   See *intrinsic value.*

Intrinsic goods   See *Epicurus.*

Intrinsic value   See *Epicurus* for intrinsic goodness, which is one kind of intrinsic value. Sometimes the term *intrinsic value* is used to mean intrinsic goodness, but strictly speaking, intrinsic value includes both intrinsic goodness and intrinsic badness. Thus something has intrinsic value if it is good *or* bad in itself apart from its use or consequences. By contrast, something has instrumental value (or extrinsic value) if it is good or bad as a means to getting something else.

Clarence Irving Lewis   (1883–1964) An American philosopher who taught at the University of California and Harvard. He made important contributions to logic (e.g., a system of modal logic), epistemology or theory of knowledge, and metaphysics. In his book *An Analysis of Knowledge and Valuation,* he argues that value is an aspect of sense presentations. The only thing that is intrinsically good is a liked or wanted experience, and the only thing that is intrinsically bad is a disliked or unwanted experience. An experience may also have a contributory value if it adds to the total value quality of conscious life. So the contributory value of an experience is different from its intrinsic value.

John Locke   See *social contract theory.*

Karl Marx   (1818–1883) The German revolutionary social and economic theorist who is the father of modern socialism. Along with his friend Friedrich Engels, he wrote the important and influential *Communist Manifesto.* This book gives an analysis and critique of capitalism, an account of true socialism (as distinguished from false socialism), and a call for revolutionary action. Marx is also known for his theory of historical materialism, according to which the material conditions of life determine practically everything in human consciousness and society.

Metaphysical Relating to metaphysics, the branch of philosophy that answers questions about reality. In Glover's article, however, metaphysical means something transcendental or beyond the sensible world.

Thomas Nagel An American philosopher who is currently Professor of Philosophy at New York University. He is the author of *Mortal Questions, The View from Nowhere,* and, most recently, *What Does It All Mean?* Two of his most well known and widely reprinted articles are "What Is It Like to Be a Bat?" and "Brain Bisection and the Unity of Consciousness."

Natural law The term *natural law* usually refers to prescriptive moral laws that are supposed to be derived from human nature, as distinguished from descriptive laws of nature such as those found in chemistry and physics.

Necessary and sufficient conditions A necessary condition for something is one without which the thing would not exist or occur. The presence of oxygen is a necessary condition for human life. Being alive is a necessary condition for being a person. A sufficient condition for something is one given the occurrence or presence of which the thing does exist or occur. Prolonged absence of oxygen is a sufficient condition for human death. Being a United States senator is a sufficient condition for being a person. Something can be a necessary condition and not a sufficient condition and vice versa.

Negative rights Basically, rights that require others to *not* do something to you. They are sometimes called rights of noninterference. Thus the right to life is a negative right if it implies that others have a duty to not interfere with your life. The right to liberty is a negative right if it implies that others have a duty to not interfere with your exercise of freedom. Negative rights are contrasted with positive rights, which require others to do something to some good or service. Thus the right to life is a positive right if it implies that others should give you the basic necessities for life such as food, water, housing, and medical care. Sometimes positive rights are called entitlements because they entitle you to goods or services. The view of Hospers is that the rights to life, liberty, and property are only negative rights, or rights of noninterference.

Ontology The philosophical study or investigation of being and nonbeing, existence and nonexistence. For example, see Jean Paul Sartre's classical existentialist book *Being and Nothingness,* which distinguishes between two types of being, being in-itself (*en-soi*) and being for-itself (*pour soi*). According to Sartre, human consciousness has an existence for-itself rather than in-itself.

Paradigm An ideal or standard example of something. In the philosophy of science, the term is used to refer to a pervasive way of regarding phenomena which dictates the way phenomena are explained.

Positivism As applied to ethics, logical positivism is a view which holds that ethical statements are meaningless because they are neither true nor false by definition nor susceptible to empirical verification or falsification. Some logical positivists go on to hold an emotive theory of ethical statements. On this theory, ethical statements about right, wrong, good, or bad are merely expressions of emotion. The terms *right* and *good* express positive emotions, while *wrong* and *bad* express negative emotions. But as expressions of emotion, ethical statements are neither true nor false, and there are no genuine or factual disagreements in ethics. Critics of this theory agree that ethical statements can be used to express emotions, but maintain that they can have other uses as well such as advising, recommending, evaluating, and so on. Furthermore, they deny that meaningful statements must be either definitions or empirical statements subject to verification or falsification.

***Prima facie* duty** A moral duty or obligation which everyone has unless it is overridden by some other duty. *Prima facie* means literally on the face of it. The basic idea is that one *prima facie* duty (say the mother's duty to save her own life) can override another *prima facie* duty (say the mother's duty to preserve the life of the fetus). By contrast, an absolute duty is one that cannot be overridden by any other duties.

***Prima facie* right** A moral right that can be overridden by another right. For example, some would say that the fetus' right to life overrides the mother's right to self-defense. To be contrasted with absolute right, which is a right that cannot be overridden by any other right.

Jean–Jacques Rousseau   See *social contract theory.*

Henry Sidgwick   (1838–1900) An English philosopher who was Knightsbridge Professor of Moral Philosophy at Cambridge University. His most important work is *The Methods of Ethics,* in which utilitarianism is given an intuitive basis. The duty to promote the greatest good for the greatest number is supported by a fundamental moral intuition, and more specific duties can be justified as ways of satisfying this basic duty.

Slippery slope arguments   In general, an argument that one cannot draw a line or avoid certain consequences. For instance, if one allows some sick people to be killed, then one must allow all sick people to be killed—one will slide down a slope of killing. In the abortion controversy, one finds the argument that if an infant is a person, and the development of the infant from the zygote is a slippery slope, that is, a smooth, continuous curve of development without any sharp breaks or discontinuities so that no lines can be drawn, then the zygote is a person, too. This argument is attacked by Thomson and defended by Finnis in the readings.

Social contract theory   The basic idea of social contract theory is that morality arises from an agreement or contract made by people so that they can live together. In his book the *Leviathan,* the British philosopher Thomas Hobbes (1588–1679) says that people living in a state of nature apart from society would find life "solitary, poor, nasty, brutist, and short." To avoid such a life, people live together in a society. But social life is possible only if people agree to follow moral rules such as "Don't murder," "Don't steal," and so on. Another philosopher who is associated with this theory is Jean–Jacques Rousseau (1712–1778). In his work *The Social Contract,* Rousseau asserts that humans living in a state of nature are stupid animals; they become intelligent beings only when they live together in a civilized society. The British philosopher John Locke (1632–1704) made an important contribution to social contract theory in his work *Two Treatises of Government.* He argues that in the state of nature humans are free and equal, but this does not mean that they can do anything they want. There is a law of nature, established by God, which gives each person certain natural rights. There is a right to life, a right to liberty, and a right to property. But to enjoy these rights,

humans must live together under a social contract which establishes a government to protect these rights and settle disputes. Without a government, humans in a state of nature would infringe on each other's rights.

Socrates   (470–399 B.C.) The Greek philosopher who was the teacher of Plato. Socrates wrote nothing himself, but an account of his life and teachings is found in Plato's dialogues, particularly the *Apology, Crito,* and *Phaedo.* According to Plato, Socrates was convicted of impiety and corrupting the youth, and sentenced to die by drinking hemlock. In philosophy, Socrates is known for a method of questioning, the Socratic method, where one elicits a conclusion from a person by patient and penetrating questions, and not by just telling the person the conclusion. In the *Meno,* for example, Socrates' questions are supposed to enable Meno's slave to see or remember the conclusion of Pythagoras' theorem even though the slave has not been taught it previously.

Stoic   One who accepts stoicism, a Greek philosophy which taught, among other things, that one should live in harmony with the universe. Doing this produces *apatheia,* a state of spiritual peace, well-being, and indifference to things beyond one's control. While in this state, one's actions are benevolent and rational.

Subjectivism   A theory of moral values holding that values are relative to a person's subjective feelings or emotions. If a person approves of an action, then it is morally right; if the person disapproves of an action, then it is morally wrong. This theory should not be confused with the factual thesis that different people have different feelings about moral values. No doubt this factual thesis is true, but it does not follow that moral values are different for different people. An act might be right even if a person disapproves of it, and an act might be wrong even though a person approves of it. This is simply to say that people might be mistaken about what is right or wrong. If such mistakes are possible, and most philosophers insist that they are, then subjectivism cannot be true. Another standard criticism of subjectivism is that it fails to recognize the fact that there are genuine moral disagreements. Pro-life and pro-choice advocates disagree about the wrongness of abortion, but this disagreement is not just a disagreement in feeling or emotion. Both sides could emotionally disapprove of abortion, and yet still disagree about its wrongness in some cases, say rape.

Sufficient condition See *necessary and sufficient conditions.*

Supererogation That which is morally good but not morally required. For example, action which is morally good but goes beyond the call of duty such as giving all your money to the needy. Distinguished from that which is required by moral duty such as treating people with respect.

Teleological theory A theory that determines moral rightness or wrongness by looking at consequences of actions. The standard teleological theory in ethics, as we can see in the readings, is utilitarianism. Utilitarianism takes different forms, depending on what view about the good is adopted (for example, hedonism or some nonhedonistic view), but all versions agree that the consequences for everyone should be considered. Unlike utilitarianism, ethical egoism is a teleological theory that considers the consequences only for the agent and ignores the consequences for others. A third teleological theory is altruism; it considers consequences for others but not for the agent. More teleological theories can be formulated, depending on who is given moral consideration. One might be concerned, say, only with one's family or one's religious group.

Teleological theories are usually contrasted with deontological theories that do not look at consequences in determining moral rightness or wrongness. Kant's theory and the divine command theory are examples of deontological theories. Another example is situation ethics, where one is supposed to decide what is right or wrong in concrete situations without using abstract rules for guidance. Appeals to conscience or moral intuition would also be classified as deontological.

Index